'*THIS IS UNCOOL* BEGINS IN DECEMBER AND WORKS CHRONOLOGICALLY THROUGH THE YEARS UP TO THE PRESENT DAY. IT SETS OUT TO TELL THE STORY OF HOW POP MUSIC HAS CHANGED AND HOW OUR WORLD HAS CHANGED IN THE LAST QUARTER OF A CENTURY. AS WITH ALL PERSONAL LISTS, THE DESIRE TO PROVOKE A BARNEY – WITH ME, WITH YOUR FRIENDS – IS MORE IMPORTANT THAN TRYING TO BE DEFINITIVE. IF WE ARE ALL HONEST WITH OURSELVES FOR A MOMENT, WE KNOW THAT THE MAJORITY OF ALBUMS WE OWN CONTAIN TWO, MAYBE THREE TRACKS THAT WE REALLY LOVE; AND GUESS WHAT? THEY'RE MORE OFTEN THAN NOT THE SINGLES . . .'

GARRY MULHOLLAND

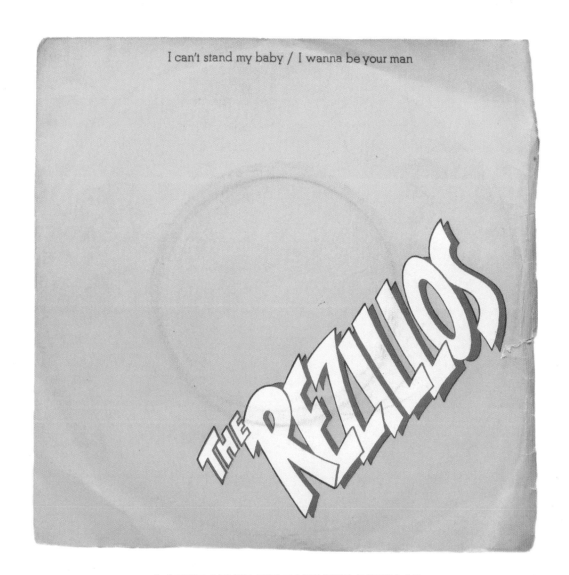

I can't stand my baby / I wanna be your man

I CAN'T STAND MY BABY/THE REZILLOS
PAGE 40

"THIS IS UNCOOL"

THE 500 GREATEST SINGLES SINCE PUNK AND DISCO

GARRY MULHOLLAND

CASSELL ILLUSTRATED

First published in Great Britain in 2002 by Cassell Illustrated, a division
of Octopus Publishing Group Limited
2–4 Heron Quays, London E14 4JP

Text copyright © Garry Mulholland, 2002
Commissioning Editor: Ian Preece
Editor: Victoria Alers-Hankey
Design: EkhornForss
Photography: Andrew Sydenham

A CIP catalogue record for this book is available from
the British Library.

ISBN 0304 631860

Printed and bound in Italy

JOSEF K/IT'S KINDA FUNNY

ACKNOWLEDGEMENTS

Apart from *The Complete Book of British Charts* by Tony Brown, Jon Kutner and Neil Warwick, there is no doubt at all about the major source of information for this book. Take a bow, Martin C. Strong, whose 5th edition of *The Great Rock Discography* and its eccentric twin *The Great Alternative & Indie Discography* (both *Mojo* Books) certainly saved me from at least six months of painstaking research. The breadth and detail contained within the two volumes is mind-boggling, and I heartily recommend both to anyone researching anything about rock and pop.

Although Strong covers quite a bit of hip hop and dance music, there is sadly no equivalent of his glorious tomes that I could locate for soul, reggae, hip hop, disco or the many forms of post-house dance music. *The Penguin Encyclopedia of Popular Music*, edited by Donald Clarke, and *The Faber Companion to 20th Century Popular Music* by Phil Hardy and Dave Laing filled a few of the '70s soul and reggae gaps, but two particular internet websites – www.sonicnet.com and www.allmusic.com – saved my bacon when it came to disco obscurity and more contemporary black and dance music, from Hi-Tension to Missy Elliott. They sell the stuff they write about too, some of it wonderfully obscure, so I recommend a visit.

From there, I just need to acknowledge and express my gratitude to the writers of various books and mag features, plus the websites and the individuals who contributed info on the acts that fell through the gaps, or additional background for various entries. They are:

Rose Royce/'Car Wash' – www.artistdirect.com

The Trammps/'Disco Inferno' – www.aaeg.com/trammps.htm

The Clash/'Complete Control' and 'Armagideon Time' – 'Inside Stories (1976-1982)' by Kosmo Vinyl from the booklet inside the 'Clash On Broadway' boxed set (Epic/Legacy 1991)

Richard Hell & The Voidoids/'Blank Generation' – '1-2-3-4! Punk & New Wave 1976-1979' Boxed set booklet by Pete Gardiner (Universal)

David Bowie/'Heroes' and Iggy Pop/'The Passenger' – 'Trans-Europe Excess' by Stephen Dalton; magazine feature from Uncut Take 47, April 2001

Bee Gees/'Stayin' Alive' – 'You Lookin' At Me?' by Johnny Black, magazine feature from Mojo No. 90, May 2001

Sylvester/'You Make Me Feel (Mighty Real)' and Lipps Inc/ 'Funkytown' – www.andwedanced.com

Nick Lowe/'I Love The Sound Of Breaking Glass' – Ross Fortune

The Cure/'Killing An Arab' – *England Is Mine* by Michael Bracewell

Wire/'Outdoor Miner' – 'New Pop U.K.' by Paul Morley originally published in issue 20 of New York Rocker. Reprinted in *The Penguin Book Of Rock & Roll Writing*, edited by Clinton Heylin

The Jam/'The Eton Rifles' – *The Jam: A Beat Concerto* by Paolo Hewitt

Funky Four Plus One/'That's The Joint' – www.jayquan.com

ESG/'You're No Good' – Uncredited sleevenotes for 'ESG: A South Bronx Story' album (Universal Sound/Soul Jazz)

Laurie Anderson/'O Superman' – Sleevenotes for 'Talk Normal: The Laurie Anderson Anthology' (Warner Archives/Rhino) by Gillian G. Goar

Duran Duran/'Girls On Film' – 'A Salmon Screams' by Paul Morley; from *The Faber Book Of Pop* (Faber & Faber)

Trouble Funk/'Drop The Bomb' – www.warr.org/trouble.html

Grandmaster Flash & The Furious Five – Sleevenotes from 'Back To The Old School' boxed set by Grandmaster Flash, The Furious Five and Grandmaster Melle Mel, written by Lewis Dene

Odyssey/'Inside Out' – The Seventies Dance Music Performers Database at Http://izan.simplenet.com/odyssey.htm

Explainer/'Lorraine' – www.calypso-music.com

Afrika Bambaataa/'Planet Rock' – Sleevenotes from 'Tommy Boy's Greatest Beats' boxed set (Tommy Boy) by David Toop

Tenor Saw/'Ring The Alarm' – www.ReggaeFusion.com

Phuture/'Acid Tracks' – Sleevenotes for 'The House That Trax Built' (Trax) CD by Tim Barr

Whigfield/ 'Saturday Night' – http://amyl.simplenet.com/whigfield

Primal Scream/'Loaded' – Chris Salmon

Blueboy/'Remember Me' – Julie Bland at 9PR, Jeff Barrett at Heavenly, Kelvin Andrews at Pharm/Guidance

MJ Cole/'Sincere' – Angela Robertson at Talkin Loud, Tuse at Rhythm 'n' Business

Ol' Dirty Bastard/'Got Your Money' – Peter Hall at East West

Artful Dodger/'Re Rewind The Crowd Say Bo Selecta'
David Silverman at Slice

Finally, some more general thank yous. Firstly, to the various editors and journalist colleagues who've provided advice, support and conversation down the years without which this book etc, etc. Chris Wells, Adam Mattera, Adam Higginbotham, Andrew Perry, Laura Lee Davies, Dominic Wells, Ross Fortune, Peter Paphides, Chris Salmon, Arwa Haider, David Hutcheon, Charlotte Raven and David Peschek.

Secondly, I only began to write about music because I was so thrilled by the best writing about music. So thank you to Greil Marcus, Jon Savage, Charles Shaar Murray, Paul Morley, Ian Macdonald, Julie Burchill, Steven Wells, Sylvia Patterson and the late great Lester Bangs for inspiration.

Obviously, this book really would not have been written if it wasn't for *The Heart of Rock and Soul* by Dave Marsh. It is, for myself anyway, The Bible of rock journalism.

And finally, the slushy personal stuff. My mother Samantha, my son Matthew and my best friend Martha . . . I owe you, as always.

Last, but not least, to my wife Linsay, who put up with the obvious ill-effects of living with someone who could only talk in pop lyrics for four months, and still had enough generosity left over to help, advise and counsel me through the writing of this book. Cheers, Dollface.

If you have any comments or observations on, or corrections or criticisms of *This Is Uncool* – or you just want to tell us who J. Walter Negro is – you can reach the author on garrymulholland@aol.com.

GRANDMASTER AND MELLE MEL/WHITE LINES (DON'T DON'T DO IT)

THE STONE ROSES

ORE T 13
Featuring Fools Gold 9.53
**Includes special
limited edition
full colour
print**

WHAT THE WORLD IS WAITING FOR

FOOL'S GOLD/THE STONE ROSES

INTRODUCTION

In 1989, Penguin published a book called *The Heart of Rock and Soul – The 1001 Greatest Singles Ever Made*, by American rock critic and journalist Dave Marsh. The book attempts the near-impossible – a list, from 1 to 1001, from 1952 to 1988, of the single releases Marsh feels best represent the aesthetics and foundations of rock and soul music, with each entry accompanied by a short essay analysing its charms. It's a wonderful, nostalgic, inspiring read. But for this British boy from a younger generation, it felt incomplete. In short – where was my version of the story?

As an American child of the 1950s who lived through the upheavals and progressions of the '60s, Marsh understandably concentrates on American music. Indeed, *The Heart of Rock and Soul* stands as the ultimate primer for anyone who wants to know more about '50s and '60s rock 'n' roll, doo-wop, southern soul, country, gospel, Motown, garage rock and rhythm 'n' blues. But, as the book approaches the era that has shaped my attitude to pop, it runs aground. The Bowies and Ferrys of this

world are dismissed as arch art-rockers; punk's flurry of activity is largely summed up by the Sex Pistols, Clash and Elvis Costello; disco is there, but treated with suspicion; slop like UB40 and 'We Are the World' enters the pantheon, but The Smiths, the Pet Shop Boys, New Order et al. are ignored; and the whole enterprise struggles to come to terms with the impact of machine-driven dance music – a music that was already revolutionizing the British pop scene as the book was published. Marsh even admits, in his introduction, that he never understood funk. It's the singles book your dad would have written . . . a very hip and knowledgeable dad, but your dad nonetheless. *This Is Uncool* is both a response to Marsh, and something different.

The title comes from a 1977 entry in the book by The Rezillos. If the 23 or so years since the release of 'Anarchy in the UK' have seen one single transformation in the way Britain consumes pop culture, it is the corporate colonization of the word 'cool', a beatnik term that has come to be applied to

ADAM & THE ANTS/ANTMUSIC
PAGE 140

everything from internet gimmicks (cool tools) and grinning prime ministers (Cool Britannia) to anything that enables us to feel we're keeping up with current consumer trends, no matter how facile. The vast majority of the singles and artists in this book were brave enough to break out of the increasingly stultifying grip of 'cool', and reshape style, language and/or performance in their image. Usually, of course, this led to another narrow definition of cool that was co-opted and exploited until another adventurer or two happened along. But that's business, and anyway, the way The Rezillos' Fay Fife intones those three words lets the listener know that she's having the coolest time of her life. A contradiction that helped to make punk's best moments so thrilling.

The major difference between the Marsh book and this one lies in its order. Marsh produced an order of merit and simply began at No. 1 and worked down. *This Is Uncool* begins at 'Anarchy . . .', released in December 1976, and works chronologically through to December 1999 (I stop there because I think it takes at least 18 months before you can judge whether a single is truly timeless, or just an entertaining noise that has quickly dated). There are a few reasons for this. Firstly, the thought of trying to subjectively judge 500 records, coming up with a concrete reason why No. 361 is better than No. 362, seems like a hellish nightmare that would have probably, knowing my own propensity for procrastination, put another six months on the writing of the book. Which is also another factor, less important than the shorter period of time dealt with and the opportunities lent by design, in making it a list of 500 rather than 1001.

Secondly, the Marsh book seems to run slowly out of steam towards the end – why should we care about the 943rd best single ever? But thirdly, and most importantly, ordering the singles by their release dates enables me to tell a story. A story about how music has changed, how our *world* has changed in a couple of decades; about how bands reach a peak and dominate the art of the pop single for a few years – even months – before disappearing off the cultural map; about how certain records – 'Anarchy . . .', 'Planet Rock', 'Blue Monday', 'Smells Like Teen Spirit' – shout a message so powerful that pop culture has to face up to the challenge, or shrivel in the face of the new information. Pop and its surrounding language, codes and styles drive and are driven by society and politics, and listing the singles chronologically gives me the opportunity to put the noises in context – because pop without cultural context simply does not exist.

One obvious result of this approach is that certain years end up dominating the discussion. For reasons that I hope become apparent as we go along, the periods 1977–81 and 1987–90 produced many more thrilling singles than, say, 1992–95. Of course, this is one person's opinion and therefore entirely open to accusations of bias based on rose-tinted nostalgia. But then, laying into my obvious attachments to rave, rap, The Specials and The Smiths will hopefully be the most enjoyable bit. As with all personal lists, the desire to provoke a barney – with me, with your friends – is more important than trying to be 'definitive'.

This Is Uncool does echo Marsh in one important respect – the manner in which the chronological entries are laid out. First line: title and artist. Second line: production (with any remix/additional production details in brackets) and writing credits. Third line: record label, month and year of release, and highest UK chart position (with any reissue details in brackets). All chart info is taken from the year 2000 edition of *The Complete Book of the British Charts – Singles & Albums* (Omnibus Press) by Tony Brown, Jon Kutner and Neil Warwick. After that, it's down to the whys and wherefores. Another departure from Marsh is that the chronological order gives me a chance to write a short intro to each year's selections, in an attempt to put the singles into some form of political, musical and personal context.

Again, there were three major factors in the decision to begin with the December 1976 release of the Sex Pistols' 'Anarchy in the UK'. The first is down to the timing of particular changes in the singles market. The 12-inch single, with its wider grooves for louder volume and potential for extended playing time, made its first impact upon the British music scene in 1976/77, although limited edition 12-inch singles had been a staple for more progressive club DJs for a couple of years by then. Though most closely associated with disco, punk also used the 12-inch as a way to snare a burgeoning collectors' market hooked on the one-upmanship of limited editions. The same marketing ambition also led to the introduction of coloured vinyl and, eventually, picture discs. As The Television Personalities put it in their 1978 classic of satirical disillusion 'Part Time Punks': 'They want to buy the O Levels' single/Or "Read About Seymour"/But they're not pressed in red/So they buy The Lurkers instead.'

The second is generational – punk is where my own relationship with pop changed from liking stuff on *Top of the Pops* to complete obsession. I was 13 years old in the year that this book begins, and everything I now know about the pop that went before comes from retrospective reading, rather than contemporary involvement. I probably do listen far more to Dylan and Curtis Mayfield than the Buzzcocks or Abba now, but this is mere hindsight. These are the records that hit me as they happened, from the years I feel qualified to write about.

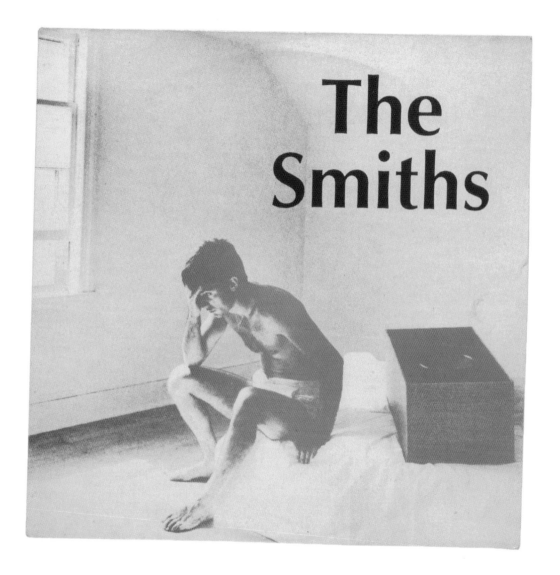

The Smiths

WILLIAM, IT WAS REALLY NOTHING/PLEASE, PLEASE, PLEASE, LET ME
GET WHAT I WANT/HOW SOON IS NOW?/THE SMITHS

The third is entirely personal. In 1976 my own life changed completely when, just as the youth culture movement that has meant most to me was boiling up nicely in various pockets of my London birthplace, my mother moved our family to a vapid, stereotypical 'New Town' called Peterborough. She had good reason. We'd been living in a rodent-infested flat in a house near Turnpike Lane in north London where the bath doubled as a kitchen table thanks to a piece of plywood, and we were suddenly in a brand-new three-bedroom house with a garden and central heating and *two toilets* and everything. But the city itself was a cultural vacuum. Nevertheless, my bitterness at not hanging out with Johnny and Malcolm down the King's Road is balanced by the knowledge that punk meant so much to me because I had absolutely nothing else going on. This was also the reason why I lived a second youth culture life as a disco boy – rejecting that as too mainstream would have meant halving any teenage wildlife Peterborough provided.

But all of this still begs the obvious question – why singles and not albums? There are, again, a few reasons, but I can't resist beginning with Marsh himself, in the opening of his introduction to *The Heart of Rock and Soul*:

'Why don't you write a book about the 1001 greatest albums?' somebody asked me before I'd barely begun. 'Because nobody goes around humming albums,' I answered without a pause.

That may seem glib, but it isn't. Our worship at the altar of the long-playing record is a distortion of music appreciation concocted by the music business itself. It is cheaper to manufacture albums, particularly on CD. To fit with this fact of business life, we've allowed ourselves to be convinced by two not entirely unrelated value judgements. Firstly, an album is a more 'serious' work, giving us a complete picture of where the artist is creatively and emotionally at time of release. Secondly, that cultural life is expensive and, as consumers, we must shop around for the value-for-money deal, and 70 minutes of music for £15 is obviously better value than £4 for 15 minutes.

If we're all honest with ourselves for a moment, we know that the majority of the albums we own contain two, maybe three tracks that we really love. And guess what? They're more often than not the singles. Apart from the depressing idea that consumers may see music in terms of yardage these days, there is also the simple truth that the great pop artist can tell you many more creative and emotional truths in three minutes than a mediocrity can in 70. Particularly as the single is specifically created to be played on the radio and reach people, which usually means that the artist has to stop contemplating his/her navel for a while and make some music *for us*. The only people whose favourite albums aren't greatest hits collections are music journalists and blokes who work in second-hand record shops. And I should know, having been both.

So what makes a great single? Well, I'm glad you asked. A great single stands alone from and transcends an artist's usual work. It uses every production trick in the book, without fear of accusations of gimmickry or novelty, to get on the radio or the club DJ's decks, to make it more than just a recording of a live performance. It must have hooklines, even when those hooklines subvert or ignore the singalong chorus norm. It should, whether it means to or not, say something striking about its chosen theme, even if it's an instrumental (music *does* talk). It should want to be a hit, even if it fails. It should, almost without exception, be made for people to listen to, rather than the artist to indulge themselves with. It should, when heard for the first time, induce the previously inattentive listener to stop what they are doing and exclaim, 'What the *fuck* is that?' It must be more than just an ad for an album, even when that is exactly what artist and record company intend it to be. It must *speak directly to you*.

Add to this my own personal Theory One of pop: *Everybody has one good single in them.* Yes, even me, probably. And it's those one-shots, ignored in the official histories of rock, that make pop the unpredictable, shocking, frighteningly stupid, and stupendously clever spectrum of communication that it is. Though it may be uncool to say so.

My final reason for wanting to write this book comes back to the incomplete feelings I mentioned earlier. When I go into a shop to buy a book about music, I find dozens of learned tomes by great American writers, delving into the history of their music and working out its meanings. I find hundreds of books by British writers, content to do no more than profile a currently popular rock band, as if the band in question exist in complete isolation from the world that created them. Outside of wonderful exceptions like Jon Savage's *England's Dreaming*, Paul Morley's *Ask*, Michael Bracewell's *England Made Me* and Simon Price's study of the Manic Street Preachers, I can rarely find a book that takes British pop seriously. Although this book doesn't just contain UK acts, the singles inside are the ones that built the rock, pop and dance landscapes that make Britain a music capital of the world, that provide a foundation, a reason, for a Radiohead, Spice Girls or Fatboy Slim to exist.

I want to go into a bookshop and find something that takes our pop history as seriously as Americans take theirs. If I can hum along to it, so much the better.

Garry Mulholland

I FEEL FOR YOU/CHAKA KHAN
PAGE 220

DEEE-LITE/GROOVE IS IN THE HEART

BEASTIE BOYS/INTERGALACTIC

PAGE 414

1976-77

1976-77

I wanna see some history.

In December 1976, the month that 'Anarchy in the UK' by the Sex Pistols was released, Jimmy Carter was elected President of the United States. Joan Baez joined a 30,000-strong peace march in central London organized by the women of the Ulster Peace Movement, who would win the Nobel Peace Prize the following year. Benjamin Britten died. The last episode of *Dixon of Dock Green* was aired. An angry visitor to the Tate Gallery poured blue dye over Low Sculpture, which consisted of 120 fire bricks laid in a rectangle. American guru of free-market economics Milton Friedman was awarded a Nobel Prize. Winnie Mandela was released from prison as South Africa got riots for Christmas. The year's biggest hit singles in the UK were revealed to be 'Dancing Queen' by Abba, 'Don't Go Breaking My Heart' by Elton John and Kiki Dee, and 'Save Your Kisses for Me' by The Brotherhood of Man. And Bill Grundy was suspended for his part in the *Today* show Sex Pistols fiasco. I'm sure various types of chocolate bars, kids' programmes, fashion horrors and fads in children's toys had an *enormous* cultural impact on various smug future C-list talking heads, but I don't remember them, and really couldn't give a shit. Call me an irony-free old fuckwit, but trying to raise one eyebrow just gives me face cramp, and I'm sure you're as bored as I am with that 'weren't we crap?' way of looking at the world. I mean, we probably were, but not for reasons that were anything to do with Spangles.

No, it's that boring old serious stuff that provided a context for sweeping changes in popular culture in the late 1970s. Although you may need a useful book of facts and a degree of hindsight to see it. When watching *The Filth and the Fury*, Julian Temple's brilliant, moving documentary on the Sex Pistols that came out in 2000, the only bit that didn't ring true to me was the beginning. Temple presented us with a near-apocalyptic vision of Britain in the mid-'70s that seemed like pure artistic licence. But I was only 12 in 1975 and probably too young to notice a country – a planet – in turmoil. In Britain, an impotent minority Labour government led by 'Uncle' Jim Callaghan was being bullied by still-powerful trade unions. Difficult to imagine now, I know. But a series of lightning strikes by workers from nationalized industries for astonishing pay rises (the miners wanted 63 per cent) reached blackly comic levels of symbolism in '77 when TV workers blacked out the state opening of Parliament, and undertakers went AWOL, leaving 800 bodies piled up in mounds. Cops clashed with secondary pickets at the Grunwick Film-Processing Plant, and public sympathy swung inexorably away from the unions, providing the foundations from which Margaret Thatcher's Tories would grind the unions into dust in the '80s. As always with the British, we didn't see what this really meant until it was far too late.

Meanwhile, as 1977 celebrated the Queen's Silver Jubilee, the first riot shields appeared on London's streets as police fought to protect National Front Nazis from the people they wanted to maim. The chief of strike-hit British Leyland resigned after making a speech referring to 'bribing wogs'. Oil-rich Arabs began buying up the parts of London the British establishment could no longer afford. The IRA bombed London. The Scots beat the English at Wembley and joyfully pulled up the hallowed turf as outnumbered police looked on, helpless. The English were feeling 'invaded' and I remember them talking about it. One thing I also recall is seeing National Front posters and stickers at Hornsey station near my home, and not grasping what it was they were getting at, with their stuff about fighting the IRA, and a better deal for the British working man. Punk might not have really achieved all we imagined it would, but the great thing it did achieve was to galvanize a significant part of the youth to join the Anti-Nazi League and Rock Against Racism, and not let (self-confessed) racists into positions of power by stealth. They still exist, of course. But, at this point, as the Tories lurched rightward and won by-election after local election, the racists were as close to a serious breakthrough as they would ever get.

So while records like 'God Save the Queen', 'Less Than Zero' and 'White Riot' talked about this England with a dread and honesty that pop had never heard before, the more salient point is that punk provided a safety valve, both for 'us' (jump around! Shout a lot! Form a band! Be too knackered and distracted to cause trouble!) and 'them', because swearing, spitting teen tribes made for better, easier-to-deal-with outrage than fascism, decay and the Yorkshire Ripper at home, or Pol Pot, Amin and Palestinian terrorists abroad. And, as for disco, well, it may not have been outrage as such. But the music and its makers did as much to educate us about black and gay culture in a less confrontational way. No one, as far as I know, ever used disco as a vehicle for fascist propaganda, unlike punk. And the massive *Saturday Night Fever*, with all its class confusion and underlying themes about the nature of masculinity, was a punk film with disco music anyway.

It's also strange how many icons of the old ways died in 1976–77. Elvis and Bolan, of course. But also Joan Crawford, Charlie Chaplin, Bing Crosby, Agatha Christie, Groucho Marx, Maria Callas, and dear old *Dixon of Dock Green*. An old world was passing away before our eyes, and although the young knew that change was desperately needed, no one had much faith that the new world would be any better.

Oh yes. *Star Wars* came out, and we were introduced to a new world of fake spectacle and merchandising dressed up as art. Many men of my age feel Chewbacca was more important than Johnny Rotten. And, as things turned out, they are probably right.

Honourable mentions: Ian Dury/'Sex & Drugs & Rock & Roll' (Stiff); Blondie/'Rip Her to Shreds' (Chrysalis); Deniece Williams/'Free' (CBS); Stevie Wonder/'I Wish' (Motown); Marvin Gaye/'Got To Give It Up' (Motown); David Bowie/ 'Be My Wife' and 'Sound and Vision' (both RCA Victor); The Commodores/'Easy' (Motown); Eddie and The Hotrods/'Do Anything You Wanna Do' (Island); Subway Sect/'Nobody's Scared/Don't Split It' (Braik); The Saints/'This Perfect Day' (EMI); Keith Rowe/'Groovy Situation' (Island); Odyssey/'Native New Yorker' (RCA Victor).

ANARCHY IN THE UK

SEX PISTOLS

PRODUCED BY CHRIS THOMAS/WRITTEN BY
PAUL COOK, STEVE JONES, GLEN MATLOCK AND
JOHNNY ROTTEN
EMI/NOVEMBER 1976
UK CHART: 38

The best thing about 'Anarchy . . .' – the thing that makes it so other, so removed from the rock of the time (hell, the rock of *now*) – is that it's really very, very funny about very serious stuff. I mean, Johnny Rotten ushers us into a brave new world with, of all things, a Sid James cackle. He may go on to tell us that he is an antichrist, but he could just as easily be goosing a passing nurse.

The opening of the record is genius – a testament to the awareness of all concerned (but particularly Rotten, guitarist Steve Jones and producer Chris Thomas) that live hard rock would not be enough to turn the heads of rock fans brought up on The Who, or Bowie, or Roxy Music (whom Thomas also produced). So the wall-of-sound guitars possess a primordial filth that was more or less ditched for later recordings, Lydon's voice is abnormally high in the mix, full of now-or-never ('Rrrright! NOW!') sore-throat relish, and the first few lines are black comedy, on the edge of cartoon: 'I am an antichrist/I am an anarchist/Don't know what I want but I know how to get it/I wanna DES-TROY . . . [pause] . . . PASSERS-BY!!!' Having established the knowing humour with that infamously wrong Christ/chist rhyme, the chorus is an agonized teen wail more in keeping with the unrequited-love anthems of the '50s than the kind of violent machismo needed to destroy people in the street. Even though 'Anarchy . . .' contains the roughest din (the muddy disco handclaps that enter around two minutes in, Jones's endless swooping bomber overdubs, Rotten's vocal levels all over the place) of all the Pistols' singles, it is also the catchiest tune, the friendliest beckoning-in, the closest they came to High Camp. Which makes it all the more perfect to usher in an era where the arm-wrestles between commerce and credibility, integrity and cynicism, glamour and grit, analysis and dancing, rebellion and acquiescence, sincerity and irony, saw pop – in the famous words of the former *NME* journalist David Quantick – eat itself.

CAR WASH

ROSE ROYCE

PRODUCED BY NORMAN WHITFIELD/WRITTEN BY
NORMAN WHITFIELD
MCA/DECEMBER 1976
UK CHART: 9

Oh, how I wished – in the spirit of the perfect punk/disco starting-point and all that – that my mind had played tricks on me and that 'Anarchy in the UK' and Donna Summer's 'I Feel Love' had been released on the same day. Sadly, nothing in history or pop is ever that simple. Still, this orchestral disco anthem from a blaxploitation movie soundtrack isn't a bad place to begin talking about the birth of a new dancefloor language. Disco might not have been exactly new by the end of 1976 (take your pick from George McRae's 'Rock Your Baby', anything by Barry White, anything uptempo from Gamble & Huff's Philadelphia International label, or even James Brown's 'Sex Machine' as disco's alma mater), but the next few years would bear witness to both its commercial and creative heights, and its apparent downfall from a mix of over-exposure, fickle fashion and the (homophobic, I still think, but more about disco and queerness later) antipathy of rock fans that manifested itself in America's 'disco sucks' backlash. Of course, disco didn't die. It just called itself house instead and rock fans were too thick to notice.

The reason that 'Car Wash' fits the new-thang bill is because of that extraordinary handclap intro. It may be a simple, almost football-crowd-friendly clapalong riff, but no matter how many times I hear this, I'm still taken by surprise when the band and orchestra kick in. Obviously, it fits. But it doesn't. It deliberately fucks with the feet of the ordinary dancer, throws you off course, revels in its syncopation sophistication, much like the R&B of 2001. And Kenji Brown's mean, impatient-to-get-on guitar – a mix of flicked wah-wah growls and stabbed yelps – ain't giving any clues.

From then on it's post-Motown funk ecstasy, as you would expect from the great psych-soul innovator and Motown alumnus Whitfield, and a Los Angeles band that learned their chops backing Edwin Starr and The Temptations. The movie was a sly and good-natured ghetto comedy set in, you know, a car wash, and the first line sets the film's scene, makes you laugh, and, in the smiling soul tones of vocalist Gwen Dickey, stands alone as a deadpan poor man's joke: 'You might not ever get rich/But let me tell you it's better than digging a ditch.' Not that far, in comic timing if not in attitude, from John

ANARCHY IN THE UK/SEX PISTOLS

Rotten's outrageous opening rhyme on 'Anarchy . . .'. Indeed, contrast the two and you have a neat summing-up of the 'political' difference between punk and disco. Rotten seeks to transcend squalor and disillusion through in-your-face rebellion and the assertion of his strength as an individual; Whitfield and Dickey seek to survive them through resigned good humour and the physical and/or communal release of dancing.

Rose Royce had a few more big UK hits – the best of which was the graceful ache of 'Love Don't Live Here Anymore' – and were inevitably swept away by younger, harder dance noises. They pop up on disco nostalgia package tours, forever pickled in kitsch. But that's OK. Let me tell you, it's better than digging a ditch.

SPIRAL SCRATCH EP

BUZZCOCKS

PRODUCED BY MARTIN 'ZERO' HANNETT/ALL
COMPOSITIONS WRITTEN BY HOWARD DEVOTO AND
PETE SHELLEY
NEW HORMONES/JANUARY 1977
DID NOT CHART

Although Jake Riviera and Dave Robinson's Stiff label had already established itself as a punk independent in London, this seminal (and that's a word I'm going to be trying to avoid from now on, I promise) collection of four short, sharp, rough-arsed fits of hysteria from Manchester truly kicked off the burst of post-punk activity we came to know as 'indie'. This isn't simply because Richard Boon's New Hormones label was entirely separate from the dominant major record companies, but because the record is so lo-fi, so radio-unfriendly, yet so incendiary in form and content, that it still sounds like another music from a very different kitchen even now. It also launched three separate pop careers that play prominent parts in this book, at least in the early chapters.

Singer/lyricist Howard Devoto (formerly Howard Trafford) is the star of the show. A rapidly balding nerd with a distant, creepy, I-know-what-you're-thinking demeanour, what Devoto seems to take from the Pistols (he and Pete Shelley were famously responsible for organising a Sex Pistols gig at Manchester's Lesser Free Trade Hall that was attended by all of Joy Division/New Order, Morrissey, Mark E. Smith, Tony Wilson and almost everyone else who went on to make Manchester the music capital of Britain) is the testimony of a man forever doomed to wait while life passes him by. He

twitches and jerks and waits for the phone to 'ring-a-ring-a-ring-a-fucking-ding' until left with no option but to twitch and jerk some more. His bookish intellectualism, which would be given freer rein in his next band, Magazine, is there in the precocious wordplay of second track 'Time's Up', but on these four songs it's buried beneath a sexual rage and amphetamine energy that transforms Rotten's confident fury into a comedy of stained-sheet neurosis. None of the songs are actually about wanking exactly, but, if you've ever tried to masturbate while on a speed comedown and emerged three hours later with nothing but a cramped claw where your hand used to be, then you'll know what Devoto sounds like on this record.

Guitarist/tunesmith Pete Shelley (formerly Peter McNeish), as the sleeve informs us, plays something called 'starway guitar'. He makes melodies here out of barbed wire and rusty tin, reaching a peak on the EP's anthem 'Boredom', where, somehow, deliriously happy pop is created out of something that sounds exactly like boredom. I still don't know how he did this, but that definitely sarcastic and self-deprecating two-note guitar solo has more than a little to do with it.

Producer 'Zero', who would later become an urban Manc Phil Spector, producing Joy Division, Magazine, Happy Mondays and many more under his own name before his death in 1991, takes the barely coherent insanity of 'Breakdown' and 'Friends of Mine' and creates a trebly maelstrom of collapsing pop, somehow keeping together a new noise that is being driven by the bizarre, tumbling punctuations of John Maher, one of rock's most original and underrated drummers. Put it all together and you get the start of something seamier, seedier, yet far more personal and definitively pop than the Pistols, The Clash and the rest of London's art-punk. It still sounds like nothing else on earth.

MORE THAN A FEELING

BOSTON

PRODUCED BY JOHN BOYLAN AND TOM SCHOLZ/
WRITTEN BY TOM SCHOLZ
EPIC/JANUARY 1977
UK CHART: 22

Nope, nothing to do with punk and disco, everything to do with standing straddle-legged in a private place, tossing back your imaginary blond mane, and deciding whether to take lead or rhythm duties on your trusty air guitar tonight. This monstrous power ballad anthem also serves as a timely reminder that punk

didn't sweep away air-brushed radio rock (oddly, it took hip-hop to do that), and that, when it's done right, AOR remains one of the most joyous sounds ever produced in the name of driving down the open freeway of the mind.

Tom Scholz was a 30-year-old muso whiz from Ohio who set up his own studio in – wa-hey! – Boston, and set about making perfect session-muso rock. Everything else he and his mates did was bloody horrible. But for one memorable moment, he concocted a tableau of non-specific big-rock angst that invented Nirvana's 'Smells Like Teen Spirit' and every other rock record that has a crunching, ever-circling A-B-C-B-constructed guitar riff that you can't get out of your head. The best bit could be the way the elegant acoustic guitar fades in at the beginning with pretty portent; or the second that the powerchord riff divebombs in; or the moment when the ludicrous baroque twin-lead solo rears up like a spooked nag before stopping dead; or the bit where Brad Delp's castrato morphs into another screeching lead; or the way those harmonies bliss out over the fade while an unsung session hero called Jim Masdea becomes The World's Greatest Funk Rock Drummer for just a few seconds or so. And then there are the handclaps. Note to producers: do you have any idea how many great records get made even better by robotic handclaps? Switch on the handclap machine. Go on. You know you want to.

Admittedly, my irrational love for this record has led me to try to find a hidden meaning behind all the guff about Mary Ann and slipping away and that line that sounds a bit like 'When I'm tired of taking coke' but clearly isn't. But there really isn't one. It just rocks.

BOOGIE NIGHTS

HEATWAVE

PRODUCED BY BARRY BLUE/WRITTEN BY
ROD TEMPERTON
GTO/JANUARY 1977
UK CHART: 2

You'd be forgiven for thinking that Heatwave were just another bunch of disco bods in Crimplene flares who had their few novelty moments before riding off into the supper-club sunset. But you'd be very wrong. Not only were this Brit-based, multiracial big band a breeding-ground for future top-rank writing and producing talents (Rod Temperton went on to write for Quincy Jones, Michael Jackson and George Benson, while later members J.D. Nicholson and Derek Bramble joined The

Commodores and worked with Bowie respectively), but their history was blighted by tragedy. Guitarist Jesse Whitten was stabbed to death, while bassist Mario Mantese and bandleader Johnny Wilder both quit performing after serious car crashes.

The weirdest Heatwave fact, though, is that their finest moment was produced by third-division early '70s glam pop star Barry Blue. Which means we have to forgive him for 'Dancin' on a Saturday Night', because this is a wonderful, deft pop-funk groove – muscular yet swish, right from its suave brush-jazz intro, through its deliciously silly Moog solo, to the overall feeling of sexy disco danger that it effortlessly creates as soon as needle hits the groove. They named a film after it, and they were right.

NEAT NEAT NEAT

THE DAMNED

PRODUCED BY NICK LOWE/WRITTEN BY
BRIAN JAMES
STIFF/FEBRUARY 1977
DID NOT CHART

This is where I cite my own personal Theory One concerning The Pop Single. Which is that, given the right time, place, producer and level of enthusiasm, anyone can make a classic single. Yes, you. Even me. Anyone. You don't need the musical talent, nor the all-round composing skill, nor even the big wodge of record company cash needed to make a great album or be a transcendant live act. You need one brilliant idea and someone to give you a platform and a shot of confidence. Exhibit One for the defence: this bunch of London pub rock cabaret bandwagon-jumpers, who not only beat the Sex Pistols to the making of the first UK punk single (the jolly 'New Rose' from November 1976), but gave us a second single that stands as one of punk's many outstanding one-offs – a pure burst of malevolent, magnificently styled rock 'n' roll mania.

Dave Vanian's vocals are little more than a nasal yap. The drums of Rat Scabies (we 14-year-olds were impressed by such names. It was a very unsexy time) are a Keith Moon blur of pissy cymbals. Captain Sensible's hypnotically thrusting two-note bassline underwrites the whole venture. But guitarist Brian James is the star, thrashing a bewildered Chuck Berry to within an inch of his life, speed-freaked, lunging forward at the end of each line, unleashing a solo that seems to release every minute spent practising into a headlong blur of joyful fury and ambition. It sounds as if influential pub rock don Lowe's job here was to stop the truck tipping over the cliff.

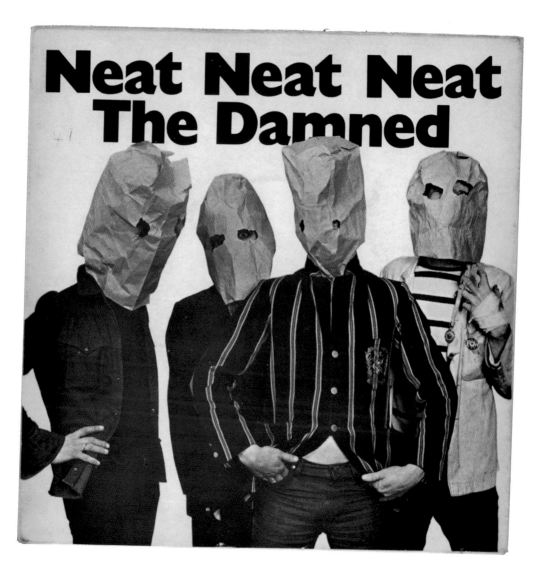

NEAT NEAT NEAT/THE DAMNED
PAGE 26

The Damned, together and separately, had bigger hits, but no comparable masterpieces. Possibly because 'Neat Neat Neat' wasn't the sound of their running jump into the future, but ours.

KNOWING ME, KNOWING YOU

ABBA

PRODUCED BY BENNY ANDERSSON AND
BJÖRN ULVAEUS/WRITTEN BY BENNY ANDERSSON,
BJÖRN ULVAEUS AND STIG ANDERSON
EPIC/FEBRUARY 1977
UK CHART: 1

A-ha. Oh, don't groan at me like that. You know that as soon as you read the title that's what you yelped in your head. It's a mark of good comedy that it can take something already so famous and recast it as something profoundly silly. But the achievement of Steve Coogan as Alan Partridge is all the more notable when you remember that the first line of this beautiful tragedy is: 'No more carefree laughter/Silence ever after.' Transfer that into the body of, say, Joy Division's supposedly more serious 'Love Will Tear Us Apart' and you wouldn't miss a beat.

Divorce pop – invented by Fleetwood Mac circa *Rumours*, picked up later by The Police and Phil Collins – was taken to defeatist extremes by Abba. Andersson's and Ulvaeus's sublime skills as arrangers, producers and writers means that, no matter how sumptuous this swirling tapestry of warm bass, cold keyboards and the occasional crashing guitar gets, it never distracts too much from the elegant agony of the theme. The Valium-dulled resignation of the pay-off line – 'Knowing me, knowing you, it's the best I can do' – still sighs with the effort of having tried and failed to keep a dead thing breathing, like a nurse switching off a life-support machine. And one shouldn't forget the glassy-eyed vocal perfection of Agnetha Fältskog and Anni-Frid Lyngstad, strolling through their empty house while gently nagging internal voices – 'This time we're through – we're *really* through' – taunt them in disbelief at the failure and waste of it all. You can keep your Leonard Cohen, friend. It doesn't get any sadder – lyrically or sonically – than this.

LESS THAN ZERO

ELVIS COSTELLO

PRODUCED BY NICK LOWE/WRITTEN BY
ELVIS COSTELLO
STIFF/MARCH 1977
DID NOT CHART

I had no awareness of this record when it came out. Punk, at this point, was just something about spitting, swearing and swastikas that turned up in the tabloids, and it would be another few months before 'God Save the Queen' opened a door I didn't know was locked, was even there, and made me obsessed with everything labelled 'punk'. Even now, you don't have to be a musicologist to hear that this strikingly gawky, prematurely old, terrifyingly bright Irish Liverpudlian from a musical family had little to do with angry three-chord thrashings. His first single begins with a clean, clear Latin-pop riff straight out of a half-remembered Ritchie Valens number. It is, despite label and producer, definitely not The Damned. The backing-band, Clover, later found fame as Huey Lewis and The News, which has some weird circular Bret Easton Ellis logic that you'll appreciate if you've read both *Less Than Zero* and *American Psycho*.

Anyway, I digress. And that's partly because, after more than 20 years, I don't really understand this song. It turns up at a tidy No. 203 in Marsh's *The Heart of Rock and Soul*, and he writes, in the confident manner of someone who knows it as fact, that 'Less Than Zero' is about a young couple making out in one of their parents' houses while 1930s British fascist leader Oswald Mosley and his sister babble poison on TV, angling for a comeback in the era of the National Front. From there, as Costello (originally named Declan McManus) sings with an ever more skilled desperation, we get the queasy feeling that the boy is snapping at Mosley's line, as he seethes, 'There is a vacancy waiting in the English through-and-through.' There is a catchy, almost celebratory hookline chant of 'Hey red', like some weasly mutation of Harry Belafonte's calypso. It's a kitchen-sink scenario pregnant with fear for the future, oozing bad sex and grasping at straws. It's essentially, I think, the same warning as 'God Save the Queen', but with shinier shoes, a bigger love for perfect garage pop, a bleak cynicism worthy of Graham Greene, and an even greater, more timeless sense of dread.

WHITE RIOT/THE CLASH

PAGE 30

MARQUEE MOON

TELEVISION

PRODUCED BY ANDY JOHNS AND
TOM VERLAINE/WRITTEN BY TOM VERLAINE
ELEKTRA/ASYLUM/MARCH 1977
UK CHART: 30

Tom Verlaine, Richard Lloyd, Fred Smith and Billy Ficca emerged blinking from the punk womb gloom of New York's CBGBs and, like fellow NY cellar-dwellers Blondie, Talking Heads and Patti Smith, made a music that has little to do with punk as we think we know it (the one recognizable punk in the band, dissolute, ripped-T-shirt poet poster-boy Richard Hell, had already gone his own way). Indeed this – their most famous song, the title track of their first and best album, their Big Footnote in rock history – had to be split in two for a 7-inch single, being over nine minutes long. Punk heresy.

It begins with one of the most insidious twin guitar riffs in history – Lloyd just chopping two chords reggae style, Verlaine telegraphing a glowing, chiming fanfare – before Verlaine yelps, panic stricken: 'I remember how the darkness doubled/I recall that lightning struck itself/I was listening, listening to the rain/I was hearing, hearing something else.'

I bought this from the bargain bin at Boots some months after its release because the equally punk-obsessed music press told me to. And, frankly, I was bewildered, especially at the first break into the intensely lovely jazz-ballad melody before the chorus. Where was the shouting? The anti-authoritarian tantrums? The ramalamadingdong geetars? I mean, weren't these guys from the same place as the Ramones? Where wuz da brat and da baseball bat?

But slowly, surely, I extracted myself from my small, raucous world and placed myself in Television's dark but pretty one. I recognised the Patti Smith influence, especially in the halting but harsh way Verlaine sang the word 'hesitating'. And I fell in love with 'Marquee Moon', as all (mainly) boys did who were grateful for punk, but still weren't entirely convinced that progressive rock really had to be boring. This song, more than any other, made sure the . . . ahem . . . thinking man's rock circle remained unbroken.

I was never entirely sure what a marquee moon was, or what, exactly, the song was about. I've never read a Verlaine explanation of the stark, slightly surreal, Dylanesque lyric, and after 25 years, don't want my version ruined now. But, considering the stuff in the third verse about entering graveyards in Cadillacs, I've always figured it's about rock 'n' roll's

relationship with dem nasty drugs and the art of choosing life over death. The reason the protagonist decides to reject the death trip is here in Verlaine and Lloyd's guitars, driving each other to a constantly climbing, at first hesitant and then uninhibited (but still restrained – no pointless from-the-crotch twiddling here) state of grace, as the long improv engulfs you with its gradually evolving ascending scales, aiming for the sky. In the long version, it dissolves, and begins all over again with the funky strut of the song's opening, lending that feeling of an endless rumination, but only once the guitars have left you communing with merrily chirping birds of paradise. It's a high-art conceit, but one the song, the performance and the sound easily sustain.

'Marquee Moon' is one of pop's greatest journeys from darkness to light, a perfect example of why hard rock doesn't have to be either aggressive or grim. A tough trick and a legendary record that, despite inventing the first three Echo and The Bunnymen albums, remains a balance of virtuosity, mood and melody that no other band has managed to pull off in quite the same way. Not even Television themselves. The quartet never quite recovered, split too soon, reformed, became ordinary.

WHITE RIOT

THE CLASH

PRODUCED BY MICKY FOOTE/WRITTEN BY
JOE STRUMMER AND MICK JONES
CBS/MARCH 1977
UK CHART: 38

The weirdest thing about listening to 'White Riot' now is the speed thing. Nah, not that. I mean that, at the time, it seemed recklessly, comically, manically fast. Yet now, after the coming and going of everything from speed metal to gabba techno to breakneck breakbeats, The Clash's first step into legend sounds almost sedate. Almost.

Unlike the clued-in hipsters – and even Joe Strummer, Mick Jones and Paul Simonon themselves – it was The Clash who indirectly led me to the Pistols, rather than vice versa. I heard 'White Riot' on Capital Radio.[1] I was stunned by the din, frightened by the intensity, and perturbed by the use of the word 'white'. Remember the swastikas? I decided to find out more, read the music press instead of the tabloids for info, was reassured it wasn't all some kind of Nazi pop, bought 'God Save the Queen'.

Taking part in an anti-police riot in the counter-culture centre that was west London's Notting Hill provoked Strummer's guttural howl of white-boy frustration. This, quite aside from the straining-at-the-leash two-chord thrash and the *Dixon of Dock Green* police siren, was something new in British pop, the first jealous whine of the wigga (Mick Jagger and Rod Stewart just convinced themselves they were black. When it suited them). The punks smoked dope, listened to reggae, saw Jimmy Cliff's definitive outlaw-chic martyr performance in the *The Harder They Come*, and worshipped Jamaicans for, supposedly, being everything white people (or, more accurately, their mum and dad) weren't. In Clashworld, whitey is servile and compliant, while supercool and fearless black men whup cop arse. So now it was our turn. Naïve, simplistic, deluded . . . yeah, probably. And no, The Clash never fought our class war for us and Strummer turned out to be John Mellor, public school-educated son of a diplomat and lapsed hippy, and Mick Jones still lived with his gran. But, with the addition of *that* sleeve – the trio lined up facing a wall in waiting-to-be-frisked pose, working man's overalls sprayed with slogans including the immortal 'STEN GUNS IN KNIGHTSBRIDGE' – this record encapsulated a young boy's rebel fantasies in grimy '70s England just as Brando had done for the white teen back in *The Wild One* in the '50s. Every time I feel I'm getting too cynical, I put this on and regress happily to a time when I could, maybe, have had the guts to do what it asked of me.

'1977', the even more stentorian B-side, is included for the pained howl 'No Elvis, Beatles or The Rolling Stones – IN 1977!!!' Which, in hindsight, was stoopid, funny and necessary.

TRANS-EUROPE EXPRESS

KRAFTWERK
PRODUCED BY RALF HÜTTER AND FLORIAN SCHNEIDER/WRITTEN BY RALF HÜTTER AND EMIL SCHULT
CAPITOL/APRIL 1977
DID NOT CHART

So, while punk garage bands rose to meet the Sex Pistols' challenge, and disco's producers worked on a new pop perfection, what was happening to the old guard? Specifically, those who had already established a very European kind of art-rock and, even if they did have to adapt to survive an incoming rush of new ideas, weren't about to pretend they couldn't play and shake a rather-too-elegant fist at The Man nor learn The Disco Duck?[2] The answer lies with this single, which, despite being, arguably, the single most influential record in this book,

initially sank without trace. Because, as so few of us were aware, one of the oddest yet most inspiring instances of cultural exchange in pop history had already ensued, and the 'Trans-Europe Express' single and album was/is the central point where all these past and future lines crossed. I'll try and keep it brief.

Ralf Hütter and Florian Schneider from Dusseldorf, Germany, form an 'experimental' electronic band in 1971. Along with other progressive (in the best sense of that much abused word) German groups such as Can, Faust, and Neu!, their mission is to forge an indigenous rock music that relies less on American blues and more upon a specifically European musical tradition. The first internationally successful product of this 'Krautrock' (and that's the only time I'm ever gonna use that horrible term) movement was 'Autobahn' by Kraftwerk themselves. A 22-minute epic on the delights of speeding on a motorway, complete with gently undulating, fully electronic instrumentation, distant and precise android vocals, and a soothing melody pitched halfway between Euro classicism and classic rock hook, it was distilled into three beautiful minutes for radio purposes, and was a 1975 hit in both Britain and America.

David Bowie, among others, was smitten. Having tried a bleached take on American soul for *Young Americans*, he reacted immediately and pinched some of Kraftwerk's distant Eurocentrism for the following year's *Station to Station* album, particularly on the title track, which begins with an electronically generated impression of a chugging train. Kraftwerk nicked the idea back for 'Trans-Europe Express'. Bowie and his friend Iggy Pop, realizing that they would probably die if they stayed in Hollywood's decadent cocaine hell any longer, decamp to Berlin to find a new *modus operandi* for their next records. They invite Brian Eno, formerly of Roxy Music, to help out. Having formed a mutual admiration society by proxy, the Bowie clan and Kraftwerk hang out. As Hütter informs us rather proudly here: 'From station to station to Dusseldorf city/Meet Iggy Pop and David Bowie.' Chuffed at the tribute, Bowie and Iggy promptly go and make some of their best-ever music, both standing out from the punks (to whom both were heroes of very different kinds) and helping the more ambitious punks locate a left turn ahead. Eno removes the beats from Kraftwerk's lustrous sweep and invents ambient.

Meanwhile, some black kids from The Bronx get hold of 'Trans-Europe Express' and are beguiled by its glistening take on their own funk backbeats. It becomes an underground fave on the emerging hip-hop scene before a white hippy producer, Arthur Baker, steals the whole thing, beefs it up, gets some local faces to holler over the top of it, and gives it back to black America as 'Planet Rock', inventing beat-box electro and helping inspire house in the process. At the same time, some other black kids from Detroit also fall in love with 'Trans-Europe . . .'. But to them it is the sadness in the machine melodies, rather than the beat, that fascinates, seeming eerily reminiscent of the sadness of their own city as it reels and dissolves in the wake of the death of its car factories. The music sounds like the boarded-up buildings, like the cars that aren't built anymore. They go away and invent techno.

And then there are the futurists. And the new romantics. And an Italian pop genius called Giorgio Moroder who had obviously been listening real hard all along. And the fact that every piece of synthetic dance music produced in Europe now gets labelled, not 'trans', but 'trance'. And if you really need me, after all that, to tell you how awesome this record still actually *sounds*, then you must be one of those old-fashioned guitar dinosaurs my mother used to warn me about.

SHEENA IS A PUNK ROCKER

RAMONES

PRODUCED BY TONY BONGIOVI AND T. ERDELYI/
WRITTEN BY THE RAMONES
SIRE/MAY 1977
UK CHART: 22

Fuck. Not just handclaps, but tambourine and sleigh-bells *and* handclaps, bub. NY's Johnny, Joey, Dee Dee and Tommy Ramone may be the ultimate punk band, but they were also the punk band that made their music out of an undying love of, rather than a sneering contempt for, Great Radio Pop. Despite the unfortunate fact that radio at the time really didn't want pop that sounded like the malformed runt at the end of your street herding buffalo through a sweet shop. I mean, what the hell is a 'pung roggher' anyway?

The Ramones' own greatest single creases up with joy at how many bits of The Beach Boys and Phil Spector it manages to round up and pummel the living shit out of. It is about simple outsider heroism, of course, because when the gorgeous Sheena saw those sick kids greasing up their surfboards and trooping off to the discothèque (probably Annabelle's in Peterborough. You had to wear a tie. The girls were nothing like Sheena), well, she just couldn't stay. She had to break away. Don't you see? It was a matter of survival.

GOD SAVE THE QUEEN

SEX PISTOLS

PRODUCED BY CHRIS THOMAS/WRITTEN BY
PAUL COOK, STEVE JONES, GLEN MATLOCK AND
JOHNNY ROTTEN
VIRGIN/MAY 1977
UK CHART: 2

Huh – No. 2, my arse. But, whatever, as I mentioned before, I bought 'God Save the Queen' on spec, felt dead hard, took it home, put it on, and said, 'Go on – you've got three minutes – say something outrageous.' And then I was utterly shocked. This enormous fucking wall of guitar just kept going 'WUH WUH-WUH WUH!!!' over and over again like some heavy-duty military torture implement. Then, after about two minutes of stroking my chin and trying to like it, I realized that the needle was stuck. I blushed a blush that still makes my face hot, nudged the arm, and stood there while my life was irrevocably changed.

It was the voice, mainly. I guess I'd expected something macho and bullying. But instead there was this . . . *man-child*, this harbinger of hitherto unseen doom who had this gift for letting you know that, in fact, you'd known this stuff all along. This wasn't his wisdom, or insight, or prophecy . . . it was yours, go on, take it. *Use* it. Just in a voice. Weird.

And those words. 'The fascist regime/That made you a moron/Potential H-bomb.' How could anyone have imagined he meant Liz? For the rest of the song – aided by Jones who we now know didn't have a clue what Rotten was on about and didn't much care as long as he got his dick sucked and got off the dole, but Jesus, that sound, that solo, is so fucking *mean* – Rotten faces up to a brick wall of history, politics, apathy, class fear, a whole country still suffering from an imperial hangover, and just crashes right through, grinning, fearless, not burdened but liberated by what he's discovered about it all. 'We mean it, *maaaan*,' he sneers at a stray hippy as he speeds past. You failed. We won't. Who knew? And then the punchline. No future. No future for you. Who, me? Them? Her? Why does he sound so inspired by such a dire warning?

The safety pin through Liz's nose on the sleeve, courtesy of Jamie Reid. Glen Matlock going the extra mile to make it as catchy as Slade. Chris Thomas's mighty production, oft-copied, never matched in a rock 'n' roll context. McLaren's and – yes! – Richard Branson's brave, foolish timing as Britain celebrated something called a Silver Jubilee that Rotten exposed as a contemptuous insult. The beatings Rotten and Cook took for saying the unsayable and refusing to back down. This stuff

GOD SAVE THE QUEEN/SEX PISTOLS

really used to mean something, you know. But you had to meet it halfway. Give the needle a nudge, and not get embarrassed when you realized you were laughing, and crying too.

If punk and disco did start to talk to each other – and, in the music of 1979–81 and intermittently thereafter, they undoubtedly did – then here is where the conversation began.

DISCO INFERNO

THE TRAMMPS
PRODUCED BY RON KERSEY/WRITTEN BY
LEROY GREEN AND RON 'HAVE MERCY' KERSEY
ATLANTIC/MAY 1977
UK CHART: 7

In 1966, the black community of Watts in Los Angeles, provoked by yet another violent episode with the L.A.P.D. and the general misery of their environment, set their neighbourhood on fire. White riot, I wanna riot. A local DJ called The Magnificent Montague, playing soul and R&B as the streets burned outside his studio, kept uttering three words, his established catchphrase: 'Burn, baby, burn.' The three words spread like brushfire from coast to coast through a black nation that was as close to armed uprising as it ever had been or would be. As copycat riots broke out, and the Black Panthers and the Nation of Islam organized, 'Burn, baby, burn' became a not-so-secret catchphrase in the Afro-American ghetto.

Just over ten years later, a Philadelphia soul big band formed in 1972 around the nucleus of Jimmy Ellis, Harold 'Doc' Wade, Stanley Wade and Earl Young recorded their biggest hit. 'Disco Inferno' was picked for, rather than plucked from, the *Saturday Night Fever* soundtrack, which wasn't released in the UK until March 1978. Among all the elegant dancefloor confections on the soundtrack, it stands out like a subversive sore thumb. 'Burn, baby, burn,' it hollers triumphantly, to another time and place. 'BURN, BABY, BURN!'

Of course, it could just be fond imagining from an old punk's perspective. Having had a few hits and jobbed around the Philly scene with Philadelphia house band T.S.O.P. and the equally disco-influential Salsoul Orchestra, The Trammps and writers Green and Kersey might have just have recalled a catchphrase and cynically recycled it for pop hook purposes. But Jimmy Ellis's gruff, thrilled passion and the words he sings with a wild glee suggest otherwise: 'Satisfaction/Came in a chain reaction/I couldn't get enough/So I had to self-destruct/The heat was on/Risin' to the top/That is where the spot got hot! . . . Burn the mutha down!' The second time he screams 'SAAA-TIS-FAC-SHUN!!!', fear and desperation infuse the joy for just a second. You can smell the smoke from 1966, and it's no hallucination.

ALISON

ELVIS COSTELLO
PRODUCED BY NICK LOWE/WRITTEN BY
ELVIS COSTELLO
STIFF/MAY 1977
DID NOT CHART

Costello's name, look and angry young man stance might have allowed him to catch a ride with punk, but releasing the new wave's first love ballad put clear blue (eyed soul) water between himself and the garage band maelstrom unleashed by the Sex Pistols. From its ringing, romantic guitar intro to the final 'My aim is true' fade-out, this is based on an already ancient idea of American soft rock. But the story of Alison is anything but soft, as Costello sets the template for what would become his peak years' major theme – failed or failing relationships and what he later called 'emotional fascism'. The unrequited love here turns to pure bile and, even worse, pity, as the tenderness in the delivery becomes increasingly cruel in its self-righteousness. And of course, there are unforgettable lines, of which 'I don't know if you are loving somebody/I only know it isn't mine' just happens to be the best.

CHINESE ROCKS/BORN TO LOSE

THE HEARTBREAKERS
BOTH PRODUCED BY SPEEDY KEEN AND THE
HEARTBREAKERS/'CHINESE ROCKS' WRITTEN BY
RICHARD HELL, DEE DEE RAMONE, JERRY NOLAN AND
JOHNNY THUNDERS/'BORN TO LOSE' WRITTEN BY
JOHNNY THUNDERS
TRACK/MAY 1977
DID NOT CHART

Even The Heartbreakers' only truly great moment was a bloody mess. Having already misplaced serial band-dumper Richard Hell, drummer Jerry Nolan quit in protest at the muddily inept sound of their first album *L.A.M.F.* (apparently down to bad mastering rather than Keen's talents), from which these two tracks are taken. Nolan and bandleader Johnny Thunders had

ROADRUNNER/JONATHAN RICHMAN AND THE MODERN LOVERS

PAGE 36

been in early '70s glam-punk legends The New York Dolls, and this single introduced punk England to a seamier side of NY than that represented by the Ramones, Blondie, Talking Heads, et al. Indeed, former Sex Pistols still mutter bitterly about how it all went wrong when the New Yorkers brought smack onto the ill-fated Anarchy tour, and introduced Sid Vicious to one Nancy Spungen.

'Chinese Rocks', co-written by and name-checking Ramones bassist Dee Dee (Richard Hell later insisted that the song was entirely the work of himself and Dee Dee – but then, if you hang out with junkies they'll nick anything that isn't nailed down), is the ultimate in self-pitying smack anthems. The flip 'Born To Lose' (or 'Born Too Loose' if you believe some accounts) drips of the same without saying it. Both boogie so swaggeringly they blow away your dislike of the whole junkie schtick, even before you clock just how much Steve Jones stole from Thunders' supercharged-Chuck Berry guitar style, or, indeed, how sludgy the sound is. Despite a career of increasingly futile smack-rock kept going by a bizarrely sentimental and misguided cult following, Thunders died of a heroin overdose in April 1991. But check out the whiney whitey mirror image of Rose Royce's cheerful stoicism, as Thunders sings on 'Chinese Rocks', reeling with bitter surprise: 'I shoulda bin rich!/But I'm just digging a Chinese ditch.' Maybe, on some level, The Heartbreakers were listening to Dickey and co. Maybe they should've listened harder.

ROADRUNNER

JONATHAN RICHMAN AND THE MODERN LOVERS

'ROADRUNNER (ONCE)' PRODUCED BY JOHN CALE/'ROADRUNNER (TWICE)' PRODUCED BY MATTHEW KING KAUFMAN AND GLEN KOLOTKIN/BOTH WRITTEN BY JONATHAN RICHMAN
BESERKLEY/JUNE 1977
UK CHART: 11

A garage-rock legend well before it entered the UK chart, the A-side was recorded back in 1972 and featured future Talking Heads keyboardist Jerry Harrison and future Cars bassist Ernie Brooks. The band split and Velvet Underground legend Cale's demos were shelved for four years, finally released as *The Modern Lovers* in 1976 and becoming an immediate inspiration and influence on both New York and UK punk, despite hailing from Boston, Massachusetts. Both retro and ahead of the band's

time, 'Roadrunner's' speeding car tempo, swirling garage organ, droning and unforgettable two-chord riff and drawling, minimalist vocals were/are so perfect that it sounds – like, say, 'Louie Louie' or The Velvet Underground's 'Sweet Jane' – as if the band had found it buried in a cave, just waiting to be discovered. Its chanted hook of 'Radio on!' and Richman's sleepy, innocent declaration, 'I'm in love with the modern world!', seemed to meld the naïve '50s with the cynical '70s, America with England, rock experiment with the simple pleasure of dancing. It rings through the years, pealing out the meaning of this whole rock 'n' roll thing – fun, *serious* fun.

Richman's re-recorded and preferred flipside version was cuter, even more danceable, but less wired and eccentric. Not that Richman didn't go on to be the most eccentric and loved of underground singer-songwriters. But his singles would be self-conscious novelties, and the best stuff tucked away on albums. We should forgive him though, because 'Roadrunner's' blissful chuckle is always ready to forgive us far worse things.

SPANISH STROLL

MINK DEVILLE

PRODUCED BY JACK NITZSCHE/WRITTEN BY WILLY DEVILLE
CAPITOL/JUNE 1977
UK CHART: 20

At this point punk had become so hot so fast that anyone not wearing spandex trousers quickly cut their hair and attempted to surf the 'new wave'. AOR hack-in-disguise Willy Deville had the added cachet of being a native New Yorker who had played at CBGBs, so, somehow, this beefed-up early '60s throwback was considered à la mode. Still, if Capitol hadn't had their marketing chops together the charts of '77 would've been all the poorer for missing out on this pristine, swaggering slice of Latin rock. The guitars shimmer and crunch, the girls (coloured or otherwise) go doo-der-doo, and Deville mixes and mellows Lou Reed's and Springsteen's differing brands of street-punk observation before strutting into a sexy Spanish bridge with all the brassneck you'd expect of someone who'd be making records with Mark Knopfler a decade later. Nitzsche had worked with Spector and the Stones, crosses the two here, and produces an irresistible confection.

SPANISH STROLL/MINK DEVILLE

PAGE 36

I FEEL LOVE

DONNA SUMMER

PRODUCED BY GIORGIO MORODER AND
PETE BELLOTTE/WRITTEN BY DONNA SUMMER,
GIORGIO MORODER AND PETE BELLOTTE
CASABLANCA/JULY 1977
UK CHART: 1
(REISSUED AND REMIXED NOVEMBER 1982: REACHED
NO. 21; RE-RECORDED AND REISSUED SEPTEMBER
1995: REACHED NO. 8)

Kraftwerk, Bowie and the German art-rockers might have come up with a working blueprint for a non-American dance sound, but it took two less credible visionaries to invent a globally recognized European dance-pop. The record they achieved this with is so beautiful and extraordinary, it presents a tough-to-challenge argument that Europop's first major cut is, after almost 25 years, still its deepest.

'I Feel Love' takes aural sex where pop had never taken it before. Male funkers and rockers made it a macho matter of urgency; female singers largely aimed for needy romance. But 'I Feel Love's' mesmeric sequenced synth undulations took the physical pleasure of love-making on a journey as endless and scenic as Kraftwerk's travels down autobahns and train tracks. The Summer–Moroder–Bellotte team's much banned and discussed 1976 hit 'Love To Love You Baby' also blatantly exploited synths and sex. But, inspired by Serge Gainsbourg and Jane Birkin's artfully cheesy 'Je T'Aime', Moroder simply made Summer impersonate the after-effects of a particularly bad bellyache and trusted that enough soft-porn users would get the picture, while the machines replicated fairly standard boudoir soul. There's no need for Summer to hammer the point home here. Her skyscraping blend of American gospel (she uttered her first notes in church in her Boston hometown) and light opera (she had found some success in European musicals and met Italian Moroder in Munich) soars in a dreamy delirium – sex as ecstatic worship, as narcotic trip, as the experience to end all experiences.

On the radio, 'I Feel Love's' insistent ethereality smothered the orchestral funk of US disco, and stood out so completely you found yourself riveted by its awe and its glowing ache. On the dancefloor, the effect was even more profound. For the first time we were taken out of our tacky pick-up joints and onto another planet, engulfed by what was the first truly hallucinatory dance record, and given prior notice of what house and techno would aim for more than a decade later. For the gay community (whose influence on the UK's proto-disco scenes of mod and northern soul remains a fascinating and deliberately ignored foundation of British pop mores), 'I Feel Love' became the template for an enduring love of churning hi-tempo Hi-NRG and Eurodisco, with Moroder's and Bellotte's speedy, bass-heavy electronic hyper-pulse perfectly replicating the euphoric, dick-hardening rush of sniffing amyl nitrate. Particularly as, in either its initial three-minute version or 1982 15-minute Patrick Cowley remix, it felt as if it – you – could last all night, forever topping the last sensation, 'falling free' through floods of physically generated emotion, through crashing waves of orgasmic ecstasy . . . and . . . uh . . . excuse me, will you? I'll be back in . . . um . . . a few minutes.

ALL AROUND THE WORLD

THE JAM

PRODUCED BY VIC SMITH AND
CHRIS PARRY/WRITTEN BY PAUL WELLER
POLYDOR/JULY 1977
UK CHART: 13

The triumphant pure rock 'n' roll power of the second Jam single is usually ignored, as the band's sudden ascent to hero status was still a couple of years away. The 19-year-old Weller's first theme – The Kids Are Alright, basically – might have turned out to be a cul-de-sac, but at this point the suburban kid, unable yet to match the city sophistication of Strummer, Rotten and Costello, but even more infused with desperate energy, simply updates his fave early Who records with every last ounce of pious passion he can muster. Beginning with drummer Rick Buckler literally knocking before they come in, and Weller's guitar bouncing off the walls before he thuggishly bellows 'OI!!!' (and how we'd all come to regret *that* use of cockernee patois), this is all mod-memory buzzwords and Pete Townshend windmills added to a dash of machine-gun riffing inspired, one suspects, by Wilko Johnson of Brit amphetamine-blues heroes Dr Feelgood. Its bridge – 'What's the point in saying destroy?' – reveals the song as a reaction to punk, and it all reaches a peak of outrageous power when Weller shoots his fingers down the fretboard with a cattle-prod shriek in the feedback-drenched, chaotic middle eight. It was a while before Weller aspired to poetry, but the 'fire 'n' skill' that Weller's manager dad used as The Jam's marketing slogan was all here, and let us know that a new British beat boom had truly arrived.

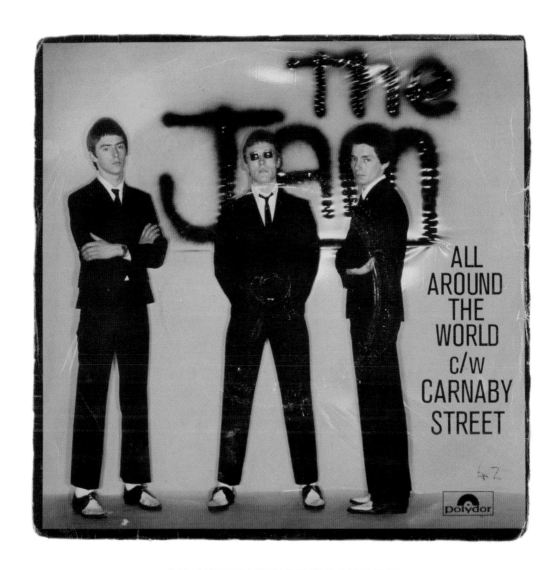

ALL AROUND THE WORLD/THE JAM

PRETTY VACANT

SEX PISTOLS

PRODUCED BY CHRIS THOMAS/WRITTEN BY
PAUL COOK, STEVE JONES, GLEN MATLOCK AND
JOHNNY ROTTEN
VIRGIN/JULY 1977
UK CHART: 6

If you're a sensitive, thinking kind of boy, you often find yourself looking at instinctive, force-of-nature types with admiration and envy, despite their obvious shortcomings. I always suspected that that's the way it was for Johnny Rotten with Steve Jones. It was Jones who gave Bill Grundy what he wanted and swore on TV, propelling the Pistols into infamy while Rotten acted like a schoolkid being bullied by a teacher. It was Jones who just got on and enjoyed the sex, drugs and rock 'n' roll while Rotten endlessly fretted about what the deeper meaning could be. It was even Jones who wore the knotted hanky on his head for the 'Pretty Vacant' video (the first time most of us got to see them actually 'perform') and said more about the uselessness of England's adult working classes than even Rotten's entire hunchback cool could muster. Which is perhaps why, as Julian Temple's superb *The Filth and the Fury* seemed to prove, Rotten was more deeply hurt and bemused by Jones's shrugging betrayal at the band's end than by McLaren's hapless mix of manipulation and ineptitude.

Just a theory, of course, brought to mind by listening to 'Pretty Vacant' again, and figuring it to be the one great Pistols song where Rotten sang from his guitarist's who-gives-a-shit perspective, rather than his own desire to prick everyone's sleeping conscience. This record is deliberately thick in more ways than one, and its taunting nihilism joined with Weller's 'OI!' (initially hollered by The Clash on 'Career Opportunities') and Sid Vicious's forthcoming celebrity to invent the arse-end of British punk that developed from dumb-fuck misanthropy into the fascist drones of Skrewdriver and their repellent ilk.

Not that that is Rotten's fault, per se. Rock fans always have and always will use records for purposes the artist never intended. But even though this is still a fantastic and funny rock 'n' roll record, the eager acceptance it got from a young, reactionary male audience who weren't remotely interested in the attendant irony pretty much signalled the end of punk's initial rebellion and impact. Oddly, the writer of the tune, soon-to-be-sacked bassist Matlock, insisted that the instantly classic, tolling-bell opening guitar fanfare and most of the melody were nicked off Abba's 'S.O.S.'. (Believe me, I've tried and tried to find the link and come up blank, which proves that Matlock is either a pop genius, or a good wind-up merchant, maybe both.) And of course, the BBC didn't ban it despite the fact that Rotten was quite plainly hollering 'CUNT!' at us on every chorus. The Beeb were right, though. That was nowhere near as offensive to the British way of life as the dark prophecy inside 'God Save the Queen', and nowhere near as dirty as the hoarse and ragged crawl through Iggy's 'No Fun' on 'Pretty Vacant's' flipside.

I CAN'T STAND MY BABY

THE REZILLOS

PRODUCED BY TONY PILLEY AND THE
REZILLOS/WRITTEN BY LUKE WARM
SENSIBLE/AUGUST 1977
DID NOT CHART
(REISSUED AUGUST 1979: REACHED NO. 71)

GARY GILMORE'S EYES

THE ADVERTS

PRODUCED BY THE ADVERTS AND LARRY
WALLIS/WRITTEN BY T.V. SMITH
ANCHOR/AUGUST 1977
UK CHART: 18

WHOLE WIDE WORLD

WRECKLESS ERIC

PRODUCED BY NICK LOWE/WRITTEN BY
WRECKLESS ERIC
STIFF/AUGUST 1977
DID NOT CHART

And, as the last Summer of Punk lurched muggily on, out of Britain's pubs they crawled. Rockers old and new, jolted awake by the Pistols' youth revolution, took their three chords into studios and, in a magical manifestation of Garry Mulholland's Theory One, mustered enough inspiration to produce their One Great Moment before slinking back into the primordial closing-time slime from whence they came.

Actually, that's a bit harsh. All three of these acts did worthwhile things further down the line. But these were their defining moments, the sort of bursts of eccentric, declamatory

PRETTY VACANT/SEX PISTOLS

energy that made the late '70s such a fantastic time for lovers of the three-minute (or less) pop single. And, although all three are influenced by the pub rock scene and the Pistols, they each found a different path to follow from punk's credo of idea-first-technique-later.

The title of this book is taken from 'I Can't Stand My Baby' for the reasons mentioned in the introduction, but also simply because I loved it so much, and still do. Beginning with The Damned's manic jab-thrash taken to even more ridiculous extremes, singer Fay Fife forgets about her baby about 30 seconds in and, double-tracked and androgynous, presents us with a mystery born of negation, Scottish colloquialism (it took another 20 years and marrying a Scottish woman before I was told that 'I'm gonna go radge!' meant 'I'm going to go a wee bit mental, if that's OK') and ancient goof-rock madness. Keeping under tightly bemused control despite the ringing, clanging background, Ms Fife appears to be here against her will and regressing by the second: 'I can't take the tempo/I can't take the noise/I wanna be a baby/I wanna touch toys/I . . . AM . . . UNCOOL.' Fay (imagine one of The Shangri-Las after six months with a bullworker) was my first real punk sex icon. Poly Styrene was too weird; The Slits too scary; Debbie Harry too impossibly perfect; Siouxsie too cool. Fay was *un*cool and could almost certainly drink her weight in pints before doing The Loco-motion, proper steps and all. Although, of course, she might prefer the toys to me.

The Adverts also had their own punk princess in bassist Gaye Advert, who hit big with punk boys by wearing leather, having kohled-up panda eyes, and standing blankly behind T.V. Smith playing really, really badly. Too cool for me, naturally. The melodramatic Smith had a grim, sub-Clash view of grey old Blighty, and his finest moment was a short story. What if they gave you an eye transplant, and the eyes belonged to a notorious serial killer? Would you see what he saw? Smith delivers this unintentionally hilarious scenario with the po-faced zeal of some reborn left-wing folkie delivering the fearsome truth behind the dangers of . . . um . . . well, eye surgery I guess, while the band desperately struggle to keep up and somehow create a momentous charcoal and sepia tension that Smith's hysteria probably doesn't deserve.

Dave Marsh, while writing about the Sex Pistols' 'Holidays in the Sun' in *The Heart of Rock and Soul*, insists intriguingly that ' . . . the real text of almost all Sex Pistols songs is Rotten's utter loathing of his own physicality', a judgement that could also be made of Costello's and Devoto's early lyrics. Rotten famously declared that sex was '30 seconds of squelching noises', and this self-flagellating fear and suspicion of rock's most common

theme fuelled many of punk/new wave's most inspired, funny and honest moments. Wreckless Eric (real name: Eric Goulden) made one of the period's best creepy love songs out of his nerdish wheedle of a voice, an old-school 'Where's the one for me?' scenario, and, yet again, Lowe's deceptively simple, let-the-song-speak-for-itself production. The Wreckless One goes all Adam Faith-nasal and plays the ugliest man in the world to the hilt, as he swears undying love to a girl he's never met in a place you know he'll never go to, the creeping two-chord guitar climbing from a chilling stalk to a gleaming declaration of hope, as his dreams become more fevered and impossible.

Goulden never really made it but emerges every now and again, a much treasured mini-cult. Smith never quite got there either and – heh-heh – did turn out to be a hippy folkie, doing the worthy lefty circuit with the likes of Tom Robinson and Billy Bragg. Gaye Advert stayed with Smith, but as a non-professional partner. Luke Warm of The Rezillos was really Jo Callis, who left the band after their *Top of the Pops* hit and literally took the tunes with him, co-writing 'Don't You Want Me', among others, for The Human League. Fife and co. carried on their cartoon pop with the more definitively retro The Revillos. Last time I saw a picture of Fay, just a couple of years ago to promote a Revillos show, she looked exactly the same. Still gorgeously uncool. Sigh.

NO MORE HEROES

THE STRANGLERS

PRODUCED BY MARTIN RUSHENT/WRITTEN BY
THE STRANGLERS
UNITED ARTISTS/SEPTEMBER 1977
UK CHART: 9

Yet more grist to my Theory One mill, can I hear a hiss and a boo for punk's nastiest villains, the new-wave equivalent of hired goons from Hollywood central casting. Hugh Cornwell, Jean Jacques Burnel, Dave Greenfield and Jet Black were ageing pub-rock hippies who saw punk's foul-mouthed graffiti on the wall, brushed up their third-rate Doors riffs, and smeared their trad rock with a sneering sub-Nietzschean bully-boy cod-intellectualism. Most of their lyrics consisted of a brutal misogyny dressed up as rebellion (hmm . . . wonder if many post-gangsta rappers checked for them?), which, along with the name, amounted to an argument that, yep, the feminists were right and all men are potential rapists and isn't it cool? Sadly, they went on to be among the most commercially successful

I can't stand my baby / I wanna be your man

I CAN'T STAND MY BABY/THE REZILLOS
PAGE 40

bands of the time, with post-prog rock boys checking for the pomposity and musicianly soloing while sniggering at the 'gurls smell' lyrics, and girls themselves continuing their masochistic relationship with rock by fantasizing about being used and abused by luscious-lipped bassist Burnel. The fact that they actually did, at one point, kidnap a female journalist and scare the shit out of her only seemed to add to the allure.

Anyway, their Theory One contender is still a fantastic, atmospheric piece of sly and slick hard rock. As Cornwell imperiously recites a list of scholarly 'heroes', from Leon Trotsky to 'the Shakesperoes', Rushent pushes Burnel's muscular, rubbery bass (including the flailing, 'listen up!' intro) to the fore and fashions a sound as instantly recognizable as that of any of the more talented artists in this book. The implication, of course, was that there were no more heroes – except The Stranglers themselves. The record is almost tough enough to back up their misguided arrogance.

COMPLETE CONTROL

THE CLASH

PRODUCED BY LEE PERRY AND MICKY
FOOTE/WRITTEN BY JOE STRUMMER AND MICK JONES
CBS/SEPTEMBER 1977
UK CHART: 28

Things were moving too fast. In mid-'76 bands were playing to a handful of scenemakers down the 100 Club. By the end of 1976 they were signed to major labels. By early '77 they were making world-changing records. By Autumn '77 they were making world-changing records about how shit being signed and making world-changing records was turning out to be.

After the release of the first Clash album in April '77, CBS wanted to give it another sales boost. They released, very strangely, the uncharismatic 'Remote Control' as a single, against the band's wishes. Having already applied for the job as punk's conscience and quickly finding themselves drowning under the contradictions of being socialist rebels signed to a huge multinational, The Clash freaked at this public humiliation. But – and this always marked The Clash out – they made great art out of the contradictions of their position and image, and, ironically, this was the first Clash recording that suggested the well-produced, big-in-America, hard rock powerhouse they were soon to become.

The only rock record, as far as I know, to be co-produced by reggae legend Lee Perry, it contrarily has nothing in common with the white reggae The Clash made before or after. Perry and early Clash producer Foote just seem to turn everything up, light the blue touchpaper and, apart from some outrageous dubwise echo applied to Strummer's middle-eight moan of 'I don't trust you – why do you trust me – Huh?', stand well back. Written almost entirely by guitarist Jones in honour of a pub comment from manager Bernie Rhodes, Strummer rants on his behalf about 'Remote Control', the kids they can't get into the shows anymore, the truth about rock and money and the band's lack of importance within the biz machine. He barks, groans and accuses with the confused and quizzical air of someone who is suddenly understanding why people tell you to be careful of what you wished for. 'You're my guitar hero,' he taunts Jones as he breaks into one of his weeping, overwrought solos, knowing that, whatever his friend may say, that's exactly what he wants. 'I don't understand,' he wails, bewildered, before looking at his paymasters and finding a moment of clarity: 'Complete control – now I see your upper hand.' By the massive minor-chord charge of the coda, Joe is lost in his own fury, gabbling with incoherent anger while the guitars and backing vocals shower him in tears of frustration. Innocence lost. From now on, it was a fight to the inevitable death.

BEST OF MY LOVE

THE EMOTIONS

PRODUCED BY MAURICE WHITE/WRITTEN BY
WHITE/MCKAY
CBS/SEPTEMBER 1977
UK CHART: 4

No such public rails at CBS for Teresa Davis and the Hutchinson sisters (Pamela, Wanda and Sheila), even though the veteran R&B vocal group could probably have told The Clash a thing or two about control after being Isaac Hayes and David Porter protégées at Stax, and making this, their biggest hit, under the supervision of Earth, Wind & Fire's Maurice White.

Endorsing my feelings about 'I Feel Love', this big-band/soul-disco stomper provides more proof that, when it comes to portraying pure, unadulterated joy in a pop song, it's the women who come up trumps every time. Even if White's blaring horns, high-stepping funk beats and tumbling melody and The Emotions' alternately chirping and whooping harmonies and testifying lead weren't such a blast, 'Best of My Love' would probably be here just for one of pop's most spine-tinglingly ecstatic moments. On the second bridge, close now to the finish,

GARY GILMORE'S EYES/THE ADVERTS

there's a sudden climb into an ascending hiccup of 'do-doo-do's, and then – pause – a shocking 'OW!' – pause – a kittenish coo . . . and finally a wave of delirious close-harmony cries, born out of church but speaking here of an emotional/physical release that is anything but holy. Or, thinking again, perhaps it is. Why should the Devil get all the best love?

THE BLANK GENERATION

RICHARD HELL AND THE VOIDOIDS
PRODUCED BY RICHARD GOTTEHRER AND
RICHARD HELL/WRITTEN BY RICHARD HELL
SIRE/SEPTEMBER 1977
DID NOT CHART

New York dollyboy Hell (originally Richard Myers from Lexington, Kentucky) was, on the face of it, the Pete Best of punk rock. Quite apart from being in Television and The Heartbreakers before they achieved what little success they did, it was Hell's name, ripped T-shirt chic, and elegantly wasted demeanour that one Malcolm McLaren clocked during his short-lived management of The New York Dolls, and apparently stole and applied to his later British project (although John Lydon still bitterly denies that he was styled by McLaren, Viv Westwood, or anyone else). Still, in the end, it ain't who does it first but who does it best, and Hell's bruised sex appeal remains the most interesting thing about most of his own musical, literary and acting career.

As Hell was always at pains to point out, his finest moment (originally given a limited release the previous year) wasn't a proto-slacker anthem. The 'Blank' meant fill your own word in – we're a blank canvas. Like Television, this is a musicianly proposition behind the punk attitood, with an elliptical take on a Bo Diddley riff quickly giving way to a swaggering rockabilly with rude, wild, slashed guitar interruptions that bands like Gang of Four must have figured are pretty cool. It's Hell's poisoned yelp and the doo-wop 'whee-ooh's that truly make the song stick though, undercutting his own insistence that he 'can take it or leave it each time'. Nevertheless, the public took his advice, at least as far as Hell was concerned. Since then, his greatest leap from obscurity was when he appeared as the boyfriend of that ultimate punk/disco offspring Madonna in *Desperately Seeking Susan*. Blink and you'd miss him, though, which seems to be the story of his life.

HEROES

DAVID BOWIE
PRODUCED BY DAVID BOWIE AND
TONY VISCONTI/WRITTEN BY DAVID BOWIE AND
BRIAN ENO
RCA/VICTOR/OCTOBER 1977
UK CHART: 24

THE PASSENGER

IGGY POP
PRODUCED BY THE BEWLAY BROS/WRITTEN BY
IGGY POP AND RICKY GARDINER
RCA/OCTOBER 1977
DID NOT CHART
(REISSUED MAY 1998 (VIRGIN): REACHED NO. 22)

The UK singles chart may be a total mess these days, but it was always pretty weird. How else can you explain why two such enduringly classic records had so little impact as hits? Actually, as far as Iggy's best-known anthem is concerned, it was killed at birth, being tucked away on the flip of the silly 'Success'. Both were plucked from *Lust for Life*, Iggy's second Bowie-produced (The Bewlay Bros is a Bowie pseudonym), get-clean-in-Berlin album. And yes, it took 19 years and a popular film about Scottish junkies before the monumental title track was released as a single at all.

'The Passenger's' circular ska riff, post-Motown strut and radio-crackle 'la-la-la's ensured that it became a hardy perennial at every student/indie disco in the land. But it also introduced us to the former James Jewel Osterberg as occasional basso profundo crooner (he's a big Sinatra fan), and revealed a joyful humanism that had never been obvious in him before. His rock 'n' roll travelogue is as romantic as Kraftwerk's, though evocative not of distance, but of cramped chaos – 'the city's ripped backsides' that have to be reclaimed by those of us oppressed by it. An anthem as generous as it is artful, then, and as catchy as a Queen song.

As Stephen Dalton reveals in his excellent 'Trans-Europe Excess' feature for *Uncut* magazine (Issue 47; April 2001), 'Heroes' was not inspired, as Bowie explained at the time, by seeing two young strangers kissing by the Berlin Wall. He was covering for his then-married producer Tony Visconti, who had a crafty snog with backing singer Antonia Maass by the wall between recording sessions. Must have been some kiss, because

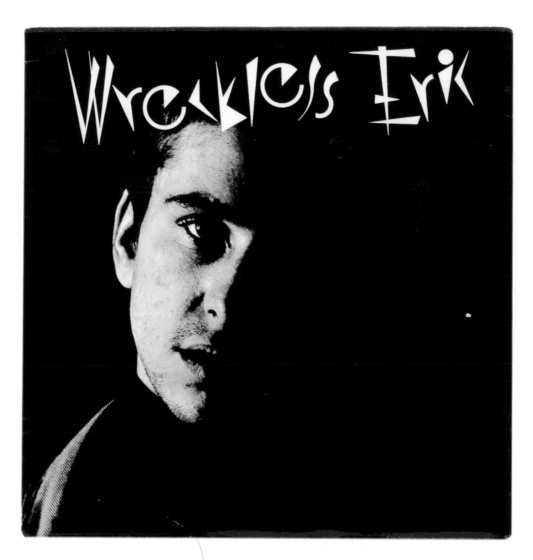

WHOLE WIDE WORLD/WRECKLESS ERIC

it provoked Bowie's most heartfelt love song and a glowing testament to us-against-the-world defiance, made all the stronger by the touch of despair in Bowie's increasingly desperate vocal. The other-worldly blend of Spectoresque, wailing wall-of-sound and rock muscle had to be on the money to make you believe in an opening line as Mills & Boon as 'I, I wish we could swim/Like dolphins/Like dolphins can swim.'

The importance of these two singles, and, of course, the albums they came from, can't be overstated. Punk was already smashing against its own Iron Curtain, and Bowie, Iggy, Eno et al. provided the mutant soul feel that would help the best of them pole-vault right over.

HOLIDAYS IN THE SUN

SEX PISTOLS

PRODUCED BY CHRIS THOMAS/WRITTEN BY
PAUL COOK, STEVE JONES, JOHNNY ROTTEN AND
SID VICIOUS
VIRGIN/OCTOBER 1977
UK CHART: 8

The Sex Pistols' last great single is also their best, although it wasn't seen as such at the time. The pop melodies left with Glen Matlock, and Jones took over by nicking (and improving) the opening riff from The Jam's 'In the City' (provoking a legendary altercation in a London club between Vicious and Paul Weller, where poor old Sid apparently learned what the word 'vicious' really meant), and making a heavy metal record that blew the Sabbaths of this world out of the water. Of course, the pursuit of transcendant rock power is considerably aided by a voice and lyric in a language that defies every rock cliché that had gone before.

'Holidays in the Sun' entered Rotten's fevered mind when England became too dangerous to live in after the Jubilee, and the band decamped first to Jersey (they hated it) before moving on hastily to, of course, bleak, bohemian Berlin. So perfect for Rotten's worldview you can almost hear him rubbing his hands with relish. The tension between East and West, squalor and decadence, oppression and freedom implicit in Bowie and Iggy's songs is made explicit here.

Many writers have heard fear and dread in the Pistols' greatest song, but that was never how it struck me. The 'cheap dialogue, cheap essential scenery' is what he's losing patience with back home, and he's wondering if there's a new challenge, even allowing for the grim authoritarianism, on the other side.

But how much is at stake? Could he start World War Three? Will they be waiting for him? The repeated declaration of 'reason' sounds like an attempt to see sense – don't go over the wall. 'And they're LOOKING AT ME!!!' he screams, as if waking from a nightmare. OK. There's *some* fear and dread.

And even if I'm just the latest to make no real sense of Rotten's escape – both real and imagined – then I'll just declare that no one else could've come up with the gleeful comic timing of 'I wanna go to the new Bel-sen/I wanna see some his-tor-ree-ah/'Cos now I gotta reezunuble econo-mee-ah!' And that no one ever impersonated a tank invasion like Mr Steve Jones.

BRICK HOUSE

THE COMMODORES

PRODUCED BY JAMES CARMICHAEL AND
THE COMMODORES/WRITTEN BY
THE COMMODORES
MOTOWN/OCTOBER 1977
UK CHART: 32

Yep, brick walls were certainly big in 1977. But when you got tired of figuring out how to get over or under 'em . . . then you just got over or under 'em anyway, in a manner of speaking.

It would be a decade or so before some enlighted young guns reshaped hard black funk for a new audience. But this hangover from the pre-disco era hit in the clubs, partly because of the awareness of the band caused by Lionel Richie's burgeoning country-soul balladeering, and partly because it was crass enough to pass as disco's dirty underbelly. As you'll remember, Richie and co. like their ladies stacked. And, even though referring to a woman as a brick house would have just got me soaked in Brandy and Babycham round my way, those of us who empathize remain totally convinced by the wiggling and grinding bassy beats and the 'shic-a-dow-shic-a-dow-now' take on the age-old exhortation to shake it down. It all comes crashing down for a second halfway through, however, when Richie declares that said brick house's winning hand is '36-24-36'. Where do you live, Mr Chinny? Skinnyville?

COMPLETE CONTROL/THE CLASH

ORGASM ADDICT

BUZZCOCKS
PRODUCED BY MARTIN RUSHENT/WRITTEN BY
PETE SHELLEY AND HOWARD DEVOTO
UNITED ARTISTS/OCTOBER 1977
DID NOT CHART

OH BONDAGE! UP YOURS!

X-RAY SPEX
PRODUCED BY FALCON STUART/WRITTEN BY
POLY STYRENE
VIRGIN/OCTOBER 1977
DID NOT CHART

Or: 'Sure, Mister, we can do that chartbusting thing. But there's something we need to get out of our system first.'

Despite Devoto's departure to form Magazine, the Buzzcocks' first major-label single is a Devoto/Shelley collaboration, a hysterical paean to masturbation sung by Shelley in a fey yelp that we would all come to know and love. The opening screech of 'Well you tried it just the once/Found it alright for kicks/But now you've found out that it's a habit that sticks/'Cos you're an orgasm addict!' still snaps your head back and makes you gasp and guffaw, as does Shelley's whey-faced wimp parody of a climax, the dance-crazed heavy breathing, and the pair's comic imaginings of who we're wanking about: 'Butchers' assistants and bell-hops . . . Children of God rejoicing and international women with no body hair.' Two minutes that almost define British punk's desire to say the unsayable and make it funny. We'll put the bit about schoolkids down to Devoto's fondness for Nabokov.

Before X-Ray Spex signed to EMI and made surreal pop-metal satires on modern consumerism that actually charted, they recorded their theme song as a one-off for Virgin. Roared by the 19-year-old queen of punk eccentrics Poly Styrene (once plain old Marion Elliot from Brixton) like Julie Covington (of 'Evita' and 'Rock Follies' fame) with a cattle-prod up her arse, played and produced as if saxophones were kazoos and guitars were rocket science, it furiously declares a teen feminism (via a furious anti-consumerist rant), which, in the wake of girl power and Britney Spears, really does make you feel that we've travelled backwards these last 20 years. Naturally, as punk was quickly being marketed in macho rock terms, Stranglers fans thought it was about S&M. Then they saw Poly's teeth-brace, heard the hate and arrogance in her nice-girl-parodying spoken-word intro, and grew very frightened. Her voice on this record remains one of the most liberated/liberating noises in rock's misogynist history, and is still guaranteed to send men of good taste running out into the street, holding their ears and crying for Mummy, in a way that bully-boy rockers can only dream about.

After the band's short-lived success, Ms Styrene joined a Hare Krishna sect. I used to see her around Brixton when I lived there, looking dreamy and content. Like I said, maybe she just needed to get it out of her system.

WATCHING THE DETECTIVES

ELVIS COSTELLO AND THE ATTRACTIONS
PRODUCED BY NICK LOWE/WRITTEN BY
ELVIS COSTELLO
STIFF/OCTOBER 1977
UK CHART: 15

PSYCHO KILLER

TALKING HEADS
PRODUCED BY TONY BONGIOVI, LANCE QUINN AND
TALKING HEADS/WRITTEN BY DAVID BYRNE,
CHRIS FRANTZ AND TINA WEYMOUTH
SIRE/DECEMBER 1977
DID NOT CHART

While the punks howled their last howls of rage and slapstick, those who'd come along for the ride pursued a different kind of tension. Our last two new-wave singles from 1977 are ostensibly murder mysteries sung by geeks – one always vengeful, the other always perplexed. Both opt out of straight-ahead rock and explore their creepy fantasies using black dance rhythms and as much room to breathe, to think, as they can afford.

Costello's two reggae-based singles (see 'I Don't Want To Go To Chelsea' p. 60) are so transcendent you still wonder why he dumped the direction so quickly. Nick Lowe had an amazing year, but never produced a record better than this, with its distorted Jamaican drum breaks, restless, speaker-straining bass and tense-as-taut-wire, Duane Eddy guitars. Costello sounds as if he's delivering the words just to get the taste of venom out of his mouth, as he inhabits a film noir scenario as yet another way of representing his terror of women – or at least, the power they

THE BLANK GENERATION/RICHARD HELL AND THE VOIDOIDS
PAGE 46

can have over him. You could even see it as a kind of sequel to 'Less Than Zero' – same couple, same couch, but this time her favourite cop series is on TV and she's having none of it, even though 'She looks so good that he gets down and begs.' Our man gets more desperate as her indifference melds with the cold violence onscreen – 'She's filing her nails as they're dragging the lake' – until he loses reason, snaps, is the killer in the show. 'It only took my little fingers to blow you away,' he sneers down at her, relishing the double entendre. Whichever way, this is Costello's high water mark, an object lesson in blending style and content; mystery, metaphor and everyday madness.

The first great Talking Heads single is actually not a murder mystery, but a mysterious song that mentions murder. Utilizing a mix of Stax soul ('Fa fa-fa-fa-fah'), psychedelic soul and a bleached, flailing funk, 'Psycho Killer' invents mutant disco, a phrase coined by some other arty Yanks a couple of years later. It shares the same, pre-David Lynch feel as most of Byrne's early work – the small, quiet nerd in the flat below who seems nice but keeps twitching violently and is maybe going completely radge (Byrne always resembled Anthony Perkins as Norman Bates in 'Psycho'). In the early part of the song, Byrne's stilted, pompous vocal implies that the idea that this impatient know-all ('Say something once/Why say it again?' indeed) might actually kill someone is ridiculous. But his growing hysteria, his wailing in French, the building clang of the guitars suggest it's the quiet ones you should watch out for. 'I hate people when they're not polite,' he yelps helplessly, as if that's the worst thing in the world. And if your world is small enough, then maybe it is.

UPTOWN TOP RANKING

ALTHIA & DONNA

PRODUCED BY JOE GIBSON/WRITTEN BY ERROL THOMPSON, ALTHIA FOREST AND DONNA REID
LIGHTNING/DECEMBER 1977
UK CHART: 1

It was January 1978 and one of the trendier teachers set a competition in my school. Translate the lyrics of current No.1 'Uptown Top Ranking' and win a prize. I have no recollection of what I won, but I do remember this half-caste boy feeling the epitome of pseudo-Jamaican cool when I handed in my word-for-word dismantling of Althia & Donna's patois classic. No need to tell 'em that I copied the whole thing from a recent piece in the *NME*.

On one level, 'Uptown . . .' is simply classic black pop music, an ebullient mix of bass and treble with two girls who can't really sing reciting catchy bollocks over the top. But, on another, it was an open letter to Britain's JA community about gender relations back home, and a friendly but defiant statement of female freedom. You see, Althia & Donna like to show off uptown, cruising in a Benz (you thought that was new?), popping the latest styles, flaunting what they got. Unfortunately, the local rastas, who prefer their women barefoot and breeding babies, are making that sucking noise with their teeth and snubbing them as sell-outs to Babylon. And how does that affect our heroines? They laugh at them ('See me in me 'alter-back/Say me gi' you 'eart attack'), knowing full well that the guys ain't averting their eyes when they dance ('Let me wine out me waist!'), and that their attitude smacks of hypocrisy. What's more, they reckon they're more conscious than the dreads anyway ('I strictly roots!'). And as the horns and clavinets and wibbling keyboards lay down pure joy, the girls whoop with pure pleasure at the end of just the right lines, sending the whole testimony into girl-group heaven.

Of course, reality bites. Forest and Reid disappeared into obscurity, and legendary JA producer Joe Gibbs (Joe Gibson is a pseudonym) got most of the credit. Pop records – even ones this perfect – can't change the world all by themselves. But there's a purely feminine joy in 'Uptown Top Ranking' that still sounds taunting and tough, that still shows up men who use religion – or any other spurious cult – as an excuse for misogyny. Which was especially useful at the time, as a generation of impressed white boys glorified everything about Rastafarianism without bothering to look at the small print.

1978

1978

The world went to war in 1978. Not officially, in terms of Western leaders identifying what the world was fighting over and asking for volunteers. But covertly, as the US and the USSR fought 'secret' CIA- and KGB-funded wars in Ethiopia, Afghanistan, Nicaragua and Cambodia. Meanwhile, the activists of the 1960s civil rights movements had hardened into terrorists: Baader Meinhof in Germany, Red Brigade in Italy, the IRA in Britain, the PLO in the Middle East. Their attacks were audacious in a way that seemed unthinkable (at least, until September 11th 2001) – the Red Brigade kidnapped and murdered former Italian Prime Minister Aldo Moro, Japanese protesters set fire to themselves with Molotov cocktails over the building of a new airport, and the Middle East conflict was played out in the streets of London as the PLO's Said Hammani was shot dead in the West End, and machine guns and grenades sprayed an Israeli airline bus at Heathrow.

Death and violence grew weirder and weirder in 1978. In a remote part of Guyana, almost 1000 people commited mass suicide at the behest of cult leader Jim Jones. A woman called Joyce McKinney disappeared in London as she was being found guilty of kidnapping and sexually abusing a Mormon missionary. A Bulgarian defector was killed in London with an umbrella laced with poison. And then there were Iran and Zaire and environmental disaster and the *Rainbow Warrior* and the Turin Shroud and the first test tube baby and Pik Botha and the evocation of the blitz spirit as the Brits did their Christmas shopping in the midst of an IRA bombing campaign and Sid accused of murdering Nancy and the Oregon man cleared of raping his own wife and Argentina's dubious World Cup victory in a stadium used to brutalize dissidents and Jeremy Thorpe accused of conspiring to murder Norman Scott and a new twist on Cold War paranoia when Soviet defector Viktor Korchnoi lost to staunch Communist poster-boy Anatoly Karpov in the world chess final, and blamed his defeat on 'hostile Soviet thought-waves'. It would all be funny if the death toll weren't so huge.

It's sometimes said that great pop periods happen in times of social content and consensus, but 1978 proved the theory wrong. Artists who were pretty damn good in 1977 became extraordinary in 1978, and invaded the charts with new forms of pop – exotic, passionate, worldly but personal, implicitly political rather than preachy, and at odds with the prevailing right-wing wind. Both Britain and America were playing out the end of liberal left consensus; as Carter attempted to negotiate peace in the Middle East at Camp David and became locked in a no-win situation that would end Democrat power for years to come; and Callaghan warned the unions that their demands would determine the next election. The Winter of Discontent proved him right. Thatcher spoke of being 'swamped by people with a different culture', articulating, in one foul swoop, a growing feeling among the ordinary Brit that 'they' (immigrants, the TUC, Arabs, the IRA, Communists, foul-mouthed punk rockers, whoever 'they' were) were sending us spinning out of control, that nothing was certain anymore. The most popular TV show was the award-winning *Upstairs, Downstairs*, a pseudo-historical soap about Edwardian servants that shamelessly purveyed a nostalgia for old class certainties. My grandmother, who was born into service, watched with a glowing pride as the loyalty and deference of her early life was turned into a kind of heroism by the characters of Hudson and Mrs Bridges. There was comfort, a sense of duty, in doffing the cap and bending the knee. After all, someone 'strong' has to be in charge. Or, as The Clash put it, 'If Adolf Hitler flew in today/They'd send a limousine anyway.'

Honourable mentions: David Bowie/'Beauty and the Beast' (RCA Victor); Swell Maps/'Read About Seymour' (Rough Trade); Earth Wind & Fire/'Fantasy' (CBS); The Mekons/'Where Were You?' (Fast); A Taste of Honey/'Boogie Oogie Oogie' (Capitol); Buzzcocks/'Love You More'/'Noise Annoys' (United Artists); Donna Summer/'Macarthur Park' (Casablanca); X-Ray Spex/'The Day the World Turned Day-Glo' (EMI); Jilted John/'Jilted John' (Rabid); The Rezillos/'Top of the Pops' (Sire); TV Personalities/'Part Time Punks' (King's Rd); Abba/'The Name of the Game' (Epic); Steel Pulse/'Ku Klux Klan' (Island)

STAYIN' ALIVE

BEE GEES

PRODUCED BY THE BEE GEES, KARL RICHARDSON
AND ALBHY GALUTEN/WRITTEN BY BARRY, ROBIN AND
MAURICE GIBB
RSO/JANUARY 1978
UK CHART: 4

'You can tell by the way I use my walk/I'm a woman's man – no time to talk.' This may be a book about *listening* to records, but it remains impossible to hear the outrageous camp of disco's (and the Bee Gees') most famous moment without seeing John Travolta seduce the world with that camp macho strut, and remembering the feeling of seeing *Saturday Night Fever* for the first time. But tear yourself away for a second, because 'Stayin' Alive's' pure grace and majesty makes closing your mind's eye and just listening a total pleasure. Those falsettos (the Gibbs' trademark was a recent development for these '60s veterans, discovered when great soul producer Arif Mardin asked Barry to 'scream in tune' on 1975's 'Nights on Broadway'). The snaking, unforgettable guitar line. The slow, sensuous build of horns and queasy strings. The million and one hooklines. The easy swagger of Dennis Byron's definitive disco drums. Those defiant lines about living to see another day and the weird protest that is 'The *New York Times* don't make a man.' The way the voices rise into panic, as if drowning under the weight of expectation and urban stress, the stuff you can't just dance past. Pop music at its best – a deliberate mix of ear candy, creative ambition and the feeling of a greater meaning beneath the surface – does not get much better than this. From now on, disco was King – until it very abruptly wasn't.

WHAT DO I GET?

BUZZCOCKS

PRODUCED BY MARTIN RUSHENT/WRITTEN BY
PETE SHELLEY
UNITED ARTISTS/JANUARY 1978
UK CHART: 37

SHOT BY BOTH SIDES

MAGAZINE

PRODUCED BY MICK GLOSSOP AND
MAGAZINE/WRITTEN BY HOWARD DEVOTO AND
PETE SHELLEY
VIRGIN/JANUARY 1978
UK CHART: 41

So the Buzzcocks split and what did we get? Two extraordinary, era-defining bands for the price of one. The reasons why Shelley and Devoto had to part are in these two distinctive definitions of their separate muses.

From the 'Cocks, we get an introduction to Pete Shelley, the punk Smokey Robinson. Painfully wise love poetry both sardonic and impassioned, 'What Do I Get?' begins the great run of Shelley love singles with Rushent's wall of fuzz-buzz and a bedsit take on the frustrated heart fatigue of Bacharach/David's 'I'll Never Fall in Love Again'. Add Maher's breathless gallop-beat and that big two-chord call-and-response turning tears into laughter towards the end ('What do I get?' *CHUNG-CHUNG!!!*), and you have a key example of the new wave's blend of rawness and pop sophistication, even before you get the double-edged joke of the blissfully crooned pay-off line: ''Cos I . . . don't . . . *get* . . . you.'

Devoto's new, more austere, less pop-friendly group scored their biggest hit first time out, which tells you why they finally gave in after four albums of attempting to seduce the mainstream with Howard's creepy high-brow pop. Devoto's freaky Buzzcocks yelp becomes an ominous, superior growl at odds with British punk's 'commoner than thou' self-image (as were the obvious, grown-up musical skills of bassist Barry Adamson and guitarist John McGeoch), making a song already more influenced by both heavy metal and John Barryesque spy themes even more aloof and inky-black.

Interpreted by some as a plea for political moderation, by others as sheer misanthropy, it still strikes me as one of the great expositions of the self-satisfaction gained from feeling different

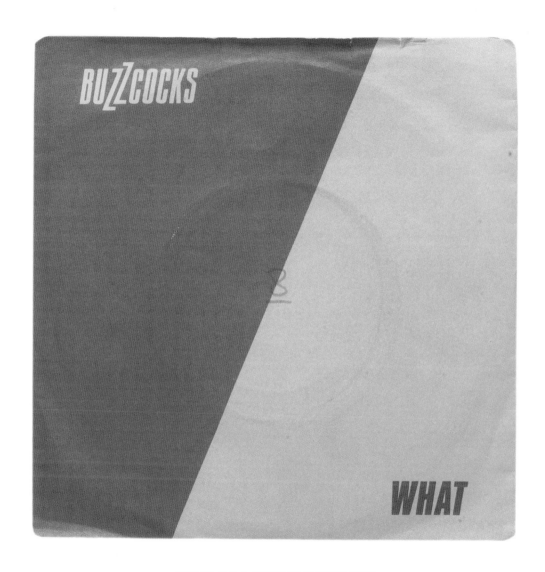

WHAT DO I GET?/BUZZCOCKS

(superior?) to those around you. Great movie script lyrics are sprayed like warning fire – 'Why are you so itchy, kid?'; 'You live and learn – you have no choice.' A storm of claustrophobic sheet-metal noise erupts in the bridge. And when Howard sneers, 'I wormed my way into the heart of the crowd/I was shocked to find what was allowed,' you know full well that he wasn't shocked at all, that nothing a human being could sink to holds any surprises for him. At one point he wonders aloud who is doing the shooting. Like we haven't seen the lump in his overcoat.

TAKE A CHANCE ON ME

ABBA

PRODUCED BY BENNY ANDERSON AND
BJÖRN ULVAEUS/WRITTEN BY BENNY ANDERSON AND
BJÖRN ULVAEUS
EPIC/JANUARY 1978
UK CHART: 1

Just (just?!) peak-period Abba, like some heavenly union of girl groups, electro-disco, doo wop and The Beach Boys. Every detail is so charming and charmed that you even want to believe in the proto-stalker 'love me – I'm a psycho obsessive!' lyrics. Still – it would take some pretty hot poetry to match the might of 'Tekkachance-tekkachance-tekkatekkachance-chance'.

T.V.O.D./WARM LEATHERETTE

THE NORMAL

PRODUCED BY DANIEL MILLER/WRITTEN BY
DANIEL MILLER
MUTE/FEBRUARY 1978
DID NOT CHART

Less a pop record, more a visionary dipping a toe in the water, The Normal's one and only single remains one of Britpop's most startling and accomplished records. Sadly, Londoner Daniel Miller decided not to pursue his solo electronic career, and instead signed Depeche Mode, Yazoo, Erasure, Nick Cave and Moby. His Mute label remains one of the few independents that has never gone cap in hand to a major, while also managing to run the careers of loyal artists big and small by the novel means of paying them fair royalties and leaving them to their own devices. Nevertheless, Mute 001 is one of the best things the label has ever made, an electro-punk record that is harsh and

sexy, rudimentary and futuristic. It might not have been a hit, but you can bet that The Human League, Gary Numan and John Foxx were taking notes.

Both sides of the single take sci-fi author J.G. Ballard's techno-fear and set them to . . . well . . . music, of a sort. 'T.V.O.D.'s' twiddly-bonk symphony is self-explanatory (the narrator is such a TV addict he just sticks the aerial into his skin, and the record ends with a long ear-splitting tone – end of tonight's programmes, end of viewer). But 'Warm Leatherette' is a scream and a work of genius, setting Ballard's *Crash* to an asthmatic, hypnotic, abrasive, one-note dance noise that makes Kraftwerk and Moroder sound as old-school as Slade. Miller's words are then delivered in debonair, poet-in-residence tones, making lines like 'A tear of petrol/Is in your eye/The handbrake/Penetrates your thigh/Quick – let's make love/Before you die' much funnier than they should be. No, really.

Better than the David Cronenberg movie, then. And a helluva lot shorter.

I AM THE FLY/EX-LION TAMER

WIRE

PRODUCED BY MIKE THORNE/WRITTEN BY
COLIN NEWMAN AND GRAHAM LEWIS
HARVEST/FEBRUARY 1978
DID NOT CHART

And in another part of London, more art-punks were sneering at the television. 'There's great danger . . . stay glued to your TV set,' Wire wheedled exasperatedly on 'Ex-Lion Tamer', the nearest they were prepared to go to the usual punk concerns. They might have begun as the most notoriously inept musicians to feature on the 'Live At The Roxy' showcase, but Hornsey Art College students Newman, Lewis, Bruce Gilbert and Robert Gotobed were quick learners. Doomed to commercial failure despite having the commercial might of EMI behind them, they split, re-formed, and have become pointlessly avant garde, while their early records have slowly made them into British punk's most directly influential group. One American band formed in the '80s to do nothing else but play the entirety of Wire's first album, *Pink Flag*.

Newman's vocals remain the ultimate in cockney nagging, and Wire concocted a music to fit. Influenced by Syd Barrett-era Pink Floyd, but too original to be pinned down to it, they made records like 'I Am the Fly' – gleefully imagining themselves spreading disease, subverting the glam-metal stomp, inventing

SHOT BY BOTH SIDES/MAGAZINE

the guitar sounds that invented Blur and Elastica, and writing choruses that broke every known rule about scanning and rhyming while simultaneously worming their way into your head until you pleaded for mercy.

'I Am the Fly' also has fantastic handclaps.

I LOVE THE SOUND OF BREAKING GLASS

NICK LOWE
PRODUCED BY NICK LOWE/WRITTEN BY NICK LOWE, ANDREW BODNAR AND STEPHEN GOULDING
RADAR/FEBRUARY 1978
UK CHART: 7

(I DON'T WANT TO GO TO) CHELSEA

ELVIS COSTELLO AND THE ATTRACTIONS
PRODUCED BY NICK LOWE/WRITTEN BY ELVIS COSTELLO
RADAR/MARCH 1978
UK CHART: 16

WHAT A WASTE/WAKE UP AND MAKE LOVE WITH ME

IAN DURY AND THE BLOCKHEADS
BOTH PRODUCED BY CHAZ JANKEL, PETER JENNER, LAURIE LATHAM AND IAN DURY/
BOTH WRITTEN BY IAN DURY AND CHAZ JANKEL
STIFF/APRIL 1978
UK CHART: 9

Who else in Britain had the ability and vision to cross punk and disco but the Stiff Records crew? Though sonic architect and veteran pop-dabbler Lowe and his friend/protégé Elvis Costello had made the first of several label moves to Radar, ' . . . Breaking Glass' was sheer Stiff skulduggery. The label's stars had applied a knowing irony to the whole rock-rebel shebang from day one, but nothing poked fun at the idea of riot and revolution with quite the same relish as this odd little song, co-written with the rhythm section from pub-rock heroes The Rumour.

While the meticulously detailed rhythm (sliding octave bass, swishing tambourine, more handclaps!) blends the early, bubblegum Bo Diddley disco of Shirley & Company's 'Shame Shame Shame' with a hint of carnival calypso, the gently sung lyrics find the ultimate metaphor for pointless rebellion as comfort food for the young. Rather than being inspired to start a riot of his own, Lowe finds the sound of breaking glass all around makes him feel 'Safe at last.' As the piano gets increasingly tricksy and teasing, Lowe simply intones, 'Nothing new – the sound of breaking glass.' And he was right, but maybe wrong too, because the radio and the public wouldn't have made this playful weirdness a hit without punk having broadened the subjects that pop could be about.

While Lowe was all unashamed novelty, Essex boy Ian Dury had a more edgy ambition and an incredible backing band to match. Led by Jankel (who went on to work with America's best, including Quincy Jones) and honed by years on the pub circuit, The Blockheads established a brand of bar-room disco, capable of lush virtuosity but muscular enough to see off the most pissed of hecklers. Now that a new audience wanted to hear English accents, Dury saw his chance and took it. A former art lecturer partially crippled from polio, he became one of new wave's most charismatic performers, the irony being that, while the able-bodied Stiff performers played on their weaknesses, Dury (already 36 by this time) presented himself as a charming street thug and ladykiller. In some ways he was the personification of punk's reinventive celebration of the everyday person with extraordinary ideas and star presence.

The contrast of beauty and dirt, of Dury's leery sexism and music hall/cockney rhyming slang humour with the gentle adoration of the object of his lust, is perfectly contained in B-side 'Wake Up and Make Love with Me', a disco epic of such graceful flourish that it's hard to believe the band are British. 'What a Waste', with its bubbling funk-reggae lope, is a good old-fashioned list song that warmly but emphatically explains Dury's love of the rock 'n' roll lifestyle. The startling bravura musical interludes force you to believe the singer's romantic fascination with 'Trying to play the fool in a six-piece band', and made Dury an overnight star after all those years as a respected face in pub-rockers Kilburn and The High Roads. Both sides still make me smile and fill my heart with a strangely personal affection for someone I've never met, and now, sadly, never will.

As for Costello, he gives us a continuation of the 'Watching the Detectives' sound that is to 'What a Waste' what meths is to vodka. A bitter sneer at the Kings Road set and the dying remnants of the swinging '60s (a deluded fashion clique that Malcolm McLaren and Vivienne Westwood still traded heavily for and upon), the apparent pointlessness of the tantrum is given weight by cutting black jokes ('They call her Natasha when she looks like Elsie,' he observes of one hapless model type), and the

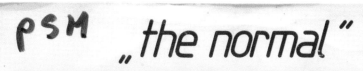

T.V.O.D./WARM LEATHERETTE/THE NORMAL

sinister backing of Steve Naïve's piping Farfisa organ and Pete and Bruce Thomas's ongoing claim to be the best rhythm section in town. Costello's huff is pure, green-eyed 'If you can't join 'em – beat 'em'.

SATISFACTION (I CAN'T GET ME NO)

DEVO
PRODUCED BY DEVO/WRITTEN BY MICK JAGGER AND KEITH RICHARDS
STIFF/APRIL 1978
UK CHART: 41

Yup, Stiff again. Having cornered the UK market in wry new wave eccentrics, the label found themselves putting out pre-major-label singles by Ohio quintet Devo, one of the most successful attempts to infiltrate mainstream pop with creepy art-house ideas. Having come up with the theory of de-evolution – that is, the human race is actually regressing back to the apes, so hey, why not enjoy it? – they proceeded to make an off-kilter, nerd-celebrating electronic rock that oozed disgust for the consumerism, machismo and nostalgia of modern America. They were promo-video pioneers too, and all this provided some neat ironic ballast when they started making student-friendly dance-pop in the '80s, and MTV made them stars.

Their version of the Stones classic can only be described as the original turned inside-out, like the unfortunate baboons at the beginning of David Cronenberg's *The Fly*. The strangely lumpy, brilliantly inelegant groove (a sort of belching skank with bells attached) follows a logic that both extends and subverts the Stones' trance-rock, while singer Bob Mothersbaugh replaces Jagger's laconic misogyny with true sexual frustration . . . a wheedling desperation that at one point just becomes a tongue-twisting chant of 'baybeebaybeebaybee' that finally ends in such a totally *wrong* place that Mothersbaugh has to leap back onto the song like a silent-era comic hanging onto the back of a speeding bus. By the time a sneering shadow of Keef's famous fuzz-guitar riff enters, you know the guy's too damn weird to ever get laid, and you've been treated to the first of new wave's great cover versions, which balance a love of the originals with a desire to rip them out of the pantheon and provide a whole new idea of what they might mean to another, less optimistic, generation.

And, on top of all that, Devo's 'Satisfaction' is also one of the most unlikely dance classics you'll ever shake a leg to. Really. Try standing still to it.

NIGHT FEVER

BEE GEES
PRODUCED BY THE BEE GEES, KARL RICHARDSON AND ALBHY GALUTEN/WRITTEN BY BARRY, ROBIN AND MAURICE GIBB
RSO/APRIL 1978
UK CHART: 1

No record has ever expressed the bittersweet thrill of going out dancing like this. The calm grace of the strings, the ecstatic thrill of the voices, that brilliant, hypnotic wah-wah guitar that plays around the edges of the dancefloor; but, just as importantly, the ever-present knowledge that this pleasure is fleeting, that the mundane greyness of everyday life is waiting to reclaim you, that this peacock display is just an animal mating game, and that the human race outside this place doesn't give a fuck how the music moved you or how indecently sexy you were. If the night is a fever, the next day is probably a dull headache, lifted only by the memory of this song's accompanying group dance, and its communal grace under pressure.

(DON'T FEAR) THE REAPER

BLUE OYSTER CULT
PRODUCED BY MURRAY KRUGMAN, SANDY PEARLMAN AND DAVID LUCAS/WRITTEN BY DONALD ROESER
CBS/MAY 1978
UK CHART: 16

Rock and suicide. A match made in heaven for the US anti-rock wing and their fundmentalist redneck partners in crime who still believe that previously stable teens will do whatever their fave guitar records tell them to do, particularly if they mention death. All very convenient, of course, for the continuing outlaw cred of a genre that lost any sense of threat sometime around, well, when this record came out, I guess. Maybe I missed something, but the only record I've ever heard that truly sounds like an incitement to suicide has never seen its Long Island makers dragged through the courts or even denounced from the PMRC (Parents' Music Resource Center) pulpit. Yet here it is, echoing down the years, saying, with a Byrdsian beauty that seems to fill the air with a benign-yet-chilling twilight glow . . . come on baby, don't be scared, death is like flying, like psychedelic transcendence, just do it, just kill yourself. Harmonized with such mellow seduction, played with a breathy, swooshing, cowbell pulse, the effect is mesmerizing, as the heroine of the song sees that she 'can't go on' and joins . . . her lover? The grim reaper? Are they one and the same? . . . in flight. It's the only time a band characterized as heavy metal have moved me to tears repeatedly, yet I'm forced to conclude that this record is possibly very evil. No one should be able to – should *want* to – make suicide so tempting, so *pretty*. But, if subversive pop is what you want, then this is as persuasive and deviant as it gets.

HI-TENSION

HI-TENSION
PRODUCED BY CHRIS BLACKWELL AND KOFI AYIVOR/WRITTEN BY HI-TENSION ISLAND/MAY 1978
UK CHART: 13

Read the official histories of rock, and you'll see little mention of something that some people quite reasonably call punk-funk. And, if you do, you'll see its invention credited to Talking Heads or Gang of Four or New York no-wavers like James White, who were all great and important. But you won't see any mention of an 11-piece London funk band who grew up, not through art-punk circles, but the dancehalls of black London. Their debut single and the first of just two hits still stands as the most weird, wired and abstract of funk records, and I just don't believe that none of the British punk-inspired popsters who attacked funk with gnarly relish through the late '70s and early '80s didn't listen to Hi-Tension very carefully indeed.

In fact, 'Hi-Tension' is the perfect starting point to describe this monstrously powerful Lost Classic. Because what you hear is some talented but inexperienced musicians attempting to play the smooth jazz-funk of Herbie Hancock or a smaller Earth, Wind & Fire and, when realising they can't, simply beating disco fusion to a bloody pulp. The call-and-response horns and vocal chants wilt in the face of a double-tracked performance by a guitarist called Paul Phillips – one channel twitches with manic scratch-funk malevolence, the other sketches a dark and prowling riff that coils like a cobra. Chris Blackwell (probably the most important white figure in the development of black British music, the man who brought over and rocked-up Bob Marley and forced reggae into the international spotlight) and co-producer Ayivor hear this incredible noise and give it pure dub colour, fill it with a spidery fire and a crucial sense of being 'out there' on the edge of a different noise entirely. By the end,

David Joseph has picked up on his guitarist's mania and turned his keyboards into an irate motorist at a roadblock and everything becomes unhinged, teetering on the edge of chaos until abruptly stopping, leaving a whispered chant of 'Bless the funk/Bless the funk.' And leaving you to recover and wonder what the fuck *that* was, and why Hi-Tension, despite getting another hit with the silly disco cash-in 'British Hustle' and even re-forming in the mid-'80s, didn't go on to be funk's greatest surrealist vandals. Still, they left this behind, and I thank them from the soles of my dancing shoes.

(WHITE MAN) IN HAMMERSMITH PALAIS

THE CLASH
PRODUCED BY THE CLASH/WRITTEN BY JOE STRUMMER AND MICK JONES CBS/JUNE 1978
UK CHART: 32

The single as gig review is a relatively small sub-genre, and for good reason. But, once Strummer gets a disappointing reggae night out at the Palais out of his system, he makes a leap of logic, faith and intellect that took The Clash to a new plateau. By this time, the Pistols had split, The Jam had writer's block, The Banshees and Slits had problems getting records out at all, and the punk nation wanted The Clash to be the leaders of the new revolution. But Strummer knew that, as far as punk really changing anything politically (or even in terms of the music biz) was concerned, the game was up. Instead of putting out another rabble-rouser, the band summed up the futility of the entire punk enterprise over an inappropriately jaunty yet haunting white reggae. Basically, he just told us it was over, most famously in the rhyme: 'The new groups are not concerned/With what there is to be learned/They got Burton suits/Ha! You think it's funny?/Turning rebellion into money.'

Voice cracking with the weight of carrying these unpalatable truths to us, Joe retires to a quiet corner of the dancehall, out of place among the black faces, suddenly feeling like Babylon's representative after all, pleading for nothing more than safety. 'Oh please mistah! Just leave me alone/I'm only looking for fun,' he explains to one suspicious face, grimly, apologetically aware that the National Front is the only white riot in town.

YOU MAKE ME FEEL (MIGHTY REAL)

SYLVESTER

PRODUCED BY PATRICK COWLEY/WRITTEN BY
S. JAMES AND J. WIRRICK
FANTASY/AUGUST 1978
UK CHART: 8

Like 'Car Wash' (see p. 22), this was a record that sorted the *dancers* from the dancers, simply because it was so bloody *fast*. And, even more than 'I Feel Love' (see p. 38), this expression of ecstatic desire was instrumental in establishing an explicitly gay disco in the mainstream. Hell, you couldn't mistake where Sylvester James was coming from, from the flamboyant clothes to the unashamedly androgynous TV(!) appearances to the sky-scraping, girlish falsetto. Which is perhaps why James and his production genius Cowley don't even get a fleeting mention in books purporting to be encyclopaedias of popular music, despite their influence being obvious in every uptempo commercial house or trance record you'll ever hear.

'You Make Me Feel' is more than just a great, ahead-of-its-time pop-dance record, taking its cue from Giorgio Moroder, but blending its hypnotic synth generations with the oomph of a traditional band. The emphasis here is a striking testament to what love means – when Sylvester's lover touches him on the dancefloor, only then does he 'feel real', which is profound personal shit when you think about it. The record also speeds with the joy of open sexuality, a celebration of and with a community making giant strides towards long-overdue acceptance. But, within three years, Cowley and James's homobase of San Francisco would be ravaged by something more destructive than the usual homophobic oppression and violence. Within four, Cowley was dead. Within ten, Sylvester was gone too. All the more reason, if any were needed, to give them the respect and status in pop history that they deserve.

PICTURE THIS

BLONDIE

PRODUCED BY MIKE CHAPMAN/WRITTEN BY
DEBBIE HARRY, CHRIS STEIN AND JIMMY DESTRI
CHRYSALIS/AUGUST 1978
UK CHART: 12

Blondie transcended punk or anything to with CBGBs because they knew that no cool scene can ever match a perfect pop record. This was their first perfect pop single, and is a key example of both the band's subtlety and power, and Ms Harry's planet-slaying sense of how to blend trad girl-group boy adoration and the erotic poetry that can only come from a fully grown woman. 'I will give you my finest hour/The one I spent watching you shower' and 'All I want is a photo in my wallet/A small remembrance . . . of something more solid' conjure sexual imagery worthy of a Cole Porter before the choruses transform want into need. Both boys and girls were smitten as they glimpsed a world of distant and beautiful lust.

HONG KONG GARDEN

SIOUXSIE AND THE BANSHEES

PRODUCED BY NILS STEVENSON AND
STEVE LILLYWHITE/WRITTEN BY JOHN MCKAY,
KENNY MORRIS, SIOUXSIE SIOUX AND
STEVE SEVERIN
POLYDOR/AUGUST 1978
UK CHART: 7

The first Banshees single is a testament to the wisdom of waiting. Though one of punk's most famous names (it was Siouxsie who provoked Bill Grundy into getting leery on the *Today* show; their first gig was at the legendary 100 Club punk fest with Sid Vicious on drums and future Adam Ant partner Marco Pirroni on guitar; every clued-in punk girl already modelled herself on Sioux), the former Susan Dallion and fellow Bromley Contingent (see The Cure/The Members p. 78) face Severin took time to find the right collaborators, write material, sign the right deal. But the results remain startling – a sound so strange and singular it pretty much invented 'post-punk' overnight.

Beginning with a xylophone, ending with a gong, 'Hong Kong Garden' as a lyric is little more than a set of exceedingly dodgy Chinese stereotypes, inspired, apparently, by Sioux's and

(WHITE MAN) MAN IN HAMMERSMITH PALAIS/THE CLASH

Severin's local Chinese takeaway. But the aura created by the darkly chiming art-thrash is not one of loathing or suspicion, but mystified fascination – a desire to break out and be something more exotic than suburban white that the band later perfected on the likes of 'Israel' (see p. 140) and 'Arabian Nights'.

But the biggest thrill still comes from John McKay's bizarre guitar – a mixture of duelling banjo and tolling bell that reinvented the guitar solo as a set of elastic, funky dischords taking the minimal post-Velvets beat 'n' bass on a journey . . . well . . . to the Orient on one level, but also to somewhere pungent, inky, kinky, sexy with a tang of S&M . . . places where a few chords just shouldn't be able to go. Unlike the vast majority of singles in this book, it really was a completely new sound, and an announcement of endless possibilities. Even more than Bowie's Berlin period, it showed everyone a place that the new music could travel to. Unfortunately, that turned out, in many cases, to be a place called goth. But don't blame The Banshees. You can invent it, but you can't control what the less imaginative do with it.

EVER FALLEN IN LOVE (WITH SOMEONE YOU SHOULDN'T'VE)?

BUZZCOCKS

PRODUCED BY MARTIN RUSHENT/WRITTEN BY
PETE SHELLEY
UNITED ARTISTS/SEPTEMBER 1978
UK CHART: 12

TEENAGE KICKS

THE UNDERTONES

PRODUCED BY THE UNDERTONES/WRITTEN BY
JOHN O'NEILL
SIRE/OCTOBER 1978
UK CHART: 31

Love, love, love. 'It's easy,' reckoned John Lennon, but The Kids knew different. Especially those of us who were spotty, awkward and rushing with ugly hormones that drove us to desperate measures both public and private. So, while the Sex Pistols and The Clash remain more IMPORTANT in the punk pantheon, these two records command more true affection among those of a certain age. Because, no matter how much you agreed with Rotten's or Strummer's view of the world, Sten

guns and anarchy meant nothing if Allyson Bird had just mugged you off and you couldn't sleep at night because of the shameful dreams about Miss Jeffreys in Home Economics. Or was that just me?

These two records redefined the British pop love song. Do you think I'm sexy? Well, no, you big-nosed twat, and what's more I don't feel I'm too sexy either. Pete and Feargal understand, and are dealing with it in the only logical ways: weeping and wanking. 'You spurn my natural emotions/You make me feel like dirt/And I'm hurt.' That, Mr Shelley, remains very beautiful. And now I notice that you're actually gay, I appreciate what you were saying when you remark that 'We won't stay together much longer/Until we realise that we are the same.' That rangy guitar lick, the one that tells me that things won't change because *it* never changes, still makes me feel better about Ms Bird somehow, even after all these years.

And Mr Sharkey, I know you didn't write these words. But it's the way you howl the word 'Awlrigheet!', the sordid glee in the admission that tonight's dirty fantasy is 'The best I've ever had', the so-young-yet-so-old grain of your white soul voice, that makes those rolling and tumbling wall-of-garage guitars hit all the way home. Handclaps must have been tough, though, under the circumstances.

Why were so many punks obsessed with wanking? Someone should write a book.

PUBLIC IMAGE

PUBLIC IMAGE LTD

PRODUCED BY PUBLIC IMAGE LTD/WRITTEN BY
PUBLIC IMAGE LTD
VIRGIN/OCTOBER 1978
UK CHART: 9

You know, there's a lot to be said for competition in rock 'n' roll. Because, just a few weeks after 'Hong Kong Garden' had stunned us new-wavey types, Johnny Rotten returned from the chaotic Pistols split and beat The Banshees, hands down. 'Public Image' is one of the most astounding debuts – one of the most astounding records – in rock's rich tapestry. It takes everything key about rock 'n' roll – defiance, self-definition, dance groove, guitar heroism, joy out of despair – and bends it into a shape barely recognizable as rock at all. Jim Walker's rock-hard, swaggering beats; Jah Wobble's booming bass, a two-note thrash with dub's reckless low-end; the neo-classical beauty and power of Keith Levine's ringing, climbing, swandiving guitar; and

HONG KONG GARDEN/SIOUXSIE AND THE BANSHEES
PAGE 64

Rotten, now just plain old John Lydon, saying goodbye to the Pistols' descent into hell with every sinew straining for escape, the liberation of saying 'no'. It was head music from the heart, pop music from another planet, a whole new thing and, despite its influence on a number of musicians, it remains a challenge that no one could take up. It was, is, simply too good.

As for Lydon's lyric, sung in an eerie high-register whine that we'd never heard before, it was aimed at Malcolm McLaren ('You never listened to a thing that I said!/You only see me for the clothes that I wear,' he begins, hurt and vengeful) but could easily be aimed at us. 'I'm not the same as when I began,' he sings in a lower key, his voice drenched in spooked memories of the Pistols' American debacle, betrayals, police raids on his home, beatings in the street from 'patriots', his best friend's descent into heroin addiction, and rises back to defiance for 'I will not be treated as property!'

As the record hit the charts, Sid Vicious was arrested for the murder of Nancy Spungen. Lydon turns his back, as he did to the audience during the early PiL shows. 'GOODBYE', his voice echoes at the death, with one creepy breath over the fade, like he'd just woken, exhausted, from a nightmare.

DOWN IN THE TUBE STATION AT MIDNIGHT

THE JAM
PRODUCED BY VIC COPPERSMITH-HEAVEN/WRITTEN BY PAUL WELLER
POLYDOR/OCTOBER 1978
UK CHART: 15

Play this, 'Public Image' (see above) and '(White Man) in Hammersmith Palais' (see p. 63) together and you can hear punk's death rattle, as the genre's three major idols succumb to disillusion, but each face up to and find their own ways out of it, onwards and upwards. While Lydon rejected rock and challenged what his audience would accept, and Strummer embraced trad rock but rubbed the fans' noses in their shortcomings, Weller looked at the crowd, didn't like what he saw and wrote a short story about them. 'They smelt of pubs/And Wormwood Scrubs/And too many right wing meetings.' Was this really the moody mod boy who went on about voting Conservative and insisted that the kids know where it's at?

Well, not exactly. Weller had done too much too soon – two albums in six months, endless touring – and suffered premature burn-out and writer's block. Chastened by the experience, he re-emerged, aged just 20, a much older man, with all the bitterness that suggests. In particular, he'd realized that the London he idealized so much in his teens that he would catch the train from Woking and carry a tape recorder around the capital just to be able hear the streets over and over again, can be an unforgiving place for the vulnerable. So he wrote a song from the perspective of an ordinary working man on his way back to his suburban home who is beaten senseless by skinheads. The result was The Jam's great leap forward, and one of the most intelligent and detailed pieces of poetry anyone would ever place within a pop song.

The tube station is 'Cold and uninviting, partially naked.' 'I fumble for change/And pull out the Queen/Smiling, beguiling.' The attack comes, and that astonishing line about right-wing meetings prefaces the victim's heartbreaking, vivid pleading. 'I've a little money and a takeaway curry/I'm on my way home to my wife/She'll be lining up the cutlery/You *know* she's expecting me/Polishing the glasses and pulling out the cork.' To no avail. 'The smell of brown leather/It blended in with the weather.' And as he lies in his own blood, picking out strange details from the walls, the final horror – 'They took the keys and she'll think it's me' – undercut by a born storyteller's pathos . . . 'The wine will be flat and the curry's gone cold.'

Weller's voice had changed too, a cockney-tinged blue-eyed soul replacing the stentorian bark of before. Coppersmith-Heaven gives it all the kind of space that allows the skittering funk light and shade, sweetening the bitter pill. Suddenly, The Jam had their finger on everybody's pulse, had mainlined all our fears, and were on their way to being Britain's biggest, most related-to band.

DAMAGED GOODS/LOVE LIKE ANTHRAX/ARMALITE RIFLE

GANG OF FOUR
PRODUCED BY GANG OF FOUR AND BOB LAST/ WRITTEN BY GANG OF FOUR
FAST/OCTOBER 1978
DID NOT CHART

More handclaps. More punk-funk. More sexual inadequacy. More provincial students reinventing rock in their own apparently unglamorous image. Another strange kind of guitar hero. More music that made you stand back from the radio and whisper, 'What the bloody hell was *that*?'

DOWN IN THE TUBE STATION AT MIDNIGHT/THE JAM

On the title track of this debut EP from Leeds's finest, lead singer Jon King inhabits the idea of being already soiled by sex with yelping hysteria, but guitarist Andy Gill gets the best lines as he puts down his funk-meets-Dr-Feelgood-riff discord and explains, in the voice of a crumbling middle-aged man, how fucked he feels. 'Damaged goods/Send them back/I can't work, I can't achieve/Send me back/Open the till/And refund the change you said would do me good/Refund the cost/You. Said. You're. Cheap. But. YOU'RE. TOO. MUCH!' I tried, at the time, to tease out every dimension of these words. Still do, and I hope to succeed before I die.

'Love Like Anthrax' unleashes a monstrous feedback guitar sound, like a man trying to play 'The Star Spangled Banner' while being electrocuted, before this loping tribal beat appears and someone just . . . coughs. And then, while King has another go at explaining this love thing ('I feel like a beetle on its back!'), Gill explains the record production process. In this dry, contemptuous way. What was this? An onward process of demystification, yeah, I know, but, I guess what I'm trying to say is that this was a new rock language completely, one almost too real, too cold. Yet so thrilling combined with this bass-driven, guitar-overdriven noise. It was bleak and industrial, as the journalists said at the time. But they meant it as a compliment.

Oh – and 'Armalite Rifle' is a stomping mid-tempo rock song protesting at the army's presence on the streets of Northern Ireland. 'Used against you/Like Irish jokes on the BBC . . . I disapprove of it/So does Jon,' Gill intones with an off-hand grumble that just seems to make everything more passionate.

LE FREAK

CHIC

PRODUCED AND WRITTEN BY NILE RODGERS AND
BERNARD EDWARDS
ATLANTIC/NOVEMBER 1978
UK CHART: 7

While the punks were trying to get the funk, those who already had it were upping the ante. Calling 'Le Freak' a disco record is like calling *Taxi Driver* a film about cabbies. It is the greatest moment of disco's greatest band, and perhaps the greatest pop ever made out of balancing sublimely joyful and muscular musicianship with chilly, contemptuous cynicism. After all, Chic were from New York.

While the best of 'Le Freak' is in Bernard Edwards's bassline – so complete, so full of sinew, blood and bone you could feel it,

inside you, as if it were being injected straight into your thighs – the rest is also all gold . . . or rather, cold steel. Tony Thompson's drums always lag instinctively behind the bass, pushing it, sending Edwards's horny bass asides spinning, preparing you for handclaps that suck on the beat rather than simply adding to it. Nile Rodgers plays an itching rhythm guitar that Hi-Tension would recognise, but in a language that even they would struggle to understand. The strings glide towards some distant disco cloud, particularly on the epic instrumental bridge. And Luci Martin's and Norma Jean Wright's deliberately anonymous, clipped vocals spit doubt at the whole enterprise. 'Just one try', they sneer, 'and you too will be *sold*.' And, as disco's four-to-the-floor crossover populism almost wiped out all traces of black soul, sold is exactly what Chic, black musicians and the traditional soul audience were. History is here too, but Chic, with Rodgers already a veteran of talent nights at the Harlem Apollo, pour sarcastic scorn on any idea of progress for Afro-America. 'Like the days of stompin' at the Savoy/Now we freak – oh what a joy!' As for any kind of dance that 'Le Freak' may be, 'freak' in the Afro-American vernacular refers to a promiscuous woman or a man who loves giving cunnilingus. Filthy street slang plus wry French sophistication equals . . . well, they don't bother running through the steps anyway.

So Chic's sex boogie comes with the irony of US disco's preoccupation with white European 'class', and disco's peak moment gets it edge from a detached disgust for the 'liberation' of dancing's weekend escapism. But then Rodgers, Edwards and Thompson had already been in a failed punk band called Allah and The Knife-Wielding Punks. If you still insist that punk and disco were natural opposites, listen to 'Le Freak' again and check the serrated edge hidden inside the elegant threads.

DAMAGED GOODS/LOVE LIKE ANTHRAX/ARMALITE RIFLE/GANG OF FOUR

PAGE 68

I'M EVERY WOMAN

CHAKA KHAN

PRODUCED BY ARIF MARDIN/WRITTEN BY
NICKOLAS ASHFORD AND VALERIE SIMPSON
WARNER BROS/NOVEMBER 1978
UK CHART: 11

If disco all but wiped out soul (check out Nelson George's *The Death of Rhythm & Blues* for the definitive account of that process), it didn't mean that soul had no place in disco. It was left to vocalists to adapt and to keep alive a sort of soul without the blues/gospel band format, and ain't nobody did that better than Ms Chaka Khan.

Raised in blues-drenched Chicago and renamed by her local chapter of the Black Panthers (her real name is Yvette Marie Stevens), Khan brought both erotic maturity and a churchy ecstasy to disco vocals, cementing the idea of the 'disco diva' aimed originally at women, and worshipped to this day by gay men hooked on the blend of sexual energy and romantic melodrama. The producer and writers here were all-time-great soul veterans at Atlantic and Motown, and can't resist pinning down the showboat strings with the odd shot of stuttering funk while Ms Khan sings a descending, bluesy 'Whoa, whoa, whoa' in a way that gives the word 'maneater' a whole new, chewier dimension. She's making some claim for herself, of course. But I've never found a reason here to argue.

SEPTEMBER

EARTH, WIND & FIRE

PRODUCED BY MAURICE WHITE/WRITTEN BY M.
WHITE, A. MCKAY AND A. WILLIS
CBS/NOVEMBER 1978
UK CHART: 3

Whenever I read something by some ancient rocker complaining about disco's 'mechanical' beat, I always wanted to play them Earth, Wind & Fire and hear them try to convince me that Ringo knew more about rhythm. Maurice White might have been a purveyor of daft new-age platitudes in the lyric department, and the live shows might have been a cleaned-up and blanded-out version of Sun Ra's and George Clinton's mothership connections. But no one else in this book played drums with John Coltrane, or Ramsey Lewis, Booker T, Curtis Mayfield or half the classic Motown roster for that matter.

All of which provides a reasonable grounding for becoming the Duke Ellington of disco and funk, which is exactly what White was.

The joy of orchestra, brass section (*the* brass section) and falsetto harmony finds sublime expression here, driven as it is by the toughest virtuoso small-band funk this side of James Brown. It's the sound of pure inexplicable happiness – always the hardest thing to do in pop without becoming syrup – and the way White growls 'Yowww!' remains one of the finest and funniest moments of the period, a lascivious wink to all of us who knew that the cosmic jive was just there to give falsetto singer Philip Bailey something to attach his angel's wings to.

GIVE ME EVERYTHING

MAGAZINE

PRODUCED BY TONY WILSON/WRITTEN BY
HOWARD DEVOTO
VIRGIN/NOVEMBER 1978
DID NOT CHART

So the charts of 1978 to 1982 opened up to all manner of inspired weirdness but remained resolutely closed to Devoto and Magazine. Everything about this single screams 'I am important' – from the baroque eastern guitar that later serves as a . . . um . . . I guess you'd call it a chorus, through the 'pay attention' thunk-funk of the bassline, to the grandiose synth fanfares – and resembles Roxy Music after a month at an army boot camp. But perhaps the self-loathing posing as arrogance was the problem, as those without strong stomachs didn't want to hear 'a baldy little pain' (as Nick Kent called him in an *NME* review so hostile it inspired the amused Devoto to send the writer a five-pound note) sneering, 'You're gonna receive punishment . . . Oh so oblique and easy/Oh you're so bleak and easy . . . now you're gonna feel like I feel.' This was Costello's emotional fascism taken to (un)necessary extremes, unsweetened by conventional hooklines, dripping with carefully administered poison. It still expresses fear of love . . . of women . . . brilliantly, because it exposes the feelings men don't want to acknowledge.

Never a contender for Simon Bates's 'Our Tune', as far as I recall.

LE FREAK/CHIC
PAGE 70

ONE NATION UNDER A GROOVE

FUNKADELIC

PRODUCED BY GEORGE CLINTON/WRITTEN BY
GEORGE CLINTON, GARY SHIDER AND
WALTER 'JUNIE' MORRISON
WARNERS/NOVEMBER 1978
UK CHART: 9

The greatest dance record ever made? Well, you know, that's a tough one. One thing is for sure: there have been many attempts since to give us a vision of the dance as Utopia – a blessed, transcendental state where life is communal perfection, as long as you never sit down – but none has convinced as much as George Clinton's commercial peak.

Though not a disco record in the narrowest terms, it remains the greatest argument against disco's supposed monotony. Because, while the pin-down beat is just four-to-the-floor kick-drum and handclaps, it's just the ballast while the world's greatest musicians fly above, below and around it (disproving the statement of the track's opening line) in a disciplined but virtuoso form of jazz polyphony. Everything here is playing a different tune or variation on the rhythm, yet all somehow lock together in a community of sensual overload. Clinton begins the song howling but, once assured of our attention, croons his Utopian vision with all the gentle optimism of a song at bedtime: 'Here's your chance to dance your way/Out of our constrictions/Gonna be freakin' up and down the hang-up alleyway . . . do you promise to funk?' Promise? Why would you turn down a chance like that, as percussion, vocals, squelching bass and playful surprises tickle the edges of the mix, the whole breaks down into the gorgeous, almost religious 'Lo-lodi-oh-doe' chant, and the band, slowly, almost imperceptibly, get louder, wilder, funkier?

HIT ME WITH YOUR RHYTHM STICK

IAN DURY AND THE BLOCKHEADS

PRODUCED BY CHAZ JANKEL, IAN DURY AND
THE BLOCKHEADS/WRITTEN BY IAN DURY AND
CHAZ JANKEL
STIFF/NOVEMBER 1978
UK CHART: 1

We bid farewell to Dury's part in this book just as The Blockheads reach their peak. Because, although there was still some great music to come from him and them, Jankel was on his way to leaving at a crucial time (he later returned), which left Dury without a melodicist capable of writing and producing great singles. It's almost as if '. . . Rhythm Stick' used up too much magic.

While Ian Dury recites another life-enhancing list, The Blockheads play the funk like trickles of perfumed rain until snapping into choruses that ring with pop triumph and a drum/bass/sax break that sneaks free-jazz into the charts with brash and smooth surety. Dury's words sound great, but, for the one and only time in his career, they have to surrender to the majesty of his backing band. Despite all the technology and production knowledge that's come since, this remains the best funk a British band has ever made because it *is made by a band*, and perfectly ends a year that saw groups taking early steps to resolve snotty white punk and fluid black dance. It does it with love, grace and a generosity born of channelling all that skill without an ounce of self-indulgence. Jankel knew they couldn't top it, and maybe Dury, in his heart of hearts, knew it too.

1979

1979

Welcome to My Favourite Year.

1979 was, in pop music terms at least, gloriously nuts. Though anything can be applied to anything through the benefits of hindsight, it seems as if artists from all sides of the spectrum understood that things would soon change, and made hay while the last rays of the sun were still shining. Punk and disco had taken the music industry by surprise and, as they struggled to understand what kind of strange noises and voices pop fans wanted, they allowed artists a degree of freedom and adventure that echoed the joy and tumult of the mid-'60s. 1979 saw the peak and the end of that process.

The strongest sounds were varied and implausibly brave, and usually got into the charts. Arty ironists produced one-shot pop marvels that took the piss out of the whole process, and sold. Punk's and disco's finest became sharper and better, and sold. Women sang things they'd never sung before and would rarely sing again, and sold. Mavericks in the margins ranted, raved, pushed the envelope as far as they could without tearing it completely, and, to a lesser extent, sold too. The Specials and The Police took contrasting roads to fusing rock and reggae, one rough 'n' ready, politically concerned, anti-star; the other impeccably clean, solipsistic, filled with the contrivance and distance that would provide a template for a more organized and deliberate kind of transatlantic success. The sound of the suburbs had a more submissive and resigned feel than the urban new wave, displayed a different kind of ambition. And, towards the end of the year, a new noise that seemed like novelty began a long journey to becoming pop's dominant cultural and commercial force.

Many of the singles below ooze either dread or an almost hysterical happiness, as if they know what's round the corner and need to express something vivid, spooked and forbidden before the inevitable clampdown begins. Of course, songwriters don't look at things like the Tories' election victory or America's hostage crises, see the writing on the wall, and write songs accordingly. But pop, especially good pop, did and does reflect the world around it, and the end of the '70s did preface a new era where the advances of the '60s – practical and emotional, real and imagined – came under relentless attack. From 1980 onwards, musicians, just like everyone else, were forced to define themselves and their work in relation to this new reality. 1979 was pop's last year of gleeful irresponsibility, the last year in the playground before it was forced to grow up.

Honourable mentions: Donna Summer/'Hot Stuff' and 'Bad Girls' (both Casablanca); The Jam/'When You're Young' (Polydor); Spizz Energi/'Where's Captain Kirk?' (Rough Trade); Neil Young with Crazy Horse/'My My Hey Hey (Out of the Blue)'/'Hey Hey My My (Into the Black)' (Reprise); Blondie/'Dreaming' (Chrysalis); Janet Kay/'Silly Games' (Scope)

I WILL SURVIVE

GLORIA GAYNOR

PRODUCED AND WRITTEN BY DINO FEKARIS AND
FREDDIE PERREN
POLYDOR/JANUARY 1979
UK CHART: 1

New Jersey's Gloria Gaynor had already played a major part in disco's rise with 1974's 'Never Can Say Goodbye', an ornate slice of hi-NRG orchestral Vegas soul (co-produced by Tony Bongiovi, who was by now sculpting its sheet-metal opposite with the Ramones). A good record it was too; but as nothing compared to this, the ultimate female anthem of defiance out of heartbreak, of dancing all over the pain of rejection.

As piano, strings and even harp try desperately to keep 'I Will Survive' at the level of showbiz melodrama, Ms Gaynor triumphs with a vocal of great subtlety. She could have roared it or wailed it, instead she combines the two with a true interpreter's instincts, one line tough and imperious, the next breaking slightly to reveal the cost of what she sings. Because she still loves him. You can tell. And the only reason she mentions survival at all is because she strongly considered the option to 'lay down and die'. The difference in her demeanour is not in depth of feeling, but in the lessons learned about self-preservation. 'I'm not that chained-up little person still in love with you,' she warns, reminding us that slavery isn't just a racial scar. The fact that the song was written by two men only makes the generation-to-generation timelessness of 'I Will Survive' more remarkable. And that's before you get to its adoption as a gay anthem, and what the song could come to mean to them – to anyone – in the wake of AIDS. To make this stick to so many for so many different reasons, the cheesiness of this music wasn't just acceptable, but essential.

HEART OF GLASS

BLONDIE

PRODUCED BY MIKE CHAPMAN/WRITTEN BY
DEBBIE HARRY AND CHRIS STEIN
CHRYSALIS/JANUARY 1979
UK CHART: 1

Harry's greatest moment is not altogether different from Gaynor's. Thought blokey was God's gift, turned out he wasn't, better move on. But, whereas Gloria is still on the verge of breakdown, Debbie is all ice. Her heart of glass is double-glazed. 'Once I had a love/And it was a gas/Soon turned out/To be a pain in the ass': less the innocence of Monroe than the seen-it-all of Lauren Bacall.

'Heart of Glass' was the first, massively successful on every level, 'punk' band attempt at pure disco pop, all boom-tit drums and drifting and pulsing Giorgio Moroder sequencers and ironic octave bass runs. You sure can't hear the stomp-pomp that producer Chapman was doing with The Sweet et al. just a few years before. Harry's schizophrenic take on lost love – one minute cooing plaintiveness, the next glacial sneering – perhaps explains why, despite her platinum-slut sexuality, Harry was more of an icon to girls than boys. Her heart got broken like everyone else's, but she swaggered out of the debris, retouched her lipstick, placed her hands on her hips, and distracted the next passing sap so much he smacked into a lamp-post, while she just smiled that cold, knowing smile. Woman Power, with dramatic split-ends.

KILLING AN ARAB/
10.15 ON A SATURDAY NIGHT

THE CURE

BOTH PRODUCED BY CHRIS PARRY/BOTH WRITTEN BY
ROBERT SMITH, LOL TOLHURST AND
MICHAEL DEMPSEY
FICTION/JANUARY 1979
DID NOT CHART

THE SOUND OF THE SUBURBS

THE MEMBERS

PRODUCED BY STEVE LILLYWHITE/WRITTEN BY
JEAN-MARIE CARROLL AND NICKY TESCO
VIRGIN/JANUARY 1979
UK CHART: 12

While the first punks were inner city kids, their followers were largely suburbanites. The Pistols' inner circle – Siouxsie, Steve Severin, Billy Idol – were The Bromley Contingent, the kind of terminally bored and alienated, thrill-seeking lower-middle-class youth going up to London for the day that dashing urbanites still dismiss airily as 'weekenders' even now. For these characters, conformity was a more insidious pressure, reinforced by their home environment of identical streets and ordered

HEART OF GLASS/BLONDIE

lawns, the Friday night after-pub violence they were usually on the receiving end of, the quietly desperate commuting workers they were expected to become. Those kids – The Jam, The Banshees, Sham 69, Generation X – grasped punk like a lifebelt. These two records from archetypal suburban new-wave bands took punk for contrasting but complementary kinds of ride.

In *England Is Mine*, Michael Bracewell's idiosyncratic study of English pop, the author fingers Crawley's The Cure as 'the musical expression of suburbia itself' as frontman Robert Smith 'moans his lyrics about blood, death and loneliness with all the plaintive weariness of a person whose library books are eternally overdue'. The most overdue book under Robert's bed was that guidebook to existential nihilism *The Outsider* by Albert Camus. The trio, producer Parry (who had tried and failed to sign the Pistols and The Clash and ended up with a band that shifted more units than either put together) and up-and-coming engineer Mike Hedges fashioned a maverick masterpiece out of its blank amorality, a playpen lo-fi whizz of splashing symbols and nervy bass, Smith's mock-Arabic guitar lines and fizzing fuzzbox interjections overcoming – no, reinforcing – the basic ridiculousness of it all. The B-side was even better, a boring night in the house as water torture and teen neurosis. Like Howard Devoto in 'Boredom', Smith is waiting for the telephone to ring, but there's a girl involved and he's getting paranoid. I mean, what else is there to do in Crawley? He then unleashes the most brilliantly inappropriate tinny-metal guitar solo before the bass drowns everything in clumsy misery.

Meanwhile, down the road in Camberley, Nicky Tesco is too busy taking in his surroundings to settle for bedroom angst. Planes rend the air overhead, Broadmoor's sirens wail, and the 'Youth club group used to wanna be free – now they want ANARCHY!' 'The Sound of the Suburbs' is a witty and busy riposte to Smith's solipsism and a sly parody of The Clash's apocalyptic London, contrasting Carroll's churning and jangling Clashchords and Gary Baker's clean Duane Eddy lead, looking at everything from Mum's Sunday roast to a neighbour's death with the same boisterous sympathy. The suburbs may be crap, but it's Tesco's crap, and its endless normality is as worthy of our attention as the fashionable and cosmopolitan capital. And anyway, Nicky can get the train to Chelsea at the weekend.

Smith hated the in-a-tin-box sound of his early stuff, made the whole thing into distant gothic melodrama, and The Cure cleaned up, despite being complete rubbish compared to their vivid and hilarious opening shots. It was the trick Wire, Gang of Four and other small-but-beautiful post-punk noisemakers couldn't pull off, probably because they just weren't tasteless and cynical enough. Smith even played with suburban queen

Sioux and her Banshees for a while, before hoovering up her fans too. The Members were just too proudly ugly and jocular to survive, as Britpop prettied up and got a proper business plan together in the '80s.

OUTDOOR MINER

WIRE

PRODUCED BY MIKE THORNE/WRITTEN BY COLIN NEWMAN AND GRAHAM LEWIS
HARVEST/JANUARY 1979
UK CHART: 51

The nearest thing Wire got to a hit because, despite no radio play and little promotion, it was so glorious in melody and texture that the few who heard it had to buy it. There are many who think that all pop should have turned out like this, the apotheosis of what *NME* writer and future pop-propagandist Paul Morley labelled 'New Pop' ('a rock music that retains all the myths, imagination, romance and ambiguities of rock & roll whilst simultaneously insisting upon honesty, simplicity, adventure and relevance'). Elusive in meaning (maybe some kind of hymn to evolution, maybe not), allusive in sound, graceful and warm almost despite its maverick ambition, 'Outdoor Miner' proved that punks could do the beauty thing too.

OLIVER'S ARMY

ELVIS COSTELLO AND THE ATTRACTIONS

PRODUCED BY NICK LOWE/WRITTEN BY ELVIS COSTELLO
RADAR/FEBRUARY 1979
UK CHART: 2

Having crafted the pop template for Pat Benatar's 'Love Is a Battlefield' (accidents will happen), Costello turned his attention to battles outside the bedroom. 'Oliver's Army' casts an educated eye, through a series of slogans and arch puns, at the connections between imperialism, exported war and the cannon fodder that is the British working-class male without education and prospects. It said 'No future' in such a subtle way that radio didn't notice; they were too interested in the dramatic piano line, the unforgettable chorus and the wet wall of sound, pinched, Costello later admitted, from Abba. It remains Costello's biggest British hit, despite the line, 'It only takes one itchy trigger/One

OLIVER'S ARMY/ELVIS COSTELLO AND THE ATTRACTIONS

more widow/One less white nigger.' Note one: it was around this time that a drunk Costello fell foul of the US music scene when, in an argument in a bar with some hippy rockers, he called Ray Charles 'a blind, ignorant nigger'. Note two: when my friend Faz and I went busking on the London Underground a few years later, I ended up singing this line just as a young black guy walked past. He gave me a look that froze my blood. I sang 'one less white hero' for the rest of the day.

Now you can't move without hearing the word 'nigger' out of the mouths of young black men sponsored by the white US music scene. How things change; and not always for the better.

MONEY IN MY POCKET (PART 1)

DENNIS BROWN
PRODUCED AND WRITTEN BY JOE GIBBS
LIGHTNING/FEBRUARY 1979
UK CHART: 14

'Can't Buy Me Love' made into a sensual plea with a light-but-propulsive rhythm. It was reggae-soul crooner Brown's biggest hit, and I don't suppose he had more trouble getting love than money after the ladies heard him sing like this.

STRANGE TOWN

THE JAM
PRODUCED BY VIC COPPERSMITH-HEAVEN/WRITTEN
BY PAUL WELLER
POLYDOR/MARCH 1979
UK CHART: 15

Paul Weller was now a master composer/arranger of classic singles. But this didn't stop him from being one bitter suburbanite. Having been rejected and ridiculed by the Pistols/Clash in-crowd, he decides that London isn't a city now, but a *town*, with all the narrow-minded claustrophobia and conformity that implies.

'Strange Town' gives his storm-in-a-teacup anger authority simply by being packed with information and great *bits* – the chiming machine-gun intro, the northern soul stomp of the verse, the dynamic breakdowns and crash-ins, the multitude of jump-cut hooklines that a lesser writer would be saving for other songs. It's as impatient as Weller, who is so pissed off that no one will help him read his *A–Z* that he ends by demanding we break

the whole place up. From now on, Jam singles almost always demanded something urgent and barely possible of us. His ever-growing army of Harrington-clad fans punched the air in agreement and had another beer.

HORRORSHOW

SCARS
PRODUCED BY BOB LAST/WRITTEN BY SCARS
FAST/MARCH 1979
DID NOT CHART

Before we get on to 'Horrorshow', a quick word about Fast and its far-sighted boss, Bob Last. Last discovered The Human League, Gang of Four, The Mekons and The Fire Engines, and put out a set of singles between 1978 and 1981 so extreme, prophetic and *whole* that you imagined Fast as some self-contained planet located conveniently in Edinburgh. It was as important an indie label as Rough Trade, Postcard or Creation, and Last certainly had more adventure and foresight than Alan McGee.

Scars were four Edinburgh teens (Bobby King, Paul Research, John Mackie and Calumm MacKay) who remain utterly obscure. This is probably because, when they signed to a major label after this single's initial impact, they bewildered even the most open-minded new waver by reciting nuclear panic poems over rubbery jangle-pop while smothered in a riot of new romantic clothes and make-up that even Adam Ant would have rejected as a bit too panto. Nevertheless, their first single is the single most violent record of the post-punk era – as eloquent a summing-up of Kubrick's film of Burgess's *A Clockwork Orange* as The Normal managed for J.G. Ballard. Based on a malevolent mix of strolling beat, stalking bassline and toothache string-bending one-note guitar, it goes through as much of the story as it can manage in three minutes while occasionally descending into a haze of screaming threats in Scots accents and glistening guitar chaos. Kubrick would probably have banned it too, given the chance.

MONEY IN MY POCKET (PART 1)/DENNIS BROWN
PAGE 82

HE'S THE GREATEST DANCER

SISTER SLEDGE

PRODUCED AND WRITTEN BY BERNARD EDWARDS
AND NILE RODGERS
ATLANTIC/MARCH 1979
UK CHART: 6

Chic weren't just geniuses for Chic. By now, they were guns for hire, and this first hit for Kathie, Debbie, Kim and Joni Sledge is one of their most adorable confections, a shining girl-group classic led by Tony Thompson's rolling thump, rabbit-in-headlight strings and the motto for living that is 'A Wop Do WOW!'

I guess Bernard and Niles were playing it straight for these Philly sisters. Except . . . well . . . the disco that our heroine and her gang are at is in San Francisco. She mentions, almost casually, that at first it isn't her thing. Maybe she isn't the Gucci-clad Gene Kelly's thing either. You know, that line 'He had the kind of body that would shame Adonis/And a face that would make any man . . . *proud*.' I know. There are plenty of dance-pop records that really don't have hidden meanings. But, with Chic, they always *feel* as if they do.

AT HOME HE'S A TOURIST

GANG OF FOUR

PRODUCED AND WRITTEN BY GANG OF FOUR
EMI/MARCH 1979
UK CHART: 58

The story goes that Jon King, Andy Gill, Dave Allen and Hugo Burnham missed their big chance of rock stardom due to principle. The Four were invited onto *Top of the Pops* to perform '. . . Tourist' but, at the last moment, Auntie Beeb bothered to listen to the song, tutted, and shook her head. The key lines were: 'Down on the disco floor/They make their profits/From the things they sell/To help you cover/And the rubbers you hide/In your top left pocket.' Auntie insisted that you can't say 'rubbers' to a family audience. The Four suggested 'packets'. Auntie sighed and huffed and demanded 'rubbish'. Aware that this rendered the line nonsensical, and of the credibility fall-out (a massive issue at this point for all post-punk bands, particularly as many of the cred police had already raised eyebrows at a 'Marxist' band signing to EMI, of all people), Gang of Four refused. Bang went *TOTP* and the band never got close to a hit single again.

The story is a perfect illustration of the sexual paranoia among broadcasters at the time. We can project all sorts of political reasons onto the banning of and conspiracy against 'God Save the Queen', but, even allowing for the timing of the Silver Jubilee, I still wonder if it would have been banned at all (and provoked the rupture in British society that it did) if it hadn't been by a group called the SEX Pistols. But, as far as 'At Home He's a Tourist' is concerned, I doubt if its barely controlled disgust and slabs of bleached funk-rock concrete would have made the Gang into Blondie overnight. Possessed of one of the all-time-great intros – ominous, circling and pumping bass and drums under Gill's itchy and freaked guitar slashes, the sound of a man at the end of his tether, unable to fully unleash his rage – the song is an anti-melodic hard-rock sprint through domestic alienation and the unconscious oppression of consumer fun and culture, which closes with 15 false endings, each louder and more blankly final than the last. It's a record so arrogantly dismissive of everything about pop culture that it almost amounts to a negation of itself. Actually, it would have been perfect for *Top of the Pops*.

POP MUZIK

M

PRODUCED AND WRITTEN BY ROBIN SCOTT
MCA/MARCH 1979
UK CHART: 2

Robin Scott went to Croydon College of Art with Malcolm McLaren, and had the same situationist, media-scam interests. Having somehow been left out of punk, he turned it to his advantage. While everyone else on the UK scene was struggling with the contradictions of 'turning rebellion into money', Scott just turned up in a suit on *Top of the Pops*, looking a bit smug and knowing and Ferry-oily, barking out his slogans in Lennon–Bowie style over heavily processed disco-pop. It was a one-shot deal – M's follow-ups made little impact – but 'Pop Muzik' can be seen in hindsight as the basic template for Heaven 17, ABC, Frankie Goes to Hollywood and any other '80s ironists who made arch pop records about pop records. Marketing gimmicks had become de rigueur by now, and Scott's was a version of the single with a 'closed groove' at the end. Leave it on, and it just repeated 'Clear!' over and over again until you removed the stylus.

None of this prevents 'Pop Muzik' from being genius. From its Radio Euro organ fanfare opening, through its chunky

DANCE AWAY/ROXY MUSIC

electronics and buzzing Bowie sax, to the girls cooing 'Shoobeedoobeedoowop' in all the right places, it makes joy out of cynicism, while Scott fills every line with a new delight, juxtaposing satire and gibberish, affection for and distrust of pop, until they become one and the same. It was the missing link between the high-art aspirations of Kraftwerk and Bowie's 'Station to Station', and the more grubby-fingered British electro-pop that characterized the early '80s.

It also crystallized a growing anti-rock feeling among the Brit music cognoscenti, as the punk bands they'd thought were the harbingers of a new aesthetic started to resemble the various Stones and Zeppelins they were supposed to replace. 'Wanna be a gunslinger?/Don't be a rock singer,' Scott wisecracks excitedly. And a whole bunch of post-punk kids hanging out in chintzy nightclubs agreed, and dug out their old Roxy Music records for clothes and attitude references.

DANCE AWAY

ROXY MUSIC
PRODUCED BY ROXY MUSIC/WRITTEN BY
BRYAN FERRY
POLYDOR/E.G./APRIL 1979
UK CHART: 2

More wonder out of cynicism. The Roxy that re-formed in 1978 were without Brian Eno and without any of the pop-art edge and threatening ambiguity that made them so extraordinary in the early part of the decade. The music they made from now on was a sumptuously produced continuation of Ferry's alternative crooner solo career, because no one bought Ferry records that didn't have 'Roxy Music' on the front. As I write this, Ferry, Phil Manzanera and Andy Mackay are trooping around the arenas of the world again, wheeling out 'Virginia Plain' to make them a deal once more, this time with their pensions manager.

Yet, although 'Dance Away' was essentially a goodbye to the essence of Roxy Music, it was a fond farewell. It begins with Ferry lighting a fag and sighing, before that familiar vibrato leer sums up his entire 'alone at the cocktail party' schtick: 'Loneliness is a crowded room', and, of course, the spectacular 'She's dressed to kill/And guess who's dying?'

The lounge-rock gently morphs into old-folk's disco, and the whole thing gets a vague prick of sincerity from Ferry's public humiliation at the hands of Jerry Hall and Mick Jagger. It suffered with insouciant elegance, and, like 'Heart of Glass', made being dumped seem as desirable as an Antony Price suit.

BOYS KEEP SWINGING

DAVID BOWIE
PRODUCED BY DAVID BOWIE AND
TONY VISCONTI/WRITTEN BY DAVID BOWIE AND
BRIAN ENO
RCA VICTOR/APRIL 1979
UK CHART: 7

This last great Berlin-era single is one of Bowie's funniest. With a glam-stomp compressed into a jangling, ragged polyphony, it exhibits the first signs of the self-parody that would come to dominate Bowie's future career, but the pompous, pom-titty-pom voice he chooses here is perfect for the two levels of piss-take. Firstly, there's the whole homoerotic undertone, all that swinging and other boys checking you out. But, more pointedly, 'Boys Keep Swinging' baldly states that which was patently untrue . . . that young men still ruled the world. With unemployment rocketing and Thatcher on her way, the teen male faced a bleak and uncertain future, wooed by extremists and the armed forces ('You can wear a uniform'), pressured to conform ('You can buy a home of your own/Learn to drive and everything') by economics rather than desire. No future, yet again. '*You'll get your share*,' he taunts, well aware of what it may cost you to get it, and how dreadful that share could turn out to be if you refuse to pay. Robert Fripp's guitar howls in hysteria and grovels in choking pain, shedding wild light on both sides of the poisoned choice. Black comedy, but pretty damn funny nonetheless.

JIMMY JIMMY

THE UNDERTONES
PRODUCED BY ROGER BECHIRAN/WRITTEN BY
JOHN O'NEILL
SIRE/APRIL 1979
UK CHART: 16

The 'Tones always insisted that 'Jimmy Jimmy' had nothing to do with the Troubles in Northern Ireland. Yet a few years later O'Neill was writing very direct anti-Brit agitprop with That Petrol Emotion, with none of this record's subversive blend of the rambunctious and the chilling, so make up your own mind.

If you recall, as a queasy organ pipes (!) in the rollicking Glitter Band-meets-Ramones stomp, we're introduced to Jimmy, a small, easily led boy who felt ignored. He wouldn't let go . . .

ARE 'FRIENDS' ELECTRIC/TUBEWAY ARMY
PAGE 88

of tradition? Peer pressure? Whatever. It was silly, and disastrous because 'No one saw the ambulance that took little Jim away.' It could've just been his 19th nervous breakdown, I guess. But what would make you so nervous in a little place like Londonderry?

ARE 'FRIENDS' ELECTRIC

TUBEWAY ARMY
PRODUCED AND WRITTEN BY GARY NUMAN
BEGGARS BANQUET/MAY 1979
UK CHART: 1

Heavy metal played by the Smash robots. Oh how I love those inverted commas.

LIFE BEGINS AT THE HOP

XTC
PRODUCED BY STEVE LILLYWHITE/WRITTEN BY
COLIN MOULDING
VIRGIN/MAY 1979
UK CHART: 54

Not all small-town bands were hawking misery, and not every pop song about pop was bathed in cynicism. Swindon's finest's first chart showing is one of the Great Lost Hits of the period, a celebration of the church-hall disco with pubescent punters and band 'too young for the bars at the hop' and happily making do with crisps and fizzy pop, which is exactly what Moulding's affectionate nostalgia creates. Producer Lillywhite was soon to be the stadium rock choice of the New Celtic Bluster generation, but it doesn't show here, as the twin guitars shake, rattle and roll in subtle but ebullient complexity over Terry Chambers's northern-soul thump. Andy Partridge's ringing disc(h)ords give the jolliness a shot of hormonal thrill, as the boys and girls sneak their first snog while the vicar isn't looking . . .

WE ARE FAMILY

SISTER SLEDGE
PRODUCED AND WRITTEN BY NILE RODGERS AND
BERNARD EDWARDS
ATLANTIC/MAY 1979
UK CHART: 8

BOOGIE WONDERLAND

EARTH, WIND & FIRE WITH THE EMOTIONS
PRODUCED BY MAURICE WHITE AND
AL MCKAY/WRITTEN BY J. LIND AND A. WILLIS
CBS/MAY 1979
UK CHART: 4

AIN'T NO STOPPIN' US NOW

MCFADDEN AND WHITEHEAD
PRODUCED AND WRITTEN BY EUGENE MCFADDEN,
JERRY COHEN AND JOHN WHITEHEAD
PHILADELPHIA INTERNATIONAL/MAY 1979
UK CHART: 5

. . . before flushing with excitement and shaking a leg to these. While rock reflected the stressful, fragmented, violent society around it, disco just kept on getting happier and happier. These three singles run on the adrenalin of hope, community and the ideal of a better place where everyday struggle surrenders to the joy of physical and communal release. The perennial dance music theme, in fact, which is why rock fans often dismiss dance as bland or escapist. But what kind of life is there without pure joy, or, just as importantly, the feeling that, if we just join hands, support each other, surrender to feeling rather than anything more rational, then we'll be taken to a higher place? The best dance music is a glimpse of paradise. These three records are that very thing.

All these singles also represent the end of something. Disco was on the verge of falling from favour. McFadden and Whitehead's one hit was also the last major success of Gamble and Huff's Philly sound, as samplers and electronics rendered their magisterial orchestral arrangements old-fashioned. There were more great EW&F and Sister Sledge singles to come, but the albums this pair came from were the bands' highpoints – Maurice White, Philip Bailey and co. took their big-band

HOMO SAFARI

XTC

LIFE BEGINS AT THE HOP

TERRY CHAMBERS=D
DAVID GREGORY=G
ANDY PARTRIDGE =G+V
COLIN MOULDING=B+V

VS 259

LIFE BEGINS AT THE HOP/XTC
PAGE 88

formula to heights they never reached again on the *I Am* album, while the Sledges found writer/producers Chic a hard act to follow. But there was a new beginning for 'We Are Family' too, as it became an anthem for US gay activists, who sang the line 'I've got all my sisters with me' with an especially defiant glee. I mean, I love punk and rock 'n' roll as much as anyone could. But I know no one's ever gonna stand in the street with their community singing 'Pretty Vacant' or 'Purple Haze' in protest against oppression. Bland? Escapist? Black dance music has always meant more to a greater variety of people than rock, and it always will.

I FOUGHT THE LAW

THE CLASH
PRODUCED BY THE CLASH AND
BILL PRICE/WRITTEN BY SONNY CURTIS
CBS/MAY 1979
UK CHART: 22

The lead track from *The Cost of Living* EP was a cover of an ancient rock 'n' roll tune by The Bobby Fuller Four. More evidence, it seemed, that The Clash had lost it in the wake of *Give 'Em Enough Rope*, their near-disastrous attempt to make a US rebel-metal album with Blue Oyster Cult producer Sandy Pearlman. It did reinforce the fact that The Clash had become a conventional rock band with a cool macho image and transatlantic ambitions. It also proved how good at it they would come to be.

Even so, its full-pelt (and erratically produced) charge through the lyric's fundamentally depressing outlaw mythology (the law won, if you remember) might not have got in here if it weren't for drummer Topper Headon's greatest moment. Strummer: 'Robbin' people with a . . .' Topper: BUP BUP BUP BUP BUP BUP!!! Strummer: 'SIX-GUN!!!' Band: CRUNCH!!! Listener: 'YAHOOOO!!!' The bit lasts for just two bars yet says everything great about rock 'n' roll – the suspense, the power, the sonic wit, the moment of resolution when the band drag it all back from the brink of chaos, the whole spine-tingling, indescribable, language-defeating X-factor of it all – that you'll ever need to know.

HUMAN FLY

THE CRAMPS
PRODUCED BY ALEX CHILTON/WRITTEN BY LUX
INTERIOR AND POISON IVY RORSCHACH
ILLEGAL/JUNE 1979
DID NOT CHART

NAG NAG NAG

CABARET VOLTAIRE
PRODUCED BY CABARET VOLTAIRE, GEOFF TRAVIS
AND MAYO THOMPSON/WRITTEN BY CABARET
VOLTAIRE
ROUGH TRADE/JUNE 1979
DID NOT CHART

Two influential records (and bands) that retooled ancient rock 'n' roll with surreal new parts and labour. The Cramps were New York trashhounds obsessed with sex, B-movies, sex, garage, rockabilly and sex. Cabaret Voltaire were Sheffield art schoolers obsessed with Burroughs, electronica, socialist politics and the avant garde. Both had been freaking out live audiences with their different forms of outrage since before the Pistols' emergence. Both came down very different roads and arrived, for their first singles, at roughly the same conclusion – the benefits of irritation.

'Human Fly's' bonehead rhythms and twangy rockabilly guitars strut beneath fizzing white noise while Lux Interior plays with his ghoulies. 'I'm an unzipped fly an' I don' know why,' he hiccups and leers. The Cramps dispense with bass. All the better to itch you with.

Richard H. Kirk, Stephen Mallinder and Christopher Watson's fizzing white noise drowns out a queerly plopping Motown drum machine while Mallinder berates the listener with the title and little else coherent. Radio messages flicker, machines go pish, everything gets sucked down and spat out like paper in a wind tunnel. The only conventionally musical thing is the needling bass. All the better to nag you with.

Both records make something funny, even danceable, out of disease and decay and an itch you can't scratch. Which made these pre-punks more punk than the punks, apart from . . .

I FOUGHT THE LAW/THE CLASH

DEATH DISCO

PUBLIC IMAGE LTD
PRODUCED AND WRITTEN BY PUBLIC IMAGE LTD
VIRGIN/JUNE 1979
UK CHART: 20

Despite turning his back on the Sex Pistols' audience, John Lydon could've farted into a paper bag and made the British charts in early 1979. The more he told us to fuck off, the more we loved him, at least, for a while longer anyway. So he pushed it as far as it would go.

This record did just about everything a punk rocker was not supposed to. It was long. It had no shoutalong choruses. It had a disco beat, of a sort (the *NME* originally announced that it was called 'Death to Disco', in a fit of punk-reactionary wishful thinking). It was based on a diseased Arabic mutation of Tchaikovsky's 'The Dying Swan' from *Swan Lake*. And it was about his mother, who was dying of cancer. The result was disturbing, blackly comic, moving, profound and so far removed from anything resembling punk, pop or anything else that it had the desired effect – it got rid of the punks.

It's less a song, more an exorcism. He sees death (his mother's, maybe his own too) in her eyes, admits that he didn't realize what he was losing until now, and screams a wailing formless lament for the next six and a half minutes, terrified of her silence, teetering on the edge of the abyss. Jah Wobble repeats the same subsonic liquid bassline endlessly, while Keith Levine unleashes what I still believe is the greatest guitar performance since Hendrix . . . an improvised trail of slashes, burns, and spidery runs that possess sadness, anger, resignation, grief . . . he meets Lydon emotion for emotion. I made the mistake of first listening to 'Death Disco' on headphones late at night and couldn't sleep for a week.

Lydon played it for his ma before she died. She apparently thought it was funny. So that's where he got it from.

GOOD TIMES

CHIC
PRODUCED AND WRITTEN BY BERNARD EDWARDS AND NILE RODGERS
ATLANTIC/JUNE 1979
UK CHART: 5

Trust Chic to capture a moment perfectly. While their most famous anthem is, on the surface, just another exhortation to shake your tush at the local Locarno, it gleams with both their trademark faux sophistication and a desperate, almost frightened, maybe misanthropic prophecy of the '80s clamp-down. Conform or suffer the consequences, it coos sweetly, as Norma Jean Wright's and Alfa Anderson's clipped harmonies insist you have no choice but to embrace 'Our new state of mind.' 'Don't be a drag – participate,' they order, before dismissing any possibility of rebellion: 'You silly fool/You can't change your fate.'

This is all easy to miss, of course, as Bernard Edwards rolls out the most loved, sampled and shamelessly plagiarized bassline of all time (begin at 'Rapper's Delight' (see p. 110), 'Another One Bites the Dust' and the first Grandmaster Flash hit (see p. 170), and continue with any bass riff that slides from three insistent notes into an ascending rumble) and the strings screech in shock during the prowling, ultra-influential 12-inch dub section. It's sonic bliss where even the rhythm guitar and the handclaps sound deeply significant and slightly cruel.

KID

THE PRETENDERS
PRODUCED BY CHRIS THOMAS/WRITTEN BY CHRISSIE HYNDE
REAL/JUNE 1979
UK CHART: 33

Sex Pistols acolyte Chrissie Hynde emerged fully formed from the chaos of punk and was immediately everything punk was not. Born in Akron, Ohio, she relocated to London to write for the *NME* in 1973, sojourned and sang in Paris, returned to hang out with Johnny and Sid, and then wrote songs that were blatantly and unfashionably in love with Classic Rock history. Her biker-diva look, at once tomboyish and almost indecently sexy, fused perfectly with her tough and tender love songs, played with Brit musicians who brought an anti-thrash blue-eyed soul feel to her Stones/Kinks/Sandie Shaw reinventions.

DEATH DISCO/PUBLIC IMAGE LTD

PAGE 92

The Pretenders' second single, 'Kid' is a mystery weepie that could be addressing a child or a lover. As the drum and guitar-heavy backing mixes power and elegance with a dreamy, breathy ambience, Hynde confesses her flaws in a manner that suggests she has done unspeakable damage ('You think it's wrong/I can tell you I do/How can I explain?/You don't want me to,' she pleads, refusing to give the listener any more information, as if we're eavesdropping). This is a world where what is not said heightens the pain, where her 'kid' simply letting go of her hand unveils another silent tragedy. The Byrdsian, country-rock guitar solo's attempt to brighten the mood only brings more pathos to the internal drama, as if Hynde is attempting to cheer 'kid' up by changing the subject and is failing miserably. The sultry tremble of her voice hangs awkwardly and unforgettably over tightrope chord changes, yet still you're never told exactly what she did that was so terrible. It's both one of the most enigmatic and gorgeously sad songs you'll ever break your heart to.

IS SHE REALLY GOING OUT WITH HIM?

JOE JACKSON
PRODUCED BY DAVID KERSHENBAUM/WRITTEN BY
JOE JACKSON
A&M/JULY 1979
UK CHART: 13

Now this is classic Theory One stuff. Midlander Jackson was a music college graduate and cabaret arranger before he discovered pub rock, nicked Elvis Costello's clothes and Graham Parker's vocal stylings, and hitched a ride on the new wave. He went on to inexplicable international successes, particularly in America, by pretentiously updating a range of ancient styles including jump-jive and sub-Cole Porterisms. But he made this single before revealing too much of his hand, and it remains an absolute classic of all-age male angst.

Jackson was not, shall we say, the most outwardly charming of men, and he must have poured every ounce of bile from every humiliating rejection into his best shot. Blending his old cabaret moves with a sparse, 'My Aim Is True' production, he opens with the magnificent 'Pretty women out walking with gorillas down my street', which still plays in my head at least a dozen times when I walk down a busy London road on a summer's evening. Our anti-hero makes no attempt to solve the mystery of why so many beautiful women sleep with hideous wankers. He just becomes slowly more seething and frustrated until he finally tries to bully it out. 'I get so mean around the scene,' he sings

through gritted and yellowing teeth, but you know he won't really punch anyone. He'll just go home alone, cry in front of the mirror, and wonder why him and not me. Sad, I suppose, but it always made me happy that someone else had noticed and had put it so well.

ROWCHE RUMBLE

THE FALL
PRODUCED BY OZ MCCORMICK AND THE
FALL/WRITTEN BY MARK E. SMITH, MARC RILEY AND
CRAIG SCANLON
STEP FORWARD/JULY 1979
DID NOT CHART

Mark E. Smith perhaps remains the ultimate punk rocker for no other reason than sheer persistence. Just as you imagine he's finally had enough of grumbling to himself, here comes another album and tour, another gnarly rush of garage, rockabilly and art-drone, another set of baffling non-sequiturs that no one notices except John Peel and a shrinking army of obsessives who all seem to work in record shops.

This third single from the Manchester Marvels concerns drugs. Ro(w)che are the Swiss pharmaceutical company that developed Valium, and who better to rant about addiction to prescription downers than the archetypal speed freak, a man who sings as if he's perpetually chewing gum and warding off comedown? 'Menopause wives are hard to handle,' he observes, but the genius lies in the no-fi whirling dervish riff, the tribal drum breaks and Smith's yelping, malevolent chant ('Well it's-a vali-arm KISH-KISH!!!'), and Yvonne Pawlett's insane fairground-sickness organ. Sorry to harp on, but this does make modern rock sound so *tame*.

JOE JACKSON

IS SHE REALLY GOING OUT WITH HIM?

IS SHE REALLY GOING OUT WITH HIM?/JOE JACKSON

ROCK LOBSTER

THE B.52'S

PRODUCED BY CHRIS BLACKWELL/WRITTEN BY FRED
SCHNEIDER AND RICKY WILSON
ISLAND/JULY 1979
UK CHART: 37

Yup, organs sure were groovy in 1979. Actually, groovy does not do this justice. 'Rock Lobster' is a rack 'em up, knockdown, stone cold classic – a record so enormously complex in form yet monumentally stupid in essence that it should be awarded (booby) prizes for bop literature.

The Athens, Georgia, quintet and producer Blackwell were, initially at least, cleaning up The Cramps' monster mash for pop consumption. But then 'Rock Lobster' leaves this far behind, as Schneider's fairground bark, Kate Pierson's and Cindy Wilson's acrobatic trills, an incredible dance-rock rhythm section, a bunch of crap jokes about beach parties, and the everlasting wonder that is the obscure-crustacean-dance-craze go off on a sub-aquatic cartoon odyssey that contains a meaning that mere mortals can barely . . . ahem . . . fathom. Indeed, they'd created a sound so immediately unique and pleasurable that, despite some later and bigger hits, they could neither truly escape it nor truly take it anywhere.

Sadly, I've only just worked out that, when Schneider hollers, 'That's satanic butter!' near the end, he's actually saying 'Pass the tanning butter.' No matter. I still believe that satanic butter exists and is the crucial ingredient in the preparation of a Rock Lobster.

GANGSTERS

THE SPECIAL A.K.A.

PRODUCED AND WRITTEN BY THE SPECIAL A.K.A.
2-TONE /JULY 1979
UK CHART: 6

THE PRINCE

MADNESS

PRODUCED BY CLIVE LANGER/WRITTEN BY LEE
THOMPSON
2-TONE/AUGUST 1979
UK CHART: 16

All this, and 2-Tone too. If one moment marked the breakdown of the fascist wave of the late '70s, it was the moment that the first single by an unknown multi-racial ska band crashed into the Top Ten. The skins now had their very own bands that could actually play a brand new take on the black music they traditionally checked for. Except that they all had black people in the bands (well, OK, Madness didn't. But it felt as if they did), and the odd denial involved in loving Jamaican music but hating Jamaicans could not be sustained anymore. Although, as both The Specials and Madness would attest, some of the more pathologically misanthropic still attempted to stick with it. Virtually all punk-associated gigs around this time involved taking your chances and hoping you could outnumber (or run faster than) the skins, and none more so than those by the 2-Tone sound's most visible standard-bearers.

'Gangsters' is a tribute to Prince Buster's ska classic 'Al Capone' beginning with a hail of noise, a holler of 'Bernie Rhodes knows don't argue!' (the man who introduced Rotten to the Pistols and Strummer to The Clash had been their manager), and a guitar- and organ-driven punk-reggae sound both ancient and modern, with Terry Hall's sardonic wail topping it off. It was the revenge of every failed provincial youth club band. 'The Prince' was another Buster tribute, but friendly where The Specials were accusatory, rhythmically complex where The Specials were flat-out, wearing a come-hither grin rather than an insolently blank expression. The two records twinned naturally and began the single most politically valuable pop movement Britain has ever produced.

ROWCHE RUMBLE/THE FALL
PAGE 94

STREET LIFE

THE CRUSADERS

PRODUCED BY WILTON FELDER, STIX HOOPER AND
JOE SAMPLE/WRITTEN BY JOE SAMPLE AND WILL
JENNINGS
MCA/AUGUST 1979
UK CHART: 5

Sugar-coated poison. The Crusaders were veterans from The Modern Jazz Sextet who helped define that least interesting of all hybrids, jazz-funk – a pretentious term for a blanded-out, rather pompous take on disco. Yet their one mainstream hit is one of the most evocative dance hits of all time, a horrified cultural critique that comes in sweet, sophisticated packaging. Much like Chic, in fact, but without the irony. The Crusaders didn't like the masochistic decadence that had taken over black street culture, and played it straight.

The star of the show is vocalist Randy Crawford, despite the fact that she is not credited anywhere on my copy. She keeps her churchy, supple, nervous wail under strict control, hitting the words home, friendly, maternal even, yet deadly serious. Here, the hustling and posing of nightlife is 'a ten-cent masquerade'. 'You'd better not get old', she warns as the pretty hustlers ignore her observations. And then, another accidental prophecy of AIDS, as she looks despairingly on at the urban street theatre: 'There's a thousand parts to play/Until you play your life away.'

The beautifully arranged brass and strings succeed in distracting from the bitterness of it all, but Crawford's authority and subtly building anger is unmistakable. Black America has lost its sense of community, is drowning in a desperate individualism, a dangerous denial. 'Street Life' is a song that never dates, because nothing since has changed.

DON'T STOP 'TIL YOU GET ENOUGH

MICHAEL JACKSON

PRODUCED BY QUINCY JONES AND MICHAEL
JACKSON/WRITTEN BY MICHAEL JACKSON
EPIC/AUGUST 1979
UK CHART: 3

No such disco misgivings for the Boy Who Would Be King. The record that transformed Jackson from child star to adult supernova remains one of the most joyful and thrilling examples of naked ambition ever made – a noise of such energy and virtuosity that it made the thrashiest punk seem lethargic.

Here, veteran genius Quincy Jones and Jackson understand perfectly where minimalism and complexity meet and create magic. The Morse code bass, glitterball strings, and Earth, Wind & Fire-influenced funk percussion force you to move. Indeed, MJ's falsetto is obsessed with 'the force', presumably inspired by *Star Wars*. It's all about sex, and an androgynous, anxious and jumpy reaction to imminent fuck action, of course. Nevertheless, there's something disquieting about the triumphalism in some of the first verse, even though Jackson is almost incoherent with anticipation of his future superstardom. 'Power . . . ah, power . . . is the force, the vow/That makes it happen/It asks no questions why.'

MONEY

THE FLYING LIZARDS

PRODUCED BY DAVID CUNNINGHAM/WRITTEN BY
BERRY GORDY JR AND JANIE BRADFORD
VIRGIN/AUGUST 1979
UK CHART: 5

A hustler's anthem that helped Michael Jackson's former boss Berry Gordy establish the Tamla Motown empire, 'Money' was a hit in 1960 for Barrett Strong before being famously covered by The Beatles, provoking one of John Lennon's most desperate and extraordinary vocal performances. The Flying Lizards' unforgettably bizarre and droll version, coming three months after the election of Margaret Thatcher, turned the street-tough classic versions inside out, and captured a moment as perfectly as 'Good Times'.

Kent-based Irish exile David Cunningham specialized in conceptual excavations of pop hits, but this was the only one that sold (both here and in the US) because it was the only one that had more to it than smartarse sarcasm. The noise is unique: barrelhouse piano offset with a subsonic disco pulse and what sounds like tea-trays crashing upon the heads of anyone who doesn't get the point, all barely in time with each other. The blank debutante spoken tones of one Deborah Evans recite a passionless version of the need for filthy lucre in a shadowy echo of Maggie at her most sanctimonious. The backing vocals sound like muzzled dogs. A ridiculous guitar solo fizzles and crackles before Evans ends up talking the old soul ad libs with hilarious lack of soul, musical or otherwise. A disembodied bleep finishes off a record so cold and brittle you can only marvel at its

GANGSTERS/THE SPECIAL A.K.A.
PAGE 96

unashamed contempt for everything, and wonder how Cunningham and co. made it so catchy and infectious. But then, soul-less greed was The Next Big Thing, and The Flying Lizards were only warning of the coming infection.

CARS

GARY NUMAN
PRODUCED AND WRITTEN BY GARY NUMAN
BEGGARS BANQUET/AUGUST 1979
UK CHART: 1

Yup, old Gazza was Bowie for thickos and his suburban sci-fi alienation as daft as a brush – but what a great noise. No wonder he's been re-evaluated as an influence on everyone from Blur to Marilyn Manson – if someone this unattractive with a voice this silly and keyboards this boxing-gloved could reinvent himself as a pop cyber-god and make great singles while doing it, then anyone could. The endlessly spiralling one-finger synth hooks, sub-J.G. Ballard misanthropy and autobahn agoraphobia make this 'Warm Leatherette's' (see p. 58) less educated twin . . . the cuddly runt of the post-Kraftwerk litter.

LOST IN MUSIC

SISTER SLEDGE
PRODUCED AND WRITTEN BY BERNARD EDWARDS
AND NILE RODGERS
ATLANTIC/AUGUST 1979
UK CHART: 17

After money and cars – what else but girls? 'Lost in Music' is yet another Chic tragedy masquerading as celebration. 'Have you seen some people lose everything? First to go is their mind,' the song begins. Responsibility is a tragedy, they explain, as the music biz sells both artist and consumer a pop-dream of escape from mundane nine-to-five realities. The melody carried by the piano is hauntingly melancholic and tense – undercutting what the singer sings with the underlying truth, making Kathie Sledge into the unreliable, self-deluded narrator in a great *noir* novel. Chic know that neither Sister Sledge, nor the popularity of Chic's own sound, will last forever. They're all caught in a trap of diminishing returns, being dropped by labels, playing old hits to smaller crowds in dodgier venues. There's no turning back.

Still dancing?

STAR

EARTH, WIND & FIRE
PRODUCED BY MAURICE WHITE/WRITTEN BY
M. WHITE, E. DEL BARRIO AND A.WILLIS
CBS/SEPTEMBER 1979
UK CHART: 16

Over to disco's greatest positivity junkies. To White, Bailey and co., we're all stars under their divine cosmic guiding light, or something, and when you've got The Phoenix Horn Section to argue the case, it's hard to disprove, even when they started blabbing on about the children of the world, which is always the last refuge of the American pop scoundrel. It's a massive, strutting, supreme funk epic of course, but is pushed into the realms of the immortal by the spine-tingling late entry of the best – and uncredited – mute trumpet solo of all time sliding gracefully into Bailey's star-struck falsetto ad libs. Pop ecstasy is made of moments like these.

EMPIRE STATE HUMAN

THE HUMAN LEAGUE
PRODUCED BY THE HUMAN LEAGUE AND
COLIN THURSTON/WRITTEN BY PHIL OAKEY,
IAN CRAIG-MARSH AND MARTYN WARE
VIRGIN/SEPTEMBER 1979
DID NOT CHART
(REISSUED JUNE 1980: REACHED NO. 62)

The early Human League were an arty, jokey bunch of Sheffield electronica press darlings. Less than a year after the inexplicable commercial failure of this single, Craig-Marsh and Ware left to form the ironic, conceptual and somewhat oily Heaven 17, while Oakey and visuals man Adrian Wright pursued their own purer pop vision with songwriters Ian Burden and Jo Callis, and two unknown girls who couldn't sing or dance and did it so brilliantly the entire under-25 female population of Britain wanted to be them for about 18 months. The initial clash between Oakey's minimalist naïvety and Craig-Marsh's and Ware's arched-eyebrow artiness produced its finest moment on this Great Lost Hit.

Over a martial electronica inspired more by Ron Grainer's *Dr Who* theme than Kraftwerk, Oakey regales us with a first-person children's story about wanting to be the tallest person in the land. The 'Tall tall tall as big as a wall wall wall' chorus is

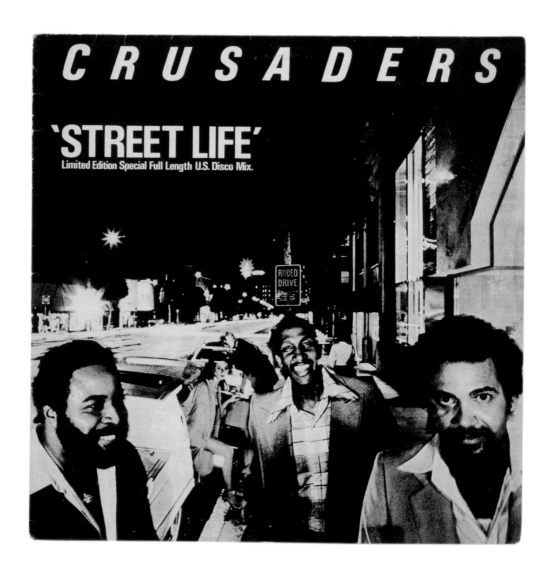

STREET LIFE/THE CRUSADERS

magnificent, and there's more pleasure to be had in the detail, as Oakey drops to a bluff spoken word to tell us that he has willed himself to become '14 storeys high', and a set of chipmunk voices add, 'At least!' The synth backing is both pretty and punchy and, whether taken as a cute joke or a light satire on the 'you can be anything you want to be!' self-determinism of the time, the single is a delight and one of the best examples of that old music-hack cliché: the huge hit in a parallel universe.

MESSAGE IN A BOTTLE

THE POLICE
PRODUCED BY NIGEL GRAY AND THE POLICE/WRITTEN BY STING
A&M/SEPTEMBER 1979
UK CHART: 1

An overnight sensation in America before they truly broke in Britain, Sting, Andy Summers and Stewart Copeland were already clever fusionists by the time they made their best early single. While all were serious jazz-scene musos, they happily cut and bleached their hair, cut short all excess musical baggage, and worked out a way to make a blend of rock and reggae that would clean up commercially. Face it – Summers and Copeland had to be fantastic musicians to take the weight of Sting's ludicrous Jamaican accent and deliberately dumb lyrical concerns. It seemed he could hardly sing a line without wailing the word 'lonely' ('LAWN-LEH!') inna sub-Marley stylee.

'Message . . .' is that shtick taken to logical extremes and driven by a hard-rock attack that just seemed to overwhelm everything else on radio. Listening to Copeland transforming rock and reggae drums into abstract and wilful jazz improv is a blast in itself. Sting's conceit – the testimony of the lawn-lehest man in the world who finds, in the last verse, that everyone else is lawn-leh too – is delivered too powerfully to sneer at, even when he howls, 'Seems ah'm not a-lawn in bein' a-lawn' in true wigga style, presumably as an aside to his accountant. 'Message in a Bottle' was, like 'Don't Stop 'Til You Get Enough', so forceful in its contrivance and blatant in its ambition, it brought mainstream pop to a whole new level of precision professionalism, preparing us for the cynical, pre-programmed horror of the MTV-sponsored '80s mainstream.

TYPICAL GIRLS/I HEARD IT THROUGH THE GRAPEVINE

THE SLITS
A-SIDE PRODUCED BY DENNIS BOVELL AND WRITTEN BY THE SLITS/B-SIDE PRODUCED BY THE SLITS AND REMA AND WRITTEN BY NORMAN WHITFIELD AND BARRETT STRONG
ISLAND/SEPTEMBER 1979
UK CHART: 60

Hmmm. I'd never previously noticed the profound influence that Motown's Barrett Strong brought to bear on British alternative pop circa 1979.

By the time they finally released a debut single, The Slits were no longer punk's most notorious and admired all-girl band. The awesome future Banshee Budgie had replaced Palmolive on drums, which gave them a sounder foundation for their unique mutations of reggae and funk, but somewhat blunted their feminist challenge and their shambolic yet striking live performances. They would shudder to a disappointing halt in little more than two years, but they left behind a few great recorded moments, of which this single was the best and most successful.

'Typical Girls' is a mercurial, shape-shifting taunt that lurches repeatedly from atonal chant to the loveliest of piano lines. The song's fury at the stereotyping of femininity – especially the obsession with cleanliness, echoing some of Poly Styrene's most memorable rants – was aimed at women as much as men, which is perhaps why it was all too close to home to change the world as it deserved to. But everything that later turned up in the short-lived but influential 'riot grrl' movement started right here.

The flipside Marvin Gaye revival is the best of all post-punk cover versions. Rejecting the spooked dread of the original for an excited brashness, it transforms quintessential male soul into funky female joy by virtue of an unforgettably prowling and ringing dub-disco backing, and the quivering yelp of Ari Up's extraordinary voice. It would be foolish to claim it as better than the original – what is? But in terms of reinvention, dance power, unlikely sunshine and supreme confidence, it's every bit as complete in a completely different way. Besides, it's an incredible celebration of a bunch of hairy and unkempt white Rasta girls being *allowed* to play music in public. And, if you think that's an odd thing to say, look around you in 2002 and count how many successful women musicians you can name who are neither in heavily styled, manufactured groups nor 'sensitive' – but shaggable and heavily styled – solo singer-songwriters.

EMPIRE STATE HUMAN/THE HUMAN LEAGUE

MEMORIES

PUBLIC IMAGE LTD

PRODUCED AND WRITTEN BY PUBLIC IMAGE LTD
VIRGIN/SEPTEMBER 1979
UK CHART: 60

John Lydon had successfully distanced himself from the Sex Pistols so quickly that his singles now charted no higher than those of Ari Up, his girlfriend's daughter. With the release of the astonishingly dark and different *Metal Box* album, PiL became a cult – much admired by arty types and future musicians, ignored by the general public. The superior 12-inch version of 'Memories' is mutant Arabic speed-disco-gone-flamenco, a deep, warm, sleek ride, another mean Wobble bassline, more virtuoso Keith Levine guitar, and Lydon raving furiously, this time about the futility of nostalgia. It's a beautiful record, almost perfect in its wilfully obscure way. But ironically, Lydon's obsession with burying the past fell on deaf ears. His public had already moved on.

MAKING PLANS FOR NIGEL

XTC

PRODUCED BY STEVE LILLYWHITE/WRITTEN BY
COLIN MOULDING
VIRGIN/SEPTEMBER 1979
UK CHART: 17

Say what you like about him – and believe me I wish you would – but no one put more faith in and money behind Britain's New Pop than Richard Branson. It's incredible to clock just how many of 1979's best records came out on Virgin. He would even occasionally allow his flop bands chance after chance to come good. And lo and behold – XTC, after a bunch of good-but-too-quirky false starts, finally did.

The secret lay in blending the maverick noises in leader Andy Partridge's head with bassist Colin Moulding's pure pop sensibility – commonly known as the Lennon–McCartney syndrome. The breakthrough result was a vibrant cross between the globally informed experiment of bands such as The Slits and PiL and classic '60s songsmithery. '. . . Nigel' sounded like The Kinks backed by Afro-reggae drum fusioneers Ras Michael and The Sons of Negus and produced by Bowie. Its tale of well-meaning but pushy middle-class parents came over as uncomfortably personal for Moulding, and the dub-flecked rumble of the music plays off the tension between a shrugging good humour and the maelstrom inside poor Nigel's pressured head. The rhythm track – and Lillywhite's production – is monumental and, like Timbaland's beats now for the likes of Missy Elliott, so strong that it forced a reluctant daytime radio to accommodate it.

THE ETON RIFLES

THE JAM

PRODUCED BY VIC COPPERSMITH-HEAVEN/WRITTEN
BY PAUL WELLER
POLYDOR/OCTOBER 1979
UK CHART: 3

'The Eton Rifles' is not The Jam's best tune nor performance, but it is their greatest moment. While the rest of 1979's most pointed references to the times were couched in irony, Weller gave it to us straight. The Tories wanted class war and we were going to lose. When a statement so bald went Top Three, without any of the controversy that aided 'God Save the Queen', it was like suddenly discovering Sting's hundred million bottles washing up on the shore.

According to Paolo Hewitt's *The Jam: A Beat Concerto*, Weller had been badly beaten by a bunch of rugger buggers while touring to support *The Modern World* in 1978. Weller expanded on this as class-war metaphor with a force and bitterness that took your breath away. But his seething hatred wasn't aimed at the ascendant upper middle classes, but a working class that he portrays as weak, disorganized, laddish, childish and masochistic. Which we were. It's an astonishing – and depressing – analysis from someone who was, lest we forget, just 21 years old. And I still feel chastened and chilled every time I hear it. After all, we bought the record, agreed, and then ran off home for our tea.

TYPICAL GIRLS/I HEARD IT THROUGH THE GRAPEVINE/THE SLITS
PAGE 102

WE ARE ALL PROSTITUTES

THE POP GROUP
PRODUCED BY DENNIS BOVELL AND
THE POP GROUP/WRITTEN BY THE POP GROUP
ROUGH TRADE/OCTOBER 1979
DID NOT CHART

MIND YOUR OWN BUSINESS

DELTA 5
PRODUCED BY ROB WARR AND DELTA 5/
WRITTEN BY DELTA 5
ROUGH TRADE/OCTOBER 1979
DID NOT CHART

ON MY RADIO

THE SELECTER
PRODUCED BY ERROL ROSS AND THE
SELECTER/WRITTEN BY NEOL DAVIES
2-TONE/CHRYSALIS/OCTOBER 1979
UK CHART: 8

A MESSAGE TO YOU RUDY

THE SPECIALS
PRODUCED BY ELVIS COSTELLO/WRITTEN BY
R. THOMPSON
2-TONE/CHRYSALIS/OCTOBER 1979
UK CHART: 10

Urgent missives from the Bristol and Leeds politico-punk frontlines. The Pop Group, despite the ironic name, were deadly serious about melding punk, funk, free jazz and Marxist politics. They made one of the most remarkably unpleasant noises ever, and it was free and splendid. Influenced strongly by Gang of Four, Delta 5 were proto-riot grrls with a twin bass attack and authoritatively strident femme vocals. Both bands were an acquired taste and didn't last long once the late '70s free-for-all abruptly ended, but their best early records were mesmeric if you wanted to open your ears.

'We Are All Prostitutes' is self-explanatory. Mark Stewart doesn't so much sing as attack his own voice with a machete. It might not have sold millions, but the chaotic funk breakdowns led to every college long-raincoat band introducing scratchy and chattering funk elements to their punk music. Everything here gibbers and bleeds and it seems extraordinary now that music like this ever existed, never mind became influential and critically acclaimed.

'Mind Your Own Business' was a more streamlined beast. John Peel played it to death because it was a fantastic dance-pop record (disco reduced to its trace elements and rudely interrupted by frustrated Andy Gill guitar), albeit a dance-pop record too lo-fi and bewildering to pick up daytime radio play. Vocalists Julz Sale, Ros Allen and Bethan Peters ask and answer their own questions: 'Can I lick the crumbs from your table?/Can I interfere in your crisis?/NO!!!' And you can guess the rest of the reply. It's the sort of record that some US punk type occasionally mentions as the foundation of their entire approach, and is further proof that Rough Trade was the best and bravest record label in the world at this point.

So confident were 2-Tone that, once they'd hooked the label up to major label Chrysalis, they happily put out singles that directly competed with each other for space in the Top Ten. So confident were Brummies The Selecter, in fact, that their debut single hit by playing a none-too-sly joke at daytime radio's expense. Pauline Black's skipping Jamaican vocal and a beatific disco-ska rhythm gives us that old pop standby – 'I love to love but my baby just loves to dance' – before bully-boy backing vocals slam into the pay-off: 'It's just the same old show!' 'On my radio,' Black trills back, in one of the most atonal and awkward choruses the charts have ever accommodated. Not now it wasn't.

The Specials' second single was the polar opposite of the violent energy of 'Gangsters' (see p. 96). Laurel Aitken's ska peace-message classic was covered with careful reverence, all harmonicas and horns and warm persuasion. Having already seen too much trouble on their own streets, at their own shows, The Specials knew that working-class violence had turned in on itself, rather than on the powers-that-be. Clash-style glorification of the Rude Boy black outlaw was right out. The voices of white Terry Hall and black Neville Staples and Lynval Golding meld in persuasive harmony over Costello's retro production. 'A Message . . .' pleads for a tradition of tolerance and community that maybe never existed. But the point was beautifully made.

MEMORIES/PUBLIC IMAGE LTD

PAGE 104

TRANSMISSION

JOY DIVISION

PRODUCED BY MARTIN HANNETT/WRITTEN BY
IAN CURTIS, PETER HOOK, BERNARD SUMNER AND
STEPHEN MORRIS
FACTORY/OCTOBER 1979
DID NOT CHART

Joy Division, even more so than the Sex Pistols, reshaped rock 'n' roll. In only their second single, everything is already in place: punishing rhythm, endless melody and hook from just two chords, space both brittle and ornate from Hannett's unique production and . . . that voice. Jim Morrison was the usual comparison, but Ian Curtis reminds more now of Johnny Cash – a voice so deep, complete and other that it sounds like it was hewn from ancient ground. 'Transmission' implies that dancing to the radio could be the last joy that you will ever feel, and that the desperation to move is both a matter of survival and the action of a drowning man. Play loud when unhappy and it feels like exorcism.

CALIFORNIA ÜBER ALLES

DEAD KENNEDYS

PRODUCED BY JIM KEYLOR AND DEAD
KENNEDYS/WRITTEN BY JELLO BIAFRA AND
JOHN GREENWAY
FAST/OCTOBER 1979
DID NOT CHART

Contrary to what we were being told at the time, some Americans did 'get' punk. Indeed, Jello Biafra of San Francisco (formerly Eric Boucher of Boulder, Colorado) dedicated his life to anti-establishment activity in a way that no British punks could match – standing for Mayor of San Francisco (he came fourth); putting out spoken-word albums laying into American double standards with a Bill Hicks-like ferocity; making a record with Ice T; taking on the entire US establishment when taken to court for a poster given away with an album (it had penises on it – he won, but it effectively ended the band). The story got a familiar epilogue when the rest of the band sued Biafra for non-payment of royalties from their own Alternative Tentacles label.

'California . . .' is a blistering attack on Jerry Brown, California's Governor at the time. It introduces the idea of the hippy fascist to youth culture over hyper-loud, melodramatic,

mock-operatic speed-metal. Biafra had the John Lydon gift of being hysterically angry and morally righteous in a friendly, funny way, his voice a blend of quivering rage and wiseass stand-up comic.

Jerry Brown seemed a remote figure to Brits even then, and a strictly non-hippy former Governor of California turned out to be the greater threat. But the best part of the song reminds you of someone closer to home, closer to now. The music breaks into a slowed-down, comically sinister middle section as Biafra goes hilariously over the top. 'Now it's 1984/Knock-knocking at your front door/It's the suede-denim secret police/They have come for your uncool niece!' Ha! Anyone for a rousing chorus of 'Cool Britannia Über Alles'?

BRASS IN POCKET

THE PRETENDERS

PRODUCED BY CHRIS THOMAS/WRITTEN BY
CHRISSIE HYNDE AND JAMES HONEYMAN-SCOTT
REAL/NOVEMBER 1979
UK CHART: 1

Must be a bastard when you define yourself – musically, vocally, lyrically, thematically – on only your third single. But that sounds like I'm trying to put some kind of negative spin on this, and that is an impossibility which is not worth pursuing. 'Brass in Pocket' is, surely, the greatest female seduction song of all time – drenched in sex without even a smudge of porn, oozing lust without ever relinquishing control, poetic without lurching towards hearts and flowers, thrillingly public and open about its desire. It co-opts funk and reggae trademarks yet doesn't possess an ounce of wigga clumsiness. Its existence means you'll never have to actually take a warm bath in asses' milk because the chiming swagger does it for you. Every guy at the time wished Chrissie had been singing to him, and every girl wished she could be this sure of herself. Play it again and those feelings haven't changed one iota.

CALIFORNIA ÜBER ALLES/DEAD KENNEDYS

MY FEET KEEP DANCING

CHIC
PRODUCED AND WRITTEN BY BERNARD EDWARDS
AND NILE RODGERS
ATLANTIC/NOVEMBER 1979
UK CHART: 21

Chic's disco reign was almost over. But before their subtlety and sophistication fell dramatically from favour, they put out their weirdest single yet, the ultimate metaphor for their own arch distrust of dance escapism.

Again, like 'Lost in Music' (see p. 100), 'My Feet Keep Dancing' hides behind an unconvincing tale of 'making it' in the pop world. But the first verse sets up the real premise, as the vocalists list a bunch of ridiculous ambitions they could fulfil, if only they could stop dancing. 'My Mom said that my brains are in my feet,' they coo submissively. From then on the music overwhelms and pushes the point home. The usual funky Chic elasticity is dumped for a monotonous staccato so insistent it becomes a hypnotic drone. The breakdown consists of Edwards impersonating a machine on his bass, and a complicated handclaps riff that sounds like tap shoes (the whole record constantly reminds you of Powell/Pressburger's lavish, death-dance, 1948 movie melodrama *The Red Shoes*) before falling away exhausted. The strings clinch it: an endlessly climbing loop of staccato screeches, trapped in an unending circle. Dancing was never made to sound so much like a nightmare.

Disco fans found this one too uncomfortable to dance to. Chic made a few more increasingly grim, formulaic albums, but had effectively finished themselves. They split for pro-duction and session work, all of which sounded too knackered to keep dancing.

RAPPER'S DELIGHT

THE SUGARHILL GANG
PRODUCED BY SYLVIA INC/WRITTEN BY
BERNARD EDWARDS AND NILE RODGERS
SUGARHILL/NOVEMBER 1979
UK CHART: 3

WE GOT THE FUNK

POSITIVE FORCE
PRODUCED BY SYLVIA INC/WRITTEN BY
EDMONDS, WILLIAMS AND REYNOLDS
SUGARHILL/DECEMBER 1979
UK CHART: 18

'Rapper's Delight' is a massively important record that came to exist through a murky blend of opportunism and total surprise. The young New York blacks of The Bronx, Queens and Long Island had no idea that what they had borrowed from Jamaican sound systems to liven up local block parties – talking in rhyme over the DJ's microphone to the instrumental passages of popular dance records – had an ounce of commercial potential. This enabled veteran music biz hustlers Sylvia and Joey Robinson to see the money-spinning possibilities in the burgeoning urban youth culture, start a new label in New Jersey, and contrive a record that would both clean up commercially, and introduce a delighted world to the wonders of 'hip-hop'.

Rap's first hit is one of the most controversial and bitterly fought-over singles of all time. Even the credits are a minefield. According to my 1989 reissue 12-inch, the song is simply written by 'Robinson'. There is no original production credit. However, on Rhino's recent Sugarhill-label *Best of . . .*, 'Rapper's Delight' is credited to Chic's Bernard Edwards and Nile Rodgers, whose 'Good Times' famously provides the backing-track. The producer is listed as 'Sylvia Inc'. The music was not Chic's original, but was recreated by the house funk band Positive Force. I'm treading through this minefield as carefully as I can.

To add to all this, the world-changing rhymes of Big Bank Hank, Master Gee and Wonder Mike were revealed years ago as blatant steals from local-scene rap pioneers. The 'Hip-hop-de-hip-hip' opening belonged to DJ Hollywood and Lovebug Starski, while almost all of Hank's Casanova routine was cribbed from a still bitter Grandmaster Caz of The Cold

Crush Brothers. As I said, their mistake was simply failing to understand the pop potential of their lyrics and vocal styles before the Smart Family Robinson.

Not that 'Rapper's Delight' was even the first rap record. The term 'rap' dates from a bittersweet mid-'60s patriotic ramble called 'America Is My Home' by, who else, James Brown, and had been used to describe everything from the boudoir groans of Isaac Hayes, to the black-consciousness rants of Gil Scott-Heron and The Last Poets. Hell, it wasn't even the first hip-hop-styled rap recording. That honour belongs to 'King Tim III (Personality Jock)' by The Fatback Band, which came out as a B-side earlier in 1979. The difference is that 'King Tim . . .' is awful, and 'Rapper's Delight' remains utterly irresistible.

The rest truly is history, as 'Rapper's Delight' became an international hit, establishing a singles market for rap and inspiring a small explosion of indie hip-hop labels such as Enjoy (formerly a legendary independent soul label run by Harlem's Bobby Robinson) and Tommy Boy. It's one of those rare records still guaranteed to send any party – trendy or cheesy, young or not-so-young – into dancefloor ecstasy. It also rolled right over Chic's ambivalence and aspirational Euro-sophistication, and introduced us to the dubious but immediate delights of the macho, materialist brag.

Sugarhill's other success of the time, 'We Got the Funk', was a joyful, old-school, call-and-response funky disco throwback with background party noises, ringing chicken-scratch guitar, big handclaps, infectious femme vocals and a light, bouncy touch. Its modest magic marked the end of one black dance style, just as The Sugarhill Gang ushered in the new. Positive Force themselves are a mystery, with even that ultimate tool for trainspotters, the Internet, failing to come up with much info. The trusty All Music Guide (AMG) site does say that they performed songs by Nate Edmonds (choose your spelling – my 12-inch says Edmunds), Bert Williams and B. Reynolds, but rather undercuts that by insisting their only album was called *We Got the Punk*. Oh, if only.

MY GIRL

MADNESS

PRODUCED BY CLIVE LANGER AND
ALAN WINSTANLEY/WRITTEN BY MIKE BARSON
STIFF/DECEMBER 1979
UK CHART: 3

After introducing themselves as 'nutty' purveyors of slapstick ska revival, and having already left 2-Tone for the label of their biggest influence, The Blockheads, Madness didn't take long to show their hand. 'My Girl' is, in its self-deprecating and unpretentious way, one of the most progressive records in this book – and not just because of its stuttering, elasticated rhythm, jazzy piano and elegant melody. Keyboardist Barson was Madness's best songwriter and resident melancholic, and this matter-of-fact tale of everyday relationship breakdown is still striking in its downbeat honesty and lack of misogynist angst. Graham 'Suggs' McPherson, always the embodiment of the most popular bloke down your local, sings it as if a joke is always round the corner. But the joke never comes, and the song ends with everything messy and unresolved, except the music, which, as the couple fail to talk the problem out, ends exactly where it begins. 'My Girl' introduced a whole new, anti-macho male perspective on girl trouble to the charts.

LONDON CALLING/ARMAGIDEON TIME

THE CLASH

A-SIDE PRODUCED BY GUY STEVENS AND WRITTEN
BY JOE STRUMMER AND MICK JONES/
B-SIDE PRODUCED BY THE CLASH AND WRITTEN BY
WILLIE WILLIAMS AND JACKIE MITTOO
CBS/DECEMBER 1979
UK CHART: 11

The Clash reinvented themselves as an eclectic, ambitious but traditional hard-rock band by making a double album with veteran biz maniac and alcoholic Guy Stevens, the svengali behind Mott the Hoople (Ian Hunter's glam-dabbling rock romantics were Mick Jones's favourite childhood band). The title track revealed a giant leap in virtuosity and rock power, while its B-side was the greatest of their many interpretations of roots reggae. The single almost went Top Ten with little TV or radio exposure, a word-of-mouth hit that crackled through what was left of the punks like an urgent message from an old friend you thought you might not see again.

'London Calling' is a defiant fist in the wake of an impending nightmare apocalypse. If the Cold War hasn't appeared as a concern in this book thus far, it's because the most socially concerned songwriters were largely looking at more immediate matters. The Reagan administration put nuclear warfare back on the agenda with a cavalier misanthropy in the early '80s, and, though it seems so distant now, ordinary people lived with a constant fear of the war to literally end all wars. The Clash saw it coming and, though full of dread, stared into the abyss and wrote a song that refused to give in easily.

Over fanfare bass, rock-reggae rhythm strut and slashed, battle-tough guitars, Strummer looks out of his window and sees a capital both chaotic and demoralized. Police brutality dominates, smack addiction grows and people are looking for leaders. 'Now don't look to us,' Strummer croaks, exasperated. 'Phoney Beatlemania has bitten the dust.' Like Lydon and Weller, he wants us to take responsibility for our own lives but doubts whether we've got the balls. So he attempts to provoke us with the ultimate horror: 'The ice age is coming/The sun's zooming in . . ./A nuclear error/But I have no fear/'Cos London is drowning and I . . . I LIVE BY THE RIVER!' That last line is delivered from somewhere between panic and defiance, and 'London Calling' is as much about The Clash's refusal to settle for the escape of rock stardom as it is about the possible breakdown of civilization. The fact that it manages to convey the latter at all without seeming crude and hysterical is a testament to the commitment and fury in every atom of its three minutes and 19 seconds.

The flip is a cover of an underground reggae anthem by Willie Williams. According to the Rastas, Armageddon was just around the corner, and the Jamaican scene teemed with musical prophecies of Babylon's Judgement Day, when only the righteous would be spared. Lacking the comforting surety of religion, The Clash took the original and made it into a dark lament, the shift into minor chords doubling the original's power. The sound of fireworks is chillingly juxtaposed with Strummer's moans for food and justice, as the band play the best pure music – largely improvised – that they ever played. The moment when it breaks and a voice crackles before Strummer wails and then barks, 'OK, OK – Don't push us when we're HOT!' is not a reference to the anger of The Kids, but the singer ordering engineer Kosmo Vinyl not to switch off the tape while they're jamming so good. With its religious feel and jingling sleigh-bells, it was like some kind of alternative Christmas record, and a broken, weeping look into the New Year, the new decade.

1980

1980

I began my first proper job on the December day that John Lennon was shot. I was 17 and had decided that working as a 'trainee manager' at Peterborough's only 'cool' record shop would smooth my passage to immortality as a rock singer. In truth, this move smoothed my passage to working in record shops for most of the next 15 years.

It's arguably more significant to remember that 1980 stood between two huge developments in pop production and consumption. In 1979 an electronic instrument designed by two Australians called Peter Vogel and Kim Ryrie became available to wealthy studios. It was called the Fairlight CMI and it enabled a producer to take sounds from an external source, say an existing record, and edit, loop, and/or mix them in digital format. The first sampler would irrevocably establish pop's increasingly post-modern, remake/remodel tendencies.

In August 1981 MTV, the first dedicated music TV channel, was launched on US cable TV. Since Queen's 'Bohemian Rhapsody' in 1975, the promo video had become an increasingly influential marketing tool for pop singles. Many of the best-selling acts of 1980 – Blondie, Madness, The Boomtown Rats, Adam and The Ants, Michael Jackson – had become the first masters of the form. As well as providing a sales tool to work alongside radio, the growth of video brought a more insidious change in the way we consumed pop. Previously, the song played and we made our own pictures in our own heads. Now the images were defined for us, by artist, promo director, stylist, record label. Commerce was overpowering imagination.

In 1980 the Cold War began to seem less of a sci-fi nightmare and more of a real possibility, as a long year of sabre-rattling over the invasion of Afghanistan and the US boycott of the

Moscow Olympics ended with the presidential election victory of Ronald Reagan. Cruise missiles were set to be deployed at Greenham Common and we realized that Britain was a possible 'theatre of war'. The country settled in for a nuclear winter, with the bunker mentality that implies, as unemployment climbed over two million for the first time since 1935.

Someone shot J.R. and we found out it was Kristen. Some cop killed London teacher Blair Peach at an anti-Nazi rally and we never found out who it was. Someone shot J.L. and another piece of '60s optimism died with him.

Honourable mentions: Cristina/'Is That All There Is?' (Ze/Island); Teena Marie/'Behind the Groove' (Motown); Diana Ross/'Upside Down' (Motown); The Clash/'Bankrobber' (CBS); Robert Wyatt/'At Last I Am Free' (Rough Trade); David Bowie/'Scary Monsters (and Super Creeps)' (RCA); Elvis Costello and The Attractions/'Clubland' (F Beat); The Fall/'Fiery Jack' (Step Forward); XTC/'Wait 'Til Your Boat Goes Down' (Virgin); Odyssey/'Use It Up, Wear It Out' (RCA)

(NOT JUST) KNEE DEEP

FUNKADELIC
PRODUCED AND WRITTEN BY GEORGE CLINTON
WARNERS/JANUARY 1980
DID NOT CHART

Not just knee deep in . . . aw, you get the picture. Funk Deluxe from George Clinton's floating line-up of jazz-rock-funk renegades, '. . . Knee Deep' is, with its never-ending circle of riffs and insane, gonzo-opera vocal chants, like 'Rock Lobster' (see p. 96) with epic muso bells on. It's all about another 'freak' too, but, in the midst of the squelching monster-movie synth and piano basslines and group celebration, Clinton keeps injecting a note of negation. This big ole freak of the week just keeps on stumbling as she tries out different moves: 'It didn't work – no/It wasn't funky no more.' '. . . Knee Deep' marks the end of Clinton's Parliafunkadelicment thang as one of America's biggest black bands and, although Clinton went on to make some good records, his chaotic business sense led him into endless litigation as he attempted to obtain control of his back catalogue. Another layer of chaos was added around a decade after his most influential record, when, having exhausted the possibilities of James Brown beats, a generation of rap producers/artists, including Dr Dre, EPMD and De La Soul, made Clinton the man to sample. The delirious, monster-movie sleaze of '. . . Knee Deep' seemed to crop up somewhere on every hip-hop single, a sonic shorthand for sex and sin.

AND THE BEAT GOES ON

THE WHISPERS
PRODUCED BY LEON SYLVERS/WRITTEN BY
L. SYLVERS, S. SHOCKLEY AND W. SHELBY
SOLAR/JANUARY 1980
UK CHART: 2

More disco positivity, although, with its mellow vocals and warm glow of love, 'And the Beat Goes On' is more comforting than inspiring. The Whispers came from LA's notorious Watts district, but there's no disco inferno here – more the pleading tone of another black LA resident imploring everyone to get along many years later.

The implacable four-to-the-floor kick-and-claps beat does, indeed, go on, and slick, slippery guitar, clavinet, synth and string hooks and the sweetest falsetto ad libs all have something

soothing to say on the subject of getting over the blues. But I have to admit that the main topic of conversation at school was how they got away with the line 'Just like pissing in the ocean' on daytime radio. The word was 'fishing', of course, but you make what you want out of all sorts of unlikely stuff, especially when you're working up the courage to ask someone to dance at Annabelle's 15 minutes before closing.

ATOMIC

BLONDIE
PRODUCED BY MIKE CHAPMAN/WRITTEN BY
DEBBIE HARRY AND JIMMY DESTRI
CHRYSALIS/FEBRUARY 1980
UK CHART: 1

Giorgio Moroder meets surf instrumental in this epic hit. For once in Blondie's career the song is almost non-existent – it's all about Clem Burke's hissing hi-hat, Nigel Harrison's burbling bass breakdown, the thrill of the signature guitar lick, and Blondie's transformation from post-modern classicists to video-led fusion futurists.

A SONG FROM UNDER THE FLOORBOARDS

MAGAZINE
PRODUCED BY MARTIN HANNETT/WRITTEN BY
MAGAZINE
VIRGIN/FEBRUARY 1980
DID NOT CHART

Manchester-scene producer Hannett cooled and deepened the Magazine sound for their third and best album *The Correct Use of Soap*, but none but the loyal Devoto heads were listening. The opening line here – 'I am angry I am ill and I'm as ugly as sin' – probably explains why this wasn't toppermost of the poppermost down at Radio One, but Hannett and the band create great beauty from Devoto's self-loathing, with drums clashing and echoing around the edges of the mix, and Barry Adamson's skipping, emotional bass worthy of an essay in itself. In fact, that series of basslines and the dramatic three-note opening guitar fanfare make 'A Song . . .' a kind of 'Atomic' for angry bookworms, as Devoto gives us a précis of Franz Kafka's 'Metamorphosis' – man as symbolic insect and all – that reaches a heartrending peak of lonely self-absorption when he

ATOMIC/BLONDIE
PAGE 116

announces, 'Then I got tired of counting all these blessings,' before Adamson's bubbling low-end sets up the punchline, 'And then I just got tired,' which is sung in an understated method daze. Big and clever ideas played with a virtuoso grace and imagination – Magazine's stock-in-trade.

IN THE STONE

EARTH, WIND & FIRE

PRODUCED BY MAURICE WHITE/WRITTEN BY
M. WHITE, D. FOSTER AND A. WILLIS
CBS/FEBRUARY 1980
UK CHART: 53

It was some dark day around the beginning of the '90s when I took my mum and my son – both visiting for the day – to the Museum of the Moving Image in London. I was broke, struggling, and spent money on the day out that I didn't have. Neither of them seemed to notice, or particularly enjoy it, or even say a thank you. They just spent my money and went on their way.

I came home afterwards to my shitty Brixton flat and found my girlfriend of the time with my flatmate in the kitchen. They'd known each other before my girl met me and seemed to be having a good time, so I explained that I'd had a bad day and needed a little time on my own to unwind, and went into the sitting-room. I decided loud music was the best way to get out of my frustrated black mood, and put on some Sex Pistols and some Clash. No good. I didn't need more anger or rebellion. Of course. I needed uplift. I reached for the Earth, Wind & Fire records, found the *I Am* album, and played 'In the Stone'. Its ecstatically funky big-band delirium threw me round the room, its sophisticated yet manic and unyielding mystical optimism made me cry and then laugh, as it explained to me, benevolently but firmly, that I was being unreasonable and petty and that my mum and son had problems too. The song ended and I bounded into the kitchen a different person, only to be greeted by a face I knew only too well. It seems that my angst hadn't fitted in too well with my girl's evening plans, and that the 30 minutes or so Maurice White had spent sorting me out were selfish, insulting and rude. She left.

Amazingly, this relationship carried on in this manner for another four dysfunctional years before finally crashing and burning in spectacular style. The woman in question decided to hold my record collection as some sort of hostage. I eventually got it back, but, as I went through the *e*s, I knew immediately that something was missing. Everything was there except *I Am*. All I could do was play 'In the Stone' in my head and chalk one up to my ex.

GARBAGEMAN

THE CRAMPS

PRODUCED BY ALEX CHILTON/WRITTEN BY
POISON IVY RORSCHACH AND LUX INTERIOR
ILLEGAL/MARCH 1980
DID NOT CHART

'Garbageman' was on the flip of a predictably silly run through Peggy Lee's 'Fever'. But almost every halfway decent 'alternative' club I went to for at least ten years played 'Garbageman' and offered thanks and praise to The Lords Of Tasteless Trash for this rabid retooling of everything wild and unhinged about ancient rock 'n' roll. Sod yer three chords, kid, The Cramps needed just one to cause an infection; or, as Mr Interior put it in the first desperate lines, 'You ain't no punk you punk! You wanna talk about the real junk?' A truck and a lion roar, a toilet flushes, windows break, and it could all be about smack, except that Lux is too horny by the end and who can fuck on skag? 'Do you understand?' he keeps demanding while guitars squeal in protest at their ill-treatment. Cult depressive Chilton produces a monstrous murky din that seems completely at odds with his past in The Box Tops and Big Star, and one Nick Knox on drums gives one of the all-time heroic drum performances by playing the disco anthem that only he can hear. Much as 'Hong Kong Garden' (see p. 64) invented goth, 'Garbageman' invented psychobilly, a strange case of alchemy in reverse.

THAT'S THE JOINT

FUNKY FOUR PLUS ONE

PRODUCED BY SYLVIA ROBINSON/WRITTEN BY FUNKY
FOUR PLUS ONE, SYLVIA ROBINSON AND C. CHASE
SUGARHILL/MARCH 1980
DID NOT CHART

Despite still being seen as a sexist genre, rap took just a couple of months to show that women could rock the mic too. The pioneer's name is Sha Rock, she's the Plus One in the crew's name, and her smoky tones knock the guys here out the box.

A SONG FROM UNDER THE FLOORBOARDS/MAGAZINE

'That's the Joint' boasted a more cred line-up than The Sugarhill Gang, featuring Lil' Rodney C, Jazzy Jeff, Keith Keith and KK Rockwell and Ms Rock, a genuine Bronx party-rockin' crew. An old Taste of Honey riff – played, I suspect, by The Sugarhill house-band comprising future Tackhead/On-U Sound adventurers Keith LeBlanc, Doug Wimbush and Skip Macdonald – provides the backing, and all go on to create one of the key jams that established hip-hop in the pre-electro days, a tune that was played to death on the disco-rejecting, rapidly developing underground warehouse-party scene in the UK. As was usual with old-school rap groups, they split before even making an album, and Jazzy Jeff, sadly, was not the same Jazzy Jeff who DJ'd for Will Smith. The track's best rhyme? 'Let's go to work! Now I got money and I can jerk!' Hell, The Cramps would've been proud of that.

GOING UNDERGROUND

THE JAM
PRODUCED BY VIC COPPERSMITH-HEAVEN/WRITTEN BY PAUL WELLER
POLYDOR/MARCH 1980
UK CHART: 1

'Going Underground', famously, went straight into the charts at No. 1 (note to younger readers: once upon a time, before record companies got too clever, records very rarely did this. The last band to pull it off with any regularity before The Jam were Slade, way back in the early '70s). It remains, without too much doubt, the most bleak and angry record ever to achieve this.

'Going Underground' features Weller attacking the public with unrestrained disgust. Over dense and spiked guitars, he looks at a new era of militarism, of youth and working class in complete denial and going for safe options, politically and as consumers, and decides to head for the bunker and leave us to it. It sounds as if poor old Bruce Foxton and Rick Buckler can barely keep up with him. The irony of the record's dramatic success only seemed to make Weller more sullen. After all, if you have such contempt for what the public wants, how do you feel if what they want is you?

GENO/BREAKING DOWN THE WALLS OF HEARTACHE

DEXYS MIDNIGHT RUNNERS
BOTH PRODUCED BY PETE WINGFIELD/
A-SIDE WRITTEN BY KEVIN ROWLAND AND KEVIN ARCHER/B-SIDE WRITTEN BY SANDY LINZER AND DENNY RANDELL
LATE NIGHT FEELINGS/EMI/MARCH 1980
UK CHART: 1

Yeah, No. 1s ones sure were weird and wonderful in 1980. Everything about Dexys' second single – the old-fashioned puritan soul production, the lurching rhythm and tempo changes, Kevin Rowland's weeping, overwrought vocal – should have marked it as an obscure curio in the making. Instead, it struck an unconscious chord with everyone who felt bored with punk and disco, and was already rebelling against pop's encroaching trip into escapist glamour.

'Geno' is, on one level, a tribute to a British pub-scene soul man called Geno Washington, and the effect his live shows had on Rowland as a young man (Rowland happily owns up to his age – he really was old enough to be in sweaty clubs in 1968). But it's also a song about avoiding the tricks nostalgia plays because, while Rowland acknowledges the inspiration he might have received, he then refutes that inspiration and admits that Washington 'sounded so tame'. It's his world now, he insists: 'And now just look at me while I'm looking down on you/No I'm not being flash it's what I'm built to do.'

'Geno' conveyed the aura of an all-nighter soul scene that had become buried by other fashions, which is how it got explicit drug references – Dexys and bombers, the speed that the punks would not be so specific about – on daytime radio. It was also a complete dismissal of the hippy-rock hegemony that punk had set itself against. For this Birmingham boy, as in the lives of many provincial '60s kids, the Summer of Love and its offshoots never existed at all.

'Geno' and its B-side – a magnificent version of Johnny Johnson and The Bandwagon's soul melodrama 'Breaking Down the Walls of Heartache' – introduced a bunch of guitar- and synth-fixated kids to the power of brass (Earth, Wind & Fire had horns – Dexys had *brass*). Incidentally, while Rowland barely endured the peaks and troughs of one of British pop's strangest careers, Geno Washington kept right on doing what he does. You can still catch him on the pub circuit, apparently doing more blues-oriented material.

GENO/BREAKING DOWN THE WALLS OF HEARTACHE/DEXYS MIDNIGHT RUNNERS
PAGE 120

MIRROR IN THE BATHROOM

THE BEAT
PRODUCED BY BOB SARGEANT/WRITTEN BY THE BEAT
GO-FEET/APRIL 1980
UK CHART: 4

Brummie 2-Tone alumni The Beat made the punk-meets-reggae feel of The Specials and Madness more explicit. Everett Morton's kinetic drums held down the bottom, Saxa's light, humanizing calypso sax sang soothingly at the top, and in between everything thrummed and thrashed, all cold steel as juddering percussion. In retrospect, the star of their finest record is guitarist David Steele, his rhythm Morse code way up in the mix, darting into Banshee-ish discord for the breaks. Dave Wakeling sings a disturbing paean to narcissism, but you are always too busy dancing like a twat to worry too much about his state of mind. In fact, dancing like a twat remains the best method for fighting vanity that I know.

POLICE AND THIEVES

JUNIOR MURVIN
PRODUCED BY LEE PERRY/WRITTEN BY
JUNIOR MURVIN AND LEE PERRY
ISLAND/APRIL 1980
UK CHART: 23

'Police and Thieves' was originally released in 1976. Its mixture of prophecy, protest and plea became the theme of the 1976 and 1977 Notting Hill Carnivals, which, like most Carnivals of the '70s, were a flashpoint for the West Indian community's growing anger at perceived police racism and harassment, and ended in mini-riot at the 'frontline' of All Saints Road. Its rerelease saw it finally become a pop chart hit in May 1980.

    Though The Clash famously covered 'Police and Thieves' as a howl of rage on their first album, inventing punk-reggae in the process, it's the original's plaintive cool that hits harder. Murvin's lovely and eerie Smokey Robinson falsetto and Perry's languid, liquid reverberations transform everyday reality into the stuff of myth and legend here. It's also easy to forget that the song is aimed at the rebel outlaw that the punks worshipped as much as it is the State thug. Both are characterized as 'fighting the nation' – whether that be Jamaica or England – and Murvin goes on to warn that if no decent people lift a finger to stop this, then self-appointed leaders will take advantage. Add the

incandescent Moment when Perry suddenly turns up the crunching hi-hat as Murvin trills a gorgeous scat vocal ('A-dutten-day-dudden-day!'), dislocating and relocating the sound, making it fly to a spliff paradise far above the heavy manners below, and you have a masterpiece of sanity, made all the more profound by the sonic surrealism.

TALK OF THE TOWN

THE PRETENDERS
PRODUCED BY CHRIS THOMAS/WRITTEN BY
CHRISSIE HYNDE
REAL/APRIL 1980
UK CHART: 8

Or: what if the supercool maneater from 'Brass in Pocket' got turned down? A public humiliation as erotic dream, it seems, as cymbals ring, guitars cascade and the whole song makes like one long sensual sigh. Hynde's masochistic poetry on the subject of unobtainable objects of desire reaches heights of magical realism and check out the franglais as she breathes 'wish' as 'weesh'. 'Talk of the Town' is just too sexy for its hair shirt.

RESCUE

ECHO & THE BUNNYMEN
PRODUCED BY IAN BROUDIE/WRITTEN BY
WILL SERGEANT, IAN MCCULLOCH, LES PATTINSON
AND PETE DE FREITAS
KOROVA/APRIL 1980
UK CHART: 62

At this point, Classic Rock had been rubbed from the landscape. I guess it had to take a band from Liverpool to paint it back. The Bunnymen mixed their heroes – The Beatles, The Doors, Bowie, The Velvet Underground – with a slippery subtlety *and* an arrogant self-confidence that, despite their gestation with Liverpool-scene faces (Julian Cope, Holly Johnson, Pete Burns, Bill Drummond and Pete Wylie among many others) at punk club Eric's, ignored punk almost completely. They quickly became one of the world's best rock bands, and certainly one grossly underrated in British rock's history.

    The second Bunnymen single was their big introduction to the music obsessive's world. A psychedelic angst song that, like everything else at the time, incorporated funk, but in this case

POLICE AND THIEVES/JUNIOR MURVIN
PAGE 122

unselfconsciously, in guitarist Sergeant's ukulele flails and bassist Pattinson's post-Magazine thunks and plunks. McCulloch's voice was all heroic power and druggy melodrama, with that Chrissie Hynde gift for suspending his voice over notes you didn't realize were there. 'Things are going wrong/Can you tell that in a song?' he asks rhetorically, as he begs some girl to come on down to his level and make him better. 'Of course you can,' we answered. 'Isn't that all you luscious-lipped rock gods ever do?'

CHRISTINE

SIOUXSIE AND THE BANSHEES
PRODUCED BY NIGEL GRAY AND SIOUXSIE AND THE BANSHEES/WRITTEN BY SIOUXSIE SIOUX AND STEVE SEVERIN
POLYDOR/MAY 1980
UK CHART: 22

In 1979 original Banshees John McKay and Kenny Morris abruptly left mid-tour. Drummer Morris was replaced by Siouxsie's soon-to-be lifelong romantic and musical partner Budgie of The Slits. But the departure of McKay began a long-term Banshee guitarist problem worthy of Spinal Tap. The guitarist here, Magazine's John McGeoch, eventually joined on a (sort of) permanent basis. But the lack of a full-time strummer for the *Kaleidoscope* album freed the band up, and saw them become a lighter, less torrid psych-pop proposition.

'Christine' is one of Sioux's observation songs about a girl with multiple personality disorder. As usual, you get her voyeuristic fascination but little insight, especially when she reports that 'Now she's in purple/Now she's a turtle.' The reasons why the single remains so hauntingly lovely are to be found in Siouxsie's newly discovered sex-coo, McGeoch's slashing and galloping acoustic guitar, and Police producer Gray's spacey, phlanged and phased, sunset-hued production. To be honest, it could have been about a purple turtle and it would still have made this list.

FUNKYTOWN

LIPPS INC.
PRODUCED AND WRITTEN BY STEVEN GREENBERG
CASABLANCA/MAY 1980
UK CHART: 2

'Funkytown' is one of those perfect novelties that only the sick of heart do not love. Play it at a disco-revival party, a cool house club or a student indie night, and the reaction will be the same – spazzy dancing complete with air guitar on the chorus. It's a one-shot so unique that no one, not even Steven Greenberg, could copy it.

Greenberg was a Minneapolis musician and disco fan who never got to hear any black music on his local radio. 'All you heard here was Neil Diamond and Anne Murray,' he explained some years later to disco-tribute fanzine *And We Danced*, surely enough to drive anyone to vocoders and chipmunk synths. One day, Minneapolis's Prince would come but, in the meantime, Greenberg decided to do it himself and played everything on this immortal number with a little help from singer Cynthia Johnson.

The track's blend of Eurodisco, girl-group teen twaddle, garage gobbledegook and minimalist synth novelty was the taste-rejecting result, and the world laughed its nuts off and adored it anyway. Its . . . ahem . . . 'theme' of escape to a funkier place was, of course, all about the Funkytown in your own head. Steven Greenberg went into computer design and never left his hometown.

FINAL DAY

YOUNG MARBLE GIANTS
PRODUCED BY YOUNG MARBLE GIANTS/WRITTEN BY STUART MOXHAM
ROUGH TRADE/MAY 1980
DID NOT CHART

The shortest song in this book is about the long Cold War. 'Final Day' is a 90-second vision of nuclear holocaust performed as a lullaby. A trio from Wales, Philip and Stuart Moxham and Alison Stratton, produced a tiny noise of spiny playroom synths, percussive guitar and a female voice as cold and blank as a wrecked landscape. In its three short verses, a pastoral world of animals, babies and innocents who 'never had their say' is painted in minimal but sharp detail, and the song is so claustrophobic in sound, so chilling in its matter-of-fact

LOVE WILL TEAR US APART/JOY DIVISION

prettiness, that you find yourself checking out of the window for mushroom clouds. In the YMGs' world, at least the bomb brings an end to the chaos of waiting: 'As the final day falls into the night/There is peace outside in the narrow light.'

LOVE WILL TEAR US APART

JOY DIVISION
PRODUCED BY MARTIN HANNETT/WRITTEN BY IAN CURTIS, PETER HOOK, BERNARD SUMNER AND STEPHEN MORRIS
FACTORY/JUNE 1980
UK CHART: 13

'Love Will Tear . . .' came out a month after singer Ian Curtis hanged himself in his old Macclesfield home. He was 23. The single came out in a picture sleeve that looked like a gravestone. Why, thank you, Factory.

After Curtis's suicide, every Joy Division song sounded like a suicide note. He was one of rock's first 'cult' victims to have departed not because of an excessive lifestyle, but because of the depth and nature of his depression. Moreover, the details of his pain were all there in his lyrics. Groovy for ghouls, I guess, but I reckon 'Love Will Tear Us Apart' would have been an even better record if he'd lived to make more like it.

'Love Will Tear . . .' is a beautiful battle of wills between Curtis's conciliatory, but exhausted, seen-too-much-too-soon words and voice, and the blazing summery energy and melody of the music. Curtis had an astonishing gift for words, steering well clear of the usual 'Ma bay-bee done left me' of the rock relationship-breakdown song, singing words that smell of decay and tense silence, of betrayal and buried violence, in brutal detail. The band seem intent on turning this all into a celebration of their skill and power, and the ensuing tapestry of trans-cendent power-pop produces conflicting emotions of release and regret. The opening six bars alone crash through Curtis's earthly concerns as if trying to break him through a wall to a place where his pain simply doesn't exist. 'Poignant' doesn't do it justice.

MAN NEXT DOOR

THE SLITS
PRODUCED BY ADRIAN SHERWOOD AND THE SLITS/WRITTEN BY JOHN HOLT
ROUGH TRADE/JUNE 1980
DID NOT CHART

The Slits had already been labelled too unruly and, you know, *female* for stardom. But they staggered on a little longer, long enough to make their second great maverick cover version. Holt's neighbour-slagging reggae classic 'Man Next Door' had been performed most famously by Dennis Brown and Dr Alimantado – hard acts to follow, but no tougher than Marvin Gaye (see p. 102). The Slits' version is Lee Perry-tributing alt-dub madness with production from Sherwood, the future king of London's dub revival scene. The vocals whisper and wail like ghosts through the debris of the original tune, with spaghetti western hoots and a whole new Middle Eastern feel borrowed from PiL. No one ever brought such a childlike wonder to the act of singing as Ari Up, and it's therefore no surprise that the original's plea for peace and quiet becomes a wish for late-night noise.

THERE THERE MY DEAR

DEXYS MIDNIGHT RUNNERS
PRODUCED BY PETE WINGFIELD/WRITTEN BY KEVIN ROWLAND AND KEVIN ARCHER
LATE NIGHT FEELINGS/EMI/JUNE 1980
UK CHART: 7

Dexys' early music always burned with a fierce pride. It was there, not just in Rowland's talk of new soul visions, but in the tight organization of the brass, the bullish power of Archer's melodies. On 'There, There . . .', Dexys get so proud of themselves they feel it's their moral duty to lecture every other band about their flabby fashion sense and lame logic. It was years later before we found out that all this grandstanding came from a debilitating insecurity on Rowland's part.

Nevertheless, this record still resounds as one of the proudest, toughest charges unto the breach you'll ever hear. The breakdown – where those horns creep through the expectant bass undergrowth as Rowland gabbles about his symbolic pop star 'Robin' (as in 'robbing' – man, did you expect Shakespeare?) hiding his young soul rebels – is one of the most ridiculous and rousing moments in the whole of pop.

HOLIDAY IN CAMBODIA/DEAD KENNEDYS

HOLIDAY IN CAMBODIA

DEAD KENNEDYS

PRODUCED BY GEZA X/WRITTEN BY DEAD KENNEDYS
CHERRY RED/JUNE 1980
DID NOT CHART

Grand Guignol satire in Biafra & co.'s finest moment, as the world was learning just what Pol Pot and the Khmer Rouge had done in the spirit of 'Year Zero'.

Biafra took his fury at America's part in the genocide and turned it on the American middle-class college kids, the kind that play 'Ethnicky jazz . . . on your five-grand stereo', and impress their mates by 'Braggin' that you know how the niggers feel cold/And the slums got so much soul.' There is a monumental horror-rock intro, hyper-speed disco drums, and a singer driven to spitting, maniacal loathing by liberal apathy and college kids playing at rebellion before straightening out and up. After all, under the Khmer Rouge, 'You'll work harder with a gun in your back/For a bowl of rice a day' . . . it's 'What you need, my son.' It's the kind of unpalatable, politically incorrect truth Brit punks dabbled in but never pulled off (see the Pistols' repulsive 'Belsen Was a Gas'), perhaps because of our shock-horror tabloid mentality and the whole mess with the scene's parent-baiting (ab)use of the swastika (the Kennedys later had an underground hit with a little ditty called 'Nazi Punks Fuck Off', in case anyone had any doubt where Biafra stood). But never mind. 'Holiday in Cambodia' wasn't just about America or Cambodia, and Biafra deserved an agit-prop medal for saying the unsayable, and taking 'a cheap holiday in someone else's misery' to its unbearable conclusion.

OOPS UPSIDE YOUR HEAD

THE GAP BAND

PRODUCED BY LONNIE SIMMONS/WRITTEN BY
LONNIE SIMMONS, RONNIE WILSON,
CHARLES WILSON, ROBERT WILSON AND
R. TAYLOR
MERCURY/JULY 1980
UK CHART: 6

FUNKIN' FOR JAMAICA

TOM BROWNE

PRODUCED BY DAVE GRUSIN AND
LARRY ROSEN/WRITTEN BY TOM BROWNE AND
TONI SMITH
ARISTA/JULY 1980
UK CHART: 10

After June's little lot we were, just like you, in need of a little light relief. 'Oops . . .' was the first pure dance 12-inch I ever bought. It goes on for eight and a half minutes, which made it perfect for The Dumbest Group Dance of All Time. When The Gap Band's ode to getting a slap round the chops got played in discos all over Britain, the entire crowd would sit on the floor in vertical lines and mime . . . um . . . rowing. Like in a boat. Sometimes you'd be expected to rock sideways, like the boat was overturning. And no, I don't know why we didn't do The Rowing Dance to The Hues Corporation's 'Rock the Boat'.

The brothers Wilson's George Clinton rip is still an awesome, vivacious noise though. Huge operatic horn breakdowns, lithe Latin guitars, Charlie leering nursery rhymes like they were secret porn stories, dirty funk for clean kids.

'Oops . . .' would often be followed in proceedings by a second-rate jazz-fusion trumpeter's footnote in disco history. Browne's wailing horn, jive talk and mighty bassline intro always caused a stampede onto the dancefloor with many a Rowing Dance straggler tragically spiked like a cocktail sausage beneath four-inch stilettos. Still, they were unavoidable casualties in the sacrifice we made for future disco generations.

OOPS UPSIDE YOUR HEAD/THE GAP BAND

THE WINNER TAKES IT ALL

ABBA

PRODUCED AND WRITTEN BY BENNY ANDERSSON
AND BJÖRN ULVAEUS
CBS/JULY 1980
UK CHART: 1

Um . . . about that light-relief thing.

I was pretty oblivious to the charms of Abba at this point. Too busy dodging stilettos and booking holidays to Cambodia, I guess. It was only a couple of years ago that I heard this, for the first time in a long time, in a taxi cab. As Londoners know, all black cabs play Heart FM all day, every day. It's the law. Occasional renegade cabbies try switching to Capital Gold, but they are soon hunted down and cast out into the cabbie wilderness. So one gets used to a depressing hangover of Simply Red and M People after a drunken night out. But on this particular evening, some Smashey and Nicey type played 'The Winner Takes It All' and, with nothing to distract me, I listened. Properly. By its end I was hoping the driver couldn't see that I was weeping like a big Jessie.

The ever-circling classical piano and vocal line. The first words of 'I don't wanna talk' before Agnetha spills her guts. The endless layers of detail both musical and lyrical, as her marriage disintegrates and falls into the control of superior outside forces. 'The judges will decide/The likes of me abide,' she croons wearily, but all her former partner can do is shake her hand, as he tries to look away from 'Seeing me so tense/No self-confidence.' Agnetha sings the song with almost too much empathy to bear (the relationships within Abba were famously falling apart), one moment all dramatic protest, the next drained resignation. I know it's ridiculous to keep comparing Abba and Joy Division – they have so little in common musically and culturally they may as well come from different planets – but Andersson and Ulvaeus hit the same hope-dashing note as Ian Curtis. Except Abba's pain, like that ever-circling melody, just seems to go on forever.

KINGS OF THE WILD FRONTIER

ADAM AND THE ANTS

PRODUCED BY CHRIS HUGHES/WRITTEN BY
ADAM ANT AND MARCO PIRRONI
CBS/JULY 1980
UK CHART: 48
(REISSUED IN FEBRUARY 1981: REACHED NO. 2)

C30, C60, C90 GO!

BOW WOW WOW

PRODUCED BY MALCOLM MCLAREN/WRITTEN BY
MALCOLM MCLAREN, MATTHEW ASHMAN,
LEROY GORMAN AND DAVE BARBAROSSA
EMI/JULY 1980
UK CHART: 34

In 1979, a handsome Londoner called Stuart Goddard decided to pay Malcolm McLaren for advice on how to become a pop star. He'd changed his name to Adam Ant after the Pistols had supported his band on their first gig and he became the first musician to see the light. He'd even adopted a bunch of S&M stage trappings and appeared in Derek Jarman's *Jubilee* movie with Toyah Wilcox. But, alas, he was seen as a third-division joke on the London scene. On the one hand, McLaren gave him lots of next-big-thing guff about pirates and native-American imagery and African tribal gubbins and various other historical rebel poses that Malc and Viv Westwood were fascinated by. On the other, he persuaded Adam's brilliant musicians to dump the loser and form a band with a 14-year-old Burmese schoolgirl he'd discovered in a launderette. Adam was now broke and utterly humiliated.

But never fear. Adam tracked down early Banshee Pirroni and formed a band to implement all McLaren's ideas. Within less than two years they were the biggest band in Britain.

Bow Wow Wow, despite Annabella Lwin's jailbait charisma and some of the most astonishing rhythm tracks ever cooked up by an English band, were seen as too clever and, due to the age of Lwin, too sleazy by half. Their fantastic debut single used speeded-up Burundi tribal drums, stop-start riffs and guitar thrash to promote home taping – McLaren still being on his kill-the-music-industry trip. Adam used Burundi tribal drums, Glitter Band guitars and spaghetti western vocal chants to do nothing else but big himself up and make us dance. Adam went on to be one of Britain's most fondly remembered pop stars. McLaren went on to advertise Richard Branson's airline.

START!/THE JAM
PAGE 132

DRUG TRAIN

THE CRAMPS
PRODUCED BY ALEX CHILTON/WRITTEN BY POISON
IVY RORSCHACH AND LUX INTERIOR
ILLEGAL/JULY 1980
DID NOT CHART

What – them *again*? Look, bub, no one was more surprised than me when I saw how many Cramps singles cropped up in this here list, like suspiciously smelly pennies. I mean, they didn't even have a proper hit, which is most of the point of a single after all. But believe me, I relistened to them all again and again, stroking my chin, being objective, trying to forget my personal rockabilly fetish. And guess what? Everyone was a stone-cold classic, and I can prove it, at home, on an Etch-a-Sketch.

On 'Drug Train', a supercharged Cramps implore you to get on board. 'You put one foot up, you put another foot up, you put *another* foot up/And you're on board the drug train.' See? Don't be shy, 'You'll see Elvis and your mother.' Reassuring, huh? This is irresponsible, facile, chaotic, decadent, goddam space-trash. B-side 'I Can't Hardly Stand It' is all of the above but dumber. What more recommendation do you need?

ASHES TO ASHES

DAVID BOWIE
PRODUCED BY DAVID BOWIE AND TONY
VISCONTI/WRITTEN BY DAVID BOWIE
RCA/AUGUST 1980
UK CHART: 1

'I've never done good things/I've never done bad things/I never did anything out of the blue . . . I wanna come down right now.' As disclaimers go, you don't get many with a better tune.

Bowie was, indeed, an earthbound artist from his next album on, his music suffused with the relief of not having to try so hard anymore. But, if 'Ashes to Ashes' is the end of something, it's also the beginning of something else. The self-reference. The tasteful white funk. That 'orrible video with Bowie and various clubland stooges – including Steve Strange – in daft clothes doing 'meaningful' mime. The ironic goodbye to an audience who might expect more than Bowie as Rock Icon. Welcome to the 1980s. Bowie has given his permission.

START!

THE JAM
PRODUCED BY VIC COPPERSMITH-HEAVEN AND
THE JAM/WRITTEN BY PAUL WELLER
POLYDOR/AUGUST 1980
UK CHART: 1

In which Paul Weller crawls out of his bunker, strips away as much bitterness and misanthropy as he can manage, and tries to look on the bright side. Admittedly, it may take a bit of time when you're trying to 'Love with a passion called hate', but it's a . . . Start! Weller's sleek and clean paean to a one-off conversation that can forge a lifelong connection is based upon the riff from The Beatles' 'Taxman', a return to basics for a man who'd taken impatient misanthropy as far as it could go.

REQUIEM/CHANGE

KILLING JOKE
BOTH PRODUCED AND WRITTEN BY KILLING JOKE
EG/SEPTMEBER 1980
DID NOT CHART

Killing Joke were four Notting Hill nihilists who crossed punk with Black Sabbath and produced one of the most thrillingly nightmarish noises of the early '80s. Like that of The Stranglers, their persona was a blend of intellectual doom-mongering and thuggish, journo-scaring threat. They knew kung fu, apparently. Unlike The Stranglers, there was no sexism – actually, no sex at all – involved. Just good old-fashioned apocalypse paranoia, war dance pseudo-shamanism and a guitar sound like a churning in the bowels of hell. They were a real laugh.

The magnificent 'Change' invented funk-metal . . . for better or for worse. It's based on the crunchingly insistent riff of a great old funk tune by War called 'Me and Baby Brother', and singer Jaz Coleman doesn't so much sing as impersonate a sergeant major's morning drill. 'You're waiting!' he hollers exasperatedly, as Youth's bass and Geordie's guitar git on down at fuzzed-up hyperspeed. 'Requiem' is a grunging dirge that invented '80s 'industrial' . . . for worse. By now we understand that we are all worthless scum ignoring our impending doom, just 'cattle for slaughter'. 'When will it start worrying you?' Coleman asks before going back to his parade ground routine. The Joke were perfect for all those nice, black-clad middle-class kids who felt

ROUGH
TRADE

a: Totally Wired

The Fall

RT 056
Rough Trade Music

Music: Riley,Scanlan,Hanley,Smith
Words: Smith   3.25

The Fall

ROUGH
TRADE
RT 056

A: TOTALLY WIRED
B: PUTTA BLOCK
FORTHCOMING NONE-SELECTIONS
FROM NEXT L.P. 'AFTER THE GRAMME'

TOTALLY WIRED/THE FALL

pop music was too much fun, and happily colluded with the band on the subject of humanity's rubbishness and their own guilt-ridden masochism. Blinding guitar sound, though.

STEREOTYPE/INTERNATIONAL JET SET

THE SPECIALS
BOTH PRODUCED BY DAVE JORDAN AND
JERRY DAMMERS/BOTH WRITTEN BY
JERRY DAMMERS
2-TONE/CHRYSALIS/SEPTEMBER 1980
UK CHART: 6

For the second album, *More Specials*, Jerry Dammers chucked out the ebullient youth-club ska-pop and replaced it with a new-found fascination. Remember those old Casio keyboards, beloved of seaside cabaret entertainers, that made a cheesy sing-song noise over built-in beats like the cha-cha-cha and the polka? Dammers did, and decided to write an album around them, displaying an interest in 'muzak' a full 15 years before the dance scene's rediscovery of lounge and easy-listening sounds. The Specials' audience was understandably bemused but went right along with it, mainly because of the double-edged power of the narrative of this first single.

'Stereotype' is an ambitious, bravura blend of gypsy flamenco, reggae and a dramatic movie score, making epic tragedy out of one typical male's pointless death. Dammers's idiot protagonist 'drinks his age in pints' before catching a sexually transmitted disease and being ordered not to drink for 17 weeks. On the first night in the clear, he heads out, downs 17 pints, gets in a fight, and gets in his car to escape the police. A 'fluorescent jam sandwich' gives chase until the inevitable disaster: 'He's wrapped round a lamppost on Saturday night.' The final twist represents The Specials' cynical ambivalence towards the British working-class male. 'He doesn't really exist,' Terry Hall whispers, and you're not sure whether the point is political or philosophical. By now, Hall's blank, dispassionate croon carries Dammers's narratives so perfectly that it's difficult to believe that the words are not his own. Neville Staples's reggae DJ toast on the album/12-inch version wilfully misunderstands, lifting the idea of being a type who likes his stereo to heights of benevolent craziness, the band inventing a whole new kind of reggae behind him.

The bizarre 'International Jet Set' takes the airport muzak joke as the starting point for a languorous, disturbing discourse on the dislocation of air travel and life on the road. Hall, again,

is superb. 'Will the muzak never end?' he asks as the softly hallucinogenic sound eventually drowns him. At this point, The Specials were the funniest, most deadly serious pop band in the world.

TOTALLY WIRED

THE FALL
PRODUCED BY THE FALL/WRITTEN BY MARC RILEY,
CRAIG SCANLAN, PAUL HANLEY AND
MARK E. SMITH
ROUGH TRADE/SEPTEMBER 1980
DID NOT CHART

'I drank a jar of coffee/And then I took some of these!' Smith's greatest three and a half minutes is a hilarious celebration of speedfreakery over clumping drums, garage guitars made of hubcaps and spark plugs, and heroic fingerpop bass by the future Lard, Marc Riley. 'You don't have to be strange to be strange/You don't have to be weird to be weird,' Smith declares mysteriously, before ending by confessing that he's always worried. Like, *duh*.

DOG EAT DOG

ADAM & THE ANTS
PRODUCED BY CHRIS HUGHES/WRITTEN BY
ADAM ANT AND MARCO PIRRONI
CBS/SEPTEMBER 1980
UK CHART: 4

No one, perhaps, in Britpop history, ached to be a star as much as Adam Ant. On the sublime 'Dog Eat Dog', Adam's talent, vision and skill finally matched his desperate ambition. The further away you get from this record's initial release, the more audacious, unlikely and visionary it seems. Adam came up with pop's best manifesto – 'Ridicule is nothing to be scared of' – in a manifestly inferior record the following year, and the way he saw that beautiful idea through on 'Dog Eat Dog' leaves you gasping in admiration. The Moment: a set of huge beats and an ultra-butch spaghetti western 'AWWWW' that set new levels for pop camp while sounding as tough and thrilling as any of the more 'serious' noises of the time. I know little about producer Hughes, but I do know that his organization of a million disparate ideas – Burundi drums, thin twangy guitars, Ennio

JOY DIVISION

ATMOSPHERE/SHE'S LOST CONTROL/JOY DIVISION

Morricone atmospherics, beatnik exclamations and party-on-down whistles and yelps – is one of the most inspired desk jobs in this book. Adam also knew that younger pop kids were getting a little fatigued at being castigated by the likes of Weller and Dammers. He cleverly took the opposite tack, ending the song by crooning, 'It makes me proud to smile at you/And see innocence shining through.' I still have no idea what that really means, but it still makes me glow with nostalgic gratitude.

ATMOSPHERE/SHE'S LOST CONTROL

JOY DIVISION

BOTH PRODUCED BY MARTIN HANNETT/BOTH
WRITTEN BY IAN CURTIS, PETER HOOK,
BERNARD SUMNER AND STEPHEN MORRIS
FACTORY/SEPTEMBER 1980
DID NOT CHART
('ATMOSPHERE' REISSUED IN JUNE 1988: REACHED
NO. 34)

This 12-inch double A-side failed to follow the chart success of 'Love Will Tear . . .'. Partly because 'Atmosphere' had already been available to Joy Division fans on a French import single earlier in the year, partly because 'She's Lost Control' was a remix of a track on first album *Unknown Pleasures*, and mainly because neither received any radio play. Nevertheless this, along with posthumously released LP *Closer*, revealed to the newcomer just how extraordinary Joy Division had become by the time of Ian Curtis's death.

'She's Lost Control' is Joy Division at their most punishing and surgical. Over brutal industrial beats, Hook's definitive melodic and skidding bassline, and Sumner's mix of ornate synth-strings and ugly, tuneless guitar, Curtis taps into his experience as a hospital worker and an epileptic, as he watches a young girl have a fit. He is alternately tender and panicked, but too fascinated to turn away. The song is written and sung in such a way that it could be someone watching their lover suffer a mental breakdown. The subject feels like a butterfly on a pin, as she screams and kicks and the music cries and crashes.

'Atmosphere' is Joy Division at their most spectral and classically beautiful. As producer Hannett uses a synthetic orchestra playing droplets of Spring rain and a splashing tambourine to realize all his Phil Spector fantasies, Curtis finds an ever richer, deeper voice in his attempt to match the beauty of the surroundings. His pleas to a departing lover are gentle and restrained, until he rears up and breaks for the bitter 'People like

you find it easy.' The 'it', we now know, must be life as well as love, and the hookline is the most overused when his suicide is written about: 'Don't walk away – in silence.' The music is slow and ancient and reminiscent of a hundred half-remembered pop romances, all elegantly doomed. Do I need to mention Abba again?

ACE OF SPADES

MOTORHEAD

PRODUCED BY VIC MAILE/WRITTEN BY
IAN 'LEMMY' KILMINSTER, FAST EDDIE CLARKE AND
PHIL TAYLOR
BRONZE/OCTOBER 1980
UK CHART: 15

Lemmy split from cosmic rockers Hawkwind when they got too intellectual and formed the ultimate power trio spewing out a malevolent cartoon blend of punk's and metal's worst (best?) excesses. They created a riffage-overkill, paint-stripping, throat-shredding, dandruff-redistributing, biker-outlaw, wish-fulfilment masterpiece. No housepoints for pinpointing The Moment: it goes (you'll see where the guitar fits in), 'I *SLAM!* I'm born to lose/And *SLAM!*bling's for fools/But that's the way I like it baby I DON'T WANNA LIVE *FOREVER*!!!' Cue mayhem. And don't forget the Joker.

FASHION

DAVID BOWIE

PRODUCED BY DAVID BOWIE AND
TONY VISCONTI/WRITTEN BY DAVID BOWIE
RCA/OCTOBER 1980
UK CHART: 5

This is one of Bowie's greatest pop marvels. The best way to listen to it is to clamp on the headphones and concentrate on the multi-layered rhythm skills of Dennis Davis (drums), George Murray (bass) and Carlos Alomar (guitar) as they stalk and stab at each other like hoods in a knife-fight. Robert Fripp's guitar interrupts rudely like only Fripp can, lashing out at everything with wry, accusing, shrieking derision. Bowie's glib dismissal of political extremes here is very '80s, but is suitably crushed by the groove and his own playful, pop-adoring doo-wop harmonies. From 'Ch-ch-ch-changes' to 'Fa-fa-fa-fashion' seems too deliciously circular to be true.

ACE OF SPADES/MOTORHEAD

PAGE 136

WHIP IT

DEVO

PRODUCED BY DEVO AND ROBERT
MARGOULEFF/WRITTEN BY MARK MOTHERSBAUGH
AND GERALD CASALE
VIRGIN/NOVEMBER 1980
UK CHART: 51

The dance-rock era had now truly arrived. Certainly in Britain more and more kids reared on punk and disco wanted to club, and when they did so they wanted to dance to – let's put it bluntly – white music. The synth technology pioneered by Kraftwerk and Giorgio Moroder made it increasingly easy for white boys to git fonky without having to learn those complicated drum and bass riffs. 'Whip It', one of the prime alt-disco records and one based on mighty speed-disco drumming (from Alan Myers) and crisp, modernist production rather than programming, gained its modest chart entry almost purely on club play.

Built around a cut-up bluesy riff from Roy Orbison's 'Pretty Woman', Devo's set of slogans takes the piss out of America's get-up-and-go mentality in the wake of Ronald the Raygun's election. I can't say whether the Yanks got the irony, but it made Devo alt-pop darlings for preppy US students, so decide for yourself. For us Brits, we chucked ourselves about at the futurist disco and sniggered at its possible references to S&M. Which was fine, although that line about breaking yo' momma's back was surely taking that interpretation to rather disturbing sado-oedipal lengths.

EMBARRASSMENT

MADNESS

PRODUCED BY CLIVE LANGER AND ALAN
WINSTANLEY/WRITTEN BY MIKE BARSON AND
LEE THOMPSON
STIFF/NOVEMBER 1980
UK CHART: 4

Madness are generally labelled as lovable comedians, largely because of those wacky videos. But there's nothing too funny about my favourite Madness single, an irresistible Motown-based kitchen-sink drama that tries to hide its anger and sadness behind a wall of pop ebullience.

The two sets of parents in 'Embarrassment' are monsters, and having made his girlfriend pregnant, Suggs staggers beneath the

force of their rejection. His voice is so understated that you can taste the bewilderment at their petty-minded disgust. The only support comes from the sassy, emphatic swing of the music, which suggests to the listener that the young couple's 'mistake' will be the making of them. But the damage is done and the final reiteration of the title is pronounced with all the defiance Suggs can muster. 'At least we'll be better parents than you've turned out to be' is the line he doesn't need to sing.

The other thing about the band's nutty image is that it obscured the fact of their often astonishing musicianship – the sort of densely arranged big-band swing that more lauded rock musicians are and were incapable of matching without hiring in black sessioneers. Madness were the absolute best at what they did.

HUNGRY HEART

BRUCE SPRINGSTEEN

PRODUCED BY BRUCE SPRINSTEEN, JON LANDAU AND
STEVE VAN ZANDT/WRITTEN BY
BRUCE SPRINGSTEEN
CBS/NOVEMBER 1980
UK CHART: 44

RUNAWAY BOYS

STRAY CATS

PRODUCED BY DAVE EDMUNDS/WRITTEN BY
BRIAN SETZER AND SLIM JIM MCDONNELL
ARISTA/NOVEMBER 1980
UK CHART: 9

Odd that these two records should enter the charts in the same week, like the dying gasps of the rock dinosaur before it all went glam, ironic and proudly synthetic. Odd too that the Stray Cats' debut sold more than Springsteen's umpteenth, which came complete with speeded-up vocal in an attempt to get that elusive hit (it succeeded across the pond). Both songs start from the same hoary old rock point – how do I escape my trapped and tedious life? – and end up at entirely different destinations.

The Cats turned out to be nothing more than a rockabilly revival band, but 'Runaway Boys' briefly suggested they could find some thrilling meeting-point between The Cramps and The Clash. Carried by an unforgettably vicious bassline, Setzer's lyrics and guitar make the prospect of running away from home at 15 seem like the sexiest thing ever, crashing straight through

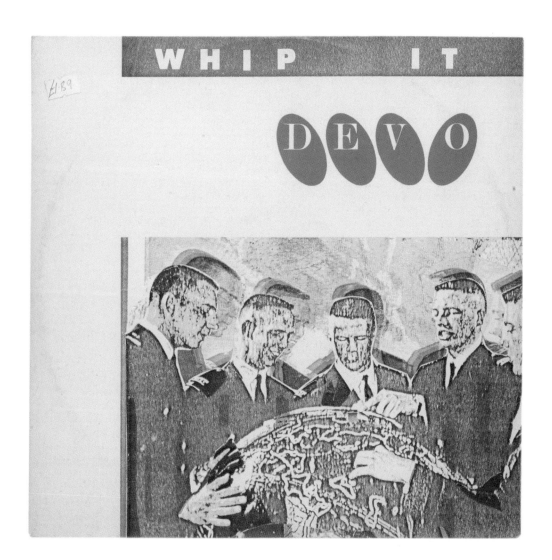

WHIP IT/DEVO

the darker implications of hanging out in gambling dens with guys who 'don't treat you like a child'. The cocksure and sassy way he sings 'steal a coupla bucks' suggests he's never going back to Mom and Pop, whatever the consequences.

By contrast, Springsteen was always the rock rebel who knew you could never escape the need for home, family, community, reconciliation. The protagonist in this grand Beach Boys-meets-blue-eyed-soul ballad dumps his wife and kids for quick thrills and finds nothing but a void. He's nuthin' but alone and there ain't no going back. As usual, the band and tune and vocals are so heroic that it all sounds comforting rather than bleak. But then, that's why Springsteen's audience is, according to his detractors, a bunch of middle-class mortgage-payers punching the air with The Boss in celebration of things they're never gonna do. He reinforces, rather than challenges, their most conservative choices, whether he means to or not.

ISRAEL

SIOUXSIE AND THE BANSHEES
PRODUCED BY NIGEL GRAY AND SIOUXSIE AND THE BANSHEES/WRITTEN BY SIOUXSIE AND THE BANSHEES
POLYDOR/NOVEMBER 1980
UK CHART: 41

In 1981 a friend and I went to a Banshees gig in Bracknell. As the band went on, the hall was invaded by a relatively large and particularly vicious bunch of skinheads. The first song was begun, the first *Seig Heils* competed for attention. You may remember that, as a member of punk's first in-crowd, Siouxsie had been especially fond of wearing the swastika. She had some making up to do and, by the shocked look on her usually inscrutable face, she knew it. The room was awash with evil vibes. Security was conspicuous by its absence.

The song was abruptly ended, and Siouxsie left the stage. Chaos ensued and the meatheads scented blood. Just as my mate and I were deciding whether to cut and run, a cheer went up. Siouxsie bounded back onstage, resplendent in a Star of David T-shirt. 'This one's called "Israel",' she hollered into the void, 'and you cunts' – she picked out some bald heads in the centre of the room – 'CAN JUST KISS MY FUCKING ARSE!!!' The song began and, to a man and woman, every frightened skinny goth-type turned and stared at said cunts. Now these Nazi scum were obviously not the brightest sparks you ever met. But they were bright enough to realize that, pale and straggly as most of us

were, we outnumbered them about 20 to 1. They slunk out. The gig was wonderful. 'Israel' is still my favourite Banshees song.

ANTMUSIC

ADAM & THE ANTS
PRODUCED BY CHRIS HUGHES/WRITTEN BY ADAM ANT AND MARCO PIRRONI
CBS/NOVEMBER 1980
UK CHART: 2

Entering the charts just before Christmas 1980, Adam took his best shot at seeing out the year, calling on us to reject the last dregs of the punk rock that had so cruelly rejected him. The Kids happily agreed, electing Adam the leader of a new escapist glam-rock, and making him the biggest British pop success of 1981.

'Antmusic' is The Ants' weirdest record, the intro all rickety-tick rimshots, the verses a jangling, almost atonal form of music hall, before the choruses come on all Gary Glitter. Irritant catchiness out of borderline chaos, it celebrates Adam's triumph with an I-can-get-away-with-*anything* arrogance. 'Ant Rap' proved that assumption wrong a year later, but that's another story.

BURN RUBBER ON ME
(WHY YOU WANNA HURT ME)

THE GAP BAND
PRODUCED BY LONNIE SIMMONS/WRITTEN BY LONNIE SIMMONS, CHARLIE WILSON AND R. TAYLOR
MERCURY/DECEMBER 1980
UK CHART: 22

If George Clinton really thought it just wasn't funky no more, then this was The Gap Band putting up a pretty fierce argument, and winning.

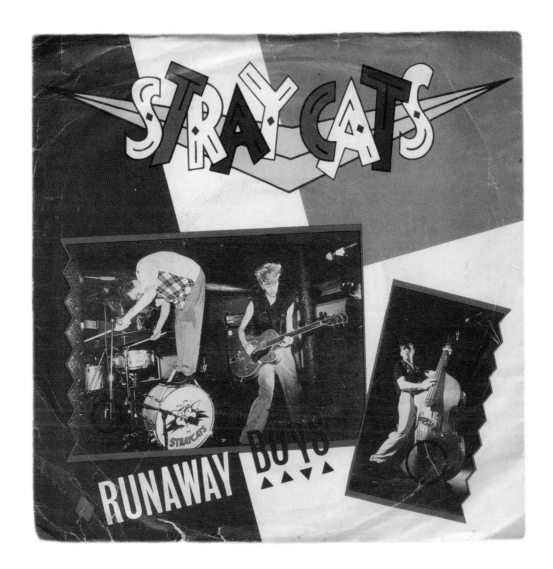

RUNAWAY BOYS/STRAY CATS

PAGE 138

IT'S KINDA FUNNY

JOSEF K

PRODUCED BY JOSEF K/WRITTEN BY PAUL HAIG
POSTCARD/DECEMBER 1980
DID NOT CHART

No word is so guaranteed to mist the eyes of the early 'indie' fan as the word Postcard. Alan Horne's label pastiched Motown with the phrase 'the Sound of Young Scotland' and gave us exactly that: a small, perfectly formed bunch of smart, charismatic, mainly Scottish bands trying to make blue-eyed soul out of jangly guitars, angular rhythms, hit 'n' hope production, and wry songs of well-read romance and mysterious edge. Postcard was the 'Spiral Scratch' (see p. 24) ideal doubled and made into a scene. It was some shock, then, when I played my way through my small stack of Postcard singles and found that only one had truly stood the test of time. Perhaps a few too many other guitars have jangled artily in the last 20 years.

Named after the accused in Franz Kafka's *The Trial*, Josef K were the slipperiest, funkiest, least chart-friendly band in the Postcard crop (which included Orange Juice, Aztec Camera and Australia's Go-Betweens). 'It's Kinda Funny' is a sophisticated ballad played and produced with an utter lack of sophistication, world-weary, enigmatic, still begging to be covered by some wiseguy. The too-heavy beats, inappropriate synth-drum bloops, alternately delicate and flailing guitars, and constant discovery of increasingly sweet new melodies buoy Paul Haig's distant croon and resigned lyricism, like some lo-fi cross between Joy Division and the Velvets' third album. The band split after one disappointing album and Haig never became the star everyone expected him to. Things were changing, and you cleaned up your act or got left behind. It's kinda funny how Josef K and Postcard defined British indie, but just a little too soon to reap the benefits.

1981

1981

In 1977, the Queen's Silver Jubilee inspired a new counter-culture. In 1981, the Royal Wedding inspired Lady Di haircuts. And that was just the boys. As pop writer Dave Rimmer put it in the title of his book about Culture Club and the '80s, it was 'like punk never happened'.

Except it wasn't. Not quite. The punk-inspired fusion of black and white music continued apace, in new forms of electro-pop, mutant disco and New York's twinning of arty post-punk and ghetto hip-hop. 1981 was the first key year in the development of what we now understand as dance music – as opposed to pop music you could dance to, which was a different thing. Almost everything good about the year was based on some form of dance rhythm purloined from either disco, funk, reggae or jazz. It inspired a lot of cynical, bloodless crap too, which the *NME*'s Julie Burchill, in her column for *Time Out* magazine, labelled 'beige' music – a wigga recipe so white-sliced it couldn't even manage wholemeal brown.

But from here on in, traditional rock became increasingly marginalized in British pop. 'Crossover' was the US business mantra, the aim of which was to sell your product to the traditionally segregated black and white audiences, and which would reach its world-changing, MTV-endorsed peak in 1983. It all seemed reasonable enough – until you heard The Thompson Twins. The process segregated and ghettoized 'alternative' rock to a degree that it has never entirely recovered from. If much of the arch, conceptual pop of 1981 leaves you cold, well, I won't argue with you. This was the beginnings of the 'high concept first – music later' pop world we're still largely stuck with. But, for this fan, the adventures in mixing image and intellect, and black and white, in the likes of Scritti, PiL and Tom Tom Club, still sounds like a thrilling discovery.

The record of the year was a black and white fusion that remained rooted in grim reality. The nationwide riots that 'Ghost Town' so accurately analysed did not suddenly emerge from a vacuum. In January 1981, 13 black Londoners died when a petrol bomb was thrown into a West Indian party in south-east London. Police were reluctant to view the New Cross fire as a racially motivated crime, and a demonstration in March became a violent battle between police and protesters. In addition, the day before the riots in Brixton, a pitched battle was fought between 300 racist skins and 400 Asian youths in Southall, north-west London. I'm writing this in July 2001 and wondering what exactly has changed in the ensuing 20 years. Thankfully, we don't have Norman Tebbit now – although the inheritor of his Chingford seat, Iain Duncan-Smith, is doing an increasingly good impression. The self-styled Tory thug's infamous 1981 quote – 'My father did not riot. He got on his bike and looked for work' – ominously summed up the Tories' contempt for the disenfranchised.

In the midst of all this – and the deaths of Bob Marley and IRA hunger strikers, the shootings of Reagan, the Pope and Egypt's leader Anwar Sadat, and the beginnings of a new kind of protest when anti-vivisection activists attacked the homes of scientists in January – pop became a riot (sorry) of colour. New mags *The Face* (for cool 20-somethings) and *Smash Hits* (for cool teenies) brought fashion and trivia into pop's frontline, and the TV show of the year was *Brideshead Revisited*, in which

spoilt but beautiful toffs suffered elegantly and let everyone else eat cake. For a short while, even the most macho blokes risked Britain's violent night-time streets, slapped on the Max Factor and aspired to a camp hedonism, like stars of some low-budget, Brit provincial version of *The Great Gatsby*. If 1981 wasn't pop's greatest year, it might well have been its strangest.

Honourable mentions: Defunkt/'Razor's Edge'/'Strangling Me With Your Love' (Hannibal); Grace Jones/'Walking in the Rain' (Island); The Clash/'The Magnificent Seven' (CBS); Siouxsie and The Banshees/'Spellbound' (Polydor); Elvis Costello and The Attractions/'Psycho' (F Beat); Depeche Mode/'New Life' (Mute); Gang of Four/'To Hell with Poverty' (EMI); Bow Wow Wow/'Go Wild in the Country' and 'Chihuahua' (RCA); Luther Vandross/'Never Too Much' (Epic)

DO NOTHING/MAGGIE'S FARM

THE SPECIALS

BOTH PRODUCED BY DAVE JORDAN AND
JERRY DAMMERS/A-SIDE WRITTEN BY
LYNVAL GOLDING/B-SIDE WRITTEN BY BOB DYLAN
2-TONE/CHRYSALIS/JANUARY 1981
UK CHART: 4

1981 would see The Specials produce the ultimate pop-hit synergy between art and real life. Yet the briefest of listens to their first single of the year reveals that 'Ghost Town' was no accident. 'Do Nothing' sums up the times and the coming year so cogently it hurts. The fact that it was written by bassist Golding rather than leader Dammers serves to remind what a *collection* of talents The Specials were.

'Do Nothing' is archetypal pop subversion – abject misery dressed in mellifluous pop plumage, a band inviting their audience to sing along to their own doom, complete with infectious reggae rhythm, Dammers's ironically cheesy seaside synthetic strings, and a vocal hook nabbed from Keith West's equally disturbing epic '60s one-off 'Excerpt from a Teenage Opera'. Terry Hall and Golding sing together in rough unison from the perspective of an inhabitant of Britain's teenage wasteland, endlessly walking but going nowhere, resigned, passive, an unquestioning consumer of things that fail to fill the void – 'Fashion is my only culture,' they admit. 'I talk and talk – say nothing.' Rico's lilting trombone attempts to fill the empty space, before the cruel pay-off. 'Policeman comes and smacks me in the teeth/I don't complain/It's not my function.' Not for a few months, anyway.

The B-side drags Dylan's '60s classic of political symbolism forward 20 years and makes its point as clear as a bell. Underneath the sardonic understatement, you can almost taste the relish The Specials felt when they remembered the name of the song.

RAPTURE

BLONDIE

PRODUCED BY MIKE CHAPMAN/WRITTEN BY
CHRIS STEIN AND DEBBIE HARRY
CHRYSALIS/JANUARY 1981
UK CHART: 5

Beige at its very best. Old-school rap pioneers still tell affectionate stories of Debbie Harry's sojourns into Bronx and Harlem hip-hop clubs, the blonde white pop star among the black ghetto kids (Harry had been around and seen everything supposedly scary that New York had to offer. It was her obvious fearlessness that made her persona so much more than cheesecake for the lads). She was instrumental in dragging early hip-hop into the arty downtown NY clubs, along with a British ex-model from Peterborough called Cool Lady Blue (and if anyone knows the whereabouts of her brother Bud, my former best friend, bandmate, and writer/producer of hits for The Rocksteady Crew, you'll find an email address at the front of this book. Cheers).

There were many attempts made at rapping by white pop stars over the next couple of years, but the rap in 'Rapture' is the only one that is not cringingly embarrassing. She'd done the homework, made sure she name-checked the right scene heroes, didn't take herself remotely seriously, and drawled her fly nonsense rhymes with casual ease and sexy vowels. The day 'Rapture' hit No. 1 in the States was hip-hop's first step from cult to cultural phenomenon.

SHACK UP

A CERTAIN RATIO

PRODUCED BY A CERTAIN RATIO AND
TONY WILSON/WRITTEN BY J. CARTER AND
M. DANIEL
FACTORY/JANUARY 1981
DID NOT CHART

The 12-inch EP that featured 'Shack Up' was actually a cheap-priced US import, and therefore one of this book's small cheats. But ACR's cover of a 1975 underground funk classic turned out to be their one definitive single, and a key meeting-point between chin-stroking post-punk and mutoid wannabe-funk throwdown. This Manchester band's original five-piece line-up is one of the most undervalued influences on British pop's dance-

A Certain Ratio *Do the Du* (casse), *The Fox*
Detail from *Facus 4*, 1980
Flipside produced by Martin Hannett at Graveyard Studios, Prestwich and Cargo, Rochdale.
Hipside produced by A Certain Ratio and M24J at Graveyard, Prestwich.
45rpm, a Factory Records (US) Inc. Product, pressed and distributed by Rough Trade

SHACK UP/A CERTAIN RATIO

fusion future, mixing an unlikely set of influences and introducing a great many previously po-faced studes to the pleasures of going to 'rock' gigs in baggy shorts and blowing whistles to Latin percussion solos.

Obscure Washington DC band Banbarra's single was a gleefully sexist tribute to living 'in sin'. ACR cop on to the original's edgy metallic weirdness and gorge on it. It's a funny, funny record, and that's almost entirely down to Simon Topping's dolorous, Manc-accented, sub-Ian Curtis vocal, grumbling all this stuff about love not being forever and not believing in alimony with all the lust of a eunuch at a church social. The Factory house-style production is all brittle reverb and teeth-on-edge guitar, Martin Moscrop's Miles Davis trumpet chants shriek in what-the-fuck protest, and best funk drummer in the world Donald Johnson drives everything to the edge of meltdown, constantly whipping the song up and then slapping it down. Banbarra's attempt to get the girl to move in would've brought a slap in the face. ACR's would've had her calling the local psych ward and running for the hills.

REWARD

THE TEARDROP EXPLODES
PRODUCED BY CLIVE LANGER AND
ALAN WINSTANLEY/WRITTEN BY ALAN GILL AND
JULIAN COPE
MERCURY/JANUARY 1981
UK CHART: 6

Horns were big in 1981, but 'Reward' is where they were biggest. Julian Cope and co. took less than three minutes to blast their way out of being a 'Liverpool-scene' band and imprint themselves on our pop consciousness with a noise so desperate and vivid that they could never reproduce it. In fact, no one could, and after years of catching up with all the '60s artists they were compared to – Love, Scott Walker, The Doors – I still can't find a precedent for 'Reward's' blaring soul action. 'Bless my cotton socks I'm in the news!' is how Cope put it in the opening line, and by the time trumpeters Ray Martinez and Hurricane Smith had blown a hole through the radio, he was utterly vindicated.

THAT'S ENTERTAINMENT

THE JAM
PRODUCED BY VIC COPPERSMITH-HEAVEN AND
THE JAM/WRITTEN BY PAUL WELLER
METROGNOME/JANUARY 1981
UK CHART: 21

Another import, this time from Germany. It was a mark of The Jam's popularity that this relatively out-of-character acoustic state-of-the-nation address was played everywhere and almost made Top 20, despite being available on the previous year's *Sound Affects* album.

As the music shuffles gently but emphatically, conjuring up a pastoral vision Weller would later become obsessed with in his solo career, King Mod paints a chillingly accurate picture of our everyday lives in the form of a list, taking in everything from 'Two lovers missing the tranquillity of solitude' to 'Lights going out and a kick in the balls.' 'Wishing you were far away' is what he imagines we're all doing, and what British pop would increasingly do over the next few years. With Foxton and Buckler (on light percussion) reaching their peak of interpretive subtlety, and Weller summing up everything he'd complained so vividly about over the previous four years, the generous and battle-hardened poetry of 'That's Entertainment' is the perfect place to leave the period's most fêted singles band. Weller was never as good nor relevant as this again.

ONCE IN A LIFETIME

TALKING HEADS
PRODUCED BY BRIAN ENO/WRITTEN BY
DAVID BYRNE, BRIAN ENO AND TALKING HEADS
SIRE/FEBRUARY 1981
UK CHART: 14

I may find myself admitting that it took me a long time to truly appreciate the wonders of this record.

I may find myself remembering that, at the time of its release, a friend I greatly admired remarked that Talking Heads were now the band that every other band had to match up to. I may have found myself agreeing eagerly without having a clue what he meant.

I may find myself going back to a night, many years later, when another friend invited a small group of us round to play their favourite singles and explain why they loved them, and

"You're No Good"

E·S·G

YOU'RE NO GOOD/U.F.O./MOODY/E.S.G.

then vote for the night's best. Somebody played 'Once in a Lifetime' and the vote was unanimous – it had blown away The Beatles, Elvis, the Sex Pistols, Public Enemy, everything. And I may find myself thinking that 'Once in a Lifetime' is as close as anyone has come to summing up The Big One – The Meaning of Life – in a pop song you can dance to. And not just because of the eccentrically told truth of David Byrne's mid-life crisis lyric, but because the perfect rhythm, the way the music carries the flow of water and life that carries us, the feeling of infinity generated by the whole-world-in-their-hands chorus, makes something proud, even noble, out of our stumble through life's events.

I may find myself marvelling at its willing wrestle with nature, time, age, money. The sudden exclamation – 'My God – WHAT HAVE I DONE?' – could . . . *should* . . . be schlocky. Yet it still chills with the horror of facing up to the repercussions of our stumbles, because the drums have been preparing you for that moment, and because the deep blue funk of the bass and the vivid daybreak colours of the chorus remind you that it's *better* to face up, and that great art is at its most life-enhancing when it *forces* you to face up, and then makes it alright by showing you that you're not alone in feeling empty, and that we are defined by our ability to not be swallowed by the darkest truths, and that you may be small but you are a part of something bigger. Because facing up to that is what separates good humans from bad.

And I may find myself thinking that 'Once in a Lifetime' is one of the greatest things I know, same as it ever was.

MESSAGE OF LOVE

THE PRETENDERS
PRODUCED BY CHRIS THOMAS/WRITTEN BY CHRISSIE HYNDE
REAL/FEBRUARY 1981
UK CHART: 11

From The Meaning of Life to The Meaning of Love. The most adventurous of all Pretenders singles entered the charts on Valentine's Day, and remains the most evocative love letter ever scrawled in the language of rollicking glam drums and hard-rock garage guitars. Hynde and Thomas eschew their usual classic verse-chorus craft and cascade of twangs for a wall of mud and blood, which reminds you that, to truly lose all love inhibitions, you have to get your hands a little dirty. Chrissie's sultry tough-tenderness looms over and above the band's awesome crunch, bigging up Bardot, quoting Oscar Wilde, reinventing every romantic cliché that she truly believes in. As her gorgeous

harmonies run their fingers through your hair, she ends the song with a simple plea: 'Talk to me, darlin',' sung over and over again with a dreamy, creamy pleasure. Unsurprisingly, darlin' is lost for words.

YOU'RE NO GOOD/U.F.O./MOODY

E.S.G.
PRODUCED BY MARTIN HANNETT/WRITTEN BY E.S.G.
FACTORY/FEBRUARY 1981
DID NOT CHART

Of all the mavericks featured in this book, Emerald, Sapphire & Gold are the most wonderfully unlikely. The Scroggins sisters formed the nucleus of an Afro-American all-girl band (plus conga player Tito Libran) hailing from the poverty-stricken birthplace of hip-hop, the South Bronx. They were virtually formed by Ma Scroggins, who figured that playing in a band would keep her daughters off the streets. The music they made – a guitarless cross between Public Image Ltd and Tamla Motown – sees E.S.G. stand at the cusp of as many future pop developments as Kraftwerk.

This first, definitive three-track single was released on Manchester's Factory after the band had supported A Certain Ratio in New York. The bass-heavy 'You're No Good's' crawling, dislocated sex-sleaze appealed to the post-punk underground, and further cemented the ongoing punk-funk love affair. The four brittle synth-notes that dominated 'U.F.O.' became a fave breakbeat for hip-hop DJs and went on to be sampled by as many future hip-hop producers as James Brown's 'Funky Drummer'. Indeed, E.S.G.'s career exemplifies the downside of sampling culture. Not only did it take years for the band to get their just financial desserts from the endless steals, but their recording career was all but ended when their indie label, New York's 99 Records, decided to sue Sugarhill for the use of 'Cavern' by similar mutant funkers Liquid Liquid, on Grandmaster Melle Mel's 'White Lines'. 99 won, but Sugarhill had gone bust and couldn't pay, leaving 99 unable to survive the court costs.

Meanwhile, 'Moody's' dark, propulsive Afro-funk was played to death at New York clubs such as Paradise Garage and The Gallery, and Chicago's Warehouse – the clubs that invented a new underground dance scene called 'house'. So adored were E.S.G. by the up-and-coming cognoscenti that it was they who played live on the legendary closing night of Paradise Garage, just as house spread its wings to travel the world.

PLAN B

Dexys Midnight Runners

You've always been searching for something
But everything seems so so-so
Tightly close your eyes
Hold out your hand
We'll make a stand
Forget their plans
and their demands
PLAN B
They're testing you—but don't worry
PLAN B
This week I'm strong enough for two

I'm coming
I'm running
I'm burning
I wouldn't sell you anything

It starts off just joking
and then they stop talking to you
and that's the worst thing of all
The worst thing of all

Whispers more than loud enough
Try to make you feel not good enough
Try this
Don't believe your eyes
Hold out your hand
We'll make a stand
Forget their plans
and their demands
PLAN B
Bill Withers was good to me
PLAN B
Pretend I'm Bill and lean on me

I'm coming
I'm running
I'm burning
I wouldn't sell you anything

PLAN B
Hold on to me
PLAN B
I'll be your friend if you'll let me

I'm coming
I'm running
I'm burning
I wouldn't sell you anything

PLAN B/DEXYS MIDNIGHT RUNNERS

And the records? Futuristic, catchy, menacing, other-worldly, sensual, a key influence on all hip-hop's and house's most abstract and innovative moves. You won't find E.S.G. in too many rock history books – no group are hidden from pop history as much as black women – but you will find a stunning compilation (*E.S.G.: A South Bronx Story*) of their brave and visionary music on Universal Sound/Soul Jazz in your local quality record shop.

IT'S A LOVE THING

THE WHISPERS

PRODUCED BY THE WHISPERS, DICK GRIFFEY AND LEON SYLVERS III/WRITTEN BY SHELBY AND MEYERS
SOLAR/MARCH 1981
UK CHART: 9

A slight song but a mighty way of singing it by LA's Whispers, as they throw down one of the chunkiest, funkiest two-chord riffs in the late disco canon, and then spin and twirl around it until you're convinced that it is, indeed, a love thing. This is an agitated, expectant, *new* love, where the sudden leaps of joy when you think of little details about her are represented by shock clusters of falsetto harmony and guitar and orchestral headrush. If you can sit still to this and not be touched by its happy anticipation, then you're obviously immune to love or the funk or both. I recommend dance therapy.

PLAN B

DEXYS MIDNIGHT RUNNERS

PRODUCED BY ALAN SHACKLOCK/WRITTEN BY KEVIN ROWLAND AND JIM PATERSON
PARLOPHONE/MARCH 1981
UK CHART: 58

Yep, horns *were* big in 1981. But the band largely responsible for the rediscovery of brass was in deep shit. 'Plan B' was a one-off single released just after most of the group had left, unable to cope with Rowland's mood swings and dictatorial tendencies. The image-obsessed Kev dressed the replacements in a bizarre ponytails and boxing boots get-up, but got them to play up a storm on this tour de force curio.

'Plan B' begins with the traditional Rowland theme of me-and-you-against-the-world. Except the typical brassy soul reinvention is treacle thick and claustrophobic, with Rowland yelping like a drowning man. The Moment comes early: a dead stop, Kev yelling 'Jimmy!', and Big Jim Paterson forcing out a staccato one-note fanfare before playing a warm and wonderful solo. But Rowland is gibbering underneath: 'They start off joking . . . and then they stop talking to you – and that's the worst thing of all – *the worst thing of all*.' Because 'Plan B' is not about the wicked outside world but his departed bandmates, and Rowland is not heading onward and upward but dwelling on it bitterly. 'I'm not selling anything,' he assures us at the end of each chorus, and a quick glance at the chart position shows how right he was. Dexys fanatics loved the record, but everyone else might have picked up on what we knew for sure years later: that Rowland was on the verge of breakdown and finding out that he was one of those people not psychologically designed for fame. His biggest success, most ridiculous fashion statements, and most ambitious album were all to come. But as a singles band, Dexys never topped the freaked and soul-baring intensity of 'Plan B' again.

FLOWERS OF ROMANCE

PUBLIC IMAGE LTD

PRODUCED BY PUBLIC IMAGE LTD/WRITTEN BY KEITH LEVINE AND JOHN LYDON
VIRGIN/MARCH 1981
UK CHART: 24

PiL's last stand remains the strangest chart record of the last 25 years, maybe ever. A one-note drone led by a naked, rudimentary pseudo-African drum riff, stiff rimshots and occasional hi-hat, no bass or guitar, Lydon needling and niggling valiantly in a complete rejection of anything we recognize as melody, and synths, violin and cello humming and shrieking like gremlins in a haunted house. It still waits in vain for pop to catch up with its gleeful dismissal of every rule in the book. 'Behind the dialogue/We're in a mess,' Lydon wails before Levine's eerie gypsy-violin dervish dance goes gloriously insane, and everything ends before you can grab on properly.

The lyric is the usual Lydon stuff rejecting sentimentality and the past. But the last line, 'I'll take the furniture/Start all over again,' reminds you that he'd already fired Jah Wobble, would soon dump Levine, and spent the next few years playing godawful versions of 'Pretty Vacant' and 'Anarchy . . .' to gobbing punk nostalgists with the aid of Armani-suited session musos, beginning a musical run of limp sub-stadium new wave (with occasional reminders of his former glories), and a career as 'Johnny Rotten – pantomime dame' (a moment of spot-on insight from, of all people, *The Word*'s Terry Christian) that reached its inevitable trough with the truly depressing Pistols reunion of 1996. But, I tell you, kid, he used to be good. The best, in fact.

(WE DON'T NEED THIS) FASCIST GROOVE THANG

HEAVEN 17

PRODUCED BY IAN CRAIG-MARSH AND MARTYN WARE/WRITTEN BY IAN CRAIG-MARSH, MARTYN WARE AND GLENN GREGORY
VIRGIN/MARCH 1981
UK CHART: 45

At first, it seemed like a bargain that The Human League split and we got two smart pop groups for the price of one. As it turned out, Heaven 17 became everything bad about beige – over-produced, coldly ironic, piling on the female black vocals with a trowel, desperate for hits but hiding it beneath their empty sub-PiL we're-a-limited-company parody of big business, hideously smug (Glenn Gregory's look-aren't-I-clever? grin sums up the worst aspects of the 1980s as perfectly as Spandau Ballet's fashion sense). But, before all that, they made a debut single (and album, to be fair) that was brave enough to make social comment while pastiching the wigga mores of the new white-boy funk. What's more, it sounded new and fantastic: a tough new kind of electro-funk, topped off by Gregory's friendly authority. The true star of '. . . Fascist Groove Thang', though, is session bassist and guitarist John Wilson, whose virtuoso buzzes and thrums ensure the whole enterprise doesn't slump into total glibness. His bass solo is an eight-bar thrill. And it was pretty great dancing to a song that was right about Reagan and included a wry joke about Cruise missiles.

THE SOUND OF THE CROWD

THE HUMAN LEAGUE

PRODUCED BY MARTIN RUSHENT AND THE HUMAN LEAGUE/WRITTEN BY IAN BURDEN AND PHILIP OAKEY
VIRGIN/APRIL 1981
UK CHART: 12

Meanwhile, Phil Oakey hired a new band, including Jo Callis from The Rezillos and two girls he met in a Sheffield nightclub, Joanne Catherall and Susanne Sulley, and promptly became 1981's biggest and brightest new thing. The electronics stayed, but the sci-fi and arty jokes were replaced by a celebration of disco tackiness and the extraordinariness of being ordinary that, with Phil in the floppy-fringe haircut and girlie make-up that he was too butch for, and the girls with their hard blank faces and gimpy dancing and non-voices, had a ring of truth that was immediately lovable. The League were the representatives of the glammed-up working class before everything became about pretending to be rich and bourgie, bourgie. Being proud of your roots *and* bleaching them until they were straw – the things that dreams are made of.

While retaining just enough of the early League's darkness to both drag post-punks in and suggest the ever-present danger of early '80s nightlife, Rushent and co. mingled Kraftwerk with Moroder and kept it sparse, almost military. Get out and enjoy this while you can, Phil insisted, perhaps to himself as much as us: 'No need to stand proud/Add your voice to the sound of the crowd.' It managed to be both uplifting and sinister, and made 1981 the League's miracle year.

TREASON (IT'S JUST A STORY)

THE TEARDROP EXPLODES

PRODUCED BY CLIVE LANGER AND ALAN WINSTANLEY/WRITTEN BY JULIAN COPE, GARY DWYER AND MICHAEL FINKLER
MERCURY/APRIL 1981
UK CHART: 18

Weird to think now that, for a few short months, Julian Cope vied with Adam and the Durans in the battle for UK teen girls' pop hearts. At least, it is after 20 years of bad hair, crusty fashion, witty psych-pop, druggy plot losses, eco agit-prop, and an amazing reinvention as a maverick raconteur, writer and ancient Brit historian. But on 'Treason' (which had initially been released on Liverpool's Zoo indie a year earlier) he was a handsome and skilled crooner of ornate pop-rock deluxe, this time as humble and self-questioning as 'Reward' (see p. 148) had been emphatic and triumphant. The song catalogues his own and our hang-ups and reasons, simply, that maybe we shouldn't take ourselves so seriously, and once we loosen up we can be whatever we want to be. Which I guess is exactly what Copey went on to prove.

ABOUT THE WEATHER

MAGAZINE

PRODUCED BY JOHN BRAND AND
MARTIN HANNETT/WRITTEN BY HOWARD DEVOTO AND
DAVE FORMULA
VIRGIN/MAY 1981
DID NOT CHART

Even Howard Devoto went beige in 1981. But once this, with its relatively clean production, faux Motown rhythm track and trilling girlie backing vocals bombed, Magazine had no choice but to throw up their hands and give up the ghost.

It was the chart's and daytime radio's loss. Based on the gorgeous '60s soul chords of Dave Formula's piano, 'About the Weather' balances Devoto's lofty head-games and a pure pop prettiness with deft colour and humour. Naturally, it's not about the weather, but about being dumped and Devoto's wordplay on the 'women are always changing their minds' cliché. 'I will study your change of heart in depth . . . I hope you learn to live with what you choose,' he pronounces with great superiority, before giving his real feelings away by shuddering and stuttering in bewilderment and fear by the end. I suppose Wham! *were* more comforting. More's the pity.

PAPA'S GOT A BRAND NEW PIGBAG

PIGBAG

PRODUCED AND WRITTEN BY PIGBAG
Y/MAY 1981
DID NOT CHART
(REISSUED MARCH 1982: REACHED NO. 3)

DER MUSSOLINI

D.A.F.

PRODUCED BY CONNY PLANK/WRITTEN BY
ROBERT GÖRL AND GABI DELGADO-LOPEZ
VIRGIN/MAY 1981
DID NOT CHART

Two massively influential underground dance hits – one from Bristol, one from Düsseldorf – that both defined two very different types of 'alternative' clubbing and pushed their respective genres as far as they could, providing future adventurers with a blueprint to follow.

Former Pop Group member Simon Underwood formed Pigbag on his Y label to accentuate the funk side of his former band's sound collisions. Their only major success turned out to be the shock dance hit of the era, a breakneck tempo big-band funk throwdown that nicked its main riff from the ancient theme of the *Tarzan* TV series, and blended it with finger-bleeding bass, chaotic percussion and ecstatic, comedic free-jazz horn solos. Despite being almost too fast to dance to, it percolated on the nascent warehouse funk *and* alternative club scenes for a year before bursting onto radio and into the consciousness of a thousand fledgling breakbeat merchants.

'Der Mussolini' was a more problematic, but even better, record. Deutsch Amerikanische Freundschaft were a duo of sexy black-leather-clad boys who mixed brutal minimalist synth backings and guttural vocals that obliquely critiqued sex and politics in their native Germany. Former Kraftwerk producer Plank gave them a speaker-blowing sound that was the polar opposite of Ralf's and Florian's gently undulating classicism, but 'Der Mussolini', with its one relentless riff, clubbing disco drums, horror movie vocal effects and sweaty, working-on-a-chain-gang exhortations to 'Dance The Mussolini', 'Dance The Adolf Hitler' and 'Dance The Jesus Christus' (the rest was in German), made them pop stars in their native land. The record felt, from a British perspective, like a liberating yet deadly serious attempt to confront the tensions and guilt that still

CANDYSKIN/THE FIRE ENGINES

surrounded Germany's past and stomp them underfoot. But then, I was stunned by the music and went along with the artists' intentions purely on trust.

'Der Mussolini' took electro-dance out of the hedonist clouds and into the dirt of manic tempos, sonic aggression, and sledgehammer sarcasm – like the hooligan cousin of Heaven 17's first single. Which made it partly responsible for lots of good things, but largely responsible for much future sub-Teutonic electro-metal crud too. Nonetheless, it's still a reckless and breathtaking attack on everything smug and safe in Euro culture, and stronger and deeper than almost anything inspired by it.

CANDYSKIN

THE FIRE ENGINES

PRODUCED BY BOB LAST/WRITTEN BY
RUSSELL BURNS, DAVEY HENDERSON,
GRAHAM MAIN AND RUSSELL SLADE
POP AURAL/MAY 1981
DID NOT CHART

Now *this* was a sign of the times. Inspired by our fearless leaders the *NME*, and particularly New Pop definer Paul Morley, we still believed at this point that all pop music would come to sound as crabby and odd and instinctive and trashed and cuddly and wired and irresponsible and *New* as The Fire Engines. We were wrong. But 'Candyskin's' blaring approximation of a seaside singalong played by drunken anarchists still sounds fresh and thrilling and full of bare-faced cheek. What's more, mainman Davey Henderson learned to sing properly and headed up two other groovy outfits, the Bolan-meets-Prince Win (in the rest of the '80s), and the still magnificent Bolan-meets-Prince-round-at-Captain-Beefheart's-place Nectarine No. 9. To a select few of us he is a mega-famous pop star, and this is his 'Like a Virgin'.

GHOST TOWN/FRIDAY NIGHT, SATURDAY MORNING/WHY?

THE SPECIALS

PRODUCED BY DAVE JORDAN AND
JERRY DAMMERS/'GHOST TOWN' WRITTEN BY
JERRY DAMMERS/'FRIDAY NIGHT, SATURDAY
MORNING' WRITTEN BY TERRY HALL/'WHY?' WRITTEN
BY LYNVAL GOLDING
2-TONE/CHRYSALIS/JUNE 1981
UK CHART: 1

The most famous slice of life imitating art in this book is actually a rewriting of history. Legend has it that 'Ghost Town' went to No. 1 in Britain as the first Brixton riots raged. In fact, the riots provoked by the Met's 'Operation Swamp '81' crackdown in Brixton happened at the beginning of April. But 'Ghost Town' entered the charts as riots hit Peckham in south-east London, and made its eerie way to the top as 'copycat' street battles were fought in Liverpool, Birmingham, all over the ghettos of England. Its analysis of the times, the wailing chants, the dark beauty of its hypnotic roots-reggae prowl and wistful melody, Neville Staples intoning 'The people getting angry' – all still bring back as clear as day the mixed emotions of being 18 and frightened of what this would all mean. There's nothing new I can say about the masterpiece that is 'Ghost Town'. But the largely forgotten B-sides of the last Specials single are worthy of bigging up, particularly as the three songs, in themselves, suggested the band had said everything they needed to say, probably more.

Golding's 'Why?' is a simple, carnivalesque plea for racial tolerance that turned out to have all the prescience of 'Ghost Town'. Just as the single was released, Golding was hospitalized by racist thugs. Despite being on the critical list for a while, he was interviewed in his hospital bed and spoke of forgiveness and feeling sorry for his assailants. He seemed like some kind of saint, and 'Why?'s' balance of Golding's plaintive bewilderment ('Do you really wanna kill me?') and the determined aggression of toaster Staples became positively anthemic.

Hall's 'Friday Night . . .' sees the singer inhabiting Dammers's teenage wasteland so completely that you can hardly see the join. Over a pointedly pretty reggae muzak, Hall has another lousy night out in a small town, treading warily through urine and vomit and blood, glumly watching bouncers bounce and girls dance round their handbags. The detail is poetry, the deadpan jokes kill ('I'm going to watch my money go/At The Locarno . . . no'), the contempt for working-class cattle-market

GIRLS ON FILM/DURAN DURAN
PAGE 160

routine is a hollow laugh at how little we demand from our lives. 'Wish I had lipstick on my shirt/Instead of piss stains on my shoes,' Terry sighs from the taxi queue at the end, explaining why someone so smart is there at all.

PULL UP TO THE BUMPER

GRACE JONES
PRODUCED BY CHRIS BLACKWELL AND
ALEX SADKIN/WRITTEN BY KOOKOO BAYA,
GRACE JONES AND DANA MANO
ISLAND/JUNE 1981
UK CHART: 53

But for some, nightlife was a very different thing. Grace Jones's *Nightclubbing* album was the hippest record of 1981. A reinvention of Roxy Music's too-much-too-soon ennui, with sublime reggae and funk rhythms from *the* rhythm section of the era, Jamaica's Sly Dunbar and Robbie Shakespeare, it gave an arty ambiguity and muso muscle to the growing rejection of the everyman realities of The Jam and The Specials. Grace Jones, an intimidatingly androgynous and Amazonian New York model – born in Jamaica – had already travelled the world and had an open invite to the kind of parties that Terry Hall could only dream of. She looked like a sleek, purpose-built alien, and spoke-sang her lyrics with a dominatrix-like authority, developing and transcending her early career as a gay-scene disco diva. Jones established and defined the growing relationship between catwalk and club cognoscenti, for better or for worse.

'Pull Up to the Bumper' remains her finest moment, a driving-as-shagging double entendre as bald as anything a *Carry On* film could come up with ('I've got to blow your horn!'). Apart from the expansive urban-tropical funk setting, the (knowing) fun lies in how terrifying her come-ons are. Pull up to this bumper and you may end up a write-off, unless your motor's been thoroughly MOT'd recently.

WORDY RAPPINGHOOD

TOM TOM CLUB
PRODUCED BY CHRIS FRANTZ AND
STEVE STANLEY/WRITTEN BY TINA WEYMOUTH
ISLAND/JUNE 1981
UK CHART: 7

Which is where I take back what I said about Debbie Harry. White New York girls were pretty good at this rapping thing.

The second hippest rhythm section in the world was Chris Frantz (drums) and Tina Weymouth (bass) from Talking Heads. Their side project was also on Chris Blackwell's Island and further established the label's pioneering two-way link between uptown Jamaica and downtown New York, based around the state-of-the-art Compass Point studios in the Bahamas. Crisp pop-funk production and a vibe of smart fun defined a sound that looked set to take over the world. Again, it proved to be another false dawn, for reasons far more difficult to fathom than the sudden death of Britain's New Pop adventure.

Kicking off with chattering typewriters, a drum effect that makes you jump out of your skin, and cutesy girls trilling a terrible pun ('What are words worth?'), Weymouth makes like a particularly intense supply teacher while Oriental chants mingle with chipmunk voices and percussion workouts. Inspired disco fluff that seems to add up to more, it briefly made Frantz and Weymouth more popular than the band they were becoming increasingly sidelined in.

THE MODEL

KRAFTWERK
PRODUCED BY RALF HUTTER AND
FLORIAN SCHNEIDER/WRITTEN BY HUTTER, BARTOS
AND SCHULT
CAPITOL/JUNE 1981
UK CHART: 36
(REPROMOTED IN DEC 1981: REACHED NO. 1 IN
JANUARY 1982)

The influence of club play on the pop charts had stretched far beyond the confines of conventional disco tunes. The original A-side, 'Computer Love' from the new *Computer World* album, made little impact on initial release. But some wise DJ forever lost to posterity must have flipped it at some point, because the stately, ambivalent B-side from 1978's *The Man Machine* album

INTERNATIONAL

SCRITTI POLITTI
The "Sweetest Girl"
Lions After Slumber

45

LONDON · TOKYO · NEW YORK

THE 'SWEETEST GIRL'/SCRITTI POLITTI
PAGE 162

became ubiquitous on the burgeoning new-romantic/futurist club scene, and gave the German electronic legends their only UK No. 1 in the more appropriately frosty January of the following year.

As the engulfing run of twinkling melodies unfolds, you are, as always with Kraftwerk, unsure of how they *feel* about their beautiful subject. 'I'd like to take her home/That's understood' seems positively rabid in the context of their studious asexuality, but the passionless 'That's understood' suggests that this is nothing more than a comment on what Hutter – every man – is supposed – programmed – to feel about the model. But there was little irony, I suspect, in the way the glammed-up girls and Bowie-suited boys posed and preened to this, all hoping that a little of the model's effortless incandescence would rub off on us. The fact that this was never meant to be an A-side suggests that Kraftwerk didn't realize they'd be taken so literally.

GIRLS ON FILM

DURAN DURAN

PRODUCED BY COLIN THURSTON/WRITTEN BY
DURAN DURAN
EMI/JULY 1981
UK CHART: 5

But then, what chance did German irony have in the face of good old-fashioned British lust and greed? Adam might have been the most desperate star, but Le Bon, Rhodes and the various unrelated Taylors were the most sure, their fevered anticipation of their future celeb lifestyles only slightly offset by the flash of fear that occasionally surfaced in Le Bon's flat, nasal foghorn of a voice. Their bare-faced ambition and self-love inspired the best and most prophetic pop feature of the time, when they yapped blithely at Paul Morley about Lady Di and how much smoked salmon they could afford in the future as an anti-police riot threatened to cancel their homecoming show at the Birmingham Odeon. *This* was the New Pop, and, no matter how much we may sneer now at the part it played in the death of English pop as rebellion or provocation, its irresponsibility and cheap glamour was undeniably exciting at the time.

'Rio' may stick in the mind as the definitive symbol of Duran's ruthless escapism. But that is, very appropriately, because of the ridiculous video (for every musician that tells you earnestly that they wanted to play because of The Clash/Public Enemy/Nick Drake/Detroit Techno, there are a dozen who started because of that champagne and those girls on that boat). 'Girls on Film'

remains the ultimate Duran single because its tacky soft-porn sexism perfectly reflects the sleazy, tabloid trivia-driven marketing machine that mainstream pop would come to thrive upon (Duran, of course, had no doubts at all about taking models home. That's understood). But the single also sweeps away all disquiet with sheer rock-disco energy, in a way that the other major players in the Second Great British Pop Invasion of America – Culture Club, Wham!, Spandau – could never get close to. This fusion fuelled the dance-rock explosion that drowned uncompromised black music in the States for the next half-dozen years, and led Duran to describe themselves as a cross between the Sex Pistols and Chic. They may have been deluding themselves as artists and musicians, but, as the distillation of what those two bands were warning us about, they had no idea how right they were.

A PROMISE

ECHO & THE BUNNYMEN

PRODUCED BY HUGH JONES/WRITTEN BY
WILL SERGEANT, IAN MCCULLOCH,
LES PATTINSON AND PETE DE FREITAS
KOROVA/JULY 1981
UK CHART: 49

Strange to think now that the major Big Rock, Stones v Beatles/Oasis v Blur-style battle of this era was between U2 and Echo and The Bunnymen. If Blur still carry a few bruises from their commercial beating, they should wonder how Ian McCulloch manages to sit down and then count his blessings. I've never quite forgiven the masses for letting the Irish blusterers trample all over The Bunnymen's shimmering sensuality, but that's honestly not the reason U2 do not appear in this book. I just don't think their singles are very good.

Anyway, the single from the Bunnies' finest album flopped, 'cos money was too tight to mention and we all bought their *Heaven Up Here* album. But it's still a thing of vaporous beauty, guitars droning, chugging and singing across vistas of sad space, Mac's voice immaculately stoned and free and tearful and at the peak of its elemental power before the silly sod discovered Frank Sinatra and started understating everything to the point of sleepwalking. The usually ignored Jones's production is a crucial element, harnessing a glistening, dubby gush that took it to a place more dreamlike and exotic than trad rock would normally allow.

EVERYTHING'S GONE GREEN/NEW ORDER

TAINTED LOVE

SOFT CELL

PRODUCED BY MIKE THORNE/WRITTEN BY
ED COBB
SOME BIZARRE/PHONOGRAM/JULY 1981
UK CHART: 1

You know, I didn't notice that Marc Almond was gay at the time. How crap is that? I mean, he didn't exactly have to dress up like Sylvester or do Tom Robinson covers, did he? So I took this second single and first massive global hit from the Leeds electro-pop duo a lot . . . um . . . straighter than I do now. And so did almost everyone who bought it, I guess. Because now it sounds like the best description of the fallout following a relationship between two men – one of them sexually confused – that anyone's ever written, despite being a cover. The other, much sadder, fact that gives 'Tainted Love' its twist is that the original was sung in 1964 by one Gloria Jones, who went on to achieve a tragic kind of pop infamy by crashing the car that killed her husband Marc Bolan. The pain you drive into the heart of me.

LOVE ACTION (I BELIEVE IN LOVE)

THE HUMAN LEAGUE

PRODUCED BY MARTIN RUSHENT AND THE HUMAN
LEAGUE/WRITTEN BY PHILIP OAKEY AND
IAN BURDEN
VIRGIN/JULY 1981
UK CHART: 3

Proof that one note in the right place at the right time can carry enough memories to fill a biography. My attempts at not getting too nostalgic on your ass are floored by the lonesome, repeated, synthetic 'BEOW' at the beginning of this record, which instantly reminds me of everything great about being 18, having cash, preparing for a flat of my own, and falling in love truly and utterly on an almost weekly basis with lovely Peterborough girls (the League's Ian Burden was, it was rumoured, from Peterborough too! Though no one had ever met him).

If 'Love Action' wasn't to be the League's biggest, it was their finest, with every detail – from the rumbling Linn drum and bass to the giggling high-end synth loop, from Phil's sincerity and wit and the weird bum note at the end of the first verse, to the girls doing that daft dance on *Top of the Pops* and unwittingly inventing Bananarama – absolutely perfect. Trivia? The old man whom Phil believes turned out to be Lou Reed. And the B-side 'Hard Times' gave its name to a much talked-about feature in new style magazine *The Face* about socialist clubbers who showed their disgust at Thatcher's monetarist policies by wearing expensive jeans with holes in them. Great days.

THE 'SWEETEST GIRL'

SCRITTI POLITTI

PRODUCED BY ADAM KIDRON AND
GREEN GARTSIDE/WRITTEN BY GREEN GARTSIDE
ROUGH TRADE/AUGUST 1981
UK CHART: 64

On 'The "Sweetest Girl"', an obscure Welsh squat-punk eccentric called Green instantly reinvented himself as a honey-voiced, Lady Di-coiffeured, beige-pop eccentric. One of a new breed of anti-rockist musicians, as well as an intimidatingly well-read intellectual, Green believed that the only progressive way to convey his post-modern analysis of pop was to make immaculately produced love songs about the clichés and stocks-in-trade of immaculately produced love songs. Hence the inverted commas. He went on to achieve his own wildest blue-eyed soul dreams, getting enough respect in black American muso circles to work with the likes of Marcus Miller and the great Miles Davis himself.

'The "Sweetest Girl"' both explains why he got what he wanted, and puts most of his later over-fussy and mathematical confections to shame. An airy, dub-inspired production featuring the keyboard talents of lefty pop's Grand Old Man, Robert Wyatt, it is so winsomely lovely that birds suddenly appear every time it is near. A rudimentary drum machine hisses and sighs in reggae time as Green coos and caresses his echo-soul tribute to female strength and male weakness. Mysterious stuff about 'the sickest group' ruptures the reverie with enigmatic portent, before Green gets off the subject completely and croons one of the most stunning and strange couplets in pop history: 'Politics is prior to the vagaries of science/She left because she understood the value of defiance.'

Almost five years later, Madness, struggling for hit tunes after the departure of their best writer Mike Barson, heard the hit potential of the song and covered it for a single. Poor Suggs does OK until he gets to these lines, and then falls flat on his face in an unintentional comedy of incomprehension. The single bombed and Madness split six months later.

GENIUS OF LOVE/TOM TOM CLUB

RELEASE THE BATS

THE BIRTHDAY PARTY

PRODUCED BY THE BIRTHDAY PARTY AND
NICK LAUNAY/WRITTEN BY MICK HARVEY AND
NICK CAVE
4AD/AUGUST 1981
DID NOT CHART

Australia's The Birthday Party were the most intense rock 'n' roll proposition of the time. A bunch of wasted and malevolent-looking cowboy junkies led by a back-combed streak of piss called Nick Cave, they sounded like the noise that would result if Elvis dragged The Cramps to the electric chair for crimes against Mom's apple pie, and performed as if hell were freezing over and they were desperate to get in before it sealed up. The only gig I've ever been truly terrified at – even allowing for racist skins at punk and 2-Tone shows – was a Birthday Party shindig in Camden where band and the majority of the audience seemed hell-bent on mutually assured destruction, egging each other on to greater and greater levels of random violence masquerading as dancing.

Having said all that, their fourth single 'Release the Bats' is one of the funniest records I know, and even after meeting the mordant Mr Cave for interviews a couple of times and talking about his former band, I still don't know if the comedy is intentional or not. Imagine a shock therapy Elvis impersonator being beaten by baseball bats in a horror movie sex scene and . . . well, that's the best I can do. It rocks so rabidly it just can't help being funny as fuck.

EVERYTHING'S GONE GREEN

NEW ORDER

PRODUCED BY MARTIN HANNETT/WRITTEN BY
NEW ORDER
FACTORY/SEPTEMBER 1981
UK CHART: 38

Can I just say, before we go any further, that, despite the uncritical adoration that the surviving members of Joy Division continue to enjoy, I still truly despise the name they gave themselves. And the whole flirting-with-fascism side of the Factory clan to boot. Ta.

New Order, more than any other band, sum up the dominant belief among '80s Brit musicians that rock was essentially all used up – taken as far as it could go by the Sex Pistols and Joy Division themselves. The bereaved Mancs were fascinated by Eurodisco, and 18 months before they made a record that would change everything in 'indie' pop, they released this haunting, brittle and totally original introduction to the band they would become. No one took any notice of the flip of this double A-side once they'd been amazed and intrigued by 'Everything's Gone Green's' proto-acid house with guitars. Especially Peter Hook's at first flailing and then singing bass-as-lead-instrument, which, as Hannett fixed each swirl of wandering echo to an exact point where darkness meets light, conjured up visions of endless space and renewed strength through the sweetest sadness. As the song moved smoothly into polyphonic dance frenzy, Barney Sumner whooped wildly, and you could sense the band's relief and joy at throwing off the cloak of grief and misery that had almost suffocated them.

WHERE DID YOUR HEART GO?/ WHEEL ME OUT

WAS (NOT WAS)

PRODUCED BY DON AND DAVID WAS AND
JACK TANN/WRITTEN BY DON AND DAVID WAS
ZE/ISLAND/SEPTEMBER 1981
DID NOT CHART

The dubious honour of Most Dramatic Fall From Grace covered in this book belongs to New York's Ze Records. The rock-rejecting music and style press of 1981 went gaga for the various mutant-disco eccentrics (Kid Creole, Alan Vega of Suicide, No Wave funk renegade James White, black rock fusioneer Bill Laswell) on the label. Yet, in the wake of its failure to deliver the deluge of weird hits it promised, Ze has disappeared completely from the pop encyclopaedias and discographies. Even the Internet draws a blank. Which, apart from making me regret throwing out my *NMEs* every week, shows how much '80s hipsterism in the music press came to be despised by the end of the decade. Basically, the writers chucking all this black music from other countries at us were committing the basic crime of telling the reader that their own culture was second-rate (which, apart from a few bands, it was). They and their jazz-soul-funk-rap-reggae music had to go, before the white male middle class starting wearing baggy trousers and talking in Brixton patois . . . uh . . . hang on a minute . . .

Anyway, I eventually discovered that Ze was the brainchild of Michael Zilkha, heir to the Mothercare fortune and the man (or

SHOOT THE PUMP/J. WALTER NEGRO AND THE LOOSE JOINTZ

one of the many men, it would seem) who discovered Madonna. The brothers Was (really David Weiss and Don Fagenson from Detroit) went on to be the biggest successes of the Ze stable, mainly as wily but vapid mainstream producers, sadly. Their finest early single is an awesomely sophisticated blend of power rock, beatnik satire and freaky romantic drama, both sides as great as each other. George Michael, of all people, went on to cover the subversive Broadway balladry of 'Where Did Your Heart Go?' (sung beautifully by soul man Sweet Pea Atkinson), bringing a whole new unintentional truth to its line about two lovers sharing 'a rusty can of corn'. 'Wheel Me Out' is squalling funk-rock therapy, as a collection of different spoken voices all insist that they are 'a former scientist' whose every attempt at personal growth meets a brick wall of cruel discouragement by 'You! You who never pushed the wheels.' The sickly harsh harmonies and chopping guitars amp up the paranoia as this all-powerful Bringer of Negativity closes in for the kill: 'You did it to him – and I'm next!' the voices accuse helplessly. It's comic, but comedy with a chill, as you remember every person in your life that ever poured cold water on your dreams.

Apparently, after the European success of Kid Creole aka August Darnell tipped the Ze label into a chaotic demise, Zilkha's big new idea was gay cowboy songs. Presumably, Mothercare intervened.

GENIUS OF LOVE

TOM TOM CLUB
PRODUCED BY STEVE STANLEY, TINA WEYMOUTH AND CHRIS FRANTZ/WRITTEN BY TOM TOM CLUB
ISLAND/SEPTEMBER 1981
UK CHART: 65

The year's most fulsome tribute to black music began a reciprocal love affair. The girl-group funk of 'Genius of Love' was used by Grandmaster Flash and The Furious Five for a rap called 'It's Nasty' the following year, and remains a staple in many a hip-hop DJ's old-school set to this day. The low chart position is the fault of a radio no-no line: 'We went insane when we took cocaine.' Its dreamy dayglo summer stroll through affectionate Sly & Robbie rhythms and dub tricks, and a roll-call of black music legends from Marley to Smokey to Hamilton Bohannon, is all in honour of The World's Greatest Boyfriend, which maybe explains why Frantz and Weymouth continue to live happily ever after.

SHOOT THE PUMP

J. WALTER NEGRO AND THE LOOSE JOINTZ
PRODUCED BY FRED MILLER, HANK O'NEAL AND QUESTAR/WRITTEN BY J. WALTER NEGRO AND PABLO CALOGERO
ZOO YORK/ISLAND/SEPTEMBER 1981
DID NOT CHART

As I write this in July 2001, New York is the cool thang. Too much great hip-hop to mention, plus a new CBGBs-influenced rock wave led by The Strokes and including Moldy Peaches and the wonderful Hamell on Trial. Exactly 20 years ago, New York was the cool thang, too. Endless adventures in black pop-fusion from Sugarhill to Talking Heads. There are riots everywhere too, as I write. Excuse me while I get a Time Tunnel shudder out of my system.

Who the hell *was* J. Walter Negro? I was beginning to think that, like Ze Records, I'd made him up for something to do until I went to this music mag party a few years back and, as I walked in the joint, the DJ put on 'Shoot the Pump' and a small but significant proportion of the revellers went joyfully mental. And quite right too, because 'Shoot the Pump' is a work of complete genius, and a pop anthem in that same parallel universe in which Davey from The Fire Engines is bigger than Madonna.

Negro's tilt at greatness is a meeting between flute and wah-wah Latin barrio-funk and the new hip-hop culture played at breakneck speed, produced like a street party and delivered with a hyperactive hysteria that makes The Pop Group sound like The Lighthouse Family. Our hero has a hobby he's burning to tell you about. It involves using a monkey wrench, an aerosol can and some minor vandalism to make New York fire hydrants hose passers-by in the heat of the Summer. And the police shoot the punk, 'cos they think the monkey wrench is a gun, 'cos a monkey wrench was as deadly a weapon in the hands of young black men in NY in 1981 as a cigarette lighter is in Brixton 2001. But Negro is a bulletproof Superman. 'Man – that was fun,' he sneers at the cops before getting on with soaking nubile young women. Mr Negro – who are you?

WHITE CAR IN GERMANY

WHITE CAR IN GERMANY/THE ASSOCIATES

PAGE 168

O SUPERMAN (FOR MASSENET)

LAURIE ANDERSON

PRODUCED BY LAURIE ANDERSON AND
ROMA BARAN/WRITTEN BY LAURIE ANDERSON
WARNER BROTHERS/OCTOBER 1981
UK CHART: 2

Chicago's Laurie Anderson was already the toast of New York's art community before she moved from the visual arts to music and performance art in 1977. It was her female co-producer Roma Baran who heard Anderson perform 'O Superman' at a soundcheck and insisted they record it as a single. The result was the UK's shock hit of 1981 and a noise so unique and charged with meaning that no other record in this book is as intimidating to critique.

Well, here goes nothing. What I hear in 'O Superman' (which is based on the aria 'O Souverain' from *Le Cid*, an opera by French composer Jules Massenet) is the slow death of civilization at the hands of America and America's calm acceptance of its inevitability. I'm not saying that that is what Anderson intended, or that that is what the thousands of others who bought something that was eight minutes long and anti-pop and *disturbing* heard. It's simply what I hear.

The backing track, you'll recall, largely consists of Anderson's voice saying 'Ah', looped into infinity and softly bleeping like a radar scan. Anderson sing-talks through a vocoder and what begins as an ansaphone message from Mom becomes a conversation with a threatening presence. It comes with a warning. Go home to Mom because the planes are overhead. No need to worry because, 'They're American planes . . . smoking or non-smoking?' She is told to go, but if that threat is real, where can you go? And who is speaking, please? 'This is the hand . . . the hand that takes.'

But what does it take? And what does it take to make this all right? And who guides the hand? Anderson explains, in the most soothing voice in this book, "Cos when love is gone, there's always justice/And when justice is gone, there's always force/And when force is gone, there's always Mom . . . So hold me Mom . . . in your long arms . . . your military arms.'

Mom's apple pie is poisoned. Superman is not coming to save the day. Technology is talking softly, making up its own rules, lulling us into an endless sleep.

Fuck. Anyone got any Duran Duran?

DON'T YOU WANT ME?

THE HUMAN LEAGUE

PRODUCED BY MARTIN RUSHENT AND THE HUMAN
LEAGUE/WRITTEN BY JO CALLIS, PHILIP OAKEY AND
ADRIAN WRIGHT
VIRGIN/NOVEMBER 1981
UK CHART: 1

Well, here we still are. In fact we survived long enough to celebrate, if not the greatest Christmas No. 1 ever, then the best Abba tribute ever. Oakey's semi-autobiographical *A Star Is Born* fantasy about what the League's girls might do to him seemed deliciously revealing and inevitable (not so – the trio are still together while everybody else left), and made working as a waitress in a cocktail bar the career choice of our whole generation. Even the girls.

WHITE CAR IN GERMANY

THE ASSOCIATES

PRODUCED BY THE ASSOCIATES AND
MIKE HEDGES/WRITTEN BY BILLY MACKENZIE AND
ALAN RANKINE
SITUATION TWO/NOVEMBER 1981
DID NOT CHART

Forgive the generalization, but: when British pop groups want to make money, they reach out to America. When British pop groups want to make *art*, they turn to Europe.

Blessed with one of the most impossibly beautiful voices in all of pop, the cheeky, eccentric, flirtatious Billy Mackenzie and his hugely talented multi-instrumental partner, Alan Rankine, came out of Dundee, Scotland, with a flyaway avant-pop noise that bridged the post-punk, electro-pop and white-funk impulses. Before their short, sharp burst of chart success, they released a set of extraordinary singles on the fledgling Situation Two indie label, of which 'White Car . . .' is the best.

Coming on like the dream collaboration between Kraftwerk and Berlin Eno/Bowie, complete with the obligatory namecheck for Düsseldorf, the song showcased two talents at what turned out to be the peak of their imagination and adventure. Pinned down by a martial electronic pulse and fleshed out with swirling echo and grandiose melodies, Mackenzie reports on a fantasy travelogue through chilly northern Europe. You can almost see the moon glinting on the snow and the icy breath escaping his

CRISTINA
THINGS FALL APART

mouth, as Billy's operatic tones swing between swelling tenor and hyper-soprano, and he indulges his penchant for oblique conversational gambit – 'I'm not one for surgery' – and mood-shattering, childlike humour: 'If some prat annoys you/Do what's felt impromptu/*Kick* them in the . . . OW!!!' No need for Robert Fripp's screeching guitars, as Billy unleashes a falsetto vocal solo that attracts his beloved whippets over distances of a hundred miles or more. The record ends with an unwitting prophecy of what future hip-hop 12-inchers would often do – a short instrumental reprise of the record's sinister bloops and marching beats. The Associates would be bigger the following year, but never as pregnant with possibility.

THINGS FALL APART

CRISTINA

PRODUCED BY DON AND DAVID WAS/WRITTEN BY CRISTINA AND WAS (NOT WAS)
ZE/ISLAND/DECEMBER 1981
DID NOT CHART

I used to be the most miserable Christmas Grinch. Thankfully, I kept watching *It's a Wonderful Life* and lightened up. But my fave Christmas record of all time remains, without a doubt, the most depressing Christmas record of all time. What can I say? I love happy records, but hit Christmas songs are the opposite of comfort and joy to me. They're so fucking desperate to please. The rictus grins are always hysterical and remind me of skulls.

No, if you want a *real* Christmas record, one that, like Jimmy Stewart's nightmare in Capra's classic, shows a genuine Goodwill to All Men by understanding and facing up to the ghosts of Christmas Past and the pressure of being HAPPY!!!, then 'Things Fall Apart' is the one. Cristina Monet, like most of the rest of NY's Ze label, is lost out there somewhere. But she left a musical short story, an arthouse movie with grunging guitars and funk beats, mainly spoken with an actor's grace and restraint, that pinpoints perfectly the experience of feeling lonely and alienated while everyone ostentatiously enjoys themselves, and, far worse, being wise enough to know that they are as desperate as you are while finding it impossible to connect with them.

Each verse puts the singer in a different, familiar situation from her recent past, and you learn that, for Cristina as for many of us, Christmas is the harbinger of bad memories. In the first verse, her mother attempts to hold a family Christmas together with a recognizable mixture of nostalgia, defiance and fear of the future. 'Once a year let's have the past,' she pleads. In the second, Cristina is spending a poverty-stricken holiday with a lover: 'We trimmed the cactus with the earrings that I meant to pawn.' And things are fine until he leaves her. '"I can't stand in your way," he said. "Way of what?" I asked. But he was gone.'

In the final verse we are in the present day and she is partying with friends. They wander, desperate for more thrills. They drink too much, laugh too loudly. Cristina is too removed to give herself up to hedonism. 'They killed a tree of 97 years and covered it with lights and silver tears,' she observes, before slinking home, unnoticed, to count the cost of the past alone.

It didn't give Slade any sleepless nights.

THE ADVENTURES OF GRANDMASTER FLASH ON THE WHEELS OF STEEL

GRANDMASTER FLASH

PRODUCED BY SYLVIA AND JOEY ROBINSON JR/WRITTEN BY J. CHASE, M. GLOVER, G. JACKSON AND S. ROBINSON
SUGARHILL/DECEMBER 1981
DID NOT CHART

If you want to know why the next generation of hip-hop acts was so ruthlessly obsessed with getting paid, then get an eyeful of those writing credits. It's fascinating to discover how many people helped compose what was essentially a collage of 12-inch singles, especially when you clock that Flash himself – real name Joseph Saddler – wasn't one of them.

The plain facts of this epochal record are as follows: the wheels of steel are Flash's twin turntables, and his adventures consist of him mixing together excerpts from Chic's 'Good Times', Blondie's 'Rapture', Queen's 'Another One Bites the Dust', The Sugarhill Gang's '8th Wonder', fellow Sugarhill rapper Spoonie Gee's 'Monster Jam', Flash and The Furious Five's 'Birthday Party' and an uncredited Disney-like playlet. This was topped off by Flash manoeuvring the vinyl back and forth, making the noise of a stylus hitting the sounds contained within the grooves into an added form of percussion. It was called scratching and it was the first time anyone out of New York had ever heard it. It was rude, ugly, syncopated, definitively DIY . . . and we went nuts for it. This record also invented that now ubiquitous figure, the Superstar DJ. And, although the way club culture has got *that* idea out of *all* proportion has often turned out bad, as far as 'Adventures . . .' was concerned, it was all good.

1982

1982

War – what is it good for? In 1982 Mrs M. Thatcher answered Mr E. Starr's famous question – it wins general elections for the most unpopular and divisive government in living memory. When most 30- and 40-somethings complain about the worst aspects of the 1980s, they will often focus on bad fashion, bad music, maybe yuppie greed, perhaps the crushing of the unions or the dishevelled Left. For me, the worst of the decade is contained within three words: the Falklands War.

On 19 March, an Argentinian scrap-metal dealer stabbed his country's flag into the soil of a forgotten Imperial outpost in the South Atlantic. By 14 June, over 900 young men had died and Britain had won a war. In those three months, the political landscape of Britain had been turned on its head by working-class patriotic fervour. Margaret Thatcher screeched 'Rejoice! Rejoice!' as the Royal Marines reclaimed South Georgia and Brits young and old did just that, blithely ignoring the sinking of the *Belgrano* as it sailed in independent waters and the fact that this military triumph had been scored over a bunch of barely trained Argentinian teens thrust into battle by a tinpot dictatorship on its last legs. I watched friends I'd thought were perfectly reasonable people degenerate into bloodthirsty monsters as they laughed at and drank to the defeat of the 'Argies'. They had got a taste of old Brittannia ruling the waves, and invoking the spirit of the Blitz was easy when the Exocets were flying around 9000 miles away. Those of us who found the taste unpleasant huddled together and began conversations about where else we'd like to live, as three million unemployed and economic meltdown were forgiven and forgotten. With Labour split and stunned by the national enthusiasm for war, the Tories had already won the next general election and Thatcher was seen as a heroine, a real leader who'd break the unions and the namby-pamby liberals and the IRA with the same brute force and shameless enthusiasm that she had broken those cowardly swarthy Latin types. And they gladly handed her a mandate to do just that.

Of course, not everybody felt this way. But this was when the tabloids truly came into their own. Rupert Murdoch's *Sun* hollered 'Gotcha' as we killed some school-leavers, and embarked on their now well-established crusade to lead and exploit the worst instincts of the disenfranchised. By the end of the year, the women of Greenham Common, Ken Livingstone's GLC and the new Channel Four had been identified as a new 'enemy within' and were treated . . . not with the fear that had greeted the Sex Pistols or 'race' rioters, but a shrieking, hysterical contempt. They were the 'Loony Left', idiot weaklings that didn't understand the new realities of personal ambition and patriotic pride. And yes – the pop music of the time reflected these new realities with aspirational encouragements to Go For It! and increasingly weak and watery (pop) or blustery and lumpen (rock) noise, designed to go down big in America, which it did.

All of which makes the best singles of 1982 even better. Though few met the political climate head on, all the singles below offered different directions and realities, mostly based on the rise of new forms of black music. They were aided by new technologies that were transforming our lives, as the 'microchip' became the new business and leisure buzzword. The satellite age had arrived, and the digital age was hard on its heels, as the microchip changed the way we produced (samplers, sequencers, computerized recording) and consumed (the Walkman, affordable and compact hi-fi and video) pop. Talking drums and wires told us of different ways of living, and we were ready for a brand-new beat.

Honourable mentions: The Valentine Bros/'Money's Too Tight to Mention' (Bridge); Elvis Costello and The Attractions/'Man out of Time' (F Beat); Kate Bush/'The Dreaming' (EMI)

SAY HELLO, WAVE GOODBYE

SOFT CELL

PRODUCED BY MIKE THORNE/WRITTEN BY
DAVE BALL AND MARC ALMOND
SOME BIZARRE/PHONOGRAM/JANUARY 1982
UK CHART: 3

A bittersweet little New Year mystery from the '80s own sleaze-fixated Judy Garland.

As Dave Ball's Fisher-Price Spectorisms swirl around Marc Almond's theatrical croons and camp dismissals, the puzzle deepens. For a start, why was Marc seeing . . . *a girl*? OK, OK, that's none of my business, and anyway, pop singers are allowed to write themselves fictional characters, right? But the more this rather brutal dumping of his 'sleep-around' goes into detail, the more mysterious it becomes. Why did the two have to go out in a cocktail skirt and a suit if it just wasn't them (although that might have had something to do with the door policy at The Pink Flamingo)? Why were they such a joke to those around them? Why is he insulting her and wailing 'Take your hands off me' one minute and being so gentle to her the next? Who is he kidding when he insists he's going to find himself, 'A nice little housewife who'll give me a steady life/And won't keep going off the rails'? And, most of all, there's the sneering line: 'To keep you secret has been hell.' Who were they hiding from? And is a cocktail skirt really much of a disguise? The self-styled Sex Dwarf was giving nothing more away. He just grinned impishly and wandered off into a long career of black-clad art-camp tragedy and apocryphal rumours about buckets of spunk.

THE BOILER

RHODA WITH THE SPECIAL A.K.A.

PRODUCED BY JERRY DAMMERS/WRITTEN BY
THE BODYSNATCHERS
2-TONE/CHRYSALIS/JANUARY 1982
UK CHART: 35

A great single is something you can play over and over again – that's the main point of a single's existence. This great single is the exception. I played it when I bought it, freaked, and put it away until writing this chapter. I've now put myself through it and, having placed it at the back of the box, will maybe never play it again.

With most of The Specials having left (Terry Hall, Lynval Golding and Neville Staples to the Funboy Three, guitarist Roddy Radiation to his own Tearjerkers), Jerry Dammers set about making a series of political issue singles. The first, 'The Boiler', was written by the (mainly) all-girl 2-Tone band The Bodysnatchers, and was spoken (not sung) by their vocalist Rhoda Dakar. It is about rape, and was released into a national landscape where a rape victim had been accused by a judge of 'contributory negligence' for hitch-hiking alone before the attack. 'The Boiler' was unplayable on radio or at clubs, and its relatively high chart placing can be put entirely down to the loyalty of Dammers's audience. Obviously, many of them reacted to the single as I did. The next release, the haunting but odd 'War Crimes', did not chart at all.

The 'Boiler's' instrumental intro is initially atmospheric, even jolly, with its spy thriller guitar and '60s beat with a touch of ska. Then Rhoda tells her story.

She is in a clothes shop. A 'hunk' comes up and offers to pay for her gear. You learn all about her painful lack of self-esteem and desperation for love early on, because she accepts. 'The Boiler' is not a simple story of evil overwhelming good. 'The Boiler' is about people who say that some women 'ask for it' and what that judgement might mean in the light of sexual attractiveness, self-image, innocence, vulnerability, trust and even economics.

He asks her out that night, and as she gets ready in her new clothes she looks at herself and the excitement and flattery of male attention is completely submerged by her self-loathing. 'But in my mind I knew I was still an old boiler.' At the end of a night of dancing, he asks her to come back to his place. She refuses, politely. 'Listen here, girl,' she impersonates gruffly, '*I* bought the gear you've got on . . . *I* bought your drinks all night.' He storms off and, half convinced of his moral rights, she chases after him. But the mood and the setting have turned even darker. She's running to keep up with him and they are walking near a bleak set of alleys and railway lines. And then he rapes her. The moment when your horror becomes heartbreak is when she gabbles about being beaten by this physically powerful man, and pleads, 'There was nothing I could do – *honest*,' still trying to convince us – herself – that she didn't deserve this. And the rest of the song consists of her horrifying, guttural, animal screams and, finally, her broken, childlike sobs as the music skitters away, leaving the scene of the crime without a backward glance.

There may be some details I have missed but I'm not going to listen to it again.

THE BOILER/RHODA WITH THE SPECIAL A.K.A.
PAGE 174

I CAN'T GO FOR THAT (NO CAN DO)

DARYL HALL & JOHN OATES

PRODUCED BY DARYL HALL AND JOHN OATES
(REMIXED BY ROBERT WRIGHT)/WRITTEN BY
DARYL HALL, JOHN OATES AND SARA ALLEN
RCA/JANUARY 1982
UK CHART: 8

Time for a warm bath. 'I Can't Go for That' shows that the American mainstream was gearing up for change, getting a grip on the dynamics and techniques of these new-fangled electro beats. Daryl Hall's beautifully sung explanation that he'll do anything for love (but he won't do that) is written with a subtle edge that could only come from people with experience. The 'that' is the loss of independence, self-control, honesty – his 'soul', as he puts it – within a relationship. And that (and Hall's graceful falsetto 'an-y-thing' on the bridges) would probably have been good enough even without the swishing, slap-back drum machine and the new way of spinning an old soul line in the body-rocking bass. It was all so easy that no one saw it as cutting-edge at the time. Then De La Soul sampled it for their 'Say No Go' seven years later, and the penny dropped.

POISON ARROW

ABC

PRODUCED BY TREVOR HORN/WRITTEN BY ABC
NEUTRON/MERCURY/FEBRUARY 1982
UK CHART: 6

It was a marriage made in pop heaven when Trevor Horn's crashing, widescreen production met Martin Fry's arch pop vision and everyman croon. ABC's *The Lexicon of Love*, the great post-modern pop album of the era, is still revered even by those who rubbish their own '80s pop past. Blending Ferry's knowing melodrama and awkward glamour, Costello's glittering wordplay, and a grandiose, gold lamé, orchestral funk-soul power that got its humour from the fact that Fry and co. were so ordinary (those Temptations dance routines on *TOTP* were magnificent because ABC *couldn't* dance, and knew it, and let us know that they knew it), ABC were like a trip from Detroit to Las Vegas if you went via Sheffield.

Of course, Martin's fighting a losing battle against the Wisdom of Womankind in 'Poison Arrow', and, when he finally gets shot down just before the last chorus, it's the treacherous Horn who provides the ammunition. Thunder claps. Rain pours. Martin: 'I thought you loved me but it seems you don't care.' Lady archer: 'I care enough to know that I could *never* love you.' God's Own Drum Kit: BUDDA-BUNKBUNKBUNKBUNK . . . *CRAASSHHHH!!!* Martin lies in pool of blood. Curtains close. Crowd screams for more.

'B' MOVIE

GIL SCOTT-HERON

PRODUCED BY GIL SCOTT-HERON AND
MALCOLM CECIL/WRITTEN BY GIL SCOTT-HERON
ARISTA/FEBRUARY 1982
DID NOT CHART

By the time '"B" Movie' was released, Chicago's Scott-Heron was a 12-year veteran of black activism in poetry and song. This track, a spoken-word political speech/stand-up comedy routine over a prowling funk backing, was actually the British B-side to a dull and worthy tribute to Marley and reggae called 'Storm Music'. But '"B" Movie' crackled through the Wag Club/warehouse party new-funk underground, introducing Scott-Heron to a young and multi-racial set of fans, and providing the political text for the scene's left-wing, anti-racist, globally informed style-with-attitude.

Scott-Heron's voice – a seductive deep chocolate burr worthy of Barry White – begins with the obvious. America has elected a right-wing second-rate movie star who will fuck up the world. 'Mandate my ass!' he sneers, pointing out that only 26 per cent of the registered voters handed Reagan power (sound familiar?). He then gives you an informed and intellectual and wickedly funny and scary and thrillingly *right* rundown of America's place in the world and the reasons Reagan is a reality, taking in Bob Dylan, the Middle East, cowboy mythology, The Village People, the Cold War, 'voodoo' economics, selective amnesia, *Mutiny on the Bounty*, and America's nostalgia for a time when 'movies were in black and white – and so was everything else'.

The band, The Amnesia Express, slowly turn up the heat under their steely horn-funk and Scott-Heron sings 'This ain't really a life' in disbelief as the music becomes harder and the chants more spooked until it reaches a boiling, hallucinogenic pitch of hysteria, twisting and denying and reinforcing the truth that the poet has told. '"B" Movie' is full of great jokes, but no one was laughing anymore.

I CAN'T GO FOR THAT (NO CAN DO)/DARYL HALL & JOHN OATES

PARTY FEARS TWO

THE ASSOCIATES
PRODUCED BY MIKE HEDGES AND
THE ASSOCIATES/WRITTEN BY BILLY MACKENZIE AND
ALAN RANKINE
ASSOCIATES/WEA/MARCH 1982
UK CHART: 9

The more interesting production techniques used on The Associates' only hit album, *Sulk*, perhaps explain why Billy Mac and the music industry didn't always see eye to eye. Pissing in hired drums and guitars and turning up to the studio with fish pinned to their lapels were just some of the ways Billy and Alan attempted to find the sounds in their heads, which also helps explain the surreal noise that is 'Party Fears Two'. True, it *is* a catchy tune. But those of us who already loved the duo were dumbstruck when Billy's lunatic paean to neurotic fear of commitment went Top Ten. That brittle, trebly, Joy Division-out-of-a-tranny-in-a-wind-tunnel production; the completely over-the-top angst about nothing comprehensible (I'm guessing about the fear of commitment); and Billy's self-parodying, in-the-shower croon, barely in control or in tune during most of it. But the children of the hairspray-and-wearing-your-mum's-curtains revolution lapped it up *and* came back for more. This year belonged, more than to anyone else in British pop, to ABC and The Associates – New Pop's last stand.

I LOVE ROCK 'N' ROLL

JOAN JETT & THE BLACKHEARTS
PRODUCED BY RITCHIE CORDELL AND
KENNY LAGUNA/WRITTEN BY JAKE HOOKER AND ALAN
MERRILL
EPIC/MARCH 1982
UK CHART: 4

Or: where the seductress out of 'Brass in Pocket' (see p. 108) finds she's getting nowhere with all that winking and imagination, and resorts to flick-knife and bicycle chain.

Philadelphia's Jett patented her Suzi Quatro-on-steroids shtick as part of Kim Fowley's semi-manufactured all-girl proto-punk band The Runaways in the mid-'70s. Her only great moment was 1982's best unreconstructed rawk anthem, notwithstanding Joan's surface hardnut feminism, which, with all that black leather and kohl-eyed lip-curling, was pure male dominatrix

fantasy. It's great because it has the loudest guitar and drums this side of nothing, and the happiest '50s nostalgia chorus in the world. Trivia: the song was originally performed by American teeny rock band The Arrows, who had their own series on Brit TV in the early '70s, and were the surprise punters at the Sex Pistols' legendary Soho strip club gig. After The Runaways split, Jett worked briefly with the Pistols' Cook and Jones. I don't know what this means, but it seems important somehow.

THE EMPIRE SONG

KILLING JOKE
PRODUCED BY KILLING JOKE AND
CONNY PLANK/WRITTEN BY KILLING JOKE
EG/MARCH 1982
UK CHART: 43

'The Empire Song' entered the lower reaches of the UK chart on 20 March, two weeks before Argentina invaded and took the Falkland Islands. It hovered there for four long weeks, as war was declared and battle came down. It even copped the Joke the weirdest of *TOTP* appearances, as the band mimed to the horrible, churning splodge of sound without their leader, Jaz Coleman, who had had some kind of breakdown and fled suddenly to Iceland (a popular move among Notting Hill-based rockers of the time – Joe Strummer had done the same thing a few months earlier). Coleman was replaced by a roadie in a grinning mask prancing insanely behind a keyboard. Who remembers how *TOTP* followed this sore-thumb eruption of bad vibes?

Plank had transformed the Joke's already doomy-but-funky sound into a mudbath of atonal yet insidiously catchy metal grunge, with tribal war drumming and distorted vocals. 'Back to square one,' Coleman yells, 'And the old school – backfire!' The music roars like a blitzkrieg heard from an underground bunker as Coleman spits his relish, 'It's been a long wait for this moment!' The most immediately chilling moment is when, somewhere beneath and through the maelstrom, a multi-tracked Coleman trills a one-time-only, three-note, 'La-la-la' harmony, its cute coo winking at us through the ugly swirl, laughing at the implications of England's decline. But the true chill, in retrospect, comes from his vision of the 'old school' shrugging their shoulders and soldiering on. 'Tighten the grip', and then a whispered, 'Getting tighter', as the music descends even further into aural claustrophobia. 'The Empire Song' caught the mood of my least favourite time of being British perfectly,

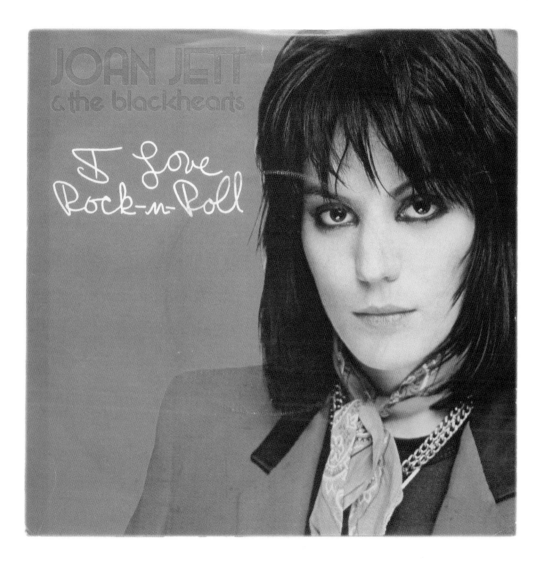

I LOVE ROCK 'N' ROLL/JOAN JETT & THE BLACKHEARTS
PAGE 178

and even more so because, as the track had been recorded months before, Killing Joke had stumbled upon our present by complete accident.

DROP THE BOMB

TROUBLE FUNK
PRODUCED BY REO EDWARDS/WRITTEN BY
ROBERT REED, TAYLOR REED JR, TONY FISHER,
JAMES AVERY, EMMETT NIXON AND
TIMOTHY 'T-BONE' DAVID
SUGARHILL/APRIL 1982
DID NOT CHART

The hip new thang on the new radical funk scene was Go-Go. Hailing from Washington DC, it involved a great many musicians playing a muscular, super-syncopated, Latin-influenced funk with raps for the verses and unison chants for the choruses. Reagan used to regularly nip out of the White House to visit go-go shows and . . . oh, OK, no he didn't. Go-go failed to catch on as a mainstream genre, partly because the songs were not *songs* as such, but mainly because the magic of the sweaty communal four-hour live throwdowns, with classics and hits of the day incorporated into elongated jams in the muso version of Grandmaster Flash's collage techniques, was impossible to capture on record.

'Drop the Bomb' is the closest go-go came, and became a warehouse club staple in those pre-house years. It's a huge, rolling, joyful, tough blend of old-school funk, party chants, and swooping synthetic bloops, that, with its relentless name-checking of various Washington crews, made you feel like you were a super-streetwise Afro-American. Its wry title remains a fave hip-hop term for the best way to do funky damage to a dancefloor.

THE LOOK OF LOVE

ABC
PRODUCED BY TREVOR HORN/WRITTEN BY ABC
NEUTRON/MERCURY/MAY 1982
UK CHART: 4

For when the world is full of strange arrangements, and gravity won't pull you through.

CLUB COUNTRY

THE ASSOCIATES
PRODUCED BY MIKE HEDGES AND
THE ASSOCIATES/WRITTEN BY BILLY MACKENZIE AND
ALAN RANKINE
ASSOCIATES/WEA/MAY 1982
UK CHART: 13

So, the world might have been turning to shit on a shovel in late Spring of '82, but the charts were pure gold. Our last Associates entry rode to glory on the itchy synthesized buzz of Rankine's high-speed acoustic guitar and Billy's magical voice – all rich lounge croon on the verses, and fucked-up, glass-demolishing shriek on the choruses. The mix of glamorous insouciance and indefinable panic captured the mood of British youth: let nightlife fiddle while Rome burns. As for the duo, cocaine did the usual damage, they split, they couldn't reach the same heights separately. Billy struggled with his mental health until finally committing suicide on 22 January 1997, two months before his fortieth birthday.

HOUSE OF FUN

MADNESS
PRODUCED BY CLIVE LANGER AND
ALAN WINSTANLEY/WRITTEN BY MIKE BARSON AND
LEE THOMPSON
STIFF/MAY 1982
UK CHART: 1

Love may be the one thing that still holds true, but only teenage lust could provoke the adolescent, rubber-johnny trauma that is 'House of Fun'. It's the kind of loving joke that has an empathy with its audience of which only Madness were capable. Yet it spelled the end of The Nutty Boys as, from here on in, they ditched the music hall comedy and became wistful mourners of their – and our – more optimistic youth. After all, this is a chemist's – not a joker's shop.

DROP THE BOMB/TROUBLE FUNK

THE MESSAGE

GRANDMASTER FLASH AND THE FURIOUS FIVE
PRODUCED BY SYLVIA INC/WRITTEN BY
E. FLETCHER, M. GLOVER, S. ROBINSON AND
J. CHASE
SUGARHILL/MAY 1982
UK CHART: 8

Rap's very own 'Subterranean Homesick Blues' proved the power of the new breed of DJ. It was club, not radio play that saw 'The Message' create a monumental buzz until it finally entered the charts at the end of August '82 and went Top Ten. But, more than this, it changed our perceptions of hip-hop overnight. Up until then, it was seen even by its fans as a vibrant street culture/fad with vocalists that rhymed in cartoon fashion about girls and money and how great their DJ was. After 'The Message' rap was taken very seriously indeed. The accompanying aspects of B-boy/girl culture – graffiti, breaking, scratch DJing – were overwhelmed and eventually forgotten by all but the diehards.

Yet 'The Message' almost never happened at all. When rapper Melle Mel (Melvin Glover) suggested that the crew record Duke Bootee's set of rhymes about the realities of ghetto life, Sugarhill, Flash and the other members of The Furious Five freaked. It was black kids who bought rap, and black kids would not want their noses rubbed in the shit in their own backyard. Presumably, everyone but Mel had forgotten how '70s reality soul from Sly Stone, Stevie Wonder ('The Message's coda, which sees The Furious Five arrested for hanging on a street corner, was pulled straight from Wonder's 'Livin' for the City') and Curtis Mayfield crossed over to both black and white punters. Mel pushed and the rest is crossover history. From the moment he roars 'Broken glass everywhere/People pissing on the stairs you know they just don't care', you *knew* that rap as what Public Enemy's Chuck D would call 'the black CNN' had arrived. Moreover, the commercial acceptance of that 'pissing', of the image of a prison inmate being used as 'an undercover fag', and of the voices of black men threatening 'Don't push me 'cos I'm close to the edge' had changed black music's relationship with the pop marketplace forever.

INSIDE OUT

ODYSSEY
PRODUCED BY JIMMY DOUGLASS/WRITTEN BY
JESSE RAE
RCA/JUNE 1982
UK CHART: 3

A NIGHT TO REMEMBER

SHALAMAR
PRODUCED BY LEON SYLVERS III/WRITTEN BY
D. MEYERS, C. SYLVERS AND N. BEARD
SOLAR/JUNE 1982
UK CHART: 5

Two records that entered the chart on the same day and proved that disco wasn't quite dead – yet.

Put together by biz mogul Dick Griffey, LA's Shalamar were a prototype for the modern-day manufactured band. Jeffery Daniel, Jody Watley and honey-voiced Howard Hewett had a string of disco hits and momentarily went ballistic in Britain when Daniel – dressed in a bizarre, archetypically '80s chaos of pastel-shade headbands and dungarees topped off by his Afro hair pasted into a Phil Oakey fringe – introduced us to the delights of body-popping. Even harder to copy than breaking, it involved a blend of robotic jerks and fluid glides that defied the laws of physics. 'A Night to Remember' was Shalamar's best, with its sugar-coated harmonies, tough beats and guitar, and lovely opening line, 'When you love someone it's natural – not demanding', sung with all the excited sincerity Hewett could muster.

'Inside Out' was an altogether more subversive affair. New Yorkers Lillian and Louise Lopez and Bill McEachern were another pop-soul vocal group whose string of earlier, eclectic disco hits almost all made it into this list. But the wild card here is the semi-legendary figure of Jesse Rae, a profilic maverick Scottish soul composer who had his own sadly unsuccessful career consisting of Rae 'singing' smooth funk songs in the manner of Andy Stewart performing 'Donald Where's Yer Troosers?' while dressed in full Highland battle regalia.

Anyway, how Rae became known in the world of major-label New York R&B is a story lost in the mists of pop time. But Odyssey grabbed a huge hit with this song which, despite its conventional – and movingly pretty – pop-funk melody, is tragic and masochistic to the point of near insanity. Because the

Associates–CLUB COUNTRY

CLUB COUNTRY/THE ASSOCIATES

lead singer is addressing her lover who she knows is having an affair, and, rather than expressing anger, shame or even disappointment, she is telling him that she understands why he can't resist the other woman, and offering . . . not competition . . . but comfort. She punishes herself with her visions of their lovemaking – 'You can feel her tightening grip' – but seems to be enjoying her suffering to a disturbing degree. She wants to be turned inside out by all this. It's all sung with an eerily calm, sexed-up androgyny, but the weirdest thing is that, while this guy is torturing her, she insists that, 'Like the words here in this song we'll go on and on and on with our love.' And you begin to wonder if she split up with him ages ago, maybe even never went out with him, and is just watching him, through a window, lying with his girl while she lies to herself.

LORRAINE

EXPLAINER

PRODUCED BY RAWLSTON CHARLES AND
WINSTON HENRY/WRITTEN BY WINSTON HENRY
CHARLIE'S CALYPSO CITY/JULY 1982
DID NOT CHART

For the white world the music of the West Indies is reggae, pure and simple. But any visit to the Notting Hill Carnival brings you a more traditional Caribbean creation. Calypso hails largely from Trinidad and Tobago, and is a supremely upful, speedy but butt-grinding dance music featuring steelpan drums and often topped by regally monikered comic vocalists making song out of the issues of the day. Calypso's bastard offspring was soca, a soul-calypso fusion that briefly threatened to make a reggae-style global impact in the early 1980s. Ask your average pop fan in the street, black or white, and chances are the only soca record they can name is Arrow's 'Hot Hot Hot', a Carnival anthem for more years than I care to remember. But the best soca record I've heard – and this judgement comes with all due acknowledgement of my limited knowledge – is 'Lorraine' by Explainer, aka Winston Henry. It's an amazing, raucous, horny roughhouse of a tune, which, like many of the great soul records of the '60s, takes its inspiration and much of its power from the global diaspora of the African people.

In 'Lorraine', Explainer is a resident of New York. It is freezing in Brooklyn and our man is homesick for Trinidad. He knows what he must do, and is thrilled by the simplicity of the solution. 'Taxi, Taxi! Airport Kennedy!!!' he hollers, as tyres skid and the horns blare in celebration, and the infectious funk-

guitar riff continues its soul-searing minor-chord journey. He's already back home in his head, but has to stop off to explain to his girl why he must leave. He paints her a picture of blissful heat and 24-7 partying, an illusion of home as paradise. Because Trinidad is not a rich country – after all, why else has he left paradise for the cold of New York?

But there's no time to think about that. His case is packed even as he's apologizing to his weeping girl. He says she can come visit, but it's a distracted, half-hearted offer. The music just charges through any lingering doubt, and you, like Lorraine, suspect that he's never coming back, despite the harsher realities he might find there.

'Lorraine' is probably the most intensely joyful record in these pages, because its excitement and dreaming comes at a cost that you feel in the blue holler of that charging horn riff. It also, I swear, repeatedly tells us of a kind of party that features a 'psychedelic steelpan', a concept that I wish Explainer had stopped to explain.

PLANET ROCK

AFRIKA BAMBAATAA
AND THE SOUL SONIC FORCE

PRODUCED BY ARTHUR BAKER/WRITTEN BY AFRIKA
BAMBAATAA, ARTHUR BAKER, JOHN ROBIE AND THE
SOUL SONIC FORCE
TOMMY BOY/POLYDOR/AUGUST 1982
UK CHART: 53

WALKING ON SUNSHINE

ROCKERS REVENGE FEATURING
DONNIE CALVIN

PRODUCED BY ARTHUR BAKER/WRITTEN BY
EDDY GRANT
LONDON/AUGUST 1982
UK CHART: 4

Oh Lordy. In truth, you could give up an entire book to these two singles. Just an hour's listen to British radio, from daytime Radio One to specialist dance stations to underground pirate, will confirm that we now live in a pop world that these two records – and the visionaries involved in their production – built out of street-smarts, artistic instinct and a whole lot of guesswork. And great, great dance music, of course.

INSIDE OUT/ODYSSEY

PAGE 182

So, to condense this: Kevin Donovan (Afrika Bambaataa) was a South Bronx hip-hop DJ with the most eclectic music taste on the scene. His sets sliced up everything from The Clash to The Monkees to instrumental obscurities like The Incredible Bongo Band's 'Apache' to hoary old FM rock tracks like Babe Ruth's 'The Mexican' to James Brown to Kraftwerk. The one thing these records had in common were The Breaks – a section when the main instrumentation would break and leave just drums, maybe some bass, which would then be elongated (by having more than one copy) and scratched so the B-Boys and B-Girls could get on with the serious business of breakdancing. He was a huge, intimidating former gang member who used his street respect to form the Zulu Nation, a collective of young black rappers, DJs and artists. His aim was to channel disadvantaged local youth away from street violence, through music, community events and the learning of black history.

Tom Silverman was a young white entrepreneur who knew the nascent hip-hop scene well enough to realize that, clever though Sugarhill had been, they were not the Real Deal. He put his money where his mouth was and started Tommy Boy records.

Arthur Baker was a white disco DJ with long hair who looked more like a Led Zep roadie than a glitterball Don. He was a whiz with technology, and the speed with which he understood the possibilities of the Fairlight sampler and its drum-sequencing buddies made him the first modern superstar dance producer, and THE pioneer of remix culture. He went on to remake and remodel tracks by artists as disparate as Dylan and Diana Ross, and to cement the growing relationship between the US and UK alternative club scenes through his work with New Order and Tottenham jazz-funkers Freeez.

Together the three made a record that changed the course of music. 'Planet Rock' was a group rap over a roughed-up, Fairlight-enhanced version of Kraftwerk's 'Trans-Europe Express', with hints of 'Apache'. The low end was so loud it made *all* your cheeks wobble. Everything squelched like acid sex. Ghosts in the machine freaked you out, shrieking in terror or ecstasy and then disappearing. Its blend of pure electronica and the voices of Bam and The Force – which, in direct contrast to the Sugarhill productions, sounded like they were being delivered from another room . . . hell, another *dimension* – invented the black beat-box-and-synth sci-fi noise of electro, which in turn begat techno. It gave hip-hop the confidence to be what it really was, rather than a pop version of what was developing all over New York and beyond. It prefaced the hard, hypnotic machine-soul of house, 'Planet Rock's' most lovable, unforgettable moment, when a rapper called Pow Wow suddenly exclaims, 'ZUMZUMZUMZUMZUM-ZUMZUMZUM!' as

the beats crash and push him on, was pure accident. He forgot the words. The visionaries kept it in and zum-zummed all the way to immortality.

Baker's 'Walking on Sunshine' is less revered, but equally important. 'Planet Rock' swept the underground, but this blaring, dubbed-to-fuck, ska-tinged cover of an Eddy Grant pop-dance song slayed the mainstream and was the year's most ubiquitous disco hit. Again, Baker knew the importance of the voice, and Donnie Calvin's throaty gospel roar and the flirtatious femme chants sent the whole shebang tumbling into delirium. On the stark intro, Calvin's grammatically challenged 'Meet me to the mountain top!' echoed into infinity and you felt like you were dancing all the way up that mountain. And the *handclaps* – like 'Car Wash' on the Moon! Funky drummers and bass players heard 'Planet Rock' and 'Walking on Sunshine' and got their coats.

NIGHT NURSE

GREGORY ISAACS

PRODUCED BY GREGORY ISAACS AND
FLABBA HOLT (REMIXED BY GODWIN LOGIE AND
PAUL 'GROUCHO' SMYLKE)/WRITTEN BY G. ISAACS
AND S. WEISE
ISLAND/AUGUST 1982
DID NOT CHART

Odd now to see that the most popular song by one of the world's greatest singers didn't chart at all. 'Night Nurse' was everywhere in the late summer of '82. Which makes this a good place to mention the mysterious world of the chart return shop, and remind yourself that the chart is not made up of universal sales, but sales from selected outlets. Despite Island's major-label clout, the reggae hit of the year almost certainly sold best in inner-city specialist shops. Though the choice of return shops has been widened in recent years, it's still very rare that a reggae-scene No. 1, no matter how massive, crosses over to the UK pop scene, unless, like a Shaggy or Beenie Man, it is bolstered by American marketing and musically fused with contemporary R&B.

Anyway, if you've only heard the Mick Hucknall version, please put that narcissistic travesty out of your mind. Isaacs' metaphor for female comfort, over a mellow but tough backing that blends state-of-the-art synth and trad roots rhythm, is sung with such a stoned, languidly lustful, utterly persuasive ache that it makes a legendarily scary man (and I've interviewed Isaacs,

PLANET ROCK/AFRIKA BAMBAATAA AND THE SOUL SONIC FORCE
PAGE 184

and he *is* scary) into the embodiment of male submissiveness, albeit with an ulterior motive. Its theme pre-dates, by just a couple of short months, a more infamous tribute to the medicinal properties of making lurrrve. But Gregory pulls the sweet scenario off as persuasively as Marvin, and I can think of no greater compliment.

SHIPBUILDING

ROBERT WYATT

PRODUCED BY ELVIS COSTELLO, CLIVE LANGER AND ALAN WINSTANLEY/WRITTEN BY CLIVE LANGER AND ELVIS COSTELLO
ROUGH TRADE/AUGUST 1982
DID NOT CHART
(REISSUED APRIL 1983: REACHED NO. 35)

By 1982, Elvis Costello didn't seem too interested in the possibilities of the pop single. But, despite having begun his rather disappointing journey into arthouse dilettantism and rock-masterclass collaborations, Costello was still angry and it was still with a woman. Our glorious PM had replaced the various Alisons and Elsies as the object of his ire, and the socialist Liverpudlian became the one British artist of the era willing and able to respond instantly to current events. With 'Shipbuilding', Costello reached the high water mark of his politically motivated songwriting.

Robert Wyatt's uniquely moving cockney choirboy tones were perfect to front this virtual summit meeting of Stiff label alumni, which features Madness's Mark Bedford on upright bass and The Attractions' Steve Nieve on piano, as well as Langer (organ) and Costello (backing vox) themselves. Here, Costello avoids the impulse to rant about the Falklands conflict, and inhabits a quiet, resigned world where the consequences of right-wing politics are a matter of personal survival, doused in unbearable irony.

The plaintive wail of Wyatt (a man still proud to call himself a Communist, and a former jazz-rock drummer until a fall from a window left him permanently paralysed) embodies the darkest days of a character caught between economics and morality. The shipyards have closed, leaving him – and his entire community – out of work. A sudden war means work and money and 'a bicycle on the boy's birthday', even as the community's mothers are waving off their own sons, maybe never to return. While he tries to cope with the news that one of his own sons is going to war, he hears that 'Someone got filled in/For saying that people get killed in/The results of their shipbuilding.' And yes, I *saw* stuff like that happen in the summer of '82. The music brushes and softly weeps, falling like a stone through water as Wyatt contemplates a life where we are 'Diving for dear life/When we should be diving for pearls.' The mixture of despair, disillusion and dreamy hope in Wyatt's graceful delivery of that bitter pun, was – and still is – absolutely shattering.

Costello did his own version the following year, and it was fine. But it was made in a modest way that acknowledged the mastery of interpretation and restrained emotion in Wyatt's definitive take. There are a few records in this book that have the power to make me cry. But none as unavoidably and as much as 'Shipbuilding', because it sums up Britain in 1982 – a year in which we lost more than we can ever regain.

LIONS IN MY OWN GARDEN (EXIT SOMEONE)/RADIO LOVE

PREFAB SPROUT

PRODUCED BY HAL REMMINGTON/WRITTEN BY PADDY MCALOON
KITCHENWARE/AUGUST 1982
DID NOT CHART

Of all the 500 singles here, the presence of this indie debut from Durham's foremost smarm-pop smartarse is the biggest surprise. As I was listening through stuff to make my final choice, I chucked this on more out of curiosity than judgement. And then found myself amazed and intrigued by its awkward preciousness all over again. You hear the beginnings of McAloon's perfectionist craft and self-indulgent over-egging here, but it's undercut by the rudimentary production and the sense of ambition overreaching itself, of wonder at being allowed to do this at all. In this sense, both of these oblique, quizzical, jangling, slightly desperate, romantic, nerdy, precocious, naïve, melody-packed, extravagantly soul-jazz-tinged and truly original songs are a last glance back at the whole Rough Trade/Fast/Postcard world of failed revolutionaries. And not a raised eyebrow in sight.

NIGHT NURSE/GREGORY ISAACS

SHOULD I STAY OR SHOULD I GO/
STRAIGHT TO HELL

THE CLASH
PRODUCED BY THE CLASH AND GLYN
JOHNS/WRITTEN BY JOE STRUMMER AND
MICK JONES
CBS/SEPTEMBER 1982
UK CHART: 17
('SHOULD I STAY . . .' REISSUED IN FEBRUARY 1991:
REACHED NO. 1)

And if the way those song titles run together looks like the end of a heated conversation, it probably was. The legs akimbo rock of 'Should I Stay . . .' was all Jones, and the swaying, percussive world music ruminations of 'Straight to Hell' all Strummer, as The Clash finally imploded under the weight of dem old rock star contradictions. In 1983 Jones was booted out for, ostensibly, becoming a guitar hero. The egos had landed. Topper Headon had already gone, the drummer's heroin addiction making him impossible to work with. Although Strummer and Simonon formed a new Clash that it's best not to talk about, The Clash proper split at the best or worst possible time, depending on your punk point of view. The Clash were massive in America, a stadium band on the verge of becoming the new Rolling Stones. Personal problems aside, maybe they just got scared.

So, the final Clash single we're concerned with encompassed all the band's contradictions. 'Should I Stay . . .' was a Stones-copping love anthem, which, sung in a hilariously fey voice by Jones, now sounds like an open letter to Strummer. 'Straight to Hell' is a beautiful study of the links between Vietnam, smack addiction in the American ghettos and the closed and rusting steel mills of Corby, England, from a dreamily abstract international socialist perspective Strummer has never abandoned. Its shuffle of ironies is immense, but not as immense as the irony that saw 'Should I Stay . . .' become The Clash's only UK No. 1 nine years after they split, on the back of an ad for, of all things, an American multinational maker of cool trousers. Crushed by the wheels of industry, as some '80s wag put it.

BACK ON THE CHAIN GANG

THE PRETENDERS
PRODUCED BY CHRIS THOMAS/WRITTEN BY
CHRISSIE HYNDE
REAL/SEPTEMBER 1982
UK CHART: 17

Country rock doesn't play much of a part in this book. But who better to turn this most album-oriented of genres into classic single material than the heroic Ms Hynde? 'Back on the Chain Gang' is glowing rootsy car-pop, from the ringing guitars, to the driving rhythm, to the Sam Cooke-quoting chorus (no one used male backing vocals as brilliantly as Chrissie) to the exquisite, almost mythical sense of loss in her words and voice. OK, so The Great Pretender, like most of the other products of punk, drifted on into increasingly shallow waters in a desperate quest to hang in there. But, if I'd written 'Brass in Pocket' (see p. 108), 'Message of Love' (see p. 150) *and* this, I'd still expect the world to kiss my feet. Even though the boots are leather, which always seemed a bit off for a radical vegetarian.

THE DAY BEFORE YOU CAME

ABBA
PRODUCED AND WRITTEN BY BENNY ANDERSSON
AND BJÖRN ULVAEUS
EPIC/OCTOBER 1982
UK CHART: 32

The final episode of Abba: The Divorce Years was released to promote a Greatest Hits collection. Bum move. The two couples were now, officially, two ex-couples, and their last album proper, December '81's *The Visitors*, picked through the miserable debris to the point where even their most recent fans couldn't cope with the girls effectively singing words that were none-too-subtle digs at them from their former partners. It was their greatest artistic statement, an elegantly cruel and frigid career suicide note.

Unlike 'The Winner Takes It All' etc., 'The Day . . .' doesn't even sweeten the poison with a catchy chorus. This is black Brechtian humour written and performed in the theatrical style of the stage musical, a world which Benny and Björn would later conquer with *Chess*. It ain't no game, though, as over mechanical disco beat and coldly trilling synth, Anni-Frid goes through the minutiae of a daily routine, just living in a life

BACK ON THE CHAIN GANG/THE PRETENDERS
PAGE 190

without meaning. The music swells melodramatically, implying that the 'you' is a lover who saves her from the emptiness. But the last scene she describes – rain rattling on the roof as she goes to bed early and alone – and the music's lack of resolution, suggests that the visitor is no more than a momentary distraction from her dulled and loveless existence.

Bye, Abba. It was real.

SEXUAL HEALING

MARVIN GAYE

PRODUCED BY MARVIN GAYE/WRITTEN BY M. GAYE
AND O. BROWN
CBS/OCTOBER 1982
UK CHART: 4

Now what *you* need, love, is some of what this has in mind. After all, if you listen *very* closely to the final fade of this soul masterpiece, you'll hear some controversial but persuasive advice, as Marvin sobs, 'Please don't fascinate/It's no good to masturbate.'

The Motown master's passionate plea for sexual salvation is made no more or less extraordinary by his shocking death, 18 months later, at the hand of his own father. Gaye re-emerged from his wilderness years in Belgium with a sound as new as 'Planet Rock' (see p. 184), yet carried by that ancient soul tension between the sacred and the profane. To Gaye, great sex was a religious experience, a movement towards God, and this comforting yet intimidating belief informs every last note of longing in that unique voice. You could hide from 'Shipbuilding's' world in here (see p. 188), and sometimes you need that.

'Sexual Healing's' black futurism stood alone from the proliferation of beige pop but, for the next few years, every soul ballad came with a softly swishing drum machine and a spacey, boudoir ambience. But one small . . . ahem . . . thing: I know everyone is supposed to fuck to this. But don't you all find what it promises a little hard to match up to?

OUR HOUSE

MADNESS

PRODUCED BY CLIVE LANGER AND
ALAN WINSTANLEY/WRITTEN BY CARL SMYTH AND
CHRIS FOREMAN
STIFF/NOVEMBER 1982
UK CHART: 5

And it's goodbye, too, to the Madness crew. Not that most of their final, grown-up ruminations weren't great, or even that their '90s re-formation was too undignified. But this, I think, is the last *big* Madness single, a summing-up of all they'd achieved in just three amazing years.

A sentimental, nostalgic love of childhood and working-class culture was always one of the band's key themes, and here, with Chas Smash's recollections of the family home and music of shining, irresistible strength and dexterity, they sum up the happy sadness of their pasts, and the inevitable passing of time and tradition. The verse where Suggs suddenly gabbles to a childhood friend about their carefree origins and the belief that 'Nothing can come between us' is suffused with all the things – relationships, work, economics, lessons learned and minds changed – that probably have come between them. And it hurts, but then the music urges you to get over it, because shit happens and our lives, like our memories, can still be great. Listen. It's all there in those cheesy, beautiful strings.

BUFFALO GALS/MALCOLM McLAREN AND THE WORLD'S FAMOUS SUPREME TEAM

BUFFALO GALS

MALCOLM MCLAREN AND THE WORLD'S FAMOUS SUPREME TEAM
PRODUCED BY TREVOR HORN/WRITTEN BY
MALCOLM MCLAREN, ANNE DUDLEY AND
TREVOR HORN
CHARISMA/NOVEMBER 1982
UK CHART: 9

As Johnny Rotten went off to America and a career in stadium-punk panto, who should be heading in the other direction bearing a big bag of goodies but his old bête noire? Having tired of Bow Wow Wow as soon as Anabella reached the age of consent, McLaren brought Rainbow Coalition hip-hop to us monochrome Brits in much the same way as Raleigh gave us the potato. Because, although all the hip-hop records I've mentioned thrilled the dazzling urbanites in ripped jeans and zoot suits, the Brit small-town majority (or at least those who didn't work in record shops) had little access to this stuff unless they read the music or style press. The 'Buffalo Gals' video brought a technicolour explosion of breaking and bombing and scratching into every pop kid's living room. And they loved it.

Not that the promo would've worked without a fantastic, funny, outrageously arranged and produced noise to back it up. Who else but Malc could see a link between black Bronx culture and the country square dancing of the white South? And who else but Horn and Dudley could organize his surreal vision into something resembling music? The mess of raps, disembodied quacks, crashing edits, fanfare synths, synthetic scratches and McLaren's dozy-doe daftness became the blueprint for Horn's and Dudley's massive impact on the mid-'80s, as the two joined up with McLaren's spiritual heir Paul Morley, formed The Art of Noise and ZTT records, and plotted the dramatic rise and fall of Frankie Goes to Hollywood. And, if that post-modernism-gone-mad wasn't enough, the Led Zeppelin drums and blaring orchestral stabs of The Art of Noise became the biggest single influence on late '80s hip-hop. A bit like Raleigh showing the natives how to make chips.

1983

1983

You might already have noticed the beginnings of a change in this book. First and most obvious, the years 1982–87 show a marked drop in quantity of entries per year. This is not a matter of personal taste, but a sign of the times. Pop post-punk and pre-dance boom was not very good. Over-produced, synthetic in a bad way, cynically escapist, obsessed with half-naked bimbos and eager to please, the mid-'80s became so devoted to racial and generational crossover that it lost any feeling of roots, of relevance, and, yes, of rebellion. This simple fact makes the records that do stand out all the more heroic and poignant; even though they are shared largely by a shrinking band of artists who effectively kept the spirit of pop alive during the years dominated by Live Aid, dance-rock, the beginnings of the mutual love/hate relationship between tabloid and celebrity, and bad haircuts. The alternative rock sector? Almost non-existent, as the class of 1977–79 folded under pressure from the new pop realities, and the rest slunk into their various narrow sub-cultures – OI!, anarcho-punk, goth, psychobilly. No more Lydon, Harry or Hynde, Madness, Human League or Clash. The relatively new 'indie' charts were a charisma-free musical wasteland.

Another new feature that you might have noticed is the slew of reissues of certain singles. If punk had drawn some sort of line in the pop sand with its ironic comments on and packaging of the past, The Biz took that line as an opportunity to celebrate yesterday as if it were only yesterday. The new skill of remixing and the rumblings of sample culture offered them the chance to scrub up something old and sell it to us as new, and who's going to turn that down? It was around this time, too, that the 12-inch single began to rival the traditional 7-inch as the preferred singles format. Dance culture had hit hard, and what had previously been a DJ tool became a consumer fetish item for the more obsessive dance fan or rock collector. You'll also notice fewer B-sides being considered from here on in. Club cool plus remixers plus new technology equals instrumental B-sides – dub, scratch or bonus beats that were sometimes genuinely exciting, but more often than not just the original with the vocals removed and a few dodgy echo effects. In 1982, The Human League went Top Ten with a whole album of this stuff. The critically acclaimed (but now utterly unlistenable) *Love and Dancing*, released under the Barry White-tributing League Unlimited Orchestra moniker, proved that there was really no need for artists to do that difficult songwriting stuff, especially to waste on B-sides. Just give it to a computer expert, give it a new name, and you have extra royalties with no work. This doesn't mean there are no good remixes. Just that the new development took more and more of the onus off bands to come up with new material to keep their profiles ticking over, or provide value for money.

Last but not least, the new digital format, the compact disc, had become available at the end of 1982, and, despite its high retail price and the even higher cost of the CD player, it was making real inroads by the end of 1983. The CD single didn't come into play until 1986, but all those dodgy unused B-sides would sure come in handy to fill up the CD album's longer playing time. Not only that, but the compact disc's major selling-points – easy storage, supposedly better sound, no more damage from your worn-out stylus – changed the nature of record consumption, taking the emphasis away from the artistic worth of the entire sleeve-art package to sound for sound's sake. So your fave band planned the album to play in a certain order for a reason? Tough. I bought it, I'm in control, and now I can put the thing on shuffle and sit back without the annoyance of having to get up and make things happen manually. CD was – is – a more passive consumer experience, although my main memories of its coming involved kicking and chucking Dire Straits CDs around Andy's Records to test whether they were truly indestructible. I'd left by the time they all came back faulty.

Meanwhile, back in the real world, Thatcher won a landslide and the US became more blatant about bullying any South American country that dared to swing left of Attila the Hun. Reagan raised the Armageddon stakes by announcing the 'Star Wars' defence system, playing up to all those wet dreams about Han Solo swooping through the skies to defeat the forces of darkness. The Campaign for Nuclear Disarmament became the official opposition, in the absence of something called the Labour Party, which remains missing in action to this very day. You could look at the records below and note that only one refers specifically to any of this. But maybe you'd be wrong. When pop is in a conservative phase, it generally retreats to the safety of the love song. 1983 is no exception – but, boy, what a bunch of twisted and paranoid love songs they were. Blokes slagging off pregnant women in night-clubs, comparing women to cars and horses, being stood up on beaches, stalking, flashing, and crooning loving odes to bicycles and cocaine, while the only female voice writes her man a ticket to spray his seed around like a demented share-cropper. Half the electronic effects sound like bombs. Good pop artists can't help summing up the times.

Honourable mentions: Funboy Three/'Our Lips Are Sealed' (Chrysalis); Yello/'I Love You' (Stiff); Indeep/'Last Night a DJ Saved My Life' (Sound of New York); The Three Johns/'A.W.O.L.' (Abstract); The Birthday Party/'The Bad Seed EP' (4AD); Afrika Bambaataa & The Soul Sonic Force/'Looking for the Perfect Beat' (Tommy Boy/21); Man Parrish/'Hip-Hop, Be Bop (Don't Stop)' (Sugarscoop); Eurythmics/'Love Is a Stranger' (RCA); The Police/'King of Pain' (A&M); Frankie Goes to Hollywood/'Relax' (ZTT/Island)

BILLIE JEAN

MICHAEL JACKSON
PRODUCED BY QUINCY JONES/WRITTEN BY
MICHAEL JACKSON
EPIC/JANUARY 1983
UK CHART: 1

Where do you begin to assess the impact of this single and its parent album, *Thriller*?

For a start, *Thriller* became the biggest-selling album of all time, and made the mysterious former child prodigy the biggest star in the world. Eddie Van Halen's guitar solo on 'Beat It' became the ultimate symbol of black/white music crossover, and the previously whites-only enclave that was MTV was forced not just to play it, but to put it on heavy rotation, forever changing the black=soul/white=rock split that had formed the foundation of American pop for over 30 years. The John Landis-directed 'Thriller' video, with its teen horror storyline, 15-minute length and big-budget special effects and cast of thousands became the first promo to be hyped – and received – as a global event. And 'Billie Jean'? 'Billie Jean' invented what we now know as R&B. Its stalking computer rhythm, seamlessly blending funk, disco, rock and electro-pop, its slick, clean, Quincy Jones production, Jackson's boyish, agitated delivery, and its self-referential gender-war scenario prefaced a thousand black male pop songs about the castrating manipulations of money-grabbing bitches. No wonder the video and the transcendent performance of the song at the Motown's 25th anniversary show featured much Michael crotch-grabbing – part macho display, part self-defence.

Time has not diminished 'Billie Jean's' strangeness. We're used, now, to Jacko's welter of multi-tracked whoop!s, whee!s, and ow!s, the sound of a man getting a good slapping, or maybe just a man for whom language is never quite enough, forever trying to shed its limitations, his own skin. But it's also strange to note that the song that made Jackson as big as Elvis and The Beatles was asking us to side with a superstar millionaire over a young single mother. And that it worked.

1999

PRINCE
PRODUCED AND WRITTEN BY PRINCE
WARNERS/JANUARY 1983
UK CHART: 25
(REISSUED JANUARY 1985 (DOUBLE A-SIDE WITH 'LITTLE RED CORVETTE): REACHED NO. 2; DECEMBER 1998: REACHED NO. 10; DECEMBER 1999: REACHED NO. 49)

Despite having the life sucked out of it by millennium parties and TV shows, the first classic Prince single still stands. The Minneapolis Midget had hitherto been an underground funk maverick, singing brittle post-P-funk jams and eccentric pop nuggets about his dirty mind and ambivalent sexuality and looking like Little Richard after an accident in an Ann Summers store. With slight adjustments to clothes (increasingly psychedelic soul Hendrix), stance (increasingly hetero) and music (increasingly electronic and radio-friendly), Prince Rogers Nelson made his leap and, with the help of both quantity and quality of records, became the unarguable musical genius of the 1980s. His influence remains tougher to pin down. People did and continue to copy him but generally fall flat on their arses. He was just too good – at everything from guitar to production to dancing to Jagger-meets-Curtis Mayfield falsetto – to boil down to a few generic gestures and trademarks.

'1999' is the single most thrilling of all Cold War records, its apparent hedonistic disregard for the future overplayed to the point of satire. That signature drum clunk and those fizzing synth fanfares, the vocal interplay between Prince and band members Lisa Coleman and Dez Dickerson, all coming in from different angles, the fantastic line about the lion in his pocket . . . all added up to rebellion against our rulers, rather than resignation to our doom. When you danced to this record, you thumbed your nose at the whole bastard lot of 'em, and felt like you were gonna live forever. Sometimes sheer joy is the best defence you've got. Remember that other Minneapolis guy who dreamed about escaping to Funkytown? Prince built that city right here, and, just as Steven Greenberg never left his hometown, we didn't have to travel farther than our stereo to escape there.

BLUE MONDAY/NEW ORDER

PAGE 200

SWEET DREAMS (ARE MADE OF THIS)

EURYTHMICS

PRODUCED BY DAVID A. STEWART/WRITTEN BY
ANNIE LENNOX AND DAVID A. STEWART
RCA/JANUARY 1983
UK CHART: 2

GET THE BALANCE RIGHT!

DEPECHE MODE

PRODUCED BY DANIEL MILLER AND
DEPECHE MODE/WRITTEN BY MARTIN L. GORE
MUTE/FEBRUARY 1983
UK CHART: 13

These archetypal '80s electro-pop singles say almost the same thing in a similar way. Using moody synths and a touch of disco, both purvey pessimistic designs for life while attempting to offer some comfort to the listener, taking from and feeding into black dance music as they try to make some sense of our futures.

Basildon's Mode have survived drugs, defections, alcoholism, critical brickbats and their lead singer believing he was the King of Siam or something, and *still* make good records. Quite a few of their singles fell just outside this list, but the one Mode single that still compels me is 'Get the Balance Right!', the first to suggest that they were more than synth poppets.

This warm and wistful yet sharp and satirical list-song shows that, while the shiny Brit pop competition were all oblivious aspiration, Martin Gore knew exactly what was going on with his audience. The burden they would have to carry as they grew up – being everything to everybody, learning how to compromise while retaining some sense of integrity, of identity – was almost too much to bear. 'Help the helpless/But always remain ultimately selfish . . . It's almost predictable,' Gahan croons sadly in his first – perhaps best – genuine vocal performance. The Miller/Mode sound is tough but blue, a seamless blend of futurist electro and candy pop. If the title to this single was partly aimed at themselves, then they rose to their own demands with grace and generosity, and affected people that none of us suspected were listening. In less than ten years, various dance producers – mainly black Americans – proclaimed themselves unlikely Mode fanatics and acknowledged them as a key influence on techno and house.

The Eurythmics' breakthrough single is even more powerful, a sinister anthem of loner pessimism and search for meaning buoyed by Lennox's demands that you 'Keep your head up' and present the world with a moving target. The synth riff is once-heard-never-forgotten, and remains a staple for remixers and samplers. Its stark restraint and soulfulness makes it all the more puzzling that Stewart and Lennox became everything self-satisfied, lazy and sickly beige about '80s pop, taking their own advice in the most superficial way they could manage.

BLUE MONDAY

NEW ORDER

PRODUCED AND WRITTEN BY NEW ORDER
FACTORY/MARCH 1983
UK CHART: 12
(REISSUED AUGUST 1983: REACHED NO. 9; JANUARY
1984: REACHED NO. 52; REMIXED AND REISSUED
APRIL 1988: REACHED NO. 3; REMIXED AND
REISSUED JULY 1995: REACHED NO. 17)

Rock retooled. Indie redirected. Euro-disco rebooted. Electro redefined. The 12-inch single reinvented. Manchester re-established as Britain's Music City No. 1. A legendary band reborn without the ghost of Ian Curtis in the room. The Factory label's dance future revealed. Even an ancient Fats Domino song title revived. 'Blue Monday' re'd so many things on its way to becoming the biggest-selling 12-inch of all time (it remained available on no other format until 1988) that it throws a matt-black shadow over all of British pop until the indie-dance boom it inspired revitalized Britpop at the turn of the '90s. The bass-drum intro alone is perhaps the most instantly recognizable sonic signature of the decade, aside maybe from the chung-chung-chung of Peter Hook's bass or the moment when the hi-hats cause an electro-shock explosion or the words 'How does it feel?' or the relentless synth-riff or the pseudo-Gregorian chant or . . . well, anyway, we can talk influence and historical importance and musical detail until we're blue in the face. But hearing Barney's existential love crisis – the student-satirizing version of Ian Curtis's genuine pain – and finding myself laughing and flinging myself around as if I'd heard the funkiest joke anyone ever told, is still one of the most vivid and unlikely memories of my pop life.

GIMME ALL YOUR LOVIN'/ZZ TOP
PAGE 204

JUST BE GOOD TO ME

THE S.O.S. BAND

PRODUCED BY JIMMY JAM AND TERRY
LEWIS/WRITTEN BY TERRY LEWIS AND
JAMES HARRIS III (JIMMY JAM)
TABU/MARCH 1983
UK CHART: 13

The clinking electronic perscussion and awesome waterfall-synth intro of this song marked the missing link between trad soul and disco, and the new swingbeat/R&B sound that would dominate Afro-American pop in the '90s. Jam and Lewis hailed from Minneapolis and were in the seminal band The Time with Prince. They went the backroom route and forged an expansive nu-funk sound that challenged their old friend and Jacko for soul supremacy, and made them into the late '80s equivalent of Chic's Nile Rodgers and Bernard Edwards. This dramatic, stuttering headrush funk ballad announced them, rather than The S.O.S. Band, with a flourish, and was later craftily welded onto The Clash's 'Guns of Brixton' by Norman Cook's Beats International for the hit 'Dub Be Good to Me', before he went on to weightier sampling success. The crunchy synth-bass, crashing crescendos and Chic-style melody give a strange strength to every masochistic word of this doormat testimony, sung by a woman almost as keen on being kicked as the nutter in Odyssey's 'Inside Out' (see p. 182). That woman was the tremulous Mary Davis, who went solo in 1987, signalling a dip in the fortunes of Atlanta's The Sound of Success Band. They still exist though, complete with the prodigal Ms Davis, and if you go to www.online.talent.com you may even be able to book them. Jam and Lewis have fared rather better. They knew what they were doing when they retreated to that backroom.

DIN DAA DAA (TROMMELTANZ)

GEORGE KRANZ

PRODUCED BY CHRISTOPH FRANKE AND
GEORGE KRANZ/WRITTEN BY GEORGE KRANZ
FOURTH & BROADWAY/APRIL 1983
DID NOT CHART

Opening with a terrifying, 'r'-rolling yell from DJ/producer Kranz, this insane German proto-house record made use of maddeningly repetitive and nonsensical rhythm chants and blaring synth over disco-rock beat. But all that was just preparation for its magnificent extended middle section, where Kranz and the anonymous drummer make magic from a complex call-and-response routine. 'Brrrrrily Boppa Brrrrily Boppa!' Kranz hollers. 'Brrrrrily Boppa, Brrrrilly Boppa!!!' the metallic drums reply, and so on and so forth until it all hovers on the brink and the drrrrums rrrrrroll and the crescendo tension is unbearable and everything smashes back in like a wrecking ball through the wall of disco's decline – tasteless, gratuitous and monumentally bleedin' loud. It remained underground over here but was a massive hit in the States, where it hit hard in the new Europhile electro-boogie scene, despite being a blatant, and rather tardy, disco-novelty one-hit wonder in true 'Funkytown' (see p. 124) style.

LITTLE RED CORVETTE

PRINCE

PRODUCED AND WRITTEN BY PRINCE
WARNERS/APRIL 1983
UK CHART: 54
(REISSUED NOVEMBER 1983: REACHED NO. 66;
REISSUED JANUARY 1985 AS DOUBLE A-SIDE WITH
'1999': REACHED NO. 2)

If Grace Jones's 'Pull Up to the Bumper' was car/sex metaphor as high-class *Carry On*, then 'Little Red Corvette' is Anais Nin as classic rock nostalgia. Once you heard this surrealist soul take on FM rock balladry, you knew Prince was far more than funk novelty, and that he could turn his hand to any kind of pop he wanted and make it sound natural, organic, and more-than-slightly freaked out.

Prince's bizarre, fearless mix of motor and . . . um . . . horse/jockey metaphors make it the dirtiest song he's ever written. Yet the easy radio melody and his own astonishment at the night's events make it far less droolingly sexist than his later stuff, despite the fact that the Little Red Corvette in question is his pick-up's vagina. Indeed, Prince is so submissive you can almost see it as the mix of panic and pleasure you might feel if you took the intimidating Ms Grace up on her bumper offer.

Once the slightly disturbing observation about the lady parking her pussy sideways has been made, our short but ever ready hero notices that she has 'A pocket full of horses/Trojan and some of them used.' For the one and only time in his entire back catalogue, Prince worries if he can match up to 'The jockeys that were there before me.' But, when the delirious chorus noise finally breaks and Prince hits that falsetto, all

TOUR DE FRANCE/KRAFTWERK

doubts melt. 'Girl got an ass like I've never seen,' he gasps with lascivious grace. 'And the ride . . . *and the ride* . . .' and then, in a orgasmic squeal, '*YOU MUST BE A LIMOUSINE!!!*' He got away with all this on radio under cover of trad-rock night, the kind that suggests to anyone listening casually that this is all about love, rather than two sluts having it away like it's 1999.

EVERY BREATH YOU TAKE

THE POLICE

PRODUCED BY HUGH PADGHAM AND
THE POLICE/WRITTEN BY STING
A&M/MAY 1983
UK CHART: 1

By now The Police were the world's biggest band, so a record that defined their place in pop history was long overdue, and came just before they split the following year, and Sting embarked upon a preposterous solo career that makes The Eurythmics appear the soul of modest integrity.

'Every Breath You Take's' disturbing power as a stalking song (courtesy of that nasty chord that hovers darkly at the end of each refrain) and, in hindsight, presence as a divorce song (Sting's first marriage had recently disintegrated) have both been well documented. It serves the purposes of the critic (and artist) even more thrillingly if interpreted as a message to our political leaders. But if we take this song as a straight love note, just for a moment, it is still majestic in its simplicity (Summers and Copeland submerge all their technical virtuosity and concentrate it on the intensity of the ever-circling riff and each careful note), and haunting and true in acknowledging, with those dark chords and that borderline psychotic obsession, the cost and the danger of loving someone that much. Sting is both tyrant and victim in 'Every Breath You Take'. After all, if you focus on somebody this much, how would you have time and space to keep a hold on your life, your sense of perspective, your very soul? Sting *could* go for that, or at least convince you that he could, which is a part of what makes him one of rock's less appealing characters.

GIMME ALL YOUR LOVIN'

ZZ TOP

PRODUCED BY BILL HAM/WRITTEN BY
BILLY GIBBONS, DUSTY HILL AND FRANK BEARD
WARNERS/JUNE 1983
UK CHART: 61
(REISSUED SEPTEMBER 1984: REACHED NO. 10)

Mum – look at the funny old rock men! The huge beards! The flasher macs! The formation dancing! The comedy names (Ham! Gibbons! The clean-shaven one called Beard!!!). I bet Warners were laughing too, when a 13-year-old redneck bar-boogie band struck global gold by incorporating throbbing disco beats and subliminally swelling synths and taking the piss out of Duran Duran's soft-porn videos. Sure – it was cynical stuff on one level. But this was much needed comic slyness at a time when rock was taking itself way too seriously. And anyway, the monster dance-rock sound was *no* pisstake. It was loud, proud and righteously chooglin', and knocked another nail in the coffin of 'disco sucks' homophobia by cavorting gleefully with the macho rawk fan's sworn enemy. Gawd love 'em.

TOUR DE FRANCE

KRAFTWERK

PRODUCED BY RALF HUTTER AND FLORIAN
SCHNEIDER/WRITTEN BY HUTTER, SCHNEIDER,
BARTOS AND SCHMITT
EMI/JULY 1983
UK CHART: 24
(REMIXED AND REISSUED AUGUST 1984: REACHED
NO. 22; REISSUED OCTOBER 1999: REACHED NO. 61)

CONFUSION

NEW ORDER

PRODUCED AND WRITTEN BY NEW ORDER AND
ARTHUR BAKER
FACTORY/AUGUST 1983
UK CHART: 12

A bit of give and take. As electro became America's hippest dance sound and transformed the Eurodance underground, so the arty pioneers gave themselves a funk makeover, entirely

COUP/23 SKIDOO
PAGE 206

suitable for break-dancing. Ironically, neither of these tunes caught on in club circles as much as New Order and Kraftwerk's less self-consciously danceable frontier moves. But both are still gleaming future-funk moments that have not dated. In fact, both fit in with current musical surroundings more cosily than they did then.

Kraftwerk's tribute to *the* annual bicycle race was originally commissioned for the Tour's TV coverage, then rejected, then used when it became a hit. It's more energetic and syncopated than anything the 'Werk had done before, and its tapestry of climbing music-box melodies, aerobic breaths and vocal exertions is pure tone poetry. The 12-inch's 'bonus beats' buzz and crackle, much as a rider's head must sound after his daily performance-enhancing drug cocktail.

The New Order–Arthur Baker summit meeting seemed too obvious after the inky glide of 'Blue Monday', but now sounds like wonderfully over-the-top tinny machine funk with a band and producer making hooligan art out of having fun. The moody Mancs even indulge in some ridiculous 'Ra-ta-ta-ta-hey!' chanting, and an equally incongruous heavy metal guitar solo, like kids unleashed into a big disco sweetshop. Barney's voice is lost in Baker's deluge of beatbox special FX, but, if what I can catch of the words is anything to go by, it's probably just as well.

COUP

23 SKIDOO
PRODUCED BY 23 SKIDOO AND
SIMON BOSWELL/WRITTEN BY 23 SKIDOO
ILLUMINATED/NOVEMBER 1983
DID NOT CHART

'Coup' is perhaps the high point, and certainly the summation, of Britain's alternative punk-funk scene. Huge and horn-driven, Afrocentric and sexy, if it had got one small smidgin of daytime radio play it would surely have been a Pigbag-style crossover – an opinion The Chemical Brothers obviously shared when they sampled it for their 1997 No. 1 'Block Rockin' Beats'.

23 Skidoo were Johnny and Alex Turnbull and Fritz Haaman, three arty London adventurers who made records that crossed Cabaret Voltaire-ish, industrial electronica with African and Asian percussion dance. The sound had a spooky, tropical bushmen feel that complimented Brian Eno's and David Byrne's hugely influential 1981 *My Life in the Bush of Ghosts* collage-funk set. Having added future Current 93 cult multi-instrumentalist David Tibet and the more surprising Sketch from

poppy Britfunk heroes Linx, they brought their sound out of the avant-closet and onto the underground dancefloor to dazzling effect on this, their one truly transcendent moment. An instrumental flecked with wild screams and chain gang chants, everything here is so damn skilful it blows your mind, from the hip-hop breakbeat-anticipating bucket drum ricochets and Sketch's hypnotic twin-bass interplay, to the rousing, ecstatic horn hook and the scattershot gun samples. So ahead of its time it makes the likes of Kraftwerk and New Order seem quaint. And if that isn't enough to convince you of 'Coup's influence on future British dance mores, then maybe the news that Skidoo gave one Andy Weatherall his first taste of recording the following year will twist your arm.

THIS CHARMING MAN

THE SMITHS
PRODUCED BY JOHN PORTER/WRITTEN BY
MORRISSEY AND JOHNNY MARR
ROUGH TRADE/NOVEMBER 1983
UK CHART: 25

It felt much bigger than a No. 25. Jesus, it felt seismic. Everyone I knew (who wasn't a black-music obsessive) fell instantly in love with 'This Charming Man', and then whimpered like The S.O.S. Band for the attentions of Morrissey and Marr. At last – a band that had image, aesthetic, tunes, playing, a great singer, wit, attitude, politics, an odd kind of sex appeal . . . and had absolutely nothing to do with punk rock or stadium rock or any of their offshoots. 'This Charming Man' was one of those rare records that convinces you of all that in just three or so minutes.

Moz's heady brew of kitchen-sink movie lines and homoerotic (but winkingly enigmatic) sexual longings are, along with his anti-rock matinée idol croon and agitated shrieks, still the bee's biscuits. But the big question about it all lies in Johnny's spidery, impossibly complex yet completely melodic and to-the-point guitar and Andy Rourke's thrusting, melodic bass. Because Moz's ambivalent attitude toward black music would pretty much do for him (at least in the UK) further down the line, yet Marr's guitar is pure African hi-life with the tiniest touch of Nile Rodgers funk, and Rourke is having a game go at James Jamerson's purest Motown bass. Did Morrissey never notice?

THIS CHARMING MAN/THE SMITHS

WHITE LINES (DON'T DON'T DO IT)

GRANDMASTER AND MELLE MEL

PRODUCED BY SYLVIA ROBINSON, MELLE MEL AND
JOEY ROBINSON JR/WRITTEN BY SYLVIA ROBINSON
AND MELVIN GLOVER
SUGARHILL/NOVEMBER 1983
UK CHART: 60
(REISSUED IN FEBRUARY 1984: REACHED NO. 7
NOVEMBER 1984: REACHED NO. 73; REMIXED AND
REISSUED IN DECEMBER 1993 (WGAF): REACHED
NO. 59)

Cocaine, cocaine – so good they told us don't twice.

Flash and The Furious Five had split into two warring factions by this time, hence the absence of Flash from the band name. But as court battles raged over who owned what, Sugarhill released this all-time classic ad for class-A gear . . . sorry . . . classic anti-drug anthem. Let's put it this way – a quick listen to this and you had some idea where 'The Message' millions were going. And it wasn't in their ears.

So, if you need reminding, this is 'White Lines': a deep and insistent two-note bassline nicked from NY art-funkers Liquid Liquid; sarcastically sweet backing vocals cooing the lyrics into your head; ironic Christmas snow keyboards; mean, horn-driven electro-funk; the delicious rhythm of the 'Something like a phenomenon' line; a pisstake of Bowie's 'Let's Dance' in the 'Higher, baby' bridge; sniffs as percussion; stuttering samples of 'Don't do it' turning into 'DO IT, DO IT, DO IT!'; a set of puns on the words 'bass' and 'freebase'; and Mel's proto-gangsta visions of gibbering Charlie meltdown, which tread a fine (and deliberate) white line between deterrent and rubbing your nose in it. 'Cos you wouldn't get hooked on it unless it was as thrilling and funny as this record, now would you? At least, so I'm told. I got more than enough pleasure from the BBC repeatedly broadcasting a handy rundown on current dealer terminology while believing they were performing a quite different public service.

1984

1984

1984 was the year I moved back down to London, on my 21st birthday. In Brixton, where I stayed, everything moved to the pulse of black music – the underground soul, reggae and early rap that made up the playlists of London's illegal stations Horizon, JBC and, particularly, Kiss. The rhythm of Brixton's streets were a shock after eight years in a sleepy New Town, the perfect backdrop for a year that matched 1978 in its potential for apocalypse. Except that the late '70s chaos was anarchistic . . . unions and terrorists and punks and an assault on old certainties. In 1984, it was almost as if the right-wing clampdown – the final rejection of the 1960s – was being buttressed by natural forces. AIDS, the first warnings about acid rain and the Greenhouse Effect, child leukaemia near Sellafield, a radioactive tanker capsizing in the North Sea. The Ethiopian famine, like nuclear power, wasn't a natural disaster – it was our fault. But those horrifying pictures touched the same nerve. The world was getting biblical on our ass.

As Reagan won another election and promised 'You ain't seen nothing yet', the Tories now had the confidence to get on with the job of breaking 'the enemy within'. Police were blank-eyed paramilitaries laying into miners at Orgreave and backing up bailiffs as they cleared Greenham Common. When Bob Geldof began Band Aid, he unwittingly helped the powers that be by channelling protest into charity, distracting from community towards a distant victim, replacing self-help with celebrity benefactors. We could feel better than our rulers without risking our own necks. Just consume and revolt. When the IRA attempted to blow up the entire Conservative Party in Brighton, their failure just made Thatcher and co. seem more indestructible and heroic.

Marvin Gaye was shot by his own father, Tommy Cooper died onstage with the audience thinking it was a gag, and the man who invented jogging, one Jim Fix, snuffed it while jogging. We bought British Telecom shares and convinced ourselves that this was People Power. Rock moaned and mourned, soul wept and lusted, and pop geared up for its ultimate triumph – the event

that would rub out all dissenting voices, buff any rough edges, force us to celebrate its flabby thinking and lack of courage, make it legit. Hey, don't complain. They did it for charity.

Honourable Mentions: The Three Johns/'Do the Square Thing' (Abstract); Time Zone/'World Destruction' (Tommy Boy); Chuck Brown and The Soul Searchers/'We Need Some Money' (Master Mix); Jocelyn Brown/'Somebody Else's Guy' (Fourth & Broadway)

WHAT DIFFERENCE DOES IT MAKE?

THE SMITHS

PRODUCED BY JOHN PORTER/WRITTEN BY
MORRISSEY AND JOHNNY MARR
ROUGH TRADE/JANUARY 1984
UK CHART: 12

The Smiths' third single and second hit is not a benchmark Smiths record. Morrissey, used to the hard work of making tapes of Marr's spidery, complex guitar lines into proper songs, barely bothers here. His exaggerated clichés of undying love are sung with lazy, horizontal insincerity, reflecting the shrug of the title. Without the comic self-dramatization of his best lyrics to work with, he opts for a nasal monotone which isn't helped by the faint echo applied to his voice (The Smiths' early producer, John Porter, never quite figured out how to showcase Morrissey's odd blend of flat northern bluntness and croony narcissism). One of the band's favourite gimmicks – the sound of shrieking kids in a playground – arrives two-thirds of the way through for no good reason. So why's this record here, then? Two words. Johnny Marr.

That's not strictly fair, as drummer Joyce and bassist Rourke are Watts–Wyman heroic here, effortlessly pushing the rock strut hard while still applying the band's trademark light, anti-macho touch. But it's Johnny's record, transforming the simplest three-chord tricks into pugilistic charges (no, nothing as crass as solos – are you insane?) with an instinctive sense of dynamics, harmonizing with himself until you're drawn into the centre of the deftly controlled, jangling, ringing and humming hurricane. If 'This Charming Man' sold Morrissey, fey and funny and sexually ambiguous, to the pop public, then this record did the job of introducing Marr's rock 'n' roll arrogance, and delivered that section of us who will always love playing air guitar in the private stadium gig that faces the speakers in our bedrooms.

Being Morrissey, though, the sweet and tender hooligan still contributes great bits. The line 'And now you make me feel so ashamed because I've only got two hands', delivered with the timing (and accent) of a top northern light entertainer. The bizarre falsetto at the song's coda, the most ridiculous-yet-lovable high voice since fellow Billy Fury fan Martin Fry first gave us his golden throat. And what the hell *is* the truth about Moz that convinces his lover not to see him anymore? The mystery is soon forgotten though, as Marr ignores him and takes his headlong leap into guitar godhood. There's more to life than this, you know. But not much more.

THE KILLING MOON

ECHO & THE BUNNYMEN

PRODUCED BY ECHO AND THE BUNNYMEN,
DAVID LORD AND GIL NORTON/WRITTEN BY
WILL SERGEANT, IAN MCCULLOCH,
LES PATTINSON AND PETE DE FREITAS
KOROVA/JANUARY 1984
UK CHART: 9

The great Bunny single is also the biggest and boldest rock single of the time – an Eastern-tinged orchestral love epic draped in a cloak of dramatic psychedelia. It was the moment Mac's ever-bragging mouth had promised since the band's beginnings, and it invented every Brit-rock band who've since gone for adult-rock glory by ringing up the local Philharmonic, particularly The Verve.

McCulloch's deliciously doomed romance rides the mountainous peaks and doomy drops of this awesome music with feline grace. In essence, there's this bird, right, who's too tasty to turn down, but Mac knows she's just randy and really loves someone else. But this seedy story is High Gothic Romance in the hands of a band at the peak of their arrogant powers, and when Mac falls hopelessly in celestial love and wails, 'Fate up against your will,' before letting us know that her true love is just biding his time before stealing her back, it feels like Man v The Gods – and you know how that scrap always turns out.

The single was balanced beautifully by its B-side. The answer to that age-old question – 'What's the best gig you ever went to?' – is always 'Echo and The Bunnymen, Royal Albert Hall, 18 July 1983' for me, and the encore from that show, a frantic, mercurial, Doors-in-the-garage version of old B-side 'Do It Clean' is here for posterity. As drummer De Freitas and guitar genius Sergeant wreak havoc, Mac pulls one of his fave live tricks, mixing a bunch of bizarrely juxtaposed classic pop songs into the moody breakdowns. 'All You Need Is Love', 'Sex Machine', 'Bony Maronie' and 'When I Fall in Love' make the magic here, and every time I hear 'Do It Clean' I see Mr Lips doing his groovy knock-kneed go-go dance, looking stoned to the bone.

We all believed that they could only get better. Instead, we got a horribly blank, cocaine-bleached career-suicide LP, splits, dull solo projects, a pointless re-formation, and a set of recent records that reinforces the general opinion that The Bunnymen were just another rock band. In truth, they were *the only* rock band that mattered between The Clash and Joy Division peaks and the birth of The Smiths.

ECHO & THE BUNNYMEN

"THE KILLING MOON" ALL NIGHT VERSION

THE KILLING MOON/ECHO AND THE BUNNYMEN
PAGE 212

JUMP

VAN HALEN

PRODUCED BY TED TEMPLEMAN/WRITTEN BY
EDWARD VAN HALEN, ALEX VAN HALEN,
MICHAEL ANTHONY AND DAVID LEE ROTH
WARNERS/JANUARY 1984
UK CHART: 7

One rock band that truly didn't matter was this bunch of poodle-rockin', fret-wanking, sexist Californian pop tarts. But Theory One holds yet again. For a few short minutes, Van Halen tapped into the Meaning of Rock *and* mourned the passing of its ability to matter with heartfelt passion, reinforcing the point of their greatest song by submerging Eddie's guitar under banks of blaring dance/prog-rock synth.

David Lee Roth revives Joan Jett's jukebox-soundtracked rock 'n' roll pick-up joint. But the usually rampant stud-muffin is not so sure of success here, and is almost buried by the triumphal synthetic din around him. The scenario is old, the moves pure nostalgia, the times have changed. It was a sadness that was hard to pick up beneath the music's piping bluster, but one young Brit heard it loud and clear. It was the wistful and quiet live acoustic version performed by Postcard-label graduate Roddy Frame of Aztec Camera that made me realize what a moving double-edged sword 'Jump' is, the singer backed up against the record machine as if under attack. The pounding plastic flash of Van Halen just keeps on assaulting him, as he shrugs, 'I ain't the worst that you've seen . . . You might as well jump.' But into what? A future that just isn't as appealing as the past?

NELSON MANDELA

THE SPECIAL A.K.A.

PRODUCED AND WRITTEN BY JERRY DAMMERS
2-TONE/CHRYSALIS/MARCH 1984
UK CHART: 9
(REMIXED AND REISSUED JUNE 1988: DID NOT CHART)

NO SELL OUT

MALCOLM X

PRODUCED BY KEITH LEBLANC/WRITTEN BY
MALCOLM X AND KEITH LEBLANC
TOMMY BOY/ISLAND/MARCH 1984
UK CHART: 60

As political comment in pop stopped being the norm, the few who refused to go with the escapist flow turned to direct agit-prop. These two very different singles did as much as any other material to reintroduce their subjects into mainstream discussion, which led to the adoption of Malcolm and Mandela as political pin-ups for the young and politically aware. To achieve that much, they had to be good records as well as worthy ones. And that they were.

Former Sugarhill house band drummer LeBlanc simply hitches cut-up speeches from the assassinated former Nation of Islam spokesman onto hardcore computer beats, in the style established by massively influential NY producers Double D and Steinski and later taken up by Londoners Coldcut. It is persuasive, inspiring and suspenseful, although you know where it ends – with a gunshot and echoing silence. It is the only track in the book co-written by someone who had been dead for 19 years.

'Nelson Mandela' is probably the most familiar and accessible protest song ever made in England. It rounded off the extraordinary career of Jerry Dammers perfectly, as later that year, the greatest singles artist of his day called it a day, and became a full-time anti-apartheid activist and sometime DJ. He had always hated touring and the trappings of fame, and anyway, he had achieved, through 'Nelson Mandela' and 'Ghost Town' and 'The Boiler' and 2-Tone's war against racism, everything you could possibly achieve through the medium of the pop single. His greatest career epitaph remains the voices of black South Africans, singing his song in celebration when Mandela was finally released from Robben Island on 11 February 1990.

Most books have some kind of hero. And if this one does too, then it is Jerry Dammers.

JUMP/VAN HALEN
PAGE 214

SHE'S STRANGE

CAMEO
PRODUCED BY LARRY BLACKMON/WRITTEN BY
BLACKMON, SINGLETON, LEFTENANT AND JENKINS
CLUB/MARCH 1984
UK CHART: 37

Larry Blackmon and his fellow Atlanta funkateers were already jazz-funk cult heroes before fashioning their electro update of George Clinton's P-funk. Blackmon's 'hi-top fade' haircut, cherry-red codpiece and big-eyed grin is one of the best memories of the '80s – his entire persona representative of someone who didn't take themselves remotely seriously while taking their music very seriously indeed . . . which is perhaps the key component necessary to have the generosity of spirit to make great pop.

Blackmon was, like Earth, Wind & Fire's Maurice White (whose trademark, barking 'OWW!' he borrowed to great effect here and in the future), an accomplished drummer, producer, and veteran live-show bandleader, which explains why Cameo's synthetic drum and handclap grooves cooked until they boiled over. This, their first UK chart hit, is delicious sex play, all spaghetti western steals, self-parodying old-school raps, edgy whistles and teasing hooklines. 'She's my Twilight Zone, my Al Capone/She's my Rolling Stones and my Eva Peron,' Larry explains, among a slew of ultra-articulate metaphors and easy witticisms, and she sounds – strangely – like the girl from 'Little Red Corvette' crossed with George Clinton's Freak of the Week. But then, you suspect all funky sex songs are about variations on the same crazy girl.

AIN'T NOBODY

RUFUS AND CHAKA KHAN
PRODUCED BY RUSS TITLEMAN/WRITTEN BY
DAVID 'HAWK' WOLINSKI
WARNERS/MARCH 1984
UK CHART: 8
(REMIXED AND REISSUED JUNE 1989:
REACHED NO. 6)

Chaka had begun her career in the early '70s as the black female singer with white male soulsters Andre Fischer and Kevin Murphy, aka Rufus. Unsurprisingly, her ball-of-fire sexual charisma and gospel vocal power transcended the band, and she embarked on a legendary solo career. 'Ain't Nobody' was the lead single from the last Rufus and Chaka album, one that they were contractually obliged to make. But, boy, no one would've known, as this soul love anthem exploded all over UK radio and dancefloors, raising the roof with its stuttering electro-groove and hollering testimony to infinite (physical) love. Its interlocking, almost Glass/Nymanesque synth riffs and crunching guitars hit home Chaka's ribald lust, and the underlying feeling of both panic and imminent loss in the bluesy notes and her sudden grungy howls created trad-soul nirvana, in an '80s boogie style.

LOVE WARS

WOMACK & WOMACK
PRODUCED BY STEWART LEVINE/WRITTEN BY CECIL
AND LINDA WOMACK
ELEKTRA/APRIL 1984
UK CHART: 14

The brother and sister-in-law of the great soulman Bobby Womack were already a successful songwriting team before they embarked on a performing career. Teddy Pendergrass's definitive boudoir ballad 'Love T.K.O.' had already proved their ability to write heartbreaking adult love songs, but their incendiary first UK hit was something else again.

From the gospel choir and acoustic guitar opening, through the establishing of its rough and rugged disco groove, to the grinding, spooky bassline and almost folky synth following Cecil's gruff, quietly pained lead vocals, this record is a work of redemptive art that should be hung in Tate Modern. 'I promise to stop boxing you round/So don't scratch my face,' is how Cecil warily approaches his partner, letting you know just how godawful things have become, even before he tells us about her sleeping with his best friend. But, every time you think you can take no more of this misery, the bridge climbs to a sunnier plateau – 'We need to get our act together/Take it off the streets/Bring it on home/And drop those guns on the floor,' Cecil and Linda implore each other, as reverbed percussion crashes and clunks and boxes Cecil around, and synth, bass and guitar squabble at each other. And then . . . *then* . . . well, I'm in floods of tears every time, as an awe-inspiring choir of gospel harmonies attempts to lift the couple above the whole vicious mess, swelling the title with a sacred faith in the final victory of tenderness over emotional fascism. The record seemed to be beamed in from another planet, a world where the scarred adult-

NO SELL OUT/MALCOLM X
PAGE 214

soul landscape of James Carr's 'Dark End of the Street' and Otis Redding's 'I've Been Loving You Too Long' still provided solace that every damaged lover could relate to, and had been brutally, brilliantly modernized to stop everyone regressing into moon and June and perpetual adolescence.

If you ever want to find a novel way of torturing me, tie me down and play this back-to-back with 'Shipbuilding' (see p. 188), and watch me slowly dehydrate.

PEARLY-DEWDROP'S DROP

COCTEAU TWINS

PRODUCED BY COCTEAU TWINS/WRITTEN BY ELIZABETH FRASER, ROBIN GUTHRIE AND SIMON RAYMONDE
4AD/APRIL 1984
UK CHART: 29

And then, as an experiment, put this on and watch me slowly rehydrate again.

The most extraordinary voice of her generation, Liz Fraser redefined pop singing as a set of erotic and gorgeous vocal effects – diving between nonsensical language and tremulous noises, between folk and soul, between meaning and the rejection of meaning. Guthrie and Raymonde took Banshee John McGeoch's surreal guitar sound, Peter Hook's melancholy bass, and half-remembered Sonny and Cher hits, and overloaded it all with mountainous reverb until it became a Spector-wall of drum machine-backed hallucination, swirling gracefully around the singer's virtuosity. It was, as every ageing pop hack now affectionately pisstakes, a sonic cathedral, routinely stuck with the adjectives 'ethereal', 'ghostly' and 'meaningless'.

It's hard to pick one Cocteaus song that stands out. But this one, the first to chart, got elected because of its series of Moments, where, in the second and fourth line of each verse, Fraser suddenly reaches up for some impossible thirteenth note, a freaked shriek that comes and goes and rips the fabric of the ringing reverie and knocks you flat on your back wondering what the fuck kind of person makes a noise like *that*. Whatever it was that Fraser was singing about, if the memory of it provoked that leap right out of her body, it must have been very, very good, or very, *very* bad.

PERFECT SKIN

LLOYD COLE AND THE COMMUNICATIONS

PRODUCED BY PAUL HARDIMAN/WRITTEN BY LLOYD COLE
POLYDOR/APRIL 1984
UK CHART: 26

The Orson Welles of British pop (there's even a facial resemblance, if not one in girth), bookish Scots swot Lloyd Cole began with an album of witty, wordy and wry country-soul classics that slew student bohemians everywhere, and, by his own admission, he could never match it. 'Rattlesnakes' soundtracked my first two great love affairs: the first particularly poignant because she lived near the album's 'Charlotte Street' and quickly proved to me that I wasn't ready to be heartbroken; the second leading to the birth of my only son. So every time I think back to that intense, life-altering year, my head plays the ringing Pretenders guitar fanfares, the Stevie Wonder 'Uptight' bassline and the wobbly Lou Reedy conversational love gags of Cole's first single, 'Perfect Skin'. 'She's got cheekbones like geometry and eyes like sin/And she's been sexually enlightened by *Cosmopolitan*.' There's no shame at all in not being able to top that, or the tune it rode in on.

WHEN DOVES CRY

PRINCE

PRODUCED AND WRITTEN BY PRINCE
WARNERS/JUNE 1984
UK CHART: 4

When True Love Number One broke my heart, it was True Love Number Two and a steady shower of *Purple Rain* that got me over it. The album, movie and over-the-top, guitar gross-out song of that name made Prince a global superstar, and, despite the grandiose gestures of the whole shebang, the album (especially 'The Beautiful Ones') possessed both a pop ebullience and a strange kind of soul pain that lifted me above the morose self-pity involved in being alone and dumped in a big city. The lead single remains a monument of pop futurism, sparse and brave and detailed where almost everything else was blustery and vague and chickenshit. Even though the words are explicitly linked to the movie's daft '50s-throwback storyline, you couldn't help but wonder – like you wondered with the 'Love Wars' marital drama – whether the 'They screw you up, your mum and

SHE'S STRANGE/CAMEO

dad' scenario was dredged from the singer's own bitter experience. But then, the black electric power of this music could've made a lyric about Prince's experiences as a seven-foot white basketball player sound like a documentary.

WILLIAM, IT WAS REALLY NOTHING/ PLEASE, PLEASE, PLEASE, LET ME GET WHAT I WANT/HOW SOON IS NOW?

THE SMITHS

PRODUCED BY JOHN PORTER/WRITTEN BY
MORRISSEY AND JOHNNY MARR
ROUGH TRADE/AUGUST 1984
UK CHART: 17
('HOW SOON IS NOW?' REISSUED AS A-SIDE
JANUARY 1985: REACHED NO. 24;
SEPTEMBER 1992: REACHED NO. 16)

What difference did they make? For a start, they were the only unashamedly English voice in the charts, and their music rang with a freedom and defiance of the outside world that sounded like a crusade. They also stuck with indie Rough Trade, when a move to a major would've made them so much more money (although they were on the verge of leaving when they split). Also, in absolute contrast to everyone else, they not only wrote B-sides, but made them so good that the material on their albums (with the exception of *The Queen Is Dead*) struggled to match up. Such was their confidence, their swagger, their *difference*, that they felt they could afford to stick two of their greatest recordings on the back of the 12-inch version of their fifth single.

Not that 'William . . .' wouldn't have got in here without its B-sides. A short, sharp sympathetic jangle through his audience's humdrum lives, Moz gets furious on William's behalf and introduces us to the solution for all ills – narcissism and celibacy – that defined his image, as he parodies the words of a grasping girl: 'Would you like to marry me/And if you like you can buy the ring/I don't dream about anyone/Except myself.'

Then 'Please . . .' undercuts this solution completely. An acoustic reverie boasting Johnny Marr's loveliest melody, here the singer is on the edge of finding the love of his life and desperate for it not to end in tears. The ringing pastoral mandolin gives Moz a chance, despite the feeling that he wants it all a little too much.

But the monster – The Smiths' masterpiece – is the glowering psychedelic funk of 'How Soon Is Now?' Again, you wonder how Morrissey missed his partner's love of black music, as Marr's Bo Diddley guitar becomes a mesmerizing, chugging funk drone, and Andy Rourke's bass goes all thump-plunk in time-honoured jazz-funk fashion. Morrissey's dreamy vaults between self-pity, fury and a dramatic pleading to be loved felt – still feels – like exactly what you wanted to say to anyone who ever said you should be satisfied with your lot, and that you were alone because you didn't make enough effort to conform. Marr's elliptical squeals rearing out of the mix, and The Moment when everything drops out and leaves Johnny's awesome, shuddering, depth charge riff , let you know that they're wrong, you're right, fuck 'em. Quite simply, this is *the* rock 'n' roll performance of the whole post-punk '80s.

I FEEL FOR YOU

CHAKA KHAN

PRODUCED BY ARIF MARDIN/WRITTEN BY PRINCE
WARNERS/OCTOBER 1984
UK CHART: 1

Normally, intergenerational pop or soul summit meetings flatter to deceive (see any duet by Aretha Franklin and a deluded '80s British pop star). But this was as epochal as it should've been. 'I Feel for You' featured not only the glorious Chaka pipes, the writing talents of Prince, and the production skills of legendary Atlantic soul veteran Mardin, but the tongue-twisting rap of Melle Mel and the unmistakable harmonica trills of Stevie Wonder. Quite some cast, and quite some contemporary reinvention of dancefloor soul; all crunchy speed-drums and fizzing crash edits, loud, proud and introduced by the chocolate-voiced Mel gibbering 'Chaka Khan? Chaka Khan?' like a robot love-slave that, despite being a supposedly soulless mass of wires, can't help imploring the magnificent Chaka to feel a little bit for him, too. 'It's mainly a physical thing,' Chaka confesses coyly. Oh, really? Well, I guess I could put myself through that, if I really *had* to . . .

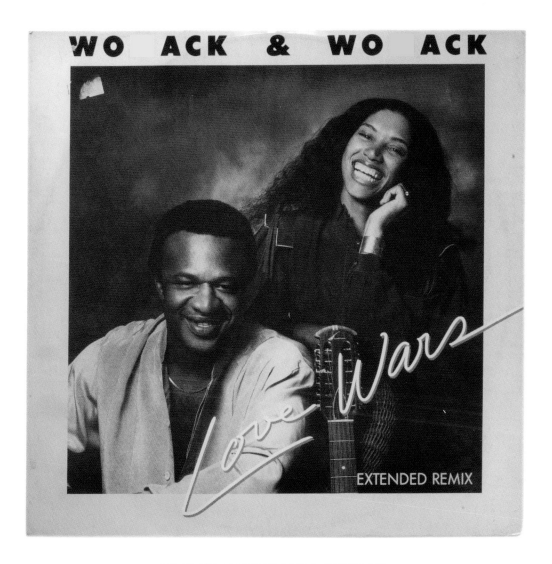

WO ACK & WO ACK

Love Wars

EXTENDED REMIX

LOVE WARS/WOMACK & WOMACK
PAGE 216

LIKE A VIRGIN

MADONNA

PRODUCED BY NILE RODGERS/WRITTEN BY
BILLY STEINBERG AND TOM KELLY
SIRE/NOVEMBER 1984
UK CHART: 3

GET OUTTA THE WAY!!! 'COS HERE SHE COMES!!!
The Monster from the Beige Lagoon! The woman who makes
Joan Jett seem like Shirley Temple! The ultimate self-created pop
product, carrying her graduation papers from the Michigan
School of Post-Modernism! *HERE'S MADDY!!!*

You know, when she was doing those cute lil' disco ditties
about holidays and burnin' up, we had absolutely no evidence to
even imagine what she would become. The ultimate punk-disco
love child, Madonna Louise Veronica Ciccone got her first break
singing and dancing behind Patrick Hernandez of 'Born to Be
Alive' mini-fame, and picked up her early taste in junkyard chic
and hairy armpits from supporting The Slits in New York. She
took all this gay/feminist info, mixed it with her love of black
music and Marilyn Monroe and Nile Rodgers of Chic, added the
fact of her own steely ambition, and became indestructible, the
unlikely and ultimate white trash triumph.

The irresistible come-on that is her sixth single let us know
just how sexy a funny, clever female pop star could be, and 'Like
a Virgin' is just so what we all love about her that it still amazes
that she didn't write it. Admittedly, her voice is still a helium
squeak, and 'Material Girl' provided a better text for Marxist
analysis and essays on pop subversion. But not even Niles could
make that song into a great noise, in the way that he makes her
hysterical amateurishness into classic girly sex-pop here. True –
the damn thing invented Britney Spears. But you can't always get
what you want.

YOU SPIN ME ROUND (LIKE A RECORD)

DEAD OR ALIVE

PRODUCED BY MIKE STOCK, MATT AITKEN AND
PETE WATERMAN/WRITTEN BY DEAD OR ALIVE
EPIC/NOVEMBER 1984
UK CHART: 1

GET OUTTA THEIR WAY!!! 'COS HERE THEY COME!!!
The three-headed Hydra beast of handbag pop! The Nabobs of
Naff! The scourge of all serious rock types! The musical
equivalent of Margaret Thatcher's Greatest Hits! *HERE'S
STOCKY, AITKENY AND WATERMANY!!!*

To recap: Pete Waterman was a veteran northern-soul DJ and
lover of Hi-NRG, Motown and unashamedly empty-headed pop
who teamed up with two computer whizz producers and built
what he was proud to call a 'Hit Factory' out of a couple of
endlessly repeated reductive dance-pop formulas. Pete Burns
was an extravagant Liverpool-scene gender-bender who'd had
no success at all with his sub-Bunnymen goth pop, and some
with a terrible cover of KC and The Sunshine Band's 'That's the
Way (I Like It)', aimed squarely at the gay dance scene. They
joined forces, killed Burns's career and sent S/A/W into infamy.

I know there are many who hate this record and all it stands
for. I would not let these miserable gits babysit a goldfish. 'You
Spin Me Round' is disco-diva exultant, miles more fun than
bombastic and proudly insincere fellow Scousers Frankie, a
queer-as-fuck, unselfconscious whirl of joy and a perfect
showcase for Burns to briefly be the Boy George who would
rather rip your balls off than have a nice cup of tea. True – the
damn thing invented Steps. But if you try sometimes, you just
might find that it's easy to ignore that and love this for the
delirious din that it is.

PEARLY-DEWDROP'S DROP/COCTEAU TWINS
PAGE 218

UPSIDE DOWN

THE JESUS AND MARY CHAIN

PRODUCED BY ALAN/WRITTEN BY JIM AND WILLIAM
REID
CREATION/NOVEMBER 1984
DID NOT CHART

GET OUTTA THE WAY!!! HERE THEY CO . . . uh, perhaps
not. Although the immediate response of the music press to East
Kilbride's Brothers Grim was Sex Pistols-hysterical, especially
when one of their 15-minute, feedback-drenched early gigs at
North London Poly provoked an old-fashioned punk-rock riot,
the Mary Chain didn't change the world or have an ounce of the
lasting effect that Madonna or S/A/W would have. Partly,
perhaps, because these quiet and uncharismatic back-combed
boys couldn't live up to the cartoon shock of the early records.
But mainly because those early records were so extreme they
caused a black hole that the band could never climb out of.
Where can you go when you've only got three chords, nothing
much to say with them, and you've already made the most
terrifying rock noise of all time?

Still, 'Upside Down' did put Alan McGee's Creation label on
the road to infamy. Don't know whether that's good or bad?
Hmmm. I know how you feel.

But what a fucking genius leap in the dark 'Upside Down'
was. Twenty-two-year-old Jim Reid's breathy whisper sounds as
old as the hills, but it doesn't really matter 'cos it's all about
William's hellish sonic vision – The Ramones playing in the
middle of a *real* Blitzkreig. It is amp feedback as firestorm art,
and if it is inspired in part by Hendrix's Vietnam-slaughter take
on 'The Star-Spangled Banner' it also did provoke a whole
bunch of soon-come bands to mess with the same idea, the best
of them being Creation's own My Bloody Valentine. When I first
heard it my head fell off. Still does, rather inconveniently.

THE BOYS OF SUMMER

DON HENLEY

PRODUCED BY DON HENLEY, DANNY KORTCHMAR,
GREG LADANYI AND MIKE CAMPBELL/WRITTEN BY
DON HENLEY AND MIKE CAMPBELL
GEFFEN/DECEMBER 1984
UK CHART: 12

Hippies, eh? Give 'em an inch and they'll drag you miles back
into the rosy-coloured past, when we were all gonna be free –
except for the wife, who was gonna be cooking dinner while you
fucked her little sister. Still, they dared to dream. And the sad
thing about dreams is that you wake up and everything is
exactly the same as it was before, except you're a little bit older.

The former Eagle's slice of hippy nostalgia stands out because
it's the only one that faces up to the truth . . . which is that, if
the '60s dream failed, well, whose fault would that be? The
Eagles' brand of soothingly morbid country rock made them the
biggest-selling rock band in American history, and they had
soundtracked the death of the dream in the '70s. Here was
Henley's take on it all, and it was weird and haunting.

Over those terribly modern synth triplets and a spacey '80s
drum sound, Henley goes on a quest. He drives to an old
girlfriend's house. She's long gone, of course, but he begins to
reminisce, 'I don't understand what happened to our love.'

And that could be that, if Henley didn't drop us a line to let
us know what he's really singing about. The light music grows
darker as he explains that he recently caught sight of 'a
Deadhead sticker on a Cadillac/A little voice said "Don't look
back you can never look back."' He still doesn't understand
what happened to the love of The Grateful Dead's generation, so
he gives in looking and drives home, presumably to count his
millions and give thanks to The Boys of Big Business. It's a sad,
unresolved little tale with no happy ending and no easy cop-out
from its author. How his hippy guilt ties in with the report, in
the August 2001 issue of *Mojo*, that Henley and his fellow
Eagles had finally dropped a three-year lawsuit against an eagle
conservation foundation for their use of the web address
www.eagles.com is a matter for his own conscience. But it sums
up the hippy legacy better than Johnny Rotten ever could.

1985

1985

So, Live Aid. Sigh. Here goes nothing.

What I want to say about 13 July 1985 is that Bob Geldof deserved every bit of praise and glory that came his way subsequently. Because going from watching some pictures of starving children on TV to putting on the world's biggest charity event revealed that the man was a true force of nature, even if he was never much of a force of music. It was an awesome, truly altruistic individual achievement. And I need to remind myself, at this point, that Live Aid was watched by 1.5 billion people and raised at least £40 million for Ethiopia. And what can be wrong with that?

Except I need to say that the majority of Live Aid stank. Not just of bad music and millionaire hippies who could hardly be bothered to tune up before going on (hello Keef and Bob!) and clapped-out comedy rockers reviving their careers off the backs of Africans fucked over by the West just a few years after they had played Sun City, South Africa (that's you, Queen and Quo). But of smug self-satisfaction and a whole bunch of white people celebrating their economic triumph over black people, and actually making those people believe they should be *grateful*. There were famously *no black acts at all* in the UK line-up, and at certain points of the day it seemed as if the purpose of the exercise was to prove you could get Phil Collins to play drums on both sides of the Atlantic, and get Mick Jagger and David Bowie's colossal egos onto one video set without the mutual back-slapping causing a tidal wave. Again, whenever it got too repulsive, in came Geldof. 'Just give us your fucking money!' And no, he wasn't speaking on behalf of Freddie Mercury's accountant.

It turned out to be a disturbing year for what I could see from the comfort of my own home. Live Aid bookended by live TV pictures of Italian football fans being crushed to death in the Heysel Stadium in May, and a real-life Brixton riot right outside my window in September. Still, these horrors proved an unwelcome distraction from the radio and my stereo, because 1985 remains the worst pop year I can remember (there were fewer classic singles in some years in the '90s, but a lot more good music generally). It was almost as if the entire music business had been waiting for their ultimate vindication – the world's most inescapable promotional video. It just sat back and waited for the world to say thank you for the homogeneous music from pop's new official Royal Family. The singles here, therefore, are an eclectic and unconnected bunch . . . a few brave missives from those who didn't get an invite to the global garden party, and a misunderstood old rock bloke.

Honourable mentions: Kate Bush/'The Big Sky' (EMI); Prince and The Revolution/'Raspberry Beret' and 'Pop Life' (Warners); Nick Cave and The Bad Seeds/'Tupelo' (Mute)

HERE I COME (BROADER THAN BROADWAY)

BARRINGTON LEVY

PRODUCED BY JAH SCREW/WRITTEN BY
BARRINGTON LEVY
LONDON/JANUARY 1985
UK CHART: 41

Ebullient, emphatic, rude and often harshly modern, dancehall reggae came out of the Jamaican underground in the mid-'80s, bringing an entirely different perspective from the roots and consciousness of Marley and the Rastas. It was JA's response to hip-hop, with machines taking over the work of some of the best musicians on the planet, and vocalists who mixed the DJ toast with sweet singing voices suffused with gimmicky vocal trademarks. This extraordinary record was the midway point, and a magical single in its own right.

Kingston's Levy had been a JA dancehall face for seven years before he and producer Screw broke with 'Under Mi Sensi' and this passionate mystery of a song. The record begins with rock-hard rhythm, squirming synth squeaks and a giddy run of onomatopoeic nonsense wails from Levy – 'Shidderley-wop! Shudderley-wop! Widdley-diddley *whoah-eeoh*' – as he hollers out an unforgettable dancefloor invitation with a barely controlled mania. From there, as the rhythm breaks down into repeated staccato stomps, Levy tells us about his girl having a baby and him running to her side with roses. Two months later, the girl's had enough and wants him to take the little girl off her hands. 'Because you are old/And I am young/And while I'm young/Yes I wanna have some fun.' The crisis is soon forgotten, though, because Barrington just heads to the dancehall and starts gabbling about the DJ, and declaring that he's extra-broader than Broadway, and extra-sizer than Sizeway. All the serious stuff about errant Jamaican fathers and suffering babymommas is left unsaid, submerged between the bravura double-tracked vocals and the vivid joy of a brand-new sound. One that would last, as reggae began to speed towards the digital age, for all of a few months.

HANGIN' ON A STRING (CONTEMPLATING)

LOOSE ENDS

PRODUCED BY NICK MARTINELLI/WRITTEN BY
CARL MCINTOSH, JANE EUGENE AND STEVE NICHOL
VIRGIN/FEBRUARY 1985
UK CHART: 13

The struggle for recognition of black British music has, as I write, taken its single biggest step forward through the block-rocking fusions of UK garage. But it still remains difficult for any talented black Brit to forge a musical career on an equal footing with the more glamorous and 'authentic' voices of America and Jamaica. By rights, for example, Loose Ends leader Carl McIntosh should be a star now – the visionary missing link between the '70s/'80s UK pop-funk scene of Heatwave, Imagination, Linx, etc. and the Great Leap Forward of Soul II Soul. But he isn't, despite a later production style that prefaced the urban machine-funk of two-step by a good ten years.

Nevertheless, 'Hangin' on a String' was a massive hit in America as well as Britain, and used Marvin Gaye's beatbox soul with a deft difference. The five ringing notes of electro-percussion wormed their way into your skull, the song's adult love theme develops easily and seductively, to the point where the vocal weaknesses of the band cease to matter. It's all about the creamy groove, the blend of slink and staccato, the slow unfolding of melodic and rhythmic detail. Not a sonic cathedral, maybe. But definitely a candlelit shrine, probably in the bedroom.

NEVER UNDERSTAND

THE JESUS AND MARY CHAIN

PRODUCED BY THE JESUS AND MARY CHAIN/WRITTEN
BY JIM AND WILLIAM REID
BLANCO Y NEGRO/FEBRUARY 1985
UK CHART: 47

'Upside Down' (see p. 224) with The Ramones swapped for The Beach Boys and the Panzer Division swapped for a swarm of furious radioactive bees torturing a man in a cellar. Also notable for the introduction to recorded rock of one Bobby Gillespie, clumping his Mo Tucker drums in a trance and figuring out what kind of primal scream might come next.

THE JESUS
AND
MARY CHAIN

NEVER UNDERSTAND/THE JESUS AND MARY CHAIN
PAGE 228

A PAIR OF BROWN EYES

THE POGUES

PRODUCED BY ELVIS COSTELLO/WRITTEN BY
SHANE MACGOWAN
STIFF/MARCH 1985
UK CHART: 72

The former Pogue Mahone (Gaelic for 'Kiss my arse') shortened their name and shortened the distance between Camden Town and Brendan Behan's Dublin. Led by the songs and the . . . um . . . unique vocal stylings of Shane MacGowan (who, in another life, had been famous for 15 minutes for getting his earlobe bitten off at a Clash gig and starting a lousy band called The Nipple Erectors), their penny whistle-led Irish shanty sound brought folk back into the British mainstream – albeit a gnarled, Clash-tinged, drunken and very Irish brand of folk. They were, along with the Mary Chain, the only thing left of punk that mattered a tinker's cuss by 1985.

MacGowan's greatest song is, fittingly, a dirge permanently swaying off a teetering bar stool. It concerns an alcoholic in a pub driven to drink by war. The only thing that had got him through the carnage was the girl he would come back to. But by the time he returns, a shell of a man, she has gone to another. The story is told in such timeless language and with such ageless authority that you cannot tell whether these were events from last week or a generation ago, until you note that the songs from the jukebox are by Johnny Ray and Philomena Begley – the pre-rock '50s. It ends with the old soldier, staggering home alone, ranting at the walls, the love songs from the pub jukebox and even the wind laughing at his pain. It is beautiful and ugly and performed with a simple truth that defies the obvious potential for melodrama.

KING OF ROCK/ROCK BOX

RUN-D.M.C.

PRODUCED BY RUSSELL SIMMONS AND LARRY SMITH ('KING OF ROCK' MIXED BY ELAI TUBO; 'ROCK BOX' MIXED BY DJ STARCHILD)/WRITTEN BY LARRY SMITH, JOSEPH SIMMONS AND DARRYL MCDANIELS
FOURTH & BROADWAY/MARCH 1985
DID NOT CHART

Oh baby. So *this* is what we'd been waiting for.

Run-D.M.C. are the single most important act in hip-hop history. The trio from New York's Hollis, Queens – rappers Joe Simmons (Run) and Darryl McDaniels (D.M.C.) and DJ Jason Mizell (Jam Master Jay) – changed the sound and attitude of rap in one fell swoop with their 1983 single 'It's Like That'/'Sucker MCs'. Their voices declaiming roughly over little more than basic beatbox rhythms, they also got rid of previous rappers' preoccupation with '70s-style Village People/loverman glitz, striding forth in black leather, trilbies, and sneakers (trainers to you and me) with the laces undone. They were unpretty, wild, funny and finished each other's sentences in declamatory unison LIKE THAT!!! And crucially, their manager and Joe's brother Russell (who would soon start hip-hop's equivalent of Motown, the Def Jam label), wanted to get paid and not get shafted by the biz old guard. As soon as you heard and saw them, you knew that rap's days as novelty were over.

This 12-inch packaged their recent US underground hit 'Rock Box' and the title track from their second album, *King of Rock*. Put very simply, it changed the world by grafting heavy-metal guitars onto rap. But this was a different – though obviously related – ballgame to Jacko's 'Beat It' ('It's not Michael Jackson/And this is not THRILLER!!!', they raged on 'King of Rock', just in case you were in any doubt). This sounded like the hardest of hard rock and the blackest of black music. The boasts on 'King of Rock' are bold and breathtaking, a revisiting of black power made all the more thrilling by the music's theft of white-boy rawk. Moments: the shouted intro, 'I'm the King of Rock!/There is none *higher-higher-higher*', snapping you to attention with the outrageous slapback echo that would be their trademark; and one of my fave jokes in pop history, 'Every jam we play, we break two needles/There's three of us but we're not The BEATLES!!!' By feigning ignorance of the line-up of rock's most famous band, while juxtaposing the joke with the mechanics of the hip-hop DJ, they were doing their level best to wipe rock right out of history, while the cheesiest rock guitar solo you ever heard screeches in protest in the background.

KING OF ROCK/ROCK BOX/RUN-D.M.C.
PAGE 230

THE WORD GIRL

SCRITTI POLITTI WITH RANKING ANN

PRODUCED BY SCRITTI POLITTI/WRITTEN BY
GREEN GARTSIDE AND DAVID GAMSON
VIRGIN/MAY 1985
UK CHART: 6

The angriest record of the year came dipped in the sweetest sugar – the proverbial wolf in sheep's clothing. Green Gartside's ongoing love affair with slick black pop and ongoing attempt to deconstruct the word 'girl' and sneak academic feminism into the Top Ten reached its peak on this, his biggest UK chart hit. Over a reggae lope played with gossamer touch and the idealized summer feel of a small child skipping through a meadow, Green sings with a caressing androgyny that reminds you just what an amazing singer he is. But his words hit home, beneath the friendliness. The word 'girl' is 'A name for what you lose/When it was never yours.' And all male lost-love songs, perhaps all male complaints about impossible girls, are reduced to one harsh statement. 'She stands for your abuse/The "girl" was never real.' The chorus is a pop-reggae joy that even Sting could never have stumbled upon, and the sleeve juxtaposes the label of Aretha Franklin's 'Chain of Fools' with a bleached shot of Shirley Maclaine, that paragon of celluloid female suffering, looking like the saddest bride that ever said 'I do'. They really don't make 'em like this any more.

THE PERFECT KISS

NEW ORDER

PRODUCED AND WRITTEN BY NEW ORDER
FACTORY/MAY 1985
UK CHART: 46

It's impossible to hear this without seeing Jonathan Demme's strangely moving promo – a straight film of the four playing the song in the studio, concentrating on pressing the right button on the right keyboard, close-ups of their faces revealing shy, embarrassed and excited swapped glances, as they coax the warmest melodies out of the coldest tools (and, of course, Hooky's ever more twanging bass).

Only New Order could get away with a chorus as gauche as 'I know/You know/We believe in the land of love', especially after (or perhaps because of) some classic Barney Sumner pretentiousness-pricking. 'Tonight I should've stayed at home/Playing with my pleasure zone,' he yelps hilariously, before pondering whether the friend he's taken out clubbing is 'deranged' and 'pretending not to see his guilt'. Still, the evening ascends with the bliss of New Order's singing, ringing electro-pop, which – and I realize this is heresy to any raincoat types who may be reading – is not really that different to anything by Stock, Aitken and Waterman, when you get right down to it. Also, as a big fan of 'The Perfect Kiss's parent album *Low-life*, I really wish they'd released 'Love Vigilantes' and introduced electro-country and western to a wider world.

I'M ON FIRE/BORN IN THE USA

BRUCE SPRINGSTEEN

PRODUCED BY BRUCE SPRINGSTEEN, JON LANDAU,
CHUCK PLOTKIN AND STEVE VAN ZANDT/WRITTEN BY
BRUCE SPRINGSTEEN
CBS/MAY 1985
UK CHART: 5

It's well documented that the *Born in the USA* album and the rather laughable dance-rock compromise of the 'Dancing in the Dark' single and video transformed The Boss from respected rock star into global pop superstar. It's also well documented that Ronald Reagan claimed that 'Born . . .', Springsteen's furious post-Vietnam protest rant, was in fact a patriotic anthem from a true all-American boy. For many a hipster, Broooce has never quite thrown off either of these labels, even in the wake of all those stark and downbeat roots records he's made since. Shame, really, 'cos 'Born . . .' is one of the great fire 'n' brimstone rock 'n' roll performances, glowering and vengeful and doused in the irony of both the military drums and synth fanfare, and his final drowning howl, 'I'm a cool rocking daddy in the USA!' No wonder that, after this, he both ignored the pop charts and stopped giving his audience any credit for understanding sarcasm.

As for the nominal topside of this double 'A', 'I'm on Fire' makes Bruce sound both as horny as hell and tortured by it. I once read a book called *Elvis – The Novel*. Sadly, I don't own it anymore and forget the author's name. But it was a bittersweet comic fantasy about how Elvis would've turned out if he hadn't gone into the army, hadn't done everything Tom Parker told him to, had taken some uppers instead of all those downers, had worked with Lennon, etc. Every time I hear 'I'm on Fire', I imagine it's the sound *that* Elvis would've gone on to make if he'd lived.

RING THE ALARM

TENOR SAW

PRODUCED BY WINSTON RILEY/WRITTEN BY
CLIVE BRIGHT
GREENSLEEVES/JULY 1985
DID NOT CHART

UNDER ME SLENG TENG

WAYNE SMITH

PRODUCED BY PRINCE JAMMY/WRITTEN BY W. SMITH
AND L. JAMES
GREENSLEEVES/JULY 1985
DID NOT CHART

The smooth changeover between reggae old and new.

Clive 'Tenor Saw' Bright's anthemic taunt to inferior Kingston sound systems spliced together deep and moody digital dub for the intro and instrumental coda, and high-stepping reggae throwback for the infectious vocal sections. Saw signals the first changeover with an incredible, high-pitched animal call, and then makes the song much more than a local skirmish with his beauteous Desmond Dekkerish croon. A great talent passed in its prime when Tenor Saw was killed by a speeding car in Houston, Texas, just four years later.

'Ring the Alarm' was based on the rhythm from a track called 'Stalag 17'. Reggae had always recycled popular rhythms, but dancehall took this to extremes, putting out whole albums based on the same tune with different vocalists. No rhythm became more ubiquitous than that of 'Under Me Sleng Teng', which marked the dawn of the digital reggae era. Smith gives worship to the weed (but 'No cocaine – I don't wanna, I don't wanna go insane!') over one unchanging computer beat, buoyed by an ultra-basic and synthetic bassline borrowed – perhaps not consciously – from 'Anarchy in the UK'. The result is mesmeric and had the same effect on human rhythm sections from Jamaica as 'Planet Rock' did on their American counterparts . . . although the best of them, including Sly and Robbie, simply adapted to the new realities.

THE SHOW/LA DI DA DI

DOUG E. FRESH & THE GET FRESH CREW

PRODUCED BY DENNIS BELL, OLLIE COTTON AND
DOUG E. FRESH/WRITTEN BY DOUGLAS E. DAVIS AND
RICKY WALTERS
COOLTEMPO/OCTOBER 1985
UK CHART: 7

Run-D.M.C. might have served noticed on the serious business that hip-hop was becoming, but the rap novelty wasn't dead yet. 'The Show' introduced the UK pop charts to the joys of the human beatbox, whereby the guy in question makes the music with his mouth. Which would seem an odd thing to do, until you remember that hip-hop developed on the street corners and in the parks of ghetto America, and not every kid could afford those flash beatboxes. You want it bad enough, you improvise with what you've got, which, in some cases, was nothing but the body you were born in.

Doug E. Davis was the human beatbox and the guy with his name on the record. But the thing that really made this single – and particularly its massively influential B-side – was the rapping of one Slick Rick Walters. Walters, at this point known as MC Ricky D, was a British-born Bronx kid with a rap style like no other – drawled, nasal, light, debonair, jokey, possessed of all the time in the world. Future rappers heard this new style and hailed Rick as rap's future. He was a huge influence on the coming deluge, and especially one Snoop Doggy Dogg, who covered 'La-Di-Da-Di' (renamed 'Lodi Dodi') on his first album, and reintroduced the master's style to a young rap audience. The jury is still out as to whether Rick or Rakim holds the official title of rap's all-time best (but, for what it's worth, I'm a Rakim man myself).

The A-side hit big in pop with its monster-movie synths and Doug's bizarre throat and tongue manipulations bouncing off a real drumbox (dominated by a momentarily fashionable, twitchy bean-shaker effect that sounded like someone snorting coke in time to the beat) in an avalanche of percussion. The B-side slayed the underground with its deliciously detailed tale of Rick getting ready to parade his sexy body round the neighbourhood, before a mother and daughter end up fighting on the street for his favours. It was also pretty misogynistic and the beginning of everything dubious in X-rated rap.

Rick signed to Def Jam but found his career constantly interrupted by violent incidents followed by stretches in prison. This began another strange rap trend – an enormous sympathy, even sentimentality, for rappers who fell foul of the law, even

THE SHOW/LA DI DA DI/DOUG E. FRESH & THE GET FRESH CREW

PAGE 234

when their guilt was unquestionable and their deeds repulsive. Fresh's decline was more usual. Court cases for non-payment of royalties took precedence over making new music, human beatboxes went out of fashion, subsequent attempts at career revival failed. His mouth-music lives on in a sampler called the Oberheim Emulator, which has a Doug E. Fresh button for that authentic old-school cluck 'n' pop effect.

CAN YOUR PUSSY DO THE DOG?

THE CRAMPS
PRODUCED BY THE CRAMPS/WRITTEN BY
LUX INTERIOR AND POISON IVY RORSCHACH
BIG BEAT/NOVEMBER 1985
UK CHART: 68

While other less inspired and intelligent rock bands insist on getting more – spit – *sophisticated*, The Cramps regressed to a state of slavering base instinct. The last classic Cramps single was from an album, *A Date with Elvis*, that was nothing more than a bunch of obsessive scuzz-rock tributes to the power of the pussy. Who needs *The Vagina Monologues* when you've got under three minutes of pummelling, twanging fuckabilly that consists of Lux Interior pleading and drooling while his girlfriend's guitar sits right on his face?

The magical thing about The Cramps was their heroic refusal to accept that anything could be smarter or more liberating than the original point of rock 'n' roll – that is, say exactly what you feel *right now* and find the simplest way to say it, and if all that amounts to is yelping like a rabid dog and shouting 'HULLY – HULLY GULLY!!!' for no logical reason, then this primal expression of dribbling hormonal craziness is worth more than a thousand stairways to heaven or careless bloody whispers because it is the essence of the lifeblood of the meaning of the whole goddam motherfucking *point*.

And at that, we leave Lux and Ivy ending 'Can Your Pussy . . .' with a glorious 'CHA-CHA-CHA!!!', making like the dance band on the rock 'n' roll *Titanic*.

WEST END GIRLS

PET SHOP BOYS
PRODUCED BY STEPHEN HAGUE/WRITTEN BY
NEIL TENNANT AND CHRIS LOWE
PARLOPHONE/NOVEMBER 1985
UK CHART: 1

Here comes the pop cavalry. And not a moment too soon.

If *Smash Hits* journo Tennant and his shy synth-mate Lowe had been big before Live Aid, I'm sure they would've done it. But they would've stood out like the Pope at a bar mitzvah by bringing some quiet dignity to proceedings, and would also have managed some tiny gesture or word which would have slyly put all the worst excesses about the event into sudden perspective. Only someone who actually cares about pop music, rather than just a pop career, can manage things like that. And PSB's great strength has always been their ability to be part of the pop parade and somehow separate, some kind of midway point between the differing ambitions of The Smiths, New Order and Duran Duran.

'West End Girls' had already come out on Epic Records in the spring of 1984, produced by their initial mentor, Hi-NRG producer Bobby 'O' Orlando. I've never heard that flop version, but its hard to imagine quite how Orlando could've screwed up such a natural hit. Wistful, wise, young but world-weary, it's strange now to realize that Tennant 'raps' the majority of this piece about accusatory conversation and mysterious dramas and the bittersweet joys of Soho's all-human-life-is-here weekend twilight zone, of bits of rough and bits of posh, of clicking high heels and sex in the air and black cabs in the rain and The Dive Bar in Gerrard Street and the constant threat of violence and losing it. The electro-disco is at once comforting and familiar but somehow new, bigger, more organic, almost as if Hague and PSB had never heard 'real' instruments and thought this was the only way you made music. It rendered every piece of 1985's white British pop redundant with one sweep from its chorus, reaching for something intangible that had nothing and everything to do with the real world of greed and duplicity.

1986

1986

They say news travels fast, but when it finds somewhere it likes, it just won't take the hint and sod off. 1986 saw the beginnings of three stories that still dominate the headlines as I write: Mike Tyson became the youngest ever world heavyweight champion in November, the NSPCC announced a disturbing rise in cases of child abuse just before Christmas, and Jeffrey Archer resigned as Deputy Chairman of the Conservative Party in October, amid allegations that he had paid a prostitute to leave the country. At the time, these stories were dwarfed by the *Challenger* space shuttle disaster, Chernobyl, Boy George's smack habit, Oliver North, the burgeoning civil war in South Africa, Wapping, Gorbachev, Maradona's Hand of God, and the British Government's tardy AIDS awareness campaign. It was one of those years when accidents and disasters and morons in positions of power exposed the true state of the world, from the endgames of apartheid and Communism, through nuclear and tabloid fallout, to Edwina Currie's blithe comments about people in the north of England being too thick to feed themselves properly. The cracks in hegemonies old and new were beginning to show.

And so it proved in pop too. Live Aid did, despite the sneering of old rockers, turn out to be our generation's Woodstock. That is, the end of something rather than the beginning, once all the self-congratulation was out of the way. The Pop Royals kept on selling, but were quickly being made irrelevant by young, (mainly) black men and their machines. They had things other than charity on their minds, and weren't about to wait for handouts. Walk this way.

Honourable mentions: Fingers Inc./'Washing Machine' (Trax); The Smiths/'Ask' (Rough Trade); The Fall/'Mr Pharmacist' (Beggars Banquet); Janet Jackson/'What Have You Done for Me Lately?' (A&M); Prince and The Revolution/ 'Anotherloverholenyourhead' and 'Girls and Boys' (Paisley Park); Depeche Mode/'Stripped' and 'A Question of Lust' (Mute); Mantronix/'Bassline', 'Hardcore Hip-Hop' and 'Scream' (10); Mr Fingers/'Can You Feel It?' (Trax)

I CAN'T LIVE WITHOUT MY RADIO

LL COOL J

PRODUCED BY RICK RUBIN/WRITTEN BY
JAMES TODD SMITH AND RICK RUBIN
DEF JAM/JANUARY 1986
DID NOT CHART

KISS

PRINCE AND THE REVOLUTION

PRODUCED AND WRITTEN BY PRINCE AND
THE REVOLUTION
PAISLEY PARK/FEBRUARY 1986
UK CHART: 6

Alien noise from some parched and hostile terrain. The debut single from James Todd Smith (Ladies Love Cool James) gave me some idea of what it might have been like to be a '50s teen who switches on their radio and hears Little Richard's desperate scream for the first time. It was thrilling, scary, and you knew it was the future, whether you liked it or not.

'. . . Radio' provides our first introduction to three revolutionary entities. Firstly, producer Rick Rubin. Like Arthur Baker, another white rocker type whose sparse, parent-baiting soundscapes formalized the fusion between hip-hop and rock. Secondly, Def Jam, the label formed by Rubin and Run-D.M.C. manager Russell Simmons, whose initial splurge of rap-renegade activity changed rap, pop and rock by snagging the white kids who were finding contemporary rock and metal as dull as ditchwater. Thirdly, LL Cool J himself: the youngest and wildest of all rap voices, delivering his early missives as if he'd had a message from above that time was running out, and then, once that panic was over, proving himself the most adaptable, perhaps cynical, of hip-hop's businessmen.

In many ways, '. . . Radio' is not music. There are pounding beatbox drums, screeching, angular horn sample-stabs, and nothing else. Nothing, that is, except Cool J, strutting through his neighbourhood with a ghetto blaster on his shoulder that makes Dom Joly's mobile look diddy. His bravura rap, all machismo and acquisitiveness and sex and comedy and gold and defiance and malevolent grin, features the first mention of a 'hip-hop gangster', one of rap's earliest product placements (his 'JVC vibrates the concrete') and a feeling that nothing can stand in his way, as long as that radio stays in his hands. When he announces the arrival of his DJ, Cut Creator responds, not with turntable virtuosity, but a few rude clunks, as if showing off would be some form of compromise to all the older neighbours holding their ears and begging for mercy. This wasn't entertainment. It was street warfare.

After the faux-psychedelic experiment of 'Around the World in a Day', Prince got back to funky business and accidentally defined himself. Because, according to the sleevenotes for the *The Hits/The B-sides* CD provided by Prince's former road manager and label Vice President Alan Leeds, 'Kiss' was a distracted afterthought. Originally written as a demo for Mazarati, one of his many protégé bands, they rejected it as 'too weird'. So The Diminutive One finished it off and shoved it on the *Parade* album, although he remains so unconvinced of the song's worth that he constantly rearranges it every time it's performed live. Still, if there's one man in this book who proves the old adage that an artist doesn't know his own best work, it's Purple Boy. Because 'Kiss' sums up Prince as, say, 'Satisfaction' sums up the Stones.

Claustrophobic yet somehow free, randy but romantic, machine-driven but made magical by lovely flurries of old-school blues-funk guitar and pop-gospel backing vox, funky but surreal, dynamic yet restrained, earthy yet dreamy, playful but desperate, hetero yet sung in the sweetest falsetto. There's one Moment when he mutters, 'Think I wanna dance,' grunts, and kicks into a rolling funk-guitar solo that throws the hitherto starchy rhythm into an utterly different, fluid flush of dance ecstasy. There's another, even better Moment at the end when the lust gets too much and the coo becomes a tortured, throat-shredding howl of Little Richard-like manic lust. And then there's 'Women not girls rule my world . . . act your age not your shoe size/And maybe we can do the twirl,' which is active feminism and pure pop poetry all rolled into one.

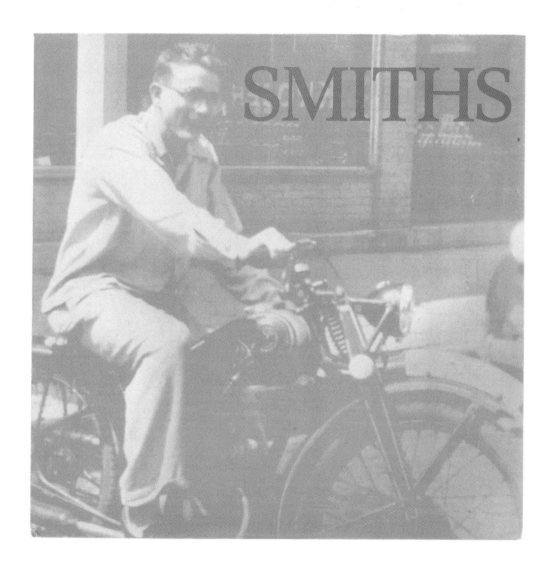

BIGMOUTH STRIKES AGAIN/THE SMITHS

HOUNDS OF LOVE

KATE BUSH
PRODUCED AND WRITTEN BY KATE BUSH
(MIXED BY JULIAN MENDELSOHN)
EMI/FEBRUARY 1986
UK CHART: 18

The previous year's big Bush hit, 'Running Up That Hill', still gets all the kudos. But for me, the title track from the Bexleyheath Ballerina's finest album is her masterpiece. If a more revealing and ecstatic song – and performance – has ever been given in the name of love and the illogical joy and fear of falling in it, its name escapes me right now. It comes down to A Moment – two Moments, actually – that turn me into a blubbering mess every time. The thundering, awkward drums hesitate, and she howls, 'Here I go!' and the juddering Beatles cellos move everything up, up and away and you can suddenly see the forest and her shoes sailing into the lake and feel the utter helplessness of giving your heart and body over to someone else and the masochistic giddy weightlessness of being truly touched and . . . uh . . . anyway . . . it's . . . ahem . . . not a *bad* record, if you like that sort of thing.

PUT YOUR FILAS ON/
P.S.K. 'WHAT DOES IT MEAN'?

SCHOOLY D
PRODUCED AND WRITTEN BY SCHOOLY D
RHYTHM KING/APRIL 1986
DID NOT CHART

By now, rap was moving so fast that each record you heard made the last one seem redundant. But it took some kind of voice to make LL Cool J sound like a pop pantywaist. Ladies and gentlemen, let me introduce to you, for one time and one time only, Mr J.B. Weaver, the harbinger of gangsta rap.

With hip-hop's history having been predictably rewritten around the preoccupation with hit records, the impact of Schooly D is almost forgotten. But the man was responsible for a great many firsts, and not all of them good. His was the first rap voice most of us had heard that did not hail from New York, but the rap boondocks of Philadelphia. He was the first rapper to introduce a malevolent, taunting slur to the rap vocal, deliberately sounding drugged to fuck and calmly psychopathic. On Schooly's self-titled first album, you heard the profane,

woman-hating, self-loathing street language that maybe some of us had heard on Richard Pryor's live performance records – 'nigga', 'ho', 'motherfucker', phrases like 'bust me a nut' meaning 'I would like to have sexual intercourse with a person of the female persuasion.' You heard rival black males threatened not with microphone virtuosity, but guns. Drugs got took and no one said 'Don't do it.' This music was threatening and violent and sexist and proud of it. It tapped perfectly into that part of you – particularly if you are male – that wanted vicarious thrills and petty crime dressed up as rebellion. It carried all the sense of danger that rock 'n' roll had ceased to possess since the demise of the Sex Pistols. But here, it was individual domination, not societal revolution, that provided that danger.

And the music? Still astonishing. 'Put Your Filas On' (more product placement, another step away from home-made style towards consumer fetishism) was nothing but beats and handclaps bathed in echo, Schooly's stoned taunt of a voice, often rapping around, rather than to, the beat, and DJ Code Money's astonishing flood of florid scratches. It introduced one of rap's most popular trademarks, a hard male 'UNGHH' followed by a woman's shrill giggle, falling in time to the beat. The B-side was even meaner and weirder, a tapestry of unresolved tension. 'P.S.K.', incidentally, didn't mean a helluva lot . . . 'P' for 'People'; 'S' for 'Scream and Shout'; 'K' for the way Code Money 'Kuts'. You felt that a secret, more ominous message lay somewhere between the party lines, just as Schooly's minimalist marketing – just one grainy amateurish photo of him and Code Money in shades and carrying a massive beatbox – felt like a mystery you weren't sure you wanted to investigate. Which is exactly why you did. There goes the neighbourhood.

BIGMOUTH STRIKES AGAIN

THE SMITHS

PRODUCED AND WRITTEN BY MORRISSEY AND
JOHNNY MARR
ROUGH TRADE/MAY 1986
UK CHART: 26

'Sweetness, sweetness, I was only joking when I said by rights you should be bludgeoned in your bed.' And that's the nearest Morrissey could ever get to an apology.

MOUNTAINS

PRINCE AND THE REVOLUTION

PRODUCED AND WRITTEN BY PRINCE AND
THE REVOLUTION
PAISLEY PARK/MAY 1986
UK CHART: 45

'Mountains' bombed because 'Kiss' encouraged everyone to go buy the wonderful *Parade* album. But it is too good to overlook, a rumbling gospel extravaganza with its head in the clouds and its feet on Stevie Wonder's higher ground. The horns and the choir sing out their praise to transcendent love, the geetars git down and dirty, the instrumental coda goes all Earth, Wind & Fire-meets-free-jazz, and you almost forget that *Parade* was the soundtrack to *Under a Cherry Moon*, very possibly the worst movie ever made, and the first sign we got that the guy was human after all.

PAPA DON'T PREACH

MADONNA

PRODUCED BY MADONNA AND
STEPHEN BRAY/WRITTEN BY BRIAN ELLIOT AND
MADONNA
SIRE/JUNE 1986
UK CHART: 1

'Papa Don't Preach' reconciles two conflicting ambitions with supreme skill. On the one hand, make the novelty disco babe into a proper album-shipping superstar by getting rid of the slut clothes, giving her a classy '50s retro image, and reintroducing Maddy as an adult, with a straightforward inner strength. On the other, get her to sing about teen pregnancy with all the empathy and sense of the price of young love she can muster. Maybe there's another great pop record that presents the reality of babies making babies as anything other than a society-threatening tragedy. But I can't remember one, and if it exists, I don't recall it being the key text in something some smartarse would later label Girl Power.

This, of all Madonna records, is the one that grows with age. The deft and detailed arrangement. Her transformed voice, now sure and achingly soulful where it had been shrill and amateurish. The subtle lack of trust it reveals in the baby's father and the friends insisting that while the girl's young she should wanna have some fun. The down-to-earth desperation in the plea to her father: 'What I need right now is some good advice.'

It was a record made for the benefit of young girls by a woman who knew how they felt. Suddenly, the blonde ambition showed its roots.

PANIC

THE SMITHS

PRODUCED BY JOHN PORTER/WRITTEN BY
MORRISSEY AND JOHNNY MARR
ROUGH TRADE/JULY 1986
UK CHART: 11

So which analogy shall we pin to this one, eh? The boy with his finger in the dyke? A man pissing in the wind while blithely unaware of what that inevitably leads to? White student rock's King Canute trying to hold back the tide of beats and black music and getting his tutu all wet? All lead to the same whiff of rising damp in The House of Moz. Yet, as we've already discussed, Johnny Marr adored black music, going on to make dance-pop with New Order's Barney Sumner as Electronic. And Moz and Marr always insisted that the infamous kiddie choir 'Hang the DJ!' chorus was inspired by listening to Steve Wright on Radio One.

Oh yeah . . . almost forgot. The song is here because it's great – a glam-rock reincarnation packed with sublime sepia small-town imagery and delicious use of the affectionate term 'honey pie'. If the implications of burning down the disco make me squirm, I just think of superstar DJs and *Ibiza Uncovered* and strange people staring in worship at a bloke playing records on a stage when the initial point of rave was that there were no stars . . . and persuade myself that Moz had seen the less appealing side of the clubbing future.

WHEN I THINK OF YOU

JANET JACKSON

PRODUCED AND WRITTEN BY JAMES HARRIS III,
TERRY LEWIS AND JANET JACKSON
A&M/AUGUST 1986
UK CHART: 10

Around this time I was DJing at a gay pub in Brixton called The
Prince of Wales. I did an 'alternative night', which basically
meant I could play anything that wasn't Hi-NRG or Eurodisco.
This consisted of some glam, some punk, some indie, and a
whole bunch of new black music that said everything to me
about my life. Nobody tried to hang me, but no one gawped at
me and offered me trips to Spain and all their drugs either, the
ungrateful bastards. But anyway, the next three singles got
played a lot, because they burned down the disco. Or rather,
they filled the dancefloor, before some homophobic fuck really
did try to burn down the place.

'When I Think of You' is my fave *Control*-era Janet/Jam &
Lewis collaboration, because it's just so damn *happy*, which is a
tough thing to pull off without just being sugary. It's the giggly,
two-chord, disco-pop, no-fear-at-all take on 'Hounds of Love's'
(see p. 242) freefall into giddy romance, especially in the bit
where she orders 'Break!', borrows some of her brother's scatty
rhythm grunts, and then this cup-runneth-over sonic boom
crashes in and she just forgets herself and roars, bursts into
laughter and trills 'Feels so good!' with a delirious amusement,
as if caught unawares by the power of her own sexuality. No
wonder she moved out from that weird family of hers.

WORD UP

CAMEO

PRODUCED BY LARRY BLACKMON/WRITTEN BY
LARRY BLACKMON AND TOMI JENKINS
CLUB/AUGUST 1986
UK CHART: 3

In which Lord Larry of the Ancient Codpiece took EW&F,
Prince and Clinton, turned them into dancing robots, shovelled
in a load of hooks he'd nicked from rap records, added a touch
of spaghetti – western-style, naturally – and rode the whole kit
and caboodle to fairground-barking funk glory. 'We don't have
no time for psychological romance,' he informed us, bizarrely.
Yeah. Whatever. Just turn the drums up, big boy.

WALK THIS WAY

RUN-D.M.C. FEATURING AEROSMITH

PRODUCED BY RUSSELL SIMMONS, RICK RUBIN,
JASON MIZELL AND JOSEPH SIMMONS/WRITTEN BY
STEVEN TYLER AND JOE PERRY
LONDON/AUGUST 1986
UK CHART: 8

Hey! Mozzer! Put your wellies on!

When Run-D.M.C. broke through that wall in the infamous
video and hollered Aerosmith's words back into their faces, it
was the single most deliberately symbolic act in recent pop
history. MTV had ignored rap until then, but played 'Walk This
Way' to death. They had to start the first dedicated rap show,
Yo! MTV Raps! And, more generally, hip-hop had finally made
The Great Breakthrough, as a deluge of noisy black rebels
followed Run-D.M.C. right through that hole, and replaced
rockers as the white adolescent's pop-rebel faves. From this
point onwards, rap was big mainstream business. And the more
taboos it romped all over, the more omnipotent it became.

Rick Rubin let the genie out of the bottle as Darryl 'D.M.C.'
McDaniels tells it. Because, although the trio knew the opening
guitar riff of 'Walk This Way' well because of its use as a hip-
hop breakbeat, when Rubin suggested they cover the whole
thing, the image-conscious black boys muttered something
about hillbilly shit and thought he'd gone insane. All logic
dictates they should've been right. I mean, radio playing a record
where black men are ranting about 'Goin' down on the muffin'?
You've got to take some pleasure from the fact that radio
programmers' inability to understand rap voices or obscure
references to cunnilingus played a major role in the now
inexorable rise of rap culture.

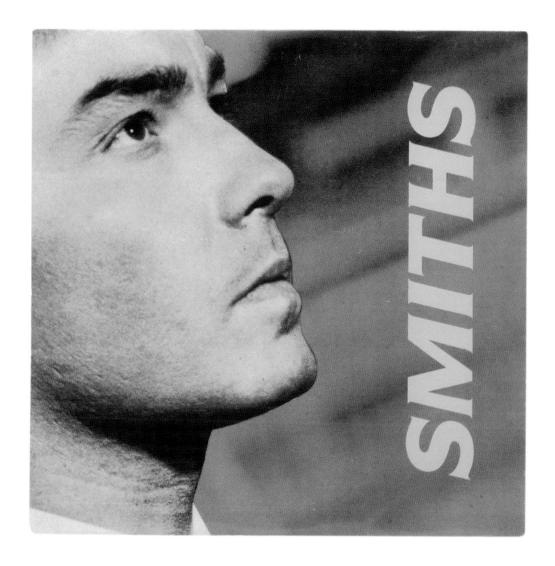

PANIC/THE SMITHS

SUBURBIA

PET SHOP BOYS

PRODUCED BY STEPHEN HAGUE (REMIXED BY
JULIAN MENDELSOHN AND PET SHOP BOYS)/WRITTEN
BY NEIL TENNANT AND CHRIS LOWE
PARLOPHONE/SEPTEMBER 1986
UK CHART: 8

So Tennant and Lowe revisited all that suburban punk angst, dressed it up in Madonna's disco gear, and ate The Cure for breakfast. Except that that wasn't what they were trying to do at all. As Neil Tennant explains in the sleevenotes of the 2001 reissue of the debut *Please* album, 'Suburbia' was inspired by the Brixton riots, and the forgotten fact that this inner-city powder-keg had once been a London suburb . . . the dream of perfect modern living. The juxtaposition of Tennant's grim vision of decay, boredom and violence with the beautiful, ringing optimism of the chorus piano line is almost matched by the skill of his imagery, particularly, 'Listen – a siren screams/There in the distance/Like a roll-call/Of all the suburban dreams.'

CANDY

CAMEO

PRODUCED BY LARRY BLACKMON/WRITTEN BY
LARRY BLACKMON AND TOMI JENKINS
CLUB/NOVEMBER 1986
UK CHART: 27

'Word Up' Part Two, pretty much. Apart from all the reasons why I like it more. Firstly, it's sexier and funnier, especially when Lazza tries to convince Candy he's shy. Secondly, the endlessly repeating thunk-funk riff is more slyly insidious. But thirdly, and especially, there's The Moment towards the end when everything climbs and Charlie Singleton kicks into a side-splittingly inappropriate and magnificent screeching metal-guitar solo and, just as the air fills with a bright rawk light and you spring to your feet and take position then . . . clunk. Over and out. And you're left holding the air guitar with nowhere to plug in. It was almost as if it had served notice on all screeching metal-guitar solos, having had the last word.

I WANT YOU

ELVIS COSTELLO AND THE ATTRACTIONS

PRODUCED BY NICK LOWE WITH
COLIN FAIRLEY/WRITTEN BY DECLAN MACMANUS
IMP-DEMON/NOVEMBER 1986
DID NOT CHART

Like 'The Boiler' (see p. 174), 'I Want You' makes no concessions to the radio nor any of the other novelty demands of the pop single. It is as dark as a power cut, as bleak as dry bones and is constructed more like a suicide note than a popular song. But it stands as Costello's last contribution to this list, simply because it is a work of broken genius, a private hell set to music, the thrilled fear of 'Hounds of Love' (see p. 242) gone sour and diseased.

In 'I Want You', the protagonist's lover has become his enemy, and the love he still feels has turned to agony and the desire for revenge, with emotional collapse hiding behind an arrogant disdain as he tries, and fails, to convince himself that he still has some measure of control. The woman is loving somebody, he only knows it isn't his (see 'Alison' p. 34). His voice is whispering the words right up in your face, drenched in jealousy and helplessness and self-loathing. The music's funereal Beatles riff – it is loosely based upon Lennon's 'I Want You (She's So Heavy)' – just circles gently, teetering on the verge of release, of complete loss of temper, but never quite opening the safety valve. The singer is malevolent and hateful – not because he's a monster but because his every sneer and implicit threat of violence is utterly familiar to anyone who has ever been rejected like this. 'Go on and hurt me – then we'll let it drop,' he begins to plead, after all the previous insults, before the inevitable and masochistic digging for the sexual details. The crawling music and Elvis's voice dies with the relationship as, hoarse and drained, he breathes, 'I'm gonna feel this way – until you kill it,' and you know exactly how that feels, when the possibility of starting again, of needing someone's approval this much, hurts more than the final rejection. When. You. Can. Start. To. Get. Over. It.

After this, the endless bright carousel of the pop singles chart was probably better off without Costello, and you suspect that the feeling was mutual.

1987

1987

In a year that was one second shorter than usual – something about an adjustment in the Gregorian calendar – a killer storm hit the south of England with unnatural force. In a pop year that was a whole lot better than usual, two American music-storms hit the north and south of England with unnatural force. The hurricane left. Hip-hop and house stayed and changed British popular culture for good.

1987 was a year of symbolism, most of it tragic, all of it blackly comedic. The *Herald of Free Enterprise* capsized at Zeebrugge as the anarchy of the stock market collapsed into Black Monday, and the newly identified 'yuppie' took the rap. Black power inspired a new generation as the golliwog was excised from the books of Enid Blyton. Fred Astaire, Andy

Warhol and Liberace died as club culture dressed down and opened up the boundaries of sexuality, race, fashion exclusivity. Michael Ryan went on a killing spree in Hungerford as pop continued to get to grips with images of gunplay and small-town panic. Riots raged in Mecca as rap went Islamic. As Gorbachev talked of a new openness – 'glasnost' – a West German teenager flew a light aircraft through Soviet air defences, landed in Red Square, signed autographs, and got four years in a labour camp for taking satire too far. A right-wing Tory admitted having sex with teen male prostitutes as a gay Englishman sang about being 'rent'. Thatcher won another election and then announced the coming of a 'poll tax', signing her own political death warrant. British customs seized cocaine with a street value of £51 million, upping the yuppie misery ante, as ecstasy began to flood working-class clubland. This new brand of clubber began to party like it was 1999 as Reagan and Gorbachev signed the first nuclear-arms reduction treaty. Mary Whitehouse accused *EastEnders* of 'the height of irresponsibility' after showing a homosexual embrace while three soul DJs, Paul Oakenfold, Danny Rampling and Nicky Holloway, brought Ibiza's gay club culture back from their holidays and saw it become the disco choice of the discerning hetero football hooligan.

And, as a by the by, *This Is Your Life* presenter Eamonn Andrews died on 5 November. A constantly chuckling, consummate telly professional, it was Andrews who was the first-choice presenter of London's *Today* programme in the late '70s. Bill Grundy covered when he wasn't available. I wonder how different this book might have been if sober, cuddly Eamonn had interviewed the Sex Pistols?

Honourable mentions: Run-D.M.C./'It's Tricky' (London); Rick Astley/'Never Gonna Give You Up' (RCA); Beastie Boys/'No Sleep 'Til Brooklyn' (Def Jam); Mel & Kim/'Showin' Out (Get Fresh at the Weekend)' (Supreme); The Proclaimers/'Letter from America' (Chrysalis); Sterling Void/'It's Alright' (FFRR); Alexander O' Neal/'Criticize' (Tabu); Big Daddy Kane/'Raw' (Cold Chillin'); The Smiths/'Sheila Take a Bow' (Rough Trade)

WHO IS IT?

MANTRONIX
PRODUCED BY MANTRONIK/WRITTEN BY MANTRONIK
AND MC TEE
TEN/JANUARY 1987
UK CHART: 40

Like Grace Jones, Kurtis Kaheel was a beautiful Jamaican-born New Yorker who contrived to become an alien entity. Unlike Ms Grace, Kurtis Mantronik was fascinated with his studio drums and wires, rather than stage and catwalk, and wanted to create a sound that fused the man with the machine. The extraordinary music he made with his rapping partner Tee (born Tooure Embden) between 1986 and 1988 provided the missing link between the Kraftwerk/Arthur Baker-developed electro, and the techno that would make electronica the choice of a new pop generation. The pair also headlined 1986's benchmark UK Fresh festival at Wembley Arena, the first proof that hip-hop was hitting on Britain as a cultural wave, rather than a novelty pop noise. They are still the best live hip-hop act I ever saw.

'Who Is It?' is a perfect example of Kurtis's innovations. The drums insinuate and cajole rather than crash and thunk like electro. The echoing bass is a subsonic feeling deep in your chest rather than a set of audible notes. Everything shimmers and glides but remains funky and tough. The mournful synth horns and clinking bells and subtle use of echo create an infinite space for the rhythms to work between the beats. It felt fine on the dancefloor, but was an equal-but-different experience on a set of headphones, where the sharp modernism and exploitation of dub-funk possibilities made it as dreamy a sonic journey as Kraftwerk or ambient Eno.

Rapper Tee was the jolliest old-school MC that ever rocked a mic, content to big up his composer/producer (as if he were a scratch DJ) in a torrent of friendly metaphors while Mantronik manipulated and buried his voice until it was just another rhythmic device. By the end of the decade, the constantly grinning Tee saw the macho and aggressive writing on the wall and quit the rap battleground for the safer environment of the US Air Force.

FIGHT FOR YOUR RIGHT (TO PARTY)

BEASTIE BOYS
PRODUCED AND WRITTEN BY BEASTIE BOYS AND
RICK RUBIN
DEF JAM/FEBRUARY 1987
UK CHART: 11

So these nice Jewish boys formed a punk band, then turned into a rap band, then made a pisstake of old sexist redneck metal songs, then woke up and found themselves playing to sexist rednecks while half-naked girls cavorted in cages around them, then came to England and got labelled 'the new Sex Pistols' and got accused of spitting at kids in wheelchairs or something, then they repented and became entrepreneurs of the new boho enlightenment and invented ironic mullets, except that they'd already invented Limp Bizkit and Eminem but didn't notice 'cos they were too busy throwing concerts for Tibet and lecturing other bands for being sexist. See where one good bonehead riff can take you?

Difficult now to see how anyone could've taken this irresistibly stupid record as anything but a joke. But I dare say some wiseacre will be saying the same thing about 'Slim Shady' in ten years' time. A fantastic boy-noise is a fantastic boy-noise and no matter how you change the emphasis or the context, it all adds up to allowing lads to work off their spare testosterone, the slam-dance safety-valve equivalent of a Jane Fonda workout. Unless you're 15, in which case it's revolutionary politics.

SHOPLIFTERS OF THE WORLD UNITE/ HALF A PERSON

THE SMITHS
A-SIDE PRODUCED BY JOHNNY MARR; B-SIDE
PRODUCED BY MORRISSEY, JOHNNY MARR AND
STEPHEN STREET/BOTH WRITTEN BY MORRISSEY AND
JOHNNY MARR
ROUGH TRADE/FEBRUARY 1987
UK CHART: 12

The Smiths were at their very best when Moz and Johnny matched each other inspiration for inspiration. But the last we hear from them (though not Morrissey) here signals a split in leadership over the two sides of this single. 'Shoplifters . . .' is all Marr – a revisit of 'How Soon Is Now?'s' (see p. 220) chugging, glowering funk-rock, plus a completely surprising and dramatic

Thin Lizzyesque twin lead guitar solo towards the end of what is one of Morrissey's least interesting and believable outsider songs.

By contrast, 'Half a Person' is a Moz tour de force. Over one of Marr's pretty but standard jangles, the singer plays with his am-I-or-aren't-I? sexuality, his wide-eyed northerner-in-London shtick, and his 'Heaven Knows I'm Miserable' image in what might just be his definitive, and funniest, Smiths performance. 'Call me morbid, call me pale,' he invites, before insisting that the story of his life would take just five seconds to relate, checking in at a London YWCA, and asking if they have a vacancy for a back-scrubber (pronounced, with an impeccable mini-pause, 'back . . . scroober'). When he catches up with the girl he's chasing, she is coldly matter-of-fact about his chances: 'In the days when you were hopelessly poor/I just liked you more.' Maybe she was speaking on behalf of Johnny Marr, who left and split up The Smiths six months later.

RESPECTABLE

MEL & KIM

PRODUCED AND WRITTEN BY PETE WATERMAN, MIKE STOCK AND MATT AITKEN
SUPREME/FEBRUARY 1987
UK CHART: 1

'TAKETAKETAKETAKET-T-T-TAKETAKETAKE!!!' Is that the sound of shoplifters uniting? Not according to pundits of the time, who reckoned a song that repeated the above vocal effect over and over again was Pete Waterman's ultimate tribute to the triumph of Thatcherism. And maybe it was. I know someone, who wishes to remain anonymous, who used to do demo, guide and backing vocals for many of the peak period S/A/W hits, and she confirms that it was all done on such a production line basis that she can't remember which ones she did. How evil is that?

Well, call me Thatch's drooling lapdog if you wish, but I loved Mel and Kim Appleby. No matter how cynical S/A/W may have been, these grinning, bouncing black girls sure didn't seem it. In fact, of all the manufactured Brit pop stars I remember, they seemed the most natural and instinctively chuffed about it all, until Mel tragically died of cancer in 1990. It all comes down to the credibility gap, I guess. For example, I'm sure many cool and credible underground DJs would rather forget that the London pair's previous hit, 'Showing Out', was played to death on pirate radio before it broke. And these were probably the same DJs who, at around this time, couldn't believe their luck when they

were sent a white-label bootleg of an obscure '70s rare groove called 'Roadblock', which they then all played out and claimed they discovered. Of course, when 'Roadblock' got an official release, and they realized S/A/W had knocked it up one lunch time and put it out to expose the dance scene's growing snobbery, it mysteriously disappeared from their sets. If S/A/W were taking anything, it was the piss out of pseuds everywhere.

SIGN O' THE TIMES

PRINCE

PRODUCED AND WRITTEN BY PRINCE
PAISLEY PARK/MARCH 1987
UK CHART: 10

Isn't it odd that Prince and The Smiths – the two finest acts of the mid-'80s – were also the era's most prolific? Kinda puts all that it-took-us-two-years-and-a-spell-in-rehab-to-make-this-album shite into perspective, doesn't it?

Despite coming so soon after *Parade*, a new Prince album felt like An Event by now. And the first single and the album's title track lived up to the billing, and how. It was the man's most self-conscious grab for greatness, a dark, tense, portentous state-of-the-world address that, by going Top Ten, proved we were all ready for some meat in pop's runny casserole again.

A slower, deeper take on the claustro-funk of 'Kiss' (see p. 240), the song mixes 'Riot'-era Sly Stone, beatbox electro and a touch of Tim Rose's '60s epic 'Morning Dew' in Prince's downward-sloping melody line. After the initial whip-crack snare and a soul-man 'OH YEAH!', the singer goes through his observations quietly, reflectively. The song doesn't preach, as it treads through the debris of AIDS, crack, smack, gang warfare, economic priorities, child poverty, the *Challenger* tragedy, Star Wars, the Cold War.

The weirdest line is the childlike use of the word 'telly' amongst all this gravitas. The best line is the thinking-out-loud revelation that 'Some say a man ain't truly happy unless a man truly dies.' The punchline is his final mumble about love and marriage and bringing a baby called Nate into the world he has just described. For once, his repeated cry of 'OH WHY?' doesn't reappear. It doesn't need to.

NUDE PHOTO

RHYTHIM IS RHYTHIM
PRODUCED AND WRITTEN BY MAYDAY (DERRICK MAY)
TRANSMAT/APRIL 1987
DID NOT CHART

In 1982, a Detroit high-school kid called Juan Atkins made an electro record, 'Clear', under the name Cybotron. It was harsh and chilly yet tuneful and pretty successful on the underground. His younger schoolmates Derrick May and Kevin Saunderson were impressed and encouraged to get some gear and dabble. Saunderson called himself Model 500. May called himself Rhythim Is Rhythim. The three were all fascinated by the new hard electronic disco beginning to creep out of Chicago and New Jersey called 'house', as well as the usual electro references: Kraftwerk, New Order, Depeche Mode, plus a brand new D.A.F.-influenced Brit industrial band called Nitzer Ebb. By 1986, May had founded his own indie label, put all those things together, and invented a new sound. They called it techno.

'Nude Photo' still sounds like the future – all sleek lines and nagging irritants, melancholy melody, factory-piston percussion and a whiff of decay in its queasy, trebly synth-string sirens; the Detroit economic collapse, perhaps, that May and co. wanted to escape without leaving their own bedrooms. A girl giggles happily and it doesn't fit this alien noise, but it *does*, for the same reasons that Kraftwerk and The Human League and Pet Shop Boys and Mantronix – from all of whom May borrows *something* – sounded so human, so liberated, beside and inside their machines. 'Nude Photo' is still so moving and beautiful that 14 years of stuff that exists in its name barely comes close.

IF I WAS YOUR GIRLFRIEND

PRINCE
PRODUCED AND WRITTEN BY PRINCE
PAISLEY PARK/JUNE 1987
UK CHART: 20

So, you make what is your best album, your creative triumph, and it turns out to be a commercial failure. You release what may well be your finest single, and it doesn't chart *at all* in America. What gives? Well, let's look at the evidence.

'If I Was Your Girlfriend' is a love song that takes on a different, yet equally valid, meaning depending on the gender or sexuality of the singer. Just to make that point, the lead vocals are credited to 'Camille', which we know is just Prince speeded up, or, if you prefer, his feminine side. 'Camille', over the loveliest, most limpid and playful electro-funk, then proceeds to wonder how his/her woman would react to him/her if he/she were a woman/lesbian/best friend. Prince then goes on to get so excited about this idea he virtually climaxes all over the track like a randy chipmunk, but you're never quite sure if the excitement comes from the thought of being her lover or her lesbian lover or her mate or a woman plain and simple or . . .

What Prince had found out was that, in the new post-AIDS hip-hop climate, America could deal with a black man threatening them, or even threatening to fuck their mothers, but not with him being effeminate, not even as a fantasy, no matter how erotic or beautiful that fantasy may be. From now on, Prince was rampant butchness personified. There's a fair argument that his music never quite recovered. Sylvester turned in his grave.

IT'S A SIN

PET SHOP BOYS
PRODUCED BY JULIAN MENDELSOHN (ADDITIONAL
MIX AND PRODUCTION BY STEPHEN HAGUE)/WRITTEN
BY NEIL TENNANT AND CHRIS LOWE
PARLOPHONE/JUNE 1987
UK CHART: 1

You know, every time a Pet Shop Boys single turns up I just want to stand up and cheer. This ultimate celebration and rejection of Catholic guilt always reminds me that, some time after its release, Jimmy Somerville of The Communards started having a go at Tennant and Lowe for not coming out. What on earth *did* he think this was about?

I KNOW YOU GOT SOUL/ERIC B & RAKIM

I KNOW YOU GOT SOUL

ERIC B & RAKIM

PRODUCED AND WRITTEN BY ERIC B & RAKIM
COOLTEMPO/JUNE 1987
DID NOT CHART
(REMIXED AND REISSUED FEBRUARY 1988: REACHED
NO. 13)

I'M BAD

LL COOL J

PRODUCED AND WRITTEN BY JAMES TODD SMITH,
BOBBY ERVIN, DWAYNE SIMON AND DARRYL PIERCE
DEF JAM/JUNE 1987
UK CHART: 71

YOU'RE GONNA GET YOURS

PUBLIC ENEMY

PRODUCED BY BILL STEPHNEY, HANK SHOCKLEE AND
CARL RYDER/WRITTEN BY CARLTON RIDENHOUR AND
HANK SHOCKLEE
DEF JAM/JUNE 1987
DID NOT CHART

On these three power-packed jams, James Todd Smith aka LL Cool J, William Griffin aka Rakim and Carlton Ridenhour aka Carl Ryder aka Chuck D represent separate sides of rap's Black Superman complex. LL rides a prowling, blaring funk interrupted by the sirens of hapless radio cops on his tail, and works himself into megalomaniacal hysteria with preposterous similes and metaphors that rain down on the listener, leaving you stunned at the sheer brassneck of his megaton ego. But somehow you want to believe that he's 'Like Jaws – My hand is like a shark's fin' because the image is so wild and his voice is so thrilling and anyway, as he says himself, 'Even when I'm braggin' – I'm bein' sincere.' Lines crash into each other, words and rhythms bend to his will, he tells us he's insane, as tasty as a biscuit, that when he retires he'll be 'worshipped like an old battleship'. At song's end the cops are bemused, terrified, calling for back-up, as even their radios have been taken over by his scabrous tones, switched to the LL frequency forever.

By contrast, Rakim is a father figure, his gruff but buttery voice dominating and rebooting the music with depth and easy authority. His and Eric's funk is a frantic, rootsy, scratched-up retooling of the early '70s golden era, the rhythm to Bobby Byrd's 'I Know You Got Soul' that led to James Brown-produced beats being everywhere in rap for many years, making the JB's rhythm section of Clyde Stubblefield and Bootsy Collins the Sly & Robbie of the era without them even meeting their employers. Whereas Cool J's music came with the space for him to declaim, Rakim had to break through the music's completeness via the gravity of his voice and of his lyrics. His blend of street boast and cerebral vocabulary made him sound almost spiritual – a tough but benevolent preacher with intellect. His opening shot – 'It's bin a long time/I shouldna left you/Without a strong rhyme to step to' – implied that he had been buried in some ancient tomb just waiting for the right moment to rise and save hip-hop. The song produced rap slogan after rap slogan – 'pump up the volume', 'fat gold chain', 'drop the mic', 'I'm wet 'cos you're sweatin' me', 'microphone fiend', 'I get hype', 'constant elevation', 'show and prove' and the final 'Rakim a-say peace'. Between times he pictures himself as helpless in the face of his destiny ('When I'm writing I'm trapped in between the lines'), he rejects rap's youth rebellion angle ('Rakim gets stronger as I get older'), and he displays wordplay of dazzling dexterity ('Whoever's outta hand I'ma give 'em handles/Light 'em up blow 'em out like candles'). He chews the words over, and raps like a great singer sings, subtly changing scan and pitch for interpretive emphasis. This and the pair's previous 'Eric B For President' raised the level of the entire game, in the same way that Hendrix or Coltrane broadened the scope of guitar and sax.

Which just leaves hip-hop's political wing. Second Public Enemy single 'You're Gonna Get Yours' shows why many labelled Public Enemy 'the greatest rock 'n' roll band in the world' in the absence of an actual rock band worthy of the title. Beginning with a roar of engines and chugging grunge-funk guitar, before crunching trebly industrial drums, shrieking tyres and thunking scratches slip straight through to top gear, Chuck D reinvents a rock cliché. The gleaming car as chick magnet becomes gleaming car as bulletproof protection against oppression and symbol of an angry community. He and co-rapper Flavor Flav (William Drayton) attack this proposition with contrasting gusto, Chuck all fire and brimstone Luther King moral strength, Flav with comic astonishment, goading his leader to increasingly incendiary proclamations of black posse power. The highpoint comes when Chuck is hauled into court for speeding, refuses to accept any law but his own, and slips in a tribute to his favourite rapper and labelmate LL Cool J and the

TRUE FAITH/NEW ORDER
PAGE 256

most over-the-top penis metaphor ever. 'So what if the judge charges me contempt?/I'll rub my boomerang 'cos I'm feeling proud/And I couldn't even hear it 'cos my radio's loud.' The band holler the double-edged joke of the title, a promise to the righteous, a threat to the suckers. The music rocks like a black Clash had been programmed into the machines.

I heard these three records and felt tall, as big as a wall.

TRUE FAITH

NEW ORDER

PRODUCED AND WRITTEN BY NEW ORDER AND
STEPHEN HAGUE
FACTORY/JULY 1987
UK CHART: 4

Another case of give and take. When the Pet Shop Boys hit big they admitted that 'Blue Monday' (see p. 200) was what had kicked them into gear – simply because they couldn't believe a bunch of supposedly dour indie Mancs had made all the sounds in their own heads. New Order realized how alike the bands' muses were, pinched PSB's producer, and tried their hand at some mellow, radio-friendly dance-pop. The finest example was 'True Faith', which nicked the bubbling sequenced bass from 'West End Girls' (see p. 236) (which had been nicked from Madonna's 'Into the Groove') but went for a vague personal love tribute, as per usual. The crashing disco beat, and a chorus of floating and fluorescent sweet sadness anchored Barney Sumner's typically 'Ooh – that'll do' lyrical wanderings, which produced yet another gem of incoherent genius, 'When I was a very small boy/Very small boys talked to me.'

IT'S THE END OF THE WORLD AS WE KNOW IT (AND I FEEL FINE)

R.E.M.

PRODUCED BY SCOTT LITT AND R.E.M./WRITTEN BY
BILL BERRY, PETER BUCK, MIKE MILLS AND
MICHAEL STIPE
I.R.S./AUGUST 1987
DID NOT CHART
(REISSUED IN DECEMBER 1991: REACHED NO. 39)

There are many serious rock types who will tell anyone willing to listen that Athens, Georgia's, avatars of alt-rock went downhill the moment Michael Stipe stopped mumbling gibberish into his fringe over tinny old Byrds riffs. Such masochists, these rock purists. R.E.M. became brilliant right about here, when they'd gathered the confidence to write about the world and reinterpret, rather than revive, the classic rock past.

This startling list-song always sounds best when played behind any bunch of TV images. They don't have to be apocalyptic news images either – the trick works even better over some ninny baking a cake, or whatever. Because the speeding joy of the music somehow makes Stipe's barked checklist of planetary chaos seem like a celebration of everything good about the world that lies between the lines. The reconciliatory last verse's juxtaposition of Lenny Bruce, Leonid Breznhev, Lester Bangs and LEONARD BERNSTEIN! is merry *and* moving, as are the million melodies Stipe seems to find in his band's buzzing blast. R.E.M.? Fun? Better start taking 'em seriously then.

STRONG ISLAND

J.V.C. F.O.R.C.E.

PRODUCED BY J.V.C. F.O.R.C.E./WRITTEN BY
B. TAYLOR, J. WOODSON AND C. SMALL
B-BOY/SEPTEMBER 1987
DID NOT CHART

Apology first. My attempts to trawl print and web for info on the makers of this key rap one-off have drawn a blank. All I know, from my rather low-budget UK copy of their debut album *Doin' Damage*, is what is written above. Extraordinary, really, considering how often this funk monster's opening fuzz-funk guitar riff and tumbling bongo beats have been sampled, and the affection in which it's held by hip-hop diehards.

Presumably, J.V.C. F.O.R.C.E. come from Long Island, the New York home turf shared by Public Enemy and Eric B & Rakim (although one of the two rappers suddenly announces he's from Brooklyn, so go figure). The track nicks its title sample from PE, that candle line from Rakim, and introduces the concept of being 'As serious as cancer' – a line that got that bloke from Euro-popsters Snap in big trouble when he used it on 'Oops Up'. The track rolls and rolls on two horn-sample stabs and the slurred, quick-quick-slow rhythms of the rhymes – just another example of rap's routine, roughhouse triumph at its 1987–89 peak.

PAID IN FULL/ERIC B & RAKIM

RENT

PET SHOP BOYS

PRODUCED BY JULIAN MENDELSOHN (REMIXED AND
EDITED BY STEPHEN HAGUE)/WRITTEN BY
NEIL TENNANT AND CHRIS LOWE
PARLOPHONE/OCTOBER 1987
UK CHART: 8

The Shoppies' success at sneaking dark real-life complexities into charts and hearts undercover of light electro-pop remains unparalleled. Despite the immediate implication of the word 'rent', the song is sung from the perspective of a kept *woman*, counting her blessings, colluding with her sugar daddy, pinpointing her ambivalence towards her life and her cynicism with both wistful regret and deadpan greed, leavened by genuine affection for her keeper. The song is slow and typically grandiose in melody and texture, but the faintly martial honk of the staccato synth-hook suggests that the protagonist has planned her life like a battle strategy. Despite her lack of economic power, she is in control, adaptable, prepared for the worst. Every war has casualties. In this case they're just little pieces of her soul.

PAID IN FULL

ERIC B & RAKIM

PRODUCED AND WRITTEN BY ERIC B & RAKIM
(REMIXED BY COLDCUT)
FOURTH & BROADWAY/OCTOBER 1987
UK CHART: 15

Or another way of saying: 'If I'm gonna get fucked by The Man, then I want what it's worth.'

Rap, conscious that early pioneers had been screwed by dodgy entrepreneurs, had already talked a great deal about the importance of financial reward. But this mellow rap-soul classic, based upon the fluid bass melody of 'Don't Look Any Further' by The Temptations' Dennis Edwards, defined rap's terms and conditions. Rather than pretending that gold and Cadillacs come easy, Rakim gives us a chocolate-coated survivalist anthem, unashamed to admit that he's struggled to get the 'dead presidents' that now fill his pockets.

Whereas the original album cut was short, low-key and thoughtful – despite its booming beats and conversational interjections and torrid turntablisms from Eric Barrier – white

Londoners Jonathan More and Matt Black, better known as Coldcut, Britain's first truly modern dance remix/production crew, made it into catchy, bright, inspirational pop by taking the streets of Long Island on a seven-minute trip through a world of found voices and Brit wit. 'This is a journey into sound,' a pompous BBC voice announced, before the sampled Arabic croon of Ofra Haza gave the track a hazy, fragrant, exotic erotica. Eric and R reportedly did not approve, until they got the royalty cheque and realized how much rent it would pay in full.

REBEL WITHOUT A PAUSE

PUBLIC ENEMY

PRODUCED BY BILL STEPHNEY/WRITTEN BY
CARLTON RIDENHOUR, HANK SHOCKLEE,
NORMAN ROGERS AND ERIC SADLER
DEF JAM/NOVEMBER 1987
UK CHART: 37

It was a hot day, sometime in the summer of '87, long before I'd heard anything by PE. Brixton High Road was clammy and chaotic as I walked up to the traffic lights opposite Brixton tube. I was heading somewhere but nowhere. Then this car pulls up at the lights and the pavement starts to shake, as if Brixton were finally giving in and falling off the edge of the world. Someone, some*thing* screamed, an inhuman shriek of pain that climbed to a shrill, tortured peak and then fell back and began all over again. A mean angry black voice hectored and bullied the crowd of shoppers, boozers and beggars. It sounded like the last voice you would ever hear. Jesus fuck! What is . . . shit . . . it's the car. The car *stereo*. A record. I began to giggle and then froze with concentration, but it was over. The car had driven off at green. What else would it do?

And that, my friends, was my introduction to PE and 'Rebel Without a Pause'. It took months of listening to pirate radio, buying their LP on spec and finding it wasn't there, getting another job in a record shop, and a belated UK release before I finally had a copy in my sweaty hands. I put it on and shivered and time stopped and I couldn't work out what was screaming (it was a JB's sax sample being strangled) or what was making the walls shake (it was the underground explosion PE called bass) or how to process everything Chuck was saying ('You're losing 'em!' as Flav rightly sneered) or . . .

Anyway, it was the second time a bit of black plastic had changed my life. How? Well, in immediate terms, it made me confront the fact that my father was Jamaican, that I was part

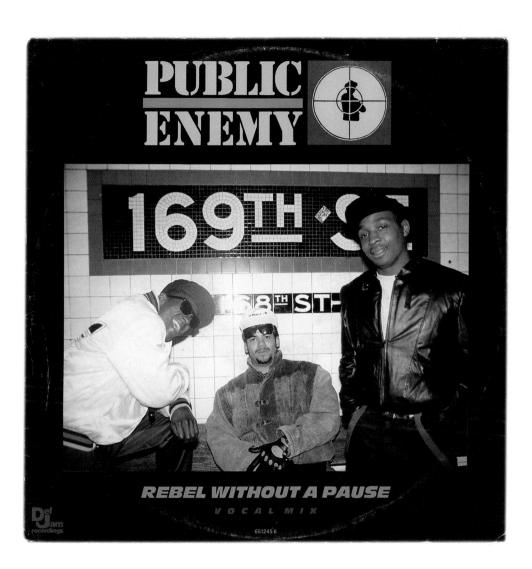

REBEL WITHOUT A PAUSE/PUBLIC ENEMY
PAGE 258

black even though I looked all white, for the first time in my life. I began to read black politics and history and tried to work out where I fitted in, why I wasn't threatened but emboldened by Chuck D's furious denunciations and declarations and awe-inspiring deconstructions of black pride.

And, on a less profound but no less exciting level, it made me fall in love with the possibilities of music again, made me truly *believe* in a group. The Bomb Squad, the PE production team, called their noise 'music's worst nightmare'. They were wrong. It was the relief and the reality of waking up.

THE ONE I LOVE

R.E.M.

PRODUCED BY SCOTT LITT AND R.E.M./WRITTEN BY
BILL BERRY, PETER BUCK, MIKE MILLS AND MICHAEL
STIPE
I.R.S./NOVEMBER 1987
UK CHART: 51

One of the most cynical and mean-minded love songs ever, 'The One I Love' got R.E.M. their first minor Brit chart placing and added another dimension to the ever-expanding enigma that is Michael Stipe. After all his early mysteries, you had to admire the brutal honesty of his telling an ex-lover that they were just 'A simple prop/To occupy my time.' The full truth about why he's saying it resides in the keening lament of his voice, the tough country-rock revisionism of the music, the longing drama in those chord changes; a sound of harsh lessons learned, of regret and loss hardened into whatever the singer needs to say and feel for the purposes of survival. Perhaps Stipe and Gloria Gaynor should have talked.

HEAVEN IS A PLACE ON EARTH

BELINDA CARLISLE

PRODUCED BY RICK NOWELS/WRITTEN BY
ELLEN SHIPLEY AND RICK NOWELS
VIRGIN/NOVEMBER 1987
UK CHART: 1

I don't hold with all that 'Men are from Mars, women are shopping for shoes' malarkey, but 'Heaven . . .' provides more evidence that the best female love songs in this book are all joy and multiple orgasms and precipitous thrill, while the best bloke

ones are all bitter castration and twisted kiss-offs. Carlisle's croon is Stevie Nicks without the pomposity and with a glowing assurance, and the way she growls 'I'm not afraid . . . anymore!' is like Kate Bush after she and her hound first did The Dog (see 'Hounds of Love' p. 242). The whole thing suggests that Belinda's heaven is a place a lot more specific, and easy to reach, than the big old Earth.

FAIRYTALE OF NEW YORK

THE POGUES FEATURING KIRSTY MACCOLL

PRODUCED BY STEVE LILLYWHITE/WRITTEN BY
SHANE MACGOWAN AND JEM FINER
POGUE MAHONE/EMI/NOVEMBER 1987
UK CHART: 2

Like Cristina (see p. 170), The Pogues found cold comfort in spending Christmas in New York. And that's good, because that idea led to the only hardy perennial Yuletide pop standard that hits home, that attempts to make sense of both the bad memories and the new starts of the season, in all their complexities.

MacGowan's 'Fairytale . . .' balances love and hate, the desire for change and the need for security, the agony of failure and the potential to overcome it, youth and old age, travel and homesickness, beauty and decay, profanity and poetry, observation and confession, the hard-boiled and the sentimental . . . all human life is here in his story of two Irish exiles and their inseparable destinies. Because Christmas here is not the reason for the song, but the backdrop to a meditation on whether a relationship can survive the weaknesses and broken dreams of its protagonists. Because Christmas has a habit of making you confront your life. My God. What have I done?

While the knockabout comedy of Shane's and the late Kirsty MacColl's traded insults stand out (and radio's casual accommodation of 'junk', 'faggot', 'scumbag' and 'yer arse' gave the first signs that our broadcasting nannies were ready to at least start letting pop out without a coat on), it's the final verse that gets you every time, with its sudden, gut-wrenchingly truthful lurch from cruelty – Shane: 'I could've been someone . . .' Kirsty: 'So could anyone' – to Shane's gentle, heartfelt plea for forgiveness: 'Can't make it all alone/I've built my dreams around you.' Blub.

1988

1988

A pop-culture comparison between 1976–77 and 1987–88 is irresistible. Both saw the beginnings of a rumble of change in the first year and the full youth-tribe explosion, complete with scene anthems, surprise mainstream hits, bandwagon jumpers and tabloid shock horror headlines in the following year. And, in a similar manner of development to punk, house The Music came from America, but it was English kids who turned it into the 'rave' lifestyle, complete with the smiley face, the popular upsurge in drug use, the love 'n' peace subtext and the applied democracy of dressing down for sweaty dancefloor action. A flood of new Brit DJ-led dance labels and acts – M.A.R.R.S, Coldcut, Bomb the Bass, S'Express, Double Trouble, Beats International (the last two featuring one Norman Cook, former bass player of worthy pop janglers The Housemartins) – rose to meet the demand.

The two major differences between acid house and punk were obvious, though. This time, the middle-English moral panic was over The Kids taking drugs, rather than dropping their trousers to the Queen. Also, if punk as an underground cult lasted just two years, between the Sex Pistols' first gig and the release of 'God Save the Queen', acid house proper lasted maybe one, before the October 1988 release of cash-in nightmare single 'They Call It Acieed' by D-Mob and a chancer called Gary Haisman made it into a pop fad overnight. Going to a Man Utd match and hearing the hard lads wailing 'AC-*IEEED*!!!' for 90 minutes might have been weird and funny, but you knew it meant the end of the original impulse, that acid house was already uncool. Over the next few years the scene would splinter into a myriad of sub-scenes and genres: deep house, techno, garage, Balearic, hardcore, indie-dance, jungle – all roughly split along the same old race, sexuality and gender lines again.

At the same time, hip-hop made a sudden leap from a mix of cult scene and novelty pop to fully fledged recorded artform and million-seller, led by Public Enemy, Eric B & Rakim and EPMD. The leap in quality and depth of these acts provided the foundation for rap's Golden Year, as the new superstars were joined by inspired one-offs and created a brief moment where black consciousness and rebellion met pure party pleasure and anything seemed possible. Simultaneously, an alternative rock scene that had slumped into a coma of twee janglings and apologetic crappiness woke up, stretched out, and prepared for a new period of glory led by the Factory and Creation labels, and this time was sussed and sharp enough to meld with the new dance wave without going beige. Even rock, pop and soul's few luddites made records that both loomed large through their defiance, and seemed to comment on what was happening around and without them. In the wider world (and despite Bush's inevitable presidential election victory) Gorbachev's dramatic Eastern Bloc reforms, the huge Nelson Mandela Birthday Concert at Wembley, even tiny Wimbledon's unlikely FA Cup Final win over mighty Liverpool, made it seem like The Year of the Underdog, and the harbinger of new, kinder, nuclear-free, optimistic times.

1988 was a pop year bettered only by, and similar in adventure to, 1979. But this time, instead of the end of an impulse, it was the beginning of everything we would love about the 1990s. The stuff we wouldn't came later.

Honourable mentions: Renegade Soundwave/'Cocaine Sex' (Rhythm King) and 'Biting My Nails' (Mute); The House of Love/'Destroy the Heart' (Creation); Sugar Bear/'Don't Scandalize Mine' (Cooltempo); Black Riot/'A Day in the Life' (Champion); Unique 3/'The Theme' (Ten); The Fall/'Big New Prinz'/'Wrong Place, Right Time No. 2' (Beggars Banquet); R.E.M./'Stand' (Warners); The Sugarcubes/'Birthday' (One Little Indian); A Guy Called Gerald/'Voodoo Ray' (Rham); Gregory Isaacs/'Rumours' (Greensleeves)

ACID TRACKS

PHUTURE

PRODUCED BY DJ PIERRE/WRITTEN BY H. JACKSON,
N. JONES AND E. SMITH
TRAX/JANUARY 1988
DID NOT CHART

When, at the end of 1987, punters started coming into G&M in Elephant & Castle where I worked and asking, 'Got any acid house, mate?' I tried not to look too uncool and just pointed towards the house import section, whereupon said punter would give me a withering look of pity and contempt before heading back out of the door. My only exposure to house of any kind had been what I'd heard at the Heaven club and the two big Chicago house hits of 1986 – Steve 'Silk' Hurley's 'Jack Your Body' and Farley 'Jackmaster' Funk's 'Love Can't Turn Around', which was fronted by a flamboyant Sylvester-on-high-cholesterol type called Darryl Pandy. I figured, like a lot of people, that it was a bit of a novelty disco throwback. Then the Phuture came into the shop and began to fly straight back out again.

Phuture were DJ Pierre, Spanky and Herb J, three young black Chicago kids who were part of the nascent house scene. Pierre DJ'd at some local clubs so, when the three got together and decided to make a track based almost entirely on the squelching sci-fi B-movie sound of the Roland TB-303 synthesizer, they had an in. They took it to scene Mecca The Music Box, house guru Ron Hardy put it on, and the dancers, who were already used to some pretty weird Euro-industrial records in the mix, went nuts. Chicago's only house label, Trax, put it out on Hardy's and young producer Marshall Jefferson's say-so. The rest is youthquake.

There were many other Trax label records out at roughly the same time doing roughly the same thing, but 'Acid Tracks' was the longest, the deepest, the headfuckingest. It fascinated anyone who wanted more than hard disco and, of course, it gave a name to the biggest pop-culture revolution in this book. Because, although punk was big news and big rebellion and big fashion, acid house democratized a dance scene that had grown moody, retro, and racially segregated since the warehouse parties of the early '80s, and, because of its largely apolitical, hedonistic, optimistic nature, affected pop far more deeply than punk ever could. On top of that, 'Acid Tracks' begat the Second Summer of Love, the taking of a new drug (at least, ecstacy was new to ordinary clubbers, despite being a fixture on the exclusive side of the US club scene for a decade), a whole bunch of parental hand-wringing, an illegal party scene, a change in the law to stop that scene, and a virtual end to dressing up to go dancing – apart from on the gay circuit, of course.

So, Acid Tracks then. A tuneless and anti-musical 12-minute instrumental machine freak-out that gave birth to everything good and bad about clubbing, drug-taking and fashion in the '90s. Not bad for three amateur kids on a tiny label in a windy city.

I SHOULD BE SO LUCKY

KYLIE MINOGUE

PRODUCED AND WRITTEN BY MIKE STOCK,
MATT AITKEN AND PETE WATERMAN
PWL/JANUARY 1988
UK CHART: 1

Lucky, lucky, lucky.

BRING THE NOISE

PUBLIC ENEMY

PRODUCED BY BILL STEPHNEY, HANK SHOCKLEE AND
CARL RYDER/WRITTEN BY HANK SHOCKLEE,
CARLTON RIDENHOUR AND ERIC SADLER
DEF JAM/JANUARY 1988
UK CHART: 32

A voice intoning the words 'Too black! Too strong!' prefaced the most famous opening lines in rap – Flavor Flav howling, 'YEEEAHHH BOYEEE!!!' and Chuck D following with the immortal 'Bass! How low can you go?/Death row – what a brother know' – as Chuck D became confident enough in PE's overnight impact to fill in more details about their aims, ideals and views. The result was a record that maybe said too much, too soon and gave the anti-rap lobby a chance to accuse them of racism, and fans like me pause for doubt.

Chuck's obsession with a racist media begins here, as critics who didn't seem to be criticizing that much get dissed, and he issues an unforgettable challenge to DJs. 'Radio stations I question their blackness/They call themselves black but we'll see if they'll play this.' The problem comes with his paranoid vision of being jailed for his rhymes, and his urgent advice that we should all listen to – even follow – the 'prophet' Louis Farrakhan. Minister Farrakhan was, and still is, the mainman of the Nation of Islam, the organization that believe the devilish

KEITH SWEAT
I WANT HER

I WANT HER/KEITH SWEAT

white man was invented in a laboratory by an evil scientist, that women should be breeding machines, that black homosexuality doesn't exist at all, and, as all the relevant evidence suggests, had Malcolm X assassinated when he left the Nation, visited Mecca, and began to question whether racial segregation was a good idea. Farrakhan had already proved himself fond of making the odd anti-Semitic statement, and PE member Professor Griff, presumably taking Chuck at his word, followed suit and was thrown out of the band before the *Fear of a Black Planet* album.

The noise the band brought us here was incendiary: fast, loud, rabble-rousing and panicked, tongue-twisting, full of incredible metaphors and bizarre references to Sonny Bono and Yoko Ono that I've never been able to work out. But my love of Public Enemy and their music and most of their message remains undercut by their success in plugging the Nation of Islam, who were suggesting that mixed-race boys like me shouldn't even exist while the legacy of apartheid was still killing black children in South Africa.

Base. How low *can* you go?

CARS AND GIRLS

PREFAB SPROUT
PRODUCED BY JON KELLY AND
PADDY MCALOON/WRITTEN BY PADDY MCALOON
KITCHENWARE/CBS/FEBRUARY 1988
UK CHART: 44

Paddy's deliberate misunderstanding of Springsteen is just an excuse for a great set of motor metaphors and a deft parody of American AOR. And, despite his penchant for irony getting the better of him with his breathily sneered 'We are deeply concerned', the Durham desperado gets his meditation on the dashing of the rock 'n' roll dream upon the rocks of reality – and his surprise roar of a Bruce impression on 'pretty streamers' – just about spot on. Any implied misanthropy in the song is cast adrift in the final verse, as the singer observes that 'Life's no cruise with a cool chick/Too many folks feelin' carsick', before ending with an affectionate, but double-edged shrug, 'Guess this world needs its dreamers – may they never wake up.' There are probably no two characters in this book as opposite as McAloon and Chuck D, but the temptation to hear 'Cars and Girls' as a footnote to 'You're Gonna Get Yours' (see p. 254) is irresistible.

I WANT HER

KEITH SWEAT
PRODUCED AND WRITTEN BY KEITH SWEAT AND
TEDDY RILEY
ELEKTRA/FEBRUARY 1988
UK CHART: 26

While the cooler kids who came into G&M wanted to hear and buy acid house and hip-hop, the slightly older majority wanted their traditional Old Kent Road fare – soul music. At one point we were flogging so much of Keith Sweat's debut *Make It Last Forever* album that it felt like sweatshop labour. And the former Keith Crier cut such an unlikely and old-fashioned figure too, with his lopsided cuddly lover grin and range of Lionel Richie knitwear and strange and unpleasant choice of sobriquet. But the New Yorker had one Teddy Riley in his corner, the man who, through his work with Guy and Wreckx-n-Effect, had invented 'new jack swing' alias 'swingbeat' – the hip-hop-meets-soul precursor to what we now know, despite its total absence of blues, as R&B.

'I Want You' is a synthetic, syncopated and agreeably cheesy slice of pop-soul, packed fit to burst with one-finger horn stabs, choppy beats, over-egged boyish harmonies (which went all doo-wop creamy on the word 'dream') and Sweat's nasal whine. But the hook was The Hook – a three-note chant on the title that stood at an atonal left-angle from the backing melody, yet somehow fitted perfectly, lodged immovably in your head, and got the moon-June love theme down into the dust of hot lust. Those three notes alone make 'I Want Her', if not the first, then definitely the best of swing's early hits.

PUSH IT/I AM DOWN

SALT 'N' PEPA
PRODUCED AND WRITTEN BY
HURBY 'LUVBUG' AZOR
FFRR AND CHAMPION/FEBRUARY 1988
UK CHART: 2

At last – rap's feminine side. But before we get on with celebrating girl group/backroom boy genius, let me explain the two record labels above.

'Push It' came out in February, with the pop-rockin' 'I Am Down', on FFRR and reached No. 41. Champion also licensed 'Push It' a few months later and coupled it with a version of old soul classic 'Tramp'. This time 'Push It' picked up UK daytime radio play on the back of enormous success in the States and, with the FFRR 12-inch still in the shops, both versions began to shift. So the chart compilers combined the sales and 'Push It' just missed topping the charts. Got it? No? It's the best I can do.

Queens's resident Hurby Azor put words into the mouths of two babes, his girlfriend Cheryl 'Salt' James and Sandy 'Pepa' Denton. Along with their DJ Pamela 'Spinderella' Greene, the pair purveyed Azor's smart, light, eclectic blend of rap, pop, rock, roll and anything else Azor could adapt to his vision of hip pop, topped by bragging, sexy lyrics tinged with a playful feminism. Their biggest and best hit revives the old is-it-dancing-or-is-it-shagging? rock riddle over an almost Brit '80s electro-pop sound buoyed by the best ever use of that shake 'n' sniff machine percussion effect. B-side 'I Am Down' rocks out sparsely on what sounds like the guitar riff from The Sweet's 'Ballroom Blitz' and, as the ladies put it, 'sticks inside your ears like wax'.

The girls, complete with a new Spinderella, later decided that being managed, produced and written for by one of their boyfriends was kinda limiting and gave Hurby the heave-ho. They did fine without him. The 'Luvbug', sadly, proved to be no Beatle.

KING OF THE BEATS

MANTRONIX
PRODUCED BY MANTRONIK/WRITTEN BY MANTRONIK AND LUVAH
TEN/MARCH 1988
UK CHART: 72

The most far-sighted tune of a far-sighted year was a B-side. A-side 'Join Me Please' was business as usual. But, on the flip of the 12-inch there was an instrumental that is still largely acknowledged as the key influence on the very British '90s genre called Big Beat.

For the first time, Mantronik takes time off from his beloved machines and splices together a collage of old funk samples – massive echoing breakbeat, a funky flute riff, wah-wah guitar – joined by wailing panic button sirens and catchphrase chants. The sound was remarkably similar to both J. Walter Negro's 'Shoot the Pump' (see p. 166) and 'The Adventures of Grandmaster Flash on the Wheels of Steel' (see p. 170), but with added turbo thrust, production power and avant garde, 'journey into sound' cheek and innovation, and, as those sirens exploded over the intro, a vibe of barely controlled mania. The track

dropped and rose in tempo, wandered miles away from where it began, went on for ages and broke every disco and hip-hop rule in the book. Various future breakbeat bods kept it canistered for future reference.

YOU GOTS TO CHILL

EPMD
PRODUCED AND WRITTEN BY ERICK SERMON AND PARRISH SMITH
COOLTEMPO/MARCH 1988
DID NOT CHART

After that bunch you need a rest, courtesy of Erick and Parrish Making Dollars. These hip-hop New Yorkers made Rakim sound hyper. Over a growling, claustrophobic meld of Zapp's P-funk milestone 'More Bounce to the Ounce' and Kool & The Gang's 'Jungle Boogie', they slurred and lisped their brags and threats with a stoned somnambulist swagger, their attempts to turn off, nod out and order a pizza rudely interrupted by K-La-Boss's vicious scratches, the off-key sampled chants, and the shotgun guitar flicks. All the rap fans getting tired of jumping around made the deep-funk E & P the new heroes of horizontal hip-hop.

GIVE IT TO ME

BAM BAM
PRODUCED AND WRITTEN BY CHRIS 'BAM BAM' WESTBROOK
SERIOUS/MARCH 1988
UK CHART: 65

Two relatively new developments in mainstream pop consumption and distribution had a negative effect on Chicago's Westbrook and his definitive acid house anthem. Firstly, by the time 'Give It to Me' had received a UK release it had been around for months on US import, meaning that two many house heads had already bought a copy for it to chart high without daytime radio play. Secondly, success on import led to one-off single deals with UK dance labels, rather than long-term, artist-developing album contracts. The house, drum 'n' bass and garage scenemakers would later make this work for them by starting their own labels. But Westbrook, after two classic singles in 1988, disappeared into the dance ether.

'Give It to Me' worked fine simply as a drum track in its opening minute or so. But then the pounding four-to-the-floor drums, crashing cymbals, swinging bongo breakdowns, and a girl's orgasmic sigh cut up and looped as a rhythmic 'AHH-AHH-AHH-OH!' are joined by the year's toughest, diving and leaping acidic bassline. The vocals consist of nothing more than a double-tracked black guy repeating the title and occasionally informing the sighing woman, 'I'm a man, baby!' in a macho Melle Mel manner. Not that she, or we, needed telling twice.

In the tiny, smoke-filled room at the Clink Street acid house jams near London Bridge, 'Give It to Me' blended with the strobe lights and gave you a premonition of Viagra. As rave became increasingly about drugs, it's easy to forget how records like this made early acid house sexy.

SIDEWALKING (EXTENDED VERSION)

THE JESUS AND MARY CHAIN
PRODUCED BY WILLIAM AND JIM REID AND
JOHN LODER/WRITTEN BY WILLIAM AND JIM REID
BLANCO Y NEGRO/MARCH 1988
UK CHART: 30

Rock 'n' roll, however, had not been unashamedly sexy for a great many years. Blunderbuss bombast on one side, twee jingle-jangle shag-fear on the other. It took the Mary Chain to remind British rock how easy and thrilling getting down and dirty could be.

The Reids are still seen as unreconstructed goth-rockers. But their finest single wore baggy pants before the fact, with its hip-hop-influenced beatbox blams and hip-grinding two-note bass. The 12-inch version is the full story though, as William unleashes a long, metallic slew of post-PiL guitar slashes over the loping rhythm, before the bass, the blues chords, and his brother Jim swagger and stagger in like zombie gunslingers of lurrrve. Unlike Chuck and Paddy, Jim ain't got no wheels and almost crawls the five miles home (at night, of course), tongue licking the pavement in anticipation of what's waiting for him. For a song that was probably inspired by missing the night bus home after the pub, it is the sleaziest fun you'll ever have with two peely-wally[3] Scots.

CHRISTINE

THE HOUSE OF LOVE
PRODUCED BY THE HOUSE OF LOVE (MIXED BY PAT COLLIER)/WRITTEN BY GUY CHADWICK
CREATION/APRIL 1988
DID NOT CHART

Guy Chadwick of Camberwell, south London, had the perfect band name for 1988. Sadly, he also had one of the least fashionable sounds. But never mind, because The House of Love made throwback classics and provided further proof that Creation was on the verge of living up to Alan McGee's blags and boasts.

Coming over like Lloyd Cole fronting Echo and The Bunnymen, Chadwick's enigmatic love songs were carried by the shimmering spangle of Terry Bickers's post-psychedelic guitar. With its running-uphill rhythm, three-note p(l)unk bass riff, soaring Bickers interjections and magical minor-key bridges, 'Christine' was less a pledge of love than a hymn to an ideal vision of love itself – a series of us-against-the-world and '60s harmony-pop clichés revived by the band's own awe at the beauty of the noises they could make. It was one of those keep-the-faith records that made you believe in rock transcendence all over again, and it still sounds timeless, partly because it was so out of time in the first place.

IT TAKES TWO

ROB BASE & DJ EZ ROCK
PRODUCED BY WILLIAM HAMILTON AND ROB BASE/WRITTEN BY ROBERT GINYARD
CITYBEAT/APRIL 1988
UK CHART: 24

YEAH! WHOO!!! The very epitome of Theory One.

Base (Robert Ginyard) and EZ Rock (Rodney Bryce) were Harlem hip-hoppers with just one great thing in 'em. But what a thing it was. 'It Takes Two' defines both rap's resuscitation of James Brown's beats and 1988's hip-hop happiness – the big splurge of doowutchyoolike before it all started to get too serious and too easy to niche market towards angry young men. The Rakims and PEs and EPMDs might have got the hardcore respect, but Base and EZ grabbed the ladies on the dancefloor, with one of those tracks that will never fail to get a body movin' at any kind of party.

YOU GOTS TO CHILL/EPMD
PAGE 267

It's a breathless rhythm underpinned by deep bass drops, as Rob's friendly come-hither boasts ride that soon-to-be-done-to-death 'Yeah-wooh!' loop from Lyn Collins's 'Think (About It)', which was produced by the Soul Brother Number One. From there on in it's flailing limbs and strange laughs, as Base gives us future catchphrases ('I'm not a sucka so I don't need a bodyguard!'), weirdness caused by speed ('Can't stand sex,' he appears to inform us, until we finally worked out he meant 'sess', yet another slang term for dope) and a magnificent slide into linguistic chaos, where hastily rhymed gibberish meets handbags-at-dawn: 'Bro'! – I got an ego! – Yo! – Talking to me? – No? – Oh!' . . . all in one machine-gun line. The long-term cred problem for Base was that he sounded about as hard as a carpet slipper. But that – and the final orgy of 'It takes two to make-a . . .' scratching – was what made the single an all-time classic.

THE KING OF ROCK 'N' ROLL

PREFAB SPROUT

PRODUCED BY THOMAS DOLBY/WRITTEN BY
PADDY MCALOON
KITCHENWARE/CBS/APRIL 1988
UK CHART: 7

'Cars and Girls''s (see p. 266) evil twin, from Dolby's self-parodying over-production, through its obvious hatred of rock and everything it stands – stood? – for, to *that* chorus, an academic's elliptical sneer at inspired rock meaninglessness. And then there are the Elvis impressions, the synth skronks and skrees, the Rik-Mayall-with-menaces insult (aimed at himself? Rock fans? Rock stars? His listeners?): 'You were never fleet of foot . . . *Hippy.*' The song was so deliberately out of time it met itself on the way back, particularly when he Elvis-croons, 'New broom, this room, sweep it clean,' a call that was being heeded by acid house hippies who *were* fleet of foot.

RUN'S HOUSE

RUN-D.M.C.

PRODUCED BY RUN-D.M.C. AND DAVY D/WRITTEN BY
DARRYL MCDANIELS, JOSEPH SIMMONS,
JASON MIZELL AND DAVID REEVES
LONDON/APRIL 1988
UK CHART: 37

As we reach our final – and finest – Run-D.M.C. entry, it's worth noting just what their career trajectory says about hip-hop. Their decline in popularity and influence had already begun by this time, as they had a go at everything from movies to sampling The Stone Roses. Their stock fell dramatically, and they learned all about the unforgiving nature of hip-hop fans who felt an act had 'fallen off'. Run got religion, Darryl Mac had voice problems caused by drink and drugs, albums came out fitfully and flopped. It took a house remix (and a breakdance nostalgia video) of early track 'It's Like That' in 1998 to revive their fortunes. But that revival was aimed at kids too young to remember 'Walk This Way', whose new metal heroes have a fetish for old-school rap. The hip-hop diehards, old and new, didn't want to know. It was almost as if the band were resented for having broken down the walls for every rap superstar since – because, I think, they had had to use white-boy rock to make that break. Hip-hop snobbery and its relationship with racial issues and crossover is a murky and confusing world, which has even stalled the career of hip-hop's blackest, Public Enemy.

The ebullient powerplay of 'Run's House' is a key example of this pit of snakes – a record forgotten by the hardcore, but one that provoked an inspired skit between the white collegiate angels played by Ben Affleck and Matt Damon in the movie *Dogma*. It's mainly Run's track, of course, and he sells the idea that he's the world's greatest superstar with never-bettered tongue-defying intensity, as those funky beatbox drums and horn stabs and dramatic slapback echoes batter down the doors of perception of how a pop record should sound. It's a bold and slightly desperate record, as if Run were screaming, 'Come back!' at a black audience streaming outta the doors of his old house.

ANYONE . . ./SMITH & MIGHTY

ANYONE . . .

SMITH & MIGHTY

PRODUCED BY SMITH & MIGHTY/WRITTEN BY
BURT BACHARACH, ROB SMITH AND RAY MIGHTY
THREE STRIPE/MAY 1988
DID NOT CHART

It's been tempting to label any number of 1987–88's house and rap landmarks as the final and inevitable melding of punk and disco . . . or even wait until 1989's 'indie-dance' coming. But this cover of 'Anyone Who Had a Heart' is the one that deserves the accolade. Not because the music has anything to do with either punk or disco trademarks – it is slow, swathed in dope fumes rather than buzzed by speed or E, and is a cover of an old soul classic informed equally by black Britain, Jamaica and hip-hop New York. It also came nowhere near hit status, despite paving the way for many songs that did. And, although it was representative of the community from which it came, it never mentions the place. The reasons why I figure this is the moment, is because it fuses pure dancehall beats and sexy femininity with a courageous punk leap-in-the-dark attitude, and because it made all those mutant disco adventures by the likes of The Slits, The Pop Group and 23 Skidoo into shimmering, sensual pop soul, with both a love, and a complete overhaul, of a classic radio pop melody. Oh yes – and it invented Massive Attack, Soul II Soul, Tricky, Portishead, Bjork, Mo wax, trip hop, The Bristol Sound, Roni Size and just about every British dance record since 1988 that has attempted to meld dub, ambient and hip-hop beats. Ladies and gentlemen, give it up for Smith & Mighty.

Rob and Ray, along with Massive Attack and Nellee Hooper of The Wild Bunch, ruled a soundsystem scene based in the regularly riot-torn St Paul's area of Bristol. Unlike other reggae-based soundsystems, Three Stripe and The Wild Bunch played punk, post-punk and 2-Tone right alongside the reggae, funk and rap basics. It was an equally black and white scene, too, and, like the DJs and dancers in the early hip-hop Bronx, the scene deemed race or genre irrelevant when searching for a good groove. The DJs began to share a collective and co-operative idea of making their own recordings, and 'Anyone . . .' was the first great product of all this low-key two-tone activity.

'Anyone . . .' is a surreal take on reggae soundsystem tradition, where a vocalist will sing their own version of a well-known favourite over a 'dubplate' instrumental. The vocal is pretty, but little more than a sketch. As the spacey beats and song begin, you're expecting a dubbed-up version of the original backing. Instead, what arrives turns everything on its head . . . a synthetic reggae-style bassline that bears no resemblance whatsoever to the singer's melody. It immediately strikes as ugly, just plain *wrong*, until the two are resolved through dark and echoing details – clinking percussion that becomes an insidious counter-melody, sliced-up dancehall exhortations, snatches of the original, dramatic orchestral interruptions, all bathed in dubwise delay. The sadness of Dionne Warwick's classic is revived not by singer or words, but by the liquid mood of the whole – the blue lines, if you will. The overall vibe was not lovelorn, but ominous, threatening, like a journey alone down a blind alley in a rough area.

The record was unclassifiable, at least five years ahead of its time, and only found an audience in some of the more adventurous British hip-hop fans. A few months later, Smith & Mighty produced and put out the first single by their friends Massive Attack.

The pair themselves were too awkward, self-contained and punkish ever to find a place in the mainstream, as one after another of their fellow travellers hopped trippily past them.

THE MERCY SEAT

NICK CAVE AND THE BAD SEEDS

PRODUCED BY NICK CAVE AND THE BAD SEEDS/
WRITTEN BY NICK CAVE AND MICK HARVEY
MUTE/MAY 1988
DID NOT CHART

On the face of it, Cave's bleak anthem of Death Row defiance is the polar opposite to the year's dancefloor revolutions. But the one thing it does share, almost unique for rock at this point, is a rush of sound that refuses to separate instruments into their usual primary-colour boxes. Its wall of white noise is almost impossible to pin down to sources, as if it had been isolated from a passing electric storm and shotgun-married to Cave's vision of the damned.

The thoughts that go through the murderer's mind as he awaits the chair are biblical, philosophical, satirical, the stuff of myth and, famously, southern Gothic literature. They play off crime and punishment, justice and injustice, damnation and redemption, fear and an unholy pride in his crimes. The music starts off dense and charged and yet builds in both tension and release, as you start to pick out violins and pianos and guitar feedback. The record's intensity and complexity are almost unmatched in this book. 'The Mercy Seat' signalled the end of self-destructive junkie punk Cave and the beginning of funny, intelligent and insightful Cave, and received the greatest testament to its stature when covered in 2000 by Johnny Cash, a man whose entire life and work had been about hovering as close to that seat as he could, without getting burned.

BREAK 4 LOVE

RAZE

PRODUCED AND WRITTEN BY VAUGHN MASON
CHAMPION/MAY 1988
UK CHART: 28

Every genre has to have its cheesy bedroom tune, even acid house. Mason and singer Keith Thompson hailed from Washington DC, rather than Chicago or Detroit, and maybe the capital still had a Barry White thang goin' on, because 'Break 4 Love' is exactly what the title says – an unforgettable and much sampled hard disco-funk break and warm circling bassline carrying Thompson's corny boudoir seductions and – surprise! – a laydee's cut-up sighs and orgasmic shrieks. It made a nice, chilled-champagne change from 'Give It to Me' (see p. 267) and, just like Vaughn and Keith with the laydees, it took its time before entry, finally getting into the charts on the last day of the year.

EVERYDAY IS LIKE SUNDAY

MORRISSEY

PRODUCED BY STEPHEN STREET/WRITTEN BY
MORRISSEY AND STEPHEN STREET
HIS MASTER'S VOICE/JUNE 1988
UK CHART: 9

His lyrical advice (see 'Panic' p. 243) to burn down the discos having spectacularly backfired, the Marr-ginalized Moz twirled his quiff – in the absence of a curly black moustache – tied the whole of England to a railway track and waited for the holiday train to Margate to finish the job. Having already written the loveliest melody his employer had ever sung, Street just hires a light orchestra and lets Morrissey weep wistfully over our parents' monochrome and windswept idea of a nice day out. The lyrical observations and pleas for armageddon were Betjeman-obvious, but his melodramatic croon and the strength of the tune made it all comically, painfully accurate, a last wave goodbye to a dying working-class tradition as we boarded the plane to Ibiza.

DON'T BELIEVE THE HYPE

PUBLIC ENEMY

PRODUCED BY BILL STEPHNEY, HANK SHOCKLEE
AND CARL RYDER/WRITTEN BY CARLTON
RIDENHOUR, ERIC SADLER, HAND SHOCKLEE AND
WILLIAM DRAYTON
DEF JAM/JUNE 1988
UK CHART: 18

FOLLOW THE LEADER

ERIC B & RAKIM

PRODUCED AND WRITTEN BY ERIC B & RAKIM
MCA/JUNE 1988
UK CHART: 21

Rebels without a pause. No sooner had we digested the last nugget of beat science and semantic complexity than Chuck and Flav and Terminator and Eric and Rakim would hit us with the next one, as if painfully aware that they would rule the rap roost for a short time before more cynical and nihilistic voices swept them away from relevance.

Don't believe Chuck's hype. His anti-media rant and insistence that he'd take all the hacks' recorders away ('No you can't have it back – Silly rabbit!' Flav added memorably) is belied by the amount of journos he's chatted up and charmed in his time. He was probably the most attentive and compliant interviewee I've ever spoken to – apart from Ol' Dirty Bastard, of course.

Anyway, 'Don't Believe . . .' overcomes its limitations by being the best example of PE's ability to make pop catchiness out of an avant-garde disregard for pop's rules. The song is too slow, too long, too repetitive, too muddy . . . and yet its churning atonal riff and shrieking sax effect and comic vocal interjections and overcooked paranoia still stick like napalm, and even made its title hook a universal catchphrase. How? If I knew their secret, I'd be making 'em not bigging 'em up.

'Follow the Leader', however, is simply one of the greatest pieces of machine-generated music ever. A sinister blaxploitation movie theme with a bassline that growls like a leashed animal, it sounded like Rakim was striding through the street followed by an orchestra *and* an army. 'Pull out my weapon and start to squeeze/A magnum is a microphone murdering MCs,' Rakim purrs, fighting a one-man battle to keep rap's sex and violence metaphorical, piling on astonishing images of third eyes and beat intellect, daring you to keep up, to decipher his cipher, knowing that you'd need to study his alliterations and linguistic games like Shakespeare before you could hope to find the full meaning of it all. It's no insult at all to Eric and R's later music to say that 'Follow the Leader' was impossible to follow, on every level.

TEARDROPS (REMIX)

WOMACK & WOMACK

PRODUCED BY CHRIS BLACKWELL AND THE GYPSY WAVE POWER CO. (ADDITIONAL PRODUCTION AND REMIX BY LEE HAMBLIN)/WRITTEN BY DR RUE AND THE GYPSY WAVE BURNER
FOURTH & BROADWAY/JULY 1988
UK CHART: 3

Cecil and Linda Womack have quite a fondness for conceptual name changes, so Rue and Gypsy Wave are the Womacks themselves. They might have looked like a cosy soul-veteran husband and wife team. But the best Womack & Womack tracks have a touch of the *weird*.

'Teardrops' is a case in point.

For a start, the song is constructed like an old soul standard, produced like a rough demo, and has a beat faster and harder than a house track. Obviously, the wife from 'Love Wars' (see p. 216) has shagged one best friend too many, and hubby's split. She sings her haunted regret in a reedy girl-group key – as if the experience had made her regress to the most agonizing times of her teenage years. The things that remind her of him are endless and inappropriate . . . 'Footsteps on the dancefloor' . . . 'Whispers in the powder-room' . . . but also a giveaway, because they reveal that she's out on the pull. A blissful, rising middle eight only confirms how empty an experience it is, and everything about the music's loose restraint – the gently ringing two-chord electric piano breaks, the choogling upright bass, the roughness of the call-and-response vocals, the spontaneous but spare snatches of Latin-funk percussion – refuse to resolve the situation for her. As the music fades, you feel the loss of someone doomed to endlessly repeat the same mistakes.

YOU MADE ME REALISE/SLOW

MY BLOODY VALENTINE

PRODUCED BY MY BLOODY VALENTINE/WRITTEN BY KEVIN SHIELDS
CREATION/JULY 1988
DID NOT CHART

Sigh. The amount of godawful shoe-gazing bollocks made in the name of Dublin's Kevin Shields and his sudden shift from anonymous indie jangler to mind-blowing sonic visionary makes me break out in hives. Somehow, the sex and violence and lysergic imagination of his original sound became, in the hands of the less extreme, a bunch of pale-faced studes with floataway voices singing about limp gurls while randomly stamping on guitar effects pedals like a clumsy dopehead trying to put out a Rizla fire. Never mind. Because 'You Make Me Realise' is a slamdance stand-off between surreal metallic male freakout and blissed-out female harmony-pop, and 'Slow' actually *slows down time*. No really! Play it and gasp when you start moving around the room like Giant Haystacks on quaaludes in a two-ton treacle jar!

GIGANTIC

THE PIXIES

PRODUCED BY GIL NORTON/WRITTEN BY BLACK FRANCIS AND MRS JOHN MURPHY
4AD/AUGUST 1988
DID NOT CHART

For years, 'indie' had been The Smiths and . . . um . . . that's it. Harsh? Well, there were some nice plain-sliced boys in plaid shirts from America who made some good albums – Husker Du and Violent Femmes in particular. Early Creation's lo-fi '60s revivalism would prove influential, the American roots-revival wave made for good live acts, and Brit indie's C86 wave (named after an NME giveaway tape) of fey, deliberately inept or wacky shamblers still has a baffling hold on former students of a certain age. But none of these impulses threw up speedy, sexy singles acts with some kind of finger on the pop pulse. And then MBV and The Pixies arrived, all at once.

Boston's Pixies were, when unplugged, so normal they were dysfunctional. Despite Goth-ishly naming himself Black Francis, singer/songwriter/guitarist Charles Thompson was a fat bloke in cheap shirt and jeans who seemed to be a complete character

EVERYDAY IS LIKE SUNDAY/MORRISSEY
PAGE 273

blank. Bassist Kim Deal was a self-confessed junkie who was always grinning cheerily and insisted on calling herself Mrs John Murphy for song credits, as if wanting to rub her own identity out completely. The other two were the other two. They played guitar and drums. That was it.

But when they began to play all primal rock 'n' roll hell was let loose. Their speciality was a quiet bass-driven bit for the verse, then some brief warning signal, then WAAAAAAGGGGGGHHHHHHHHH!!!!!! for the chorus. Nirvana liked it so much they bought the company.

'Gigantic', by Pixies standards, was a ballad, and a rare co-writing effort (tension between Thompson and Deal eventually split the band in 1992) and lead vocal by Deal. It could be about 'A big, big love', as the lighters-aloft chorus repeats, or it could, as everyone kept saying, be about her old man's cock, which Deal, grinning as always, didn't do much to deny.

BIG FUN

INNER CITY

PRODUCED BY KEVIN SAUNDERSON (MIXED BY
JUAN ATKINS)/WRITTEN BY PENNINGTON,
FOREST, SAUNDERSON AND JACKSON
TEN/AUGUST 1988
UK CHART: 8

As Kraftwerk prophetically put it back in the mid-'80s Dark Age – 'Musique non-stop – Techno Pop!'

It turned out that not all these Detroit boys were content with sci-fi instrumentals. Kevin Saunderson hitched up with diva Paris Grey and went for pop's high ground, creating a key house anthem at the first time of asking, and setting the template for over ten years of Inner City dance-pop hits, an almost unique run of recorded success for an early house act.

Nothing topped this, the 'Good Times' of the house scene, though – albeit a 'Good Times' without the dimensions and sly satire. It wasn't words or voice, but the mighty bassline, the monumental funky drums, the decaying keyboard hooks, the cheery pop-soul melody, that techno sense of scope and endless space. The bass riff was so strong that the 'Magic Juan' extended mix even survived the most hilariously inept piano solo in recorded history, evidence, perhaps, of Les Dawson's hidden role in the rise of techno.

STRICTLY BUSINESS

EPMD

PRODUCED AND WRITTEN BY EPMD
COOLTEMPO/AUGUST 1988
DID NOT CHART
(REMIXED BY MANTRONIK AND REISSUED AUGUST
1998: REACHED NO. 43)

EPMD could make anything rock. Even Eric Clapton. Actually, strike that, 'cos Clapped-Out's version of Bob Marley's 'I Shot the Sheriff' was always pretty funky, and Erick and Parrish do little to it except loop it, cut it to shreds occasionally, and slur stoned malevolence over it as they drag rival MCs into a slow-motion world of pain. Points of interest: one of the first examples of hard-boy rappers' obsession with their moms, and one of the last testimonies to abstinence in rap, when Parrish asks his partner if he takes blow, and Erick protests, 'No time to start sniffin'/My parents find out – then they start riffin'.' Also, a sign that rappers were having to venture ever further into bad taste with their similes to stay 'hardcore', when Parrish reckons he's 'As deadly as AIDS', before hurriedly adding, 'When I rock a party.'

FREAK SCENE

DINOSAUR JR

PRODUCED AND WRITTEN BY J. MASCIS AND
DINOSAUR JR
BLAST FIRST/SEPTEMBER 1988
DID NOT CHART

What's in a name? Although Mascis's Massachusetts guitar-squallers were initially presented as a punkish proposition, they turned out to be a throwback – long-hair rockists who existed to showcase Mascis's old-school fret-wankery. J.'s just-got-out-of-bed stage demeanour and can't-be-arsed interview technique saw them dubbed a 'slacker' band, the forerunners of grunge miserablism who were too lazy to reach for the shotgun. Mascis's partner Lou Barlow quit and formed the more rounded Sebadoh before it all got too like Neil Young on a *major* bummer, dude. But not before he'd contributed to the band's great punk-pop moment, the raucous and touching 'Freak Scene'.

It's a rock guitar showcase, all short-sharp pop dynamics as the song goes from a Postcard jangle, to Sex Pistols 'Holidays . . .' power chord, to juddering machine-gun shock tactics, to sweet

my bloody Valentine

YOU MADE ME REALISE/SLOW/MY BLOODY VALENTINE

acoustic lightness, to fuzz and shriek punk-metal soloing. Mascis's wry drawl details some dysfunctional relationship or another, and it all sounds like one of those drunk drama moments at a disintegrating teen party. The pay-off is so good and so sweet that Mascis finally stops the guitars and tells it straight to his lover/mate: 'Sometimes I don't thrill you/Sometimes I think I'll kill you/ Just don't let me fuck up will you/'Cos when I need a friend it's still you.' The guitars crash back in and Mascis shakes his head at the freak scene and sighs, 'What a mess,' as the guitars smash up one of the bedrooms.

CAN YOU PARTY

ROYAL HOUSE

PRODUCED AND WRITTEN BY TODD TERRY
CHAMPION/SEPTEMBER 1988
UK CHART: 14

I'LL HOUSE YOU

JUNGLE BROTHERS

PRODUCED BY THE JUNGLE BROTHERS (REMIXED BY RICHIE RICH)/WRITTEN BY NATHANIEL HALL, MICHAEL SMALL AND TODD TERRY
GEE STREET/OCTOBER 1988
UK CHART: 22

Todd Terry was the first undisputed Don of the New York house scene, and the first modern superstar DJ/producer. The Jungle Brothers were Mike G (Small) and Afrika Baby Bambaataa (Hall), two Brooklyn rappers with a bohemian, Afrocentric take on the new hip-hop mores. Together they took 1988's most ubiquitous club classic and doubled it.

Terry's 'Can You Party' looped a Marshall Jefferson Chicago house track, cut and chopped it into a series of stutters and suddenly rearing orchestrals, added sirens, 'Can you feel it?' hollers, sampled gospel howls and, most significantly, a drum track that forsook four-to-the-floor disco thump for a speeded-up hip-hop breakbeat sound with an unnaturally loud and twitching hi-hat . . . a prophecy of drum 'n' bass. The track was an immediate headrush, produced as if the musicians at a Latin street party had been plugged into machines and forced to play like sequencers. It was cosmic, street-tough, quick and, best of all, short – in, brilliant, and out before you had time to work out what had hit you.

The JBs were on the same Warlock label in the States as Terry. Someone suggested they try rapping over 'Can You Party', even though its speed and sound ran at odds to their own low-slung, funk-sampling style. This was a brave move, because, on the less tolerant parts of the US hip-hop scene, house was simply 'fag music' and therefore looked down upon. Mike and Bam not only ignored that but unleashed a sexy, sing-song, jokey, high-speed freestyle rap that actually upped their rep and popularity. It predictably gave birth to a sub-genre, the generally awful 'hip house', but, more importantly, helped clear some space for the brief moment of Rainbow Coalition rap androgyny called the Daisy Age, which was defined by De La Soul, precursored by the Jungle Brothers, and taken on by A Tribe Called Quest, who were all part of a loose boho collective called the Native Tongues. Most of all, it crystallized a moment in England when house and hip-hop and the people who liked them came together, the heavy vibe around clubland evaporated, and everybody got rehoused.

FEED ME WITH YOUR KISS

MY BLOODY VALENTINE

PRODUCED BY MY BLOODY VALENTINE/WRITTEN BY KEVIN SHIELDS
CREATION/OCTOBER 1988
DID NOT CHART

Arty New York noisemongers Sonic Youth spliced with The Buzzcocks and then forced to run downhill towards a massive wall and told not to stop so their heads go 'BLOWWBLOWWBLOWWW!!!' against the wall while Shields and Bilinda Butcher sing the chilliest sex harmonies over the resulting carnage. Not an acid house favourite.

FREAK SCENE/DINOSAUR JR

PAGE 276

LEFT TO MY OWN DEVICES

PET SHOP BOYS
PRODUCED BY TREVOR HORN AND STEPHEN
LIPSON/WRITTEN BY NEIL TENNANT AND
CHRIS LOWE
PARLOPHONE/NOVEMBER 1988
UK CHART: 4

Now *this* is what I mean about deciding for yourself what records are about. After more than a decade of being genuinely moved by my fave PSB song because I thought it really was Neil's life story, I pick up the 2001 reissue of the *Introspective* album and read his comments about the track, and it turns out that he wasn't a lonely boy as a child and the 'party animal' (writer Jon Savage, apparently) wasn't that much of a party animal and the lyrics were sort of cobbled together under deadline and, worst of all, that it was producer Horn who wanted to put Debussy to a disco beat and Che Guevara was an afterthought. *NOOOOOO!!!*

Well, I've learned my lesson. No more reading these detailed deconstructions of the artistic process, because I want to believe that every inch of drama and deadpan drollery and sadness and joy and beauty and outrageous orchestral overkill and camp innuendo and Meaning of Life in a production triumph like this was dragged from the innermost recesses of the singer's soul. And, left to my own devices, I probably could.

WHERE'S YOUR CHILD?

BAM BAM
PRODUCED AND WRITTEN BY BAM BAM
DESIRE/DECEMBER 1988
DID NOT CHART

So we got a good friend to babysit and went out to an acid jam. We were glad to get out and the vibes were good. Then some psycho DJ turned down the lights, turned up the smoke machine and this car speeds between the speakers, a baby squeals, bassless beats bump ominously, and SMASSH! . . . a window breaks. And then this Hammer Horror voice asks me and my partner, 'Where's your child? Do you know?'

We looked at each other and tried to keep dancing, as the undulating acidic synths lapped over and around each other. Then Monster Boy goes, 'Curfew! No one likes to be left alone. Especially when they don't know right from wrong. Parents – where's your child? You're all *my* children now. HARHARHARHAR!!!'

Curfew. We *ran* home. Our mate, who'd given up her time for nothing, wondered why we were looking at her funny as we checked on the kid. Thankfully, we hadn't taken any drugs, or else we'd *still* be blubbering in a foetal position inside the club. But my partner wouldn't go to any more acid jams. The Summer of Love had become a chill winter wind.

1989

1989

1989 was an intense year for me. I split from a five-year relationship and my only son, and bounced far too quickly into a rebound relationship. I moved house twice. After having worked hard to get into North London Poly as a mature student, I got too heavily into sex, drugs and dance 'n' roll and blew it after just a year. I found myself working full-time in another record shop, this time in Camden Town. My band went electronic as I continued to refuse to accept that I wasn't very good. I travelled abroad for the first time, the reasons why I didn't before still cloudy and probably down to old-fashioned working-class cowardice. As some kind of karmic reaction to all of this, my skin and senses exploded into a series of spectacular allergies. Yup, it was intense, and every record here brings another charged memory either good or bad which I'll leave to your imagination.

The brief acid party broke up, and all the various tribes started their own parties again. House became a deluge of mini-genres. Hip-hop hardened. Rock bands found a way of hoisting dance beats onto their songs without going beige, mainly by employing DJs such as Andy Weatherall and Paul Oakenfold to mix or produce. Indie-dance took over the rock world, and the music press, bewildered by house and rap, breathed a sigh of relief as they 'discovered' a bunch of guitar-toting white boys, complete with dress codes and drug lifestyles to drool over. Although it's worth pointing out here that most of the bands used hip-hop, rather than house, beats to become relevant again, and that serious groundwork had been already been done through the '80s by a series of still-maligned Brit and Irish bands, including Big Audio Dynamite, The Shamen, Pop Will Eat Itself, Age of Chance, That Petrol Emotion and – gulp – Jesus Jones.

But, more than all this, real life actually matched and overwhelmed pop fantasies as 1989 gave us the End of the Century feeling we didn't get ten years later. The Hillsborough disaster brought home to us the contempt in which the working class was held by police, government, the tabloids. For once, the victims' families wouldn't just shrug and let it drop. De Klerk replaced Botha in South Africa. Chinese students humiliated their government in Tiananmen Square. The Ayatollah Khomeini ordered the murder of Salman Rushdie and then keeled over and died. An unknown called Sir Anthony Meyer dared to challenge Thatcher for the Tory leadership, and the knives were unsheathed. And then, in November, the Berlin Wall fell down. Just like that. And a couple of weeks later, at a Bush–Gorbachev summit, a Soviet spokesman announced that the Cold War had ended at 12.45pm on 3 December.

Again, just like that. The historical and political realities that had dominated our lives, that had always seemed irrevocable and impossible to remove, began simply to evaporate. For the first time for our generation, real life promised to be better than dreaming.

Honourable mentions: The House of Love/'I Don't Know Why I Love You' (Fontana); Ten City/'Devotion' (Warners); Frankie Knuckles/'Your Love' (Trax); De La Soul/'Me Myself and I'/'Jenifa Taught Me' and 'Eye Know' (Big Life/Tommy Boy); Roxanne Shante/'Have a Nice Day' (Cold Chillin'/A&M); Tone Loc/'Funky Cold Medina' (Delicious Vinyl)

SHE DRIVES ME CRAZY

FINE YOUNG CANNIBALS

PRODUCED BY DAVID Z AND FINE YOUNG
CANNIBALS/WRITTEN BY DAVID STEELE AND
ROLAND GIFT
FFRR/LONDON/JANUARY 1989
UK CHART: 5

Despite the singer's beauty, the guitarist's top bandy-legged gimp dance, and their deft blend of Prince-pop and upfront dance beats, the two-tone trio formed by ex-Beat members David Steele and Andy Cox and Al Jolson-soundalike Roland Gift were the height of late '80s uncool. Every youthquake brings a set of new snobberies, and FYC committed the credcrimes of having a frontman who knew how gorgeous he was, doing a whole bunch of (admittedly awful) cover versions, and – horror of horrors – being mainstream big in America, especially once this song reached No. 1 over there. Me, I reckon they're much maligned, particularly as they aspired to being nothing more than a quality pop act, which is exactly what they were.

A cross between mid-Atlantic electro-pop and 'Kiss'-era Prince – unsurprisingly considering the production presence of Prince acolyte David Z – 'She Drives Me Crazy' glides infectiously on FYC's dry, sparse pop-funk formula, the fragile falsetto verses just an excuse to get to the perfect pop chorus and a bunch of minimal choppy funk-guitar hooks that lend a tense edge to the radio-friendly enterprise. It has nothing to say, but says it with crunch.

THAT'S THE WAY LOVE IS

TEN CITY

PRODUCED BY MARSHALL JEFFERSON AND TEN CITY
(REMIXED BY TIMMY REGISFORD)/WRITTEN BY
LAWSON, BURKE AND STINGILY
ATLANTIC/JANUARY 1989
UK CHART: 8

The fact that house's most soulful and ecstatic five minutes or so was relegated to the B-side of the 12-inch by an appalling 'Acieed' mix says much about the crass acid exploitation of 1989. But that's the way pop is, and anyway, no one who loved house was fooled. It was the underground mix you heard everywhere, the most glorious doo-wop/gospel tribute to love's highs and lows since . . . ooh . . . we're probably talking northern soul here.

'That's the Way Love Is' revisits 'Love Wars' (see p. 216) territory over tough soul-funk – rather than disco – drum and bass, a mesmeric orchestral loop, and a seemingly endless run of swooping and soaring counter-melodies. The words this time are not a brutal examination of a specific break-up, but an attempt to console the listener that they are not alone in the lies they've told or the promises they've broken. The vocals, courtesy of legendary deep-house singer Byron Stingily, are astonishing, shooting suddenly from an opening easy croon to his trademark – an eerie falsetto, part Smokey Robinson warmth, part the edge-of-panic shriek of '50s doo-wop prodigy Frankie Lymon. The harmony chorus melts all over you, and just as you think it can get no more beautiful and moving, it adds a minor-chord bridge complete with ominous pre-Massive Attack strings, and the joyful redemption of a churchy piano solo that makes up for Inner City's sins.

The record laid bare what I was going through in my life at the time, in all its guilt, lust, sorrow and hope. It didn't convince me that what I was doing was morally right. But it put its generous soul arms around me and reminded me that I wasn't the first, wouldn't be the last, and that maybe I'd find some kind of redemption eventually, if I worked at it hard enough. If a piece of music has never done that much for you, then I can only hope you'll find your own Ten City some day soon.

THE LAST OF THE FAMOUS INTERNATIONAL PLAYBOYS

MORRISSEY

PRODUCED BY STEPHEN STREET/WRITTEN BY
MORRISSEY AND STEPHEN STREET
HIS MASTER'S VOICE/FEBRUARY 1989
UK CHART: 6

Our final word from Moz is perhaps his most basic *and* his most misunderstood song. You get some idea of why he got fed up with the British press, as they kept asking why he appeared to have a fetish for the Kray twins, when '. . . International Playboys' is so obviously a lyric sung in character. The problem was that Morrissey had become a Rock Icon, which means every word he sings is taken as personal testimony, particularly if sung in the first person. From here on in, his audience drifted away bewildered, having grown up with their hero's self-dramatization on their behalf ('These are the ways on which I was raised,' as the song puts it). Morrissey lost his constituency,

THAT'S THE WAY LOVE IS

ACIEED MIX/EXTENDED VERSION
UNDERGROUND MIX/EXTENDED VERSION

DEVOTION
RADIO MIX

TEN
CITY

THAT'S THE WAY LOVE IS/TEN CITY
PAGE 264

dumped his second-best songwriting partner (Stephen Street), and drifted into self-parody, mediocrity, and a future career as a superstar in, of all places, Mexico.

'. . . International Playboys' is a look at an increasingly common phenomenon, whereby a disturbed individual hides in his room, reads lots of books about psychopaths, and decides that they are counter-culture heroes and people whose attention he would like to attract by killing. Keeping within his Brit '60s obsession, Moz predictably chooses the Krays, but it could have been any serial killer. The point emerges – and you can't miss it – in the last verse, when he croons, 'In our lifetime those who kill/The news world hands them stardom.' Apply it to, say, Charles Manson or Timothy McVeigh, and you realize that it hardly amounts to a love letter to Big Ron. In fact, it has exactly the same theme as Oliver Stone's movie, *Natural Born Killers*. Mind you, after the way that was treated, perhaps Moz got off lightly.

STRAIGHT OUT THE JUNGLE

JUNGLE BROTHERS

PRODUCED BY NATHANIEL HALL AND MICHAEL SMALL (REMIXED BY DJ SOUL SHOCK)/WRITTEN BY AFRIKA BABY BAMBAATAA, MIKE G AND Q-TIP GEE STREET/FEBRUARY 1989
UK CHART: 72

The Afro-pride anthemics of flipside 'Black Is Black' were more obvious, but it was on the title track of the Jungles Bros' debut album that Afro-centrism met the high end of funk innovation. Soul Shock adds softly probing double bass, swathes of psychedelic organ and African folk chants to the Brothers' already sore-thumb sound, with a staccato guitar riff and funk drums so clean and clear they sound as if they're in the room with you. Over this, Mike, Bam and A Tribe Called Quest's Q-Tip revisit Melle Mel's New York-as-jungle and reject racial conflict while declaring a new B-boy pride in their ancient origins. Anti-materialist ('I wear no gold around my neck/Just a black medallion'), yet still proud and tough, the track made explicit Rakim's idea of rap as a spiritual and intellectual odyssey, an opportunity to reject the white power structure's version of the American dream, and revive Marcus Garvey's Back to Africa campaign as a journey of the mind and soul. Sadly, the majority of soon-come rappers took the Jungle Bros' black pride as a one-dimensional element to gain hardcore cred, but weren't about to turn down white South Africa's gold.

KEEP ON MOVIN'

SOUL II SOUL FEATURING CARON WHEELER

PRODUCED BY JAZZIE B AND NELLEE HOOPER/WRITTEN BY BERESFORD ROMEO TEN/MARCH 1989
UK CHART: 5

Yup, it sure was one helluva year for uplifting messages. And none more so than this – the British anthem of the year, a club and pop classic, the most immediately recognizable drum track ever, the overdue coming-of-age of UK soul, a massive coals-to-Newcastle hit in and influence on America, a song and performance and production so perfect in every way that the Sun seemed to come out every time it played. Not only that, but the foundation it gave the early career of Soul II Soul's south London leader Beresford Romeo, aka Jazzie B, would prove that it was a black Brit, rather than an American, who pioneered the now ubiquitous hip-hop/R&B ideal of the multi-media entrepreneur. That Funki Dred logo, lest we forget, advertised records, clubs, soundsystems, recording studios, a clothing line, record shops, DJs and The Man himself – the ultimate self-made and self-styled role model, a Richard Branson for the homeboys. And didn't the cocky bastard get annoying after a while?

But, while you play the beautiful string-driven thing in your head (and don't forget the inspired country-hoedown fiddles courtesy of the Reggae Philharmonic Orchestra), let's spare a special thought for one Caron Wheeler. 'Cos I reckon it takes one amazing singer to make the words 'Yellow is the colour of sunrays' sound deep and meaningful.

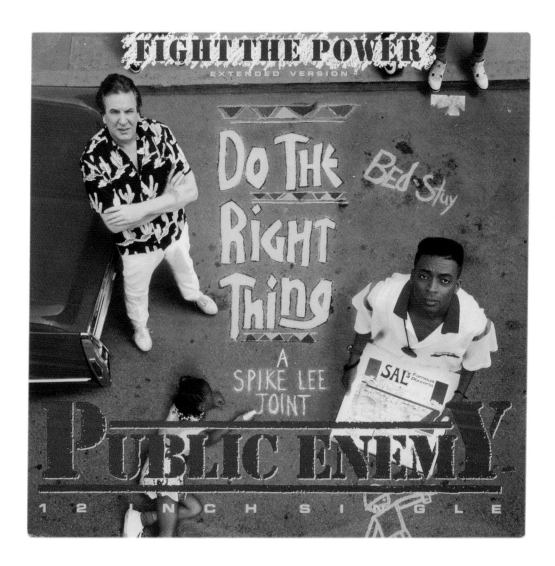

FIGHT THE POWER/PUBLIC ENEMY

LIKE A PRAYER

MADONNA
PRODUCED AND WRITTEN BY MADONNA AND
PATRICK LEONARD
SIRE/MARCH 1989
UK CHART: 1

By this time Madonna had become a pop deity – the hard-headed '80s feminist equivalent of Elvis and The Beatles. She had to finally reach some sort of creative and self-defining peak, even if she was destined to successfully reinvent herself on a permanent basis. And what else could it be for a good Catholic girl turned disco überslut turned goddess, but shagging a black Jesus? It's hard to know what was more awe-inspiring about the conceit of this song and its accompanying video – the sheer ego needed to go there, or the fact that she now had the talent and soul and imagination to pull it off so magnificently.

MONKEY'S GONE TO HEAVEN

THE PIXIES
PRODUCED BY GIL NORTON/WRITTEN BY
BLACK FRANCIS
4AD/MARCH 1989
UK CHART: 60

JUST LIKE HEAVEN

DINOSAUR JR
PRODUCED BY DINOSAUR JR/WRITTEN BY
ROBERT SMITH, SIMON GALLUP, PORL THOMPSON,
BORIS WILLIAMS AND LOL TOLHURST
BLAST FIRST/APRIL 1989
DID NOT CHART

Boy, them disco biscuits sure brought everyone closer to God in 1989. Not that these two were 'on one', I wouldn't imagine. But even the Yank kings of pro-celebrity shrugging caught the bug somehow and fancied shoehorning a bit of religious imagery into their strictly non-danceable indie-rockin' fare. Even if it meant covering The Cure.

Considering how massive Robert Smith's lipstick whinge was among fashionably alienated American studes throughout the '80s, I don't doubt, for one minute, that J. Mascis loved this poppier slice of The Cure's suburban ennui. But Lord knows what he'd do to a song he didn't like, because he destroys it, murders it, *lays waste to it*. I mean, it begins sprightly and reverential enough, all jangling acoustics and sparky electric twangs. But then J. starts singing. A drawl so lazy and half-formed you can't help but laugh. And it goes on like that for a couple of verses before one of the all-time great vandal mood changes in rock. It sounds like the entire population of Utah have broken into the studio and bawled, 'NOOOOO!!!' and turned the band into Black Sabbath. They restore order for a while and then it comes again, even more apocalyptic and murderous and the band (and the song. And The Cure) just . . . vanish. And then you spend the next hour or so attempting to get your heart back out of your mouth.

Francis, meanwhile, had more serious matters on his mind. The ozone layer is disappearing, we're all going to fry, and we didn't evolve enough to do anything to stop it. The song contrasts verses of spoken-word newspaper reports over bumping bass and Beatles cellos with a huge power-ballad chorus. In case all this eco-fear got too serious, Francis drawls a sardonic 'Rock me, Joe' before Joey Santiago's guitar solo gently weeps, and then comes up with an astonishing middle eight, where everything drops out, he explains that man is five, the devil is six, and 'If the devil is six then *GOD* IS SEVEN!!!' The impact of a Black Frank howl is best explained by a quote from the sleevenotes of the band's *Death to the Pixies* compilation, where writer Gary Smith is trying to tell his children why that screech turned him on so much. 'How am I supposed to explain to them that the world into which Black Francis started screaming still heard it like a scream and not like fashion?' And that, people, is very possibly the true story of the slow death of rock 'n' roll.

Back to life (club mix)

soul II soul

BACK TO LIFE/SOUL II SOUL FEATURING CARON WHEELER
PAGE 290

KNOW HOW

YOUNG MC

PRODUCED BY THE DUST BROTHERS/WRITTEN BY
M. YOUNG, J. KING AND M. SIMPSON
DELICIOUS VINYL/4TH & BROADWAY/MAY 1989
DID NOT CHART

Nothing more, on the face of it, than another American brother talking inspired bollocks over a loop of the infamous wah-wah guitar from Isaac Hayes's 'Shaft'. Except that its producers went on to reinvent sampledelica with The Beastie Boys and Beck, and Queens-raised Michael 'Young MC' Young was born in, of all places, Neasden.

How good is this? Well, if I'm in someone's house and hear that opening riff, I hope it's Isaac Hayes. If I'm in a club and I hear that riff, I hope it's 'Know How'.

FIGHT THE POWER

PUBLIC ENEMY

PRODUCED BY HANK SHOCKLEE, CARL RYDER,
ERIC SADLER AND KEITH SHOCKLEE/WRITTEN BY
KEITH SHOCKLEE, ERIC SADLER AND
CARLTON RIDENHOUR
MOTOWN/JUNE 1989
UK CHART: 29

In which even angry old Uncle Chuck got the positivity bug. Not that the lyric of PE's best-known track isn't as furious as anything they'd written before. But 'Fight the Power' possessed both a less ominous, more danceable, less macho musical backdrop and a chorus (borrowed from The Isley Brothers) that felt more inclusive than their previous hectorings and accusations. The use of a barrage of contrasting vocal samples is like some sort of masterclass on just how far almost subliminal details can open up a track and make it both funkier and funnier. I can't agree with Chuck's famous assertion that Elvis was a racist or a sucker or simple or plain, but I understand why he held up Presley and John Wayne as symbols of everything that held white America in a trance. And the righteous rejection – 'Most of my heroes don't appear on no stamps' – and exasperation – 'Don't worry be happy was a number one jam/Damn!/If *I* say it you can slap me right here!' – of the rest of the last verse was the epitome of Public Enemy's attempts to convince us that politics and seriousness was more *fun* than

escapism. It was all the more appropriate that 'Fight the Power' provided the musical bedrock for *the* movie of 1989, Spike Lee's B-boy microcosm of the roots of racial violence, *Do the Right Thing*, and therefore that it came out on Motown.

BACK TO LIFE

SOUL II SOUL FEATURING CARON WHEELER

PRODUCED BY JAZZIE B AND
NELLEE HOOPER/WRITTEN BY BERESFORD ROMEO
TEN/JUNE 1989
UK CHART: 1

'Keep On Movin'' (see p. 286) – The Sequel. That is, after all that dreaming and walking face up towards the sun and a brighter future, you eventually have to come 'Back from a fantasy.' Which is why it balances more love war with its exotic soul momentum, why it struts on earthier ground. When it hit No. 1, you knew that black British music had won a major battle, if not the war, with its American inferiority complex.

FRENCH KISS

LIL LOUIS

PRODUCED AND WRITTEN BY LIL LOUIS
FFRR/JULY 1989
UK CHART: 2

One synth riff. For ten minutes. What?

Well, it was all in the detail: the gradually building hi-hat and percussion, the drum rolls, the arrival of a fanfare horn and gently climbing synth lick, one sudden key change. It was deep, hot and hypnotic, Chicago acid's most obvious homage to 'I Feel Love'. It also introduced a bit of cheeky good groove rebellion with its major gimmick, as, around three-quarters in, a girl starts to do the tummyache sex sigh and Louis just slows the whole track d-o-w-n u-n-t-i-l *i-t s-t-o-p-s*. And then, while you were kicking your heels and staring stupidly at the DJ, he speeded it *very* gradually right back up again. Dancers went bananas, and the Balearic breakdown was born.

FRENCH KISS/LIL LOUIS

RIDE ON TIME

BLACK BOX

PRODUCED BY GROOVE GROOVE MELODY/WRITTEN
BY DAN HARTMAN, MIRKO LIMONI, DANIELE DAVOLI,
AND VALERIO SEMPLICI
DECONSTRUCTION/AUGUST 1989
UK CHART: 1

And the micro-genres just kept on coming. Welcome to the small world of Italo-house – it was house made by Italians. Effectively the light, cheesy, typically Euro disco take on the new club sound. This massive gospel-inflected hit, with its self-deprecating English-as-second-language title (the hook was 'You're *right* on time') was its finest and most famous moment. And that's it. Or at least, that's what the Groove Groove Melody team wanted us to think. Instead, 'Ride on Time' pointed out that all we'd been told about sampling – that it was a blow against the Empire of The Man, essentially – was a load of self-serving tosh.

'Ride on Time' was a remake of an old Salsoul label disco record called 'Love Sensation'. The composer of the original, Dan Hartman, got his credit. But the roaring female gospel voice that was making the record into a hit didn't. Loleatta Holloway, now a deserved dance scene diva legend, howled loud all over again at the injustice of it all. One can only imagine how it feels to hear your voice everywhere and see it coming out of the mouth of some busty model type called Katrin, while Ms Holloway eked out a living on the lower levels of the disco diehard circuit.

So, all the stuff that the Beastie Boys and Public Enemy had said early on about sampling being some kind of Robin Hood enterprise was exposed for what it was – a cheat that affected black music's already ripped-off pioneers all over again. The veterans crawled out of the woodwork to demand what was theirs, and 'Paid in Full' began to cut both ways.

W.F.L. (VINCE CLARKE MIX)

HAPPY MONDAYS

PRODUCED BY MARTIN HANNETT (REMIX BY
VINCE CLARKE)/WRITTEN BY HAPPY MONDAYS
FACTORY/SEPTEMBER 1989
UK CHART: 68

Call the cops! There's a madman around!

The only Brit band who've come close to living up to 'the new Sex Pistols' hype that murders every remotely interesting rock band had already made two albums before their leap into infamy. The most recent one, *Bummed*, had been a unique and surreal masterpiece made of bits of staggering (Rolling) stoned blues mixed with A Certain Ratio's mutant funk, Martin Hannett's clanging, fizzing murk production, and the surreal sleaze testimonies of one Shaun Ryder, a litany of junkie babble, sick jokes, snatches of drug movie dialogue, cutting insults, weird scenes and comedown defiance. It was the first realistic Brit response to hardcore hip-hop, not because there was any rapping or big beats, but because Ryder represented his treacherous Manchester sink estate 'hood in all its bad faith, street aggro and narcotic collapse. When *Bummed* began to get the praise it deserved, and the music press and Factory's Tony Wilson began to talk up a Manchester scene based around The Mondays, a straighter rock band called The Stone Roses, acid house, ecstasy and Factory's own Hacienda club, Ryder and co. decided that they needed to take this whole thing a step on. They called in an unlikely saviour to buff up their previous flop single 'Wrote for Luck', a symbol of everything un-rock 'n' roll, fey and tiddly-bonk about the 1980s – Basildon's Vince Clarke.

The sometime Depeche Mode, Yazoo and Erasure synth-pop maestro took the cluttered rock chunk-funk of 'Wrote for Luck' and stripped it bare. As the beat clumped and the bass synth rumbled and the dominating guitar was reined in, you could actually hear Ryder's 'singing' voice – a bizarre but instantly lovable mix of Mark E Smith, Liverpudlian rock shouter Pete Wylie and Grandpa Simpson – for the first time. It's opening gambit – 'I wrote for luck – they sent me you!/I sent for juice – you give me poison!' – was magnificent, and prefaced a slew of cleverly contradictory slag-offs that made the subject of his contempt into every thieving two-faced drug fuck you'd ever met, while slyly letting you know that Ryder was no better. The mix of catchy electro-disco and glam moonstomp was perfect for all those indie kids who were fed up with sitting in their bedrooms listening to whinge-rock while everyone else was raving it up, but weren't sure they could keep up with all that

black box ride on time

deconstruzione italiano

RIDE ON TIME/BLACK BOX
PAGE 292

funk and disco ('You were never fleet of foot – *hippy*'). Lo and behold, Madchester (after the city), or baggy (after the trousers), or indie-dance (*long* after New Order) was born.

THE SUN RISING

THE BELOVED

PRODUCED BY MARTYN PHILLIPS/WRITTEN BY STEVEN WADDINGTON AND JON MARSH
WEA/OCTOBER 1989
UK CHART: 26

Going on dance and drug holidays to Ibiza caught on quickly among the more committed house heads, and even created a micro-genre – Balearic beats. This encompassed a wider range of noises than straight house (everything from aggressive Nitzer Ebb and DAF to obscure pop nuggets from the likes of The Cure, It's Immaterial and even Mandy Smith!), as most of the point was to build to a frenzied peak around three in the morning, and then gradually mellow out until you were ready to watch the sun rise and get that Meaning of Life feeling. Unfortunately, I was both too broke and too uncool to enjoy these Ibiza moments while they were still young and innocent, but I can't believe there was ever a more perfect Balearic record than 'The Sun Rising', simply because it stated the bleedin' obvious so beautifully, with its blissed-out, whispered messages of pensive optimism, and dreamy operatic hookline.

Jon Marsh and co., incidentally, jumped on the dance bandwagon even more hastily than the Mondays, but couldn't last the pace due to their preference for twinkly electro-pop at a time of funky rock. Nevertheless, they left a lovely, timely pop moment that took us to a Mediterranean beach without a passport.

STRINGS OF LIFE

RHYTHIM IS RHYTHIM

PRODUCED BY MAYDAY/WRITTEN BY MAYDAY AND M. JONES
KOOL KAT/BIG LIFE/NOVEMBER 1989
UK CHART: 74

Originally released in 1987, I've held this back until the 1989 repackage of the ultimate Detroit techno classic, largely because the superficially minor chart placing was achieved on a tiny label and with absolutely zilch promotion or radio play – it sold just on the developing strength of the underground electronic scene and the track's legend. But also because 'Strings of Life' could be dated December 2010 and it wouldn't give its age away, so timeless, futuristic and sophisticated in its construction does it remain.

The A-side Juan Atkins remix attempts to make it more defined and dance-friendly, but I'm sure he and Derrick May knew it was missing the point. The original, famously, is perhaps the only disco milestone that occasionally lurches completely out of sync and didn't even have any bass – just an initially modest piano riff, whistling, tentative string synth . . . and then wave upon wave of churning rhythm and melody, always grabbing for something just out of reach, quizzical, hugely emotional and made with just enough punkish attitude-over-technique to remind you how brave and unique it all is, while its breaks and subtle shifts in emphasis convince you that modern jazz can be played on sequencers and drum machines. If I ever grow tired of 'Strings of Life', I'll know I've finally grown tired of music.

I'M NOT THE MAN I USED TO BE

FINE YOUNG CANNIBALS

PRODUCED BY ANDY COX, DAVID STEELE AND ROLAND GIFT/WRITTEN BY DAVID STEELE AND ROLAND GIFT
FFRR/LONDON/NOVEMBER 1989
UK CHART: 20

There's a great deal of rhythm, but very little blues, in the years covered by this book. But if R&B, in modern terms, is allowed to be more than marketing speak for 'music by black people that isn't house or gangsta rap', then this record is it. The speedy steal of the ubiquitous James Brown/Clyde Stubblefield 'Funky Drummer' break, the gospel organ and Gift's hesitant, cracking bark gave real grit and truth to this bleak confession of a

STRINGS OF LIFE/RHYTHIM IS RHYTHIM
PAGE 294

peculiarly male strain of self-loathing, as the singer stares into his bottle and sees a coward and a loser staring back, a man he hardly recognizes and doesn't want to, but has to face up to anyway. The subtle blend of boxed-in horns and James Brown guitar root the track in a history of soul testimony, even lending a touch of slave legacy when Gift wails, 'Don't know my name!' Unfortunately, Gift looked too pretty and pleased with himself on *Top of the Pops*, so, without the drama being acted out, it was all too complex and black for the new rockist orthodoxy to want to understand.

THE MADCHESTER EP

HAPPY MONDAYS

PRODUCED BY MARTIN HANNETT/WRITTEN BY
HAPPY MONDAYS
FACTORY/NOVEMBER 1989
UK CHART: 19
(REMIXED AND REISSUED JANUARY 1990: REACHED
NO. 22)

FOOL'S GOLD

THE STONE ROSES

PRODUCED BY JOHN LECKIE/WRITTEN BY
JOHN SQUIRE AND IAN BROWN
SILVERTONE/NOVEMBER 1989
UK CHART: 8
(REISSUED SEPTEMBER 1990: REACHED NO 22; MAY
1992: REACHED NO. 73; APRIL 1995: REACHED NO.
25; REMIXED AND REISSUED FEBRUARY 1999:
REACHED NO. 25)

These two came out on the same day, and, at Rhythm Records in Camden, we may as well have shut the rest of the shop and just sold the two 12-inchers out of the back of a van. It wasn't just indie studes either; 'Fool's Gold' especially was selling to everyone from rave kids to the local shop girls to black B-boys. When the Roses and the Mondays both turned up on *Top of the Pops* – loose, scruffy and arrogant – the following week, the Madchester boom bandwagon was a-rolling. By the time the wheels fell off British rock had been irrevocably altered. On the plus side, any rock band unwilling to get to grips with beats had to put up one helluva strong Luddite argument. On the minus, a uniform, 'you callin' my pint a poof?' laddishness descended

upon our rockblokes; an apolitical white sliced hetero-anxious rock conservatism that shows no sign of lifting, even allowing for the better efforts of the Manics, Pulp, Blur and Radiohead. But then, this is the inevitable result when you turn a few handy funk riffs into a design for life.

The records, though, still rise above all of that. The bandwagon-creating *Madchester* EP rivals 'Flowers of Romance' and 'Death Disco' as the most abstract, rule-breaking Top 20 record ever, a shrieking, wailing, dub-funk-blues four-track celebration of filth and contagious oblivion ('I'm Shaun Willie Ryder! Let me lie down beside ya/Fill ya fulla junk!' he howls terrifyingly on 'Hallelujah'). 'Holy Ghost', 'Clap Your Hands' and 'Rave On' were similarly chaotic, animal, insane and diseased, crashing through pop and dragging PiL, Can, Talking Heads, ACR, The Pop Group, and all that other 1979 post-punk/mutant disco into the mainstream, along with a drug dealer chic pulled straight from the windswept walkways and alleys of bombsite Manchester estates such as Hulme.

As for 'Fool's Gold', it was very simply the greatest funk record ever made by a British band – and I don't mean just a white or rock British band either. Considering the laughably overrated quartet began as third-rate Bunnymen imitators and ended up a Led Zep pub tribute band, it was as if they'd all been hanging around the studio and had suddenly been possessed by the errant spirit of Sly Stone for 9 minutes and 53 seconds, before tumbling back to earth. I still have no idea – or much interest – in what Ian Brown's mumbling about. I just know that he finds the perfect restrained and enigmatic counter-melody for the band's fluid layers of loops, breaks, bass and wah-wah, a magical and unlikely marriage of Brit psychedelia and blaxploitation funk.

I know the credits belong to guitarist Squire and Brown. But, in the wake of all their various post-Roses activities, I can't help wondering if the *credit* should have gone to future Primal Scream bassist Mani, the only one who didn't appear to have a broom stuck up his arse.

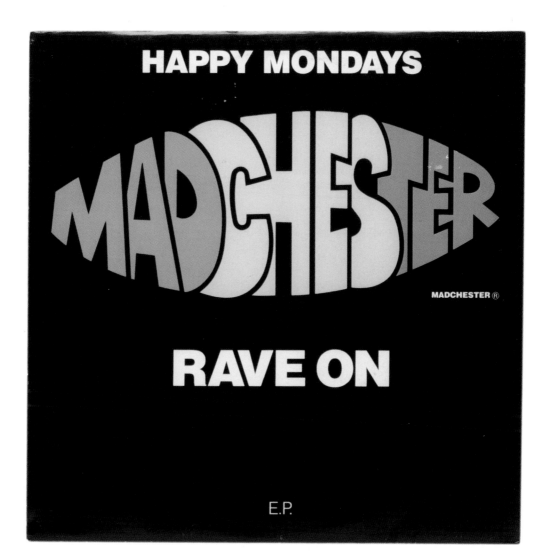

HAPPY MONDAYS

MADCHESTER

MADCHESTER ®

RAVE ON

E.P.

THE MADCHESTER EP/HAPPY MONDAYS
PAGE 296

DOOWUTCHYALIKE

DIGITAL UNDERGROUND
PRODUCED BY SHOCK G/WRITTEN BY
GREGORY JACOBS
B.C.M./TOMMY BOY/DECEMBER 1989
DID NOT CHART

By now, for the hippest hip-hop samplemeisters, James Brown was out and George Clinton was in. EPMD had taken the smoky, claustrophobic side of Clinton's spin-off projects while De La Soul grooved on the freewheeling black psychedelia of Funkadelic on *Three Feet High and Rising*. Shock G of Oakland, California, boosted the fledgling funk of West Coast rap with the help of Parliament's big beats and rude comedy. The debut result was the cheeky surrealism, different-strokes-for-different-folks, jazzy idea overload of the glorious 'Doowutchyalike'. It was weird and catchy and funky in a new way and had a fantastic piano solo and a bit, on the extended version, where it all disappeared and someone made a spoof radio announcement and it just started all over again. I heard it and thought that my beloved hip-hop was going to get ever more mad and sexually open and tolerant and druggy and progressive. However, another Californian group called Niggas With Attitude had already made two nihilistic, misogynist, childish, hate-spewing but indefensibly exciting albums, and the latest was tearing up everything else in America, beginning rap's slow descent into mean-minded machismo, internecine feuding and sexual and political conservatism. One of the background rappers on 'Doowutchyalike', a pretty black militant kid called Tupac Shakur, figured he was in the wrong place at the right time, and jumped on the bandwagon. Most bandwagons just grind to a halt. This one picked up so much speed down its dead-end street there could only be one conclusion.

1990

1990

1990 began with the arrival of a mad cow disease, and ended with the departure of a mad cow. In between contaminated beef and Thatcher weeping as she was magnificently humiliated by her own treacherous and declining party, we saw the two extremes of what politicians can symbolize and achieve – Nelson Mandela's release from jail had grown adults weeping with joy and hugging complete strangers in Trafalgar Square, and John Selwyn Gummer used his own child as a hostage to BSE fortune by feeding her a hamburger for a photo op.

The poll tax provoked a riot, 87 people perished in a fire at an illegal New York rave, Paul Gascoigne bawled like a big Jessie and made football go all touchy-feely, and it was announced that AIDS was now the major killer of women aged between 20 and 40, which really confused the homophobes ('Duh . . . dey musst awl bee dem lezbeens, bubba'). Popwise, it was the last thrilling post-rave year before the early '90s slump, as everything went dayglo and techno and dance-rock for one last time, before the splintering of the scenes led to the new decade's splurge of narrowly focused sub-genres, and an ever-increasing split between pop – a dirty word meaning manufactured music for children and housewives – and 'real' music – everything that wasn't sullied by those nasty uncool charts. From now on, this book becomes increasingly about artists who kicked, in various ways, against that split, and who had the ambition to take on pop on their own terms, as those who invented '90s music were rejected by its new realities, and replaced by acts whose media and marketing savvy were as important as the noises they made.

Honourable mentions: EMF/'Unbelievable' (Parlophone); A Tribe Called Quest/'Bonita Applebum' (Jive); The Charlatans/'The Only One I Know' (Situation Two); Public Enemy/'911 Is a Joke' (Def Jam); Kylie Minogue/'Better the Devil You Know' (PWL)

NOTHING COMPARES 2 U

SINÉAD O'CONNOR

PRODUCED BY SINÉAD O'CONNOR AND
NELLEE HOOPER/WRITTEN BY PRINCE
ENSIGN/JANUARY 1990
UK CHART: 1

A bit of a Theory One contender, this. I mean, we're all agreed Prince *was* a genius, right? And that Sinéad, while a beautiful and fascinating pop character with all her public melodramas and all that, largely makes lumpy Celtic AOR fare and sings a bit flat, yeah? So how come the Prince version of this is completely anonymous, and Sinéad's was so huge and heartbreaking? Well, I guess it has a lot to do with the spacey, empty-house Hooper production. And maybe the tear rolling down her face in the video has a bearing. But mainly it just sounds like Ms O'Connor meant every word of the song while Prince did not. Every catch in her voice lets you know that her pleading is falling on deaf ears, and that she's really just mourning the death of something that was once full of life. It's one of the greatest vocal performances in this book, because O'Connor used her limitations to make the story real.

WELCOME TO THE TERRORDOME

PUBLIC ENEMY

PRODUCED BY HANK SHOCKLEE, CARL RYDER,
ERIC SADLER AND KEITH SHOCKLEE/WRITTEN BY
KEITH SHOCKLEE, ERIC SADLER AND
CARLTON RIDENHOUR
DEF JAM/JANUARY 1990
UK CHART: 18

With Griff temporarily on his way out and the band attacked as racists, PE returned with their angle cleverly turned towards the revolutionary threat of interracial sex – the white supremacist's *Fear of a Black Planet*. The first single rivalled PiL and Happy Mondays for Top 20 sonic subversion, the whole thing based on a boiling, undulating bluesy shudder that isn't even recognizable as a riff. We then get an almost unfathomable and definitely unmatchable mix of Flav going 'Boing!' and quoting Al Pacino from *Scarface*, guitars spitting off-key venom, enormous horn sections cut off in their prime, horny female harmonies, and the best and most complex slew of metaphors and similes Chuck ever wrote. The rush of slogans and wordgames only slam into

focus when he looks back at the slaughter of two black heroes and admits, 'Every brother ain't a brother 'cos a black hand squeezed on Malcolm X the man/The shootin' of Huey Newton[4] . . . the hand of a *nigger* pulled the trigger,' his voice breaking like Sinéad's and falling agonized and weary over the last four words. It's almost as if he could see the deadly east-west rap game coming, and the truth of black-on-black violence had suddenly reared up on him, and broken his heart.

LOADED

PRIMAL SCREAM

PRODUCED BY ANDREW WEATHERALL/WRITTEN BY
BOBBY GILLESPIE, ROBERT YOUNG AND ANDREW
INNES
CREATION/FEBRUARY 1990
UK CHART: 16

The record company rep strode into the record shop I worked at, with an 'I know something you don't' air. 'Here's a white label for you, lads,' he said. 'Thanks . . . who's it by?' 'Primal Scream.' Ten minutes passed as we laughed ourselves wet and drew up plans to turn it into an art-deco ashtray. The rep waited patiently. Finally, he said, 'I think you ought to play it.' 'Why?' 'I just think you should.' So we did.

Ten more minutes later, as we tried to wire our jaws back together after the record's shatteringly sexy fusion of the Stones, Soul II Soul, wild biker B-movies, and, somewhere underneath it all, a wee smidgin of an actual Primal Scream '60s retro dirge called 'I'm Losing More Than I'll Ever Have', the rep was standing there, still smiling. 'But . . . *how can this be*?' one of us cried, as we tried to comprehend a world turned upside down. 'Remixed. By a DJ called Andy Weatherall. Called "Loaded". What do you think?' 'Great. No, *really* great. Can I have one as well?' 'HAHAHAHA!!! No. Bye.'

LOADED/PRIMAL SCREAM

THE SHIP SONG

NICK CAVE & THE BAD SEEDS
PRODUCED BY NICK CAVE AND THE BAD
SEEDS/WRITTEN BY NICK CAVE
MUTE/MARCH 1990
DID NOT CHART

The first great Nick Cave love song was a big surprise – pianos, harmonies, Spectoresque production, (relatively) straight crooning, a heartfelt tribute to love cut with Cave's newly discovered skill at leaving a barely suggested black hole into which the love will eventually, inevitably, fade and die. There was no white noise, no howling at the moon, no southern Gothic, no murders . . . although the girl does set some dogs upon him at regular intervals. Kids' stuff, after all those bats.

THE HUMPTY DANCE

DIGITAL UNDERGROUND
PRODUCED BY SHOCK G/WRITTEN BY
GREGORY JACOBS
B.C.M./TOMMY BOY/MARCH 1990
DID NOT CHART

Let's get this straight from the start: Greg Jacobs, that is, Shock G, had an alter-ego called Humpty Hump. And why not? Anyway, Humpty Hump's special characteristic was a huge false nose. This is because Humpty, that is Shock G, set fire to his real nose in a kitchen accident. Keeping up? OK. So Shock G, that is, Humpty, goes into the studio and makes Digital Underground's biggest US hit and most indefatigable P-funk anthem out of this nasal tragedy. It is called 'The Humpty Dance', and it is about how Humpty satisfies women with . . . ah, you're ahead of me now, aren't you?

KILLER

ADAMSKI
PRODUCED BY ADAMSKI/WRITTEN BY ADAMSKI AND
SEAL
MCA/MARCH 1990
UK CHART: 1
(RE-RECORDED AND REISSUED BY SEAL ON ZTT IN
NOVEMBER 1991: REACHED NO. 8)

And speaking, as we kind of are, of doomed relationships, how nuts was this one? Adam Tinley was a camp white anarchist synth-rave boffin who made a punk record on the Fast label when he was 11 and a hit called 'N-R-G' that accidentally invented Guru Josh in 1989. Sealhenry Samuel was a 20-foot Nigerian-Brazilian black dread who overcame facial scarring and a difficult childhood in north-west London to become a '90s adult-pop superstar. Yet together they made a record that only George Michael could ruin.

'Killer' was exactly that – a deadly slice of beefed-up electro-pop with one of pop's best-ever doomy basslines, twitching techno percussion, and Seal's sad honey-soul voice bringing melancholy solace to the solitary brothers and sisters in a sort of Soul II Soul-meets-'Ebony and Ivory' way. There's a great Moment when Adamski takes Seal's falsetto trill on the word 'Be' and turns it into freaked Morse code before Seal shuts it off with a Prince-growled '*Yeah!!!*' Afterwards, the white one wasn't very good and stiffed, while the black one wasn't very good and bestrode the world like a colossal 20-foot aquatic mammal.

STEP ON

HAPPY MONDAYS
PRODUCED BY PAUL OAKENFOLD AND
STEVE OSBOURNE/WRITTEN BY JOHN KONGOS AND
CHRISTOS DEMETRIOU
FACTORY/MARCH 1990
UK CHART: 5

The Mondays started to take the mainstream on a weird trip. Their dance-pop cover of forgotten '60s South African John Kongos's 'He's Gonna Step On You Again' (they'd already rediscovered ancient novelty crooner Karl Denver on 'Lazyitis' and, God help us, Donovan on their forthcoming LP) paved the way for all those future dance-scene obsessions with '60s easy

KILLER/ADAMSKI

listening and soundtrack composers. But it also established Ryder's skill at making the psychotic tyrannies of bad men sound like celebrations. That bright and bouncy Italo-house-derived fanfare introduced Ryder laughing merrily about another geezer's fascistic ability to 'make you forget you're a man', while Mark Day's guitar rang out the changes, and we were introduced to Rowetta's soul backing vox and warned not to twist Shaun's melons, man. At last, a British band capable of smuggling a secret, loaded language onto the airwaves in time-honoured, only-The-Kids-understand style.

SOON

MY BLOODY VALENTINE
PRODUCED BY MY BLOODY VALENTINE/WRITTEN BY
KEVIN SHIELDS
CREATION/APRIL 1990
UK CHART: 41

As if the Great Leaps Forward of the Mondays, Roses and Primal Scream weren't enough, even the era's leading noise terrorists briefly caught the dance-pop bug. 'Soon' was indie-dance's most cosmic and spine-tingling missive, as a wall of decaying guitars found chord changes that froze your blood and repeatedly fell, swooning, off trad-rock's radar and into a hallucinatory perversion of gravity's pull, while a bright string-loop jigged like a Morris dancer and merged, near-comatose male/female voices breathed erotic words for harmonic effect. A separate Andy Weatherall remix hit home the punk-disco marriage by blending Gang of Four and pure funk rhythms . . . making a pair of equal-but-different milestones that added up to the long overdue revenge of mutant disco.

HOLD ON

EN VOGUE
PRODUCED BY THOMAS MCELROY AND
DENZIL FOSTER/WRITTEN BY THOMAS MCELROY,
DENZIL FOSTER AND EN VOGUE
ATLANTIC/APRIL 1990
UK CHART: 5

Meanwhile, black America pressed on with a much needed alternative to all the testosterone-fuelled hip-hop He-man-isms of the era. The precursors of Destiny's Child's sassy manufactured femme-funk (and their endless line-up changes), En Vogue and their creators Foster–McElroy stripped down swingbeat's nasal teen gimmicks and hollered throaty adult sex, love and desire over tough, sparse hip-hop beats. 'Hold On' was clearly influenced by – and proved as influential as – Soul II Soul's warm beat classicisms, beginning with a stunningly beautiful a capella demonstration, before the beats slammed in and bumped mercilessly, and the new Supremes sung their bruised romance as if love were an insoluble and disturbing mystery movie – which, of course, it is. 'Hold On' proved a retro-*nuevo* revelation in the five minutes it took to reinvent real American soul.

EVERYTHING FLOWS

TEENAGE FANCLUB
PRODUCED BY TEENAGE FANCLUB/WRITTEN BY
NORMAN BLAKE
PAPERHOUSE/JUNE 1990
DID NOT CHART

ONLY LOVE CAN BREAK YOUR HEART

SAINT ETIENNE
PRODUCED BY SAINT ETIENNE/WRITTEN BY
NEIL YOUNG
HEAVENLY/JULY 1990
DID NOT CHART
(REISSUED AUGUST 1991: REACHED NO. 39)

Glasgow's most cuddly began as Dinosaur Jr with a smiley face, before their long career as Creation's resident Neil Young-worshipping record collector rock classicists. Their first single is so lovely even a production near-disaster cannot dim its light, as a mudpile of droning guitars go through a set of tearjerk chord changes, and Norman Blake establishes their easy-going, confused melancholia: 'I'll never know which way to go/Set a course for . . . I don't know.' The song simply carries on reflecting the title, piling on jangle after jangle, and flowing to fade with a few casually tossed-off Best Guitar Solos of All Time. The Fannies have continued happily in this vein with better jokes and better production, but, inexplicably, never quite convinced as much again.

London's most cuddly began as indie-dancers with a dreamy face before their long career as Heavenly's resident Neil Young-

EVERYTHING FLOWS/TEENAGE FANCLUB

worshipping record collector pop classicists. Their first single is a lovely production masterpiece, as echoing beats and piano go through their tearjerk paces, flowing to fade with vocalist Moira Lambert's sweet blankness representing the empty implications of the title and a few casually tossed-off Biggest Beats of All Time. Bob Stanley, Pete Wiggs and permanent vocalist Sarah Cracknell have continued happily in this vein with kitschier jokes, but . . . you get the picture.

COME TOGETHER

PRIMAL SCREAM
PRODUCED BY PRIMAL SCREAM
(ADDITIONAL PRODUCTION AND REMIX BY
TERRY FARLEY)/WRITTEN BY BOBBY GILLESPIE,
ANDREW INNES AND ROBERT YOUNG
CREATION/JULY 1990
UK CHART: 26

The previous two entries and this pre-*Screamdelica* anthem were all bound up with what was soon to become a Britpop mafia. PR man Jeff Barrett's Heavenly, manager and mogul Alan McGee's Creation and a loose aggregation of DJs, bloggers, movers and shakers based around a sharp, nouveau-mod music/fashion/footie/drugs/club lifestyle fanzine called *Boy's Own* became influential almost to the point of media monopoly, using long-established press goodwill, swap-around dance-rock collaborations and crossovers, and a great deal of entrepreneurial vision. Essentially, they pinpointed the fact that British rock had been a timid, fey, unglamorous, politically correct and narcotically straight alternative for far too long. The Roses and the Mondays had proved how much white Brit kids wanted something more dangerous and street, and that journalists needed some wild boys to write about. The Creation/Heavenly/*Boy's Own* axis transformed Britrock into a boy's club, and the seeds of New Laddism were sown.

The Scream's forthcoming 'Screamadelica' album was where it all came together, as this keynote single baldly states. 'Come Together' aimed at – and reached – another kind of connection, of course – the twinning of 'Let It Bleed'-era gospel junkie rock and optimistic E culture. But nevertheless, when a frontman who danced like a nelly, looked like the school nerd on smack and sang like my seven-year-old nephew after a big boy came and stole his doughnuts briefly became British rock's new Messiah, you knew that the mass appeal lay not in a revival of rock star glamour, but in a 'he's just like us!' celebration of ordinary

awkwardness. If Bobby could imagine himself as Mick Jagger, then all of us could be anything – especially if we were backed up by the power of the female gospel chorus, the nod to Elvis's 'Suspicious Minds' and the choogling 12-bar of Andrew Innes's Memphis soul guitar, the lisping, languid romance of the melody, the classic Stones piano-chord sequence, and the effortless frug 'n' roll of *Boy's Own* DJ Farley's dynamic, widescreen, gradually climbing mix.

WHAT TIME IS LOVE?
(LIVE AT TRANCENTRAL)

THE KLF FEATURING THE CHILDREN OF THE REVOLUTION
PRODUCED BY THE KLF/WRITTEN BY JAMES CAUTY,
WILLIAM DRUMMOND AND MC BELLO
KLF COMMUNICATIONS/AUGUST 1990
UK CHART: 5
(RE-RECORDED AS 'AMERICA: WHAT TIME IS LOVE?'
FEBRUARY 1992: REACHED NO. 4)

Where do you start? The sample-terrorism of The Justified Ancients of Mu-Mu, where they exposed the future of pop-theft by stealing Abba, The Beatles and Whitney Houston? The ambient/prog satire of the *Chill Out* album, which actually started a techno trend? The book they wrote about how to make a No. 1 record that they then successfully applied with the appalling 'Doctorin' the Tardis' as the Timelords? The dead sheep and the Extreme Noise Terror performance at the 1992 Brits? The Turner Prize-mirroring £40,000 worst-piece-of-art award to the ridiculous Rachel Whiteread? The did-they-didn't-they? 'art' stunt of burning a million quid on a remote Scottish island? The amount of recycling/remixing piss-take mileage they got out of 'What Time Is Love?', which had already been an underground trance hit and an entire album by the time this version became a massive pop hit? Or maybe just the fact that Echo and The Bunnymen's manager Bill Drummond and his partner-in-crime Jimmy Cauty managed to make the nation dance to their intellectually charged, situationist contempt for everything about the 'business' of art and culture? Wherever you begin, The Kopyright Liberation Front were the Chris Morris of pop, and we should worship them, for we will almost certainly never see their like again.

COME TOGETHER/PRIMAL SCREAM

WHERE ARE YOU BABY?

BETTY BOO

PRODUCED BY BETTY BOO AND KING JOHN
(ADDITIONAL PRODUCTION AND MIX BY
PETE LORIMER)/WRITTEN BY BETTY BOO
RHYTHM KING/AUGUST 1990
UK CHART: 3

Amongst all the white-boy plotting and scheming, we spared a little room, briefly, for mixed-race female kitsch. Even the sternest rock blokes seemed to fall in love with Scots/Malaysian Londoner Alison Clarkson, and her giggly rush of '60s trash-culture references, pouty lips and helium rapping. 'Where Are You Baby?' is both a preview of the Spice Girls and Girl Power, and a funnier, more rebellious proposition altogether, with its unashamed trash aesthetic and utter refusal to accept that rap was anything but talking gibberish, and pop anything but a grab bag of cheap cosmetics and a bunch of machines permanently set on 'catchy'. It winked conspiratorially at the girls, while momentarily distracting the boys from all that male bonding.

Proving even smarter than she looked, Ms Boo cashed in her pop star chips within three years and currently pursues a successful career writing songs for manufactured pop bands. If only some of these stage school fame-slaves could perform them with an ounce of her humour, gusto and sauce, then maybe we'd be able to watch teen pop TV again without vomiting.

GROOVE IS IN THE HEART

DEEE-LITE

PRODUCED AND WRITTEN BY DEEE-LITE
ELEKTRA/AUGUST 1990
UK CHART: 2

If Brit mixed-race kitsch was plastic and tinny, New York kitsch was made from only the best dayglo ingredients and roared with laughter, love and the art of the groove. But it was so much more than that. Not only is the debut single from Ohio's Lady Miss Kier, Kiev's DJ Dmitri and Tokyo's Towa Tei the greatest dance record of the years this book covers, but, if I were asked to pick just one record that summed up as many of the impulses and styles we've dealt with as possible and made them click without showing the joins, it would be this one, *the* 'Uncool' single.

Based upon the bassline from jazz-fusion great Herbie Hancock's 'Bring Down the Birds', 'Groove . . .' welds tough street groove to high-concept pop, catwalk to junk shop, sample-delia (Deee-Lite's phrase) to live party feel, hip-hop to disco, house to jazz funk, black to white, Euro to Americano, P-funk's Bootsy Collins to daisy age rapper Q-Tip (both on guest vocals), sex to slapstick, Todd Terry instrumental beat science to louche vocal comedy, space to chaos, wry New York mutant-disco aesthetic to the 1988 Summer of Love, male aggression to female sensuality, soul integrity to airy pop playfulness . . . and then dispatches it all with punk intensity. If I were ever forced to play some crazy DJ version of Russian roulette, where you had one chance and one chance only to make a roomful of disparate people dance or you die – I would play 'Groove Is in the Heart' and book my cab home. It invented Fatboy Slim and Basement Jaxx and Missy Elliott and all other recent dance music that keeps it bright and funny while pushing the funky sonic envelope. It made everything around it at the time – even all the great stuff – sound monochrome. Including the rest of Deee-Lite's career, sadly. Still, if they hadn't put all their best ideas in one kitsch '70s pot, we wouldn't have the wonder that is 'Groove Is in the Heart'.

MY LEGENDARY GIRLFRIEND

PULP

PRODUCED BY ALAN SMYTH AND PULP/WRITTEN BY
PULP
FIRE/SEPTEMBER 1990
DID NOT CHART

Strangely, a bunch of Sheffield indie blokes (and girl) were working along not entirely dissimilar lines – albeit without the hi-tech production and the hip-hop element. Pulp had jangled and yelped anonymously throughout the '80s, but refused to lose and were about to make their leap into stardom. The first sign of something stirring was this – the sound of a Yorkshire art-school dropout reinventing himself as Barry White over a sound that reclaimed the brittle '80s arch-pop that everyone else had utterly rejected.

'My Legendary Girlfriend' is a scream – a prophecy of all the sleazy sex, self-deprecating wit and Morrissey-on-E imagery we would come to love in Jarvis Cocker in a few years' time. Over a two-four Motown-style rhythm, a mighty machine-gun bassline doubled on piano, plastic strings and Isaac Hayes wah-wah stabs, Jarvis just breathes sexual desperation into his legendary girlfriend's ear until he's in a sloppy froth of lust. The choruses are all very croony '80s electro-pop – a sort of toytown

WHAT TIME IS LOVE? (LIVE AT TRANCENTRAL)/THE KLF
FEATURING THE CHILDREN OF THE REVOLUTION

Human League – but you just want them to end so we can get back to the molten groove of the verse, a loving parody of boudoir-soul cut with the irony-free frustration of Jarvis's knowledge that the champagne is Special Brew, the satin sheets smell of damp towels and asthma inhalers, and that he is, in fact, a broke and skinny white boy, and not a big black walrus of lurrrve.

THERE SHE GOES

THE LA'S

PRODUCED BY BOB ANDREWS (REMIXED BY
STEVE LILLYWHITE)/WRITTEN BY LEE MAVERS
GO! DISCS/OCTOBER 1990
UK CHART: 13
(REISSUED ON POLYDOR IN SEPTEMBER 1999:
REACHED NO. 65)

The Britpop future, Part Two. This time it wasn't an artist who would help define the mid-'90s, but a sound, as a bunch of Liverpool 'scallies' reinvented the Golden Era of English pop – that quintessential moment between Merseybeat innocence and drug-addled psychedelia when The Beatles, Stones and Who seemed to reinvent pop on a weekly basis, all the girls were gamine and panda-eyed, and the world swung in time to London's beat. The melody, the texture and the choirboy-thug singing voice on 'There She Goes' was immediately familiar – as if it had woken some dormant Britbeat beast that had been sleeping inside our heads – but glowed with a whole new freshness and innocence, as if The La's had never listened to any music and therefore thought they'd made the sound up themselves. Every time you hear its blissful, impossibly idealized tribute to another legendary girlfriend (or, according to some wags, to smack, which only goes to show how desperate some rock blokes are to ruin something beautiful) you feel nostalgic. Not for Autumn 1990 (it had originally been released as a less radio-friendly version in November 1988), but for some mythical Britpop Camelot that you were too young to visit and which probably never existed anyway.

La's mainman Lee Mavers became the Great Enigma of British rock, as he railed in interviews against the production on The La's debut album and locked himself away to find the noises in his head, a Scouse Brian Wilson in his sandpit. Ten years have passed in which La's bassist John Power formed Cast, becoming the first musician to start his own second-rate tribute band . . .

and Mavers is still in a garage somewhere, gabbling to those who track him down about alien waves and searching for the 13th note. The drugs do work. That's the problem.

KINKY AFRO

HAPPY MONDAYS

PRODUCED BY PAUL OAKENFOLD AND
STEVE OSBOURNE/WRITTEN BY HAPPY MONDAYS
FACTORY/OCTOBER 1990
UK CHART: 5

'Son – I'm thirty/I only went with your mother 'cos she's dirty/And I don't have a decent bone in me/What you get is just what you see – yeah!' Those extraordinary opening lines mark the best and last Happy Mondays entry and Shaun Ryder's most potent and problematic study of male evil. As the Beatlesesque guitar lick snaked and circled, and Ryder raged with relish about crucifying 'some brother', everyone laughed and danced and dismissed the title as some kind of kitsch joke. But, as a mixed-race kid who has never met his Jamaican dad, I can only say what I heard. Because 'Kinky Afro' struck me as the first-person testimony of the kind of black man who sprays his seed and walks away, the absent black father who was simultaneously cropping up in many US rap lyrics of the time, the nastier truth behind The Who's 'Substitute'. The fact that Ryder was brave enough both to inhabit that character and make him defiant rather than apologetic is what makes him one of the most underrated truth-tellers in British pop history. Because, as his friend and Mondays' dancer Bez got homophobic in a notorious Steven Wells *NME* interview, and the band fell heavily and druggily from grace, Ryder became little more than the subject of ribald drug stories – The Most Fucked-Up Man Alive. Having a bad habit and not having a great deal of alternative career options, Ryder went along with his court jester role. But underneath all that bollocks is the most skilled and rebellious maverick Britrock lyricist and commentator this side of Rotten and Morrissey. However, as those two also found out, there's usually more rock money and mileage in self-parody than there is in keeping it real.

WHERE ARE YOU BABY?/BETTY BOO

AFTERMATH

NIGHTMARES ON WAX
PRODUCED BY NIGHTMARES ON WAX/WRITTEN BY
GEORGE EVELYN AND KEVIN HARPER
WARP/OCTOBER 1990
UK CHART: 38

As Sheffield had been the birthplace, through The Human League and Cabaret Voltaire, of British electronic art-disco it was only fitting that UK techno's key record label and best early single hailed from south Yorkshire's (former) Steel City. Warp's set of spiky, deliberately anonymous electronicists ('faceless techno bollocks', wailed the few remaining unloved-up rockists) produced a run of futuristic instrumental singles that made the charts, but 'Aftermath' was the stunner: a black female soul voice singing of 'something unreal', looped at a horror-movie angle around pounding beats and blundering speaker-blowing bass, a Bam Bam-style bad trip hit home by tense industrial synth effects, tribal chants and dramatic, rhythmic echo on the lonely soul vocal. Amazingly, and in time-honoured fashion, the English had taken on an American noise and improved it.

MAMA SAID KNOCK YOU OUT

LL COOL J
PRODUCED BY MARLEY MARL/WRITTEN BY
MARLON WILLIAMS AND JAMES TODD SMITH
DEF JAM/NOVEMBER 1990
UK CHART: 41

After falling foul of the hardcore rap fans by way of too many weedy pop compromises, our favourite rap Bad Boy was teetering on the edge of Run-D.M.C.-style career meltdown. So he enlisted supercred producer and Cold Chillin' label mainman Marley Marl to make him a comeback. Except, famously, it wasn't. The tough beats swaggered in, a posse chanted, 'Gangsta boogie,' LL yelled, '*DAMN!*', a TV newscaster spread the news, a Sly Stone funk harmony spread ominous sleaze, and . . . SLAMMM!!! 'Don't call it a comeback!/I bin here for *years*,' roared a bigger, wealthier, more desperate version of the kid who terrorized the hood with his radio, who then proceeded to go 'maniac psycho' in violent simile and reduce the MC opposition to the repeated squeal of a baby. A veteran rapper called Kool Moe Dee had had the nerve and gall to take a pop at LL on a track called 'How You Like Me Now?', and even after spitting

venom at him, the knowledge of that slight sends LL on the rampage, his voice scarred and raging as he boils over completely: '*OOOOOoo!* – Listen to the way ah *slayyyy*/Your crew!/Damage-UH! – damage-UH! – damage-UH! –*Damage-UHH!!!*/Destruction, terror and mayhem/Pass me a sissy and sucka I'll slay them . . . I think ah'm gonna bomb a *towwwwn*!' Hilarious, breathtaking in its 'Empire State Human' delusions (see p. 100), utterly irresistible . . . he made crap records again, and rival rappers *did* take him on again. But an *un*Cool James had made his point for all time.

BEING BORING

PET SHOP BOYS
PRODUCED BY PET SHOP BOYS AND
HAROLD FALTERMEYER/WRITTEN BY NEIL TENNANT
AND CHRIS LOWE
PARLOPHONE/NOVEMBER 1990
UK CHART: 20

The Pet Shop Boys survived and thrived through the post-rave realities, simply because they had always loved and understood dance music, and, unusually for a pop group, had a loyal constituency of fans who stuck with them as a foundation to their changing tastes. Only PSB could've made a great hit album with that ultimate symbol of dodgy '80s dance production, 'Axel F'-maker Faltermeyer. Only PSB could get a hit with a slow sad song called 'Being Boring'. Only PSB could say sayonara to the '80s not with a ravey wave, but a grieving whisper, a count of the tragic cost.

Neil Tennant has never said that the deceased real-life friend he is singing to died of AIDS. Whether he did or he didn't, the lines in the last verse – when Neil quietly observes that 'All the people I was kissing/Some are here and some are missing/In the nineteen-nineties . . . But I thought in spite of dreams/You'd be sitting somewhere here with me' – pay a dignified and beautiful tribute to all those lost in what had amounted, in the 1980s, to a holocaust. As the rock and rap worlds began to write and behave as if AIDS couldn't affect *them*, 'Being Boring's' undertones of grief and controlled anger seemed all the more relevant.

1991

1991

It was like the sudden ending of a long dark journey into the very soul of misery and oppression. No, not the end of the Soviet Union, silly. But 27 October 1991, when Bryan Adams was finally knocked off the top of the singles charts after 16 weeks, and British pop emerged from its very own period of Siberian hard labour. It's a recurring theme in the world of the pop single – after every pop-culture shakedown, along comes a gi-normous and gi-normously turgid hit to remind you that things haven't really changed forever, and that there are always more of Them than there is of you. But '(Everything I Do) I Do It for You' was an extreme, the singles equivalent of the long '80s puzzle of who exactly kept voting for Margaret Thatcher. I'm still yet to meet a single human being who admits they bought this record.

In truth, though, our Canadian friend didn't have a great deal of competition. The drop in pop's standards straight after the glories of 1987–90 was far more precipitous than it had been after 1977–81. Reasons? The splintering of the rave scene, the rise of gangsta rap, and the obliteration of indie dance, as the Roses and Mondays went into sharp decline and the hundreds of baggy chancers who rose in their wake were exposed as . . . well . . . baggy chancers, and nothing more. A cold northern winter fell over the British rock scene as it struggled for a new direction – particularly as most of even the worst 'indie' bands had been signed in a major-label feeding frenzy and soon proved themselves incapable of surviving in an environment where ambition was compulsory. It may be an unfashionable opinion, in the midst of our current obsession with displays of material wealth and the banal lifestyles of empty-headed celebs, but this phase of rock failed because – Mondays aside – it had nothing of value to say . . . a state of affairs that has never really changed since. With Britrock all played out, the only bright home-grown sparks were acts from a soul and hip-hop background, who created the foundations of two much maligned genres: acid jazz and trip hop. This proved fortuitous for me a couple of years later, as I was given an opportunity to write about the alt-jazz/rap scene for black British music mag *Echoes* (believe me, there wasn't a queue). Sneer at the likes of Jamiroquai and The Brand New Heavies as much as you like (and I'll quite happily join you), but the more maverick aspects of the club-jazz scene created a space for the likes of Portishead, Tricky, Basement Jaxx and Moby to thrive. The coffee-table album – usually some form of adult dance crossover that had probably won or been nominated for the new Mercury Music Prize and provided a perfect soundtrack for that hip dinner party – was on its way.

The major events of 1991 made us feel like we'd wandered onto the set of a Hollywood high-concept war epic. The Gulf War, The IRA's mortar attack on 10 Downing Street, and, particularly, the surreal two-day Communist coup in Russia and Boris Yeltsin's subsequent public humiliation of Gorbachev, were political violence as sheer spectacle. They just didn't seem real. Perhaps we'd reached a point where what would have filled us with dread in the mid-'80s had become just more small-screen drama – we felt untouchable. Yet, just in case we felt *too* bulletproof, the death of Freddie Mercury and the revelation that US basketball's Golden Boy Magic Johnson was HIV positive proved that the rich and famous were not immune to life's horrors. In fact, one event made that bombshell feel like justice, as fat crook Robert Maxwell took a short walk off a big boat.

Honourable mentions: Nicolette/'Waking Up' (Shut Up And Dance); A Tribe Called Quest/'Can I Kick It?' (Jive); Tim Dog/ 'F-ck Compton' (Ruffhouse/Columbia); Urban Soul/'Alright' (Cooltempo); Naughty by Nature/'O.P.P.' (Tommy Boy); The Pixies/'Planet of Sound' (4AD); Blur/'There's No Other Way' (Food); T99/'Anasthasia' (XL); Pet Shop Boys/'Where the Streets Have No Name (Can't Take My Eyes Off You)' (Parlophone)

YOU GOT THE LOVE
(EREN'S BOOTLEG MIX)

THE SOURCE FEATURING CANDI STATON
PRODUCED BY THE SOURCE/WRITTEN BY STEPHENS,
HARRIS, BELLAMY AND PRINCIPLE
TRUELOVE/JANUARY 1991
UK CHART: 4

One of the most soulful and inspirational club favourites of the early '90s, 'You Got the Love' was an inspired coupling of two separate records – an a capella of a 1986 soul ballad by veteran 'Young Hearts Run Free' Alabama soul-diva Candi Staton, and the instrumental version of a 1989 underground Chicago house hit by Frankie Knuckles and Jamie Principle, called 'Your Love'. 'Your Love' was weird stand-out fare in the first place, an alternately sparse and ornate, doomy electro-pop throwback with overwrought, Princeish vocals from Principle and a beat far too slow and flat to dance to. DJ John Truelove and co. used the eerie juxtaposition of the clinking, probing, string-drenched electronica and Staton's bluesy bravura to create a gospel ballad that redefined the word 'haunting'. The title of the mix came from the track's origins – the increasingly widespread – and illegal – DJ/remixer enterprise of doing home-made mixes of tracks, playing them out as 'exclusives', and, if they worked out on the floor, pressing them up as 'bootleg' white labels for specialist dance shops. Truelove made the effort to get the appropriate permissions, make it official, and score a massive, era-defining hit.

UNFINISHED SYMPATHY

MASSIVE
PRODUCED BY MASSIVE WITH JONNY
DOLLAR/WRITTEN BY GRANT MARSHALL,
ANDREW VOWLES, ROBERT DEL NAJA,
JONNY SHARP,AND SHARA NELSON
WILD BUNCH/CIRCA/FEBRUARY 1991
UK CHART: 13

Yes . . . just Massive. As some may remember, the Bristol crew's emphatic entry into musical legend came out with their name chopped in half, lest anyone think it was some kind of comment on the Gulf War. The typical Brit media hypocrisy that insists we change an irrelevant band name, but gets off on watching the bombs on TV.

Still, that has nothing to do with the impact this heartbreaking thing had on British pop, then and now. The track's imperious meld of jingling hip-hop beats, ominous cinematic strings and Nelson's weeping soul grief made it the soundtrack to every lost love you'd ever known. Shara's astonishing vocal made sense of the title's bad pun – as her operatic falsettos and tremulous wails teetered on the verge of an incoherent hysteria, mining what seemed like a bottomless well of pain. The feeling that this was a whole new kind of soul was further reinforced by The Moment – perhaps the very best of all this book's Moments – when the turquoise gloom suddenly shifts in key, and Will Malone's strings soar blissfully upwards, the glorious light at the end of the tunnel, climbing and flying and looking forward to the better love that is always on its way . . . until, with a shudder of dark cellos, the flight is over, the light is cruelly snuffed out, you're dumped back alone and grieving. Never had so many men and women had to suddenly run to the club toilet, covering their faces, assuring you that they just had something in their eye.

APPARENTLY NOTHIN'

YOUNG DISCIPLES
PRODUCED BY YOUNG DISCIPLES AND
DEMUS/WRITTEN BY CARLEEN ANDERSON AND
MARCO NELSON
TALKIN LOUD/FEBRUARY 1991
UK CHART: 46
(REISSUED JULY 1991: REACHED NO. 13)

'Unfinished Sympathy's' more politicized and less agonized twin entered the charts on the same day – signalling a new start for British black music. Although it wasn't strictly black nor strictly British when the Disciples came together, a joining of visionary soul forces comprising a black and a white DJ from London's rare-groove scene, Femi and Marco, and the daughter of two of their heroes, Carleen Anderson, whose parents Bobby Byrd and Vicki Anderson had been vital members of James Brown's legendary funk family. Having established her pedigree and a tough-but-sunny funk-hip-hop groove intro, Ms Anderson's bleeding gospel wail hit us with this: 'A popularity of invasion/Handed down through centuries/A force of arms called gentle persuasion/What have we learned from history . . . Apparently nothin'.' If that reads as a pretty sophisticated take on the old anti-war protest song, then it sounded like the Sermon on the Mount against the backdrop of the Gulf War.

UNFINISHED SYMPATHY/MASSIVE

The Disciples quickly became the heroes of the rare groove/nascent acid jazz scene, selling records in the States and influencing black America to rediscover its jazz-soul roots. They seemed to have the world at their feet. But Femi and Marco did a Lee Mavers (without the drug paranoia, I hasten to add) and refused to follow up their *Road to Freedom* album. Carleen went solo and later joined the Brand New Heavies but could never quite find that groove again.

LOSING MY RELIGION

R.E.M.

PRODUCED BY SCOTT LITT AND R.E.M./WRITTEN BY BILL BERRY, PETER BUCK, MIKE MILLS AND MICHAEL STIPE
WARNERS/FEBRUARY 1991
UK CHART: 19

The song that vaulted R.E.M. overnight from respected '80s cult band to '90s rock megastars is an elusive, self-referential thing, with its 'That's me in the spotlight' wails and intimations of lost faith. In fact, Stipe insisted that the title and hook was a phrase that meant losing control . . . saying too much, as he tells us repeatedly. It established Stipe's soulful, rock-historical vocal skill in making lyrical conversations sound like messages to the world. He's bolstered, of course, by Buck's beatific mandolin, a great melody and the best trad-rock rhythm section on Earth.

Incidentally, in the interests of expert advice for any young musicians who may be reading, when I interviewed Stipe a few years ago and asked him why R.E.M. had survived and thrived without public spats and 'musical differences' coming between them, he pointed to the unshifting democracy of R.E.M. songwriting credits. In fact, drummer Berry had got bored with the rock lifestyle and had left by this time. But at least the remaining trio know he's never gonna sue his friends for the unpaid royalties and recognition of his rightful share of the collaborative process that so many rock egos never want to acknowledge.

WHO'S GONNA TAKE THE WEIGHT?

GANG STARR

PRODUCED AND WRITTEN BY DJ PREMIER AND GURU
COOLTEMPO/FEBRUARY 1991
DID NOT CHART

I COME OFF (SOUTHERN COMFORT MIX)

YOUNG MC

PRODUCED BY MATT DIKE AND MICHAEL ROSS (REMIXED BY DAVE DORRELL AND C.J. MACKINTOSH)/WRITTEN BY MARVIN YOUNG, MATT DIKE AND MICHAEL ROSS
DELICIOUS VINYL/FOURTH & BROADWAY/MARCH 1991
DID NOT CHART

By the end of 1991, the baggies, B-boys and ravers who frequented Rhythm Records had been almost obliterated by an odd crew of guys in goatees, waistcoats and dodgy headwear asking us to 'track' (that is, play through the tracks on) obscure and expensive jazz, funk and rap import albums. The two import 12-inch singles they all bought in such quantities that, if this was being replicated elsewhere in the country, meant they had no chance of charting once finally given a Brit release, were both New York rap records that caught a new two-tone hip-hop mood. Indeed, one starred the voice of a black New Yorker originally from Neasden, was produced by two white bohos, had been remixed by two white London DJs, and featured a backing-track pinched from the swamps of black Louisiana.

The original album cut of 'I Come Off' was cute but inconsequential pop-rap. But someone from the Delicious Vinyl label was obviously aware of this British funk revival thing, and gave Dorrell and Mackintosh carte blanche to transform it into a hip-hop masterpiece, simply by adding a few smoky effects, a couple of new backing vocals, and, crucially, the deep, awesome, dangerous bassline from 'Hercules', a '70s black-struggle soul anthem by one Aaron Neville. Young's witty brag wordplays and virtuoso vocal rhythms ('I get raw like Eddie/*Rrrrough* like Freddie/Kruger with a Luger turn the men into spaghetti!' flows likes the rolls of a Latin percussion master) were transformed into a strutting, loping exposition of black pride and intellect. Everyone on the new funk scene combed the specialist shops for Neville's 'Hercules' and found it was even better. But that's a whole other book.

CHECK THE RHIME/A TRIBE CALLED QUEST

Boston rapper Keith 'Guru' Elam probably chose the worst band name he could have before hooking up with Brooklyn beatmeister Chris 'Premier' Martin. Gang Starr's leader and future mainman of jazz-rap wanted hip-hop to rise above the gang wars and the language of violence, his deadpan wordiness and ghetto-reportage style introducing a new kind of street intellectualism to the scene. 'Who's Gonna Take . . .', a mere B-side both here and in the States, became a boho Asiatic funk anthem and remains the duo's high water mark – JB-funk cut with crackling political speeches and Guru's powerful and much loved opening-line: 'I was raised as a Muslim/Praying to the East.' Later, Elam admitted that he'd been raised a Christian, actually, but that this sounded better, and he was right. The track was sent into overdrive, though, by Premier's incredible parade of turntable effects – a high whistle scratched, spun and rewound into a series of spooked clarion calls, catchy, mysterious, superbly skilled, a hip-hop DJ version of the Asian spiritual quest in a John Coltrane solo. Except it made you dance as well as wonder what it all meant.

OPTIMISTIC

SOUNDS OF BLACKNESS

PRODUCED AND WRITTEN BY GARY HINES,
JIMMY JAM AND TERRY LEWIS (RAP WRITTEN BY
PROF. T)
PERSPECTIVE/A&M/JUNE 1991
UK CHART: 45
(REISSUED FEBRUARY 1992: REACHED NO. 28)

No chance of this lot losing their religion. Sounds of Blackness are a 40-piece Minneapolis gospel choir backed by a ten-piece orchestra and led by Gary Hines. In keeping with their classy, besuited, civil rights-era attitude to black music, Janet Jackson producers Jam and Lewis brought them into the studio and attempted to get that old-time religion in the charts – succeeding 11 times in the UK alone. Referring to a gospel record as 'inspirational' is a bit Glenn Hoddle, I know, but that is exactly what 'Optimistic' is, even to an agnostic such as myself. The blend of hip-hop, R&B and gospel is balanced deftly and without gimmick, the female lead voices are simply *profound*, and the climb in key to the so-happy-it's-too-much-to-bear million-voiced hook – 'As long as you keep your head to the sky . . . you can win!' – is like the answer to the question raised by the soaring string Moment in 'Unfinished Sympathy' (see p. 318) (yup, there's always another, better day – and yes, the absolute

passion and belief with which this homily is delivered here makes this another guaranteed tearjerker). No matter what's going on in your life, listening to 'Optimistic' makes you feel indestructible, which I guess is the major benefit of true faith.

GETT OFF

PRINCE AND THE NEW POWER GENERATION

PRODUCED AND WRITTEN BY PRINCE AND
THE NEW POWER GENERATION
PAISLEY PARK/AUGUST 1991
UK CHART: 4

'Nothing can stop . . . Prince and the N.P.G.!' shouted the sleeve of the 'Gett Off' 12-inch. Nothing except the man himself. When this less conventional Minneapolis faith healer embarked on the long war with his record company and prepared to rename himself Squiggly Thing or whatever, he ended up winning his freedom and making an important point about the amount of control record companies exert over artists. But at what cost? His descent into an endless parade of limp ballads and turgid funk jams merely proved that he couldn't edit himself, and it was almost as if the legal battle had drained every ounce of imagination and soul from his work. He continued having hit singles and albums for a while, but even his loyal and obsessive fanbase eventually lost patience. The Paisley Park shop, just a few yards up from Rhythm in Camden, opened with a lot of hoopla and closed not long afterwards, not a purple punter in sight.

His first NPG hit hit the spot, though – even if the new ultra-butch hip-hop Prince ('Let a woman be a woman and a man be a man!' Yes. All right. You're a heterosexual. You don't want to be anybody's girlfriend anymore. We *get* it.) didn't seem like much of a charmer. The Moment, when the clanking industrial-strength funk-rock grinds – and I mean *grinds* – to a halt and he droolingly leers, 'You gotta have a mutha for me *nowmoveyerbigassroundthiswaysoIcanworkonthatzipperbaybeh!*' is the musical equivalent of a cartoon dog's tongue rolling out and lolling around its private parts. Still, all the women I knew at the time loved that bit, so what do I know?

Beers, Steers & Queers (Remixes)

BEERS, STEERS & QUEERS (DROP YOUR BRITCHES MIX)/REVOLTING COCKS

ENERGY FLASH

BELTRAM

PRODUCED AND WRITTEN BY JOEY BELTRAM
R&S/SEPTEMBER 1991
UK CHART: 52

More techno turmoil – this time from New York and brutal, rather than England and soulful. 'Energy Flash' is so minimalist it makes Lil Louis's 'French Kiss' (see p. 290) sound like 'Bohemian Rhapsody', but, boy, does it prove how much one note, a backward string sample and a drum machine can rock like Prince's mutha. A whispering bloke keeps making the word 'ecstasy' seem like a threat rather than a promise. They cut it with Harpic, you know.

CAN'T TRUSS IT

PUBLIC ENEMY

PRODUCED BY STUART ROBERTZ, CERWIN DEPPER, GARY G-WIZ AND THE JBL/WRITTEN BY CARLTON RIDENHOUR, STUART ROBERTZ, GARY G-WIZ AND CERWIN DEPPER
DEF JAM/SEPTEMBER 1991
UK CHART: 22

CHECK THE RHIME

A TRIBE CALLED QUEST

PRODUCED AND WRITTEN BY A TRIBE CALLED QUEST
JIVE/SEPTEMBER 1991
DID NOT CHART

PE's pre-eminence couldn't last forever and it didn't. The *Apocalypse '91* album, with its new production team and series of single-issue sermons, began the decline in popularity and relevance. It housed one last great record, a broiling, yelping, even jaunty, monster groove aimed at reminding us why Afro-Americans were American. Chuck's discourse on slavery, on how slavery must have felt *and maybe still feels*, is leavened brilliantly by Flavor Flav's interjected parodies of Jamaican stoners and Hollywood's craven, eye-rolling slaves. It didn't prevent the band falling slowly from favour and losing their edge as, with painful irony, the only audience that kept listening was mainly white.

The opening single from A Tribe Called Quest's milestone *The Low End Theory* album suggested a new rap direction other than gangsta nihilism. Slow, laid-back, with a full and warm 'low end' bass that entered your bones, a jazzy feel to the trebly snare drum, curling horn riffs and soft organ, and the freewheeling anti-violence raps of Q-Tip and Phife, 'Check the Rhime' formalized and gave credibility to jazz-rap, made an informal connection with Brit acid jazz, and was music not for dancing or air-punching to, but for sitting happily stoned at home with, pondering the whys and wherefores of the new multi-racial bohemia.

BEERS, STEERS & QUEERS (DROP YOUR BRITCHES MIX)

REVOLTING COCKS

PRODUCED AND WRITTEN BY REVOLTING COCKS (REMIXED BY HYPO LUXA)
WAX TRAX/OCTOBER 1991
DID NOT CHART

So far this book has ignored the electronic/rock sub-genre labelled 'industrial'. This is because it was horrible, misanthropic, adolescent-boy tosh that invented everything most grim about contemporary American metal. But there was one band with a sense of humour, and they made one sparkling, largely unknown single that further proves that comedy and rock 'n' roll do mix, especially when there's a bit of good old-fashioned righteous anti-Nazi hatred in there as well.

Revolting Cocks were a loose side-project collective based around Texan industro-metal band Ministry and sometimes featuring future glum-rock superstar Trent Reznor of Nine Inch Nails. 'Beers . . .' was their funny-as-fuck and furiously assembled slag-off of rednecks, and was based upon the male rape scene in the movie *Deliverance* (hence the title of the remix). When Yankees start stereotyping Texans as incest-addled, bible-bashing, latent homosexual Klansmen loonies, it always smacks of an almost racist snobbery. When Texans themselves do it – using ahead-of-their-time distorted beats, hooligan scratches, a pretty fly fuzzed-up white rap drawl, sweary insults, spaghetti western guitar flourishes, wry snatches of commentary, barking yard-dogs, and a general rush of 'glad I got *this* shit off my chest' intensity – then I guess they must have their reasons.

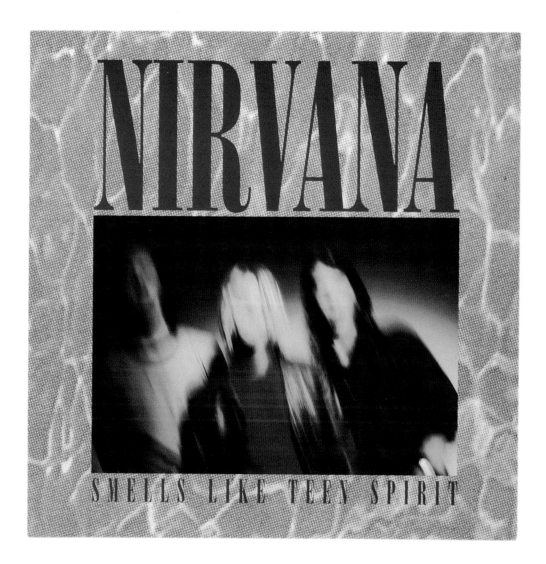

SMELLS LIKE TEEN SPIRIT/NIRVANA
PAGE 326

SMELLS LIKE TEEN SPIRIT

NIRVANA

PRODUCED BY BUTCH VIG AND NIRVANA/WRITTEN BY
KURT COBAIN AND NIRVANA
GEFFEN/NOVEMBER 1991
UK CHART: 7

Very possibly the greatest rock 'n' roll single in this book – even the Sex Pistols notwithstanding – is also the most withering negation of everything rock 'n' roll was supposed to stand for at its late '60s peak. While the music packs as much physical and visceral thrill into its time as is possible without setting fire to itself, its singer and lyricist looms over and around the whiplashing, painstakingly *organized* maelstrom, fixes the listener with a steely-eyed stare, and attempts to force us into a pact of mutual self-loathing and resigned defeatism. The attempt fails, simply because the music is too exciting, even after the singer ends by wailing 'A DENIAL – A DE-NY-YUL!!' at us over and over again, all his pessimistic insight contradicted by his own pop genius.

But this shouldn't imply that the words and the music are easily separable here. Nirvana never came close again to the absolute perfection of '. . . Teen Spirit', and the reason lies in the tension between the band's realization that they've made A Great Pop Moment, and Kurt Cobain's fear of what that may come to mean. Producer Butch Vig went on to one of the most mathematically contrived pop careers of the '90s with Garbage, and this record bears all the hallmarks of calculated pop production. Or do you think a sound this dynamic, detailed, elastic and funky comes fully formed out of Ye Olde Punke Rocke garage?

If Cobain was really as terrified of and alienated by showbiz, mainstream success and fan adulation as future events suggested (and this record insists), it's no wonder that Vig was swiftly dumped after helping to make Nirvana the most important band of their time. '. . . Teen Spirit' utterly rejects the cowardice of indie-rock snobberies. Its tightly honed pop skills hit home throughout, from the way the choppy, almost acoustic guitar riffage of the intro is suddenly (but inevitably) rocketed by Dave Grohl's explosive funk-rock drums and Cobain's overdriven guitar fuzz; through the precipitous mood swing as Krist Novoselic carries Cobain's ambivalent drawl along with stalking metallic bass (pinched wholesale from The Pixies) while the guitar rings your imagination's doorbell; into the impatient, almost jazzy spring of Cobain's angular guitar chopping, creeping around the edges of the mix, making the choruses swing instead of simply bludgeon. And then the whole shebang is finally sent into the realms of the immortal by the expertly-timed arrival of The Gimmick, as everything dives for cover and voice and guitar unite on a what-the-fuck?, deadpan 'Yay' that stands as rock's best ever stab at musical sarcasm.

Apart from The Pixies and the Pistols, '. . . Teen Spirit' nicks from 'Louie Louie', Boston's 'More Than a Feeling' (see p. 24), the early Who and the most gloriously dumb cartoon-devil drones of Black Sabbath. But, again, the real key lies in Cobain himself and his ironic shrugging about rock's power to accomplish anything in the face of the sonic evidence that it can and does. His performance veers from the straightforward vocal commitment of the anthemic chorus, to the full-on mockery of rock's guitar heroism in the anticipation-shredding, gloriously hapless guitar solo. His lyrics lurch from a beautiful summing-up of mass hysteria and What the Rock Kids Want ('I feel stupid and contagious/Here we are now – entertain us!') to sneering, blank-faced gibberish ('I found it hard, it was hard to find/Oh well, whatever, never mind') and the superb 'A mulatto, an albino, a mosquito, my libido', which, if I'm not mistaken, provides yet another riposte to all those that insist that comedy has no place in 'serious' music. A love/hate relationship with your own art and its audience has never been so incisively expressed.

I'm afraid I have an irrational hatred of rock's obsession with death cults. But for what it's worth, and despite the most analysed (and convenient for they-died-for-our-sins coffin-chasers) suicide note in recent history, I don't believe people kill themselves over their guilt at selling records and having fans who aren't as sensitive as they are. But if I *did*, then I guess the extraordinary analysis of rock's failure to change the world within this record would provide all the fuel I needed. The title, as most people know, comes from the name of an American deodorant – Cobain's wry tilt at the windmill of youth rebellion's co-option into the consumer mainstream. Whether this record or the man's suicide is the greater symbol of rock 'n' roll's fall from the forefront of the counter-culture probably depends on whether you believe in great art or the cult of the celebrity fuck-up. I'll go with the song.

1992

1992

If 1992 was the Queen's 'annus horribilis' – Charles' and Di's splits, Fergie's tits, Windsor's blitz – it was also the pop single's 'annus loadofbollockis'. Just eight singles make the grade as US rock and hip-hop became increasingly exploitative and grim, and Britain unconsciously hung around and waited for Britpop. The few that transcended comprise some black/dance music innovations and two rock bands and records that gave us a sneak preview of the anti-Britpop reaction we didn't even know we were going to need.

1992 really was a horrible fucking year – the full-on post-rave '90s euphoria comedown. Another Tory election win. The introduction of a new term for racist genocide in 'ethnic cleansing'. Racist violence in Germany. Symbols of hip-hop's loss of faith with B-boy icon Mike Tyson jailed for rape, and the Los Angeles race riots provoked by an all-white jury acquitting the cops who beat up Rodney King on camera. Fergie's tits. The only possible cheer was the presidential election triumph of Democrat Bill Clinton, a sort of trailer-park Kennedy who would come to share *some* of his funky namesake's ancient vision – One Intern Under His Desk. Still, compared to Reagan and Bush, the guy at least vaguely resembled a human being, and we could still look forward to a Cold War-free world . . . with a better soundtrack, we hoped.

Honourable mentions: Shut Up and Dance/'The Green Man' (Shut Up and Dance); Arrested Development/'People Everyday' (Cooltempo); kd lang/'Constant Craving' (Sire); Prince/'Sexy MF' (Paisley Park); Eric B & Rakim/'Don't Sweat the Technique' (MCA); Shanice/'I Love Your Smile' (Motown); Funky Green Dogs from Outer Space/'Reach for Me' (Murk)

MY LOVIN'
(YOU'RE NEVER GONNA GET IT)

EN VOGUE

PRODUCED AND WRITTEN BY THOMAS MCELROY AND
DENZIL FOSTER
EAST WEST AMERICA/MARCH 1992
UK CHART: 4

If you're fed up – and how can you be? – of all those femme R&B records wishing righteous revenge on some cheatin' no-account man in post-Oprah 'You go Girl!!!' style, then this is the record to blame. There'd been 20 years or so of mainstream female soul submissiveness before this soul-funk monster did its Sistah Pop thang, mixing a churning old-school James Brown guitar riff, (b)itchy beats tumbling underneath the tight, tough sound, and declamatory vocals buttressed by emphatic, close-harmony 'Oooooo . . . BUP!'s. Male writers Foster and McElroy cleverly pen the verses as if Dawn Robinson, Terry Ellis, Cindy Herron and Maxine Jones were ranting at some inadequate loser on behalf of another woman – *women* full-stop – and The Moment is a sheer vocal joy, as a radio announcer voice wryly says, 'And now it's time for a breakdown', before the girls harmonize a glorious a capella tapestry of 'Never gonna get it's in taunting cabaret style. No post-breakup trauma here . . . just the sound of freedom, independence and sexual control.

TENNESSEE

ARRESTED DEVELOPMENT

PRODUCED BY SPEECH/WRITTEN BY SPEECH AND
EARLEE TAREE
COOLTEMPO/APRIL 1992
UK CHART: 46
(REISSUED MARCH 1993: REACHED NO. 18)

The growth of Atlanta, Georgia, as a centre of black American music proved important in the breaking down of the increasingly gang-influenced urban east west rivalry. Artists such as TLC, Erykah Badu and Outkast were coming to bring a rootsy southern alternative to the materialist concerns of LA and New York, and Arrested Development were a key act in this process of decentralization. Their first single remains a monument to how their disappointing and short career echoed their name. Because 'Tennessee' subtly and movingly examines some of the most crucial issues in black America without, as

Todd 'Speech' Thomas's later work was apt to do, either lecturing or patronizing the listener, while making hip-hop groove and pop catchiness the main ingredients.

Speech's song – and it is sung in a reggae-influenced style, rather than rapped – is a conversation with God about the complexities and cost of the Afro-American migration to the cities, and how much of the rural history may be left flowing in his blood. As the appropriately boxed-in, horn-led backing clunks and thunks, almost like decaying machinery, the singer asks for guidance as to his place in the world, and how to cope with both personal loss and the problems of his community. He's willing to put himself in God's hands – 'I know you're supposed to be my steering wheel/Not just my spare tyre' – and finds himself driven to find a place in Tennessee, one of the centres of slavery, in an attempt to locate his roots. As the song continues, a female voice pictures a group regressing to playing traditional childhood games in order to find themselves. Speech explores the environment, even deciding to 'Climb the trees my forefathers hung from.' Although the song cops out with an 'it was all a dream' ending, the unspoken truth is that a return to Tennessee is not enough – it's just a painful stop on the way back to Africa.

What makes 'Tennessee' so profound is its knowledge and understanding of what drives Afro-American culture – the psychohistorical baggage of slavery, displacement and migration, the struggle to learn and acknowledge roots while chasing the aspirational white American Dream. The majority of black Americans are unconsciously ashamed of their own traditions (go to, say, a country blues gig in America or Britain and see how much the audience is dominated by white men who idealize those same traditions), and Speech attempts, in this song, to present an alternative to chasing the newest Black Thing, and to suggest, subtly, that his people would be less vulnerable to oppression – and less violently committed to competing with each other for the benefit of white America – if they came to terms with the defeats of the past.

All that in a pop song? Sure. This is why pop is so much more than showbiz.

ARRESTED DEVELOPMENT

TENNESSEE

TENNESSEE/ARRESTED DEVELOPMENT

PAGE 330

LANGUAGE OF VIOLENCE

THE DISPOSABLE HEROES OF HIPHOPRISY

PRODUCED BY MARK PISTEL AND
MICHAEL FRANTI/WRITTEN BY MICHAEL FRANTI
FOURTH & BROADWAY/MAY 1992
UK CHART: 68

The most powerful and ferociously incisive lyric in this book was responsible for making none other than 'original gangsta' Ice T rethink his attitude to homophobia. And no wonder. You'd have to be one sick hombre not to react emotionally as well as intellectually to Michael Franti's spot-on, bravura examination of the roots of anti-gay violence. Someone should play 'Language of Violence' to Eminem and maybe, just maybe, he could start putting his own brand of lyrical genius to a more positive use.

Franti and partner Rono Tse came out of San Francisco art-industrial band The Beatnigs. . . . Hiphoprisy was a halfway point between Franti's punk roots and the endlessly positive, jazz-influenced black pop he would later make with Spearhead. On a personal level, I guess I relate/look up to Franti more than any other musician – a politically active socialist and mixed-race man who obviously struggles with his own sense of racial identity, basically believes that everyone should be nice to each other, and occasionally gets too preachy for his own good.

His most extraordinary achievement is carried along by a slow, claustrophobic mutant funk, and begins with a queer-bashing at school. For Franti, whose deep, rich tones are a 50/50 split between the voices of Chuck D and Gil Scott-Heron, the putrid language of the insults the boy endures before his beating is not just as bad as the violence, but an infectious *part* of it – the virus that spreads a disease among men unsure of their own sexuality. As he puts it, 'Dehumanizing the victim makes things simpler . . . words can reduce a person to an object . . . completely disposable/No problem to obliterate.'

He moves on to witness an even more brutal street beating, wondering if these thugs had been sexually abused at home, unable to prove their manhood in any way but through hate and rage. But Franti is not sympathetic: 'They ran like cowards' and left the boy to die. It's here that the lyric goes well beyond agitprop, and into the realms of ironic noir, as one of the queer-bashers is caught and imprisoned. Suddenly, the school and street scenes are turned on their heads, and the tyrant becomes victim as he is gang-raped by older, stronger inmates. They use the same language, but 'The words he used before had a new meaning in here.' The end is yet more death, not literal, but

spiritual, and the violent language we use so casually – as if to be prevented from using it is a violation of *our* human rights! – is to blame. 'The power of words . . . Who is really the victim?/Or are *we* the cause and victim of it all?'

It's almost as draining a listening experience as 'The Boiler' (see p. 174). But, whereas The Special AKA offered no solace, no lessons learned, the very brilliance of Franti's insight provides hope that, one fine day, human beings may evolve beyond hate crimes and sexual violence. You end up wanting to cheer him rather than weep for humanity.

RAVING I'M RAVING

SHUT UP AND DANCE FEATURING PETER BOUNCER

PRODUCED BY SHUT UP AND DANCE/WRITTEN BY
SMILEY, P.J. AND MARK COHN
SHUT UP AND DANCE/MAY 1992
UK CHART: 2

How bloody marvellous were Smiley and P.J.? Let me count the ways. The two hard-looking black boys from Stoke Newington, London, were a vital and massively successful ingredient in Brit rave culture. Their use of speeded-up hip-hop and funk breaks virtually invented jungle (a term that the two angry young men then dismissed as racist). Their lyrics, song titles, spoken skits and eclectic musical juxtapositions both commented upon and satirized the early illegal party/pirate radio rave scene (one of their early singles was called '£10 to Get In'. The follow-up was called '£20 to Get In' and began with a mobile phone conversation where a desperate raver questions the doubling of the ticket price, and is told, 'Nah mate. It's 'ad a remix!'). But especially, their flagrant (ab)use of samples – whole chunks of a variety of hugely famous records suddenly dropped into the middle of tracks – was hilarious and fuck-The-Man brave. This gung-ho attitude broke them, in more ways than one.

'Raving I'm Raving' is one of the oddest stories in chart-pop history. A poppy, high-speed rave track, its slow beatless piano and voice hookline is a rewritten version of Mark Cohn's big 'Walking in Memphis' hit from 1991, with a bloke called Peter Bouncer (who really was a Hackney club bouncer!) crooning a wonderfully nonsensical lyric about going to Ibiza for a raving holiday, before it all goes minimalist rave mental. The previous SUAD tunes had been huge on the underground, but this was altogether catchier and funnier and more knowingly rave-exploitative, and was being played everywhere long before its

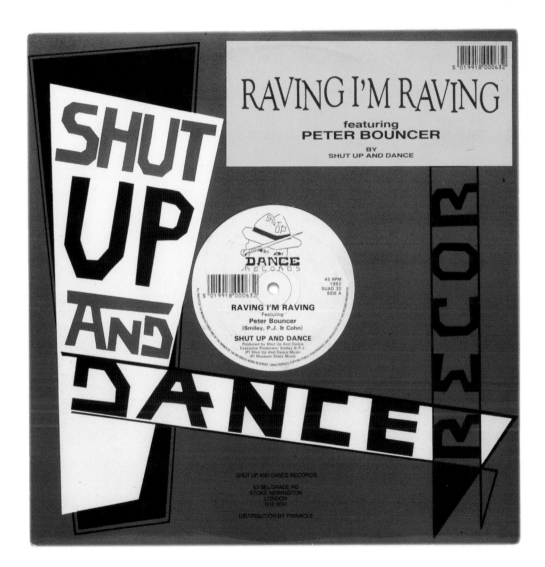

RAVING I'M RAVING/SHUT UP AND DANCE FEATURING PETER BOUNCER

official release. Oops. Cohn and his publishers did not approve. As the track had already been pressed up, they allowed SUAD to release a limited quantity as long as it was deleted the same day and all proceeds given to charity. The result was ravers' frenzy, a complete first day sell-out, and a chart entry at No. 2 before disappearing completely the next week. The furore alerted all the big cheeses they'd previously sampled and litigation chaos ensued, particularly as Smiley and P.J. were fond of telling them all to 'Sod off' whenever they were interviewed. Their successful cottage industry was soon no more, and by the time they'd extricated themselves and started again, the dance scene had moved on and left their rambunctious, rough-house, scene-referential sound without an audience.

'Raving I'm Raving' is still wonderful, though, mainly for its comic cheek. There's something brilliant – and evocative of original rave naïvety – about a black Hackney doorman crooning 'Put on my raving shoes' with a straight face, and almost getting the rest of this aggressively daft din to No. 1.

MOTORCYCLE EMPTINESS

MANIC STREET PREACHERS
PRODUCED BY STEVE BROWN/WRITTEN BY
NICKY WIRE, RICHEY EDWARDS,
JAMES DEAN BRADFIELD AND SEAN MOORE
COLUMBIA/JUNE 1992
UK CHART: 17
(REISSUED SEPTEMBER 1997: REACHED NO. 41)

When the Manics initially vaulted out of Blackwood, South Wales, looking like the aftermath of a car crash involving The Clash and The New York Dolls, they were greeted as the Future of Rock or the punchline to a bad joke, depending on where you stood on the 'rock should be queer and melodramatic/blokey and anonymous' divide. You can probably guess where I was. Even though their records were flawed and couldn't match their 'we'll sell a million then split' pronouncements, the four were a beautifully confused throwback to 'ridicule is nothing to be scared of'. But even their admirers thought they were doomed to thrash glammily and then disappear. Until we heard 'Motorcycle Emptiness'.

Richey and Nicky's sloganeering rejection of consumer culture and the false idols of teen pop culture dreaming would be cool and weird enough, but it's given weight and real sadness by the funky power-ballad dream-rock shaped by Bradfield and Moore. James's shining fanfare guitar line and throaty open-

mouthed voice duel for the title Bleeding Heart Champion of the Alienated World, even if he does treat the words as noises rather than messages. Its mid-section, where the orchestras go all Radio Two, violins pluck prettily, and James wails, 'All we want from you is the kicks you've given us,' carries the sense of the vacuum of youth consumption, and also gave a big AOR hook that led to the Clash-style irony of the song becoming a soundtrack to state-of-the-art hatchbacks cruising down open motorways. It also signalled early warning of the adult soft-rock proposition (from drag to *a* drag?) the band would become after the disappearance of Richey Edwards, the band's non-musical spirit and soul.

DON'T YOU WANT ME

FELIX
PRODUCED AND WRITTEN BY FELIX
DECONSTRUCTION/AUGUST 1992
UK CHART: 6

Londoner Rollo started out at the Acid Jazz indie label before becoming one of UK dance's most successful (and deliberately invisible) backroom boys. Prior to forming Faithless he designed the template for their inspirational adult rave-pop on 'Don't You Want Me', which is nothing to do with The Human League, and everything to do with that high, boxy, churchy synth sound that will forever be associated with the laziest of all house sub-genres: trance. Rollo/Felix's offspring may be the very embodiment of rave-bunny banality, but the original is fine – a retro-*nuevo* blend of squelchy Eurodisco and a synth riff possessed of both a fiery spirit and a built-in sadness. The answer to the title's question appeared to be 'No', but the answer from every lame house knob-twiddler and the Ibiza crowd they served was a definite 'Yes'.

THEY WANT EFX/DAS EFX
PAGE 336

THEY WANT EFX

DAS EFX
PRODUCED AND WRITTEN BY A. WESTON AND
W. HINES
EAST WEST AMERICA/AUGUST 1992
DID NOT CHART

Rap 1992 was largely a grim old business. How else can you explain this novelty rap throwback hitting hard on the underground but flopping in the mainstream? EPMD Brooklyn protégés Skoob (Hines) and Dre (Weston) dared to sound happy and carefree by way of their own special vocal gimmick – a rhythmic stammer that made every wiggity-word a higgity-hookline. Any record that begins 'Bum-stiggidy-bum-stiggidy-bum!!!' and features Pinocchio, *The Sound of Music*, 'Dem Bones', 'Shiver me timbers!!!', a hundred nursery rhymes, James Brown funk and Malcolm McLaren's ghostly 'Buffalo Gals' wail, and manages to make it all sound mystifying, funny and somehow secretly Important, is as close to the true spirit of rock 'n' roll as anything the Manics or Cobain could agonize over. The Das EFX gimmick didn't sustain itself for long, but that stammer still turns up on rap records, another smoothly adapted part of hip-hop's international language.

CREEP

RADIOHEAD
PRODUCED BY SEAN SLADE AND
PAUL Q. KOLDERIE/WRITTEN BY RADIOHEAD (LYRICS
BY THOM YORKE)
PARLOPHONE/SEPTEMBER 1992
DID NOT CHART
(REISSUED SEPTEMBER 1993: REACHED NO. 7)

How the mind plays tricks. Did this definitive hymn to adolescent self-loathing *really* first come out bang in the midst of grunge . . . not just long before Britpop, but even before its funnier, funkier twin, Beck's 'Loser' (see p. 356), was released in America? It took another year and a reissue, of course, before it hit over here, as Yorke's Oxford Dons of Despair famously got a surprise hit in the States without the Britpop press mafia's permission, and poor old Thom was introduced to the horrors of being successful and admired by *total strangers*. Yeuch.

'Creep' may be a gauche thing compared to the likes of 'Kid A', but it's still a great song. A dead ringer for The Hollies'

ancient power ballad, 'The Air That I Breathe', the first time that Yorke sneers, 'You're so fucking special,' and future guitar hero Jonny Greenwood responds with a series of epileptic machine-gun shots – like a pitbull straining at a leash – before slamming into the chorus is pure twitch-rock nirvana (with a small 'n'). The graceful, familiar melody and Greenwood's six-string vandalism give Yorke's choirboy self-pity genuine substance and drama when the lyric alone adds up to little more than a commercial for Clearasil.

1993

1993

I have to thank the symbolism of reaching my 30th birthday and a Nottingham band called Tindersticks for showing me the light. At the Rhythm Records Christmas party of 1992 my band played before the 'Sticks. We were dreadful and unfocused and I made us bottle out by playing a load of dumb covers. My fellow shopworker Dave Boulter's band were bleak and timeless and beautiful and utterly sure of where they were going. They were a *band*. Playing in front of loads of my friends and various London biz luminaries including Heavenly's Mr Barrett, I just felt painfully embarrassed. I knew I was all played out. For two months I brooded on a future spent tracking through Roy Ayers records for acid-jazz tosspots. Even Dingwalls, where I'd been doing some DJing, had shut down. Then I saw a copy of *Echoes*, thought, 'I could do that,' rang the editor Chris Wells, was told they needed a jazz columnist, and celebrated my birthday as a badly paid but proudly published writer. It was all so quick and painless and obviously right for me that it made the previous 14 years of failure and frustration seem laughable. But that's the way misguided self-love goes, I suppose.

Just to reinforce how fortuitous it all was, my debut as a journo coincided with the beginnings of a pop rebirth. G-funk, Björk and Blur heralded the real beginning of the 1990s, and short, sharp, sexy pop songs – my favourite things – were back on the agenda. After work at Rhythm we'd all go to a pub called The Good Mixer in Camden, a surreal boozer where Japanese girls would be staring in awe from one corner at Morrissey and various members of Madness and Blur getting drunk and shooting pool in the other. In a few short months, Camden Town would briefly become the centre of the pop world. Everything seemed possible.

Honourable mentions: A Tribe Called Quest/'Electric Relaxation' (Jive); R.E.M./'The Sidewinder Sleeps Tonight' (Warners)

HER JAZZ

HUGGY BEAR

PRODUCED AND WRITTEN BY HUGGY BEAR
CATCALL/WIIIJA/FEBRUARY 1993
DID NOT CHART

It's still a music press truism that Riot Grrrl – a short, sharp, early '90s burst of confrontational underground feminist indie-punk activity led by US band Bikini Kill and Brighton's Huggy Bear – was cleaned up, given some lipstick and corporate branding muscle, and re-presented to us as the slightly more commercially successful Girl Power. And I suppose it makes a nice story. But it's difficult to imagine the army of male Svengalis behind the Spice Girls clocking this band's old-school feminist rantings in the press, or seeing this chaotic racket performed on *The Word*, and making the ker-ching connection. 'Her Jazz' is prime Slits/X-Ray Spex lo-fi noise irritant mixed with some Manics sloganeering, and has about as much to do with 'Wannabe' as it had with a post-baggy music biz that did its best (and ultimately succeeded) to undermine the whole thing with derisory 'they're ugly and they can't play their instruments' rock-bloke misogyny. Pity, 'cos its howl of rage and vision of male sexuality as 'out of touch' with itself is both a liberating punk-stomp noise-thrill and strangely . . . um . . . sexy. And that is probably another reason why the Bear split in frustration after little more than a year. When it comes to a rare female rock rebel, the reaction of us guys is either fear or a desire to fuck her. Between those subconsciously sexist reactions from an art form dominated by male producers and consumers, the chances of getting any more potent message through to potential grrrls is ultimately doomed. To put it another way: unlike, say, Madonna or Courtney Love, Huggy Bear just weren't man enough.

NUTHIN' BUT A G THANG

DR DRE

PRODUCED BY DR DRE/WRITTEN BY DR DRE AND SNOOP
DEATH ROW/INTERSCOPE/MARCH 1993
DID NOT CHART
(REISSUED JANUARY 1994: REACHED NO. 31)

Compton's former N.W.A. producer/rapper Andre Young ruled the rap world in 1993. His solo album *The Chronic* slowed his former band's frantic ranting into a sexed-up, marijuana lope, as the more sleazy soul moves of George Clinton were transformed into a sound called G-funk. Though the rap hardcore had already become obsessed with the 1992 album, this single introduced G-funk, an immaculately stoned Long Beach rapper called Snoop Doggy Dogg, and Suge Knight's Death Row records to a wider British public. The eagerly seized-upon rumour was that Knight had done all manner of terrible things to N.W.A.'s Eazy E to extract Dre from his contract, and hip-hop finally had an – apparently real – shadowy Mafioso type to approach with a blend of fear and knicker-wetting excitement. Rap's growing obsession with seeing itself as a black pop version of a gangster movie, and misguided belief that violence and intimidation were the only way to achieve self-determination in the white man's world, drove Knight and Death Row to encapsulate every brains-in-their-balls drug-thug racist stereotype known to The Man, and raised the stakes of the east v west conflict by turning it from quality of music and insult into gun-toting macho dare. Although Knight, in true gangster don style, was playing chicken with other people's lives rather than his own.

Still, this was all in the future. And for now, 'Nuthin' But a G Thang' was just the most indefensibly irresistible funk fun in town. It features a sample from an old Leon Haywood track, but Dre's trick was to hire musicians to *play* his low-slung, trebly-synth-and-booming-bass coiled-snake take on Clinton's P-funk, making the sound deeper, like he and the posse were right there in the room (or, more appropriately, the jeep) with you. Snoop's and Dre's raps were a male-bonding fantasy of submissive bitches, gleaming cars and 24-7 hedonism, spiked by constant threats of violence against any uppity 'nigga' – no challenge to cops or the establishment here. Dre was, and continued to be, way too clever to play with real fire.

HER JAZZ/HUGGY BEAR

EVERYBODY HURTS

R.E.M.

PRODUCED BY SCOTT LITT AND R.E.M./WRITTEN BY
BILL BERRY, PETER BUCK, MIKE MILLS AND
MICHAEL STIPE
WARNERS/APRIL 1993
UK CHART: 7

While all America's ageing grunge dweebs were greedily exploiting teen trauma and turning Cobain's 'we' into a melodramatically miserabalist 'me', the chairmen of the board rose above such kid's stuff and provided soul solace for the masses. 'Everybody Hurts' is the most directly generous song in this book, less a comforting arm, more a big woolly blanket wrapped around the loneliest and most depressed of their audience . . . everybody, in fact, from time to time. The ageless power of Stipe's voice makes the simple sentiments move far beyond the point where it might all seem too corny – the singer pushes his own range until you hear all the personal tragedies and troughs that he has travelled through, the things that give him the authority to preach to us of holding on. Coming at a time when rock music was drowning in gratuitous misery, 'Everybody Hurts' stands as a song brave and true enough to treasure life above death, and sad enough to help you cry the hurting out.

FOR TOMORROW

BLUR

PRODUCED BY STEPHEN STREET/WRITTEN BY
DAMON ALBARN, GRAHAM COXON, ALEX JAMES AND
DAVE ROWNTREE
FOOD/APRIL 1993
UK CHART: 28

And, finally, they came. Heading over Primrose Hill with their handsome lippy singers, evocations of the swinging '60s and sneers at America's self-obsession and apparent hatred for looking good and being rich and famous, the Britpop hordes planned their new British invasion with military precision and not a little desperation. With the Brit teen ground having been prepared by comedy Bowie impersonators Suede, the first real shots were fired by an Essex band who were similarly indebted to cockney Dave, and had climbed free of the baggy wreckage sporting a neat line in Mod-meets-*A Clockwork Orange*

threads, and declaring that *Modern Life Is Rubbish*. It was difficult to disagree, but it got a bit better when Damon and co. used the glam past to head for the future.

The early Blur were only one step away from a manufactured band – complete with hasty name changes and indie-dance remixes – and 'For Tomorrow' is a tribute to how contrived they could be and still come up trumps. A 'Hunky Dory'-like beat-ballad bolstered by Mott the Hoople's girly backing vox and Radio Two orchestra, Damon's sketch of Jim and Susan holding onto each other tightly in a London spinning like a car in permanent skid sounded so fresh and inspiring (and . . . blimey . . . *southern*) after all that butch northern blankness – a new psychedelic summit meeting with teen pop. It and the *Modern Life Is Rubbish* album gave Blur critical and cult respect rather than massive sales, but the scene was now set for British guitar pop's one last gasp.

I AIN'T NEW TA THIS

ICE T

PRODUCED BY DJ ALADDIN, SLJ AND ICE T/WRITTEN
BY ICE T AND DJ ALADDIN
RHYME SYNDICATE/VIRGIN/APRIL 1993
UK CHART: 62

Tracy 'Ice T' Marrow's career is the story of gangsta rap's successes, failures, what it could have been but ultimately couldn't be. A light-skinned New Jersey black kid raised in gangland Los Angeles, he was the real ghetto pimp thing before deciding that rap might be both more rewarding and less potentially fatal. His blend of blaxploitation satire, anti-establishment insight and commercial savvy almost proved him wrong when he formed an incendiary and prescient black heavy-metal band called Body Count and released a track called 'Cop Killer' in the wake of the LA riots. The LAPD issued sinister statements, the shareholders of his record company Time Warner (including right-wing gun-lover Charlton Heston) were furious, and, after staff at Time Warner received anonymous death threats, Ice agreed to both drop 'Cop Killer' from the *Body Count* album and leave the company. This move saw him catch astonishing flak from the self-appointed rap hardliners, who seemed to expect rappers to happily risk the death of friends, family and themselves in order to perpetuate a rebellion they could enjoy from the comfort of their armchairs. Ice had exposed more than enough about the US power structure and wasn't going to play cat and mouse with his health. And, like

FOR TOMORROW/BLUR

Public Enemy, he was left with a white rock audience who were more used to rebels who, ultimately, didn't want to die or end up in prison for their audience's sins.

The first album for his new label, *Home Invasion*, concentrated on this phenomenon, playing up to the idea of the black superman brainwashing white middle-class youth. Its finest moment, though, was a battle-rap throwback that mixed Tribe Called Quest acoustic bass funk, queasy piano and whistle effects, and nigga-baiting threats that verged – deliberately – towards the cartoon, as Ice declaimed, 'Fuck fuck around you'll catch a left and a right . . . FIST!!!' while his posse made kung fu fighting noises. Ice takes a little time to spell out that he's 'The I-C-E-T-O-G the L-A-P-D-H-A-T-E-S' and inform us that the Ku Klux Klan are trying to off him, but the blend of ominous theatrics and tough-boy fun just drew more derision from his old fans. Hell – this stuff wasn't there to *enjoy*, fool. Although another controversial California gangsta or two was already bucking that trend, theirs was a more empty and dangerous rebellion that would truly enable inadequates everywhere to get their vicarious rocks off by staring at the tough boys.

THAT'S THE WAY LOVE GOES

JANET JACKSON
PRODUCED AND WRITTEN BY JANET JACKSON, JAMES HARRIS III AND TERRY LEWIS
VIRGIN/APRIL 1993
UK CHART: 2

Mind you, the new SexJanet was trying her best to grab their attention. Much though I continue to adore the (relatively) sane Jackson, there's always a suspicion that she constantly reinvents whatever Madonna is doing at the time for a black audience. But Madonna never made a record as funkily and arrogantly sensual as 'That's the Way . . .', where Janet essentially turns male boudoir-soul against itself, and, over an easy-strolling and foreplay-stroking remake of James Brown's 'Papa Don't Take No Mess', extracts satisfaction from some stud, imploring him to 'go deeper baby, *deeper*' because that is the way his love better go if he doesn't want to get put out with the milk bottles come morning.

GIVE IT AWAY

RED HOT CHILLI PEPPERS
PRODUCED BY RICK RUBIN/WRITTEN BY ANTHONY KIEDIS, FLEA, JOHN FRUSCIANTE AND CHAD SMITH
WARNERS/JUNE 1993
DID NOT CHART
(REISSUED JANUARY 1994: REACHED NO. 9)

The biggest challenge to the white-boy funk supremacy of 'Fool's Gold' (see p. 296), but this time Californian, rap-inspired, bare-chested and sporting an erection rather than a glassy 1000-yard stare. The Chillis' Jew's harp groove is potent enough, but Kiedis's staccato rap is a fantastic balance of rhyming doggerel and anti-materialist, anti-grunge uplift, checking for Sly Stone and Bob Marley, presenting sex, fun and dancing as life's magic mojo that you gotta keep right on workin'. Rubin had now become a specialist in recording bands as live, reinventing them by rejecting '80s-derived production excess, and the band respond with one of the toughest, tightest psych-funk noises that ever forced a rock fan to move dem hips. An overdriven version of 'Give It Away's rap-rock mastery would inform the coming wave of nu metal. But the new boys' adolescent mewling could never match the adult power of a band revelling in just how instinctively they understood, and could reshape, black rhythm 'n' blues.

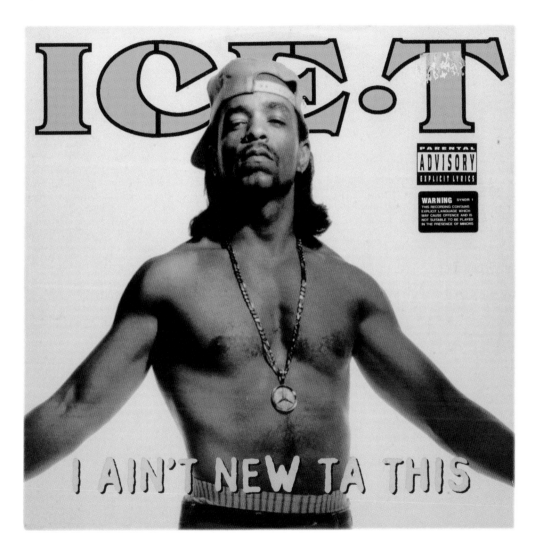

I AIN'T NEW TA THIS/ICE T

SNAKEDRIVER

THE JESUS AND MARY CHAIN

PRODUCED AND WRITTEN BY WILLIAM AND
JIM REID
BLANCO Y NEGRO/JUNE 1993
UK CHART: 30

FROM DESPAIR TO WHERE

MANIC STREET PREACHERS

PRODUCED BY DAVE ERINGA/WRITTEN BY
RICHEY EDWARDS, NICKY WIRE,
JAMES DEAN BRADFIELD AND SEAN MOORE
COLUMBIA/JUNE 1993
UK CHART: 30

Superficially bleak rock 'n' roll from the Celtic contingent. I say 'superficially' because both bands were not resigned waifs, but perma-furious outsiders . . . and that gave their best music an inner strength that suggested redemption rather than damnation. For the Manics that redemption lay in their politics and their analysis of what was wrong in the world of Young People Today. For the Mary Chain it lay in filthy fantasy sex and the sonic skills they possessed in order to suggest it.

'Snakedriver' is a scream – the dark underbelly of The Beach Boys if they ever thought to begin a song, 'I got syphilitic hetero friends in every part-a town/I don't hate 'em but I know them I don't want them hanging around.' It drones and swaggers and oozes dubious liquid discharges as it revives the oldest salvation in the rock book – 'And then I kissed her' – while its three Chuck Berry chords slowly feedback and mutate into one of the most gigantic hooligan guitar solos Will Reid ever plucked out of a sex-horror nightmare. Everything screeches and howls like lost souls in purgatory before it all just becomes one long pre-orgasmic moan. It still makes me laugh in sheer delight at just how much S&M relish they could inject into this stuff.

For the Manics, sex has always been a rather irresponsible thing to indulge in when there's an impending personal and collective working-class/youth apocalypse to worry about. 'From Despair to Where' is the highpoint of Richey's and Nicky's existential loathing and James's delivery of it, his voice looming out of the speaker, wasted and wrecked, shaking as it cries the opening plea for help – 'I write this alone in my bed/I've poisoned every room in the house' – right close up in your ear. From there a sophisticated, almost Rod and The Faces-like

organ-flecked rock strut provides some much needed ballast between the vivid snapshots of Richey/Nicky/all sensitive young people as living infections, and the contempt for, and hermetic refuge from, a brainwashed population ('Outside, open-mouthed crowds/Pass each other as if they're drugged'). The one place where 'us' and 'them' connect is in the exhausting need to put a brave face on their differing reactions to a world that sees everyone as no more than fodder: 'The weak kick like straw . . . I try and walk in a straight line/An imitation of dignity.' The bright love of rock history in the boogie groove and James's posing-in-the-mirror guitar fills help the song become a beacon of strength from pain, rather than grunge's resigned form of masochism for profit, which is probably why hiring the excellent Eringa to help them break America didn't work. It asked too much of the listener. It challenged you to travel from despair to something that required brains and hard work, rather than beer, drugs and nihilism. The other side of defining their aesthetic so vividly, sadly, was the band's magnetic pull on a fanbase who wanted to join Richey Edwards in an orgy of self-inflicted pain and 'too sensitive to live' melodrama, as Richey began his descent towards his disappearance, and Manics fans swapped 'I've attempted suicide more times than you' correspondence in a music press all too happy to encourage such '4 Real' self-damage in the name of therapy culture.

The reason why I've put together two such different records? Well, I've always felt that if you could've crossed Richey's beauty, the Manics' politics and the Mary Chain's sonic sex and black humour, we might have got the perfect '90s British rock band.

VENUS AS A BOY

BJÖRK

PRODUCED BY NELLEE HOOPER/WRITTEN BY
BJÖRK GUDMUNDSDOTTIR
ONE LITTLE INDIAN/AUGUST 1993
UK CHART: 29

By the time this was released as a single, the Icelandic former lead singer of a wacky goth band called The Sugarcubes had achieved a brand-new type of pop crossover. Her *Debut* album had been hailed as The Hot New Thing by the indie-rock mags, the quality glossies, the newly pop-obsessed broadsheets, the dance press and absolutely anyone who had ever owned or considered owning a coffee-table. And fair enough, because the pixie-faced princess of avant-pop had top tunes, a unique and

MARYCHAIN
SPEED

6083

SNAKEDRIVER/THE JESUS AND MARY CHAIN
PAGE 346

beautiful voice, the best dance producer, an effortless way of mixing and matching genres and themes . . . plus, best of all, she looked, dressed and acted like a space alien.

There are hardly any words in her most famous, Eastern-tinged love song. With that voice, she didn't need 'em. But the few blunt 'say it as it is' words that there are simply define, in the first lines, What Every Woman Wants: 'His wicked sense of humour/Suggests exciting sex.' And then she tells us exactly how exciting it is using little more than a digital reggae lope, a decaying orchestra, and a voice that swings naked from the chandelier.

GO WEST

PET SHOP BOYS

PRODUCED BY PET SHOP BOYS AND BROTHERS IN RHYTHM/WRITTEN BY JACQUES MORALI, HENRI BELOLO, V. WILLIS, NEIL TENNANT AND CHRIS LOWE
PARLOPHONE/SEPTEMBER 1993
UK CHART: 2

'Who would have thought that an obscure Village People song covered by the Pet Shop Boys would become the song of football? It's fantastic. I think it's our greatest achievement.' Neil Tennant, from the sleeve notes of the reissued (in 2001) *Very* album.

And, apart from observing that a camp and innocent '70s eulogy to San Francisco as Gay Paradise could be turned into the mournful and hope-dashing sequel to 'Being Boring' only by Neil Tennant's wistful whine and a male voice choir, I'll leave it at that.

WHAT'S MY NAME?

SNOOP DOGGY DOGG

PRODUCED BY DR DRE/WRITTEN BY SNOOP
DEATH ROW/EAST WEST/DECEMBER 1993
UK CHART: 20

'What's My Name?' was the lead single from the most eagerly anticipated album in hip-hop's chequered history. By the time *Doggystyle* (harrumph! Snurgle!) was out, Calvin 'Snoop' Broadus had been charged with murder. And even though he later beat the rap, an increasingly turned-on-by-death rap audience seemed to think the LP would feature some sort of field recording of a drive-by, complete with graphic pictures that

hovered magically above your hi-fi. If you think you're picking up a deal of personal shame in being a hip-hop fan around this time, then you'd be right. Dead right.

Nevertheless, Dre's slow and evil twinning of Funkadelic's 'Knee Deep' and Tom Browne's 'Funkin' for Jamaica', Snoop's drawling self-glorification, and the worshipful vocal tributes of Jewel *were* The Bass Buzz Bomb. Never have so many mothers been fucked in the name of sex-funk mastery. And I'd always thought it was your daughters you were advised to lock up.

REALLY DOE/MY SKIN IS MY SIN

ICE CUBE

PRODUCED AND WRITTEN BY ICE CUBE
FOURTH & BROADWAY/DECEMBER 1993
UK CHART: 66

In which Amerikkka's Most Obnoxiously Racist, Sexist and Homophobic rapper suddenly remembers that he's an intelligent college-educated man called O'Shea Jackson from a perfectly good home in Crenshaw, Los Angeles, and directs all that exploitative gangsta anger into two vivid and atmospheric dissections of both white supremacy and black defiance.

'Really Doe' is just the *blackest* humour and the *spookiest* funk powerplay. Beginning with Cube muttering distractedly, eerily, about his clothes and his hair, a sampled contrast between a guy demanding, 'An' who the fuck are you?', a fantastic girl-soul chorus asking us, over and over again, 'You gotta believe in something – why not believe in me?' and Cube's sly first line: 'To G or not to G – that is the question/And like Smith told Wesson . . .'. And what did Smith tell Wesson? That's harder to say. It's a welter of surreal simile and black superman imagery. Violent, yes. Misogynous, 'fraid so. But possessed of a threat way beyond threatening his own community, the relish of a man who can make language and cultural reference bend to his will. There's something genuinely terrifying about those girls asking you to believe in his lofty disregard for everything normal – or rather, everything normal about American morality. I could try writing down all the lyrics, but they make no sense on paper, and sound like The Death of Everything in his gum-chewing, southern parody voice and against the backdrop of this echoing back-alley funk.

The B-side is both more obvious and a more obvious single, a huge G-funk slam with one of rap's greatest lyrics. It is Cube's relish of the white racist's fear of the black man, kicking off with an unashamed adoption of racist stereotype (his bragging about

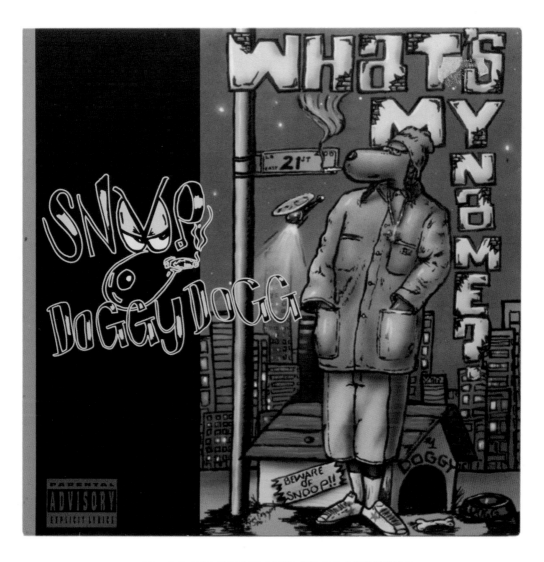

WHAT'S MY NAME?/SNOOP DOGGY DOGG

his enormous genitalia slides straight into him gobbling chicken and watermelon) before rubbing our faces in it with an incredible string of bravura puns and WASPish taunts. The entire rap is ace stand-up comedy, but lack of space means I'll have to choose a line. Let's try: 'You can't stand when I talk like that/Why do black men have to walk like that?/'Cos we swing low like a chariot/And now I got Harriet/All on my dick/'Cos my shoe size is much bigger than a motherfuckin' ten . . . My *skin* is my sin.' Nothing winds up a Klansman more than the white-woman/black-cock porno nightmare. But I don't suppose flipping this over would have equalled the success of 'White Christmas'.

the tapestry. The three-note double bassline keeps the track's discipline, a reggae MC bigs up the DJ, and it all dissolves into a dub chamber before a drum roll wakes you from your reverie and . . . really, it's just amazing and unfathomable and suggested as if for the first time what a single or hip-hop or *music* could be . . . and all you needed was a sampler, the patience to hunt second-hand shops for obscure records to sample, and the imagination to reassemble them as if you were a classical composer. Piece of piss.

IN/FLUX

DJ SHADOW AND THE GROOVE ROBBERS
PRODUCED AND WRITTEN BY DJ SHADOW
MO WAX/DECEMBER 1993
DID NOT CHART

So it took a white Californian to find a way out of hip-hop's confrontational malaise. But a white major-label *rapper* couldn't have done it – at least, not in 1993. The record that briefly made jazz/hip-hop DJ James Lavelle's Mo Wax indie the hippest imprint in underground Britain, that sparked a rebirth of interest in the 'old school' led by white kids, that invented London's trendy Hoxton, and that inspired UK dance publication *Mixmag* to coin the term 'trip hop', is a collage in true Grandmaster Flash style. Except that this time, the idea was to create an apparently seamless instrumental music that worked entirely within its own sense of time, tempo, space and texture – a hip-hop symphony, if you will. Though San Francisco's Josh Davis has continued to make music as extraordinary as 'In/Flux', the shock of the first hearing of his debut lends it a frisson that demands inclusion here.

It begins with the voice of a comedian running through a litany of the world's ills – 'Just a few things that have been running through my head' – before a flute trills, and a beat begins. It's a dragging, underwater jazz-funk beat flecked with the static and scratches of the ancient vinyl it was pulled from. The other kind of scratches rudely interrupt the easy flow, as state-of-the-nation voices litter the backdrop, and there is an uplifting jazz-piano key change. Then it stops completely, a guy says something about 'social narcotics', and it starts again. And so on, with orchestras and saxes and mournful trumpet and staccato turntable tricks reverbed until they just form part of

1994

1994

A case of 'be careful what you wish for'.

Britpop really was a piece of shit, in the end. Go on, it was a long time ago now . . . we can all own up. Four decent bands, a bunch of pub-rock no-marks, and an avalanche of delusion about the supremacy of white English (*not* British) '60s retro, untethered laddism, and 'Three Lions' jingoistic fuckwittery that went on to lay karmic waste to record labels, live venues and rock mag institutions alike. As for the prospect of a British invasion, Jamiroquai and Incognito did as well in the States as Oasis, and Blur could sell records over there only once they started sounding like Nirvana and dressing like the Beastie Boys. I mean, who do you think your beloved Beatles and Stones were trying to copy? Motown. Little Richard. Obscure rhythm & blues singers. *Black people*, you cloth-eared dolt. Multi-racial Bristol gave us Massive Attack, Portishead, Nellee Hooper and Roni Size. Britpop gave us Chris Evans, Skinner and Baddiel and Damien fucking Hirst. Well, thanks a bunch, St George.

My new job soon gave me an insight into the mindset of the time. I fulfilled my ambition to write for the *NME*, looked round the office, saw one other non-white face, and accepted my place as acid jazz/hip-hop correspondent. As soon as I realized that that was *all* my particular face was seen as fitting, I went to the newspapers. I was sent off by one broadsheet to review a particularly appalling third-rate Britpop band, and wrote about them accordingly. The review was killed because 'They're going to be huge and anyway you're not *positive enough about Britpop*.' The band in question barely managed minuscule and, boy, was I right about the obvious soon-come collapse of a 'scene' with no dress sense, no manifesto, no new ideas, and *no bands*. Still, you didn't read about it here first.

None of this is intended to deny that 1994 (and bits of Britpop's commercial peak in 1995) was a great year for pop. It's one of the very best in this book. Just that there was a little more to it than the Tremeloes revival and lad-rock. Much of the best of what was around was black, anti-retro and – whisper it – had some women in it. Indeed, it's tempting to view 1994 as the narrow world of Blair's victory grin and 'Back to Basics' and Cobain's suicide and our greatest athlete being reduced to 'Linford's lunchbox' and the National Lottery, attempting to black out the wider concerns of the age of consent for gays and President Mandela and the Rwandan genocide and O.J. Simpson

. . . alien stuff too scary and complex and *now* to fit in with dreams of Rule Britannia and lager-lout-wannabe public schoolboys who agreed with Prince Charles's pathetic comment that 'political correctness is destroying the fabric of society'.

Loaded magazine . . . meet Jug Ears. You have much in common.

Honourable mentions: Jhelisa/'Galactica Rush' (Dorado); Carleen Anderson/'Nervous Breakdown' (Circa); Blur/'End of a Century' (Food); Morrissey/'The More You Ignore Me, the Closer I Get' (EMI); Nick Cave and The Bad Seeds/'Red Right Hand' and 'Do You Love Me?' (Mute)

AFTERMATH

TRICKY

PRODUCED BY TRICKY AND KEVIN PETRIE/WRITTEN
BY TRICKY
FOURTH & BROADWAY/JANUARY 1994
UK CHART: 69

So what would you get if you crossed Björk and DJ Shadow and, of course, Massive Attack and the confusions and insecurities rappers were too afraid to show in public and 2-Tone and just a little bit of punk rock? Its name was *Maxinquaye* by Bristol's Adrian 'Tricky' Thaws and it, and its lead single, was what the world had been waiting for.

Contrasting Tricky's offhand mumble and Martina's offhand croon, the tough funk-metal with its three mean beats at the end of every loop and a lazy hallucinatory whirl of textures and details, pretty incantations with eerie dread, a vocal contribution from The Pop Group's Mark Stewart with Tricky asthmatically wheezing the lyrics of David Cassidy's 'How Can I Be Sure?', 'Aftermath' was pop from another, more open-minded planet and opened up a can of possibility worms with which to catch the directionless pop fish. Ahem. Sorry. 'Aftermath' just affects me like that.

SOUND OF DA POLICE

KRS-ONE

PRODUCED BY SHOWBIZ/WRITTEN BY L. PARKER AND
R. LEMAY
JIVE/JANUARY 1994
DID NOT CHART

My last cheat, honest. For reasons best known to themselves, the UK arm of Jive Records resisted releasing this in Britain, even as it spent most of the year as the Brit scene's most celebrated rap anthem. The American import 12-inch is here because it's a special case – one of the most important and breathtaking hip-hop records – records, period – ever made. Not least because, in the wake of the 'Cop Killer' furore and the new gangsta mainstream's refusal to engage politically, it took the same theme and did it harder, sharper, more angry, more incisive and with a weight of history and *considered* revenge that had once been the province of the now unfashionable Public Enemy.

Kris Parker was the original South Bronx gangsta whose debut album, *Criminal Minded*, had introduced the gang-thriller

lyric to rap way back in 1987. When his DJ partner Scott La Rock was shot dead soon afterwards, he turned his lyrical efforts to a teachin' 'n' preachin' attitude that gave him huge respect, if marginal sales. For 'Sound of Da Police', his sound, voice and words boiled over into barely controlled rage, and produced a masterpiece of righteous rap 'n' roll protest. The opening and recurring 'WHOOP-WHOOP!!!' siren impression hook became a clarion call to the dancefloor, a chance to dance your way out of your conceptions. And the lyric begins strongly, Kris swapping between Jamaican patois and Bronx bark, before the music makes a little space and KRS introduces his key point, asking us to repeat the name of the slavemaster over and over again, 'like a sample'. 'Overseer! Overseer! Overseer! OverseerofficerofficerofficerOfficer!!! . . . You want a little clarity? *Check the similarity!'* The evidence of Kris's slavery continues, becoming more and more exasperated, his voice breaking with the recollection of generations of institutionalized racism until he wails, 'My father had to deal with the cops/My grandfather had to deal with the cops/My great-grandfather had to deal with the cops/My great-great-great . . . *WHEN'S IT GONNA STOP!!!'* Moving but rhetorical. It won't. The war between American state and American people continues, and as long as it does, it will be shadowed and exposed by the glowering mania of 'Sound of da Police'.

GIN AND JUICE

SNOOP DOGGY DOGG

PRODUCED BY DR DRE/WRITTEN BY
SNOOP DOGGY DOGG
DEATH ROW/EAST WEST/FEBRUARY 1994
UK CHART: 39

Of course, some were just too pissed to give a 4X. Snoop's sleazy paean to male bonding over Motherfucker's Ruin features a sample of 'Watching You'. By Slave.

SOUND OF DA POLICE/KRS-ONE
PAGE 354

LOSER

BECK
PRODUCED AND WRITTEN BY BECK
GEFFEN/FEBRUARY 1994
UK CHART: 15

I suppose, in hindsight, you'd have to be pretty dumb not to see that Beck's rise-to-prominence single was a joke. The over-cooked white-trash rap mumble. The Beefheartian gift for so-wrong-its-perfect lyrical juxtapostion (my fave is 'beefcake pantyhose'). The ridiculous stream-of-poetically-inarticulate-consciousness (my other fave is 'My time is a piece of wax falling on a termite'). And the singalong chorus kinda brings in the irony sledgehammer: 'I'm a loser baby/So why don't you kill me?' indeed. But in defence of the hordes who claimed him as a slacker poster-boy and all those of us who dismissed him as novelty for the same reason, I can only say that US rock wasn't big on satire or wit or tunes or *anything* that Beck would go on to display at the time. Particularly not in the context of hip-hop blues with sitars.

ROCKS

PRIMAL SCREAM
PRODUCED BY TOM DOWD (REMIXED BY GEORGE DRAKOULIAS)/WRITTEN BY BOBBY GILLESPIE, ANDREW INNES AND ROBERT YOUNG
CREATION/MARCH 1994
UK CHART: 7

But rock is at its funniest when it doesn't know it's telling a joke.

GIRLS & BOYS

BLUR
PRODUCED BY STEPHEN STREET/WRITTEN BY DAMON ALBARN
FOOD/MARCH 1994
UK CHART: 5

What British pop needed was a dose . . . of salt, that is. Single-handedly reviving the Dammers/Weller tradition of insulting your own audience and making them like it, Blur begat Britpop with a song that sneered at and celebrated our cheap and irresponsible '90s hedonism over a decayed rock-disco that oozed sarcasm. The big break also set the terms of the later vicious backlash, as if even those who adopted it as a beer and singalong knees-up anthem must have subconsciously picked up on the withering contempt in Damon's voice and Graham's marvellous XTC-go-dancing guitar, as they're described as a 'herd' and 'battery thinkers' capable of no more than five of those thoughts at a time. It made Albarn into pop's Martin Amis – and nobody *likes* a smartarse, do they?

SUPERSONIC

OASIS
PRODUCED BY OASIS AND MARK COYLE (ADDITIONAL PRODUCTION AND MIXING BY OWEN MORRIS)/ WRITTEN BY NOEL GALLAGHER
CREATION/APRIL 1994
UK CHART: 31

Proof that bands are like buses . . .

Whereas Blur had worked long and hard before finally catching up with the Zeitgeist, the Gallaghers and Beaky, Mick and Tich sprang fully formed from the womb of all our boy-rock dreams. Alan McGee smacked their arses and they were away! With a first-time, bang-on-the-money, knock-'em-out, unputdownable rollercoaster of a ride. It's Lennon. It's the Sex Pistols. It's 'My Sweet Lord'. It's T. Rex. It's the blues on E. It's definitely the second-best lyric Noel Gallagher ever wrote, when nothing was expected and no one demanded gravitas from him. 'I know a girl called Elsa/She's into Alka Seltzer/She sniffs it through a cane/On a supersonic train.' You can almost hear Marc Bolan cheering them on. And of course it has as much deep meaning as anything by . . . ooh . . . pick your own tortured rock poet. Because when you have a singer who can make 'You got to be yourself/You can't be no one else' into soul-searing philosophical revelation, then your job is just to give him vivid, funny, rock 'n' roll smart-dumb images to chew over and spit out. It's a song that says, 'I've met some interesting people but who gives a fuck, really, because now I'm going to be a globe-humping rock god, and I can't fucking wait.' What more does a rock 'n' roll single need?

The final genius of 'Supersonic' lies in Noel's Hari Georgeson geetar bleeding all over the lazy strut at the end – no crap vocal ad libs, no Americanisms, no flab. Liam's job is done and he's already off test-driving limos.

ROCKS/PRIMAL SCREAM

NO GOOD (START THE DANCE)

THE PRODIGY

PRODUCED BY NEIL MCLENNAN AND LIAM
HOWLETT/WRITTEN BY LIAM HOWLETT, KEITH PALMER
AND J. BRATTON
XL/MAY 1994
UK CHART: 4

You wait for ages . . .

The Criminal Justice Bill – a legal attempt to stop ravers raving and travellers travelling – galvanized this Essex novelty rave band and transformed them into angry, charismatic sonic movers and shakers. The *Music for the Jilted Generation* album was an astonishing leap, from its us-against-the-cops inner-sleeve art to Liam Howlett's steely, muscular melds of techno, hip-hop, pop and rock, and made them representatives of a 'hardcore' rave scene that looked set to grow up and provide the new rebel-rock thrills for their 'jilted generation'. This never materialized, perhaps because Liam, Keith, Maxim and Leeroy retreated and turned into cartoon punk-metal. In truth, the only thing that the Prod were political about was the right to party. Once that battle was lost, they were just another Met Bar, tabloid-friendly stadium band with a crap attitude to women.

Great singles band, though. 'No Good' is one single that, for me at least, is inseparable from the promo video, where a leather-coated, grim-looking Howlett strode imperiously through a subterranean club, surveying a small bunch of wasted and blank-eyed rave waifs who seemed to have lost the will to live, never mind dance. It was like some government anti-drug ad, and was honest about a hardcore rave scene that had grown smaller and darker as the heavier drugs – and drug dealers – had moved in. The gabbling headrush turbo-powered breakbeats, doomy cathedral synth swells and riffs, percussive vocals, and the hookline sample of soul singer Kelly Charles boiled over with too-fast-to-live vibes and a terrible sense of dread, as if the hedonistic energy of a whole scene had suddenly slumped into a collective bad trip, and things were spinning violently out of control. 'Don't need no one,' the munchkin-paced hook kept on insisting, like the last shred of defiance buried within some kid's twitching and sweating comedown paranoia.

COME CLEAN

JERU THE DAMAJA

PRODUCED BY DJ PREMIER/WRITTEN BY K.J. DAVIS,
C. MARTIN, C. PARKER, F. SCRUGGS, K. JONES AND
T. TAYLOR
FFRR/PAYDAY/MAY 1994
DID NOT CHART

Another extraordinary hip-hop one-off – this time a definitive meeting between old and new. New Yorker Kendrick Jeru Davis (named Jeru after the son of Egyptian Gods Osiris and Isis, no less) was one of the first rappers to actually pronounce himself an anti-gangsta and bring the trad rap skills of verbal sparring, metaphorical imagination and freestyle (improvised) live performance back to the hip-hop hardcore. But the beats that Gang Starr DJ and production genius Premier hooks him up to are anything but traditional. An initially arhythmic, utterly abstract series of tuneless bloops – like The Clangers on 16rpm – held down by a martial drum track – no bass – and punctuated by a crackling walkie-talkie slew of rougharsed chorus scratching, Premier pushes the funk envelope so far he's breaking sound barriers like Chuck Yeager.[5]

To add to this, Jeru is simply mesmeric. His voice a confident, dirty staccato strut, taking fly liberties with the spaces behind and ahead of the beat . . . I'm not sure writing down the best of it can do justice to his rhythms, but, 'Got a freaky, freaky, freaky-freaky flow/Control the mic like Fidel Castro/Locked Cuba/So deep you can Scuba dive my jives' is too good not to give it a try. Though Premier and Jeru were no commercial threat to Dre and Snoop, the sound of 'Come Clean' stunned the hip-hop underground, forging a prophetic link between the experiment of DJ Shadow and the brash black avant-R&B of future heroes The Neptunes, Missy Elliott and Timbaland.

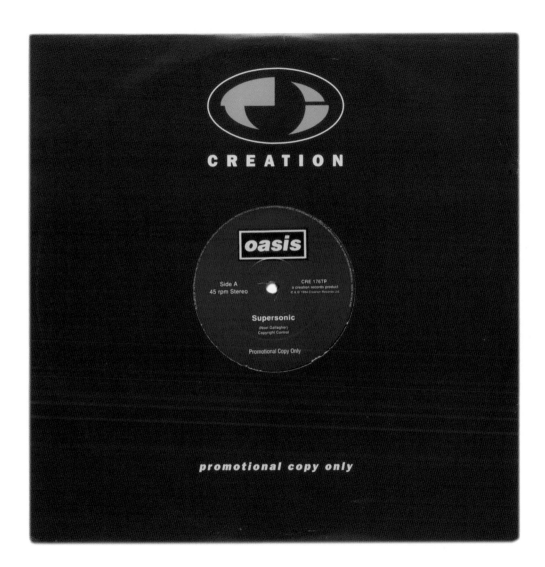

SUPERSONIC/OASIS
PAGE 356

YOU DON'T LOVE ME (NO, NO, NO)

DAWN PENN

PRODUCED BY CLEMENT 'COXSONE' DODD
(ADDITIONAL PRODUCTION AND REMIX BY STEELY &
CLEVIE)/WRITTEN BY CLEMENT 'COXSONE' DODD
BIG BEAT/MAY 1994
UK CHART: 3

In the constant search for soulful musical sustenance, the committed music obsessive of 1994 had begun to rediscover the roots and dub reggae of the late '60s and '70s. The hippest label name to drop was Studio One, Clement 'Sir Coxsone' Dodd's pioneering Kingston hit factory. As reissues and vinyl repressings of the classic Studio One albums began to shift sizeable units in specialist shops, the major digital ragga producers of the time, Steely & Clevie, located long-lost lovers' rock diva Dawn Penn and persuaded her to break her 17-year recording silence with a remake of her biggest late '60s hit. For a heart-warming, fairytale 15 minutes or so, it made Penn a housewife superstar.

The original 'You Don't Love Me' is a slow, languid, mournful rocksteady lament. Steely & Clevie decided to ignore the lonely breakup lyric and reshape it as an emphatic dancehall celebration, making Penn seem ecstatic at being free and single again. The new version, with its shattering drum, bass and guitar fanfare intro, hip-hop-style vocal interjections, and tougher, faster beat, murdered both the original and contemporary dancehall's roughneck vocal novelties. It remains that key rarity . . . the remix that shows the possibilities of the form when the knob-twiddler loves the song more than the money-for-old-remix rope.

BIG GAY HEART

THE LEMONHEADS

PRODUCED BY THE ROBB BROTHERS AND EVAN
DANDO/WRITTEN BY EVAN DANDO AND TOM MORGAN
ATLANTIC/MAY 1994
UK CHART: 55

The warm bath after the cold shower of 'Language of Violence' (see p. 332), Evan Dando's first-person plea for homophobic tolerance is one of the most generous songs ever written by a white hetero country-rock dude from Boston. How do I *know* he's straight? I'll tell you an odd story.

One day, Evan wandered into Rhythm Records, guitar in hand, and asked to play an impromptu acoustic set. Now Dando was big news at this point, as he was a very public drug fuck-up and the bookies' favourite to follow his friend Kurt Cobain into what Kurt's mum memorably called 'The Stupid Club'. He was a beautiful, high-cheekboned, smiley-faced hippy dreamboat, even though today he looked like a battered tramp. He was wearing a filthy old raincoat that the guy who brought him in insisted, breathlessly, was 'the last coat Kurt ever wore' or something. As if by magic, the shop began to fill with waifish post-grunge ghouls, the kind of people who can smell a car crash from two miles away. Unfortunately for them, the scruffy guitar didn't have a shotgun inside it, and Evan began to play and sing. And it was very nice, too, until he spotted this piece of disturbingly pretty jailbait, a blonde stringbean with enormous eyes and bee-stung lips, and increasingly directed his set directly into the ingénue's eyes. The ingénue flirted right back, sidling ever closer, and we started to feel like we were intruding in a very intimate moment and a potential police investigation.

Finally, he ends his set. Ignoring the applause and autograph hunters, he shambled up to the ingénue. 'So – did you enjoy it?' he twinkled lasciviously. 'Oh, yus,' the boy answered gruffly, 'I've got awl yor records, mate.' Evan looked like he'd just taken an uppercut, twitched, checked to see if we were watching (oh, we were), and whirled away as fast as a drug casualty's little legs could carry him. Poor, confused Evan.

So why does 'Big Gay Heart' work? Simply because Dando and the steel guitars and the easy melody and his bruised manly angel voice and his direct discussion with a homophobe are the soul of sweet reason, and he therefore finds it easy to inhabit the soul of a gay man under attack: 'I don't need you to suck my dick or help me feel good about myself' is the set-up, because the character doesn't want to be loved by the bully . . . just left alone. And 'After all it doesn't take that much and it means the Sun to me/For you to lose the part that's still afraid and not prepared to see . . . my big gay heart' is the pay-off because, like Michael Franti, Dando understands the link between hate crimes and the dehumanization of the victim. The lovely sincerity of his voice and the gentle Gram Parsons revival acoustica fill in the gaps.

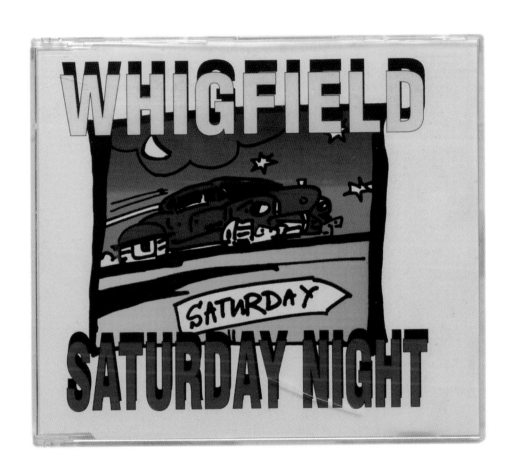

NUMB

PORTISHEAD

PRODUCED AND WRITTEN BY GEOFF BARROW, BETH
GIBBONS AND ADRIAN UTLEY
GO! BEAT/JUNE 1994
DID NOT CHART

And they all come at once.

The next piece in the Bristol jigsaw still strike me as the most innovative and, in their modest way, shocking. I still vividly recall putting on this debut single for the first time at home, trying to review it in my head (occupational hazard by this time, I'm afraid) and feeling defeated by the limits of both language and any music I'd ever heard before. The fact that Portishead soon became a cultural cliché points up both the speed with which pop had begun to chew up and spit out brand-new ideas, and the more damaging occupational hazard of making a noise so in and of itself that every subsequent tune sounds like self-parody. The hundreds of godawful girl-and-two-boffins copyists didn't help any.

What I heard that day was music as The Method. Beth's quivering soul-weep and Barrow's blank face-off between thriller keyboards, frozen drum and dislocated scratching *is* numb – a coruscating, empty and drained unhappiness worthy of Joy Division, offering solace only in the quality and originality of the noise. Still not sure how Portishead became a dinner-party favourite. Surely the sun-dried tomato bruschetta and the feisty Rioja couldn't have turned out this badly?

REGULATE

WARREN G

PRODUCED BY WARREN G/WRITTEN BY WARREN
GRIFFIN AND NATE HALE
DEATH ROW/JULY 1994
UK CHART: 5

It took a surprisingly long while for some bright spark to invent gangsta soul, but when it came, it was all good. The Long Beach sound of Snoop's cousin Warren and his partner and perennial first-choice hip-hop crooner Nate Dogg was so mellow and friendly that its male-bonding tale – the usual G-funk blend of driving, shagging and shooting with a deftly written western influence – sounded neither misanthropic nor misogynous. It was a hedonistic, cartoon-pop superhero fantasy that made no

attempt to convince you it was real, or anything but funny – silly, even – but somehow ended up soulful and inviting. Warren reacts to being mugged at gunpoint the way the rest of us might react to not winning the pools – a shame, but not unexpected. The fact that Warren and Nate have to 'regulate' the naughty boys – that is, kill them – is just a mere inconvenience on the way to a night at a motel with some lovely laydees.

This unlikely resolution of all that gang psychosis is down to Nate's authoritative but loved-up chocolate jazz-soul tones – one of the great vocal styles of the '90s – and Warren's final, smiling disclaimer: 'G-funk – where rhythm is life and life is rhythm.'

PING PONG

STEREOLAB

PRODUCED BY PAUL TIPLER AND
STEREOLAB/WRITTEN BY TIM GANE AND
LAETITIA SADIER
DUOPHONIC/JULY 1994
UK CHART: 45

Now *this* is what we wanted. Former agitprop indie janglers McCarthy giving birth to subversive Europop virtuosity. Gang of Four-style Marxist analysis of how the free market needs war to sustain the myth of the boom-bust economic 'reality' sung like an Astrud Gilberto love song by a gorgeous French female singer (Sadier) with the most casually erotic voice on Earth. Sixties beat-pop brass and Gainsbourg-meets-Getz, Gauloise-cool, bossa nova chanson d'amour a-ra ta-ta ta-ta melody and texture. London's 'Lab would obviously kick-start the revolution by smuggling dialectical materialism into the charts and the indie kids' hearts undercover of impossibly stylish sex.

Except that they then went on to stare enigmatically into the distance and blow the same sonic smoke ring 473 times until the indie kids had to tell them they'd met someone else: it's not you – it's me, I've changed – you haven't. Some songs really are more equal than others.

CIGARETTES AND ALCOHOL/I AM THE WALRUS/OASIS
PAGE 367

SOUR TIMES

PORTISHEAD
PRODUCED AND WRITTEN BY GEOFF BARROW,
BETH GIBBONS AND ADRIAN UTLEY
GO! BEAT/AUGUST 1994
UK CHART: 57
(REISSUED APRIL 1995: REACHED NO. 13)

The most elegantly heartbreaking noir rejection since the closing shot of *The Third Man*.

LIVE FOREVER

OASIS
PRODUCED BY OASIS AND MARK COYLE (ADDITIONAL
PRODUCTION AND MIXING BY OWEN MORRIS);
WRITTEN BY NOEL GALLAGHER
CREATION/AUGUST 1994
UK CHART: 10

Eagle-eyed Oasis fans might have noticed that I've neglected to include all the reissues of the Mono-browed Mancs' many entries. It wasn't until I saw the list in my trusty chart reference book that I realized just how much and often Creation and their paymasters Sony reboarded the Oasis gravy boat in the absence of any other decent bands. If *This Is Uncool* ever gets published as a ten-volume encyclopaedia then we'll list all the attempts to snatch the last penny of pocket money from the mad-for-it kids whom Creation once insisted they did it for, OK?

Anyway, any remaining doubts that Liam Gallagher was the best rock vocalist of his day were dispelled by Noel's first foray into lighters-aloft power balladry. The song is always held up as the band's most uplifting; but, if true musical life-enhancement is achieved only when the performance confronts less positive realities and transcends them, then it's Liam's vocal, rather than Noel's lyrics or wall-of-arpeggios, that carries the weight of mortality and the hopelessness of avoiding it, while carrying *the art* they create into the realms of the immortal. Whether Liam knows he's accomplishing something so huge depends on whether you believe he's an instinctive genius, or the luckiest idiot savant on God's green Earth. Me, I've been sitting on this fence so long it feels like a sofa.

DREAMER

LIVIN' JOY
PRODUCED BY LIVIN' JOY/WRITTEN BY VISNADI AND
J. ROBINSON
UNDISCOVERED/MCA/AUGUST 1994
UK CHART: 18
(REISSUED MAY 1995: REACHED NO. 1)

Talking of lucky bastards, we unrepentant disco bunnies can get our life-enhancement from anonymous purveyors of runny *fromage*, as well as credible rock gods. It's easy to forget, in the wake of the Britpop Wars, that the charts were actually still being dominated by happy-clappy dance one-offs, like this loud and ecstatic thing from Italians Venturi, Viani and wonderfully named diva Tameka Starr. 'Dreamer' is the sort of emphatic and ridiculous cathedral of cheese that makes me laugh about those drippy saddos who like to worship number-327-with-a-bullet white-bread Beatles/Byrds/Beach Boys tribute records as 'perfect pop'. Perfect pop *where*, Grandad? Some planet shaped like a giant second-hand record shop where dancing's been banned since all the women fucked off to Earth?

SATURDAY NIGHT

WHIGFIELD
PRODUCED BY LARRY PIGNAGNOLI/WRITTEN BY
LARRY PIGNAGNOLI AND DAVIDE RIVA
SYSTEMATIC/SEPTEMBER 1994
UK CHART: 1

YA-HEY!!! Squeal, indie pig, squeal!!!

If someone had told me that all the people involved in this record were teen virgins, and had actually made 'Saturday Night' about the anticipation of having sex for the first time, perhaps on their honeymoons, I would've so wanted to believe them. But, as writer and co-producer Larry Pignagnoli (Hoorah! Even his name sounds like a game you play with marbles!) and partner Davide Riva are (probably middle-aged) Italians, and Whigfield (formerly Sannie Charlotte Carlson) is Danish, and was in her mid-twenties when she 'sang' this, I'll probably have to take my cue from her quote to a Danish pop mag: 'The first time a willy is a terrible thing. But it's like cigarettes: in the beginning it tastes like hell, but suddenly you smoke 20 to 30 a day.' Ah. That must be the legendary Scandinavian sense of humour.

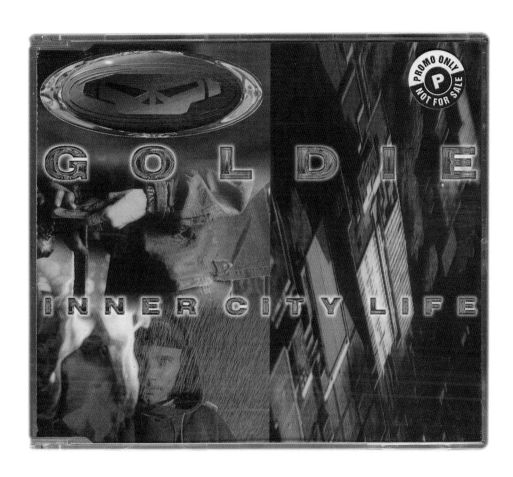

INNER CITY LIFE/GOLDIE PRESENTS METALHEADS
PAGE 368

'Saturday Night', a disco nursery rhyme with all the piano-led sophistication of 'Chopsticks', complete with surreal quacking noises, inappropriate scratches, skipping-song drums, and the most irritatingly catchy and unchanging electronic one-finger bassline ever, is here for three good reasons: it makes me feel young, innocent and happy – and at least two of those are minor miracles. A true inheritor of teen-girl line-dance novelties like 'The Clapping Song' and 'The Loco-Motion', its success is probably indirectly responsible for every terrible manufactured bimbo act since, from S Club 7 to Aqua. But The Beatles are to blame for Kula Shaker, and we don't hold it against *them*.

Whigfield, in true pop-airhead fashion, went on to make some records that sounded exactly the same and that nobody remembers, before the rainbow cane of pop yanked her rudely offstage by the neck. Even her Internet fanpage insists that 'this page is now part of my archive of old pages and will not be updated further'. Ouch.

A couple of funny things: this record was the first debut single by any artist ever to make the British No. 1 spot – a once proud achievement that now seems to happen at least four times a week. Also, the *NME* critics voted this their 15th favourite single of 1994. The *NME* readers responded by voting it the worst. Just thought I'd mention it, in case you fall foul of the popular misconception that we jaded hacks are the *real* snobs about Perfect Pop Things.

AFRO PUFFS

THE LADY OF RAGE

PRODUCED BY DR DRE AND DAT NIGGA DAZ/WRITTEN BY DAT NIGGA DAZ AND THE LADY OF RAGE
DEATH ROW/INTERSCOPE/SEPTEMBER 1994
UK CHART: 72

You might have noticed by now that the Death Row label was the home of gangsta, and that gangsta was male. Still, got to cover all the bases, right? Even the bitches (though definitely no fags, they *scare* me). So they found a token female from Farmville, Virginia, who called herself The Lady of Rage and looked pretty damn hard to boot, and let her rap her little ditty on the soundtrack of a movie called *Above the Rim*. One small thing. 'Afro Puffs' turned out to be the best thing Death Row ever released.

Much of this is down to the guys Dre and Daz shaping the most vicious, snarling, drugged-up, eerie G-funk sonic boom they could. But the rest was down to Rage's rough and rugged

rhyme skills. The Afro Puffs in question, incidentally, were not the Nation of Islam moving into the production of breakfast cereal, but this unusual Princess Leia thing she did with her Afro hair, like two burnt buns had been glued to either side of her head. Having established her trademark she then proceeds to rip her competitors to shreds. And, although it's never made explicit, you know she's throwing down a challenge in skill and intensity to the men around her as she spits, among other rapid-fire streams of verbal and rhythmic dexterity, 'I got the *tongue* that has out*done* any*one* from the ri-*sing* to the setting of the Sun.'

So what happened? Snoop was given the last word as the track fades, getting to patronize her while calling her a ho and a bitch. The single blew up the scene but was given next to no promotion, and performed accordingly. Death Row concentrated on its boys' club of death wish geezers and Lady of Rage's long-awaited album crawled out three years later, long after she'd been forgotten, and performed accordingly. There was no follow-up.

A GIRL LIKE YOU

EDWYN COLLINS

PRODUCED AND WRITTEN BY EDWYN COLLINS
SETANTA/OCTOBER 1994
DID NOT CHART
(REISSUED JUNE 1995: REACHED NO. 4)

The evening before writing this, I saw an ad for one of those tacky mail-order-only AOR compilation CDs. It was called *Drive* and featured the usual ugly parade of Clappos and De Beuurrghs aimed at fulfilling the 'Born to Run' fantasies of Brian from Accounts on the long road to the sales conference in Kettering. Suddenly, in amongst the shots of sporty saloons and snatches of dirge-rock, the voice of Edwyn and his mighty northern-soul pastiche ripped the fabric, and I was immediately taken back to an interview I did with him where he glowed with uncynical, childlike joy whenever he talked about 'A Girl Like You'. After all those years of being a clever cult, he'd finally stumbled onto the magic formula and made a worldwide hit that will be played and loved probably long after he's dead and gone, even by Brian from Accounts.

Edwyn, you see, is one of a dying breed of pop artists who truly care about the State of Pop, and was often too busy slyly analysing what it all meant to write a straight-ahead pop tune. That's why his song from 1994's *Gorgeous George* album, 'The Campaign for Real Rock', is probably the best bit of anti-grunge music journalism ever written, never mind sung, and why he couldn't resist smuggling another great pop-hack line – 'Too many protest singers/Not enough protest songs' – into 'A Girl Like You's' superficially straight love tribute. Whether Brian from Accounts noticed it is a moot point. But the point of pop subversion is to be generous enough to make sure the tune hits Brian first, and not get precious if he just wants to drive to it.

CIGARETTES AND ALCOHOL/
I AM THE WALRUS

OASIS

PRODUCED BY OASIS AND MARK COYLE (ADDITIONAL MIX AND PRODUCTION BY OWEN MORRIS)/A-SIDE WRITTEN BY NOEL GALLAGHER/B-SIDE WRITTEN BY JOHN LENNON AND PAUL MCCARTNEY
CREATION/OCTOBER 1994
UK CHART: 7

What Edwyn wants, Edwyn gets . . . a protest singer *and* a protest song.

What's that? You don't think 'Cigarettes and Alcohol' is a protest song? Well, all I can say is that I reckon it is, particularly once Liam-as-Lydon and Noel-as-Bolan-and-Steve-Jones have got through with it, and made it one of the greatest three minutes or so of Meaning of Rock ever. Because big bruv gives little bruv a song that pinpoints *exactly* why everyday slog becomes everynight body punishment, why them Communists used to call us 'the decadent West', why rock 'n' roll ever existed at all. Elvis, Jerry Lee, Little Richard? All protest singers with sly protest songs about the small world they were born into and the world of possibilities they intended to bust open, whatever the cost. And somewhere between the imperious rise-of-the-north rhyme of 'soon-shee-yine' and 'white line', and the perfect No Future throwback of 'Is it worth the aggravay-shee-un/To find yourself a job when there's nothing worth working for?' is that '50s leap in the dark remoulded for a present of consumer and leisure pleasure that the early rockers could only dream of, but that, when it came to the bottom line, had changed nothing. We still wanted to bust out of our skin. We could still feel the world shrinking to fit. What else is there, when you feel that bottom line, but fags and booze and drugs?

The hindsight that this was Oasis's peak is buttressed by the live version of their hero's surrealist masterpiece, played and sung with such peerless arrogance they pulled off the impossible – making a Beatles song their own. There's something spine-tinglingly dramatic about the way Liam changes Lennon's jumpy, bullish 'Chooga chooga' ad libs into a lofty, drawling 'Chooga choog*ahhhhh*', like a new king surveying his subjects and proclaiming himself some scruff-ball god. After listening to these, it's easy to understand why so many ended up worshipping such false idols.

FLAVA IN YA EAR

CRAIG MACK

PRODUCED BY EASY MO BEE/WRITTEN BY CRAIG MACK
BAD BOY/ARISTA/NOVEMBER 1994
UK CHART: 57

The abstract funk-rap moves of Jeru and Premier made into blistering, insidious hip-pop. Strangely, the credit for this epochal classic went neither to Long Island's raw-toned and innovative Mack nor production master Easy, but to the 'executive producer' (Question: How many executive producers does it take to change a light bulb? Answer: 'You do it and I'll sell the light bulb when you get shot') who was concurrently creating crazy mad phat flava with his new protégé, The Notorious B.I.G. Puffy. Puff Daddy. P. Diddy. No matter which way you say it, it still spells R.A.P.'S N.A.D.I.R.

INNER CITY LIFE

GOLDIE PRESENTS METALHEADS

PRODUCED BY GOLDIE/WRITTEN BY GOLDIE,
DIANE CHARLEMAGNE AND ROB PLAYFORD
FFRR/NOVEMBER 1994
UK CHART: 49
(REISSUED NOVEMBER 1995:REACHED NO. 49)

Jungle's 'Keep on Movin'' (see p. 286) remains a signifier of world-shaking potential that the drum 'n' bass scene just couldn't fulfil. It's almost as if, when even blanket press coverage and a reissue couldn't make this into a 'Keep on Movin''-sized hit, the entire scene went into a sulk that it's never come out of, becoming an insular, elitist, moody, sonically repetitive, blokey trainspotter genre that couldn't deal with the fact that it had, at the very least, invented the only brand new British music in my lifetime. It took the less suspicious and cred-obsessed UK garage producers to take many of the musical ideas and give them melody, glamour and the much needed femininity briefly lent here by Diane Charlemagne's soulful vocal.

Nevertheless, 'Inner City Life' is still a beautiful and timeless thing – a reminder of the true British pop adventure that Britpop was desperately trying to ignore, with its obsession with Luddite guitars and white boys it could relate to. The celestial space explored by Charlemagne's operatic swoops, the synths' jazz/classical sense of harmony, and the bowel-churning power of the depth charge bass and martial beats sounds like nothing on Earth. It led our metal-toothed Wolverhampton-born hero to an unlikely future as C-list celeb and *EastEnders* gangster, which I'm sure wasn't the kind of inner city pressure Ms Charlemagne was emoting about.

1995

1995

So O.J. was innocent. So some vapid Sloane declared herself 'the queen of people's hearts' and the people bought it. So a dead band (The Beatles, natch) released a dead single sung by a dead guy and people bought it. So one speccy wideboy brings down a whole company by gambling other's people money and gets played by Ewan McGregor in the movie. So a French footballer kung-fus a guy in the chest and gets . . . oh, hang on. *That* was *brilliant*.

But, anyway, 1995 was a year about class and privilege and its effects and symbols and signals. This was played out in Pop Event terms by Blur (southern, a bit posh, a bit arty, wrote songs that rhymed 'Balzac' and 'Prozac') and Oasis (northern, a bit rough, a bit thick, a bit artless, wrote songs that rhymed 'shee-yine' with . . . um . . . anything you like, really). It was handsome middle-class school prefect Damon v handsome working-class school rebel Liam and, this being rock, the rebel had to win, even though the rebel wasn't actually that working class or rebellious and was really more Rod Stewart than John Lennon. Still, it made British pop into a series of – what do they call 'em these days? – water-cooler moments again, and entertainingly exposed all our inverted snobberies without trying.

For me, 1995 was the year I got a proper job for the first time in my life. Being Assistant Music Editor at *Time Out* magazine gave me a generous mentor (Laura Lee Davies, who currently edits *Time Out*), a great writer to measure myself against (my predecessor and former Staff Writer, Peter Paphides) and an opportunity to write about music that wasn't made by black people occasionally. I learned how magazines work, too. But nothing's perfect.

It was a wonderful year to be involved with pop, as the singles below testify. Despite all my misgivings about Britpop, it had a briefly positive effect on the confidence of artists – they started writing about *things* and making short, sharp pop statements again. The biggest disappointment was jungle's refusal to go on and engage with the wider world, with its reliance on an elitist scene and a set of endlessly regurgitated sonic effects. The inability of drum 'n' bass to come to terms with the song or meet the pop fan halfway means that it has only one more entry, and that in 1999. The self-indulgence of the Goldie albums represents everything this book is a reaction against.

Although there aren't as many entries from 1995 as 1994, every one here is a classic, a big hit, a Zeitgeist definer. It was probably the last year in this book where the pop single felt very central to everyday life, rather than just a grab bag of noises. Sometimes I wonder whether it ever will again, as Britain has become such a disparate set of cultures, aspirations and impulses. A good thing for real life, on the whole. A lousy thing for pop? Yeah. Maybe.

Honourable mentions: Leviticus/'Burial' (FFRR); Shaggy/ 'Boombastic' (Virgin); Black Grape/'In the Name of the Father' (Radioactive); Moloko/'Fun for Me' (Echo); Tricky/'Ponderosa' and 'Hell Is Round the Corner' (Fourth & Broadway); Method Man/'Release Yo' Delf' (Prodigy Mix) (Def Jam)

CREEP

TLC

PRODUCED AND WRITTEN BY DALLAS AUSTIN
LAFACE/ARISTA/JANUARY 1995
UK CHART: 22
(REMIXED AND REISSUED JANUARY 1996: REACHED
NO. 6)

So, while the white English rock boys howled 'creep' as a noun drenched in hatred of their own physicality, the black American girls chirped the word as a sexually charged verb. Oddly, though, the song is written by a man and the masochism remains intact. A more crass enterprise might have seen super-producer Austin's tit-for-tat cheating song as a rallying cry for female emancipation. But 'Creep' drips with a resigned sadness, a sense of time and love wasted, as its softly chiming trumpets and almost subliminal chorus chant wend their sultry way through the debris of a relationship based on lies and mutual mistrust. The lazy, horizontal lead vocal of Tionne 'T-Boz' Watkins – this is not the virtuoso pop-gospel retro of En Vogue – makes the idea of having affairs sound about as thrilling as Morrissey's rainy seaside town. It happens only because the singer feels there is no choice, that having it out with her errant lover will only lead to even greater loss. The first line – 'The twenty-second of loneliness' – sets the tone and paints a picture of two people living separate lives in shadows and silence, as Austin feminizes hip-hop's musical and lyrical language before your very ears. To 'keep it on the downlow' may be a common Afro-American term for being discreet, but here 'down' and 'low' say exactly what they mean.

Nevertheless, the resignation turned out to just be a convincing performance, at least as far as the band's bad girl Lisa 'Left Eye' Lopes was concerned. Despite the Atlanta trio's huge international success they were almost bankrupted by an insurance claim after Lopes burned down the mansion and trashed the motors of her football star boyfriend Andre Rison, before creeping into alcohol rehab.

GLORY BOX

PORTISHEAD

PRODUCED AND WRITTEN BY GEOFF BARROW,
BETH GIBBONS AND ADRIAN UTLEY
GO! BEAT/JANUARY 1995
UK CHART: 13

Famously, both Portishead's 'Glory Box' and Tricky's 'Hell Is Round the Corner' grooved on the ever-circling strings of the graceful feline riff from 'Ike's Rap 2' by Isaac Hayes. But Geoff 'n' Beff win out through the grain of the Gibbons voice and her leap of imagination, as the mediaphobic tomboy uses those descending chords to paint herself as a jaded femme fatale – the Greta Garbo of trip hop. The chorus's pleas for love – a reason to stop seducing and begin feeling like a woman again – may be intended as most of the point, but it's the way that Beth sings 'temptress', a purred, self-deprecating, gorgeously camp '*temp-tur-ress*', that sticks in the memory, although her fragile *and* demanding 'Move over and give us some room, *yeah*' is another great rip of the superficially soothing fabric. As for where Beth's 'Glory Box' might be located and what it contains – oh, do I need to draw you a diagram?

POISON

THE PRODIGY

PRODUCED BY LIAM HOWLETT/WRITTEN BY
LIAM HOWLETT AND KEITH PALMER
XL/MARCH 1995
UK CHART: 15

From the opening thunk-funk and the ecstatic whiplash 'Yaaah!'s, the Prod's first bona fide stadium proto-Big Beat anthem begins rock-hard and then keeps on getting heavier, melding acid house, industrial, Balearic and hip-hop with a punishing relish. Palmer (rapper Maxim) sounds unhinged as he screeches about possessing the poison and the rhythmical remedy, a neat minimalist encapsulation of why people go dancing and why other people make records for them to dance to. At times he's just content to go 'Boom!' beneath Howlett's royal flush of ace crunches, happy to be just another beat bomb in the arsenal.

BACK FOR GOOD/TAKE THAT

BACK FOR GOOD

TAKE THAT

PRODUCED BY CHRIS PORTER AND GARY
BARLOW/WRITTEN BY GARY BARLOW
BMG/RCA/APRIL 1995
UK CHART: 1

More poison, vicar? Oh, go on . . . you know you love
it. Because THE That were the best modern manufactured
Brit band, and this was their best record by a zillion miles . . .
a song so sure of itself it just seemed to swagger to instant
pop glory, scattering Britpoppers and boy band rivals in its
wake. I know poor old Gary is some kind of karmic joke now,
but 'Back for Good' has all the pure pop heart that his former
dancing partner utterly lacks (and it's worth remembering that
Robbie Williams's solo career was going the same way as the Z-
list dodo until he released a shameless Barlow facsimile called
'Angels' and hit roughly the same market as Jilly Cooper's
novels). As for Gazza . . . a *fist* of pure emotion, the *twist* of
separation, doggerel as heroic tragedy. Now that's what I call
pop music.

SOME MIGHT SAY/TALK TONIGHT/ACQUIESCE

OASIS

PRODUCED BY OWEN MORRIS AND NOEL
GALLAGHER/WRITTEN BY NOEL GALLAGHER
CREATION/APRIL 1995
UK CHART: 1

By this time, every record released in Britain went straight to
No. 1 for 15 minutes, in some crazy Warholian nightmare of art
as marketing . . . or was it the other way around? Anyway, when
an 'indie' band (who sounded like every mainstream rock band
ever signed to EMI) on an 'indie' label (owned by those famous
cottage entrepreneurs Sony) debuted at the top, it was the end of
anything interesting Britpop might have developed into, and the
beginning of the Dadrock era. Dadrock? It rocks like your
collective dad: lazy, badly dressed and flecked with dandruff and
the faint odour of cheese, two World Wars and one World Cup,
turn that bloody jungle music down, fancy a pint of bloke dahn
The Pig & Bigot?, you calling my Small Faces album a poof?,
Weller, Ocean Colour Scene, it were all valve amps round here
when I was a lad. Dadrock.

The Blur v Oasis singles war in August began as a great bit of
marketing hype and went on to become a strange symbol of
class warfare – not economic class, but the tired, played-out,
only-in-England kind, where Oasis were celebrated for their
bullish inarticulacy – for reinventing the Sex Pistols' risky
rebellion as a conservative 'I'm all right, Jack' – and Blur
pilloried for having, you know, *intellectual* tendencies. Noel's 'I
hope they die of AIDS' comment drew no Happy Mondays-style
backlash. The New Lads sniggered and loved Noel for putting
what they always wanted to say about anyone with cerebral or
creative aspirations into words on their behalf.

These three songs are still fantastic, though, because Noel still
had a lust for glory if nothing else. 'Some Might Say' is Faces-
meets-Boston FM-rawk deluxe with lyrics so much less than a
feeling you could hear all Gallagher Elder's future songwriting
disasters a-coming round the bend. Noel's solo 'Talk Tonight' is
manly maudlin, you're-my-besht-mate balladry, even though it
was probably written for Meg. It's even clumsier lyrically than
'Some Might Say', which makes Noel some kind of amazing
tunesmith to overcome his vocal and lyrical limitations. The old
energy – the final dose, as it happened – is saved for the
definitive 'Acquiesce', a freaked Pistolero duet that sums up
Liam's and Noel's sibling tension and only goes to prove that
Liam doesn't have to be able to spell the song's title to sing it
brilliantly, as long as Our Big Kid don't put no poofy foreign
words in the lyric. Nevertheless, this was rock less influenced by
LSD than £.s.d.

SOME MIGHT SAY/TALK TONIGHT/ACQUIESCE/OASIS

BORN SLIPPY

UNDERWORLD

PRODUCED BY RICK SMITH, KARL HYDE AND
DARREN EMERSON/WRITTEN BY RICK SMITH AND
KARL HYDE
JUNIOR BOY'S OWN/MAY 1995
UK CHART: 58
(REISSUED JULY 1996: REACHED NO. 2)

It's entirely fitting that the record that best encapsulated the beer and skittles Britlad era came out on the label that grew out of the *Boy's Own* magazine and wasn't a Britpop record. Indeed, the reason this monumentally powerful thing initially made little chart impact is because the 'Nuxx' mix was just the B-side to a fairly anonymous piece of techno. Danny Boyle put it on the soundtrack to *Trainspotting* and, a year later, it made the impact that gave it true meaning.

The union between veteran electronic popsters Smith (from Wales) and Hyde (the Midlands via Wales) and star techno DJ Emerson (from cockney Essex) is surely responsible for the nature of 'Born Slippy's' dislocated wonder and paranoid beauty. Hyde's scattershot stream of spooked 'lager, lager, lager' and 'boy' (not man) observations and Smith's cathedral chords ride rhythm as sheer bruising, layered, Afro-industrial sensual assault, even though the beats seem (unconsciously?) based on the themes from *Stingray* and *Thunderbirds*. Its small-town boy meets terror city, southern flash meets provincial panic, the thrill of being defeated but never jaded. What Boyle heard, in its endless climbs and falls and terror and laughter and giddy narcosis, was a very male kind of loneliness, born of addiction (in Hyde's case to alcohol), of Soho's zoo parade, of sex laced with brewer's droop, of fear of and desire for violence . . . of Weller's 'Strange Town' (see p. 182) mixed with The Specials' nightmare nightclubs and 'Cigarettes and Alcohol' (see p. 367) and Morrissey's fear of dance absorbed and transformed into ecstatic surrender and Chic's marionette dancers and David Byrne's 'My God – what have I done?' expulsions that mark a sudden realization of the futility of what your life means *right now* – the moment of clarity you don't want or need but can't avoid if you truly want to live. It is not a comedown anthem. It is your true self breaking through the anaesthetized fuzz. It is the black hole at the end of hedonism and jumping in anyway. It's also the single most extraordinary song I've ever seen or heard performed live, because the trio find a way of saying all this, and yet join with their ecstatic, helpless audience in celebrating confusion and alienation as communal joy, a thing that lets us know we *are* alive, and know our fun is futile, and *do* care. But still need to surrender to impulse, to animal magic, to lights and pounding drums and clear and present danger, in order to check our own pulses. I really, *really* love this record, because it is punk's and disco's greatest, most passionate offspring, and the musical equivalent of knuckles tattooed with 'love' and 'hate'.

FAKE PLASTIC TREES

RADIOHEAD

PRODUCED BY JOHN LECKIE/WRITTEN BY RADIOHEAD
PARLOPHONE/MAY 1995
UK CHART: 20

The Bends, Radiohead's second album, came as a shock to anyone who got to hear it. What we'd thought was a Brit second-division grunge ugly duckling was now a swan. The reason the hilariously facile prog-bluster of the following *OK Computer* got all the hysterical praise and shit was because it got all *The Bends*'s good reviews. This happens a lot in an increasingly bandwagon-chasing UK rock press, most famously with the initial worship of *Be Here Now* after the initial lukewarm reception given to *What's the Story (Morning Glory)?*.

'Fake Plastic Trees' is a weeping ballad mystery (the deliberately tautological title, the lines about 'a cracked polystyrene man' who 'used to do surgery for girls in the '80s') that I prefer to take straight. Yup, you guessed it: another private funeral march for another bad breakup. What I heard was the saddest of melodies and the lovely slips from orchestra to organ and the most subtle and instinctive interpretive vocal performance, partly in Yorke's sweet leap to falsetto on 'plastic' and 'crumbles' and his general choirboy agony, but mostly in the way he sings, 'It wears her out,' broken and blank, then 'It wears him out', ending with a throaty howl of rage, and then, of course, 'It wears me out,' so exhausted, before he caresses the words 'If I could be who you wanted . . . all the time', shrinking, all defiance and bitterness gone, touching the sound of the lyric as if stroking a photograph, tender and grieving but beginning to get over it . . . even suggesting as many fond memories as painful ones. The mardy-arsed moaner can sing all right, and this still kills me softly every damn time.

BORN SLIPPY/UNDERWORLD

COMMON PEOPLE

PULP
PRODUCED BY CHRIS THOMAS/WRITTEN BY PULP
ISLAND/MAY 1995
UK CHART: 2

While Oasis and Blur symbolized the British class divide, Jarvis Cocker took a Great Leap Forward and defined it. Being smarter than both, he knew that, in the end, it's about economics . . . norms of class behaviour are just the red herrings that keep us in our places. Never has trashy, trebly synth-pop been forced to be so bitter and bilious and contemptuous and spot on, deadeyed right about everything in the world ever. It was fantastic to hear someone (apart from the less direct Underworld) able to make the personal political again, and, what's more, to do it leaving no room for misinterpretation. It was all of Morrissey's and Tennant's and Dammers's world views drawn together and howled in a way that could only have come from someone who had tasted nothing but pop failure in his last 15 years. It was Britpop's greatest (only?) three minutes by a mile, and was made all the more perfect by the production presence of Chris Thomas, who'd manned the helm when lower-middle-class Geordie Bryan Ferry imagined himself an upper-class fop and working-class Irish cockney Johnny Rotten had revelled in his – and reinvented our – underclass status. But it was Yorkshire's classless Jarvis that revealed Noel's and Damon's playground spat, and our reactions to it, as completely shallow. Which is why even The Lads loved him for his camp and his artiness and his *difference*. Even the emotionally stunted can't beat the Real Thing.

ALRIGHT

SUPERGRASS
PRODUCED BY SAM WILLIAMS/WRITTEN BY
SUPERGRASS
PARLOPHONE/JULY 1995
UK CHART: 2

Yet another in the list of Classic No. 2s, the Oxford monkey men's finest single is the happy-go-lucky flipside to 'Common People's' Very British Resentment. Well, as they keep saying, they *were* young, too young for popular Marxism. What they did have was a big barrelhouse piano and a bit of music hall and ballroom quickstep and a truly great line about keeping your

teeth clean, although, astonishingly, not everyone agrees. My lovely wife hates 'Alright', because she walked into a disco bar one day as it was playing, and saw all these *very* young people pumping their fists and stomping and shouting along in triumph, and felt like she had wandered into some sort of Nuremberg Rally on behalf of the New Ageist Order. And funnily enough (although the 'Grass, easygoing muso dopeheads to a man, are totally innocent in this), 'Alright' did seem to represent the dominant and apparently never-ending marketing religion that is eternal youth, which is just one of the nastier components of Cool Britannia, and which it would take Jarvis Cocker – who else? – to satirize appropriately in two years' time.

WATERFALLS

TLC
PRODUCED BY ORGANISED NOIZE/WRITTEN BY
MARQUEZE ETHERIDGE, LISA 'LEFT EYE' LOPES AND
ORGANIZED NOISE
LAFACE/ARISTA/JULY 1995
UK CHART: 4

TLC had been CrazySexyCool from the get-go, but we sure didn't expect no social comment from them. When it came it was, with its jazz-style mute trumpets, bubbling Sly Stone synth, suddenly stumbling martial beat and 'Sign o' the Times' religion and pessimism (see p. 251), the best song Prince Rogers Nelson never wrote, the flowing but fateful fall to the bottom of his 'Mountains' (see p. 243). Its view of drugs, gang violence and AIDS in the ghetto is heartfelt but resigned, asking the young black man to look to God, but in such a way that failure is inevitable (borne out by its use of the oft-repeated rap slogan, 'Y'all don't hear me'). The song is sung with a grainy agony, and the title metaphor is plain beautiful, running against all black music's currents, pleading for patience, warning against 'moving too fast'. Towards the end, after Left Eye's munchkin rap, it tells us that 'Dreams are hopeless aspirations', which surely makes 'Waterfalls' one of the most existential pure pop songs of all time – John, Paul, Sartre . . . and no Ringo.

HIGHER STATE OF CONSCIOUSNESS/JOSH WINK

HIGHER STATE OF CONSCIOUSNESS

JOSH WINK

PRODUCED AND WRITTEN BY JOSH WINK
MANIFESTO/OCTOBER 1995
UK CHART: 8
(REMIXED AND REISSUED JULY 1996: REACHED NO. 7)

Josh Wink was Joey Beltram and Lil Louis – The Sequel (see p. 290/324). He was American, he slayed the Brit dance underground and crossed over to the mainstream with his Great Minimalist Moment, and it was his *one* Great Moment, too. 'Higher . . .' was a shameless acid-house throwback (it seemed so long ago by this time) and sought to live up to the promise of the title by none-too-subtle shifts and expansions in the endless repetition of a one-note 303 acid riff and a speedy funk break. And it did, in this cheesy, parent-baiting way, with euphoric climbs and ear-bleed high-frequency belches and comic robot-having-a-hissy-fit gimmicks that just made you shiver with the joyous pop vandalism of it all. The dance glossies hailed the white Trustafarian Wink as a new acid Messiah. They sure hadn't learned anything from the embarrassments of the rock media.

GANGSTA'S PARADISE

COOLIO

PRODUCED BY DOUG RASHEED/WRITTEN BY ARTIS
IVEY JR, LARRY SANDERS AND DOUG RASHEED
MCA/OCTOBER 1995
UK CHART: 1

Compton's Artis Ivey was, in rap circles, strictly unCoolio. He'd been around for years, had been in rehab, had a truly silly bonsai hairdo, and essentially made Tupac Shakur's and Ice Cube's thug stylings into pop while largely preaching against the gang life he'd escaped from. This final point made him both a 'biter' of another's work and, as rap continued on its path towards killing its own, somehow 'soft'. The fact that he'd actually lived the ghetto life that so many others just exploited for profit didn't impress the hardcore. Repentance was a compromise with The Man, or some other such thing that white middle-class boys wanted to hear.

But then Coolio had a massive hit from a Michelle-Pfieffer-educates-the-savages movie called *Dangerous Minds*, a record so insidious and proud that even Britain's rap-phobic mainstream couldn't stop it reaching the top. The song, based on a sample from Stevie Wonder's 'Pastime Paradise' and buoyed by a portentous gospel choir and a chorus from soul man L.V., was slow and bleak and melodramatic and beautiful and carried a ring of truth inside its epic grandeur, particularly in its knowledge that too many young men were impressed by the lifestyle Coolio described, and that this version of the American Dream was, indeed, a hopeless aspiration. America suddenly realized it could sell non-party rap to Brit panty-waists, and that's exactly what it has done ever since. In many ways, 'Gangsta's Paradise' signalled the end of gangsta, or 'reality' rap as a cult. It lost the allure of the forbidden when your mum started singing along.

BROWN SUGAR

D'ANGELO

PRODUCED AND WRITTEN BY D'ANGELO AND
ALI SHAHEED MUHAMMAD
COOLTEMPO/OCTOBER 1995
UK CHART: 24

Hip-hop and R&B were by now overtaking rock and country as the world's biggest-selling music genres. But what we didn't have was a prodigy, a keeper of the faith, a true Soulman. Enter 21-year-old Michael Archer from Richmond, Virginia, an all-singing, all-instrument-playing, dope-smoking, rap-quoting black Adonis with a thinking-woman's six-pack and enough glowering, implied violence to impress the boys who really aren't interested in that as a homoerotic sort of thing, oh no they're not. And his music? Oh, that was just better than everyone else's, period.

By employing A Tribe Called Quest's Ali Shaheed Muhammad, D'Angelo gave his retro-*nuevo* country soul both urban sheen and deep funk foundation. The title track from his first album was like a rebirth of Marvin and Stevie and Bobby Womack and Al Green and Sly rolled into one . . . not that I'm saying it's better than all put together, because then my head would explode and there'd be no book. Just that he took tiny things from each and made them his own, as he tells the tale of his cocoa-eyed, caramel-skinned lover from Philadelphia, PA. Or is it? Because, in an odd echo of The La's 'There She Goes' (see p. 312), 'Brown Sugar' is generally seen as a loving tribute to drugs, this time the ubiquitous herb. Blunts come from Philly. Sugar's got a sister called Chocolate Thai, another dope slang term. He's generally happy to share her with his homies, but

GANGSTA'S PARADISE/COOLIO

wants this coupling all to himself. He gets high off her love, don't know how to behave. They make love so much his eyes have gone red. He sticks his tongue out before he 'hits' her ('hits' equals 'shags'. Don't be so *sensitive*). He even drops in a 'Y'all don't hear me' reference. It works both ways as a deep and dizzy aphrodisiac, so take it all your own way, so to speak.

WONDERWALL

OASIS

PRODUCED BY OWEN MORRIS AND NOEL GALLAGHER/WRITTEN BY NOEL GALLAGHER
CREATION/NOVEMBER 1995
UK CHART: 2

No record in this book has given me greater pause for thought regarding its inclusion. I mean, on one level, it pretty much finished Oasis as a rock 'n' roll band. From this moment on they were a tabloid joke, or a chorus of 'Rule Britannia', or recipients of the dubious honour of making the song most likely to be busked really badly at a shopping centre near you. On another . . . well . . . it's just rubbish, isn't it? The sound of a man running out of ideas. Title from a George Harrison album, cellos off *Sgt. Pepper*, all that Beatles bollocks about winding roads and backbeats, the lame afterthought attempt to make it funky. The joke wasn't funny anymore.

Except . . . it was. 'Wonderwall' is just undeniable, the proof that Liam could transform any old tat into something painful, sung from the edge of something you couldn't pin down, an internal angst, you couldn't help but surmise, that he could only express when singing. And the melody is just so huge, it overpowers whatever it might be about until you don't want to start looking for the beer mat it was scribbled on. As plenty observed at the time, 'There are many things that I would like to say to you/But I don't know how' is tough to beat as an honest message to your audience. Problem was, 'Wonderwall' was so high, wide and tall ('Faster than a cannonball?') that poor old Noel could do nothing but bang his head against it. You'll find him there still, surrounded by paparazzi and his brother shouting, 'Just do us another one like The Beatles, yer fooking coont!'

1996

1996

Jarvis Cocker defined Britpop – not with a bang but a wiggle. When he jumped onstage at the 1996 Brits and shook his tiny tush at the sickening spectacle of Michael Jackson's God complex, Jacko's people exposed the flimsiness of their pretensions by overreacting completely and accusing Pulp's singer of pushing the terrified (or terrifying?) stage-school children off the stage. Jarvis abusing kids? Oh, the irony. By the time they'd realized that the whole thing was, you know, *being filmed* and that the little British have lawyers too, Jarvis's tilt at the windmill was a national cause célèbre, the blunt Yorkshireman taking on the might of the American multinationals and winning a craven climbdown. The King of Pop was in the altogether. It was a great leap into the dark from Cocker. But the whole fiasco also accentuated the smallness of British pop – and not just Britpop. America continues to reject the majority of our next-big-things, and particularly our guitar bands, who are seen as work-shy fops in their unwillingness to jump through hoops for the US biz, to treat their sponsors as gods until they are awarded godlike status for sycophantic services rendered.

The event was also a symbol of something else that had taken over pop and which increasingly informs the last ten years of entries in this book. Although the plethora of new musical mini-genres gave the consumer more choice, it also allowed the biz to market pop more narrowly. To focus. To *brand*, just as Jacko was branded as a benevolent god who does it for the sake of the children. Moreover, the business had learned that the best way to sell music was to appeal to the punter's vanity and prejudices. Part of that process was an insistence that your chosen genre – whether jungle or hip-hop or nu metal or Dadrock – was *not pop*. The word 'pop' implied that people who didn't walk, talk, dress and think like you might enjoy the record in question.

Even *gurls* might like it. This was *not cool*, and had a particularly dramatic effect on all areas of dance music. For example, the Busta Rhymes record (see p. 390) is, to my ears *and* eyes, the poppiest product in the 1996 list (including the Spice Girls), in its novelty value, in the way Rhymes was marketed, in its absolute crossover ambition. If you said that to a Busta Rhymes fan, he would inform you, politely if you were lucky, that rap is not pop, because pop is Boyzone. Why? Because that's what it's called, silly. And it's easy to convince yourself that that was your own idea.

So it actually became a career-threatening move for 'cool' artists to make great pop singles. They might make big bucks, but they might consequently lose their core audience. The idea that being creatively ambitious in a mainstream context amounted to selling out had always hung around the rock world but had now become a major plank of pop marketing. The records that comprise the rest of this book are largely records that rebel in some small way against this streaming of music into cool and – hooray! – uncool; that either seek to redefine cool on their own terms or just ignore it and attempt to make the chaotic marketing-to-kiddies disaster that is the UK singles chart (another reason that the Yanks laugh at our pop) bearable again.

And the last thing I want to say about 1996 is . . . I got married, and lived happily ever after. No more breakup stories, you'll be relieved to hear.

Honourable mentions: The Fugees/'Killing Me Softly' (Columbia); Tiger/'Race' (Trade 2/Island); Tricky/'Tricky Kid' (Fourth & Broadway); Faithless/'Insomnia' (Cheeky); Livin' Joy/'Don't Stop Movin'' (MCA/Universal); Beck/'Where It's At' (Geffen); Marilyn Manson/'The Beautiful People' (Nothing/Interscope)

HYPER-BALLAD

BJÖRK

PRODUCED BY NELLEE HOOPER AND BJÖRK/
WRITTEN BY BJÖRK
ONE LITTLE INDIAN/FEBRUARY 1996
UK CHART: 8

Björk's most wonderful single takes the simple joy in intimacy of 'Venus As a Boy' (see p. 346) and adds several layers of imagery, doubt, musical adventure and complex emotion. Following its drum-'n'-bass-influenced intro's resonant purrs and swishes, a bravura impression of a person listening to themselves breathe, we're taken on a sonic ride driven by the contrast between heavily processed music and the rough, very human recording of Björk's voice, all sharp intakes and tactile grain. The singer parks us on top of a mountain where she apparently lives, and where, early each morning as her companion is still sleeping, she goes through a ritual of throwing garbage onto the rocks below – cleaning up – pausing only to 'imagine what my body would sound like/Slamming against those rocks'. The choruses then soar above even the mountain's lofty peak, the bleeps, bloops, and strings evoking a space-walk joy in being outside, and alive, and alone but not alone; a house bounce after the prowling and creeping of the verses, the embodiment of her lover's (or her child's?) waking. Hooper breaks out the heartbreak 'Unfinished Sympathy' strings (see p. 318) but keeps them submerged, just part of the fabric, not as important as rhythm track or voice.

'Hyper-ballad' is obviously related to Björk's pixie-princess ancestor Kate Bush, both in the effortless conjuring up of landscape, and the ability to convey sensual ecstasy. But there's also a smidgin of, of all people, Paul Weller here, and his career-long lyrical obsession with finding solitude and peace, away from crowds and cruel cities. The music, which sounds less like it was played and more as if it were gently coaxed from a series of benign machine entities, was obviously being closely checked out by Madonna and everyone else. We're so used now to records that put ghostly pings and parps where guitars and pianos used to be, it's easy to forget what sonic pioneers Björk and Hooper were, maybe still are. But there aren't too many of those who've copped the moves who can sing so much love and lust and fear and pondering of mortality into the simple words, 'Safe again'.

HOMETOWN UNICORN

SUPER FURRY ANIMALS

PRODUCED BY GORWEL OWEN AND SUPER FURRY
ANIMALS/WRITTEN BY SUPER FURRY ANIMALS
CREATION/FEBRUARY 1996
UK CHART: 47

More songs about travelling and loss. These prodigiously talented and intelligent Welshmen have gone on to make better and better albums since 1996's *Fuzzy Logic* debut. But their first Creation single remains my favourite, largely because it sounds like Mott the Hoople on magic mushrooms. 'Hometown Unicorn', with Gruff Rhys's tender double-tracked vocals, the almost subliminal cello flourishes, the deliciously crunchy fuzz-guitar stabs and its comically 'we are weird' opening line – 'I was lost/Lost on the bypass road/Could be worse/I could be turned to toad' – is one of those giant parallel universe hits, because it has a chorus so lovely and sad and gently funny and ridiculously catchy that only a Radio One producer could fail to love it. And, as a special bonus, the pained choirboy 'What can I do?' and the four underpinning insistent, dramatic blue chords that end every chorus condense the whole of Bowie's 'Hunky Dory' into just one bar! Beautiful – and time saving!

RETURN OF THE MACK

MARK MORRISON

PRODUCED BY PHIL CHILL AND MARK MORRISON
(ADDITIONAL MIX AND PRODUCTION BY CUTFATHER &
JOE)/WRITTEN BY MARK MORRISON
WARNERS/MARCH 1996
UK CHART: 1

Poor Mark Moz. It was the beginning of 1996, and we at *Time Out* were doing the round of interviews that constituted our 'Top Tips for '96' feature. It was picture- rather than text-led, so the disparate group of fledgling popsters had to come to the office, so we could snap them in the lift. You know. A lift. Right to the top. The very top. Oh, please yourselves.

So, having nominated Leicester-via-Florida's Mark Morrison to be Britain's first-ever major R&B artiste, I spoke to him. He came into the office on time, a short, stocky young black man hidden behind shades and wearing some over-flashy designer gear. He sat down at my desk and . . . hardly said a word. Not, as you might suspect, because he was sullen and arrogant. But

A DESIGN
FOR LIFE
MANIC STREET
PREACHERS

INCLUDES STEALTH SONIC ORCHESTRA
MIXES AND "FASTER" REMIXED BY
THE CHEMICAL BROTHERS

A DESIGN FOR LIFE/MANIC STREET PREACHERS

because he seemed terrified of me. Each question – and these were questions of the 'What's your favourite cheese?' variety – made him shrink and stiffen a little further. It was like shoving a TV camera in front of a small, shy adolescent. I cursed my choice. Good tunes, but he's just too quiet, ordinary, *nice*.

Two months later, this comes out, and he's suddenly huge. Then the album arrives, and he's on the front in pervy leather dangling a pair of handcuffs. We thought it was regrettable. How right we were. Then he's caught waving a gun or a water pistol or something by the cops, gets nicked, gets prison. Comes out, does something else, gets more prison. Then he's suddenly the toytown Brit equivalent of all those self-destructive rap bad boys, a bad joke being pooh-poohed and shunned by a UK soul community who feel he's put their cause back ten years. Then he's out, and . . . oblivion. Apart from offering to referee a fight between Liam and Robbie in a desperate bid for attention.

So every time I hear 'Return of the Mack' – which is, incidentally, a super-funky, sweet soul strut of a tune, like a reggae soundsystem singer trying to be Cameo and Bobby Womack and nearly pulling it off despite *obviously* coming from Leicester – I think of this short, stocky, timid geezer I met for half an hour one day, and wonder at what point he decided that he was, in fact, a 'Mack', and also wonder if Craig David will ever think that staging a drive-by in Southampton would be a good career move, or at least, make him more black.

FIRESTARTER

PRODIGY

PRODUCED BY LIAM HOWLETT/WRITTEN BY LIAM HOWLETT, KEITH FLINT, TREVOR HORN, ANNE DUDLEY, J.J. JECZALIK, PAUL MORLEY AND GARY LANAGAN
XL/MARCH 1996
UK CHART: 1

Man – check those writing credits! That's Liam, Keith . . . and the entire line-up of '80s band The Art of Noise! Because 'Firestarter' samples their 'Close to the Edit'! Certainly, the similarity between the two records is startling, in so much as there isn't any. Apart from that girl shouting, 'Hey!' Still, if I understood music law I'd be a very rich psychopath by now, and who would want that?

Having failed to lead the raving new hippy hordes unto a new disco-in-a-field Jerusalem, Liam introduced Keith Flint as Johnny Rotten in 'Punk – The Panto' and headed for stadia, cartoon metal, bitch smacking, The Met Bar and various thin,

blonde identical members of All Saints and TV presenters I can never remember the names of. A bit like promising a towering inferno, and ending up boiling a kettle. But reinventing Alice Cooper for the young 'uns still makes for a right rollicking mosh, and a right rollicking mosh is, in this case, hot enough.

A DESIGN FOR LIFE

MANIC STREET PREACHERS

PRODUCED BY MIKE HEDGES/WRITTEN BY JAMES DEAN BRADFIELD, SEAN MOORE AND NICKY WIRE
COLUMBIA/APRIL 1996
UK CHART: 2

The Manics are *so* uncool. At least, everybody I know, including those who used to love them before Richey Edwards vanished, thinks they're now either laughable or teeth-grindingly dull. The problem lies in their seriousness. Whereas Radiohead have such an exceptional musical arsenal to both bolster and distract from their lack of light and humour, Bradfield and Moore are old-school rockers whose traddy tiers of rawk noise or power balladry teeter and tear beneath the weight of Nicky Wire's sixth-form socialism. It often sounds like a young boy writing for a middle-aged man's band. In order to find them at all entertaining, you have to both find clumsiness endearing and be impressed by their refusal to accept that the world has moved on since George Orwell were a lad. Being an old Clash fanatic helps, in both respects.

'A Design for Life' was the post-Richey comeback single that saw the Manics move towards an all-lard diet. I still love it though, because it is the last gasp of their romantic despair, before it just became Radio (U)2 angst and bluster. Despite the melodramatic seriousness of its lyric about the failures of the working class (the hope *doesn't* lie in the proles), there's enough camp in the 6/8 rhythm, James's strip-club guitar bridge and chorus and the way Hedges keeps putting the strings in all the so-wrong-it's-right places, to keep it from becoming pompous. Again, it's the slight clumsiness (and the half-remembered '60s ballads) that makes you feel the weight of their sadness, rather than their laziness and limitations, for one last time.

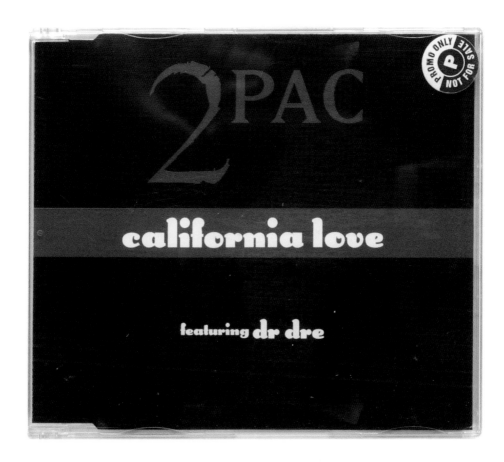

CALIFORNIA LOVE/2PAC FEATURING DR DRE
PAGE 390

CALIFORNIA LOVE

2PAC FEATURING DR DRE

PRODUCED BY DR DRE/WRITTEN BY TUPAC SHAKUR,
DR DRE, R. TROUTMAN, L. TROUTMAN, J. COCKER AND
STAINTON
DEATH ROW/INTERSCOPE/APRIL 1996
UK CHART: 6

A funk masterpiece. Not sure what else to say that doesn't either glorify, mystify or cynically dismiss what happened to Tupac Shakur just five months later. Except that . . . there's something about the unsolved murder, the way a young man seemed to push all America's conflict buttons until death was inevitable, the unending slew of posthumous releases, the manner in which Shakur has been deified and sentimentalized despite his violence and his imprisonment for sexual assault and the fact that his own death appears to lead to the murder of Biggie Smalls . . . something that makes my blood run cold at the signals it gives to black men – any men – about the nature of masculinity and rebellion and heroism. So I'm inclined to just listen to the erotic charge of this and the beautiful, wise and agonized pre-prison album *Me Against the World*, and figure that world just lost someone who was good at what they did. Why be yet another worm in the carcass?

WOO HAH!!! GOT YOU ALL IN CHECK

BUSTA RHYMES

PRODUCED BY RASHAD SMITH AND BUSTA RHYMES/
WRITTEN BY TREVOR SMITH AND RASHAD SMITH
ELEKTRA/MAY 1996
UK CHART: 8

Brooklyn's Trevor Smith was just what hip-hop needed. An alien-looking huge-gobbed nutter who pretty much did party rap, but did it with such cartoonish virtuosity and silly-goat-gruff cod-malevolence that the hip-hop hardcore didn't notice that he wasn't actually pissed off at anyone. Moreover, the comic lurch of this and much of his *The Coming* album broadened rap's range of beats immediately, bringing us towards the bizarre, angular, globally informed, anything-goes-but-straight, gleaming chrome rhythms that now fuel hip-hop's and R&B's creative and commercial dominance.

In Busta's case, it's not about what he says – which is sod all – but how he says it. Loop up tough-but-playful rhythm. Find dumb-fuck hookline, maybe even two, like 'YAWYAWYAW YAW-YAW!' or a yelping rodeo 'Woo Hah!!!'. Rap in voice of every crotchety cartoon character you ever heard, complete with slapstick staggers, jumpy quivers and tongue-twisting ragamuffin exclamations, then pick a syllable – say, 'Yo' – and rhyme as many words with it as possible until chorus, making sure you occasionally threaten something dire to no one in particular. Heat until boiling, before ending by bursting into opera, like your eccentric grandad in the bath. Bloomin' marvellous, at least until Busta's success and apparent mateyness made it illegal to make a rap record for the next five years (and counting) without him guesting and doing *exactly* the same bloody thing over and over and over again, like the office joker but in really expensive shoes.

WANNABE

SPICE GIRLS

PRODUCED BY STANNARD & ROWE/WRITTEN BY SPICE
GIRLS AND STANNARD & ROWE
VIRGIN/JULY 1996
UK CHART: 1

Lee Davies, my boss at *Time Out*, was the first person to write about the Spice Girls. *Ages* (well, quite a few weeks) before this came out. 'I'm going to do a feature about this new manufactured girl band,' she said. 'Are you? That's nice,' I said. 'I think they're going to do well,' she said. 'Do you? That's nice. Well, it will be a fun feature anyway,' I said. Which is why she is now the editor of a world-famous listings publication and I'm . . . well . . . not.

But don't waste your sympathy on me. Spare a thought for one Michelle Stephenson, who was originally in Touch (the Spicey ones' first name) but left in Summer 1994. Jeez, how do you live with being the Spice Girls' Pete Best? She was replaced by Emma Bunton, so not only did she not have to drum, but all she would have had to do for the rest of her life is grin inanely. She could even have been spared the celebrity eating disorders. She is the Unluckiest Human in the World.

Incidentally, everyone goes on about the marketing when discussing Posh, Sleepy, Bashful, Dopey and Sneezy's unprecedented and instant success, but I reckon it would have fallen flat on its face without the rather brave production of 'Wannabe' by Stannard & Rowe. Listen to it again – it's a din. A fucking unholy row. They're all over the place, barely in tune, levels constantly changing . . . and *that rap*. And 'Zig-a-zig-ahh'?

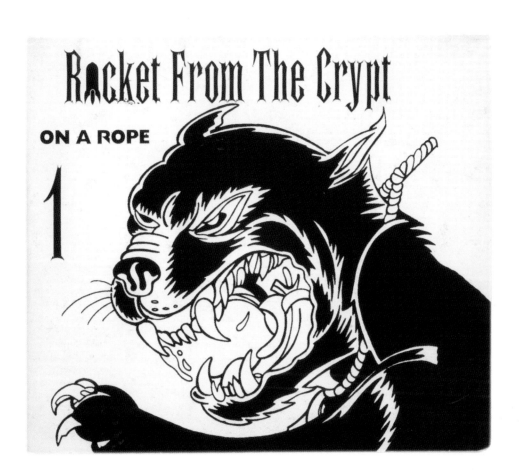

ON A ROPE/ROCKET FROM THE CRYPT

What genius knew *that* would work? The music (What music? A one-finger piano. A pissy breakbeat you can hardly hear. You can't dance or anything to it. All you can do is sing it. And we did until they were the most famous women in the world!) is totally underdone and deliberately basic. It makes Hear'Say sound like Schubert. It's karaoke. That's why it's still such a thrill. I can't believe they weren't ordered to clean it up, but some bright spark somewhere in Simon Fuller's shadowy operation must have realized that if you're gonna sell a load of desperate no-talents as a ball-breaking girl gang, then you may as well make 'em sound rough and ready for action, warts 'n' all. The gloss came from the second single on, because they'd made their point and now had to be made into singers and adult personalities.

And you think manufactured pop is easy?

BECOMING MORE LIKE ALFIE

THE DIVINE COMEDY
PRODUCED BY DARREN ALLISON AND NEIL HANNON/ WRITTEN BY NEIL HANNON
SETANTA/AUGUST 1996
UK CHART: 27

Northern Ireland's Neil Hannon provokes quite extreme reactions for one so almost famous. To a few of us, he's an oasis of intellect, satire, musical subtlety and lyrical risk in a desert of dreary 'indie' rock inarticulacy and traditionalism. To most, however, he's The Antichrist. Why? Because he's cleverer than us and isn't afraid to show off about it, imagining, quite reasonably, that a pop star's job is to exaggerate their key characteristic for our entertainment. Sadly, he's emerged into a British pop culture that truly despises intellectualism, especially when sensing that the brainbox is making a joke that we don't quite get at our expense.

Admittedly, when Hannon started writing clever-clever ditties about National Express coaches and hay fever he was cruising for a critical bruising. But before that he wrote this. It's a song from a concept album about male sexism and class conflict called *Casanova*, and it absolutely sums up Cool Britannia's journey towards the relegitimizing of misogyny as 'cool'. Trouble is that, with its jauntiness and references to New Lad icon Michael Caine's most sexist character and lines about no meaning yes, it appeared to be a foppish celebration of crap blokeness, until you looked more closely. The key bit reminds me of Joe Jackson all those years ago, lamenting the fact pretty

women go out with gorillas (see p. 94). Hannon/Alfie/Every bloke tells us that, if he wants to get laid, he must resign himself to being one of those gorillas – 'Y'know, the kind who will always end up with the girls' – even though he's smart enough to know better. Because women were going – and do go – along with this 'bastards are more fun' bollocks, creating a context in which the wider world's woman hating can happily thrive. 'Oh, *come on*!' Hannon keeps yelling over the loungey trumpets and '60s movie keyboards, daring you to disagree.

ON A ROPE

ROCKET FROM THE CRYPT
PRODUCED BY JOHN REIS JR/WRITTEN BY ROCKET FROM THE CRYPT
ELEMENTAL/SEPTEMBER 1996
UK CHART: 12

RFTC's brief bask in the Brit-chart sun was the Great Rock Red Herring of the late '90s. This San Diego sextet were pure smart-dumb adrenalin-rock 'n' roll reborn, an amalgam of Vegas Elvis, James Brown, Dexys, The Clash, Husker Du, and US hardcore punk legends The Misfits and Fugazi. The first time I saw them live it was truly as if someone had completely exposed all the time I'd wasted on *rock* bands, and, after having a good laugh at my straying from the path of righteousness, had formed a cartoon collage of everything I really wanted from *rock 'n' roll*. With horns! And formation dancing!!! I kept going back just to check I hadn't dreamt them. But there they were – sexy, ironically macho, ridiculously fast and tight, playing as if their lives depended on getting each crushing, wrecking-ball riff absolutely perfect. They spat fire (sometimes literally, in the shape of singer John 'Speedo' Reis's occasional fire-eating turn), laughed at themselves and us between songs, then executed (and I mean, *executed*) the next one with such intensity you worried for their health. And . . .

Uh, sorry. This isn't a book of gig reviews. It's just that RFTC were so what the rock doctor ordered, and so unlikely in a world ruled by Ocean Colour Scene, that 'On a Rope's' commercial success just didn't seem possible. It turned out to be a complete one-off, of course, because Speedo's genius couldn't extend to making the records look and sound like the shows. But for this three-and-a-bit minutes of stomping, chomping-at-the-bit inarticulate sexual frustration, they almost did. And it was so awesome people stopped resisting and swallowed Speedo's fire.

BREATHE/PRODIGY

NO DIGGITY

BLACKSTREET FEATURING DR DRE

PRODUCED BY TEDDY RILEY AND WILLIAMS STEWART/
WRITTEN BY T. RILEY, C. HANNIBAL, L. WALTERS AND
W. STEWART
INTERSCOPE/OCTOBER 1996
UK CHART: 9

Black America's version of manufactured pop possesses a musical depth, an aura of quality – and, yes, credibility – that the Brit version does not. The anonymous R&B vocalists who made up Teddy Riley's Blackstreet were no more artists than Boyzone, were constructed in a virtually identical manner. But not only is this irrelevant in the context of Riley's and Stewart's deep sample funk, it could also rope in that most cred of hip-hop superproducers, Dr Dre (as a rapper, strangely), for added street authenticity; the equivalent of Nellee Hooper singing on the first Spice Girls LP. Dre got something else other than spondulicks out of the deal, too – with the East v West/Death Row v Bad Boy war game now producing real casualties, this was Dre's first step towards extricating himself from Death Row and heading towards a pop audience, where the only risk was to his credibility. He floundered a little before discovering a funny white boy who could rap.

'No Diggity' is a stammer on 'no doubt', a throwback to Das EFX (see p. 335). It's just about being rich and black and wanting to have sex with a laydee. It burns because all the usual extraneous trebly swingbeat textures have been cast out, leaving just a low-slung disco stomp, a punctuating one-chord piano and a bluesy groan from soul-folk legend Bill Withers's 'Grandma's Hands', which I figure must have hit a little baldy white bloke called Moby pretty hard. It also has a tough female rap from one Lynise Walters, in case you didn't get the sexually democratic, anti-gangsta misogyny point from a lyric that is turned on as much by the honey's independence as her body.

DEVIL'S HAIRCUT

BECK

PRODUCED BY BECK HANSEN AND THE DUST
BROTHERS/WRITTEN BY BECK HANSEN, MIKE
SIMPSON AND JOHN KING
GEFFEN/NOVEMBER 1996
UK CHART: 22

The Dust Brothers' junkshop approach to sampling had already helped reinvent the Beastie Boys as the epitome of so-uncool-it's-the-coolest on their second album, *Paul's Boutique*. Now they did the same thing for Beck on *Odelay*. In this sonic world, country and garage rock and obscure jazz-funk and old-school electro could fit together with almost slapstick edits, collage as perfect low-attention-span post-modernism. Hansen's deadpan sing-talk is the dispassionate contrast to the awesome fuzz guitar fanfare here. And a 'Devil's Haircut'? In his mind? Well, Beck's particular talent for language lies in holding onto the detritus, the weird thoughts and juxtapositions you have when alone that will sometimes have you laughing or crying or simply staring into space, contemplating a meaning only you could possibly make sense of. Beck just mumbles them right out and lets the listener trip on them, hoping they connect. So you end up with 'Discount orgies on the dropout buses', which seems ridiculous, until it melds with heads hanging from 'garbageman trees' and 'a rotten oasis' and that riff and the repeated assertion that something's wrong and the final distorted yowl and a devil's haircut. And you feel the dread among the slapstick and pop referencing and paint your own picture of the America that disturbs Beck. And that's art, without the garfunkel.

BREATHE

PRODIGY

PRODUCED BY LIAM HOWLETT/WRITTEN BY
LIAM HOWLETT, KEEF SKINT AND MAXIM
XL/NOVEMBER 1996
UK CHART: 1

Keef Skint. No, I didn't make that writing credit up. That really is their idea of a punk joke. 'Breathe' is one of the all-time great rhythm tracks ever to be dragged out of a computer. As Maxim's and Leeroy's subsequent solo projects have proved it was always all about Liam the noise genius and his lucky devil's haircut mates.

1997

1997

When New Labour got elected and Diana got dead an eerie glow spread throughout the land. It seemed that having not voted Tory and having wailed hysterically about someone we'd never met made Britain feel pretty good about itself, because it apparently proved that there was such a thing as society after all. Pop stars were the new royalty in this meritocratic touchy-feely New World, as the Spice Girls went to No. 1 in America with their first single, Oasis sold 350,000 copies of *Be Here Now* in one day in Britain, Macca got knighted and Sir Elton persuaded a staggering 31.8 million people worldwide that Diana had been 'England's Rose' with an undercurrent of tragic Marilyn. Radio One had become a never-ending parade of 30-somethings pretending they were 18, and playing the music to match. What chance, in the face of all this 'middle youth' cultural hegemony, did any of the once-every-ten-years/once-every-eleven-years/when-the-year-ends-in-seven cultural youthquake theories stand?

So the best of 1997's pop had to take a distant back seat to Diana and Tony and Louise Woodward and Dolly the Sheep and 'Did you stay up for Portillo?' Fair enough, I guess. But as I write this in the week of the World Trade Center attack, I can only cast my mind back to the hideous wailing and gnashing and simpering of September 1997 – the complete halt of every other form of news or conversation or human emotion except sentimentality for what seemed like aeons – and realize that, according to the British mainstream, the murder of up to 3000 innocent people just about adds up to the accidental death of one pampered aristocrat. The only note of sanity came from an unlikely source. When someone waved a microphone in front of wizened old Keith Richards and asked for his thoughts on Diana's tragic death, he simply replied, 'I never met the chick.'

Honourable mentions: Pavement/'Stereo' (Domino); Janet Jackson/'Got 'Til It's Gone' (Virgin); Photek/'Ni-Ten-Ichi-Ryu' (Science/Virgin); Ultra Nate/'Free' (Strictly Rhythm/AM:PM); The Charlatans/'North Country Boy' (Beggars Banquet)

BEETLEBUM

BLUR

PRODUCED BY STEPHEN STREET/WRITTEN BY
DAMON ALBARN, GRAHAM COXON, ALEX JAMES AND
DAVE ROWNTREE
FOOD/JANUARY 1997
UK CHART: 1

Odd that Blur should find a way out of Britpop's dead end by ripping off The Beatles. But then, Britpop had been a remarkably unsexy micro-genre, so, when everyone was merrily grave-robbing the jaunty or anthemic or cod-mystic bits of the Fab Four, no one had gone near The Beatles of 'Dear Prudence', 'Sexy Sadie' or 'I Want You (She's So Heavy)', the ones about doing it in the road. There's no mistaking, though, where Graham's inside-out slabs of drone guitar, Dave's Ringo beat, or the overall feel of narcoleptic, narcotic sex comes from.

'Beetlebum' was also the beginning of the conjecture in British rock's ever-shrinking world that all Damon's songs were about his girlfriend Justine Frischmann out of Elastica. Particularly as everyone in Camden seemed terribly excited about rumours that all of Blur, Pulp, Suede and Elastica were living out some sort of *Performance*-meets-*Trainspotting* scenario on Primrose Hill. Call me terminally uninterested, if you like, but it's the new soulfulness of Damon's voice when he groans 'She'll suck your thumb/She'll make you come' that got me all unnecessary. Presumably enough people agreed to get it to No. 1, especially when it goes all Eno at the end, with its chattering radio voices and electronic skronks and screes, and gives a clue to what The Beatles *might* have sounded like if they'd made it in the 1990s – that is, nothing like Dadrock.

REMEMBER ME

BLUEBOY

PRODUCED AND WRITTEN BY LEX BLACKMORE
PHARM/JANUARY 1997
UK CHART: 8

Scot Lex Blackmore's inspired Big Beat one-shot is a dry run for Fatboy Slim's entire career. 'Remember Me' still delights by hooking up one of conscious soul's great divas – Marlena Shaw – to a simple three-note bassline and a harsh hip-hop beat. 'Remember Me? I'm the one who had your baby's eyes,' she cries, in a disembodied echo of the world of abandoned black mothers referred to in Shaun Ryder's 'Kinky Afro' (see p. 312), before the 'Geng-ga-ga-geng – ha!' scat vocal hook accentuates her toughness and heads for disco ecstasy, the dancing away of heartache. A joyful tune and a prophetic slice of perfect dance crossover, being a nod to the knowledgeable rare-groove head, novelty-catchy enough for the pop fan, and relentless and emphatic enough in rhythm to enable even the most club-footed lagered-up stude to strut their unfunky stuff.

INTO MY ARMS

NICK CAVE & THE BAD SEEDS

PRODUCED BY NICK CAVE AND THE BAD SEEDS AND
FLOOD/WRITTEN BY NICK CAVE
MUTE/FEBRUARY 1997
UK CHART: 53

(ARE YOU) THE ONE THAT I'VE BEEN WAITING FOR?

NICK CAVE & THE BAD SEEDS

PRODUCED BY NICK CAVE AND THE BAD SEEDS AND
FLOOD/WRITTEN BY NICK CAVE
MUTE/MAY 1997
UK CHART: 67

If I could have had any musical career in the world, I would have liked Nick Cave's. All the initial thrill of being in a wild and dangerous rock band, followed by the slow, eventual flowering into the best songwriter of my day, separate and oblivious to the vagaries of pop fashion, reflecting the inevitable ageing of myself and my audience and bringing them all along for the ride, while making more or less each album slightly better than the last. OK, I admit I'm not at my most objective when dealing with the man from Warracknabeal, Australia . . . I'm in awe of his talent and integrity. But I accept that he's never been a singles artist, even though much of my list-making process for this book consisted of reluctantly taking most of the Cave singles out.

'Into My Arms' and '(Are You) The One That I've Been Waiting For?' are too beautiful to go, despite making no concessions to radio play whatsoever. They are here together because of their musical similarity, and because their themes of fear of, redemption through, and loss of love complement each other and the rest of the classic that is Cave's *The Boatman's Call* album.

(ARE YOU) THE ONE THAT I'VE BEEN WAITING FOR/NICK CAVE & THE BAD SEEDS

'Into My Arms' is a hymn-like ballad accompanied only by Cave's piano and Martyn P. Casey's unobtrusive bass. The singer hits his adoring love song home by undercutting both the constant religious references in his work and the obviously sacred references in the music and melody. His voice is deep, resonant, but still unsure. There are plenty who don't think Cave is much of a crooner. What they mean is that his technique is not perfect. But his use of that is exactly why he's a great, great singer – because no matter how Scott Walker he attempts to get, his vulnerability always peeks through and lends the work a greater humanity.

'I don't believe in an interventionist God . . ./But if I did I would kneel and ask him/Not to intervene when it came to you,' he begins, and then pays tribute to the object of his love by using religion and the possibility of contentment to question the meaning of his own existence. As soon as the verses begin to hint at doubt and fear, he switches to the simple warmth and intimacy of the title and chorus, gently banishing his own neuroses, the part of himself – of most of us – that does not feel we deserve or can deal with quiet security. 'Into My Arms' is therefore both the embodiment and the rejection of pop's history of unhappy love songs, the calm after the storm.

As was much reported at the time, the songs on *The Boatman's Call* concern Cave's relationship with Polly 'PJ' Harvey. Presumably the woman Cave went on to marry does not have it high on her list of fave listens, and especially not '(Are You) . . .', which is as lovestruck a tribute to a specific person as anyone has written. Again, it's a slow, quiet ballad, more country-rock in style than Into My Arms and distinguished by the subtle spidery guitar shimmers of Blixa Bargeld. Cave's anticipation of the relationship is, despite his declarations of almost cosmic adoration, pained and pessimistic, his voice shot through with the prophecy that this joy and excitement cannot last. Or, as he puts it himself in the heartbreaking rise of the middle eight: 'Oh we know, don't we?/The stars will explode in the sky/But they don't, do they?/Stars have their moment . . . And then they die.' By the end of the song, the title question has become rhetorical and resigned. But in terms of communicating all the losses and gains, all the mind-melting physical and emotional thrills of a love so fleetingly perfect (and perhaps more perfect because it is fleeting), it is beautiful and complete and almost too true, and the finest moment in Cave's career of fine moments. Which only leaves me to locate the box of tissues I've managed to avoid since 'Fairytale of New York' (see p. 260).

SONG 2

BLUR

PRODUCED BY STEPHEN STREET/WRITTEN BY DAMON ALBARN, GRAHAM COXON, ALEX JAMES AND DAVE ROWNTREE
FOOD/APRIL 1997
UK CHART: 2

Muppet grunge. Nope, sadly, I didn't come up with that perfect description. It was Blur's Alex who called 'Song 2' that when I interviewed him in 1999 and asked him about the irony of Britpop's key anti-American band scoring their biggest international hit with a blatant Nirvana copy. Not that the whooping rush of distorted head-fuck rock 'n' roll is at all Muppet to my ears. But Damon's lyric about feeling heavy metal and being buzzed by jumbo jets is the deliberately meaningless antidote to all those sledgehammer social-comment character-comedies that began to grate on *The Great Escape* album, and to Kurt Cobain's pain and artistic frustration. Albarn groans 'Song 2' and even yelps its famous 'WHOO-HOO!!!'s with a sardonic, barely concealed contempt, as if to say 'This is what you want, this is what you get.' Unfortunately or otherwise, Dave and Graham (and producer Street) thrash-funk it out with such furious (relieved?) guerrilla relish that it easily wins its own argument – in exactly two minutes that reached No. 2 and comprised the second track on the *Blur* album.

SUPER BON BON

SOUL COUGHING

PRODUCED BY DAVID KAHNE AND SOUL COUGHING/ WRITTEN BY SOUL COUGHING AND M. DOUGHTY
SLASH/LONDON/JUNE 1997
DID NOT CHART

The increasingly persuasive relationship between TV/film/ advertising and pop has changed the way we've listened to and consumed pop over the last 20 years. For example, with this odd, fairly obscure throwback and update of early '80s New York art-funk and mutant disco, I owned it and liked it fine on first release, but only fell in love with its twisted angular lope when it turned up soundtracking some typically evil deed in the first series of *The Sopranos*. 'Move a . . . side and let the man go through,' New Yorker M. Doughty sneered coldly over a bowel-loosening buzzing double bass, low-tempo drums with hissing

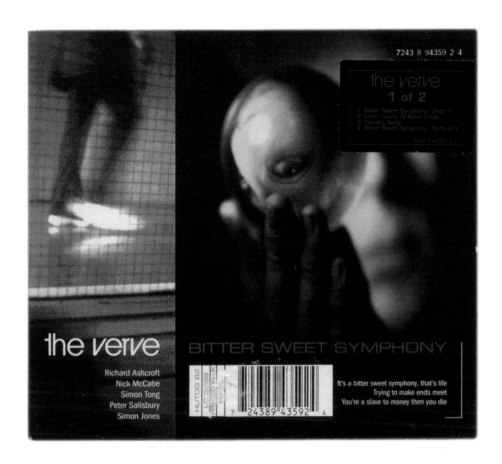

7243 8 94359 2 4

the verve
1 of 2

1 Bitter Sweet Symphony - Original
2 Lord I Guess I'll Never Know
3 Country Song
4 Bitter Sweet Symphony - Radio Edit

7243 8 94359 2 4

the verve

Richard Ashcroft
Nick McCabe
Simon Tong
Peter Salisbury
Simon Jones

BITTER SWEET SYMPHONY

It's a bitter sweet symphony, that's life
Trying to make ends meet
You're a slave to money then you die

HUTDG 82
LC 3098
PRINTED IN UK

7 24389 43592 4

BITTER SWEET SYMPHONY/THE VERVE

PAGE 402

hi-hats, and what sounds like steel drums being shagged by robots until they begin to gabble in protest. After that, the sing-rap is Beck-meets-Byrne surrealist juxtaposition and avant-freakery, but that first line with the malevolent power strut of the funk *was* Tony Soprano and all of the programme's sexy psycho-machismo made noise. Really, if you've never heard it, and if you love 'Once in a Lifetime' (see p. 148) or 'Coup' (see p. 206) or 'Give It Away' (see p. 344) or 'Fool's Gold' (see p. 296) as much as I do, then this is right up there with them as examples of what white boys can do with the funk when they transcend wanting to be black, and is available on an album called *Irresistible Bliss*.

BITTER SWEET SYMPHONY

THE VERVE

PRODUCED BY YOUTH AND THE VERVE (ADDITIONAL PRODUCTION AND MIX BY CHRIS POTTER)/
WRITTEN BY RICHARD ASHCROFT, MICK JAGGER AND KEITH RICHARDS
HUT/JUNE 1997
UK CHART: 2

Now *this* is what Chuck D and the Beastie Boys were on about. Because when an artist samples something and a struggling artist or writer gets paid, it all seems perfectly just. When an artist samples something and an old music biz player who's never played a note in his life gets paid, well, we're well into 'the ownership of ideas' minefield.

Allen Klein, former manager of both The Beatles and Rolling Stones, is an infamous figure in late '60s and early '70s rock. When The Verve's beautiful use of a loop from Andrew Loog Oldham's (the Stones's first manager) little-known orchestral version of the Stones's 'The Last Time' underpinned the Wigan band's greatest hit, it turned out that Klein owned the rights. He demanded – and got – every penny from Richard Ashcroft's song, which surely put as much strain on the soon-to-split band as Ashcroft's and guitarist Nick McCabe's personality clashes or various members' rumoured drug habits. The irony is that if Ashcroft and co. had played the riff, maybe changing a note here and there, instead of sampling it, the disaster would never have occurred. Whether it would have sounded as lovely as this remains a moot point.

The Moment when the orchestra gracefully spirals upwards and that classic Phil Spectorish beat crunches in is one of the peak thrills in modern rock. The fact that Ashcroft doesn't just carry the weight of this momentous music but defies gravity with his passionate Bunnymen-meets-Jimmy-Webb ponderings of life's inner meaning explains why Noel Gallagher wrote about Ashcroft with such generous awe on 'Cast No Shadow'. Unlike many, I still think the solo Mr Luscious Lips is pretty good, but I doubt if even he can top the feat of reinventing Jim Morrison's glamorous existential angst while completely retelling the story of the blues for a new generation of thin white blokes.

RISINGSON

MASSIVE ATTACK

PRODUCED BY MASSIVE ATTACK AND NEIL DAVIDGE/
WRITTEN BY DEL NAJA, MARSHALL, VOWLES, REED AND SEEGER
CIRCA/JULY 1997
UK CHART: 11

No such sampling chaos for Massive Attack, but plenty of confusion for me. 'Risingson' unrecognizably samples The Velvet Underground's teen ballad-tributing 'I Found a Reason' from the final *Loaded* album. The Bristolians credit Lou Reed and someone called Seeger. My copy of *Loaded* says it's entirely the work of Uncle Lou. Any advice on this matter would be much appreciated.

Anyway, I love 'Risingson' almost as much as 'Unfinished Sympathy' (see p. 318); in fact, I probably listen to it more these days. Again, it is glamorous existential angst, but, whereas Ashcroft is all grand gestures and Big Statements, Robert '3-D' Del Naja and Grant 'Daddy G' Marshall are specific, detailed and intimate. Like Bryan Ferry mixed with The Specials ('Is this the in-place to be? What am I doing here?' wailed Jerry Dammers via Terry Hall's voice on The Specials' 'Nite Klub' almost 20 years ago), they are at a party – an exclusive kind of club, you suspect – but at first are too paranoid and troubled to join in the hedonism. They stay separate, watching, wondering why they're there at all. The music is a sinister, slow-motion reggae-blues crawl, all shimmering effects, off-camera noises and enormous dubbed-up choral interjections, particularly when a wall-of-ghostliness choir chants, 'Dream on,' sounding frozen, as if playing a game of statues. There's a lover involved somewhere, giving D and G a hard time, and Del Naja uses the party as an amusing distraction – 'Toylike people make me boylike,' he sings with quiet relish. But the good times immediately turn evil. 'You're lost and you're lethal/And that's when you've got to leave all/These good people.' But they don't.

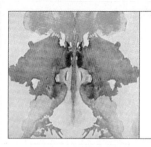

MASSIVE ATTACK
RISINGSON

RECORD 1A 1. RISINGSON (OTHERSIDE) 2. RISINGSON (OTHERSIDE INSTRUMENTAL)
RECORD 1B 1. RISINGSON (SINGLE MIX) 2. RISINGSON (MEYANDERTHAL MIX)
RECORD 2A 1. RISINGSON (DARREN EMERSON FOR UNDERWORLD REMIX)
RECORD 2B 1. RISINGSON (UNDERDOG REMIX) 2. RISINGSON (UNDERDOG INSTRUMENTAL)

WBRTDJ8 For promo use only. LC 3098 Printed in the U.K.

The music shifts to a gurgling, synthetic heavy metal, and the pair nag at the high life in front of them, seeing a lie that reflects on the relationship in question. There's no resolution – 'Risingson' is all half-formed impressions, not quite enough information. But the sense of dread and decay is overwhelming and the almost symphonic construction as much a challenge to the listener as it is to whomever they are so pissed off with. They may take their time putting out records, but it's always worth the wait.

BRIMFUL OF ASHA

CORNERSHOP

PRODUCED AND WRITTEN BY TJINDER SINGH
WIIIJA/AUGUST 1997
UK CHART: 60
(REMIXED AND REISSUED NOVEMBER 1997:
REACHED NO. 1)

This record is one of the most magical of unlikely triumphs in British pop history. It *all* just makes me grin. Firstly, it hit No. 1 on a tiny indie when everyone else felt they needed to be swallowed by majors in order to survive. Secondly, it jangled indily when indie was supposed to be dead. Thirdly, it was bought by at least some people who presumably hated British Asians, even when it heavily referenced a British Asian childhood and culture. And yeah, I know it would never have got to the top without a Fatboy Slim remix, but the original's miles better, so yah boo sucks.

And then there are the bases it covers. By highlighting Bollywood songstress Asha Bhosle and various other Indian stars and movies and contemporary political issues, it gave Asian kids a mainstream shout-out for the first time, making 'Brimful of Asha' a more useful blow against racism than Cornershop's early, shouty protest songs. By blending Bhosle with Marc Bolan and Trojan reggae it represented a *real* Britpop – one that reflected the cultural diversity that remains one of the few great things about this nation. And, for a wee bit of irony, while Massive Attack paid Lou Reed for a soundsource no listener could even locate, Tjinder, Ben Ayres and co. just sounded like the Velvets (and their eccentric nephew Jonathan Richman) and claimed that sound as their own. *And*, finally and of course, it's about the godlike wonder of the old-fashioned seven-inch vinyl single, the lifeblood of everything good about popular music. Indeed, if books had a theme tune then this one's would sing out 'Everybody needs a bosom for a pillow – mine's on the 45.'

THE RAIN (SUPA DUPA FLY)

MISSY 'MISDEMEANOUR' ELLIOTT

PRODUCED BY TIMBALAND/WRITTEN BY MELISSA
'MISSY' ELLIOTT, TIM MOSLEY, A. PEEBLES, B. MILLER
AND D. BRYANT
EAST WEST/AUGUST 1997
UK CHART: 16

Perhaps the thing that really put paid to the east v west rap wars was the rise of the south. Missy and Timbaland came from Virginia with a brand-new sound and a whole different kind of black charisma. There had been many marvellous female rappers before – Salt 'n' Pepa, Roxanne Shante, Queen Latifah, Da Brat, Lady of Rage and so on – but none that had made such a vivid and instant impression on hip-hop's and pop's consciousness. Missy was big and beautiful and mean but happy looking and possessed of all the in-your-face presence of the guys while neither compromising her femininity, nor pushing some spurious girl-power brand of feminism as financial success and the right to diet. The video for 'The Rain . . .' featured her floating in a Michelin Man suit, risking ridicule by exaggerating her body shape while neatly presenting herself as weightless – untethered by gravity's pull.

But the sound of 'The Rain . . .' is something else again. Based around the hook from soul goddess Ann Peebles's 'I Can't Stand the Rain', the initial lurch of strange, stumbling rhythm, chirping crickets and distant thunder, and Missy's own erotic drawl felt like hearing hip-hop for the first time all over again. Indeed, in Missy and Timbaland's sound, R&B and hip-hop were married once and for all, in defiance of genre, inventing a genre no one's been able to name. (There seems to be an attempt to call it . . . ahem . . . Bling Bling. I'm still yet to hear a normal person – i.e., someone who doesn't work in the media – use this term. Thank fuck.) Elliott is not an 'MC', in terms of being able to produce reams of poetry in a meaningful way. Her magic lies in her skills as a vocal stylist, a seeker of verbal effects, from her staccato stops and starts (the *anti*-flow), through her trademark kittenish 'Freakyfreaky' squeal, to the sudden bursts of echoing harmony. These don't just fit with Mosley's beat adventures, but comment upon them, stretching, punctuating, stroking, until the pair's studio relationship begins to sound like one of the all-time great romances, an instinctive flirtation of push and pull, seduce and slap. It's simply one of the most effortlessly hot and sexual noises anyone's ever made. The debut *Supa Dupa Fly* album single-handedly dragged hip-hop away from its reliance on sampling and back into electronics and experiment. The pop of the 21st century had arrived early.

BRIMFUL OF ASHA/CORNERSHOP

HELP THE AGED

PULP

PRODUCED BY CHRIS THOMAS/WRITTEN BY COCKER,
BANKS, DOYLE, MACKAY AND WEBBER
ISLAND/NOVEMBER 1997
UK CHART: 8

Jarvis Cocker's willingness to go against the grain had been amply displayed at the 1996 Brits. But rebelling, however slyly, against your own audience and an entire cultural hegemony was arguably more risky, and definitely did more damage to Pulp's chances of staying huge.

The euphoria that greeted Blair's election victory was painted as Young Britain's victory over Olde England – the very idea of youth (but not the reality. Britain remains a nation that despises children – try taking your kid into a pub) had never been so fetishized. Only Pulp would have released a post-Britpop single – a ballad! With depressing lyrics about imminent death! – that fetishized the old and infirm.

'Help the Aged' is, I think, the funniest lyric in this book. Because it's so painfully true. You need the slapstick of 'It's time you took an older lover, baby/Teach you stuff/Although he's looking rough', and the opening image of your gran sniffing glue in order to swallow Cocker's warning, delivered deadpan, 'You may see where you're headed and it's such a lonely place.' There is something very Hitler Youth about our obsession with the young and revulsion at the old. Cool Britannia stank of it. Cocker obviously thought so, and I don't think he was being glib when the band donated the proceeds to – who else? – Help the Aged. Sadly, this probably didn't help the aged that much, as reaching No. 8 these days is a whole bunch of nothing at all.

1998

1998

It was only when I looked again at the best singles of 1998 that I realized how feminine they were. It's a year dominated by female voices: some experienced and wise, some young and angry, one just plain nuts. Even the male pop of the year is largely gentle and dreamily awestruck about its relationships with women – and shimmeringly homoerotic in one case – and where it isn't, it is an enthusiastic parody of machismo. The only theory I've got is the basic 'what goes around, comes around' . . . the '90s had been dominated by various kinds of blokeishness. Maybe female pop fans and artists just got tired of being labelled as whores by guys with death wishes, or having to compete for attention with cigarettes and alcohol, and maybe a few guys began to agree. Whichever way, 1998 turns out to be the least macho year in this book, the point where the charts began to appear more female than male.

The more caring, sharing world introduced to us in 1997 manifested itself in a great many apologies (Canada to Native Americans, the Vatican to Jewish holocaust victims, the Khmer Rouge for Pol Pot, the Japanese to Britain for World War Two, the Met to the parents of Stephen Lawrence), while Monica Lewinsky proved the power of a woman by almost bringing down a president by going down on a president. As the Commons and the Lords bickered over the gay age of consent,

George Michael's willie, Welsh Secretary Ron Davies's visit to Clapham Common and the tragic suicide of Justin Fashanu, Britain's only out (and that *out* should be taken with as much italic as is possible) gay footballer all said something powerful about what happens to men when they are forced to submerge their sexuality.

And then there was the weather. Weird, destructive, scary weather the scientists called El Niño. Storm clouds gathered and found human form in August; in Omagh, Northern Ireland, and in two attacks on US embassies in Africa carried out by an Islamic terrorist called Osama bin Laden, who had, incidentally, been initially funded to fight the early '80s Soviet invasion of Afghanistan by the good old US of A. Hurricanes raged and, when the winds settled, the world we live in now had been firmly set in place.

Honourable mentions: Money Mark/'Hand in Your Head' (Mo Wax); Busta Rhymes/'Turn It Up'/'Fire It Up' (Elektra); The Beta Band/'Los Amigos Del Beta Bandidos' (Regal); Six by Seven/'88-92-96' (Mantra); Stardust/'Music Sounds Better with You' (Roule/Virgin); Rocket from the Crypt/'When in Rome, Do the Jerk' (Elemental); Doolally/'Straight from the Heart' (XL); Massive Attack/'Teardrop' (Circa); Mousse T v Hot 'n' Juicy/'Horny' (AM:PM)

SEXY BOY

AIR

PRODUCED AND WRITTEN BY JEAN-BENOÎT DUNCKEL
AND NICHOLAS GODIN
SOURCE/VIRGIN/FEBRUARY 1998
UK CHART: 13

It's comforting to view the success of Air as proof of our new pop open-mindedness as we reached the next century. But, in truth, Dunckel and Godin's impact was down to 'Sexy Boy', and 'Sexy Boy' is one of the most irresistible records in this book. Indeed, you fear for the heart and soul of anyone who does not respond to its perfection – a perfection born of the music's blend of Kraftwerk's cold classicism and the warmth of the great pop love song. Like all great pop, it is based on a snap-you-to-attention rhythm track . . . in this case, made of swishing ride symbol and talking-frog bass care of that most post-modern of rediscovered electronic instruments: the Moog synth. The other strengths of its erotic-aesthetic loveliness are in the details – a glockenspiel playing a set of gently ascending scales beneath the fragile treated voices, the synth-drums and sci-fi effects, and an unashamed homoeroticism that is cleverly sneaked in by way of a robotic vocal objectivity, courtesy of the other most post-modern of rediscovered electronic instruments: the vocoder. The reason Air are often referred to as '80s revivalists is not down to their sound, but because of their ability to make all those clever-but-sexy early '80s beige-pop ambitions into a reality without ever sounding academic or faux-black. Suddenly, those in the know acknowledged that French pop was where it was at. The ultimate Britpop backlash.

FEEL IT

THE TAMPERER FEATURING MAYA

PRODUCED BY FALOX (MIXED BY THE SHARP
BOYS)/WRITTEN BY MICHAEL JACKSON AND
JACKIE JACKSON
PEPPER/APRIL 1998
UK CHART: 1

How to cover and improve The Jacksons' 'Can You Feel It?' Easy. Be Italian and therefore insanely and tastelessly inspired enough to ignore the original's dull inspirational theme and replace it with playground violence by turning everything up to granny-torturing levels and posing the question: 'WHAT'S!!! she

gonna look like with a chimney on her?' Somewhere on the planet there is a discussion group devoted to finding the answer to this very question. And if there isn't, there should be.

RAY OF LIGHT

MADONNA

PRODUCED BY MADONNA AND WILLIAM ORBIT/
WRITTEN BY MADONNA, WILLIAM ORBIT, CLIVE
MULDOON, DAVE CURTIS AND CHRISTINE LEACH
MAVERICK/WARNERS/APRIL 1998
UK CHART: 2

As discussed many times previously, only pop women seem to do the unbridled ecstasy thing, I guess for the same reasons that male action-movie heroes never seem to actually *enjoy* sex. Think about it. It's true. Nevertheless, it's a man who is as responsible as a woman for the sheer joy expressed in the best ever Madonna single because, despite the cast of thousands involved in writing 'Ray of Light', all the mystical bollocks about zephyrs and the Universe doesn't do the business here. Nope, it's Maddy's giddy, newly light and natural vocals – complete with bravura operatic falsetto and those swooping psychedelic scales – and Bill Orbit's magnificent meld of jangle guitar (the intro *is* The Cure's 'Boys Don't Cry'), Hi-NRG disco, echoing repetitions, hard-rock mud, and, of all things, acid house, that does the trick. By the finish, you believe a woman can fly, and that Madonna has reinvented herself for the pop kids yet again. And flying is *a doddle* compared to that feat.

A ROSE IS STILL A ROSE

ARETHA FRANKLIN

PRODUCED AND WRITTEN BY LAURYN HILL
ARISTA/APRIL 1998
UK CHART: 22

Many dark rumours surround the seeming reluctance of The Fugees – makers of the most successful rap album ever, *The Score* – to work together again. Most of them revolve around the way the one woman in the band was treated by the two men. None of the three are telling (I've interviewed Ms Hill and she skirts around the subject very sweetly), so we may never know. Two things we can substantiate are that the early perception of The Fugees – that of two mediocrities being propped up by one

the tamperer
feel it
featuring maya

virgin
PRICE
£4.49

records

FEEL IT/THE TAMPERER FEATURING MAYA
PAGE 410

female genius – was spot on. The other is that Lauryn Hill took all of the frustrations into her solo career, forging and establishing a new kind of soul feminism that the likes of Kelis, Macy Gray, Destiny's Child and Erykah Badu have all benefited from. This came to full fruition on her debut solo LP *The Miseducation of Lauryn Hill* but found its first flowering here, where a woman in her early twenties manages to write and produce in the language of a legendary woman old enough to be her grandmother, giving Queen Aretha her first classic record in 25 years.

'A Rose Is Still a Rose' is a maternal feminist love song, the passing down of wisdom from Aretha to an unnamed young woman who is abused and dominated by men. Hill may be only 23, but her lyrics often sound so *old*, as if her experiences in the biz have surgically removed all traces of youth from her, leaving her weary, angry and determined that no other young female should make the mistakes she has had to learn from.

The song does not glide or slide in – the beats clunk and thunk, tough and spontaneous, letting you know immediately that this is the Real Soul Deal. Aretha skips and scats high and then moans the first verse low, before the first move on up to a subtle and beautiful bridge, adorned by strings that fill you full of hope even as Aretha *kills* the line 'She never knew what hit her', singing throaty and thick the implications of all the kinds of male violence it covers. The chorus makes plain what the title suggests – that a man cannot beat the beauty from a woman's soul either physically or mentally, that this girl will overcome. The song continues that this is as much about – and, boy, every time I switch on MTV or see a mag, do I see the truth of this – refusing to look, dress or behave in any way that compromises female independence. Other details emerge – 'He'll make and he'll *break* you' is especially scary and painful – but the rest of the song is about hearing the greatest singer of all time getting her talents around a song that is worthy of her and of a hard-won and emotive feminist authority. If Lauryn Hill had gone to work in a 24-hour garage straight after making this, then her place in soul history would still have been assured.

SINCERE

MJ COLE

PRODUCED AND WRITTEN BY MATT COLEMAN
AM:PM/MAY 1998
UK CHART: 38

One of the first mainstream successes to come from the UK garage/two-step scene, Londoner Matt Cole's 'Sincere' remains the new genre's most narcotically beautiful moment in a scene dominated by macho energy. The intro is masterly – the announcement of a whole new school of funky soul – as the opening backwards-phasing effect slowly uncovers a speeded-up voice hitting a delirious blue note joined by a hot femme groan. The effect just seems to grow in strange loveliness each time it's repeated, while the song is sung deep and throaty – almost sexually intimidating – and the verses are all 'I love you – let's shag' simplicity. But the chorus – 'Don't do it – Be sincere . . . I'm crazy' – undercuts it completely, suggesting feelings out of control, trying to hide fear of pain behind a bullish warning. The androgynous vocals belong to Nova Caspar and Jay Dee, their voices clipped from a CD of voices for sampling put together by The Cool Notes, which perhaps explains the dislocated, disturbed vibe.

Each 16 bars or so reveals another jazzy little detail – tinkling electric piano riffs, a parping sax, another subtle development of the deep disco-with-a-twist-of-the-hips beats and bass. It's a throwback to early '80s funk-boogie in many ways, but that breathtaking rush effect and the jarring dread of the singers' pleas lets you know that this sound is far more than mere retro.

EVERYBODY HERE WANTS YOU

JEFF BUCKLEY

PRODUCED BY TOM VERLAINE (MIXED BY
ANDY WALLACE)/WRITTEN BY JEFF BUCKLEY
COLUMBIA/MAY 1998
UK CHART: 43

As death cults go, the one surrounding Jeff Buckley has been a low-key, sensitive sort of death cult. Media and public alike could have had a 'he died for our sins' field day with a handsome and uniquely talented singer-songwriter who drowned in a swimming accident in Memphis in May 1997 at the age of 31, having made just one sublime album proper, *Grace*, and whose life and death so closely mirrored his father's, the even more

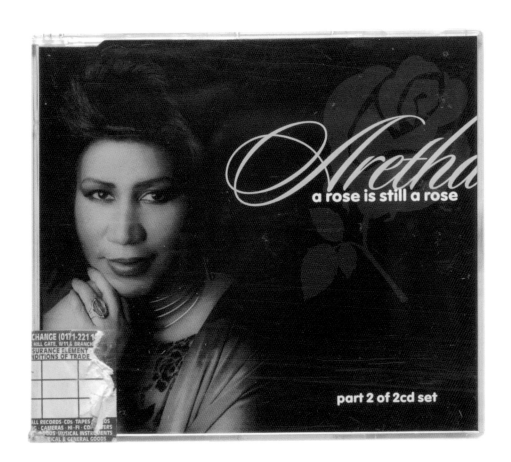

Aretha

a rose is still a rose

part 2 of 2cd set

A ROSE IS STILL A ROSE/ARETHA FRANKLIN
PAGE 410

cultish Tim Buckley. Yet the use of Buckley as some kind of dustbin for displaced angst never emerged. Maybe his death wasn't violent enough, or people were tired of it all after Cobain, Edwards, Shakur and Biggie Smalls in quick succession.

No, the dubious honour posthumously paid to Buckley is that virtually every British rock band of the last three or four years has mercilessly ripped him off. And his dad. Weird. Or cynical, considering this is what you'd call a real gap in the market. From a personal point of view, I would be happy to never again hear some lazy clod doing a choirboy falsetto while whingeing some angst-ridden doggerel over some vaguely minorish chords. But if any failed bank clerk seems to be able to do this, they most certainly can't do the posthumously released 'Everybody Here Wants You'. Because this is the kind of performance that sorts the wheat from the chaff, an unembellished, straightforward blue-eyed soul record, like Laura Nyro or Dusty Springfield or Charlie Rich used to make. The sort of thing that only the very best singers can manage without becoming Paul Young.

Truly, I can't approach being able to describe the otherworldly soulfulness of Jeff Buckley's singing here. All I can do is say that the song and performance become even more extraordinary when you realize that this is little more than a demo that Buckley would almost certainly have re-recorded. Indeed, Verlaine and Wallace make the emptiness into a virtue – very few records dare to sound as if the singer and band are in the room with you anymore. The second wonderful X-factor is the song's theme: loving someone impossibly beautiful and having to accept that there will always be backstabbers who want to take your place. Yet the impossibly beautiful Buckley embraces this submissive position with a languid intensity and a tear-jerking longing (and a love of '70s soul) that either makes him a sublime method actor, or someone who knew that his baby would never leave and is talented enough to make that self-confidence into something that burns with love.

Then again, he could have been singing to himself.

THE ROCKEFELLER SKANK

FATBOY SLIM

PRODUCED AND WRITTEN BY FATBOY SLIM
SKINT/JUNE 1998
UK CHART: 6

Norman Cook's public persona – that of the Happiest Man on Earth – can come over as both smug and blokey when divorced from his music. But when taken together with this, the record that made him a star after all those years as a crafty bandwagon jumper with The Housemartins, Beats International and Freakpower, you just gotta say good luck to the guy. Because 'The Rockefeller Skank' is surely the most fun you can have with machines, from its steals from '60s northern soulies The Just Brothers and the legendary John Barry, through its half-buried elements of Gary Glitter and The Fall and ancient '60s beat records, to the minute or so of pure noise vandalism in its breakdown (if you've ever wondered what happened to punk rock, its sonic spirit is alive and well and living in the last two minutes of this record).

Not only had dance music's recycling of old styles not thought to go back to a mythical '60s world of girls doing the milking-a-cow-while-shaking-their-hair-dance, but to then allow it to disintegrate into an ear-splitting alarm before making it crawl back up to speed and get this nightmare din on every radio and in every club . . . well, the guy just must have known his time had come. Certainly, there's not another machine-generated record I've heard that sounds so live and spontaneous.

By the way, did you know Norman's real name is Quentin? You did? Oh.

INTERGALACTIC

BEASTIE BOYS

PRODUCED AND WRITTEN BY BEASTIE BOYS AND
MARIO CALDATO JR
GRAND ROYAL/JUNE 1998
UK CHART: 5

Despite their reinvention as super-cool, globally aware, tofu-munching crusaders for Buddhism and male feminism, The Beasties are always at their best when they're being stupid. They know this, which is why they're stupid a lot of the time. The kind of playground nonsense raps they do on a record like 'Intergalactic' are not just very fly self-parody, but also their

SINCERE/MJ COLE
PAGE 412

subtle way of having a dig at hip-hop's obsession with the battling, dissing macro MC, as they take the basic 'I will BLAH you like BLAH-BLAH!!!' construction of the traditional form as far into the realms of slapstick surrealism as they can without becoming a comedy act. The music, however, is deadly serious, and it is 'Intergalactic', ironically, that has paved the way for all the Eastern-flavoured psychedelic computer-funk tunes from black America that have made the charts a better place in the last couple of years.

Like 'The Rockefeller Skank' (see above), 'Intergalactic' is the sound of machine as purveyor of pure joy, in tandem with those raps that have the . . . STYLE!!! To rip the merry piss until you . . . SMILE!!! Fave Moment: 'I'll stir-fry you in my . . . WOK!/You need to start shakin' and your fingers pop/Like a pinch on the neck from Mr Spock!' Oh yes indeedy.

CELEBRITY SKIN

HOLE
PRODUCED BY MICHAEL BEINHORN (MIXED BY TOM LORD-ALGE)/WRITTEN BY COURTNEY LOVE, ERIC ERLANDSON AND BILLY CORGAN
GEFFEN/SEPTEMBER 1998
UK CHART: 19

DOO WOP (THAT THING)

LAURYN HILL
PRODUCED AND WRITTEN BY LAURYN HILL
RUFFHOUSE/COLUMBIA/SEPTEMBER 1998
UK CHART: 3

Comparing and contrasting these two artists' and records' takes on pop feminism is irresistible. While Hill is popularly characterized as a woman used by men, Courtney Love is labelled rock's ultimate user of the rock-bloke. While Hill is so musically talented you feel she probably has to restrain herself from writing symphonic jazz operettas, Love has a singing voice like a moose having its bollocks squeezed and often gets some help from the guys (in this case, Billy Corgan of Smashing Pumpkins) in the writing of her three-chord punk-metal ditties. While Hill's take on feminism is all fire 'n' brimstone Christian moralizing – don't fuck, don't get your tits out, be strong through the rejection of sin – Love's is all about sexual power and the play-off between looking and behaving like a slut and

how that look and behaviour makes men underestimate you. And, while Hill's 'Doo Wop' is all brassy soul and jaunty persuasion, a happy and feminine music that houses her deep, almost masculine voice and a bunch of rabid criticisms of women who collaborate in their own oppression ('Niggas fucked up and you still defending them?') and men who hide their immaturity behind a wall of violent machismo ('The sneaky silent men/The punk domestic violence men'), Love's 'Celebrity Skin' is all power-chord guitar crunch and camp Joan Jett sneers, a metal throwback music that houses her deep, almost masculine voice and a bunch of rabid 'I'm so fucked' self-dramatizations ('A walking study in demonology') as she tries to convince us that she is somehow appalled by Hollywood women when we know her entire life, career and public image have been about joining the folks on the hill.

Both singles are marvellous despite and because of all those contrasting reasons. But Lauryn's music is all about her talent and voice while the song is about the wider world, and Courtney's music is all about male rock power (the star is guitarist Eric Erlandson) while the song is about and addressed to no one but herself. Make your own choice on which one adds up to feminism.

BELIEVE

CHER
PRODUCED BY MARK TAYLOR AND BRIAN RAWLING/
WRITTEN BY HIGGINS, BARRY, TORCH, GRAY, MCLENNAN, POWELL
WARNERS/OCTOBER 1998
UK CHART: 1

If Lauryn or Courtney ever need advice on how to survive in a male-dominated industry, they could do worse than approach Cherilyn Sarkasian La Pier, who has thrived on little more than . . . um . . . er . . . no, it'll come to me . . .

Still, disco glory is disco glory, and this is *true* disco glory, thanks to Messrs Taylor and Rawling. But I can't help but wonder at how it needed six people to write this slice of vocoder bleat-beat as I dwell over the mysterious sleeve credit: 'Vocal Effects in Metrovision'. Is Cher singing in tune some kind of trick with mirrors?

Incidentally, somebody at Warner Bros Records once mistakenly faxed Cher's tour requirements to the *Time Out* music section. Ha! We wet ourselves for days at the ridiculousness of the world Ms Love has so eagerly bought

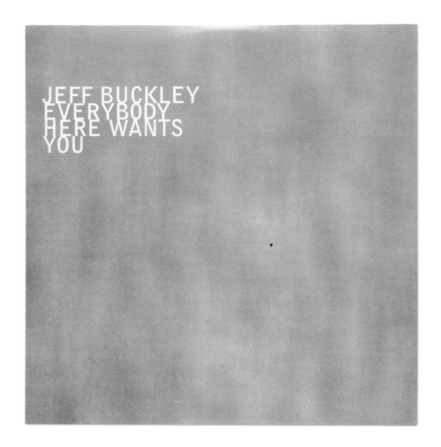

EVERYBODY HERE WANTS YOU/JEFF BUCKLEY
PAGE 412

into. What were Cher's specific gig requirements? I really can't say, but one in particular was dead funny. If you see me in the pub . . .

GODDESS ON A HIWAY

MERCURY REV
PRODUCED BY DAVE FRIDMANN AND JONATHAN DONAHUE/WRITTEN BY MERCURY REV
V2/NOVEMBER 1998
UK CHART: 51
(REISSUED AUGUST 1999: REACHED NO. 26)

THE CERTAINTY OF CHANCE

THE DIVINE COMEDY
PRODUCED BY JON JACOBS AND NEIL HANNON/ WRITTEN BY NEIL HANNON AND JODY TALBOT
SETANTA/NOVEMBER 1998
UK CHART: 49

Ah, the grandiose power ballad. The place where guys come over all sensitive and windswept, where they fearlessly wander to the very edges of the abyss of pretension, where much money is made from the sale of disposable lighters. More often than not, the power ballad is shite. But when it's good, its very, *very* good, and here are two good reasons why it should continue to exist.

Standing at opposite poles of hipness, we have Buffalo, New York State's Mercury Rev, a formerly chaotic Yank art-punk band who suddenly went all rootsy and cosmic Neil Young with 1998's *Deserter's Songs* album and became critical darlings, and Neil Hannon who, as we've previously heard, is a smart-arse fop who should be drummed out of rockworld for singing in tune, possessing a sense of his own ridiculousness and knowing three-syllable words. Both make songs here that are slow and grandiose and seem to strain for the Meaning of Life, the Rev by enigmatic suggestion, the Div by deliberate and ironic design.

'Goddess on a Hiway' is what slow rock should sound like. Gently funky, subtle and then sweeping, anthemic but full of off-kilter details, with its chilling submarine peals and underlying organs and harpsichords. Jonathan Donahue is speeding down that all-American highway with the girl of his dreams, but, like Tom Verlaine's Cadillacs in graveyards (see 'Marquee Moon' by Television, p. 30), this is less a rock dream than a failing denial of some kind of dread. The Big Arms-Aloft Hook is 'And I know

this ain't gonna last.' His goddess's eyes 'explode like two bugs on glass'. The very act of them driving is causing rivers to run dry. No matter how comforting the melody and Donahue's lovely harmonies become, the song remains an uncomfortable portent of something real bad, the lull before the coming of El Niño.

'The Certainty of Chance' is an even more spectacular tune and arrangement, and also makes explicit Donahue's feeling of being at the mercy of uncontrollable forces. For Hannon, the only thing that is certain is chaos and the ultimate triumph of fate. The rumbling and ominous slo-mo Phil Spector chord sequence throws in the loveliest curveball – the chord equivalent of 'you couldn't see it coming' – and Hannon's portentous Scott Walker croon stays cold and calm as butterflies cause hurricanes and small boys crash the world's computers and pianos and choirs and Talbot's strings go all cod-operatic on our helpless asses. But why all this philosophical pondering on the nature of chaos theory? What purpose does his detachment serve? The last verse reveals all. This is Hannon's excuse for dumping some poor hapless bint, his attempt to convince her that life, the Universe and everything is bigger than their (but mainly her) feelings, and that the split 'will bring you back to me'. Yeah, right. And I hope we can still be friends.

The undercutting of the initial premise, the sheer cruelty of it all, makes you gasp at the man's chutzpah. Because he's taken the pathetically dishonest, get-me-off-the-hook excuses we use to reject people to their logical conclusion in the most sensitive and pretty of settings, and the joke is on us. And that, in a nutshell, is why many don't take to Neil Hannon. He's just too *accurate*, especially about the nature of men.

1999

1999

And I ask myself, well, how did I get here?

To recap: CD singles have pretty much replaced the vinyl single, just as the CD has the vinyl album, except in the loyal dance market with its love of the 12-inch. The seven-inch single is bought only by indie nerds and collectors. Boo!

The limited edition coloured vinyl and picture discs of punk taught major labels how to market singles more aggressively to fans – with CD singles often split into two or three different editions featuring remixes or live tracks or – blimey trousers – a new song or two.

Singles that are made in the true spirit of the single – a short, sharp message to the listener designed to transcend the artist's own work and genre and stand out on the radio – are an increasing rarity. They mainly exist to sell albums. They always did, to some extent. But not as much. The charts are a mess. A complete irrelevance. Having said that, maybe if I were 14 again, they wouldn't be. Who knows? Just don't ask me who's No. 1 at the moment, because I haven't a clue.

Rock 'n' roll is alive and living in the machines of Dr Dre and Basement Jaxx and Aphex Twin and Underworld and Timbaland et cetera. Dance and black music now do everything in terms of challenge and innovation that rock used to, while rock is either the appalling Limp Bizkit or your grandad moaning about the rain while trying to locate his pipe and slippers. But rock 'n' roll still has the capacity to survive and surprise – see The Strokes, The White Stripes, The Hives. Hoorah!

Soul music has gone from nowhere in 1977 to everywhere in 2001, courtesy of R&B, which is becoming increasingly sonically unfathomable and fantastic.

Rock or pop rebellion used to be The Kids railing against The Man while rejecting all the clothes and records He tried to sell them. Rock or pop rebellion now is The Kids from over here railing against The Kids from over there, heavily sponsored by The Man, and dressed in whatever clothes He has a sale on this week. For rebellion, see the visual arts, movies, protest movements. This makes the odd smidgin of pop rebellion that emerges all the more heroic, no matter how subtle it may be.

Pop has almost nothing to do with the counter culture anymore. See above.

Disco and its derivatives are now pop's primary colours. They have been since *Saturday Night Fever* and I doubt it will ever change.

There is more brilliant pop music around than there ever has been before, and, because of the plethora of new media, it is easier to access, if more difficult to filter. This is not a contradiction to the stuff about rebellion and counter culture above. It's the reason why nothing can hold our collective attention for long enough to matter as much as The Beatles or the Sex Pistols.

The late, great Lester Bangs once wrote, 'We will never again agree on anything as we agreed on Elvis.' The whole of pop history since, and therefore this book, is about the truth of that statement. Elvis accidentally opened up a world, and once we'd begun to explore it, we ended up in different parts of it, agreeing on nothing. The only large quantities of people who agree about anything are people who buy Ronan Keating or Toploader or Hear'Say or Shania Twain records. Because they don't actually like music very much, and that's an easy thing to agree on.

The pop single is still one of the great inventions of the modern world. Go on, switch on the radio. I guarantee you'll hear at least one blinding record that sums you and your life up completely at this moment in time. Albums are even more dull in comparison now, particularly since the compact disc enabled them to get even longer. That's why they had to make a separate chart for all those *Now That's* . . . singles compilations. All those conceptual masterworks just can't compete.

As for the real world, part of this book was written in September 2001 as the planet seems to have accepted that it was going to war. This isn't that much of a shock when you've just looked through 23 years' worth of events that make you realize that we've always been at war – we just got better at making sure it was fought somewhere else. Pop has lost a lot of its nerve about commenting on the world outside itself, but certain sounds, styles and stances still do, almost despite the artists themselves. Of course, they are only pop records. But then, bullets are only metal, money is only paper and religion is only old books, when all is said and done. I hope you've enjoyed reading about *these* records as much as I've loved listening to them. Hell – I hope you're still here.

Honourable mentions: Underworld/'Bruce Lee' (JBO/V2); Fatboy Slim/'Praise You' (Skint); Ladytron/'He Took Her to a Movie' (Invicta Hi-Fi); Mr Oizo/'Flat Beat' (F Communications); New Radicals/'You Only Get What You Give' (MCA/Universal); Godspeed You Black Emperor!/'Blaise Bailey Finnegan III' (Kranky); Supergrass/'Moving' (Parlophone)

NO SCRUBS

TLC

PRODUCED BY KEVIN 'SHEKSPERE' BRIGGS/
WRITTEN BY KEVIN BRIGGS, KANDI BURRUSS AND
TAMEKA COTTLE
LAFACE/ARISTA/MARCH 1999
UK CHART: 3

TLC's lesson in Afro-American man-dissing slang is a wonderful record because it is such a sad record. If the Spice Girls – or even Destiny's Child – had been given 'No Scrubs', its dimensions would have been washed away by blaring production noise, girl power gimmickry and faux feistiness. But here, the resigned voices join with the stark synthetic/acoustic guitar, the moody orchestrals and the slow, swaying tempo to imply that men will never change, and that the TLC three are destined to spend the rest of their lives (or at least until they show signs of ageing) being hollered at from cars by losers. The middle eight contains the key lyric . . . a simple list of the criticisms of (a significant proportion of) black men that preoccupy black female pop at the cusp of the 21st century. They live with their mothers. They're not there for their children. They have no money. Indeed, the last of these had by now taken over from gang talk as the major topic of conversation within American black music – a seeming acknowledgement on the part of black women that money *can* buy their love, and a refusal to see what that makes them, answered in turn by bitter denunciations of 'hoes' from even the most traditionally right-on rappers. Buried in this superficially cheap and nasty gender war is a mountain of info about the legacies of slavery, economic alienation, emasculation and misogyny, and the divisive con of capitalism and the American Dream. And, although this war of words will probably never be responsible for killing any artists, each snipe kills off a little more of the spirit of community and potential unity in the face of oppression. 'No Scrubs' comments upon and transcends all this through a combination of melodic beauty, elegant weariness, and inspired and repeated use of the most valuable word in the English language – 'No'.

WINDOWLICKER

APHEX TWIN

PRODUCED AND WRITTEN BY RICHARD D. JAMES
WARP/MARCH 1999
UK CHART: 16

Many of the greatest musicians of our age are probably incapable of strumming a simple E major on an acoustic guitar. Like that matters, if you understand the possibilities of machines. No artist represents this idea as well as The Aphex Twin aka Richard D. James, who does things with drum machines, samplers and sequencers that seem to defy the laws of physics.

'Windowlicker' is the most impossible to understand noise within *This Is Uncool*. Conversely and wonderfully, it is also one of the most aesthetically beautiful. Based upon a soulful three-note bassline, James begins by groaning asthmatically before unleashing a surreal barrage of beats based roughly upon old-school electro. These beats establish themselves, then stop, leap back, leap forward, crash, stumble, freeze and rush – almost as if James had sought to represent his entire writing process in less than one minute. Now you are sitting uncomfortably, he then brings forth the major theme – a set of sampled voices singing 'ahh', 'ohh' and 'dum-da-dum' with a melting longing, all set at different tones and levels until they make a buttery meld of gracefully erotic gospel harmonies – albeit gospel from the inhabitants of the spaceship in *Close Encounters*. The record continues like this until it stops, give or take the odd wall of synthetic heavy metal.

I once listened to this on a Walkman on a tube train and honestly felt like I was floating around the carriage, looking down on my fellow passengers as they were bathed in a mellow yellow glow, while I stifled hysterical laughter and wished they could all hear and feel like this. Drugs? Well, I'd taken some hay fever tablets. But I don't think antihistamines mixed with caffeine usually produce this effect.

And then there was Chris Cunningham's accompanying video, where James's scary grin was morphed onto a series of fly hunks and voluptuous honeys in a brilliant parody of a Miami-style US rap video. The sight of that evil beardy head winding its big booty on a beach was genuinely terrifying, and by the end of the promo all notions of money, fame, physical attractiveness, sexual identity and American excess had been surgically exposed for the empty charade that they are. The counter culture isn't dead. It just replaced guitars and shouting with computers and art design.

WINDOWLICKER/APHEX TWIN
PAGE 422

MY NAME IS

EMINEM

PRODUCED BY DR DRE/WRITTEN BY MARSHALL
MATHERS AND DR DRE
AFTERMATH/INTERSCOPE/MARCH 1999
UK CHART: 2

Ever feel someone's been written about just a little too much? Still, what else could we do? In a pop world of careerists, cop-outs and mealy-mouthed stooges, all we wanted was someone who looked good, had a talent, and had the balls to say what was on their mind and fuck the consequences. Then we got The Dream. The white boy who could rap better than the black boys. The homophobe who looked like an Old Compton Street twink. The misogynist who explained, in gruesome detail and within his work, why he was a misogynist. The Detroit nerd who had the world's greatest producer in his corner. The satirist you could dance to, if you could stop laughing long enough. And, best of all, the kind of artist who put us right-on types in a constant lather and pickle of confusion – why do I love this stuff when it's so utterly indefensible? Sometimes even our best intentions have to be challenged in their complacency. What else is art for?

The debut single that made Mathers aka Eminem aka Slim Shady an overnight star is one of his most troublesome concoctions. It goes 'Hi!!! My name is . . . trickytricky . . . SLIM SHADY!!!' It hates everyone the world likes and makes it funny. It slags off his own mother so bad she sued him. Among the slapstick it uncovers the dark truths of growing up poor and alienated and inadequate and bewildered in America. Its rage at parental failure is awful and unprecedented. It has Dre music that is almost comedy yet still sounds deadly serious. It has a great joke about being shit at school. It features Mathers explaining that 'God sent me to piss the world off.' About time. It had been 22 years since He sent the last one.

TO LOSE LA TREK

CAMPAG VELOCET

PRODUCED BY CAMPAG VELOCET/WRITTEN BY
PETE VOSS, IAN CATER, LASCELLES GORDON AND
BARNABY SLATER
PIAS/MARCH 1999
DID NOT CHART

The charts have become so volatile and easy to manipulate that it is virtually impossible for any band with music-press covers and a few quid behind them not to chart. Congratulations, then, to this Portsmouth via London band who succeeded in making a record so unfashionable it bombed utterly. Crime one: Pete Voss sings/raps in a London accent. Crime two: 'To Lose La Trek' is the worst pun of all time. Crime three: 'To Lose La Trek' sounds like the bloke from baggy bandwagon jumpers Flowered Up guesting with Talking Heads. Crime four: Pete Voss looks and sounds as if he wants to kick your head in. This last crime is drenched in irony, as pop was now full of macho black Americans who looked as if they wanted to blow your head off. But that was a distant threat, a vicarious thrill. Voss is the hoolie in your local pub, the Stanley knife and the Glasgow Kiss. Too close to home.

This was made even more unlikely and unlikeable to many by the surreal verbosity of Voss's narratives. His obsessions appear to be S&M, very sleazy sex and . . . um . . . cycling. You know, riding a bike. That is what 'To Lose La Trek' is 'about', the runty vocal equivalent of the struggling-uphill odyssey of Kraftwerk's 'Tour De France' (see p. 204). It insists, memorably, that 'Nothing is painless.' The 'Once in a Lifetime' rhythm track (see p. 148) and Ian Cater's old-school choppy-funk guitar are blindingly brilliant, and it always makes me feel nostalgic for Wobble-era PiL, mutant disco and 1979.

TO LOSE LA TREK/CAMPAG VELOCET
PAGE 424

RUN ON

MOBY

PRODUCED AND WRITTEN BY MOBY
MUTE/APRIL 1999
UK CHART: 33

Richard Melville Hall's massively successful *Play* album is the key example of modern machine fusion, and how much it has altered the breadth of our listening habits. There are records previously mentioned in this book that fuse bluesy soul vocals with computer beats, but New Yorker Moby went on to make the link more explicit, and square the circle around the blues and dance music. 'Run On', which samples a record called 'Run On for a Long Time' by Bill Landford and The Landfordaires, sounds like legendary '60s/'70s blues-rockers Canned Heat remixed by Dr Dre in Eminem-lite mode. The two-chord piano vamp and deep bass simply underpins the atmospheric gospel-blues voices as they tell their story of sin, adding the odd scratch or breakbeat, but largely leaving the ancient wonder of the voices to speak for themselves. It was the first and finest track from an album destined to follow Portishead, Massive Attack and Air and become an adult dinner-party staple, a place so far removed from what Moby originally sampled as to be a satire in itself.

SIX SECS

COBRA KILLER

PRODUCED AND WRITTEN BY D'ORIO AND TROST
DIGITAL HARDCORE/MAY 1999
DID NOT CHART

Now, if someone played this at a dinner party I'd ask if I could move in. 'Six Secs' is probably the most obscure release contained within these pages, a seven-inch vinyl release on Berlin rave-punk anarchist Alec Empire's Digital Hardcore label that I didn't even see get reviewed.

The majority of Empire's and DH's music is a hilarious hybrid of high-speed 'gabba' techno and ferocious white-noise overload with added screaming. Empire and co.'s anti-capitalist, no sell-out beliefs are the nearest thing to a pop representative of the anti-globalization protesters. His flagship band is called Atari Teenage Riot and that is exactly what their music sounds like. It's the sort of stuff that makes us hacks write purple prose in praise of its commitment, originality and rabid sonic fury, before we file it and never put ourselves through the hell of actually listening to it ever again.

But 'Six Secs' is the funky and feminine exception to the DH rule. It's still pretty noisy, I'll grant you, but here the noise is balanced by a monstrous James Brown-style 'UNNNGH!!!' grunt, a claustrophobically funky '60s organ riff and hot, cooing sex – apart, that is, from the orchestras that enter playing a completely different tune for no reason, and the fabric-rupturing jumps, sticks and rude interruptions. It says little fathomable except 'Sookie Sookie, man' but says it in a strangely old-fashioned, almost '50s teen nonsense, funny, cute pop-vandal genius way. It ends much too quickly. And you can't help wondering how much more relevant Alec Empire would be as an artistic rebel voice if all his records sounded like this, rather than yet another macho man throwing the toys out of his pram.

COFFEE + TV

BLUR

PRODUCED BY WILLIAM ORBIT/WRITTEN BY
DAMON ALBARN, GRAHAM COXON, ALEX JAMES AND
DAVE ROWNTREE
FOOD/JUNE 1999
UK CHART: 11

My favourite single by my favourite '90s pop group is not just a lovely tune and a moving song, but some kind of masterclass in how to make old-school guitar pop sound fresh all over again. Admittedly, if someone had told me beforehand that this would be achieved by a song about recovering from alcoholism that sounds like a blend of Wire's 'Outdoor Miner', 'Michael Caine' by Madness, and every naïve and innocent indie jingle-jangle and '60s harmony pop novelty, I wouldn't have bought it. Until they said it was by Blur. And then I would.

Again, Graham Coxon's revealing, anti-macho, drenched-in-Camden-and-The-Good-Mixer-pub lyric about hiding from a hostile world and coming to terms with the fear of other people that drives him to drink is, like 'Windowlicker' (see p. 422), hard to separate from its milk-carton-hunts-for-missing-boy-and-dies-saintly-death video, a perfect representation of Coxon's childlike public image (I've interviewed him and frankly have no idea whether he's putting us on). The details that make the music so perfect are the tough, swinging rhythms led by Graham's triplet chords, and the fantastic Robert Fripp-plays-Bowie impression he unleashes at the end. The best performance yet from the best guitarist on Earth at the present time, because his imagination and technique are balanced and bolstered by a refusal to play a single pointless note.

SIX SECS/COBRA KILLER
PAGE 426

GUILTY CONSCIENCE

EMINEM FEATURING DR DRE
PRODUCED AND WRITTEN BY MARSHALL MATHERS
AND DR DRE
AFTERMATH/INTERSCOPE/AUGUST 1999
UK CHART: 5

The very idea of Dre playing the Voice of Reason on a rap record was irresistible to anyone who loved hip-hop and knew the part he had played in its descent into aimless violence. But with the *Abbott and Costello Meet the Mummy*-style piano riff and Eminem's relentless glorification of said aimless violence, 'Guilty Conscience' becomes a new high – and deliberate low – in irresponsible pop entertainment. Armed robbery? Check. Paedophilia and date rape? Gotcha. Murdering your cheating wife? All present and correct. But must we fling our kids at this pop filth? Well, I can only go from the personal. My son was 13 when he heard and fell in love with Eminem. Even at that tender age, he understood that this was a cartoon satire on the amount of violence and hate crime chucked at him through music and TV. Two years later he still loves Eminem and, as far as I can tell, decides for himself which parts of Mathers's shtick he approves and disapproves of. But then, there's a song on the first album called 'Role Model' that explains and refutes the entire concept of passing personal responsibility for our own actions onto celebrities, and 'Stan' gives him the other side, so Mathers himself pinned it down for my kid better than I could.

You have to smash eggs to make an omelette.

NEW YORK CITY BOY

PET SHOP BOYS
PRODUCED BY DAVID MORALES AND PET SHOP
BOYS/WRITTEN BY NEIL TENNANT, CHRIS LOWE
AND DAVID MORALES
PARLOPHONE/OCTOBER 1999
UK CHART: 14

This book is full of great singles artists who got lost. So it's especially heart-warming to still be writing about someone who didn't. 'New York City Boy', despite its reasonably high chart placing, provoked the first rumblings I'd ever heard of a PSB backlash. Even lifelong fans – hell, even lifelong gay fans – seemed to feel that the song was *too gay*. I guess it's no real surprise when you consider that gay events such as London's Mardi Gras (formerly Gay Pride, and the change in that name says a mouthful) are dominated by manufactured kiddie pop acts – (apparent) heteros who are more than happy to take the Pink Pound while singing about the most empty version of straight love imaginable. Maybe, after AIDS and Clause 28 and the Old Compton Street nail-bombings and the mainstreaming of homophobia through hip-hop, the idea of being gay as a camp but defiant celebration of a lifestyle just doesn't seem tenable. It could be worse, though. 'New York City Boy', despite being co-written and co-produced by New York superstar DJ David Morales, bombed completely in the States, heading the same way as George Michael's career. Yeah, I know George's music sucks, but they didn't seem to mind as long as they could kid themselves that he was a red-blooded pussy hound. God bless America.

Anyway, this song sums up the genius of Tennant and Lowe. Their picture of a boy who could be from an Eminem song ('Lying on your bed playing punk rock . . . Home is a boot camp') and his salvation in the streets of NY is unspecific lyrically. It's the beefed-up Village People march of the music and the drag queens in the video that make the theme explicit . . . that discovering that you're gay in your youth is more thrilling than being straight. No one wanted to hear that. But I think that's beautiful.

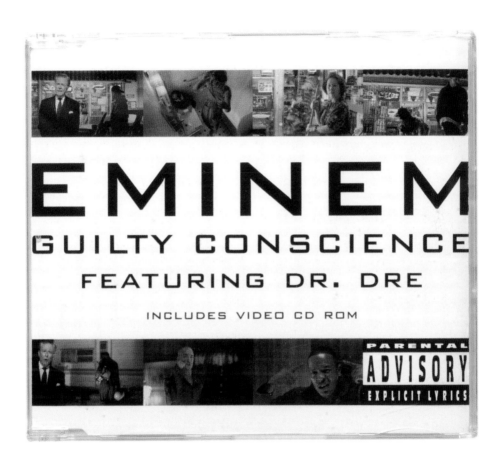

GUILTY CONSCIENCE/EMINEM FEATURING DR DRE
PAGE 428

CODED LANGUAGE

KRUST FEATURING SAUL WILLIAMS

PRODUCED BY KRUST/WRITTEN BY KRUST AND
SAUL WILLIAMS
TALKIN LOUD/OCTOBER 1999
UK CHART: 66

People might have wanted to hear 'Coded Language', but were never going to get the chance. Even in a British radio climate finally becoming more at home with cutting-edge black music, this collaboration between Bristol drum 'n' bass don and Reprazent member Krust and American boho poet Williams was too black, too strong. Nevertheless, it is a single of astonishing power, musically and lyrically, and showcased a new voice in Williams, who seemed capable of doing anything with words. His verbal virtuosity matches Eminem's, but here, as in his solo work, he is far too serious for jokes, sick, satirical or otherwise. Which is probably why he's still not a star yet, despite having the charisma to match the talent.

In the seven minutes or so that 'Coded Language' rumbles and rages, Williams tackles the connection between The Funk and displaced African people, the abuse of the language of violence, the gap between what the human mind is capable of understanding and the shit we are fed, a spine-tinglingly inspirational list of counter-cultural heroes – black, white and all points in between – *and* the terrifying flipsides that have shaped the modern world, and how music, art, and communication are the frontline against a planet that has declared an unending war on the human spirit. Quotes from the deluge of words – a vocabulary unmatched by Mathers or Chuck D or even Scott-Heron – just can't do the overall effect justice, particularly when housed within a speaker-blowing tower of crushing breaks, insidious guitar riff and restless interference. Less a pop single than an intimidating intellectual experience, it proves that, if jungle never quite came to terms with the song, it sure provides the toughest backdrop for a truly great poet.

JUMP 'N' SHOUT

BASEMENT JAXX

PRODUCED BY SIMON RATCLIFFE AND FELIX BUXTON,
WRITTEN BY RATCLIFFE, BUXTON AND JAMES
XL/OCTOBER 1999
UK CHART: 12

So we get to this stage and find records that mix together huge amounts of what has gone before. Brixton's Buxton and Ratcliffe have become Britain's best dance act by snatching equally from disco (the beats), punk (the energy), rock 'n' roll (the riffs), 2-Tone (the attitude), dancehall reggae (the vocals, in this particular single's case) acid house (the hysterical noise and hypnotic repetitions), R&B (the crafty Eastern motifs and computerized funk abstraction) and acid jazz (the smooth and funky poise, although *not* in this particular single's case). The result is manic, infectious like foot and mouth and bullishly, deliriously happy, as if every one of the city's problems can be solved by jumping and shouting and sounding like this. Slarta John's ever-climbing motormouth MCing is untouchably great, reaching a peak when discussing how rivals who can't match this should go to 'Basement Jaxx school', because 'We have di knowledge/We go a good college/A+ in a history and home economics!' If miserable Miss Jefferys had made Home Economics rock like this, I'd be the Jamie Oliver you don't want to ritually disembowel by now.

Artful Dodger
Rewind - (4.03)
Tel Relentless:
020 7432 3224

RE-REWIND THE CROWD SAY BO SELECTA/ARTFUL DODGER
PAGE 432

GOT YOUR MONEY

OL' DIRTY BASTARD

PRODUCED BY THE NEPTUNES/WRITTEN BY PHARRELL
WILLIAMS, CHAD HUGO AND RUSSELL JONES
ELEKTRA/NOVEMBER 1999
DID NOT CHART
(REISSUED JUNE 2000 'FEATURING KELIS': REACHED
NO. 11)

You'll probably know that Russell 'Ol' Dirty Bastard' Jones is a member of hip-hop collective the Wu-Tang Clan, and that his problems with drugs and child support have led him to numerous arrests and eventual incarceration. His most famous escapade involves going on the run from the cops, turning up at a Wu-Tang gig and doing a spot before heading out on the run again, and finally getting caught when he stopped to sign autographs in a McDonald's car park, where he pleaded, 'Don't arrest me here, officer. These kids see me as a role model.' All the satirists in the world could not come up with a black rapper stereotype like ODB – they'd be dismissed for being too broad.

But he's made some brilliant records, and none better than this. 'Got Your Money' introduced us to new 'I hate you so much right now!!!' R&B harpy Kelis, who trills the chorus line prettily, and to new R&B/hip-hop production heroes The Neptunes, who serve up a slice of infectious P-funk in their soon-to-be-trademark stark, almost demo-ish style with a side order of their gift for 'it's weird but I can't pinpoint why' details. The vocal is insane, a drunken Scooby Doo caricature of rap aggression, greed and slobbering sexism, which suggests, without making it plain, that ODB is demanding money as a pimp. It's even more disturbing than anything by Eminem, because it's impossible to locate *any* gap between art and life, in ODB's case, and also because the man himself is too knowing about his vicarious appeal ('Radios play this all day, every day/Recognize I'm a fool . . . and you *luurrve* me'). I've tried not to adore it and I've failed miserably.

RE-REWIND THE CROWD SAY BO SELECTA

ARTFUL DODGER

PRODUCED BY MARK HILL/WRITTEN BY CRAIG DAVID
AND MARK HILL
RELENTLESS/NOVEMBER 1999
UK CHART: 2

We still love the sound of breaking glass – though maybe not as much as 'Craig David all over your . . . BOINK!!!', which can keep me entertained for hours. The final chapter in this here tale, with its blend of disco warmth and reggae vibe, its pure home-grown London small-club ambience, its smashing-glass effects and avant-garde off-key chorus, its mix of sex and an undercurrent of violence, and its massive success on an indie label, reaching No. 2 in the midst of Christmas's traditional mix of manic marketing and maudlin mawkishness, shows just how much things have changed over the last 23 years. On the other hand, the fact that it was kept off the Christmas No. 1 spot by Cliff Richard shows just how much they've stayed exactly the same.

Party over. Oops. Out of time.

APPENDIX

THE BEST SINGLES OF 2000–01

'We've got stars directing our fate,' Robbie Williams cooed meaningfully in his 'Millennium'. And, despite all previous evidence of the cyclical nature of popular culture, the British trend of obsessing about celebrities – and obsessing most about those who have the least substance, talent or relevance to justify our curious blend of fascination and *schadenfreude* – continues to obliterate any hope of reviving a vibrant British pop culture. Add the self-serving irony of the media's 'middle youth' marketing preference (we're 'cooler than our kids'. Ha! We ain't as cool as our fucking mothers!) and you'd be forgiven for falling for the pop myth most prevalent among the chattering classes these days . . . that is, that current pop music is rubbish. With all that in mind, I was asked by my publishers to write a short appendix about the singles of 2000–01, the records that, if we take on board my contention that you need at least 18 months to judge whether a record really stands the test of time, might well have made the Uncool 500 a couple of years down the line. And guess what? It took me ages to boil it *down* to 39 singles. The problem is that you have to wade through much more bullshit these days (see above) to find them.

I figured that you might have had enough of chronological order by now, so here they are, in the old-fashioned way, starting at the bottom rising to the top. And what better way to start than with the tiniest pop genre of all – the good Christmas single.

39: A LITTLE CHRISTMAS EVE THIEVING PUDDING
WOODEN

A black comedy and the very essence of superficially silly English eccentricity hiding savage social satire. Pudding are folky vocalists Helen Pendry, Marcus Hickman and Sheila Seal, singing for mad svengali Edward Barton, a Manchester maverick best known for writing Balearic house hit 'It's a Fine Day' and his insane, shaggy-bearded, one-man-and-an-out-of-tune guitar performances of the astounding 'Me and My Mini' on *The Tube* in the mid-'80s. On the A-side, over a lone bass guitar, Pendry haughtily sings an oddly scanned song about going out to steal her family's Christmas presents and treats – 'more pressies than the whole estate gets' – but the lyric alludes slyly both to her own crap life and the pain of those whose car she breaks into.

38: MY RED HOT CAR
SQUAREPUSHER
WARP

Beardy techno bod Tom Jenkins's unlikely tribute to the glories of UK garage was not about cars. It had a vocodered vocal that went, 'I'm gonna fuck you with my red hot cock.' Whether this was a parody of sexual machismo or an allusion to the dangers of nude sunbathing, it still rocked. Electronically.

37: WINTERLIGHT/JUMBLE SAILING
CLEARLAKE
DUSTY COMPANY

The debut single from these Brit indie alchemists saw extraordinary beauty in the apparently mundane. The sky in winter, going to a jumble sale with a friend, both inspired soaring melodies and an unashamedly English voice conjuring the imagery of anticipation and the joy in small things.

36: ROMEO
35: WHERE'S YOUR HEAD AT
BASEMENT JAXX
X L

Provoked rabid dancefloor abandon on the back of punchy Latin, The Beat trying to play metal, and, in the promo for the latter single, the scariest monkey video ever.

34: BREATHE AND STOP
Q-TIP
ARISTA

2000 saw the A Tribe Called Quest rap veteran give up trying to convert the world to chilled jazz rap and go for the sexed-up and sparkling solo ground. This was an implausibly tough, rhythmic and seductive ad for his hunky charms, and made him a long overdue rap superstar in the States.

33: LET ME BLOW YOUR MIND
EVE FEATURING GWEN STEFANI
RUFF RYDERS/INTERSCOPE

Young femme rapper Eve briefly lent credibility to that woman out of No Doubt by allowing her to guest on this fine and fly sexual brag.

32: THINGS HAVE CHANGED
BOB DYLAN
COLUMBIA

The eerie bleakness of this Oscar-winning song from the *Wonder Boys* soundtrack proved beyond doubt that Dylan's 'Time Out of Mind' return to form was no fluke.

31: PYRAMID SONG
RADIOHEAD
PARLOPHONE

In which Chuckling Uncle Thom brought avant-jazz complexity to the Top three. Gagging for a Roger Sanchez remix.

30: ANY DAY NOW
ELBOW
V2

See Clearlake but even better – a passionate and haunting meld of dubby 1979 depth, churchy psychedelic stealth and wide-eyed 21st-century optimism.

29: OVERLOAD
SUGABABES
LONDON

Gave this suspiciously normal manufactured teen band an irresistible hit but failed to make them massive stars, suggesting that those who buy this kind of pop want eating disorders, vapidity and desperation as well, or they're not playing.

28: OH NO (SENTIMENTAL THINGS)
SO SOLID CREW
RELENTLESS/INDEPENDIENTE

Who used all the tricks of the formula pop trade but convinced everyone they were drug-dealing two-step gang psychos, and therefore credible. Seems a bit rich for them to complain when they attract gunmen to their shows and become black stereotype scandal fodder, even though their first single was magnificently weird *and* catchy as hell.

27: WITNESS (ONE HOPE)
ROOTS MANUVA
BIG DADA

It's faint praise to describe Mr Manuva as the best British rapper ever. He's one of the best full-stop right now, spreading his amused authority and homely intellect here over sci-fi squelching and martial beats.

26: RIDE WIT ME
NELLY
UNIVERSAL

St Louis hip-hop superstar presents all the usual trappings of conspicuous consumption. But, with the aid of a softly chugging acoustic guitar, makes it sound like a bittersweet triumph – an excess of flash, signifying nothing.

25: HERO THEME
THE INFESTICONS
BIG DADA

Alt-rap from one Mike Ladd, who reckons he's an Infesticon sent to save us from some other kind of con, namely the kind of 'playa' Nelly would recognize. Sounds like a deranged beatnik ranting in the bath while a 40-piece orchestra drown in the same tub.

24: A LITTLE BIT OF LUCK
DJ LUCK AND MC NEAT
RED ROSE

With a little bit of luck, Messrs Luck and Neat and their fellow revellers might make it through a whole night at the dance without someone getting killed. The sentiment – along with a mesmeric, opiated vocal chant – makes this surprise two-step hit a dark and starkly impressionistic reflection of the violence surrounding the garage scene.

23: CONSTELLATIONS OF A VANITY
THE NECTARINE NO.9
CREEPING BENT/BEGGARS BANQUET

Our old Fire Engine friend (see p. 156) Davey Henderson refuses to give up on that sleazy, sexy, Bolan-meets-Prince, psychedelic-guitar-pop-with-soul-and-freakazoid-lyrics type affair.

22: THE WAY I AM
EMINEM
AFTERMATH/INTERSCOPE

A terrifying outpouring of one American's fury at the price of fame that even had my Mum-in-law open-mouthed in stunned admiration when she saw the video in an Indian takeaway in Dundee. And if the above sentence doesn't sum up great pop's unmatchable *reach*, then chuck me in a car boot and call me Kim.

21: GOT YOU/F–K YOU
PHAROAHE MONCH
VIRGIN

Rap-metal redux from the soundtrack of *Training Day*. Though it's not actually in the movie. Which is a great shame, because, with its raging first-person cop-as-criminal narrative and post-Hendrix chops and squalls, it's much better and briefer and doesn't star Ethan Hawke.

20: TEENAGE DIRTBAG
WHEATUS
COLUMBIA

At last, a rocking pop song that doesn't hate everyone and want to die. If you do not shed a happy tear when he sings the girl's bit and she's got Iron Maiden tickets and she admits she's a dirtbag too, then you've become one of Them. I recommend a job at a music paper.

19: LAST NITE
THE STROKES
ROUGH TRADE

Actually the B-side to the New Yorkers' debut single, it turned out to be the one everyone liked, because no white rock 'n' roll band has rewritten Tamla Motown so completely in their own image with such swagger since 'This Charming Man'. And if I hear one person even whisper the words Phil and Collins . . .

18: FRONTIER PSYCHIATRIST
THE AVALANCHES
XL

A collage of vocal and orchestral samples taken to virtuoso comic lengths, yet somehow constructed like a song.

17: BECAUSE I GOT HIGH
AFROMAN
UNIVERSAL

One-hit wonder? Ooh, probably. Maker of the best anti-drug record of the modern era? Definitely. Joseph 'Afroman' Foreman's cautionary comedy hits on a simple truth – you can only lecture about the downside of anything when you've done it. Repeatedly. And realized how funny and selfish it is. And still want to do it.

16: E.I.
NELLY
UNIVERSAL

Stoned sex in the back of the world's biggest jeep.

15: FAMILY AFFAIR
MARY J BLIGE
MCA

Dr Dre and Ms Blige make effortless dancefloor soul magic. 'Don't need no hateration/Holleration/In this dancerie' is sheer boogie poetry.

14: TRY AGAIN
13: WE NEED A RESOLUTION
AALIYAH
BLACKGROUND

Yep, there really are a lot of US rap and R&B records here, aren't there? You know why, don't you? *'Cos black people with computers make the best, most cutting-edge music right now.* I mean, I appreciate your need for nice boys with guitars and nice girls with pianos and shit, but, well . . . Glenn Miller's been missing for some time. Sorry, that must have come as a shock.

Have a nice cup of cocoa and listen to these.

Two big things about these two records. Firstly, the producer on both is Timbaland who is pretty much responsible for all these strange and incredible noises around at present, 'cos if he didn't make them, then the way he's upped the funk ante has forced everyone else to try and match up. This is why rap and R&B rule at present. No one there is much interested in living in the past.

Secondly – and its kind of connected – Aaliyah died in September 2001 in a (unrelated to September 11) plane crash. She was barely out of her teens. No one in Britain said much about it, apart from the black music press, who mourned one of the greatest young talents around. A few months later, a man who had lived a long and full life (and who hadn't been a relevant part of our lives for 30 years) died and we had yet another baffling outbreak of national mourning. Nothing whatsoever against George Harrison, but I suspect this phenomenon has some bearing on the backward and barren nature of our supposedly 'cool' culture. I mean, Aaliyah was black, and female, and young, and made things that young people relate to now. Who gives a fuck?

12: UP WITH PEOPLE
LAMBCHOP
CITY SLANG

Of course, when you're drifting toward such misanthropic thoughts, there's nothing better than a record that loves people, warts 'n' all. Nashville's Kurt Wagner has been writing those sort of songs in a old-school country-soul manner for a few years now. But 'Up with People' was a big, bold single, with high-stepping rhythm, gospel backing and a delirious chorus. It simply says that people are shite, but then again, so am I, so best celebrate anyway.

11: DREAMY DAY
ROOTS MANUVA
BIG DADA

See Lambchop, but with an impassioned Jamaican holler replacing the offhand southern mumble, and a piano pinched from 'Macarthur Park' and transformed into something sweepingly major yet tear-jerkingly minor.

10: LAPDANCE
N*E*R*D
VIRGIN

N*E*R*D are The Neptunes, who currently run a close second to Timbaland in the 'R&B producer of the moment' stakes. This stark, stuttering, infectious thing is pure rock 'n' roll – rebellion, sex, coded messages, and political frustration set to mean rifferama and rhythm you can shag to. Oddly, actual rock 'n' roll bands seem unable to do this anymore.

9: THE REAL SLIM SHADY
EMINEM
AFTERMATH/INTERSCOPE

Motor-mouthed parent-baiting over slapstick horror music.

8: CLINT EASTWOOD
GORILLAZ
PARLOPHONE

Damon Blur and friends go 1979 under cartoon cover . . . all Augustus Pablo and PiL and early, cheeky rap. Really annoyed indie and 'keepin' it real' hip-hop snobs, which is always a surefire guarantee of quality.

7: AISHA
DEATH IN VEGAS
CONCRETE/DECONSTRUCTION

More proof that it's your dance boys that make rock 'n' roll nowadays, although DIV did cheat by hiring rock 'n' roll's very embodiment, one Iggy Pop. He recites the testimony of a serial killer in a deep, dead tone, halfway between blank humour and restrained mania. He's backed by a thunderous cross between The Stooges and Led Zeppelin. With added woodwind.

6: MS JACKSON
OUTKAST
LAFACE/ARISTA

So, you're a freaky camp kind of rap star. You've just conformed to stereotype, sired kid, dumped Mom. What do you do? Write an incredible song which – with its deliberately ancient production style, and taunting quotes from 'The Wedding March', and heartfelt (yet somehow still ambiguous) apologies to the mother of your old flame, soul star Erykah Badu – sees you come out of it looking enlightened.

5: HEARD IT ALL BEFORE
SUNSHINE ANDERSON

SOULLIFE/ATLANTIC

Well, exactly. All feckless men must quiver before the titanic force of Ms Anderson's roar, as that no-good, cheatin' man gets so thoroughly dissed you can almost hear his balls shrivel. The music – perfectly – is an update of classic soul, with a sublime suspended chord that Sunshine just keeps leaping under and over and right on through, with much holleration.

4: CAUGHT OUT THERE
KELIS

VIRGIN

Or you could just scream at him until his eardrums explode. And then round up a posse of cuckolded women to beat him up. And then come up with the best radio-friendly allusion to fellatio ever while they scrape the sucker off the floor. Whatever suits you best.

3: JUMPIN' JUMPIN'
DESTINY'S CHILD

COLUMBIA

After all that, you go on a crusade to convince all happily married women to accompany you on a mission to have as much adulterous sex as possible. You need a juddering, impossibly propulsive rhythm, thrilling nightlife imagery, and the ability to make an echoed cry of 'BALLERS! Ballers!' sound somehow ladylike, even religious. And then you smile demurely, thank God and deny everything in interviews.

2: GET UR FREAK ON
MISSY 'MISDEMEANOUR' ELLIOTT

THE GOLD MIND INC./ELEKTRA

In any normal circumstance, this would be unbeatable. It does, after all, completely reinvent the entire concept of popular music, by way of one astonishing mutant bhangra rhythm and a set of vocal harmonies, ticks, howls, croons, grumbles and purrs that combine and defy time, space, hook, line, sinker and a thousand copycat records and mobile phone tones. What's it about? The Universe? My bum? Who cares.

1: STAN
EMINEM

AFTERMATH/INTERSCOPE

But if any record suspends all normal circumstances, it is this. I even deducted points for inflicting Dido upon us, and it's still The Boss. 'Stan' has been parodied, analysed and debated over so much, it leaves little to say. Except that it is the last word on investing more in the rich and famous than you do in yourself and those who love you. Which is where we came in, and where we appear to be.

SLEEVE CREDITS

The publisher has made every effort to clear permissions for the illustrative material in this book and apologises for any inadvertent omissions that have been made.

Pages 1, 105, 123, 163, 165, 169, 189, 231, 257, 259, 269, 287, 289 **The copyright in this artwork is owned and used by kind permission of Universal-Island Records Ltd**
Page 5 **Postcard**
Pages 8, 83, 137, 181 **Licensed courtesy of Sanctuary Copyrights Ltd**
Page 9 **1989 Silvertone Records Limited**
Pages 11, 29, 49, 65, 91, 155, 277, 303, 307, 309, 357, 359, 363, 375, 388 **Courtesy of Sony Music Entertainment (UK) Ltd**
Pages 13, 191, 207, 213, 241, 245, 347 **Warner Music UK Ltd**
Pages 15, 16, 51, 97, 133, 159, 183, 201, 214, 221, 229, 265 **Courtesy of Warners Bros**
Pages 17, 37 **Capitol**
Pages 23, 33, 41, 59, 89, 93, 103, 107, 119, 139, 193, 233, 319, 345, 401, 403, 417 **Courtesy of Virgin Records Limited**
Pages 24, 61 **Courtesy of Mute Records**; 279 **Blast First/Mute Records**; 399 **Layout: Slim Smith, Photo: Christoph Dreher/Mute Records**
Pages 27, 47 **Courtesy of Stiff Records Ltd**
Page 35 **Berserkley**
Pages 39, 69, 131 **Polydor Limited**; page 67 **Artwork taken from the single released by Polydor UK, 1978**
Page 45 **Anchor**
Pages 57, 99, 121, 151, 157, 175, 275 **Courtesy of EMI Records Ltd**
Pages 71,109 **Fast Product, courtesy of Bob Last**
Pages 73, 285 **Courtesy of Atlantic Records**
Page 79 **1979 Chrysalis Records, Inc**; page 117 **1980 Chrysalis Records, Inc**; page 331 **1992 Chrysalis Records, Inc**
Page 81 **1979 Elvis Costello Ltd, issued under license from the Demon Music Group Ltd**
Page 87 **Courtesy of Beggars Banquet Records Limited, www.xl-recordings.com**
Page 95 **Courtesy of A&M Records Limited**
Page 101, 381, 305 **MCA**
Pages 125, 135, 147, 149, 161, 199, 255, 297 **Factory Communications Limited**
Page 127 **Artwork: Dead Kennedys, courtesy of Cherry Red Records**
Page 129 **Courtesy of Universal Music Group**
Page 141 **(Arista) 1980 BMG Entertainment International UK & Ireland Limited. Used by permission**; page 177 **(RCA) 1982 BMG Entertainment. Used by permission of BMG Entertainment International UK & Ireland Limited on behalf of the copyright owner**; page 185 **(RCA) 1982 BMG Entertainment. Used by permission of BMG Entertainment International UK & Ireland Limited on behalf of the copyright owner**; page 293

(Deconstruction) 1989 BMG Entertainment International UK & Ireland Ltd; page 313 **(Rhythm King) 1990 BMG Entertainment International UK & Ireland Ltd. Used by permission of BMG Entertainment International UK & Ireland Ltd.**; page 373 **(RCA) 1995 BMG Entertainment International UK & Ireland Ltd**; page 413 **(Arista) 1997 Records Inc. Used by permission of BMG Entertainment International UK & Ireland Ltd.**
Page167 **Situation Two**
Page 179 **Epic**
Pages 187, 217 **Tommy Boy Music**
Page 205 **Illuminated**
Page 219 **Club**
Page 223 **Courtesy of 4AD, www.4ad.com**
Pages 235, 253 **Cooltempo**
Page 271 **Three Stripe**
Page 295 **Kind permission from Kool Kat/Network Records, Artwork by Dexter M**
Page 311 **KLF Communications**
Page 321 **1991 Zomba Records Limited**; page 355 **1993 Zomba Records Limited**
Page 323 **Wax Trax**
Page 325 **Reprinted by permission of Geffen Records**
Page 333 **Shut Up and Dance**
Page 335 **Courtesy of Elektra**
Pages 341, 405 **Wiiija Records**
Page 343 **Produced by Stephen Street, engineered by John Smith, Sleeve artwork by Stylorouge, single released 19th April 1993, taken from the artist's album Modern Life Is Rubbish.**
Page 377 **Artwork: Tomato, courtesy of Junior Boy's Own**
Page 219, 379, 415 **Courtesy of Mercury Records Limited**
Pages 291, 365, 361 **London Records 90 Limited**
Page 387 **Columbia**
Page 389 **Reprinted by permission of Death Row Records and Interscope Records**
Page 391 **Art: Savage Pencil, Design: Savage Leisure Centre, licensed courtesy of Elemental Records Ltd**
Page 393 **Courtesy of XL Recordings Limited, www.xl-recordings.com**
Page 411 **Courtesy of Time S.R.L (Italy)**
Page 423 **Courtesy of Warp Records. Cover photograph: Chris Cunningham. Design: The Designers Republic.**
Page 425 **Design: Ian Cater. Photography: Ken Copsey. Released on (Pias) Recordings UK.**
Page 427 **Design by Henni Hell, used by permission of Digital Hardcore Ltd**
Page 429 **Reprinted by permission of Aftermath Entertainment and Interscope Records.**
Page 431 **Licensed from Relentless Records Limited**

FOOTNOTES

1. London's first commercial radio station was cabled to Peterborough through our televisions, presumably to make us exiled cockneys feel even more homesick than we already did. Capitol's antipathy to punk was legendary, and the following month (April 1977) the New Musical Express gave away a free flexi-disc of The Clash performing 'Capitol Radio', a caustic tilt at the station's blissfully unaware windmill ('They give you all the hits to play/To keep you in your place all day.'). Nevertheless, it was heroic 'Your Mother Wouldn't Like It' hard rock presenter Nicky Horne who played 'White Riot' on his late-night show.

2. The Disco Duck was a novelty disco record by Rick Dees and His Cast pf Idiots that reached No. 6 in the UK charts in September 1976. It had an accompanying dance which I don't remember but I suspect had something to do with moving like a duck.

3. 'Peelywally' is a Scottish word for pale, frail, pasty, and probably not your first choice for back up in a gang fight.

4. Huey Newton was the assassinated leader of sixties black radical 'self-defence' organisation The Black Panthers

5. Chuck Yeager is the real life Test Pilot hero of Philip Kaufman's The Right Stuff movie.

LYRIC CREDITS

1976–77

ANARCHY IN THE U.K. by Cook/Jones/Matlock/Rotten. © Sex Pistols Residuals.

CAR WASH by Norman Whitfield. © MCA Music Ltd.

BOREDOM by Howard Devoto and Pete Shelley. © Virgin Music (Publishers) Ltd.

KNOWING ME KNOWING YOU by Benny Andersson, Björn Ulvaeus and Stig Anderson. © Union Songs AB.

LESS THAN ZERO by Elvis Costello. © Elvis Costello Ltd.

MARQUEE MOON by Tom Verlaine. © Double Exposure Music Ltd. ASCAP

1977 by Joe Strummer and Mick Jones. © Sony Music Entertainment (UK) Ltd.

TRANS-EUROPE EXPRESS by Ralf Hütter and Emil Schult. © Famous Chappell Ltd.

GOD SAVE THE QUEEN by Cook/Jones/Matlock/Rotten. © Sex Pistols Residuals.

DISCO INFERNO by Leroy Green and Ron 'Have Mercy' Kersey. © Famous Chappell Ltd.

ALISON by Elvis Costello. © Elvis Costello Ltd.

CHINESE ROCKS by Richard Hell, Dee Dee Ramone, Jerry Nolan and Johnny Thunders. © Warner Bros. Music/Chappell & Co./Virgin Music.

ROADRUNNER by Jonathan Richman. © White Metal Music.

I FEEL LOVE by Donna Summer, Giorgio Moroder and Pete Bellotte. © Warner Chappell Music Ltd./GEMA

ALL AROUND THE WORLD by Paul Weller. © And Son Music Ltd.

I CAN'T STAND MY BABY by Luke Warm. © Sensible Songs Ltd.

NO MORE HEROES by The Stranglers. © Complete Music Ltd./SBK Songs Ltd.

COMPLETE CONTROL by Joe Strummer and Mick Jones. © Sony Music Entertainment (UK) Ltd.

THE PASSENGER by Iggy Pop and Ricky Gardiner. © James Osterberg Music/Ricky Gardiner Songs Ltd.

HEROES by David Bowie and Brian Eno. © Bewlay Bros. Music/Fleur Music/E.G. Music Ltd.

HOLIDAYS IN THE SUN by Cook/Jones/Rotten/Vicious. © Sex Pistols Residuals.

ORGASM ADDICT by Howard Devoto and Pete Shelley. © Virgin Music (Publishers) Ltd.

WATCHING THE DETECTIVES by Elvis Costello. © Elvis Costello Ltd.

PSYCHO KILLER by David Byrne, Chris Frantz and Tina Weymouth. © Sire Records Inc.

UPTOWN TOP RANKING by Errol Thompson, Althia Forest and Donna Reid. © Lightning/Carlin.

1978

WHITE MAN IN HAMMERSMITH PALAIS by Joe Strummer and Mick Jones. © Sony Music Entertainment (UK) Ltd.

STAYIN' ALIVE by Barry, Robin and Maurice Gibb. © RSO/Chappell.

WHAT DO I GET? by Pete Shelley. © Virgin Music (Publishers) Ltd.

SHOT BY BOTH SIDES by Howard Devoto and Pete Shelley. © Virgin Music (Publishers) Ltd.

WARM LEATHERETTE by Daniel Miller. © Mute Records.

EX-LION TAMER by Colin Newman and Graham Lewis. © EMI Records Ltd.

I LOVE THE SOUND OF BREAKING GLASS by Nick Lowe, Andrew Bodnar and Stephen Goulding. © Rock Music Co. Ltd.

WHAT A WASTE by Ian Dury and Chaz Jankel. © Melvin Blackhill Music Ltd.

(I DON'T WANT TO GO TO) CHELSEA by Elvis Costello. © Elvis Costello Ltd.

HI-TENSION by Hi-Tension. © EMI Music Publishing Ltd.

PICTURE THIS by Debbie Harry, Chris Stein and Jimmy Destri. © Chrysalis Music Ltd.

EVER FALLEN IN LOVE (WITH SOMEONE YOU SHOULDN'T'VE?) by Pete Shelley. © Virgin Music (Publishers) Ltd.

PUBLIC IMAGE by Public Image Ltd. © Warner Bros Music Ltd./Virgin Music (Publishers) Ltd.

DOWN IN THE TUBE STATION AT MIDNIGHT by Paul Weller. © And Son Music Ltd.

DAMAGED GOODS by Gang Of Four. © EMI Music Ltd.

LOVE LIKE ANTHRAX by Gang Of Four. © EMI Music Ltd.

ARMALITE RIFLE by Gang Of Four. © EMI Music Ltd.

LE FREAK by Bernard Edwards and Nile Rodgers. © Warner Bros Music Ltd.

GIVE ME EVERYTHING by Howard Devoto. © Virgin Music (Publishers) Ltd.

ONE NATION UNDER A GROOVE written by George Clinton, Gary Shider and Walter 'Junie' Morrison. © Malbiz Music

1979

I WILL SURVIVE by Dino Fekaris and Freddie Perren. © Polydor Ltd.

HEART OF GLASS by Debbie Harry and Chris Stein. © EMI Music Pub. Ltd.

THE SOUND OF THE SUBURBS by Jean-Marie Carroll and Nicky Tesco. © Virgin Music (Publishers) Ltd.

OLIVER'S ARMY by Elvis Costello. © Elvis Costello Ltd.

HE'S THE GREATEST DANCER by Bernard Edwards and Nile Rodgers. © Warner Bros. Music.

AT HOME HE FEELS LIKE A TOURIST by Gang Of Four. © EMI Music Ltd.

POP MUZIK by Robin Scott. © Midascare Productions Ltd.
DANCE AWAY by Bryan Ferry. © BMG Songs Ltd.
BOYS KEEP SWINGING by David Bowie and Brian Eno. © Bewlay Bros Music/Fleur Music/E.G. Music Ltd.
JIMMY JIMMY by John O'Neill. © West Bank Songs Ltd./Undertones Ltd.
WE ARE FAMILY by Bernard Edwards and Nile Rodgers. © Warner Chappell Music Ltd.
I FOUGHT THE LAW by Sonny Curtis. © Acuff-Rose Music Ltd.
HUMAN FLY by Interior/Rorschach. © Mediocre Music Ltd.
GOOD TIMES by Bernard Edwards and Nile Rodgers. © Warner Bros Music Ltd.
KID by Chrissie Hynde. © Hynde House Of Hits/EMI Music Publishing Ltd. T/A Clive Banks Songs.
IS SHE REALLY GOING OUT WITH HIM? by Joe Jackson. © A&M Records Ltd.
ROWCHE RUMBLE by Mark E. Smith, Marc Riley and Craig Scanlon. © Step Forward Music.
ROCK LOBSTER by Fred Schneider and Ricky Wilson. © Island Records.
STREET LIFE by Joe Sample and Will Jennings. © Rondor Music (London) Ltd./Leeds Music Ltd.
DON'T STOP 'TIL YOU GET ENOUGH by Michael Jackson. © Miran Publishing Corp. (BMI)/Warner-Tamerlane Publishing Corp.
EMPIRE STATE HUMAN by Phil Oakey, Ian Craig-Marsh and Martyn Ware. © Virgin Music (Publishers) Ltd.
MESSAGE IN A BOTTLE by Sting. © Magnetic Publishing Ltd.
MIND YOUR OWN BUSINESS by Delta 5. © Rough Trade.
ON MY RADIO by Neol Davies. © Selecter.
CALIFORNIA ÜBER ALLES by Jello Biafra and John Greenway. © Sound Diagrams/Decay Music.
LONDON CALLING by Joe Strummer and Mick Jones. © Sony Music Entertainment (UK) Ltd.

1980

(NOT JUST) KNEE DEEP by George Clinton. © Malbiz Music.
AND THE BEAT GOES ON by L. Sylvers, S. Shockley and W. Shelby. © Carlin Music/Sony Music Publishers.
A SONG FROM UNDER THE FLOORBOARDS by Magazine. © Virgin Music (Publishers) Ltd.
GARBAGEMAN by Poison Ivy Rorschach and Lux Interior. © Illegal Songs Inc./Ascherberg Hopwood & Crew Ltd.
THAT'S THE JOINT by Funky Four Plus One, Sylvia Robinson and C. Chase. © I.Q. Music Ltd.
GENO by Kevin Rowland and Kevin Archer. © EMI Music Publishing Ltd.
POLICE AND THIEVES by Junior Murvin and Lee Perry. © Blue Mountain Music Ltd.
RESCUE by Will Sergeant, Ian McCulloch, Les Pattinson and Pete De Freitas. © Zoo Music/Warner Bros Music Ltd.
CHRISTINE by Siouxsie Sioux and Steve Severin. © Pure Noise/Chappell.
FINAL DAY by Stuart Moxham. © Rough Trade.
HOLIDAY IN CAMBODIA by Dead Kennedys. © Virgin Music (Publishers) Ltd.
THE WINNER TAKES IT ALL by Benny Anderson and Björn Ulvaeus. © Union Songs AB.
DRUG TRAIN by Poison Ivy Rorschach and Lux Interior. © Illegal Music Ltd.
ASHES TO ASHES by David Bowie. © Bewlay Bros Music/Fleur Music Ltd.
START! by Paul Weller. © And Son Music Ltd.
CHANGE by Killing Joke. © Energy Music Ltd.
REQUIEM by Killing Joke. © Energy Music Ltd.
STEREOTYPES by Jerry Dammers. © Plangent Visions Music Ltd.
INTERNATIONAL JET SET by Jerry Dammers. © Plangent Visions Music Ltd.
TOTALLY WIRED by Marc Riley, Craig Scanlan, Paul Hanley and Mark E. Smith. © Rough Trade Music.
PRINCE CHARMING by Adam Ant and Marco Pirroni. © EMI Music Publishing Ltd.
DOG EAT DOG by Adam Ant and Marco Pirroni. © EMI Music Publishing Ltd.
ATMOSPHERE by Ian Curtis, Peter Hook, Bernard Sumner and Stephen Morris. © Fractured Music.
ACE OF SPADES by Ian 'Lemmy' Kilminster, Fast Eddie Clarke and Phil Taylor. © Motor Music Ltd.
RUNAWAY BOYS by Brian Setzer and Slim Jim McDonnell. © Arista Records Ltd.

1981

DO NOTHING by Lynval Golding. © Plangent Visions Music Ltd.
'Reward' by Alan Gill and Julian Cope. © Mercury Records Ltd. (London).
THAT'S ENTERTAINMENT by Paul Weller. © And Son Music Ltd.
ONCE IN A LIFETIMe by David Byrne, Brian Eno and Talking Heads. © Index Music/Bleu Disque Music Co. Inc. ASCAP/E.G. Music Ltd. BMI.
MESSAGE OF LOVE by Chrissie Hynde. © Hynde House Of Hits/EMI Music Publishing Ltd T/A Clive Banks Songs.
PLAN B by Kevin Rowland and Jim Paterson. © EMI Music Publishing Ltd.
FLOWERS OF ROMANCE by Keith Levine and John Lydon. © Virgin Music (Publishers) Ltd./Warner Bros Music Ltd.
THE SOUND OF THE CROWD by Ian Burden and Philip Oakey. ©

Virgin Music (Publishers) Ltd./Dinsong Ltd.

ABOUT THE WEATHER by Howrd Devoto and Dave Formula. © Virgin Music (Publishers) Ltd.

DER MUSSOLINI by Robert Görl and Gabi Delgado-Lopez. © Wintrup Musik.

GHOST TOWN by Jerry Dammers. © Plangent Visions Music Ltd. Why? by Lynval Golding. © Plangent Music Visions Ltd.

FRIDAY NIGHT, SATURDAY MORNING by Terry Hall. © Plangent Visions Music Ltd.

PULL UP TO THE BUMPER by Kookoo Baya, Grace Jones and Dana Mano. © Rydim Music/Blue Mountain Music Ltd.

WORDY RAPPINGHOOD by Tina Weymouth. © Metered Music.

THE MODEL by Hutter, Bartos and Schult. © Famous Chappell Ltd.

THE 'SWEETEST GIRL' by Green Gartside. © Rough Trade Inc./ASCAP

WHERE DID YOUR HEART GO? by Don Was and David Was. © Island Music Ltd.

WHEEL ME OUT by Don Was and David Was. © Island Music Ltd.

GENIUS OF LOVE by Tom Tom Club. © Island Music Ltd.

O SUPERMAN (FOR MASSENET) by Laurie Anderson. © Warner Bros. Records Inc.

WHITE CAR IN GERMANY by Billy Mackenzie and Alan Rankine. © Fiction Songs Ltd.

THINGS FALL APART by Cristina and Was (Not Was). © Island Music Ltd.

1982

SAY HELLO, WAVE GOODBYE by Dave Ball and Marc Almond. © Metropolis/Warner Bros Music Ltd.

THE BOILER by The Bodysnatchers. © Chrysalis Music Ltd./Plangent Visions Music Ltd.

POISON ARROW by ABC. © Mercury Records Ltd. (London).

THE EMPIRE SONG by Killing Joke. © The Energy Music Company Ltd.

THE LOOK OF LOVE by ABC. © Mercury Records Ltd. (London).

THE MESSAGE by E. Fletcher, M. Glover, S. Robinson and J. Chase. © I.Q. Music Ltd.

A NIGHT TO REMEMBER by D. Meyers, C. Sylvers and N. Beard. © Chappell Music Ltd.

INSIDE OUT by Jesse Rae. © Major Tom's Music/Luzuli Music.

LORRAINE by Winston Henry. © Oval/Kuti.

WALKING ON SUNSHINE by Eddy Grant. © Warner Chappell Music Ltd.

SHIPBUILDING by Clive Langer and Elvis Costello. © Plangent Visions Music Inc. (ASCAP)/Warner Bros. Music Ltd.

SEXUAL HEALING by M. Gaye and O. Brown. © April Music Ltd.

OUR HOUSE by Carl Smyth and Chris Foreman. © Nutty Sounds Ltd.

1983

GET THE BALANCE RIGHT! by Martin L. Gore. © EMI Music Publishing Ltd./Grabbing Hands Music Ltd.

BLUE MONDAY by New Order. © Bemusic Ltd.

LITTLE RED CORVETTE by Prince. © Controversy Music/WB Music Corp.

WHITE LINES (DON'T DON'T DO IT) by Sylvia Robinson and Melvin Glover. © I.Q. Music Ltd.

1984

WHAT DIFFERENCE DOES IT MAKE? by Morrissey and Johnny Marr. © Warner Music UK Ltd.

THE KILLING MOON by Will Sergeant, Ian McCulloch, Les Pattinson and Pete De Freitas. © Zoo Music/Warner Bros. Music Ltd.

JUMP by Edward Van Halen, Alex Van Halen, Michael Anthony and David Lee Roth. © Warner Bros Music Ltd.

SHE'S STRANGE by Blackmon, Singleton, Leftenant and Jenkins. © Polygram Records Inc. (New York).

LOVE WARS by Cecil and Linda Womack. © Next Flight Music.

PERFECT SKIN by Lloyd Cole. © CBS Songs.

WILLIAM, IT WAS REALLY NOTHING by Morrissey and Johnny Marr. © Warner Music UK Ltd.

I FEEL FOR YOU by Prince. © Island Music Ltd.

THE BOYS OF SUMMER by Don Henley and Mike Campbell. © The David Geffen Company.

1985

HERE I COME (Broader Than Broadway)' by Barrington Levy. © Profile Records Ltd.

KING OF ROCK by Larry Smith, Joseph Simmins and Darryl McDaniels. © Protoons Inc./Rush-Groove.

THE WORD GIRL by Green Gartside and David Gamson. © Chrysalis Music Ltd./Warner Bros Music Ltd.

THE PERFECT KISS by New Order. © Bemusic/Warner Bros Music.

BORN IN THE USA by Bruce Springsteen. © Zomba Music Publishers Ltd.

UNDER ME SLENG TENG by W. Smith and L. James. © Greensleeves Publishing Ltd.

1986

I CAN'T LIVE WITHOUT MY RADIO by James Todd Smith and Rick Rubin. © Def Jam Records Inc.

BIGMOUTH STRIKES AGAIN by Morrissey and Johnny Marr. © Warner Music UK Ltd.

PAPA DON'T PREACH by Brian Elliot and Madonna. © Elliot/Jacobsen Music Pub. Co. ASCAP

WORD UP by Larry Blackmon and Tomi Jenkins. © Polygram Music Publishing Ltd.
WALK THIS WAY by Steven Tyler and Joe Perry. © Daksel Music Corp./BMI
SUBURBIA by Neil Tennant and Chris Lowe. © Cage Music Ltd./10 Music Ltd.
I WANT YOU by Declan Macmanus. © Elvis Costello Ltd.

1987

HALF A PERSON by Morrissey and Johnny Marr. © Warner Music UK Ltd.
SIGN O' THE TIMES by Prince. © Controversy Music/WB Music Corp.
I'M BAD by James Todd Smith, Bobby Ervin, Dwayne Simon and Darryl Pierce. © Def Jam Records Inc.
I KNOW YOU GOT SOUL by Eric Barrier and William Griffin. © EMI Music Publishing Ltd.
YOU'RE GONNA GET YOURS by Carlton Ridenhour and Hank Shocklee. © Island Music Ltd.
TRUE FAITH by New Order and Stephen Hague. © Bemusic/Warner Bros Music/Cut Music/MCA Music Inc.
STRONG ISLAND by J.V.C. Force by B. Taylor, J. Woodson and C. Small. © Pisces Music Ltd.
THE ONE I LOVE by Bill Berry, Peter Buck, Mike Mills and Michael Stipe. © Chappell Music Ltd.
HEAVEN IS A PLACE ON EARTH by Ellen Shipley and Rick Nowels. © EMI Music Publishing Ltd.
FAIRYTALE OF NEW YORK by Shane Macgowan and Jem Finer. © Stiff Music Ltd.

1988

BRING THE NOISE by Hank Shocklee, Carlton Ridenhour and Eric Sadler. © Def American Songs Inc. (BMI).
CARS AND GIRLS by Paddy McAloon. © Kitchen Music Ltd./SBK Songs Ltd.
IT TAKES TWO by Robert Ginyard. © Protoons Music Ltd.
THE KING OF ROCK 'N' ROLL by Paddy McAloon. © Kitchen Music Ltd./SBK Songs Ltd.
DON'T BELIEVE THE HYPE by Carlton Ridenhour, Eric Sadler, Hank Shocklee and William Drayton. © Def American Songs Inc.
FOLLOW THE LEADER by Eric Barrier and William Griffin. © Copyright Control/UNI Records Inc.
TEARDROPS by Dr Rue and The Gypsy Wave Burner. © Island Records Inc.
GIGANTIC by Black Francis and Mrs John Murphy. © Rice And Beans Music.
STRICTLY BUSINESS by EPMD. © Beach House Music/ASCAP
FREAK SCENE by J. Mascis and Dinosaur Jr. © Copyright Control/Blast First.
WHERE'S YOUR CHILD? by Bam Bam. © Fiction Songs.

1989

THE LAST OF THE FAMOUS INTERNATIONAL PLAYBOYS by Morrissey and Stephen Street. © Warner Chappell Music Ltd./Virgin Music (Publishers) Ltd.
STRAIGHT OUT THE JUNGLE by Afrika Baby Bambaataa, Mike G and Q-Tip. © Tonk Music/Prodisc Music (BMI).
KEEP ON MOVIN' by Beresford Romeo. © Virgin Music (Publishers) Ltd.
MONKEY'S GONE TO HEAVEN by Black Francis. © Rice And Beans Music.
FIGHT THE POWER by Keith Shocklee, Eric Sadler and Carlton Ridenhour. © Island Music Ltd.
WROTE FOR LUCK by Happy Mondays. © London Music Ltd.
I'M NOT THE MAN I USED TO BE by David Steele and Roland Gift. © Virgin Music (Publishers) Ltd.
HALLELUJAH by Happy Mondays. © London Music Ltd.

1990

WELCOME TO THE TERRORDOME by Keith Shocklee, Eric Sadler and Carlton Ridenhour. © NIA Music Inc./Def American Songs Inc. (BMI).
EVERYTHING FLOWS by Norman Blake. © Paperhouse Records.
KINKY AFRO by Happy Mondays. © London Music Ltd.
MAMA SAID KNOCK YOU OUT by Marlon Williams and James Todd Smith. © Marley Marl Music/LL Cool J Pub. Inc./Def Jam Music Inc.
BEING BORING by Neil Tennant and Chris Lowe. © Cage Music Ltd./EMI 10 Music Ltd.

1991

APPARENTLY NOTHIN' by Carleen Anderson and Marco Nelson. © Phonogram Ltd. (London).
LOSING MY RELIGION by Bill Berry, Peter Buck, Mike Mills and Michael Stipe. © R.E.M./Athens Ltd.
I COME OFF by Marvin Young, Matt Dike and Michael Ross. © Varry White Music Inc.
WHO'S GONNA TAKE THE WEIGHT? by DJ Premier and Guru. © Gifted Pearl Music Inc./Almo Music Corp. (ASCAP).
OPTIMISTIC by Gary Hines, Jimmy Jam and Terry Lewis. © Perspective Records Inc.
GETT OFF by Prince and the New Power Generation. © Controversy Music/WB Music Corp.
SMELLS LIKE TEEN SPIRIT by Kurt Cobain and Nirvana. © Virgin Music (Publishers) Ltd.

1992

MY LOVIN (YOU'RE NEVER GONNA GET IT) by Thomas McElroy and Denzil Foster. © Two Tuff-E-Nuff Songs/Irving Music Inc. BMI.
TENNESSEE by Speech and Earlee Taree. © Arrested Development Music (BMI).
LANGUAGE OF VIOLENCE by Michael Franti. © Copyright Control.
£20 TO GET IN by Smiley and P.J. © Shut Up And Dance Music.
RAVING I'M RAVING by Mark Cohn, Smiley and P.J. © Shut Up And Dance Music/Museum Steps Music.
CREEP by Radiohead (Lyrics by Thom Yorke). © Warner Chappell Music Ltd.

1993

I AIN'T NEW TO THIS by Ice T and DJ Aladdin. © Warner Chappell Music Ltd./Ammo Dump Music.
THAT'S THE WAY LOVE GOES by Janet Jackson, James Harris III and Terry Lewis. © Black Ice Publishing (BMI)/Flyte Tyme Tunes (ASCAP).
SNAKEDRIVER by William and Jim Reid. © Warner Music UK Ltd.
FROM DESPAIR TO WHERE by Richey Edwards, Nicky Wire, James Dean Bradfield and Sean Moore. © Sony Music Publishing.
VENUS AS A BOY by Björk Gudmundsdottir. © Polygram Music Publishing Ltd.
REALLY DOE by Ice Cube. © Priority Records Inc.
MY SKIN IS MY SIN by Ice Cube. © Priority Records Inc.

1994

SOUND OF DA POLICE by K. Parker and R. Lemay. © Zomba Enterprises Inc./BDP Music/Soul Clay Music (ASCAP).
LOSER by Beck. © Bongload Records.
SUPERSONIC by Noel Gallagher. © Creation Songs Ltd./Sony Music Publishing.
COME CLEAN by K.J. Davis, C. Martin, C. Parker, F. Scruggs, K. Jones and T. Taylor. © FFRR.
BIG GAY HEART by Evan Dando and Tom Morgan. © EMI Virgin Songs Inc./JonBing Music Inc. ASCAP, Bug Music Inc./Dave And Darlene Music Inc. ASCAP/Moo Chewns Inc./Polygram International Publishing Inc. ASCAP.
REGULATE by Warren Griffin and Nate Hale. © Warren G Publishing/Suge Publishing.
AFRO PUFFS by Dat Nigga Daz and The Lady Of Rage. © Suge Publishing (ASCAP).
A GIRL LIKE YOU by Edwyn Collins. © Edwyn Collins.
CIGARETTES AND ALCOHOL by Noel Gallagher. © Creation Songs Ltd./Sony Music Publishing.

1995

CREEP by Dallas Austin. © LaFace Records.
GLORY BOX by Geoff Barrow, Beth Gibbons and Adrian Utley. © Chrysalis Music Ltd.
FAKE PLASTIC TREES by Radiohead. © Warner Chappell Ltd.
WATERFALLS by Marqueze Etheridge, Lisa 'Left Eye' Lopes and Organized Noise. © LaFace Records.
WONDERWALL by Noel Gallagher. © Creation Songs Ltd./Sony Music Publishing.

1996

HYPER-BALLAD by Björk. © Polygram Music Publishing Ltd.
HOMETOWN UNICORN by Super Furry Animals. © Creation Records Ltd.
BECOMING MORE LIKE ALFIE by Neil Hannon. © Damaged Pop Music.
DEVIL'S HAIRCUT by Beck Hansen, Mike Simpson and John King. © Cyanide Breathmint Music/BMG Songs Inc./Dust Brothers Music ASCAP.

1997

BEETLEBUM by Damon Albarn, Graham Coxon, Alex James and Dave Rowntree. © EMI Music Publishing Ltd.
INTO MY ARMS by Nick Cave. © Mute Song.
(ARE YOU) THE ONE THAT I'VE BEEN WAITING FOR? by Nick Cave. © Mute Song.
SUPER BON BON by Soul Coughing and M. Doughty. © Slash Records.
NITE KLUB by Jerry Dammers. © Plangent Visions Music Ltd.
RISINGSON by Del Naja, Marshall, Vowles, Reed and Seeger. © Island Music Ltd.
BRIMFUL OF ASHA by Tjinder Singh. © Wiiija Music Ltd./Momentum Music Ltd.
HELP THE AGED by Cocker, Banks, Doyle, Mackay and Webber. © Island Music Ltd.

1998

FEEL IT by Michael Jackson and Jackie Jackson. © Warner Chappell Music Ltd.
A ROSE IS STILL A ROSE by Lauryn Hill. © Sony/ATV Tunes LLC-Obverse Creation Music (ASCAP)
SINCERE by Matt Coleman. © Copyright Control.
INTERGALACTIC by Beastie Boys and Mario Caldato Jr. © Brooklyn Dust Music/Polygram International Music Publishing Inc. (ASCAP)
DOO WOP (THAT THING) by Lauryn Hill. © Sony/ATV Tunes LLC-Obverse Creation Music (ASCAP).

CELEBRITY SKIN by Courtney Love, Eric Erlandson and Billy Corgan. © Mother May I Music/Echo Echo Tunes (BMI).
GODDESS ON A HIWAY by Mercury Rev. © Mercury Rev Canaveral Pictures/(BMI).
THE CERTAINTY OF CHANCE by Neil Hannon and Jody Talbot. © BMG Music Publishing.

1999

MY NAME IS by Marshall Mathers and Dr Dre. © Chrysalis Music/Aftermath Ent./Interscope Records.
NEW YORK CITY BOY by Neil Tennant, Chris Lowe and David Morales. © Cage Music Ltd./Emi 10 Ltd./Def Mix Music/EMI Music Publishing.
JUMP 'N' SHOUT by Ratcliffe, Buxton and James. © MCA Music.
GOT YOUR MONEY by Pharrell Williams, Chad Hugo and Russell Jones. © Wu-Tang Publishing/Ramecca Publishing.
RE-REWIND THE CROWD SAY BO SELECTA by Craig David, Peter Devereux and Mark Hill. © Warner Chappell/Windswept Pacific.

ARTIST INDEX